FONDREN LIBRARY
Southern Methodist University
DALLAS, TEXAS 75275

D0064988

The Legislative Process

The Legislative Process

A Comparative Approach

David M. Olson
University of North Carolina at Greensboro

HARPER & ROW, PUBLISHERS, New York
Cambridge, Hagerstown, Philadelphia, San Francisco,
London, Mexico City, São Paulo, Sydney

1817

Sponsoring Editor: Alan Spiegel
Project Editor: Pamela Landau
Production Manager: Marion Palen
Compositor: Maryland Linotype Composition Co., Inc.
Printer and Binder: Halliday Lithograph Corporation
Art Studio: Vantage Art Inc.

THE LEGISLATIVE PROCESS: A Comparative Approach

Copyright © 1980 by David M. Olson

All rights reserved. Printed in the United States of America. No part of
this book may be used or reproduced in any manner whatsoever without written
permission except in the case of brief quotations embodied in critical articles
and reviews. For information address Harper & Row, Publishers, Inc., 10 East
53rd Street, New York, N.Y. 10022.

LIBRARY OF CONGRESS CATALOGING IN PUBLICATION DATA

Olson, David M
  The legislative process.

  Bibliography: p.
  Includes index.
  1. Legislative bodies. 2. Legislative power.
3. United States. Congress. I. Title.
JF511.O57   328'.3   79-19713
ISBN 0-06-044919-5

B-T-80-0258

Contents

Preface

One purpose of this book is to compare the world's national legislatures. This book does present much more material about the United States Congress than about any other single national legislative body because much more extensive research literature is available on it than for any other country or for the American state legislatures.

Hopefully, students will come to understand the distinctive features of the United States Congress by comparing it with other parliaments. Students can also appreciate what the Congress has in common with other national legislative bodies and thereby understand some of the generic attributes of legislative institutions—wherever they are found.

As a book of description and explanation, this book is based on a wide and diverse body of prior research. My debt to the many authors of such articles is indicated by the footnotes in each chapter. I have attempted to summarize what we know and to guess on those many matters on which research is lacking.

This book rests upon and draws from the active and critical intelligence of my students, both graduate and undergraduate. They have raised questions to which I did not have an answer or could not even make a respectable guess. They have patiently listened to my ideas and reviewed my data and then have proceeded to launch questions that forced me to do a thorough review of what I thought I had completed.

In particular, this book incorporates the work of my research assistants, all of whom have been undergraduate students. One set of students has developed bibliographies and prepared abstracts of research articles (particularly Marsha Buckalew, Ann Beaver, Maria Sanchez-Boudy, and Sandra Schmoyer). Another set has worked with me in collecting, punching, and tabulating congressional district census and election data (particularly Debbie Buie, John Constantinou, and Mike Williams). Finally, most of the tables in this book are based on the work of David Hobbs, who, with perseverance and good cheer, has ferreted out the raw statistics from elusive sources and made them intelligible. Phil Swink was instrumental in obtaining photographs of the U.S. Congress and documentation on the Energy bill. The student research assistants have been funded by a series of grants from the Research Council of the University of North Carolina at Greensboro.

Another set of students has written research papers and provided critiques of selected chapters: Paul Bell, Susan Bjork, Robert Briskin, Ken Campbell, Nancy Hope, Jeff Johnson, Bill Park, Steve Sherman, Randy Sides, Phil Swink, and Norma Wood, all at the University of

North Carolina at Greensboro. In addition, two students at Duke University have provided critiques of the whole manuscript in an earlier form—Robert Monks and Stephen Brake.

My colleagues have been a major source of encouragement and support, both for the book project itself, and in obtaining relevant sources and data. Because my ignorance of Communist political systems was the greatest, I have relied upon my colleagues in that specialization the most. Professors James Seroka and Maurice Simon have found election statistics and fragmentary accounts of legislation, have translated materials upon request, and have read and critiqued portions of the book. In addition, I have benefited from the critiques of selected chapters by B. David Meyers, Charles Prysby, and James C. Thompson of my department.

Colleagues at other universities have been generous with their time and have been precise in their critiques in reading earlier versions of this book: Charles Bell, Roger Davidson, Richard Fenno, Malcolm Jewell, Allan Kornberg, and Marvin Weinbaum.

If an army marches on its stomach, a book depends upon its typists. The skills and good humor of Maggie Davis, Betty Brown, and Lisa Claudon have been demonstrated amply in the preparation of the manuscript and its earlier versions.

David M. Olson

The Legislative Process

Chapter 1
Congresses and Parliaments in an Age of Executive Dominance

A visitor in the gallery of a nation's parliament is apt to be either disappointed or confused. Because few parliaments meet the whole year, the visitor is likely to find the chamber empty. Even if the visitor is there at the right time of the year, the parliament may not be meeting at that particular time of day. Instead, the members may be in committee or party meetings, or may be elsewhere in the building, or in the capital city. Should the visitor be in the gallery during a formal meeting of the whole parliament, he or she may find that few members are on the floor or, if many are in their seats, they do not seem to be paying attention to the proceedings. Indeed, the proceedings may be dull, technical, and incomprehensible to the outsider. If the visitor is lucky, he or she may see occasionally a major debate or a close vote. Even then, the voting procedures may be arcane to the visitor.

Although parliaments have their moments of ritual, of great debate, and of pomp and circumstance (Fig. 1.1), they are not, unlike drama in a theater, created for the spectator. Instead, they are working bodies and their procedures accommodate the working needs of their members rather than the entertainment of visitors.

The observant visitor in the gallery could easily spot the desk of

Figure 1.1 A parliamentary body in session: The U.S. House of Representatives. (National Geographic Photograph. Courtesy U.S. Capitol Historical Society)

the presiding officer who, in the British Parliament and in several former British colonies, wears a wig and robes of office. The visitor could see—even if not many members were present on the floor—the places on the floor from which motions are stated and speeches given. In all parliaments the floor and seating arrangements have a spacing pattern that designates those places from which leadership is exercised. The geography of the floor is a clue to the internal organization and leadership structure of the whole body (Fig. 1.2).

The British Parliament, by contrast with the U.S. Congress, is clearly marked off into two sets of benches facing each other. On the Speaker's right sits the party that forms the current cabinet, or the "government of the day," whereas facing them are the benches for the party forming "Her Majesty's Loyal Opposition" (Fig. 1.3). In the U.S. Congress, the president and members of the cabinet, by contrast, have no place on the floor, symbolizing the separation between the executive and legislative bodies.

To the extent that a parliament uses committees, those committees will usually met in separate rooms—or even in separate buildings, as do the political parties in many nations. The visitor would have to leave the gallery to find those rooms or buildings. If the rules of the parliament admit outsiders to a committee meeting, the visitor would find a much higher proportion of members in attendance, much less ceremony, and much more detailed discussion than would usually occur on the floor.

   This book will attempt to guide the reader into the places of work

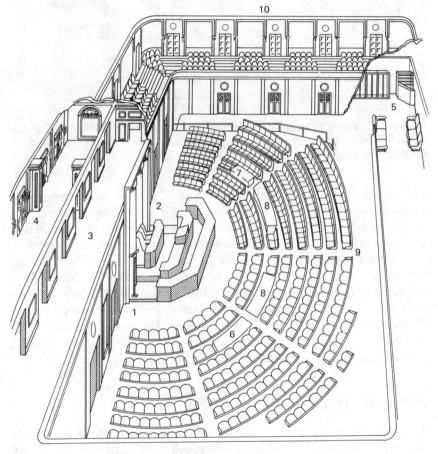

1. The Mace	6. Democratic leadership table
2. Speaker of the House	7. Republican leadership table
3. Speaker's lobby	8. Committee tables
4. Members' reading rooms	9. Center aisle
5. Republican cloakroom	10. Visitors' galleries
(Democratic cloakroom on opposite side of chamber)	

Figure 1.2   U.S. House of Representatives floor diagram. (Source: Adapted from Howard E. McCurdy, *An Insider's Guide to the Capitol*, Washington, D.C.: The American University, 1973, p. 45.)

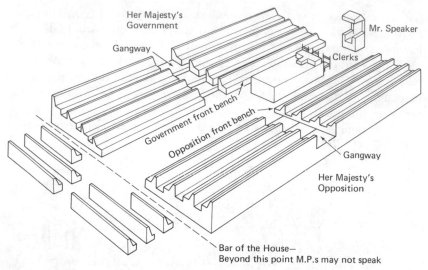

Figure 1.3 British House of Commons floor diagram. (Source: Stanley Rothman, Howard Scarrow, and Martin Schain, *European Society and Politics,* St. Paul: West Publishing, 1976, p. 255.)

of parliaments and their members. We shall explore how persons are originally elected to serve in parliament and what they do after they are elected. We shall inquire into their internal forms of organization and how they relate to the chief executives and to their electorates.

We will attempt to view all the parliaments in the world's nations, but will accomplish that task only in part. The amount of information available to us is very fragmentary. Most research on parliaments concentrates on the industrialized democracies in Western Europe and in North America. But even for these nations, the research literature is scattered and partial. Thus, this book is also a review of the existing state of knowledge—and ignorance—of the world's parliaments.

PARLIAMENTS AROUND THE WORLD

Every nation has a set of administrative agencies, and every nation has an executive authority and a judiciary. All possess power and all are continuing and important elements of their government. Although executives may be deposed, and the form of the executive office altered, that any given nation shall have someone in executive authority is rarely questioned.

Parliamentary bodies, by contrast, are neither necessarily permanent nor powerful. Although most nations at any one time have parliaments, in a wide variety of nations they are overthrown and abolished.

They do, however, come back. If not permanent, parliamentary bodies are at least resilient. Even most military coups overthrowing an elected parliament promise to restore elections and, therewith, parliament.[1]

Parliaments are essentially an European institution. Originating in Britain and Scandinavia, they have been adopted in democratic European nations beginning with the French Revolution. From Europe, parliaments have been exported around the world, but they have taken firmest hold in countries populated by European colonists, such as the United States and Australia. In Mediterranean Europe, and in most of the nations on other continents, democracy is unstable, and thus parliaments are both uncertain in existence and circumscribed in powers.

Of 138 nations in the United Nations in 1971, 30 nations did not then have parliaments. These nations were mainly Arab, together with some Mediterranean, European, African, and South American nations.[2] Since then, Chile, Argentina, and Uruguay have abolished their parliaments, whereas Greece and Portugal have newly established theirs, and Spain in the mid-1970s shifted from an appointed to an elected Cortes. India, the world's most populous democracy, at the same time emasculated its parliament over a two-year period by jailing opposition members and substituting executive decrees for parliamentary enactments.

The origins of parliamentary institutions rest in the distant past of Western Europe, but in numerous countries of the world, parliaments are abolished and created almost annually before our very eyes. The question of origins and creation is, for most countries outside the Western European tradition, a very contemporary issue.

In this book, we shall discuss parliaments in world perspective, although our main attention will be on the U.S. Congress. That body is the most active and probably the most powerful of the world's parliamentary institutions. It is also that body about which we have the great amount of information. We shall compare the U.S. Congress to other parliaments around the world when information is available, to permit the reader to place it in the context of developments in other nations. Even though Congress is a thriving institution in the United States, it is by no means settled that parliaments are or shall become important and independent centers of decision making in many other countries of the world in the contemporary period.

---

[1] Jean Blondel, *Comparative Legislatures* (Englewood Cliffs, N.J.: Prentice-Hall, 1973), pp. 9–10; Allan Kornberg and Kenneth Pittman, "Representative and Military Bodies: Their Roles in the Survival of Political Systems of New States," in Joel Smith and Lloyd Musolf (eds.), *Legislatures in Development* (Durham, N.C.: Duke University Press, forthcoming), chap. 3.

[2] Blondel, *Comparative Legislatures*, pp. 7–9.

THE CRITICAL ENVIRONMENT

Two major problems have been confronted in the long evolution of parliaments. The first has been their relationship to the executive; the second, to the electorate. In short, these two main problems concern parliaments' relationship to the two most critical elements in its environment. Parliaments are poised between the executive on one side and the electorate on the other. Parliament is an intermediary institution between executives and electorates. Its creation and its activities grow out of that dual relationship.

The first problem faced historically by parliaments was to become independent from the crown and its advisers. The British Parliament had obtained substantial independence from the royal power by the time of the American Revolution. In a way, the American "separation of powers" system defined the presidential-congressional relationship as the king-parliamentary relationship then existed. But Parliament went a step further, finally to gain control over the executive. The prime minister and cabinet, by the mid-nineteenth century, had become "responsible" to Parliament instead of to the king. That is, the crown could no longer appoint a prime minister without that selection being ratified by and acceptable to Parliament. With the growth of a two-party system, the prime minister in reality either already was or became the leader of the majority party in Parliament. Parliament could make and break the prime minister and it was he and his cabinet, not the crown, who exercised the authority of government. Thus, the crown "reigns, but does not rule." The principle of parliamentary supremacy, or of accountability of the chief executive and cabinet to parliament, was achieved in most European nations at about the time of World War I.

Some indication of the complications in the development of modern parliamentary institutions is found in Table 1.1. Thirteen European nations are listed in the order of the time at which their respective parliaments obtained constitutional recognition. Although at least some of their parliaments had a much longer period of existence (especially the British and the Swedish),[3] this particular development marks the occasion at which the crown conceded that the parliament had a constitutional right to exist, to be consulted, and in effect, to question and perhaps even modify the crown's intentions.

The next important step chronicled in the same table is the point at which the "government of the day," that is, the prime minister and the cabinet, became "responsible" to the parliament (col. 2). In 9 of the 13

[3] Gilbert Campion, *An Introduction to the Procedure of the House of Commons*, 3rd ed. (London: Macmillan, 1958), pp. 5–15; Dankwart A. Rustow, *The Politics of Compromise* (Princeton, N.J.: Princeton University Press, 1955), pp. 10–11.

Table 1.1 CHRONOLOGY OF PARLIAMENTARY DEVELOPMENT

NATION	(1) CONSTITUTIONAL BASIS FOR PARLIAMENT: YEAR	(2) GOVERNMENT RESPONSIBLE TO PARLIAMENT: YEAR	(3) ADULT SUFFRAGE: YEAR	(4) LENGTH OF TIME TO ACHIEVE RESPONSIBLE GOVERNMENT FROM CONSTITUTIONAL BASIS (2) − (1)	(5) LENGTH OF TIME TO ACHIEVE ADULT SUFFRAGE FROM RESPONSIBLE GOVERNMENT (3) − (2)
Britain	1689	1741	1928	52	187
France	1789	1792	1945	3	153
Netherlands	1796	1848	1919	52	71
Sweden	1809	1866	1920	57	54
Norway	1814	1884	1913	70	29
Belgium	1815	1831	1948	16	117
Luxembourg	1815	1830	1919	15	89
Italy	1848	1876	1946	28	70
Denmark	1848	1901	1915	53	14
Austria	1848	1918	1918	70	0
Germany	1848	1918	1918	70	0
Finland	1869	1917	1906	48	9
Iceland	1874	1922	1915	46	+5

SOURCE: Peter Gerlich, "The Institutionalization of European Parliaments," in Allan Kornberg (ed.), *Legislatures in Comparative Perspective* (New York: McKay, 1973), pp. 100 and 106.

countries, that step took an additional 40 or more years to achieve (col. 4).

The second major problem confronted in the development of parliaments concerned its relationship to the electorate. Who was eligible to select the representatives, and thus who and what was to be represented? The United States led the way in this development, for something close to universal suffrage (for white males) had been achieved by the 1820s. The major extension of the right to vote in Britain did not occur until the 1860s, and most other European nations did not obtain universal (male) suffrage until about the time of World War I. In the nineteenth century, especially in Europe, the growth of the suffrage ran parallel with the notion of representation in, and popular sovereignty through, parliaments.

The date at which the right to vote was held by the adult population, and not restricted by property, or income or sex qualifications, marks the attainment of the democratic ideal that the whole population should be represented. In six of the 13 nations charted in Table 1.1, that development took 70 or more years after the achievement of government responsibility (col. 5).

The dates of universal suffrage occur, for most countries, quite a bit later than does the attainment of government responsibility to parliament. The more recently that relationship between the government and the parliament was defined, the more rapidly universal suffrage was attained.[4]

These two major problems concerning the place of parliament in relation to the two critical components of its political environment were faced sequentially in Britain, the United States, and to a lesser degree, in France. In most other European nations, however, these questions were resolved simultaneously at around the turn of the twentieth century and on into World War I. The entire sequence of developments was stretched out over a longer period of time for those countries that started earlier than for those that commenced their parliamentary developments later.

In no country have these developments occurred without violence, bloodshed, and repression. Dynastic feuds, civil wars, and international conflict have all taken place. Dictatorship has often alternated with periods of parliamentary government and democratic elections. In general terms, the earlier a nation has started toward parliamentary government and a wide suffrage, the easier the transitions have been.

[4] Peter Gerlich, "The Institutionalization of European Parliaments," in Allan Kornberg (ed.), *Legislatures in Comparative Perspective* (New York: McKay, 1973), pp. 100–107.

The more these major changes have been compressed into a short time span, the more erratic and perhaps also traumatic have been their governmental and political events.

These governmental developments are also closely associated with the changes occurring in their respective societies and economies in the 1800s. Those nations (Austria, France, Italy, Netherlands) remaining largely rural, and at the other extreme, those nations rapidly urbanizing (Finland, Germany, Luxembourg), have had the greatest difficulty in developing a parliamentary control over the crown's ministers. In the rural societies, an urban and commercially oriented population did not become large enough to challenge the crown and the established rural aristocracy. In the rapidly urbanizing societies, however, the economic dislocations and the influx of large numbers of uneducated and unskilled farm hands into the cities posed more problems for the government than could be solved peacefully and to everyone's satisfaction. Four countries—Great Britain, Sweden, Denmark and Norway —experienced a moderate rate of urbanization in the nineteenth century, and it is those countries that most easily (in relative terms at any rate) evolved the control by parliament over the executive power of government.[5]

When the relationship of a parliament to both components of its critical environment arises and must be resolved in the same time period, the decisions and events are likely to be more dramatic and more disruptive for a nation than when they can be separated and resolved in different time periods and through unrelated events and even by different generations. Many of the newly independent nations, however, are now facing both issues simultaneously and furthermore are also wrestling with the issues of nationhood and of economic development. Under these conditions the political arrangements of a nation are likely to be strained to the limit and perhaps disrupted. In those settings parliaments may be rather fragile and not very important institutions.[6] We shall give more attention to this question in the last chapter.

The relationship between a parliament and its environment is sketched in Figure 1.4. Parliament, the chief executive, and the elec-

[5] Ibid., pp. 103–104, and 108–110. We do not imply that urbanization by itself, or any other single factor, is the key and sufficient variable to "explain" everything else. Rather, we use it as one indicator—available and measurable—of a much broader range of socioeconomic changes.

[6] This form of analysis is applied to political parties in Joseph LaPalombara and Myron Weiner (eds.), *Political Parties and Political Development* (Princeton, N.J.: Princeton University Press, 1966), pp. 427–433.

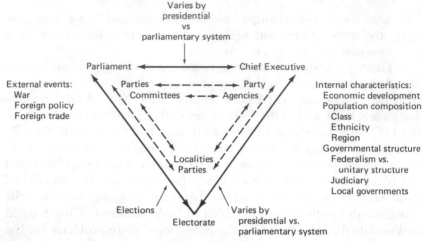

Figure 1.4 Parliament and its environment.

torate are shown as three points on a triangle, in which parliament interacts simultaneously with both the chief executive and its electorate. Each of these relationships is the subject of later chapters in this book.

We show the chief executive, too, as having a relationship to the electorate.[7] Although the claim that parliament derived from the will of the people (through elections) was a major basis for its claim to becoming responsible for the government in the place of royal authority, the chief executive too can be directly elected by the people, as the American experience discovered. The constitutional writers had little inkling that a two-party system in combination with universal suffrage would convert the indirect selection system of electoral college and Congress into a direct popular election. The Gaullist system in France is directly based upon the American precedent. Thus, elected chief executives can also claim they "represent" the people, and when in conflict with their parliaments, they can appeal directly to the electorate for support against parliament.

The interplay among parliaments, chief executives, and their electorates will provide a major theme for this book. Each is a component of the others' critical environment. For parliaments, the claim to represent the electorate and the assertion that they should participate in the governing process provide the basis and the rationale for their very existence.

---

[7] Inter-Parliamentary Union, *Parliaments: A Comparative Study on the Structure and Functioning of Representative Institutions in Forty-One Countries* (New York: Praeger, 1962), pp. 249–253.

DEFINITION AND ACTIVITIES

Definition

We shall use the term *parliament* as a generic term for all national legislative assemblies, even though the specific names vary greatly: the British Parliament, the American Congress, the German *Bundestag* and *Bundesrat,* the Swedish *Riksdag,* the French National Assembly, the Italian Chamber of Deputies, the Japanese Diet, the Russian Supreme Soviet, the Polish *Sejm,* and so on. The term *parliament* will also include state legislatures and provincial assemblies.

We use the term *parliament* in a generic and inclusive sense because the alternatives either carry national connotations (such as congress) or are too restrictively an implied definition of what these bodies do (such as "legislature"). Further, the term itself partly derives from one of its major activities—the French term *parler,* meaning *to talk.*

Functions

Parliaments have two basic and generic activities: representation and consideration of taxes. They do many other things, too, in great profusion and variation among nations, but these two activities (or "functions") are basic to all parliaments and are among the purposes for which the early parliaments evolved.

Representation is a complex concept, both in logic and in practice. One important component is that parliament has the right to speak for and to commit the whole nation in its deliberations and decisions. Kings summoned the original parliaments to obtain their agreement to a course of action, and especially to raise taxes. But that agreement was worthless to the king unless parliament could agree on behalf of the nation as a whole. Kings have rarely ruled by themselves; they have usually had councillors and advisers in their court. But a parliament had a special quality in that it was larger in size and its members came from some wider segment of society (and geographic areas) than the court itself.[8]

Another original and simultaneous activity of parliaments has been to approve taxes. Although kings have usually had their own sources of revenue, their expanding needs led them to call together those who could furnish additional funds. From these ad hoc gatherings, parliaments evolved. From such a gathering came the Magna Carta, for the power to withhold assent to taxes became the power to scrutinize

[8] Antonio Marongiu, *Medieval Parliaments: A Comparative Study* (London: Eyre & Spottiswoode, 1968), pp. 223–228.

the purposes to which the funds were put and the manner in which the king treated his subjects.[9] The original tax and finance function has been greatly expanded over the centuries into the much broader and now more important activities of considering general questions of public policy.

A third original function of parliaments has been judicial. The assemblies heard petitions from aggrieved persons against the king and his administrators. From this practice, the judiciary has evolved into a separate and complete institution in itself. But to this day, one house of the British Parliament remains the highest judicial court in the land, with the chief justice being a member of the House of Lords. The impeachment power is an example of a residual judicial function remaining with the U.S. Congress.

From these three original functions of parliament, two others have evolved: legislation and control over the executive branch. Legislation is only one function of parliaments; hence, we use *parliament* rather than *legislature* as our generic term. But legislation itself is a very broad activity, and many of the other activities of a parliament are accomplished through this one. Legislation (or an "act" or a law) essentially is a statement of governmental policy on some topic, ranging from agriculture to health through zoos. In practice, a bill as a proposed law may contain many details making it similar to "administration." It can be so vague that most of the operating principles and practices must, by default, be developed in the executive branch as the law is implemented, thereby delegating to the later the lawmaking function of the former. Perhaps we should simply say that parliaments share in the making of law. An even more modest statement is that parliaments are law-effecting bodies. They certainly do not monopolize the "making" of law.[10]

Control of the executive is a continuing and basic activity of parliaments, inhering in both its original taxation and judicial functions. Even if one views contemporary nations as highly complex, industrial, and technological societies, in which the locus of planning and decision making would rest in the expert agencies and with the powerful chief executive, to monitor, to question, and to seek modifications in executive branch activity remains a potentially important function for parliaments in every nation. The extensive exercise of this function depends on the extent and quality of information available to parliament and on the independence with which its members were elected in the first place. As we shall see, both the function of executive branch

---

[9] Ibid., p. 183; Campion, *An Introduction to the Procedures of the House of Commons,* pp. 6–8, 30–36; and Inter-Parliamentary Union, *Parliaments,* pp. 203–210.
[10] Richard Sisson and Leo Snowiss, "Legislative Viability and Political Development," in Smith and Musolf, *Legislatures in Development,* chap. 2, p. 14.

supervision and the acquisition of information are more accomplished through committees than by the whole of parliament itself (Chapter 4).

An associated activity for most, though not all, parliaments is critical: the selection of the chief executive. The "parliamentary system," exemplified by Britain, means that the prime minister is selected by parliament and is a member of parliament. In other systems, the chief executive is selected separately from and remains outside of parliament. But even in the American "separation of powers" system, Congress would select the president in the event of a non-majority result in the electoral college (Chapter 4).

A final function of parliaments is the mobilization of consent from the electorate. Even if parliaments are not independently active in the development of law, and even if they do not extensively supervise the executive branch, they can still help obtain the populace's support for the government and its policies. This function inheres in its selection process. Although representation is usually thought to be a means by which citizen preferences may be expressed to government, the same mechanism selects persons (members of parliament) who are best suited, from the government's point of view, to explain and justify its action to the citizenry. This task has been emphasized in newly independent nations, even if their leaders and single ruling parties have otherwise limited and depreciated the legislative and governing capacities of parliament.[11]

Scope of Activities

The activities of parliaments may be placed in three categories, varying in their breadth of subject matter and importance to the society. At one extreme are questions of detail, which usually concern specific persons and relate to the action of a particular government agency as it affects one citizen or locality. At the other extreme are the broad and major policy issues that face the whole society and set the general policy of the government over a long time span. The intermediate category of parliaments' activity largely concern the means and procedures by which agencies implement already adopted policies.[12]

DETAILED QUESTIONS
Parliaments, and especially their members, are often interested in the detailed implementation of a government policy and seek to modify a given government action in the interests of a constituent. This "case

[11] Newell M. Stultz, "The National Assembly in the Politics of Kenya," in Allan Kornberg and Lloyd D. Musolf (eds.), *Legislatures in Developmental Perspective* (Durham, N.C.: Duke University Press, 1970), pp. 321–323.

[12] This section is based on Blondel, *Comparative Legislatures,* chap. 6, pp. 8–10.

work" function is one of the oldest of legislative activities. It is also found, we suspect, in most parliaments of the world. Even if a parliament is excluded from "policy" questions, the individual members can still act as intermediaries between their constituents and locality on the one hand and government agencies on the other. Parliamentary members have a governmental status and physically travel to the nation's capital, and thus they have far greater opportunity than do ordinary citizens to meet with government agency officials and to intercede with them.

The bulk of such activity probably occurs individually and informally. The individual member contacts government agencies and also meets with affected constituents. But some activity in this respect can also be more formal and occur on the floor during sessions of parliament. The British practice of question time, in particular, is frequently used by members to call attention of the government ministers to local problems. The parliament does not deliberate or act collectively, but the member is able to use floor time to raise such questions publicly and to receive replies. Most parliaments differentiate between government bills and the "private member" bills; the latter are frequently opportunities to propose modifications in government practices that affect a locality or even a specific constituent. Many parliaments enact appropriation bills permitting the government to expand funds for certain purposes. Debates on this type of bill permit an individual member again to raise questions about those policies affecting his or her district.

Committees are another locale for formal legislative activity in which questions can be raised with government officials about any matter, including specific and local ones. In the Soviet Union, for example, locally oriented questions are apparently raised in the committee of the Supreme Soviet that reviews the government's major expenditure plan. The minister presenting the plan to the subsequent meeting of the Supreme Soviet will sometimes acknowledge receiving such questions and will promise that the government will, in the coming year, review the matter brought to its attention. Apparently the questions mainly seek to increase the amount of expenditures going into a local area for a particular purpose.[13]

INTERMEDIATE QUESTIONS
As the second broad category of parliamentary activity, questions of "intermediate" importance center upon the implementation of government policy. The policies are agreed upon; the questions concern how they can best be administered. If interstate highways are to be funded

[13] L. G. Churchward, *Contemporary Soviet Government* (New York: Elsevier, 1968), pp. 122–123.

by the federal government, how shall they be built and where shall they go? If the government has a public health insurance program, how can health care best be provided for a large and diverse population? Interest groups and local governments are mainly interested in this type of question and on most matters deal directly and constantly with the relevant administrative agencies. When, however, the agencies do not provide satisfaction, interest groups and local governments may turn to their legislators for assistance.

The committees of parliament can be the major arena within which such questions are raised and discussed with government officials. In the United States, agency supervision is defined as part of the continuing work assignment of its standing committees. They often hold hearings to review agency activity in fulfilling a previous legislative decision. Such questions can also be raised when a program is up for renewal and extension. Other parliaments have created a few specialized committees to review agency performance, such as the British committees on nationalized industries and on expenditures. Review of the budget, however, is the prime occasion at which parliaments and their committees may raise questions of adequate implementation of existing and already adopted policies.

This type of issue may also be raised on the floor. Question time, discussed previously, may be used for such matters. In addition, both the American and British parliaments provide time when members may address the floor with their concerns. Although not many other members will be present then, the members speaking do place their remarks in the printed journal, and do have an opportunity to attract the attention both of government officials and of the mass media.

The questions both of detail and of implementation provide wide scope within which the individual member can be active. They are matters on which committees and regionally defined groups of members may be interested. They are also usually considered to be matters unaffected by partisan considerations. They are either bipartisan or nonpartisan in character. This definition is particularly important in one-party states; members can raise questions about governmental activity that do not question either the content of the policies or the legitimacy of the government and its party system.

POLICY QUESTIONS

The third general category of legislative activity includes policies, the broad questions of major importance. Although most of the time of individual legislators and of committees may be taken with the first two categories of activities, most national public awareness and mass media reporting—to the extent there are any—concentrate on the major and broad questions of public policy. Both committees and floor sessions can be important arenas of activity in this respect. The official decisions of the parliament are made on the floor and by voting. As we shall note in the next section, the amount of time available for formal floor sessions varies greatly around the world. Committee systems also vary greatly around the world in the time available to them and in the extent of their activity (Chapter 6).

In some countries few questions are brought to the parliament's attention, little time is devoted to their consideration, and the parliament is reduced to an almost pro forma ratification of the government's proposals. At the other extreme, many questions are brought before parliament, it and its committees meet almost continuously, and a substantial proportion of such proposals are either amended or defeated. Indeed, in such parliaments, at least some policy proposals are initiated by parliament itself, not by the government, and are enacted over the government's objections (Chapter 4). Such questions are often defined as partisan and may affect the fate and fortunes of the existing governing cabinet or presidency. It is probably on questions of broad policy that parliaments show their greatest variation around the world.

CONSTRAINTS ON PARLIAMENTS

We can provide several measures of the extent to which it is possible for a parliament to be active. The length of time it meets, the time members have to speak on the floor, the proportion of members who do speak on the floor, and the number of bills introduced all indicate the limitations on parliamentary activity.

Time

Time is one of the important constraints on legislative bodies. Chief executives and administrative agencies ordinarily have a continuous existence throughout the year, and from year to year. The office of prime minister or president must always be occupied, and most countries have a means of rapid succession when such an office becomes vacant.

Parliaments, however, are not necessarily continuous. While they maintain a continuous legal existence (unless abolished by coup or decree), they are not actually in session every day. Even the U.S. Congress, which recently has adopted a schedule covering the entire year, allows for recesses of weeks and sometimes a month's duration. The number of days during which parliaments meet per year are indicated in Table 1.2. For those parliaments for which information is available, the number of meeting days ranges from three for East Germany up to 180 for Canada. The countries with over 50 days of parliamentary meetings annually are mainly Britain and its former colonies, while the countries meeting least frequently are mostly Communist party states.

Table 1.2 FLOOR TIME PER MEMBER AND NUMBER OF DAYS IN ANNUAL SESSION[a]

TIME/ MEMBER (MINUTES)	NUMBER OF DAYS/YEAR			
	LOW 3–18	MEDIUM LOW 25–44	MEDIUM HIGH 54–90	HIGH 100–180
High 140–415		Western Samoa (47) Jamaica (53)	New Zealand (80) Australia (124)	Canada (265) U.K. (630)
Medium high 90–120		Zambia (105)	Kenya (170) Uruguay (99) Chile (147)	U.S. (435)
Medium low 36–65	Yugoslavia (120) Madagascar (107) Singapore (51)	Switzerland (200) Senegal (50)	Venezuela (133) France (485)	
Low 1–7	USSR (750) Poland (460) Hungary (349) East Germany (400)			
N = 22	(7)	(5)	(7)	(3)

SOURCE: Jean Blondel, *Comparative Legislatures* (Englewood Cliffs, N.J.: Prentice-Hall, 1973), p. 59, table 6–1, and pp. 156–157, col. 2.
[a] Number of members stated in parentheses after country name.

Individual members are limited, not only by the number of meeting days, but by the duration of the meetings whenever they do occur, and also by the size of the parliament. These several considerations may be combined into a measure of the amount of floor time available per member, shown in Table 1.2 along the left side. Parliaments vary from a high of 415 minutes per member (New Zealand) to a low of one minute per member (East Germany). Four of the Soviet area parliaments are in the lowest category; they meet only a few days per year, but are all sizable bodies. New Zealand's parliament, by contrast, meets frequently and is, in addition, relatively small. Western Samoa and Jamaica are even smaller, and also rank in the highest category of the amount of floor time available per member.

Time constrains both the legislature as an entity and the member within it. Parliaments that meet infrequently are limited in the extent to which they can supervise the executive. They can hardly supervise the conduct of agencies and the administration of government policy. Nor can they closely review and consider policy proposals from the

Table 1.3 PROPORTION OF MEMBERS PARTICIPATING ON FLOOR BY TIME AVAILABLE PER MEMBER IN ANNUAL SESSION

MEMBERS PARTICI-PATING ON FLOOR (PERCENT)	SESSION TIME PER MEMBER (MINUTES)			
	LOW (1–7)	MEDIUM LOW (35–65)	MEDIUM HIGH (90–120)	HIGH (140–415)
High (90–95%)			Uruguay	Jamaica U.K. Canada Western Samoa
Medium high (77–83%)		Switzerland Zambia France		
Medium low (50–69%)		Singapore Madagascar	Kenya	
Low (8–40%)	USSR East Germany	Yugoslavia		
N = 14	(2)	(6)	(2)	(4)

SOURCE: Jean Blondel, *Comparative Legislatures* (Englewood Cliffs, N.J.: Prentice-Hall, 1973), p. 59, table 6–1, and pp. 156–157, col. 10.

government. Groups of members or whole parties may deeply oppose a government proposal, but the amount of time parliament meets limits the extent to which they can raise objections and require the government to justify itself.

Individual members are likewise limited in what they can do. If they are members of large parliaments that meet infrequently, they are not even likely to obtain access to the floor. Regardless of the merits of the opinions and information held by the members, if they are not recognized by the chair, they will not have an opportunity to express their views on the floor to their colleagues. The limits upon individual members are expressed in Table 1.3 (on the left-hand side) which shows the proportion of members who have participated on the floor, ranging from a low of 8% in East Germany to a high of 95% in Britain, Jamaica, and Canada. This progression generally varies with the amount of time the parliament is in session, calculated as minutes per member (along the top of the same table).[14] Whether floor participation by the individual member is "meaningful" or "important" remains to be seen, but this question can arise only in those parliaments permitting the member access to the floor in the first place. (Notice the discrepancy in the number of countries between Tables 1.2 and 1.3. The difference illustrates the difficulties in acquiring the same information for a variety of national parliaments. Hence, we use

[14] Blondel, *Comparative Legislatures*, pp. 59, 156–157. See also Inter-Parliamentary Union, *Parliaments*, pp. 106–111.

the countries for which we have information, even though their numbers may be small.)

Number of Bills

We have one other indicator of the extent of legislative activity and its variation among the nations of the world: the number of bills introduced. Averaged over a five-year period, the number of bills introduced annually into parliaments is presented in Table 1.4. Covering 39 countries, the lowest number of bills introduced annually has been in the parliaments of several Communist party states, while the largest number have been introduced in the U.S. Congress and the Finnish parliament. The range of 50 to 95 bills is the most common, at least for the countries and in the time included in this particular survey.[15]

From these tables, we can begin to flesh out a notion of the extent of activity by the world's parliaments. They tend to meet for limited periods of time, often measured in days rather than months. Although floor activity is perhaps not the most important type of activity for the individual member (committees could be more important), the members' access to the floor is ordinarily quite limited. And while the significance and sheer bulk and complexity of bills vary enormously, the number of bills introduced annually is another indicator of the relatively limited extent of parliamentary activity. As with floor time per member, the number of bills introduced varies with the number of days the parliament is in formal session. If it meets, it may do little; if it does not meet, it can do nothing.

These bits of data help illustrate the enormous variation among those institutions that bear the same general label of "parliaments." These data also help illustrate the variations in the extent to which parliaments are active and presumably important locales of governmental decision making.

The same broad issue may also be examined through time. Germany and Italy both illustrate the vicissitudes of parliamentary existence. In both nations, dictatorships abolished their parliaments (except for ceremonial occasions) and competitive elections. When the Italian Assembly was created after World War II, a full 73% of its members had never previously served in a parliamentary body. When the German parliament was established after World War I, 63% of its members had no previous experience, and in 1949, when its parliament was reconstituted after World War II, 96% of its members had not previously served in a parliament. In both countries the existence of parliament was episodic, and its members were largely inexperienced.

[15] Valentine Herman and Francoise Mendel, *Parliaments of the World* (Berlin: De Gruyter, 1976), pp. 12–16, 298–312.

Table 1.4 NUMBER OF BILLS INTRODUCED BY NUMBER OF DAYS PER ANNUAL SESSION[a]

NUMBER OF BILLS INTRO- DUCED	NUMBER OF DAYS			
	LOW 3–18	MEDIUM LOW 25–49	MEDIUM HIGH 50–95	HIGH 96–180
300 or more			France (490) Belgium (212) Malaysia (154)	U.S. (435) Finland (200) Sweden (349) Costa Rica (57)
200–299		Austria (183)	New Zealand (87) Netherlands (150)	Canada (264) U.K. (635) Denmark (179)
100–199	Spain (561)		Japan (491) Australia (127)) West Germany (518) Ireland (144) Rep. of Korea (219) South Africa (171)	India (524) Israel (120)
50–99	Rumania (465) Senegal (100)	Zambia (105) Tunisia (112)	Kuwait (62)	
25–49	Cameroon (120) Jordan (60) Monaco (18)	Switzerland (200)	Malta (56) Rep. of Vietnam (159)	
1–24	USSR (767) Poland (460) Hungary (349) East Germany (500) Bulgaria (400)	Czechoslovakia (200)		
N = 39	(11)	(5)	(14)	(9)

SOURCE: Valentine Herman and Francoise Mendel, *Parliaments of the World* (Berlin: De Gruyter, 1976), pp. 12–16, 298–312.
[a] Number of bills introduced is a five-year average. Number in parentheses is number of members of each parliament's lower or popularly elected house.

The British Parliament and the U.S. Congress, by contrast, have had an uninterrupted existence, and each session has usually had a large proportion of experienced members. For Britain the average percentage of newly elected members, during the years 1918–1951, has been 28%; in the United States the average has been 22%. The highest proportion of new members in the British Parliament, 53%, was elected immediately following World War II, while the highest proportion of newcomers in the U.S. Congress was 37%, elected in the depression year of 1932. Thus no country escapes the traumatic impact of war or economic calamity, but some nations, more than others, have been able to maintain their parliaments in continuous existence and to develop a large core of experienced members. In some nations the existence and activity of parliaments is more assured and is presumably a more integral part of their governmental and political practices than in others.[16]

Viewed in the comparative context of the world's parliaments, the U.S. Congress is a unique institution. It has met continuously during the nation's existence. It now meets throughout the year and it is presented with the largest number of bills to consider. It is also one of the most powerful legislative bodies and usually has far greater independence from the chief executive than is found elsewhere. Although we shall concentrate in this book on the U.S. Congress, we shall also attempt to compare it at each point with the information available to us about its counterparts throughout the world.

HOW MANY HOUSES?

The countries of the world divide almost equally between those with unicameral parliaments and those with bicameral, or two-chamber, parliaments (Table 1.5). Bicameral parliaments are more common than unicameral ones in the former British colonies and among Asian nations. The Arab and African nations, and the Communist party states, predominantly have single-chambered parliaments, whereas European nations are more evenly divided between the two types. Within the United States, only Nebraska has a single-chamber state legislature; all the others have two houses, as does the U.S. Congress. The question of the internal construction of the parliament historically has been an important one in the evolution of parliament as a governing institution.

A two-chamber structure is particularly common among federal nations, within which states or provinces have some independent constitutional stature. One house (usually the "upper" house) represents the states in some fashion, while the other (usually the "lower" house), represents the "people" directly. Although the U.S. Senate is now directly elected, its members were, until about World War I, selected by state legislatures. The members of the West German federal chamber, by contrast, are selected by the governments of each state.

[16] Gerhard Loewenberg, "The Institutionalization of Parliament and Public Orientation to the Political System," in Kornberg (ed.), *Legislatures in Comparative Perspective*, pp. 145–147.

Table 1.5 DISTRIBUTION OF UNICAMERAL AND BICAMERAL
PARLIAMENTS AMONG NATIONS

GEOGRAPHIC REGION OR DERIVATION	UNICAMERAL		BICAMERAL	
British-derived nations	Malta New Zealand		Australia Canada South Africa	Britain United States
Europe	Denmark Finland Israel Liechtenstein Monaco	Spain Sweden	Austria Belgium France West Germany Ireland	Italy Netherlands Norway Switzerland
Communist party states	Bulgaria East Germany Hungary North Korea	North Vietnam Poland Rumania	Czechoslovakia USSR Yugoslavia (several chambers)	
Asia	Bangladesh Sri Lanka	Thailand	Fiji India Japan	Malaysia Pakistan South Vietnam
Black Africa	Cameroon Ivory Coast Malawi Senegal	Sierra Leone Zaire Zambia		
Arab and North Africa	Kuwait Syria Tunisia		Jordan	
Latin America	Costa Rica		Argentina Brazil	
Total:	30		26	

SOURCE: Valentine Herman and Francoise Mendel, *Parliaments of the World* (Berlin: De Gruyter, 1976), pp. 12–17.

A very different origin for upper chambers is the European medieval tradition, in which various social classes, or "estates," were separately represented, each in its own chamber. France had five houses and Sweden four, whereas Britain retains a two-chamber parliament.[17]

Upper houses have tended to be changed in keeping with democratic practices. Either their powers have been greatly curtailed (the British Lords, for example), or the upper chambers have been abolished (Sweden now has a single house, for example). In other cases the upper house has retained its equality of powers with the

[17] Inter-Parliamentary Union, *Parliaments*, pp. 3–13; Marongiu, *Medieval Parliaments*, pp. 226–227.

lower house by becoming directly and popularly elected (the U.S. Senate is a major example).

An intermediate solution, for those chambers representing states or provinces, is to provide them with special powers on matters directly affecting the states, but otherwise to reduce their powers compared to those of the lower house. In addition, cabinets and prime ministers are usually selected by and are responsible to the lower, not the upper, house. Another ingredient of this intermediate solution is that the state governments are themselves directly elected.

Among the world's upper houses, the U.S. Senate occupies a unique status. Its members are directly elected, although each state, irrespective of its population size, has the same number (two) of senators. The Senate retains certain powers that are not exercised by the House, especially in the confirmation of presidential appointments and in the ratification of treaties. Furthermore, its members serve six-year staggered terms, while the entire House membership runs for election every two years. That is, only one-third of the Senate membership is elected every two years. Senators have longer terms of office than either their House counterparts or the president.

By and large, we shall examine those houses that are directly elected, those that have the major task in selecting the chief executive, and those that have the major responsibility for legislation. It is primarily in the United States in which these tasks are equally shared between the two chambers. In most other countries the "lower" house is the predominant chamber of the two in these respects.

THE INTERNAL ORGANIZATION OF PARLIAMENTS

Our previous comments in this chapter about members, parties, committees, and floor stage imply that parliaments are not single and undifferentiated entities but, rather, are highly complex in their internal structure. It is necessary to take the dome off the capitol building, as it were, to peer inside to learn how parliament is constituted, how it is organized, and how it functions.

The two major means by which parliaments are organized are parties and committees. Parliament accomplishes its tasks of representation of the electorate and interaction with the chief executive through its component parts. It is mainly through committees and parties that parliament fulfills its functions in relationship to its external environment (Fig. 1.4).

Political parties are unique in that they are usually found in the electorate and are also involved in the selection of the chief executive. That is, parties bridge the gaps among parliaments, executives, and electorates, as well as being an important component of parliaments' internal organization.

But executives are likewise highly differentiated internally. Although a president or prime minister is (usually) just one person, these individuals provide direction to numerous and sizable administrative agencies; furthermore, they usually have their own staff assistants and offices. The agencies, especially, are a functional counterpart to the committees of parliaments.

Electorates are also diverse and variable. While ethnic and socioeconomic class differentiations are usually important in any nation, so is locality and region, particularly over questions of the distribution of government funds, services, and projects.

These elements of the internal organization of parliament, and their links to the major actors in their external environment, are discussed separately in Chapters 5 and 6.

INFORMAL RULES AND EXPECTATIONS

Another aspect of the internal organization of legislative bodies is more informal—the expectations that members have of each other and of themselves, and how they should act toward one another. Most groups, and parliaments are no exception, develop among their participants common understandings that facilitate interaction even when there are disagreements. The informal norms within parliamentary bodies appear to fall within two broad categories: institution oriented, and interpersonal.[18]

The norms that are oriented to the institution prescribe organizational and work performance expectations.[19] "Apprenticeship" is one such norm in the U.S. Congress. Newly elected members are expected to defer to the more experienced members, both in committee and on the floor. As an illustration, members sit on committees in descending order of seniority, and ask questions of witnesses in that order. Newly elected members are expected to speak less on the floor than their more experienced colleagues.

Closely linked to the norm of apprenticeship is that of "specialization." Members are expected to become experts on matters concerning their committees and their districts. To become knowledgeable takes time, thus reinforcing the apprenticeship norm.

Both of these norms have been found in the U.S. Congress, a body of members with long tenure and with a strong committee system. A

[18] The research literature is summarized in Malcolm E. Jewell and Samuel C. Patterson, *The Legislative Process in the United States*, 3d ed. (New York: Random House, 1977), pp. 328–334, which is the source of the distinction between two types of norms.

[19] The norms of apprenticeship and specialization are discussed in Donald R. Matthews, *U.S. Senators and Their World* (New York: Vintage, 1960), pp. 92–97.

very different norm appears to operate within the Canadian Parliament—the expectation that members will follow their party leaders and the decisions of the party caucus.[20] This norm has seldom been encountered in Congress, although it does appear to operate in some state legislatures. In each instance, the informal norm reflects the reality of the way in which the legislative body is organized and functions. Apprenticeship and specialization in the U.S. Congress emphasize the committees, whereas party-oriented norms in the Canadian Parliament shows the importance of party leadership.

Interpersonal norms, found in the U.S. Congress, the state legislatures, and the Canadian Parliament, all emphasize the reduction of overt conflict and hostility among the members.[21] Interpersonal courtesy is one such norm. Members are admonished to speak on the floor with deference and respect to one another: the term *distinguished* may be overworked in the U.S. Senate, but members commonly refer to one another in that fashion. In many parliaments, members do not address one another directly, but only through the Speaker. Floor remarks in Congress begin "Mr. Speaker," while in Sweden, "Herr Talman."

Reciprocity is another interpersonal norm. Members expect of one another that they will cooperate when they can, and support one another on bills and votes on those matters not directly concerning the member's own political interests. This practice is particularly important on district-related legislation and appropriations.

These informal norms appear—insofar as we have research on them—fairly widespread, but they are subject to change. Particularly in the state legislatures, which have a high rate of member turnover, a sizable group of new freshman members can bring with them quite different expectations than characterized the same legislation in the previous session. In the Iowa legislature, for example, norms emphasizing the open expression of conflict replaced other norms existing only two years previously.[22] In the Canadian Parliament, the emphasis on party norms and the expression of conflict had both considerably increased over a six-year period.[23]

In the U.S. Congress, the apprenticeship norm seems to have

[20] Allan Kornberg and William Mishler, *Influence in Parliament: Canada* (Durham, N.C.: Duke University Press, 1976), pp. 75–79.

[21] Jewell and Patterson, *The Legislative Process in the United States*, pp. 340–342; Matthews, *U.S. Senators and Their World*, pp. 97–101; Kornberg and Mishler, *Influence in Parliament: Canada*, pp. 76–77.

[22] Ronald D. Hedlund, "Legislative Norms and Legislative Behavior: Functional Requisite Analysis and State Legislatures," paper read at Midwest Political Science Association, 1973, as reported in Jewell and Patterson, *The Legislative Process in the United States*, pp. 342–343.

[23] Kornberg and Mishler, *Influence in Parliament: Canada*, p. 79.

greatly diminished in the 1970s compared to the 1950s. Freshmen are encouraged to become involved in legislation, to offer amendments and to speak, even on the floor.[24] In part, this change may reflect the considerable increase in subcommittee activity in Congress today compared to even a decade ago.

As political conflict increases, the norms of courtesy and restraint become more important. The Senate majority leader, for example, observed that "one or two members can, when time is running out, resort to obstructionist tactics. . . . ," while a comparatively new senator said of him, "If he wants to play . . . hardball, we can play it too."[25] Perhaps the norms of both apprenticeship and of interpersonal courtesy are under attack in the contemporary U.S. Congress.

Though informal norms may, and do, change, their very existence is an indication that legislative bodies are more than a random collection of individuals who happen to be members. Those individuals who do become members enter an ongoing and complex network of organizations, practices and interactions. Much of this book is devoted to an examination of that inner life of parliaments.

ORGANIZATION OF THIS BOOK

All of the activities of parliament are interrelated. All of its activities have the potential of simultaneously affecting the other participants in its nation's politics. Thus, any plan of organization of a book on parliaments and congresses is likely to be artificial, in that it makes distinctions among activities which are simultaneous.

We shall begin with the selection process: the systems of election, nomination, and recruitment that designate a small number of citizens to represent and enact policy for the nation as a whole (Chapter 2). We shall then consider the background experiences of parliamentary members and the views they hold of their tasks in parliament (Chapter 3) as representatives of the electorate.

Although these two chapters are concerned mainly with the relationship of parliament to one of the critical components of its environment, the electorate, Chapter 4 considers parliament's relationship to the chief executive as the other critical component of its political environment.

We then turn to the two major ways in which parliaments and congresses organize their members and their work—by parties (Chap-

---

[24] David W. Rhode, Norman J. Ornstein, and Robert L. Peabody, "Political Change and Legislative Norms in the United States Senate," paper read at American Political Science Association, 1974, as reported in Jewell and Patterson, *The Legislative Process in the United States,* p. 333.

[25] *Congressional Quarterly Weekly Report,* September 2, 1978, pp. 2308–2309.

ter 5) and by committee (Chapter 6). While political parties are fairly inclusive and generalized means of relating to both the electorate and chief executive, committees are more specialized means of attaining similar objectives.

In many respects the work (and the very existence) of parliaments as a distinctive governmental body is symbolized by its floor meetings. Parties and committees are ways of organizing the members on the floor and are also arenas in which activity takes place prior to floor stage. It is at floor stage, however, that the authoritative decisions of parliaments are made through the act of voting (Chapter 7).

Finally, in Chapter 8, we shall reexamine parliaments in relationship to the components of their critical environment and try to put back together in a single, multifaceted entity what the previous portions of this book have taken apart as separate components.

Chapter 2
The Elective
Process

Parliaments and elections largely occur together. Most parliaments are elected; most elective offices in a government are legislative. Even though chief executives are elective in many nations, there usually is only one president or governor or mayor. There are, however, many members of congresses, state legislatures, and city councils. Although the oldest of our surviving parliaments—the British Parliament and the Swedish Riksdag—began as elite institutions, today they and most parliamentary bodies are elective. While many parliaments were in the past elected from narrow segments of a population, today the electorates for most parliaments include the entire adult population.

The frequent coups that abolish parliaments also abolish political parties and elections. When parliaments are restored, so are parties and elections. Within the past decade we have witnessed the restoration of parliaments and elections in Greece, and the creation anew of a whole parliamentary and electoral system in both Portugal and Spain to replace their former dictatorships. In the case of Spain, we have seen the old appointed *Cortes* actually vote to abolish and replace itself with an elected parliament and to authorize the creation of political parties to manage the electoral process.

Not all parliaments, and not all members of any one parliament, are necessarily chosen by election. Spain's Cortes, for example, was mostly appointed during the Franco regime. Some newly independent countries also place some appointed members in parliaments which are mostly otherwise elected (Tanzania). Surviving colonial-style nations, such as Rhodesia and South Africa, have appointed a small number of black Africans to represent their numerically superior populations within parliament, to which the much more numerous white members are elected by the much smaller white electorate.[1]

Some upper chambers, whose powers are now greatly reduced, contain hereditary members or members who are appointed as an honor. The British House of Lords, until World War II, was entirely the former; it now contains both hereditary and appointed members. The Canadian Senate is entirely the latter. Other upper chambers are indirectly elected, as was the U.S. Senate until World War I. That is, the members are chosen by some other body which itself is directly elected. In the former U.S. Senate case, the elective state legislatures selected members to the Senate. In West Germany, the provincial governments select members of the *Bundesrat*, the upper house in the national parliament.

Indirect elections have also been employed in the selection of parliaments when political elites judged their populations and political institutions too fragile and immature for a direct election system. The Turkish parliament, for example, was indirectly elected while a Westernized elite attempted to graft European democratic practices onto an agricultural and illiterate populace in the 1920s and 1930s. Direct elections were not instituted until 1945. Paralleling this change, the ruling single party permitted the formation of political oppositions, leading to the development of a two-party system.[2]

Since most parliaments, and most members of parliaments, are today directly elected, this and the following chapter will concentrate on those direct elections. We shall employ two organizing principles in this discussion of parliamentary elections. The first concerns the relationship, to be further elaborated in the chapter on chief executives, between the election to parliament and the selection method of the chief executive. In one pattern (a "parliamentary" system), the chief executive (termed *prime minister* or *premier* or *chancellor*) is elected by and through parliament. In the other pattern (a "presi-

[1] Kenneth A. Heard, *General Elections in South Africa, 1943–1970* (New York: Oxford, 1974).

[2] A. J. Milnor, *Elections and Political Stability* (Boston: Little, Brown, 1969), pp. 127–134; Dankwart A. Rustow, "The Development of Parties in Turkey," in Joseph LaPalombara and Myron Weiner (eds.), *Political Parties and Political Development* (Princeton, N.J.: Princeton University Press, 1966), p. 122.

dential" system), the chief executive (termed *president*) is directly elected by the same populace as elects the members of parliament or congress. The British and German systems exemplify the first pattern, while the United States and France the second. In the first, election of parliament is simultaneously the selection of the prime minister; voting for the one is a single act of selecting the other. The second set of nations have a dual election system: the election for president is separate from the election to congress. In France, the elections to the two offices are held at different times. In the United States, the elections to the two offices are held at the same time (once every four years), but the voter casts two separate votes for the two offices.

The second organizing principle used in our discussion of elections concerns the electoral cycle. Elections consist of a sequence of steps, culminating in the general election. A prior step in preparing for the general election is the decision, termed *nomination,* by the parties of those who will be the candidates in the coming general election. In most countries this decision is made by party leaders, whereas in the United States it is most often made through primary elections. An even earlier stage in the electoral cycle is termed "candidate recruitment," the process by which persons decide to become candidates in the first place. This earlier step can take a period of years or be squeezed into a day or less. The general election itself is usually for a short period— of months or even weeks. The nomination period takes longer, and in the United States, the primary elections stretch out, among the states, over the better part of a year.

We shall first look at different kinds of election systems used throughout the world to establish the context and the ground rules within which each country's elections and campaigns are conducted. We will then consider American congressional campaigns, and especially the activities of political parties in those campaigns. We can then compare elections abroad with the American ones. Since most of the comparisons will concern general elections, the succeeding sections of this chapter will consider nominations and the candidate recruitment process. We shall also take a brief look at what little is known about campaign finance as a basic resource in election campaigns. Finally, we shall consider the extent to which elections and nominations are competitive. It is through competition, presumably, that representation is best assured.

COMPONENTS OF THE ELECTION SYSTEM

Models of Election Systems

Three components help define the formal rules of an election system: the district system, the party system, and the voting method.

Table 2.1 THREE MODELS OF DISTRICT, PARTY, AND
VOTING SYSTEMS

COMPONENTS	BRITISH U.S. MODEL	EUROPEAN CONTINENTAL MODEL	SOVIET MODEL
District	Single-member	Multimember	Single-member
Party	Two	Multi	One
Voting method	Plurality	Proportional	Majority

The district system refers to the number of representatives elected from any one district, the two major types being the single-member district (as for the British Commons and the U.S. House of Representatives), and the multimember district (as in Sweden and Italy).

The party system refers to the number of parties, of which the major conventional categories are one (USSR), two (U.S.) and multiparty (France) systems.

The voting method refers to the rules by which votes are cast and by which they are counted to ascertain the winners. The major categories are plurality (U.S. and Britain), majority (Soviet Union and France), and proportional representation (most of continental Europe).

These components tend to be interrelated as indicated in Table 2.1. The British model combines single-member districts and plurality voting with a two-party system, as do most of its former colonies, including the United States. The continental European model combines a multiparty system with proportional representation and multiple-member districts. Italy and the Scandinavian countries best illustrate this model in the 1970s, although its origins are French. The Russian model combines single-member districts with a majority vote counting method and a single slate of candidates endorsed by a single or at least dominant party.

The plurality system is the original vote method used at the time the United States and European nations became democratic. (They also tended to use multimember districts.) Those nations, such as the United States and the British Commonwealth countries, that developed a two-party system have retained the plurality voting system but have evolved single-member districts. The European nations, mostly developing a multiparty system, then switched to various forms of proportional representation and increased the number of seats allocated to their multimember districts.[3]

Although there are many combinations among these electoral elements in the world's nations, the three contrasting models are very different ways of organizing political life, both for the voter and for the members of parliament. In the British-U.S. model, a party candidate

[3] Leon D. Epstein, *Political Parties in Western Democracies* (New York: Praeger, 1967), pp. 38–39.

runs in a relatively small district against only a few other candidates of the few other parties. Each participating party may nominate a single candidate in that district. The coincidence of having two major parties in a single-member district means that usually only two major candidates run, and the winner automatically obtains a majority of the votes cast. If there are more than two candidates, however (minor and local splinter parties), the winner is decided by plurality; that is, the candidate with the most votes wins, whether or not he or she has obtained a majority of all votes cast.

There is considerable variation in size of the districts in this system, but they are small relative to what they would be in a multiple-member system. Although the British district has an average of about 50,000 voters, the U.S. district averages 500,000 population, and in India the figure is 800,000. The population size of the British parliamentary district more matches that of districts in American state legislatures than the U.S. Congress. Britain has a larger House than the United States, but a much smaller population. Thus, size of district varies greatly among nations.

In the continental model, a relatively larger district has not one but some number of seats filled at large within it. There are fewer, but larger, districts than in the previous system. In the newly constituted Portuguese Assembly of the Republic, for example, the 263 seats are allocated among 24 districts, on the basis of one seat for every 25,000 registered voters.[4]

Each party can nominate as many candidates within a multi-member district as there are seats to be filled. Typically, three or more parties contest the elections. Sweden, for example, has five parties, and Denmark ten, while Israel has 13 parties in parliament and the Netherlands 12. How then do the parties organize the ballots from which the voters make their selections? Although there are many variations in detail, voters typically select among alternative party lists. The voter usually votes for the entire slate of candidates for a single party rather than voting for some candidates of one party and other candidates from other parties.

This election method is termed *proportional* because of the way in which the votes are counted. In principle, the number of a party's candidates elected from a district should match its proportion of the votes received in that district. Hence, in a ten-member district for example, if a party received 30% of the votes, three of the ten seats would be won by its candidates. In the contrasting single-member plurality system, if only two major parties had candidates, the 30% vote candidate would lose. In the multiple-member proportional

[4] Walter Opello, "The New Parliament in Portugal," *Legislative Studies Quarterly* 3 (May 1978), p. 311.

system, however, 30% is a sizable share of the vote if there are several parties, and such a party would have at least some of its candidates elected.

The Soviet Union resembles the U.S.-British model in that it uses single-member districts. The winner is decided by majority. The dynamics of the system, however, are completely different because of the single-party system. Ordinarily, a single candidate is on the ballot. Whether that candidate is declared a winner by a plurality or a majority makes little difference. Presumably, the ballot format makes little difference too, but it is organized—or so it seems to Western observers—to minimize the possibility of a vote being cast against the single candidate. That is, a voter who wishes to vote against that candidate must retire to a curtained booth and draw a line through the name printed on the ballot. If, however, the voter does not wish to register that dissent, he simply takes the ballot, and in public view, folds it, and deposits it in the ballot box. In some Eastern European nations, which formally have several parties, a single slate of candidates is nominated through the "front," which combines them all under the leadership of the ruling Communist party (which has a variety of names, differing among the countries).

Variations

Many variations exist on these three models. West Germany, for example, combines the U.S. and continental methods. Half of its lower house, the *Bundestag*, is elected from single-member districts using the plurality vote method, while the other half is elected from multi-member larger districts, using the proportional method of counting the vote. France has experimented with both methods at various times. It has also employed a majority vote method with single member districts in a multiparty system. When several French parties contest for a single seat, the plurality candidate may have a rather low vote— say 20%. To eliminate the possibility of that low proportion of the vote deciding the winner, a runoff election is held a week later in the district among the top candidates to decide the winner. In the 1958 elections, only 83 districts had two-candidate runoffs, while 240 had three candidates, and another 91 districts even had four candidates. By 1968, however, the proportions had shifted, with the bulk of runoffs occurring with only two candidates.[5] For those district runoff elections confined to two candidates, the plurality vote between them is actually a majority. The French runoff provision is very similar to that used in American southern state primaries.

[5] Howard Rosenthal and Subrata Sen, "Spatial Voting Models for the French Fifth Republic," *American Political Science Review* 71 (December 1977), p. 1460, table 13.

Most of the third-world countries have single parties. Some of them have attempted to introduce competition into their elections by having two or more candidates run for a single seat, all of whom are nominated by the dominant party. Kenya, as the leading example, emulated the Yugoslavs, who first developed that practice. Presumably, both or all of the candidates are equally acceptable to the regime. The candidates do not attack either the government or the ruling party. Rather, they compete either in asserting their loyalty to and effectiveness on behalf of the dominant party, or they claim effectiveness in defending local interests in the national government.[6]

There is also variation and experimentation among the East European nations, which we can illustrate with Poland. In form, at least, it more resembles the European continental model than the Soviet Union's electoral system. Poland's 460 seats in the *Sejm* are allocated among 80 districts proportional to their population. The districts mainly correspond to provinces, though the more populous ones are subdivided.

Beginning with the 1956 elections, more candidates must be nominated than there are parliamentary seats to be filled within each district. The nominated candidates are placed on a single list by the Front of National Unity which is a coalition of three parties under the leadership of the Polish United Workers Party. The voter receives a ballot card, on which the names of the nominated candidates appear. The voter votes for candidates by crossing out the names of candidates for whom he does not wish to vote. The winning candidates must receive a majority, among whom the highest vote winners obtain the available seats. A further requirement is that voter turnout must be over 50% for the election to be valid.

The 1976 Polish election revision provided for more voter secrecy than previously. Voters can cross out candidate names in a curtained booth, place their ballot card in an envelope (a common European procedure), and then drop the envelope publicly in a ballot box.[7] Previously, when only as many candidates were nominated as seats, to step behind a curtain or to make any mark at all on the ballot was a highly visible act. We do not know how many persons actually use the curtained booths to cross out candidate names. If no names are crossed out, the ballot is counted as being cast for the top listed candidates. Further, the candidates are listed on the ballot in the order preferred by the Front of National Unity.

[6] Raymond F. Hopkins, "The Kenyan Legislature: Political Functions and Citizen Perceptions," in G. R. Boynton and Chong L. Kim (eds.), *Legislative Systems in Developing Countries* (Durham, N.C.: Duke University Press, 1975), p. 216.
[7] Polish Interpress Agency, "Polish Parliamentary and Local Government Elections," Warsaw, February 1976 (mimeo), pp. 1–8.

It is possible, in this type of system, at least, for the relative vote standings among the candidates to change from the order in which they were placed on the ballot. In the 1961 election the prime minister received only the second highest number of votes in his district, even though he headed the ballot list. In another district the head of an independent nonparty parliamentary group received the highest number of votes, although he was placed fourth on the list. The lowest percentage received by any elected deputy was 88%, but that meant that some 37,000 voters actually had crossed out his name from their ballot.[8]

During the brief 1968 political "thaw" in Czechoslovakia, one of the reform proposals suggested the creation of two parties, both of which would have been communist, as a means of introducing a greater range of choice to the electorate. To the extent that one can judge public opinion in a chaotic time, the public-opinion polls showed considerable support for the proposition that the political parties should be equal, and low approval of their current practice of having a single slate of candidates.[9]

Additional variations are found in elections to American state legislatures. While most now have at least some degree of two-party competition, many have been dominated effectively by a single party. The greater difference among the states now lies in their district system and vote-counting methods. Almost 42% of the members of the lower house are elected from multimember districts, while about 18% of the state senators are.[10]

Although the more common single-member districts use the plurality method of counting votes, the multimember districts have several variations. In one common variation, called the general at-large system, the highest vote getters win; if, for example, a district has seven seats, the seven candidates with the seven highest vote totals would win the seven offices. In the other major variation, called the place system, each seat is numbered. Each candidate runs for one specific seat, or place. Rather than running generally for any of the seven seats, the candidate runs only for one of those specific seats. Each seat, or place, thus becomes a single-member district for vote-counting purposes, although each seat shares exactly the same electorate. The closest parallel is found in the U.S. Senate, in which each state has two seats.

[8] Hansjakob Stehle, *The Independent Satellite* (New York: Praeger, 1965), pp. 183–187.
[9] Otto Ulc, "Political Participation in Czechoslovakia," *Journal of Politics* 33 (May 1971), pp. 422–447.
[10] Samuel C. Patterson, "American State Legislatures and Public Policy," in Herbert Jacob and Kenneth N. Vines (ed.), *Politics in the American States*, 3d ed. (Boston: Little, Brown, 1976), p. 152, table 2.

One practical consequence of the two different systems is that, in the first, all candidates run against each other, thus limiting the extent to which the nominees of a single party are likely to campaign with each other cooperatively as a party ticket. In the second system, however, candidates could more easily form a party-wide campaign, for each would be competing, not against each other, but only against candidates of other parties who had filed for a specific seat.[11]

The Japanese Diet is elected by a system that is almost unique but is similar to some American state legislatures in that it employs multi-member districts. Although each district elects three to five members, each voter can only vote for one candidate. The candidates receiving the highest numbers of votes win, again being similar to general at-large state legislative systems. The requirement, however, that each voter votes for only one candidate completely alters the total number of votes cast and greatly affects the campaign strategy of the parties. This system pits not only one party against the others but each candidate against all other candidates, including those of his own party. Within the largest party, the Liberal Democrats, the several factions compete against each other in an effort to gain the most votes—and not to merely win a seat but to be elected as "number one." One observer commented that this election system "seems to have been peculiarly well designed to drive campaign managers and their candidates to distraction and despair, and which is exceptionally well-suited to exacerbating intra-party strife."[12]

Election System Consequences

THE DISTORTION EFFECT

At least one purpose of elections is to achieve "representation." Presumably elections select officials who portray in office the views and perhaps characteristics of the electors. However one may more precisely define the concept of representation, elections are not a perfectly neutral means of achieving that goal. The methods used to conduct the election, especially the vote-counting methods and the district system, have a distortion effect: The distribution of seats among parties in parliament is not precisely the same as is the distribution of the votes among those parties in elections. That is, every voting and seat allocation system distorts the vote to some degree. The most consistent effect has been to increase the share of parliamentary seats of

[11] Malcolm E. Jewell and David M. Olson, *American State Political Parties and Elections* (Homewood, Ill.: Dorsey, 1978), pp. 179–180; Lester G. Seligman, et al., *Patterns of Recruitment* (Chicago: Rand McNally, 1974), pp. 46–50.

[12] Hans H. Baerwald, *Japan's Parliament* (New York: Cambridge, 1974), pp. 54–57. The quote is on p. 54.

the largest party over its share of the votes cast in the election. In this respect, election systems tend to increase the likelihood of governmental stability by increasing the strength of the largest party (perhaps in coalition with others) in parliament.[13]

Considerable mathematical ingenuity has been devoted to the creation of vote-counting formulas that would reduce the amount of electoral distortion. All electoral systems create some distortion; they differ only in the amount of that distortion. Proportional systems, usually in combination with multimember districts, better project into parliament the ratios in the election than do plurality and single-member systems.[14]

The precise distortion effects, however, vary with the number of parties and also with their geographic distribution. The difficulty with a single-member plurality system in combination with two parties is that a 49% minority party, evenly distributed throughout a nation, would not win a single seat. If, however, that minority were concentrated in some regions, it would constitute the majority within those regions, and, depending upon the regional allocation of seats, could approach a 49% share of parliamentary seats.

Within single-member plurality systems, of which the United States and Great Britain are the main examples, the party winning a plurality of the popular vote has almost invariably won a majority of parliamentary seats. In the United States, with only two national parties, this result has meant an artificial diminution of the losing party's share.[15] In Great Britain, having a third party (Liberals) competing nationally and several regional parties as well, the result has been to increase the seat share of two major parties at the expense of all of the minor parties.[16]

The extent of the distortion effect is measured in Tables 2.2 and 2.3 for the United States and Great Britain, respectively. In both countries, the largest party has obtained 4% to 12% of additional

[13] Three different models to measure the extent of the seat-vote distortion in single-member and two-party systems are tested in Edward R. Tufte, "The Relationship Between Seats and Votes in Two-Party Systems," *American Political Science Review* 67 (June 1973), pp. 540–554.

[14] To compensate for vote distortions, the Swedish election system adopted in the early 1970s provided that only 310 of the 349 seats would be elected from districts, which themselves were large multimember ones. The remaining 39 seats would be allocated to the parties on the basis of their nationwide votes, to more precisely allocate the Riksdag seats in the same ratio as the national votes were cast.

[15] Similar effects in the two-party state legislatures are measured in Patterson, "American State Legislatures and Public Policy," pp. 153–155.

[16] Exceptions in recent British elections, however, include the Conservatives in 1951 and the Labour party in 1974. See John E. Schwarz and L. Earl Shaw, *The United States Congress in Comparative Perspective* (Hinsdale, Ill.: Dryden, 1976), p. 67.

Table 2.2 DISTORTION EFFECTS IN SINGLE-MEMBER
DISTRICT SYSTEMS: U.S. HOUSE 1968–1976

ELECTION YEAR	PARTY	VOTE (%)	SEATS (%)	VOTE-SEAT DIFFERENCE
1968	Dem	50.0	55.9	+ 5.9
	Rep	48.2	44.1	− 4.1
1970	Dem	53.4	58.6	+ 5.2
	Rep	45.0	41.4	− 3.6
1972	Dem	51.7	55.9	+ 4.2
	Rep	46.4	44.1	− 2.3
1974	Dem	57.6	66.8	+ 9.2
	Rep	40.6	33.3	− 7.3
1976	Dem	56.2	67.1	+10.9
	Rep	42.1	32.8	− 9.3

SOURCE: U.S. Bureau of the Census, *Statistical Abstract of the U.S.:
1974*, 95th ed.; *Congressional Quarterly Weekly Report* (March 19,
1977), p. 489.

seats over and beyond its share of the popular vote. The impact of the
vote-counting method on British parties is further illustrated in Table
2.4, which shows the hypothetical distribution of seats among the
parties in a recent election assuming the results had been allocated

Table 2.3 DISTORTION EFFECTS IN SINGLE MEMBER DISTRICT
SYSTEMS: BRITISH HOUSE OF COMMONS, 1970–1974

ELECTION YEAR	PARTY	VOTE (%)	SEATS N	SEATS (%)	VOTE-SEAT DIFFERENCE IN PERCENTAGE POINTS
1970	Conservative	46.4	330	52	+ 6
	Labour	43.0	288	46	+ 3
	Liberal	7.5	6	1	− 6
	Other	3.1	6	1	− 2
			630	100	
Feb. 1974	Conservative	37.8	297	47	+ 9
	Labour	37.1	301	47	+10
	Liberal	19.3	14	2	−17
	Other	5.8	23	4	− 2
			635	100	
Oct. 1974	Conservative	35.8	277	44	+12
	Labour	39.2	319	50	+11
	Liberal	18.3	13	2	−16
	Other	6.7	26	4	− 1
			635	100	

SOURCE: David Butler and Dennis Kavanagh, *The British General Election of
October 1974* (New York: St. Martin's, 1975), pp. 293–294.

Table 2.4 HYPOTHETICAL DISTRIBUTION OF BRITISH PARLIAMENTARY SEATS BY PROPORTIONAL REPRESENTATION COMPARED TO PLURALITY METHOD: ELECTION OF OCTOBER 1974

PARTY	PROPORTIONAL REPRESENTATION (HYPOTHETICAL)		PLURALITY (ACTUAL)		INDEX OF DIFFERENCE
	N	%	N	%	
Labour	254	40.8	319	51.2	+10.4
Conservative	232	37.2	277	44.5	+ 7.3
Liberal	118	18.9	13	2.1	−16.8
Scottish National	17	2.7	11	1.8	− 0.9
Plaid Cymru	2	0.3	3	0.5	+ 0.2
Total	623	99.9	623	100.1	

SOURCE: David Butler and Dennis Kavanagh, *The British General Election of October 1974* (New York: St. Martin's, 1975), p. 355, Table 15.

by proportional representation rather than by the plurality method. Although Labour would still have been the largest party, it would have lost its majority, and the difference between it and its nearest rival would have lessened. The Liberal party would have been affected the most. As the third largest party, which contests seats in most areas of the country, it is hurt the most by the existing plurality single-member system.

France has employed a different vote-counting method with single-member districts, and has, perhaps as an intended result, obtained somewhat different distortion effects. It employs a runoff system, or second election, if no candidate has won a majority in the first election. The result has been to increase the plurality party's share of assembly seats to a majority. That effect is similar to the British and American cases, but the percentage increase has been much greater in France. While the increase in percentage share of seats over votes has, in the former set of countries, rarely gone over 12 points, the rate of increase has usually been greater—up to 20 points—in France. A second difference is that a sizable party, by no means the smallest, has been greatly penalized—namely, the Communist party. Although it usually obtains no more than 10% of the seats, it has usually won no less than 20% of the vote.[17]

The location and allocation of district boundaries are neutral neither in intent nor in effect. The fine art of drawing district lines has been characterized by an ancient American contribution to political vo-

[17] Ibid., p. 68. For a discussion of France, see B. Criddle, "Distorted Representation in France," *Parliamentary Affairs* 28 (Spring 1975), pp. 154–179. The still different election system of Mexico has had a similar effect of limiting the number of seats won by the largest opposition party; see D. J. Mabry, "Mexico's Party Deputy System: The First Decade," *Journal of Inter-American Studies of World Affairs* 16 (May 1974), pp. 221–233.

cabulary: the *gerrymander*. There are two related problems in the placement of district boundaries. One concerns the precise location of the boundaries to provide advantage to one party (or faction or candidate or ethnic group) or another. The other, which is much more amenable to remedial action, concerns the distribution of districts so that they are of approximately equal population size. A fairly common practice among nations is to have higher populations within urban districts and lower numbers of persons within rural districts, thereby overrepresenting the rural populations to the disadvantage of the urban. This effect is more easily attained (or less easily avoided) within single-member districts than with multimember districts, and thus reinforces the greater partisan distortion effect of the former compared with the latter type of district.

Extensive urban-rural disparities were not eliminated in the United States until the mid-1960s. This action did not occur through legislation but through the courts. Population inequalities were judged incompatible with the constitutional requirement of equal protection of the laws. The "one man, one vote" principle led to extensive redistricting through the later 1960s for the U.S. House and for both houses of most state legislatures.[18] In the 1970s congressional redistricting plans have been challenged in, and overturned by, the courts in California, Texas, New York, and Tennessee.[19]

STABILITY AND FRAGMENTATION

The most general statement of the different effects of plurality and proportional election systems is that the former more leads to governmental stability while the latter provides representation in parliament for a larger number of parties. Plurality systems tend to produce in parliament a single majority party, whereas proportional systems lead to fragmentation within parliament among several parties. These presumed "effects" are at best statistical associations, and they indicate that the two conditions tend to occur together.

Proportional representation, however, has different effects. The purpose of this system is to reflect in the composition of the legislature the political forces of a society. This system is typically employed in nations that have three or more parties; each party can hope to achieve some degree of representation in parliament in rough proportion to its share of the vote in the electorate. One effect of proportional repre-

---

[18] The basic Supreme Court cases are: *Wesberry* v. *Sanders,* 376 U.S. 1 (1964) on congressional districting, and *Baker* v. *Carr,* 369 U.S. 186 (1962) on state legislative districting.

[19] For a discussion of the proincumbent and pro-Democratic impacts of American congressional redistricting, see Tufte, "The Relationship Between Seats and Votes," pp. 549–554.

sentation is to make less likely the emergence of a majority party in parliament. As a result, the government cabinet is either a minority or a coalition formed among two or more parties. A second effect is to splinter the opposition. To form a coalition among them is even more difficult than to form the governing coalition. The governing coalition usually is formed with a large, perhaps the largest, party as its nucleus; seldom is another large party also created in proportional representation systems.

Electoral and district systems tend to stabilize the party system existing at the time the given voting and district systems were instituted. Or so we assume. Yet we have many examples of changes in contemporary governments. West Germany is an example of a nation that had several parties in the 1950s, but by the 1970s had developed largely a two-party system. The Scandinavian countries, in the 1930–1960 period, had each developed strong tendencies toward a two-coalition system among their many parties. Even France has shown a tendency for a general left-right formation in elections and in the General Assembly. Italy is perhaps the most spectacular example of two major parties (Christian Democrats and Communists) developing out of a multiparty system using proportional representation in multi-member districts. Examples can be cited of changes in the opposite direction—of fragmentation rather than coalition. Great Britain has seen, in the 1960s and 1970s, the growth of regional parties in Scotland and Wales, while the long-term "third" party (the Liberals) continues to contest and win seats in Parliament.[20]

DISTRICT RELATIONSHIPS

Another potential difference among the election systems is that an elected representative from a single and relatively small district can have "closer" relationships with his or her electorate than can several representatives from a relatively larger one. The citizens of a single district have only one congressman to deal with, so their efforts to communicate with an elected representative are concentrated upon that one person. The elected official in turn can concentrate his attention upon a smaller number of persons than in a larger district, has a smaller geographic area to travel within, and can be more localized in his efforts. Perhaps elected representatives from the smaller single-member districts more engage in "casework" services than do those from the larger and multimember districts, and give relatively more

[20] Studies of extensive and rapid changes in vote and seat distributions in the 1970s include Great Britain and Denmark. See Hugh Berrington and T. Bedeman, "The February Election," *Parliamentary Affairs* 27 (Autumn 1974), pp. 317–332, and Ole Borre, "Denmark's Protest Election of December, 1973," *Scandinavian Political Studies* 9 (1974), pp. 197–402.

attention to the questions of details, discussed in the first chapter, than do those from the multimember districts.

MODERATION VS. EMPHASIS OF DIFFERENCES

Presumably the plurality method in a two-party system leads both parties toward the moderate center. Both parties would appeal to a majority of the voters. Within a complex society, the majority is usually fashioned from diverse (or at least generalized) appeals to a diverse population. The presumed result is policy moderation and generalized agreement between both major parties.[21] The presumed result in a multiparty system, however, is an emphasis upon differences, not upon commonalities. Each party would appeal to its distinctive electoral segment by emphasizing its distinctiveness from, and disagreements with, other segments of the society and their respective supporting political parties.

There are at least two difficulties in the real world with this presumed set of consequences. First, as we noted immediately above, we have seen a tendency toward a two-coalition formation in nations with many parties and proportional representation. The parties begin to moderate their positions to appeal to a wider segment of the electorate.

The second difficulty is found within the two-party and single-member district nations. The presumed moderating effect depends upon some degree of nationwide dispersal of the major population segments. If important political groups are regionally concentrated, appeals to different local majorities could result in a polarized parliament. If the nation is ethnically bifurcated, each party could be supported by a different ethnic group, with the election campaigns having the effect of deepening, rather than bridging, the social divisions of the population.[22]

We have discussed three components of the legislative election system: districts, parties, and vote-counting methods. Although these three components tend to exist together in certain types, the world's nations experiment endlessly, and so do the American states. All election systems distort the very phenomenon they have been invented to measure, usually increasing the largest parties' share of seats over their share of the vote. While electoral systems tend to stabilize any given party configuration, we have seen dramatic examples of change, both toward a two-party or two-coalition system out of a multiparty system in multimember districts using proportional representation, or

---

[21] A. J. Milnor, *Elections and Political Stability*. Boston: Little, Brown, 1969, pp. 36–38.

[22] Ibid., pp. 37, 102, and R. R. Premdas, "Competitive Party Organizations and Political Integration in a Racially Fragmented State: The Case of Guyana," *Caribbean Studies* 12 (January 1973), pp. 5–35.

the reverse, toward party fragmentation from a two-party system in single-member districts using a plurality vote-counting method.

It is within the context of the electoral system that parties enter and contest any given election campaign, and within which they nominate candidates. We now turn to these two topics, and in that order.

AMERICAN CONGRESSIONAL ELECTIONS

Congressional elections are unique within the American political system. Like the presidential office, Congress is a national institution, and elections are held throughout the country. Unlike the presidential election, however, there are 435 separate seats to be filled in as many different and separate congressional districts. There are, in effect, 435 different elections with 870 major party candidates, assuming each of the two major parties has candidates in each district. In addition, numerous candidates may also have run in the primaries of each party in each congressional district.

Elections to the U.S. Senate, like those to the House, involve separate electorates holding separate elections among different candidates. Only one-third of the Senate seats usually are up for election, however, in any one election year. Thus, the House provides the only office filled throughout the United States every two years.

Election campaigns are a search for votes. The conditions of the vote search vary with the circumstances discussed in the previous section and also with characteristics of each congressional district. Among the most important of those varying district characteristics is the political party. How it is organized, what it is able to do, and the assets and resources it is able to utilize in campaigns provide one of the major background circumstances for the conduct of election campaigns. Candidates tend to adapt their campaigns to the abilities and assets of the political party in their particular district.

From the perspective of the candidate, the political party is a fixed characteristic with which he must contend in an election campaign. He judges the party within his congressional district on a pragmatic and utilitarian basis: What can it do for me? Party leaders look at the congressional candidates in the same way: What can he do for us? From the perspective of the candidate, the assets and liabilities of his district party is a given long-term factor, which he must accept and work within just as much as the population and location of the district are constant, or at least long-range, factors. From the perspective of party leaders, candidates change and are changeable. The identity and personality of candidates are short-range factors. When, however, the candidate wins, he then becomes an incumbent. His own assets thereby presumably increase, and if he stays in office very long, his possession of the congressional seat becomes one of the long-range factors to which other candidates and the district party leaders must accommodate.

Unfortunately for our purposes, we have no accepted or generally used way of measuring the attributes of political parties within localities and districts. Neither do we know how different types of political parties are distributed across the United States. We do generally assume that parties are less well organized and important than formerly, and that candidates increasingly conduct independent campaigns, using mass media and personal organization as means of bypassing the party and of directly reaching the electorate. We do not, however, have adequate measures of parties and campaigns throughout the United States today, much less for some previous time.

The relationships between congressmen and their parties in elections vary among the states, and among districts within the same state. At one extreme, congressmen rely extensively upon their parties at election time, in both the nomination stage and in general elections. In one national sample, about 20% of the incumbent congressmen were in this category. Such congressmen usually come from districts in which the parties are well organized. The parties ordinarily select and endorse a set of candidates in the primary, which they usually win. In the general election, the candidates then campaign as a party unit. As one congressman in this category said, "The whole ticket campaigns for each other," and also indicated that in primaries, "the organization supports me." One important characteristic of this type of electoral relationship is that most of the parties are safe in their competitive status, as are the congressmen themselves.[23]

At the opposite extreme are those congressmen who campaign individually; they neither expect nor receive much help from their local parties. As one congressman said of the party in his district, "I leave it alone." Instead, he campaigns on his own to "build a wide base of support" for himself. A full one-third of the congressmen in the national sample were in this category. Most of them came from districts in which the parties were not well organized, and had little tangible help to provide at election time. Furthermore, candidates conducted

[23] The electoral reliance data are reported in David M. Olson, "U.S. Congressmen and Their Diverse Congressional District Parties," *Legislative Studies Quarterly* 3 (May 1978), pp. 239–264. The other national studies are Jeff Fishel, *Party and Opposition* (New York: McKay, 1973) and Robert J. Huckshorn and Robert C. Spencer, *The Politics of Defeat* (Amherst: University of Massachusetts Press, 1971). Other congressional election studies include David A. Leuthold, *Electioneering in a Democracy* (New York: Wiley, 1968) and Alan L. Clem (ed.), *The Making of Congressmen: Seven Campaigns of 1974* (North Scituate, Mass.: Duxbury Press, 1976).

individual campaigns; they would not campaign for their own party's nominees—either to the White House or to the courthouse.

One of the three intermediate types of electoral relationships between congressmen and their district parties is the factional reliance category. A few congressmen have bifactional parties, which are split into two well-organized but hostile factions. The congressmen then campaign as extensively with one of the two factions as do those congressmen who campaign with their parties. In each of the few districts in this category, the party held a safe competitive status, and thus all of the political conflict within the district could be funneled into intraparty conflict and expressed through bitterly contested primaries.

The two other intermediate categories of electoral relationships between congressmen and their parties tended to vary with their parties' competitive status. Furthermore, in neither set was the district party very well organized. If the party usually won the general elections, congressmen tended to cooperate with the other candidates of their party in the general election, but they were wary about the possibilities of contested nominations within their own parties. If the party's competitive status was more precarious in general elections, however, the congressmen would campaign individually in general elections but would also expect and receive the party's help in protecting their own renominations.

Taking these several types of electoral relationships together, about 40% of the congressmen campaign with their parties either extensively or at least in general elections. These proportions are similar to the 40% to 50% of congressional candidates who, in other studies, have also reported that they have found their district parties in general elections to be at least "somewhat" important sources of help in their campaigns.[24]

We should note, however, that party solidarity and reliance by congressional candidates upon their parties is discouraged by competitiveness. That is, a genuine competitive threat in general elections from the other party did not induce the candidates to campaign together and seek strength through unity; but rather, they reacted fearfully and attempted to separate themselves from the other candidates of their own party label. The party leaders in the district recognized this protective reaction by the candidate and understood its reason. Both the candidates and the party leaders were pragmatic: They shared the goal of winning elections.

This discussion of the electoral reliance relationship between congressmen and party organizations could apply to candidates to any

[24] Fishel, *Party and Opposition*, p. 106, and Huckshorn and Spencer, *The Politics of Defeat*, p. 134.

office. But there are at least two circumstances unique to Congress and congressional candidates. In the first place, the congressional district party is usually not a single entity. It is, rather, a derivative of county parties, and in some cities, of party units organized by assembly district or ward. Usually the congressional district shared only the single office of congressman. The district boundaries are pliable, shifting with population, while county boundaries are fixed and furthermore contain numerous offices in the county courthouse. By and large, parties are structured by the offices they seek: the county has more offices than the congressional district, and hence, parties are more organized by the former than the latter unit.[25] A related characteristic of the congressional district is that its boundaries rarely match the audience boundaries of the mass media. Either the large-city newspapers and the TV stations include many districts or the rural districts are split between several such papers and stations.[26]

Secondly, the congressional office does not seem to be very important to the leaders of the county parties. Our evidence on this point is impressionistic, but local party leaders ordinarily state, as did one: "The higher the level of government, the less I can do about it, the more my influence decreases. Thus, with limited time, I apply my efforts where I do have influence."

Congressmen generally agree that their local party officials are more concerned with other offices than with Congress. Congressmen lament the relative indifference of local party leaders at election time, but on the other hand, usually prefer their district party leaders to not get involved in the congressman's Washington activities of committee work and voting on legislation.[27]

The office of U.S. Senator might be very different in these respects from the U.S. House. The senators' electoral districts are whole states, thus coinciding with the state's party organizational units. Furthermore, the office is a valued one: Governors and congressmen run for the Senate, whereas senators run for president but usually not for governor or the U.S. House. Yet the relationship between senators and their state parties does not seem to be much closer than that of House

[25] Joseph Schlesinger, "Political Party Organization," in James C. March (ed.), *Handbook of Organizations* (Chicago: Rand McNally, 1964), pp. 787–793. Leo Snowiss observed that "Congressional districts are rarely 'natural' political units," in "Congressional Recruitment and Representation," *American Political Science Review* 60 (September 1966), p. 627.

[26] Donald E. Stokes, "Parties and the Nationalization of Electoral Forces," in William N. Chambers and W. Dean Burnham (eds.), *The American Party Systems*, 2d ed. (New York: Oxford, 1975), p. 197.

[27] Snowiss, "Congressional Recruitment and Representation," p. 629; Frank Sorauf, *Party Politics in America*, 3d ed. (Boston: Little, Brown, 1976), pp. 350–352. The quote is from a personal interview.

members and their respective county parties. Senators use what they can of state party resources, but also conduct their own independent and name-oriented campaigns. A midwestern state party chairman commented about his party's two U.S. Senators: "We have both U.S. senators but they have neither one ever shown any real interest in the party. They leave us alone and we leave them alone."[28]

In Maryland, a Democratic incumbent (Tydings) almost ran two separate campaigns in the same election: one with the party "regulars," and the other through reform-minded volunteers. In Connecticut, a Democratic incumbent (Ribicoff) had a better organized party in the state to work with, but still he developed his own campaign organization and directly appealed to the electorate for votes. An Illinois mass media campaign for a Republican senatorial candidate (Percy) was organized and conducted throughout the state, even though the Republican party is reasonably well organized and active in most areas. In all three cases, the senatorial candidates did not rely only upon the existing party organization and personnel, but also conducted independent campaigns.[29]

The relative separation of national congressional and senatorial offices from the concerns of the local and state party leaders may lessen in the next several decades as the scope and importance of the national government increase. The increasing financing by the federal government of education, welfare, medical services, highways, and energy supplies may have the effect of making congressmen and senators more visible than previously to their electorates and more important than previously to the local governments and businesses of their districts and states. As a result, the leaders of district and state parties may come to regard congressmen and senators as more important to them than previously.

One major difference between European parliamentary and American congressional elections is that ours are combined with presidential elections every four years. Since both sets of elections are to national governmental institutions, we might expect that the party candidates would campaign together. Each candidate, however, tends to react to the others in the same protective way we have described for the local party. If a presidential candidate is judged popular in a district, the congressional candidate of the same party will join his

---

[28] Robert J. Huckshorn, *Party Leadership in the States* (Amherst: University of Massachusetts Press, 1976), p. 91.

[29] The Maryland campaign is discussed in John Bibby and Roger Davidson, *On Capitol Hill*, 2d ed. (New York: Holt, Rinehart and Winston, 1972), pp. 25–51, and the Connecticut campaign in the same book, 1st ed., 1967, pp. 31–52. The Illinois campaign is discussed by Donald Osten in Robert Agranoff (ed.), *The New Style in Election Campaigns* (Boston: Holbrook Press, 1972), pp. 330–340.

campaign to the presidential one. But if the local estimate is that the presidential candidate is unpopular, then the congressional (and other) candidates will avoid joint campaigning. In states such as New York and Pennsylvania, in which Republicans had practiced ticket-wide campaigning, the 1964 Goldwater candidacy came as a severe shock. Fearing his local unpopularity, the state and county Republican units created separate campaign offices in an effort to save their own candidates. Southern Democratic congressmen and state officials had been doing the same thing ever since Truman's 1948 campaign. For them the Carter candidacy in 1976 was a major departure. For the first time in a generation, many southern Democratic candidates for congress and senate, governor and sheriff, happily ran as a Democratic "team" with Carter's name and picture receiving the most emphasis.

AMERICAN CAMPAIGNS COMPARED WITH OTHER COUNTRIES

Reliance and Centralization

American election campaigns may be compared to those abroad on two very broad dimensions. One, party reliance, is an extension to foreign settings of the concept of party reliance discussed above. The other dimension, centralization, measures the extent to which campaigns in the districts are coordinated by the national level of the party. Although precise measurements are not readily available for the two dimensions, and little empirical study has been conducted of campaigning on a cross-national basis, we can identify examples to illustrate the logical extremes of each dimension.

The combination of decentralized parties and independent campaigning is characteristic of the United States. Candidates to the U.S. Senate and House typically depend upon their own efforts and construct their own campaign organizations from volunteers, and paid staff and campaign management firms, and thus are located in Cell III (of Table 2.5), candidate-centered campaigns. French Assembly campaigns also tend to be local and candidate-centered.[30]

There are some American examples, however, of high reliance on selected local parties. Chicago Democrats, and Virginia Democrats

[30] D. B. Goldey and R. W. Johnson, "The French General Election of March 1973," *Political Studies* 21 (September 1973), p. 327, and William G. Andrews, "Presidentialism and Parliamentary Electoral Politics in France: A Case Study of Eureux, 1962 and 1973," *Political Studies* 21 (September 1973), pp. 317–320. On the other hand, French Assembly elections show considerable national uniformity rather than local variations in the voting patterns. See Howard Rosenthal and Subrata Sen, "Spatial Voting Models for the French Fifth Republic," *American Political Science Review* 71 (December 1977), p. 1449.

Table 2.5 CANDIDATE AND PARTY: RELIANCE AND CENTRALIZATION

NATIONAL-LOCAL COORDINATION	PARTY RELIANCE BY CANDIDATE(S)	
	HIGH	LOW
High	Cell I: Europe Pennsylvania Republicans Communist parties	Cell IV: Some French parties
Low	Cell II: Chicago (Democrats) Virginia (Democrats)	Cell III: Most of U.S. France

Key:
   I. National party-centered campaign
  II. Local party-centered campaign
 III. Candidate-centered campaign
 IV. Avoided centralized campaign

until the mid-1960s, illustrate the strongly led and cohesive local party organization that dominated politics and campaigns in their respective areas and operated independently of national party direction. Indeed, Virginia Democrats (the Byrd machine) defied the national party.[31] These examples are in Cell II, the local party-centered campaign, of Table 2.5.

From the American perspective, most other nations would be marked by party centralization and high party reliance by parliamentary candidates (Cell I, national party-centered campaign). In many nations, the capital's newspapers circulate throughout the entire country, and the few radio and TV stations broadcast nationally. That is, a centralized and uniform set of campaign appeals can be directed to the public more easily in such nations than the United States simply as an artifact of their already centralized mass communications system. But still, the Soviet Union and India present even greater difficulties in their geographic reach and population size than the United States, but nevertheless have more centralized party campaigns than we.

Not only are most nations smaller than the United States and more centralized in their communication media, but most of the competitive nations have a parliamentary rather than a presidential system of government. That is, the main prize of government office, that of chief executive, is allocated by and attainable only through parliament. Except in the event of deadlock in the American electoral college, congressional elections are irrelevant to the selection of the president. In parliamentary systems, however, elections to parliament are simultaneously the election of the chief executive. All of the energies, funds,

[31] Chicago Democrats are discussed in Snowiss, "Congressional Recruitment and Representation," and Virginia Democrats in V. O. Key, *Southern Politics* (New York: Knopf, 1949), chap. 2.

and publicity invested in an American presidential election are, in parliamentary systems, invested in the election campaign to parliament itself.

In at least some nations, the parliamentary election approaches the U.S. presidential election in the emphasis placed upon the identity and characteristics of the party's candidate for prime minister. Election posters in West Germany, for example, commonly picture the chancellor candidates, and a major feature of British campaigning is the daily press conference and frequent TV interview attention devoted to the parties' leaders who are the candidates for the prime ministership.

We can draw some inferences from the election returns about the relative balance of local, candidate, and nationwide factors in parliamentary elections. The British parliamentary election returns, for example, are much more uniform throughout the nation than in American congressional elections.[32] To the extent that such national trends are a product of the presidential and prime ministerial campaigns, we can infer that American congressional candidates are more independent of their presidential candidates than the British are of their parties' national candidates. Furthermore, over the past 25 years, party voting in American senatorial elections has declined, while the importance of incumbency and a combination of state and candidate influences has probably increased in importance.[33]

Most nations, unlike the United States, are either single-party or multiparty. Although the precise district and voting system is irrelevant in the former case, most multiparty nations have multimember districts and proportional representation. Both sets of circumstances make candidates dependent upon their parties. Voting is usually for the party, not for individual candidates. The chances of a candidate being elected depend upon placement on the party's list: If the candidate is placed toward the top of the party list, the chances of election are strong; if the candidate is placed near the bottom of the party list, the usual splintering of the vote among parties makes the chances of election slim. The candidate is dependent upon the party both for his placement on the party ballot and in campaigning to attract votes to the party list as a whole rather than to him as a single candidate. The combination of these circumstances makes most European parliamentary elections centralized nationally in which the candidates closely cooperate with and rely upon their parties. At least in comparison to

---

[32] Stokes, "Parties and the Nationalization of Electoral Forces," and Richard S. Katz, "The Attribution of Variance in Electoral Returns: An Alternative Measurement Technique," *American Political Science Review* 67 (September 1973), pp. 817–828.

[33] Warren L. Kostroski, "Party and Incumbency in Postwar Senate Elections: Trends, Patterns, and Models," *American Political Science Review* 67 (December 1973), pp. 1213–1234.

most American elections, European ones have far less emphasis on the personal qualities and names of the individual candidates, on the one hand, and far greater ability of the party organization to deliver tangible campaign aid to their candidates, on the other. Thus, most European elections would be placed in the upper left-hand cell of Table 2.5.

Contributing to the same result is the use of mass media. In the United States, mass media have been used by individual candidates to bypass their political parties and to also avoid being associated with other candidates bearing their same party label. In other countries, however, the political parties have developed a competence in mass media, thus drawing the candidate to, rather than driving the candidates away from, their national party organizations and campaigns.[34]

The upper right-hand cell of the chart is the least likely combination. One would not expect to find centralized parties that candidates tended to avoid in campaigning.

American and British Campaigns

Unfortunately for our purposes in comparing parliamentary campaigns among nations, the relevant studies do not ask the same questions. Instead, they ask questions that reflect the unique circumstances of each country. Thus readers have to tease out the comparisons for themselves. But let us compare the relationship of local campaigns to the national in two studies, one of the American congressional campaign of 1964 and the other of the two British parliamentary campaigns of 1974. The American study asked challenging candidates (excluding the incumbents, most of whom were reelected) to rate the amount of campaign help provided by each geographic level of their political party. Over half estimated the national level of their party to have provided either "considerable" or "some" help to their campaigns, while about half made the same estimate of their local parties. Most candidates dismissed their state parties as providing little campaign assistance.[35]

British parliamentary candidates, in both elections in 1974, were asked the extent to which they followed their parties' national campaigns. The proportions reporting they "closely followed" them varied from a low of 16% for Conservative party candidates in the February election to a high of 68% for Labour party candidates in the same election (Table 2.6). There is similar variation, though seldom climbing over 50%, in the proportions paying attention to their national leaders' speeches, to daily communications from the national party

---

[34] Richard Rose, *Influencing Voters: A Study of Campaign Rationality* (New York: St. Martin's, 1967), pp. 35–94.

[35] Jeff Fishel, *Party and Opposition,* p. 106.

Table 2.6 BRITISH CANDIDATES' ATTENTION TO NATIONAL CAMPAIGNS IN TWO ELECTIONS, 1974

ELEMENTS OF NATIONAL CAMPAIGN CLOSELY FOLLOWED	FEBRUARY 1974			OCTOBER 1974		
	CON-SERVA-TIVE (%)	LABOUR (%)	LIB-ERAL (%)	CON-SERVA-TIVE (%)	LABOUR (%)	LIB-ERAL (%)
Campaign as whole	16	68	62	29	33	27
Leaders' speeches	25	44	45	50	33	38
National office communications	33	43	37	50	44	42
Through mass media	25	54	44	45	64	49

SOURCE: David Butler and Dennis Kavanagh, *The British General Election of October 1974* (New York: St. Martin's, 1975), p. 230, Table 1.

Table 2.7 BRITISH CANDIDATES' EMPHASIS ON PARTY PLATFORMS IN TWO ELECTIONS, 1974

EMPHASIS	FEBRUARY 1974			OCTOBER 1974		
	CON-SERVA-TIVE (%)	LABOUR (%)	LIB-ERAL (%)	CON-SERVA-TIVE (%)	LABOUR (%)	LIB-ERAL (%)
A great deal	65	82	67	73	62	78
Some, little, or none	35	18	13	26	38	21
Total	100	100	80[a]	99	100	99

SOURCE: David Butler and Dennis Kavanagh, *The British General Election of October 1974* (New York: St. Martin's, 1975), p. 230, Table 2.
[a] The missing 20% is not explained in the original source.

office, or even following the national campaign through the mass media.[36] Perhaps this range of responses strikes the American observer as lower than we would have expected.

But still the British candidates largely campaigned within the policy statements of their national parties. The proportions of candidates who emphasized their national party platform was never lower than 60% (Table 2.7).[37] No study we know of has even bothered to ask this question of American candidates. But this question is not relevant for half of the American congressional elections—those occurring in presidential midterm years, for the national parties usually meet and adopt platforms only during presidential election years.

[36] David Butler and Dennis Kavanagh, *The British General Election of October 1974* (New York: St. Martin's, 1975), p. 230.
[37] Ibid.

Candidates in both countries are similar in that they will avoid the national candidates who are unpopular with their district's electorate. In the British case, neither leader of the two major parties was thought popular by the parliamentary candidates. As a result, 44% of the Labour and 63% of the Conservative candidates avoided making references in their district campaigns to their respective national leaders.[38]

Although British elections are like ours in that the parliamentary district candidates will avoid their national candidate for the prime ministership when they judge it expedient, the national impact on the constituency campaigns seems greater in Britain than in the United States, and the candidates seem more clearly identified with their national parties. Unlike the situation in the United States, a vote for a parliamentary candidate is simultaneously a vote for that candidate's party leader to become prime minister.

In both countries the national party committees supply campaign aid to local candidates, identify critical or marginal seats, and channel funds and speakers into those districts. Yet the British effort is more substantial for their parliamentary candidates than is the American. Most of the time and effort of American national level parties are invested in the presidential campaign. By contrast, all of the British national effort goes into the parliamentary campaign. In effect, Parliament acts as their electoral college through which their chief executive is selected.

In the October 1974 British parliamentary election, both national parties identified marginal districts—the ones in which a shift of a small number of votes would change the party result. In the previous summer, the Conservative party created a committee to concentrate on the marginal seats, consisting of three leading members of their parliamentary party. On the basis of visits in the districts, they developed a list of 47 critical seats that received supplemental funds, visits, and supervision from the national party staff and priority claim on big-name speakers from Parliament.

The Labour party, at the same time, was doing the same thing. It developed a list of 59 critical marginal constituencies, and attempted to staff each district with a full-time, paid party agent. Less than half of its critical districts, however, had full-time agents, whereas all of the Conservative's critical districts did.[39] By contrast, we know of few local American parties with their own full-time staff. Even the understaffed British Labour party has more organizational advantages than do either of the American parties.

The British constituency agents are less than completely effective.

[38] Ibid., p. 233.
[39] Ibid., pp. 226–228.

Both parties have difficulties in recruiting and paying them. In the October 1974 parliamentary election the Conservative party had 375 agents for the 635 districts, whereas Labour had only 125. Furthermore, most of Labour's agents were not in the marginal districts where presumably they were needed the most, but rather in the safe districts in which the local party had more funds. The lack of agents was a result mainly of small memberships in the districts and thus of the lack of local funds with which to pay the agent's salary.[40]

The relationship of candidate to party is a product of many ingredients. If the candidate is personally popular, has independent sources of electoral support, and has access to campaign funds, his or her need for the party decreases. Although we think many American legislators fit this description, the same may be true abroad as well. A study of one British constituency, for example, found that the incumbent member of Parliament was personally popular and the party organization was "minimal." Indeed, the long-term incumbent developed his own network of supporters, and did nothing to aid the development of the organization of his own party.[41]

Something of the flavor of a 1920s parliamentary campaign may be gleaned from the memoirs of Harold MacMillan, who became prime minister in the 1950s, but whose first election was in the 1920s. Television was unknown, the use of radio for campaigning was in its infancy. Even the London papers did not penetrate his rural district, nor did the national party:[42]

> Naturally pamphlets and propaganda papers were sent to us from Central Office (if we paid for them, which we were loath to do) but very few were much good to us. It was better to print short and simple messages attuned to our own needs.

And while outside national speakers were useful in the local constituency, they were hard to obtain. "Moreover, outside speakers must be carefully chosen. They could easily do more harm than good."[43] As a result, the candidates waged campaigns largely as separate contests.

MacMillan noted that, just prior to World War I, "campaigning

[40] Ibid., pp. 222–224, and Robert Frasure and Alan Kornberg, "Constituency Agents and British Party Politics," *British Journal of Political Science* 5 (October 1975), pp. 459–476.

[41] Frank J. Bealey, J. Blondel, and W. P. McCann, *Constituency Politics: A Study of Newcastle-under-Lyme* (New York: Free Press, 1965).

[42] Harold MacMillan, *The Past Masters: Politics and Politicians 1906–1939* (New York: Harper & Row, 1975), p. 168.

[43] Ibid., p. 169.

was a more leisurely affair." Not only were TV, radio, telephones, and automobiles lacking, but the electorate was much smaller.[44]

> Many of the smaller boroughs did not have more than a few thousands electors. . . . There was no question of these enormous bodies of voters with which the modern candidate has to struggle, sometimes rising to eighty or one hundred thousand.

Finally, many districts were not contested. In the 1900 election, 243 members out of the then 670 did not have an opponent. MacMillan observed, "it was almost thought rather bad form to contest a constituency where the result was obvious and the Member had been long installed."[45]

These remarks indicate that at an earlier time in a more rural society, political parties were less well organized than now, both in the constituencies and nationally, constituency elections were more independent of the national campaign, and the candidate himself had a larger part in and perhaps influence on the election. If MacMillan's observations are typical, then British and American parties have evolved differently since the turn of the century. Presumably that period was the peak of our "machines," and our parties have declined in organization and activity since that time.[46]

One important difference between American and British parties concerns the place of the district in the party structure. In most parts of Britain the parliamentary constituency is the basic unit of party organization, whereas in the United States the county often is. In Britain the party is mainly organized to contest parliamentary elections; in the United States it is mainly organized to contest the county courthouse.[47] Unless the congressional district is coterminous with a single county (very rare), the district party is an amalgam of several county parties in rural areas or a portion of one or more county units in urban areas. Whereas in Britain the parliamentary constituency is the main organizational unit of the party, in the United States the district party is derivative from, but irrelevant to, the county party. As we noted earlier, congressmen feel, and local party leaders agree, that

---

[44] Ibid., p. 28.

[45] Ibid., p. 30.

[46] On the other hand, our understanding of our own political past leaves a lot to be desired. Most of our studies of earlier American parties were conducted in cities but at a time when less than half of our population resided in urban areas.

[47] While the county is the most common local governmental unit in the United States around which parties are organized, it is not an important unit in New England, and in some states (e.g., California), county offices became nonpartisan during the Progressive era. See Jewell and Olson. *American State Political Parties and Elections*, pp. 59–60.

other offices are more important to them than is the congressional. The organizational discontinuity between the American party and the congressional district almost requires the congressman to be more independent of his or her local party (or parties) than is the British member of Parliament.

Communist Nations

Although the results of parliamentary campaigns in the Soviet Union are hardly in doubt for the single unopposed candidates, the Communist party and the candidates go to great lengths to produce a high voter turnout, which invariably is over 95%. The campaign is designed to ensure that high rate of voter participation. Those Eastern European countries that permit, and now even require, the nomination of more candidates than seats are no less insistent upon similarly high rates of voter turnout. The campaign, in both democratic and communist systems, is directed at the voter. In all systems, the election campaign is a search for votes.

The voter in the Soviet system is exhorted to show his solidarity with the motherland and to further the fight for communism. The government newspapers and other mass media give extensive attention to the campaign and to the candidates. The candidates themselves attend rallies and campaign meetings. The Communist party organizes millions of "agitators" to visit every voter in his residence to explain the campaign and to ensure his vote. Each agitator is a volunteer, and usually visits 10–30 families two if not three times. (If this goal is actually achieved, the modern Communist party is far more efficient than American party machines ever were.) The election agitator is also on duty at the polling place until all of "his" voters have appeared. One of his duties is to issue absentee ballots to those who will be away election day, which can be cast wherever the voter is—at an airport or even on a train. The campaign culminates in an election eve broadcast by the dominant party leader—most recently Leonid Brezhnev, who is both general secretary of the Communist party and president of the Soviet Union.[48]

Current thinking in communist systems about the meaning and intent of elections and election campaigns may be illustrated by citing the 1976 Political Bureau report of the Polish United Worker's Party:[49]

[48] Max E. Mote, "Soviet Local and Republic Elections," in Joseph L. Nogee (ed.), *Man, State and Society in the Soviet Union* (New York: Praeger, 1972), pp. 243–259.

[49] Poland. Polish United Workers' Party, Central Committee, Political Bureau, "Development and Consolidation of the Nation's Patriotic Unity, Consolidation of the State and Development of Socialist Democracy" (Warsaw: Polish Interpress Agency, 1976, mimeo), pp. 17–18.

The last few weeks before the elections will be filled with a great discussion with all working people, with the entire nation, on the most important affairs of the present and future. The programme outlined by the 7th Party Congress, a programme aimed at the further building up of Poland's strength and of the prosperity of our nation, will be the principal subject of this discussion.

A rather exuberant interpretation of the election results in the Soviet Union, by a Soviet commentator, further illustrates their view of the purposes of elections:[50]

The dazzling victory of the Party and non-Party bloc in Soviet elections is a clear expression of the monolithic cohesion of the Soviet people, of its faith, love and devotion to the Communist Party and to the Soviet Government, to its wholehearted readiness to march behind the Party along the road to communism.

The election campaign is no less frantic and aimed at the public in one-party nations than in competitive ones. The purpose of public appeals is not to ensure that the one candidate or party wins, but that a large proportion of the electorate actually votes. The act of voting is usually seen—or is at least intended by those in control—as a demonstration of popular support and loyalty.

The act of voting is also seen by elites in newly independent one-party nations as an education of the masses in nationhood and supportive citizenship. The ruling party generally regards itself as a (or often the only) leader of the populace who must be urged and "educated" to know of the state itself, to know and support the party, and to actively participate in the giving of that support.[51]

THE NOMINATION STAGE

With only a few exceptions, candidates' names are entered in the general election through a political party.[52] The decision of which candidates shall be entered with which party's name is termed *nomination*. Indeed, about the only activity that parties have in common around the world is the use of their name for election purposes. Although parties vary enormously in their organizational forms and electoral capacities (a point we have discussed earlier), the use of

[50] Yu. K. Filonovich, "Sovetsky deputat," quoted in L. C. Churchward, *Contemporary Soviet Government* (New York: Elsevier, 1968), pp. 108–109.

[51] Joseph LaPalombara and Myron Weiner (eds.), *Political Parties and Political Development* (Princeton, N.J.: Princeton University Press, 1966), pp. 402–440, 424–427.

[52] One American State legislature (Nebraska) has nonpartisan elections. Some countries, including the United States, permit "independent" candidates also to run in the general election along with the party-nominated candidates.

party labels in the election process is the one generic characteristic of political parties.[53] The nomination process, in effect, is the procedure by which the party's label is allocated among aspiring candidates for use in the general election.

In most countries that decision is made by the party itself. Its leaders, or a committee or a convention, or some combination of party-defined groups and procedures, decide which candidate(s) shall be nominated by that party.

American Primaries

The United States, however, is the major exception in that most nominations are made through elections. The primary election was introduced as a reform, to take the nomination decision out of the hands of party "bosses" and "machines" and to give that power "to the people." One result is that all of the elements of a general election campaign are also found in a primary election campaign. The whole campaign can take the better part of a year, the financial costs double, and the organizational and strategic problems for candidates also at least double. Nominations are mainly decided by party conventions only in Connecticut and Delaware, and frequently also in Virginia. Minority parties, especially Republicans in the South, have long used conventions, but as a result of their growth into major party status they have shifted to primary elections.

One of the most vexing problems faced by American parties is presented by the primaries: Which voters shall be eligible to participate in the primary elections? This question is decided—as are most other electoral matters—by state law. By and large, the states fall into two categories, open and closed. In "closed" primaries the only voters permitted to vote in a party's primary are those who have previously registered in that party, whereas in "open" primaries all voters are eligible to vote in the primary of any party. The closed primary presumably screens out the usual adherents of other parties, while the open primary at least permits the normal supporters of one party in the general election to "cross over" and help select the candidates of the other party. The result could be the nomination by one party of a candidate more preferred by the voters of a second party than by the voters of the first. If then elected to Congress, that candidate might not be inclined to vote with his nominal party on legislation deemed important to that party and perhaps also to its president.[54]

---

[53] Epstein, *Political Parties in Western Democracies,* pp. 9–14; Austin Ranney, "The Concept of 'Party,'" in Oliver Garceau (ed.), *Political Research and Political Theory* (Cambridge, Mass.: Harvard University Press, 1968), pp. 149–150.

[54] Jewell and Olson, *American State Political Parties and Elections,* pp. 127–130, 162–163, 294–298.

State parties—and state laws—have developed a variety of ways of coping with the near universality of primary elections as the means of nominating candidates in the United States. In several states (e.g., Colorado, Minnesota) party conventions officially endorse candidates in their own primary. In other states (e.g., New York, Pennsylvania) party organizations at both state and local levels unofficially endorse and support candidates and effectively control their nominations. This type of party was included in our earlier discussion of electoral reliance upon the party organization.[55]

In most states, however, the official party personnel, from precinct worker to state chairman, are required by state law to be neutral in the primaries. Indeed, the party leaders sometimes deliberately avoid participation in the primaries so that they will be able to cooperate in the general election with whomever is nominated by their party. National party officials and the leaders of the congressional parties must likewise be ready to cooperate with whoever wins the party's nomination.

There is, as a result, not a single or uniform nomination system for the U.S. Congress. Rather, there are many, ranging from the party convention through the open primary. The members of Congress, though holding office in a single national institution, are nominated variously through state-defined and locally implemented procedures. Though congressmen belong to the same national party, the state and local units of their party vary greatly in their nomination procedures.

In no other country do party leaders and their organizations run such risks. In all other countries one of the major decisions available to the party—nomination—is made by the party itself.

Nominations in Competitive Systems

PARTY ORGANIZATION

In most other countries parties are organizations, possessing a clearly defined leadership and an equally well-defined membership. Persons become "members" of a political party not merely by voting (even consistently) for the candidates of that party and not merely by asserting their support in a public opinion poll ("party identification" in the American studies), but by formally affiliating with and paying dues to that party. In addition, other organizations may explicitly affiliate with a party, as do trade unions in many countries with Labor parties. It is these explicit members of the party who have the responsibility of selecting the party's nominees.

[55] The Pennsylvania case is discussed in Frank Sorauf, *Party and Representation* (New York: Atherton, 1963), pp. 52–58. The national sample of 36 districts is discussed in Olson, "Congressmen and Their Diverse Congressional District Parties," pp. 249–250.

The members, in turn, elect a variety of officers and committees who ordinarily make the nomination decisions for the party. In British parties, for example, "selection committees" interview prospective candidates and present a "short list" of potential candidates to the party's governing committee. That committee's selection of the candidate is then reviewed and usually ratified in the party's membership meeting.[56]

In single-member districts, the whole membership is able, presumably, to attend a party membership meeting. Indeed, as we noted earlier, the parliamentary constituency is ordinarily the major unit of party organization in Britain. But in multimember districts, frequently corresponding to regions or provinces in size, party nominations are made by conventions or committees to which delegates are elected by lower-level party units and their memberships. The more local direct membership meeting, however, may not be much different from the regional convention. Party memberships are relatively small, and those who regularly attend are an even smaller number. Either way, the decision makers are the party activists.

Some membership parties approximate the American primary election in that they provide for a direct ballot on nominations by all party members.[57] Sometimes these are conducted by mail to reach all party members, not just those who attend a meeting. But given the relatively small proportion of the electorate who belong to a party, the European attempt to involve all party members is still far different from the American primary election. The main contrast is that where in other countries party membership is a well-defined, unambiguous status, in the United States the eligible electorate in a primary election is often as broad and diverse as is the whole electorate for a general election. The American primary election system tends to take the nomination decision away from the party—thought of as a membership and set of leaders—and even away from a party-loyal constituency. In most other countries, by contrast, the nomination is made within a

[56] Epstein, *Political Parties in Western Democracies*, pp. 216–222; Robert T. McKenzie, *British Political Parties* (New York: St. Martin's, 1955), pp. 550–556; Austin Ranney, *Pathways to Parliament* (Madison: University of Wisconsin Press, 1965), chaps. 3 and 6; Butler and Kavanagh, *The British General Election of October 1974*, chap. 9; Bealey, Blondel, and McCann, *Constituency Politics: A Study of Newcastle-under-Lyme*, pp. 99–100.

[57] Malcolm E. Jewell, "Linkages Between Legislative Parties and External Parties," in Allan Kornberg (ed.), *Legislatures in Comparative Perspective* (New York: McKay, 1973), p. 216; Jeffrey Obler, "Intraparty Democracy and the Selection of Parliamentary Candidates: The Belgian Case," *British Journal of Political Science* 4 (April 1974), pp. 163–185; James Jupp, *Australian Party Politics* (Melbourne: Melbourne University Press, 1964), pp. 62–64; C. H. Dodd, *Politics and Government in Turkey* (Berkeley: University of California Press, 1969), pp. 181–185.

well-defined organization and by a relatively small set of activists clearly separate from the rest of the electorate.[58]

DECENTRALIZATION

Parties vary in the extent of their decentralization in making nomination decisions. The main variable associated with the location of nomination decision making is the electoral system. In single-member districts (United States and Great Britain) nominations are made within those districts. In the larger multimember districts nominations are made by party units at that level. Thus the main distinction between American nominations and those in most other countries is not local vs. national level decision making, but rather the primary election system vs. the party-decided nominations.

Americans commonly suppose that national party leaders abroad have considerable influence over the nomination of parliamentary candidates. We draw that inference from the marked contrast between the high degree of party voting in foreign parliaments compared with the considerable party fragmentation in the U.S. Congress. In most democracies, however, national party leaders defer to local and regional choices of candidates, even though the national leaders have a more formal authority than in American national parties. To again cite the British example, the national parties maintain lists of approved potential candidates among whom the local parties may select for their consideration. Yet, this list is used to cull out persons with potential personal liabilities rather than to impose from the top a single type of candidate upon the local parties. Indeed, local party leaders seem jealous of their autonomy and resent any overt attempt by the national office to "dictate" their choices. The importance of the national party leadership in making parliamentary nominations seems greatest in some of the newly independent countries. But even in those countries, such as India and Zambia, national leaders exercise influence through consultation with local party leaders and by mediation of local disputes.[59]

The emphasis in European parties upon decentralized nomination decisions may be further illustrated by a survey of delegates to the

[58] Epstein, *Political Parties in Western Democracies*, p. 231. France, however, is something of an exception. While its national parties attempt to make decisions about candidacies, they sometimes convert the first of their two elections into a kind of local primary to select among rival factional candidates for the party label. See D. B. Goldey and R. W. Johnson, "The French General Election of March 1973," pp. 325, 334–336.

[59] Epstein, *Political Parties in Western Democracies*, pp. 225–230; Jewell, "Linkages Between Legislative Parties and External Parties," pp. 214–218, and Henry Valen and Daniel Katz, *Political Parties in Norway* (Oslo: Universitetsforlaget, 1964), pp. 90–98.

national conventions of the several Finnish parties. The national delegates were asked which party level should make parliamentary nominations. A majority of delegates within all six parties thought that the
constituency level should make that decision. Only a small number (a
maximum of 15% in one party) responded that the national party
should make nominations. Nevertheless, 20% to 40% of each party
replied that nominations should be made by both the constituency and
national party levels together.[60]

The decentralized nomination system of European parties contrasts with our previous finding of centralized campaigning; that is,
although candidates are nominated at constituency and provincial
levels, the ensuing general election campaign is conducted in a more
centralized manner. Both phenomena are possible because the constituency decision is made within the party, not by a large and diffuse
electorate. Furthermore, the local party activists are loyal to the
national party and want to support their parliamentary party leaders.
They want to nominate nationally loyal candidates. Their sense of
national party loyalty greatly contrasts with the local orientations of
the leaders of American parties in the states and counties. Thus the
difference in party voting on legislation in Congress and in European
parliaments does not stem from any difference in party centralization
in the nomination process.[61]

TICKET BALANCING

One important criterion of choice in party nominations, especially in
multimember districts, is ticket balancing. That is, the party seeks to
place candidates on its lists who, taken together, will appeal to the
major electoral segments within the district. The population segments
themselves are frequently represented through factions within the
party, and they attempt to place their respective candidates on the
party list and as high as possible on that list. In West Germany, for
example, the major population groups and factions within the Christian
Democrats have been refugees, youth, women, Protestants (in a
largely Catholic-oriented party), small businessmen, and governmental
officials. In Norway the parties placed candidates on their party lists
to appeal to youth, women, workers and unions, farmers, religious
groups, and different geographic areas of the constituency. To nominate
candidates of wide and diverse social appeal seems to be a consistent

[60] Tapio Koskiaho, "The Parliamentary Candidates and the Candidate Selection in
Finland." Paper read at International Political Science Association World Congress,
Munich, 1970, p. 25, table 9 (mimeo).

[61] Epstein, *Political Parties in Western Democracies*, p. 219.

effort in all countries and in all party systems, including those with single dominant parties.[62]

Single-Party Systems

In one-party systems, the degree of national centralization over nomination decisions probably varies with the degree to which support of the national party can be obtained through decentralized decisions. Decentralization may also vary with the ideological and militant character of the party. That is, we might expect an ideological and elite party, such as the Communist party, to make centralized nomination decisions, reflecting its highly centralized character in all other matters as well. The one-party systems of newly independent nations, however, apparently vary greatly in their centralization and openness on a wide range of matters, including nominations.

Well-organized single parties can have many aspirants for their nomination. In the 1965 election in Tanzania, for example, three or more candidates were proposed for nomination in 97 of the 107 constituencies. That step itself required a nomination petition supported by not less than 25 voters. To resolve the choice of which candidate would obtain the party's nomination, secret ballots were cast at a district conference of the party. The national executive committee of the ruling party, however, then finally selected the two candidates to run in the general election in each district.[63]

The nomination process is no less complicated and diverse in Soviet-area countries. Judging from their own general descriptions and from some fragmentary data relating to local government offices, the Communist party solicits candidate suggestions from its many subunits and also from private organizations. In those peoples' democracies that officially have several parties, they constitute a "united front" with the Communist party under its leadership. In such united fronts, the parties together form a single slate of candidates that is then presented to the electorate.

Several Eastern European countries now require that more candidates be nominated than can be elected to the available number of seats. This practice, which apparently originated in Yugoslavia, has since been adopted by newly independent nations such as Tanzania, to which we referred above.

[62] Loewenberg, *Parliament in the German Political System* (Ithaca: Cornell University Press, 1967), pp. 76, 98–99; Valen and Katz, *Political Parties in Norway*, pp. 59–62; Jewell, "Linkages Between Legislative Parties and External Parties," pp. 218–222.

[63] William Tordoff, *Government and Politics in Tanzania* (Nairobi: East African Publishing House, 1967), pp. 33–34.

Poland, to take one example, requires that the final list of candidates for the *Sejm* must exceed the number of seats to be filled. That excess may go up to one-half of the number of seats, but no more, "to prevent an excessive diffusion of votes." The candidates are listed on the ballot in the order preferred by the Front of National Unity.

The Front of National Unity, under the leadership of the ruling Polish United Workers' party, includes the United Peasants party and the Democratic party. In principle, at least, the ruling party consults widely through the mechanism of the Front to select candidates for nomination. Apparently, candidates are suggested "by political, cooperative, and civic organizations and other social organizations of the working people." The National Front committees "seek the opinion of voters in the residential area, place of employment, villages, or military units." The National Front then selects the final list of nominated candidates.[64] A report by the Political Bureau of the Polish United Workers' party is more blunt: "Following consultations, we placed the names of candidate Parliament . . . members on the joint list of the National Unity Front."[65]

At least one purpose of consultations in the nomination process seems to be to form a slate that will appeal to various segments of the electorate. To this extent, ticket balancing is a widely practiced political art, transcending national boundaries and ideologies. But consultation has a wider purpose, as well, to build confidence by the populace in their government. To quote from the Political Bureau report, once more, to the ruling Polish United Workers' party:[66]

> We attach great importance to the composition of the representative organs in our state. . . . In the process of selecting the candidates, we . . . assure that the names of leading workers, peasants and members of the intelligentsia, men of science, culture and technique, social activists who enjoy the respect and confidence of the electorate and are fully capable of shouldering their duties, figure on the voting lists.

The intent of the complicated consultation system is to transfer to the nomination stage many of the political conflicts which, in a Western democracy, occur in general elections. The election and its campaign are not intended[67]

> to furnish a battleground for antagonistic forces, but instead to provide a framework for a national discussion on . . . programmes. The

[64] Poland. Polish Interpress Agency, "Polish Parliamentary and Local Government Elections." Warsaw, February 1976, pp. 4–5 (mimeo).

[65] Poland. Polish United Workers' Party, Central Committee, Political Bureau, "Development and Consolidation of the Nation's Patriotic Unity," p. 18.

[66] Ibid.

[67] Poland. Polish Interpress Agency, "Polish Parliamentary and Local Government Elections," p. 4.

momentum of the political problem in the elections is shifted to the fixing of the best possible lists of candidates . . .

Candidates in the 1976 Polish parliamentary election were nominated through the National Front in the ratio of 55% for the ruling Polish United Workers' party and 33% divided between the other two parties, while the remaining 12% were independent candidates. This proportion reflected almost exactly the distribution of seats in the previous parliament. Even though more candidates were nominated than there were seats to be filled, the party ratios in the succeeding Sejm reflected almost exactly the ratios in the previous one. The continuity of party ratios between the two parliaments was thus ensured through the nomination system. From these results, and given the statement quoted above that "the political problem . . . is shifted to the fixing of the . . . lists of candidates," it is unfortunate that we know next to nothing about the interparty negotiations that produce the final list of candidates for the election ballot in Communist party states. The Yugoslavs, who originated the multiple-candidate nomination practice in one-party states, have themselves tried many different ways of initiating and screening candidate nominations. In the 1970s, however, they abandoned the whole effort, and shifted from direct elections to a complicated system of indirect ones, thereby largely eliminating the problem of nominating candidates to the national parliament.[68]

Summary

Although most mass media attention is given to general elections both abroad and in the United States, and although competition in general elections is greater than in nominations, most decisions of who shall be members of a parliamentary body are made at the nomination stage. Most seats in general elections are safe—a point to be developed later in this chapter. Thus, whoever wins the party nomination has effectively, in the safe seats, already won the election.

The election practices of the United States diverge most from other countries in the nomination stage of the election cycle. Although in most other countries and parties the nomination of parliamentary candidates is made within the party organization, in the United States most congressional and senatorial nominations are made through primary elections.

The nomination procedures between the United States and other countries, however, are similar in at least two respects. First, nominations tend to be made locally, not nationally. European party units at

[68] Susan B. McCarthy, "Gate-Keeping in the Nomination Process in Yugoslavia." Paper read at Annual Meeting of the American Political Science Association, Chicago, 1974 (mimeo).

the constituency level protect their autonomy from the national leaders and apparently regard the nomination of parliamentary candidates to belong at their respective levels of the party. Second, nominations in all systems tend to protect the incumbent. Whether by choice of party leaders or by a large and heterogeneous electorate, incumbents usually seek and obtain renomination. This point will be elaborated in a later section.

To this point we have examined general elections as the final stage of the electoral cycle and the nomination stage as an earlier stage. But an even earlier stage within the electoral cycle consists of the decisions about who will become candidates in the first place.

THE PARTY AS AGENT OF CANDIDATE RECRUITMENT

By what procedures do otherwise ordinary human beings become candidates for congressional or parliamentary office? Who do prospective candidates talk with in making that decision? Who in a society attempts to find suitable candidates for political office? That is, who and what are the "agents" of candidate recruitment?

The major question to be asked concerns the activity of the political party: Were the persons active in candidate recruitment associated with political parties, or were they acting in other capacities? The answers to this question inform us both about the background experiences of the persons who become members of parliament and also about the organization and conduct of politics within the member's home districts.

The answers to this question are probably more varied within the United States than in most other countries. The reason for this difference between the United States and other countries in candidate recruitment practices lies in the different nomination systems. As we have noted in an earlier section, nominations in most other countries are made by party organizations, whereas in the United States most nominations are made through primary elections. We also find in foreign parliaments a higher proportion of members who are full-time party officials than in the American Congress. We would guess that party leaders abroad are the ones who are mainly active in their societies in the recruitment of candidates because they control the selection process. They then select persons in their own image.

Table 2.8 shows the agents of candidate recruitment for three sets of U.S. House members and candidates in the early 1960s. Each set of legislators or candidates was asked different questions about their recruitment, with correspondingly different answers.[69] Party leaders are consistently, however, among the most common recruiters of con-

[69] Fishel, *Party and Opposition,* p. 58; Huckshorn and Spencer, *The Politics of Defeat,* p. 49. This section is drawn from Olson, "Congressmen and Their Diverse Congressional Parties," pp. 249–250.

Table 2.8 AGENTS OF CANDIDATE RECRUITMENT AMONG THREE SETS OF CONGRESSIONAL CANDIDATES

AGENTS OF RECRUITMENT	1965 INCUM-BENTS[a] (%)	1964 CHAL-LENGERS[b] (%)	1962 LOSERS[c]	
			REPUB-LICAN (%)	DEMO-CRATIC (%)
Party	45	35	65	68
Faction	8	—	—	—
Associates	6	—	56	61
Self	42	35	35	34
Family, relatives	—	—	19	15
Interest group	—	18	—	—
Combination	—	12	—	—
Total	100	100	[a]	[d]
N =	(36)	(293)	(128)	(110)

[a] Original data.
[b] Data are from Jeff Fishel, *Party and Opposition* (New York: McKay, 1973), p. 58, estimated from table 3.13.
[c] Robert Huckshorn, *The Politics of Defeat* (Amherst: University of Massachusetts, 1971), p. 49, table 3. 1.
[d] Multiple responses.

gressional candidates in all three studies. Candidacy to Congress is also often the candidates' own idea. The activity of friends, associates, and family seems to be more variable. Only one of the three studies, however, identified interest groups in stimulating candidacies to Congress. We would guess that interest group activity in this respect might be more common abroad than in the United States because of the more direct activity and open involvement of interest groups in political party affairs abroad than here.

The recruitment of candidates to state legislatures also shows considerable variation, corresponding to the nationwide difference indicated in the congressional studies (Table 2.9). States showing the highest proportion of candidate recruitment by political parties include those usually thought to have well-organized parties (Connecticut, New Jersey, and Pennsylvania), together with two states showing a revival of party organization and activity (Minnesota and Washington). States in which the fewest candidates are recruited through political parties to run for the state legislature include the safe parties (at the time of the studies) of Georgia, Tennessee, and California, together with both parties in Wisconsin and Ohio. With the exception of Ohio Republicans, these states are usually thought to have relatively inactive or fragmented party organizations.[70]

The pattern of candidate recruitment is related to the capacity and activity of political party organizations. Among the 1965 House incumbents, for example, the better organized the party, the more likely

[70] Jewell and Olson, *American State Political Parties and Elections*, pp. 87–88.

Table 2.9   STATES RANKED BY PROPORTION OF
LEGISLATIVE CANDIDATES RECRUITED BY POLITICAL
PARTIES

RANK	PERCENT	STATES
High	60–85	Connecticut New Jersey Pennsylvania Washington Minnesota
Intermediate	26–59	Iowa Oregon Pennsylvania (winners) California (Democrats) Georgia (Republicans) Tennessee (Republicans)
Low	5–25	Ohio (Republicans) California (Republicans) Tennessee (Democrats) Wisconsin Ohio (Democrats) Georgia (Democrats)

SOURCE: Malcolm E. Jewell and David M. Olson, *American State Political Parties and Elections* (Homewood, Ill.: Dorsey, 1978), p. 87, table 3.4.

its leaders are to recruit congressional (and other) candidates. That candidate recruitment varies by the organizational capacity of the district parties was also found among Pennsylvania parties' candidates to the state legislature. These findings inferentially support our guess that most candidate recruitment abroad would occur through the political party because parties are better organized, at least in Europe, than in the United States.

The activity of party leaders in candidate recruitment is even more directly associated with their ability to control their own nomination process. Of the congressmen whose initial nominations had been party-controlled, 77% were recruited by the party, while of those whose nominations were not controlled by the party, 79% were self-recruited. Again, this relationship was also found among Pennsylvania legislative candidates.

Competitive status is also related to the party role in candidate recruitment, especially among losing candidates (Table 2.10). The incidence of party recruitment of congressional candidates was 10% higher for the 1962 marginal losers (that is, the near winners in competitive elections) than for their more badly losing counterparts, at least among Democrats. For candidates of both parties, the extent of self-instigated recruitment was lower in the competitive than in the sure-loss districts. Among the 1965 incumbents, by contrast, less difference was found in the sources of candidate recruitment between safe-

Table 2.10 AGENTS OF CANDIDATE RECRUITMENT BY COMPETITIVE STATUS FOR TWO SETS OF HOUSE CANDIDATES

| | 1965 INCUMBENTS[a] | | 1962 LOSERS[b] | | | |
| | | | ALL LOSERS | | MARGINAL LOSERS | |
AGENT	SAFE (%)	COMPETI-TIVE/ MINORITY (%)	REP (%)	DEM (%)	REP (%)	DEM (%)
Party	40	50.0	65	68	69	81
Self	45	37.5	35	34	17	28
N =	(20)[c]	(16)[c]	(128)[c]	(110)[c]	(29)[c]	(32)[c]

[a] Original data.
[b] Robert Huckshorn, *The Politics of Defeat* (Amherst, Mass.: University of Massachusetts, 1971), p. 49, table 3.1.
[c] Totals do not add to 100% because, for both sets, only some recruitment agents are included and, for the 1962 losers, multiple responses were permitted.

party congressmen and those whose party was marginal. The minority-party congressmen, however, were all recruited by the party, thus confirming the finding among the 1962 losers.[71]

Party recruitment does not vary so much by competitive status as by the organizational abilities of the party itself. What do vary by competitive status, however, are the reasons for which the party recruits candidates and the means by which they recruit. The nomination is not as attractive to potential candidates in the minority as in the majority party. Recruitment in the majority party could be a matter of selecting among several aspirants, while in the minority party, the leaders would have to actively seek a candidate in order to have someone on the ballot under the party's name. One or two active leaders would be sufficient for the latter, while a sizable and cohesive organization would be required to select—and enforce that selection—among several rival candidates.[72]

While party recruitment of candidates is tied both to the organizational capacity of the party and to the ability of the party leaders to control the outcome of the nomination process, the act of party recruitment is also related to the subsequent electoral reliance relationship between the congressman and his district party. The five types of electoral reliance discussed earlier are arrayed against the sources of candidate recruitment in Table 2.11. The candidates recruited by party

[71] The data for losing House candidates are reported in Huckshorn and Spencer, *The Politics of Defeat*, p. 49. The data on the 1965 House incumbents are reported in Olson, "Congressmen and Their Diverse Congressional District Parties," pp. 249–250.

[72] Sorauf, *Party and Representation*, p. 57; Seligman et al., *Patterns of Recruitment*, pp. 75–76; Jewell and Olson, *American State Political Parties and Elections*, pp. 89–93. The same finding is reported for Belgian parties in Obler, "Intraparty Democracy and the Selection of Parliamentary Candidates: The Belgian Case," p. 169, footnote 11.

Table 2.11 ELECTORAL RELIANCE BY AGENTS OF CONGRESSIONAL RECRUITMENT

ELECTORAL RELIANCE RELATIONSHIP	AGENTS OF RECRUITMENT			
	PARTY (%)	FACTION (%)	ASSOCIATES (%)	SELF (%)
A. Party	44	67	50	0
B. Faction	6	0	0	0
C. General elections	19	0	0	27
D. Nominations	25	0	50	0
E. Self	6	33	0	73
Total:	100	100	100	100
$N =$	(16)	(3)	(2)	(15)
Gamma $= 0.671$				

and faction tended to rely heavily upon their party in subsequent elections, whereas the self-recruited candidates overwhelmingly relied upon their own efforts. It would appear that the ability of the party to participate actively in election campaigns and the ability of the party to recruit candidates are related aspects of a more general capacity of the party and its leaders to be effective participants in the electoral process within their respective districts. In addition, that ability changes slowly; it tends to persist through a series of elections, so party activity in recruitment, which necessarily occurs prior to a congressman's initial election, continues in later years in the form of active election support.

Given the recent American political speculation that our political parties are in a state of decline, the extent of party activity in candidate recruitment may be surprising. Though campaign financing is very much conducted by individual candidates, and increasingly through "political action committees," and even though the extent of policy agreement between Congress and the president may be in question, party leaders do appear to remain active in candidate recruitment. This act is one of the earliest of all election activities, occurs outside the glare of publicity, and most relies upon individual contacts and informal discussions. It is an activity in which a few individual party leaders, as contrasted with large party organizations, can participate with maximum effectiveness.

CAMPAIGN FINANCE

United States

Finances are a basic resource in an election campaign. Efforts to reach the voter are expensive, and the more campaigns turn to TV and management by professional consultants, the more expensive they become.

Table 2.12 CAMPAIGN FINANCES, U.S. SENATE GENERAL ELECTIONS, 1976: AVERAGE EXPENDITURE AND AVERAGE COST PER VOTE BY PARTY, STATUS OF CANDIDATES, AND RESULT

CANDIDATE STATUS AND RESULTS	DEMOCRATS		REPUBLICANS		
	AVG. TOTAL EXPENDI- TURE ($)	AVG. COST PER VOTE ($)	AVG. TOTAL EXPENDI- TURE ($)	AVG. COST PER VOTE ($)	NO. OF STATES
A. Democratic incumbents			Republican challengers		
Win			Lose		10
	476,770	0.73	221,303	0.66	
Lose			Win		5
	714,201	1.57	605,153	1.52	
B. Democratic challengers			Republican incumbents		
Lose			Win		4
	282,441	1.35	440,911	1.44	
Win			Lose		4
	1,008,440	0.81	1,319,670	1.12	
C. Open seats					
Win			Lose		5
	475,414	1.37	571,787	2.45	
Lose			Win		3
	904,431	2.03	1,387,310	1.25	

SOURCE: Calculated from *Congressional Quarterly Weekly Report,* June 25, 1977, p. 1293. This table excludes two uncontested elections.

The magnitude of campaign expenses is illustrated in Table 2.12 for the 1976 elections to the U.S. Senate. It shows the average total expenses, and the average cost per vote received, for three types of Senate contests: (1) Democratic incumbents contested by Republican challengers, (2) Republican incumbents challenged by Democratic candidates, and (3) open seats lacking an incumbent. In addition, the figures are averaged separately for the winners and losers within each category. In elections with senatorial incumbents, the incumbents spent more than did the challengers, regardless of whether they lost or won. Their greater expenditures perhaps indicate that incumbents usually are more able to raise campaign funds than are challengers. On the average, the lowest expenditures were about $220,000 (losing Republican challengers) while the highest average amount spent was about $1,320,000 (losing Republican incumbents). Costs were higher in the open races. The largest average amount spent was about $1,390,000 (winning Republicans), with their losing Democratic opponents spending about two-thirds as much ($905,000).

Electorates for the Senate are whole states, which vary greatly in size and hence in campaign expenditures. We have presented averages to even out the disparities among individual campaigns and their states. The same table presents another way to hold size constant: expenditures are calculated as cost per vote received by each candidate. On this basis, the cost of election campaigns still varies greatly. The lowest expenditure was $0.66 per vote (losing Republican challengers), while losing Democrats in open seats spent more than three times as much ($2.03) per vote.[73]

Winners did not consistently spend more than losers. The disparities, however, were greatest between incumbents who won (of both parties) and their loosing challengers, with the former spending almost twice as much as the latter in average dollar amounts, though the differences in their per-vote costs were not as great.

An adequate amount of campaign funds would seem a prerequisite to waging an effective campaign. Funds are translatable into the other resources needed to fuel a campaign and its organization: personnel, campaign advertising materials, TV time and production, travel, and the like. Yet we cannot claim that campaign finances, by themselves, make the difference between the winning and losing campaign. Normal party voting habits and incumbency seem to operate as powerful influences upon voter perception and upon the election results. As a result, campaign finance does appear to have a more critical function for challengers than for incumbents. The amount spent by challengers in the 1972 and 1974 congressional campaigns was associated with the number of votes they received, but that relationship was not found for incumbents. We do know from voter surveys that how people vote is related to their recognition of the names of candidates and that incumbents are better known than are challengers. It would appear that the more challengers spend, the greater the chances that voters will recognize their names and, as a result, their vote chances improve relative to that of incumbents.[74]

We cannot claim a great deal of established and verified knowledge about campaign financing, either of its sources or its effects upon elections. It is only as a result of Watergate-associated inquiries and reforms that we are now obtaining reasonably full public reporting of campaign financing. An associated development is the use of publicly provided funds in the presidential election of 1976. Up to 1979, however, Congress had refused to provide public financing for its own elections. Incumbents feared that their challengers would be advan-

---

[73] *Congressional Quarterly Weekly Report* (June 25, 1977), p. 1293.

[74] Gary C. Jacobson, "Practical Consequences of Campaign Finance Reform: An Incumbent Protection Act?" *Public Policy* 24 (Winter 1976), pp. 1–32, and Stanton A. Glantz et al., "Election Outcomes: Whose Money Matters?" *Journal of Politics* 38 (November 1976), pp. 1033–1038. See also Charles Atkin and Gary Heald, "Effects of Political Advertising," *Public Opinion Quarterly* 40 (Summer 1976), pp. 216–228.

taged, each party feared that the other would be advantaged, and non-incumbents feared that incumbents would gain undue advantages.[75] But Congress is feeling one perhaps unanticipated result of public finance for presidential elections: the private funds which formerly went to candidates for that office until 1976 now flow into the congressional campaigns. Not only are campaign costs increasing, but so are the contributions.

Campaign Finance Abroad

In many other countries with competitive elections, some form of public finance is often used in election campaigns. Public funds are alloted to parties in proportion to their votes in some previous election. In addition, some countries, of which Sweden is an example, provide public funds to political parties for their interelection organizational and planning activities.

The British have a variation in campaign finance. A number of their parliamentary candidates are "sponsored" by interest groups, which usually pay a portion of the candidates' campaign expenses and often provide subsistence or expense funds for the successful ones while in office. Table 2.13 indicates that the number of sponsored candidates is constant in each election (about 25% of the total number of seats). While they are mainly also successful candidates, the exact number of winners vary. All sponsored candidates are in the Labour party (and its affiliated Cooperative party), and thus the success rate of the sponsored candidates varies with Labour's fortunes in any one election.

Table 2.13 BRITISH SPONSORED CANDIDATES BY ELECTION YEAR AND RESULTS

ELECTION RESULT	YEAR AND CANDIDATES					
	1966		1970		1974 (OCT.)	
	N	%	N	%	N	%
Win	150	92.6	129	78.6	142	88.2
Lose	12	7.4	35	21.3	19	11.8
Total	162	100.0	164	99.9	161	100.0

SOURCE: David Butler and Dennis Kavanagh, *The British General Election of October 1974* (New York: St. Martin's, 1975), p. 217; pp. 932–934; David Butler and Michael Pinto-Duschinsky, *The British General Election of 1970* (New York: St. Martin's, 1971), p. 299.

[75] The controversies are reviewed in *Congressional Quarterly Weekly Report* (April 16, 1977), pp. 707–713. The major studies, up to 1974, are reviewed in Jeffrey M. Berry, "Electoral Economics: Getting and Spending," *Polity* (Fall 1974), pp. 120–129. State level developments are summarized in Jewell and Olson, *American State Political Parties and Elections*, pp. 205–212.

The candidates are mainly sponsored by trade unions, which are also affiliated with the Labour party itself. Candidate sponsorship was developed by unions to obtain working-class representation in Parliament, for their candidates often lacked the personal wealth or professional-business occupations that permit Conservative members to pay their own living expenses during parliamentary sessions. It was also a means of balancing the flow of business originated finances to the Conservative party and its candidates.[76]

In one-party nations the costs of campaigns can still be high, for they commonly go to great lengths to stimulate a high voter turnout. We would guess that such costs, however, are usually paid by the government, so neither the candidates nor the party need attempt to raise the funds themselves.

In Japan the campaign financing system is directly tied to the system of factions within the larger parties, especially within the Liberal Democratic party. In spite of its name, it is a conservative and business-oriented party, which since its creation in the mid-1950s has been the largest and governing party. Its candidates receive party funds, and they also raise funds locally. These two sources together provide about 75% of the needed approximately $300,000 for each candidate. For the remaining 25%, candidates approach the faction leaders, who are such because they can raise funds from outside sources. Based upon the official expense reports, several of the factions within the Liberal Democratic party had well over 20% of the total funds available to the party itself, and together they spent more than did the official party.[77]

COMPETITION, TURNOVER, AND TURNOUT

The definitive act of the citizen in an election campaign is to vote. By voting, citizens decide which parties and which persons shall enter public office and exercise the powers of government. The citizens' choices, however, are greatly constrained by all of the considerations we have discussed to this point.

Do the election campaigns result in, and are the members of parliament selected by, a competitive process? Does a system of elections also imply participation in the elections by a large proportion of the population? In most nations, the answer to the second question is

---

[76] Butler and Kavanagh, *The British General Election of October 1974*, pp. 217–218; David Butler and Michael Pinto-Duschinsky, *The British General Election of 1970*, p. 299; Richard Kimber and John D. Lees (eds.), *Political Parties in Modern Britain* (London: Routledge, 1972), p. 66.

[77] Baerwald, *Japan's Parliament*, pp. 49–50.

Table 2.14 PARTY TURNOVER IN CONGRESSIONAL
SEATS, 1914–1970

TIME PERIOD	PARTY-CHANGE ELECTIONS (%)	SAME-PARTY DISTRICTS (%)
1914–1926	11.8	62.1
1932–1940	10.6	69.9
1942–1950	11.9	74.0
1952–1960	7.8	78.2
1962–1970	8.2	76.5

SOURCE: Charles O. Jones, "Inter-Party Competition for Congressional Seats," *Western Political Quarterly* 17 (September 1964), p. 465, as reported and updated by William J. Keefe and Morris S. Ogul, *The American Legislative Process*, 4th ed. (Englewood Cliffs, N.J.: Prentice-Hall, 1977), p. 98, table 4.3.

"yes," even though the answer to the first question is much more variable. It is only in some nations—mainly those in Western Europe and its derivative nations such as the United States—that elections are competitive. Most other nations have single-party systems. Although some of the single-party nations have nominated multiple candidates, some of the two-party or even multiparty nations have relatively uncontested elections. Thus, the answers to the competition question are variable and perhaps also contradictory.

Extent of Competition in General Elections

PARTY TURNOVER

One component of competition is *party turnover*—the extent to which any given legislative seat is, over a period of time, held by occupants of different political parties. In the U.S. Congress from 1914 to 1970 the rate of party turnover decreased slightly (Table 2.14). In the period from 1914 to 1950 the party turnover rate was about 11%. Since then, however, the rate has dropped to about 8%. The percentage of congressional districts in which the same party has held the seat has slowly risen from 65% in the earliest period to 78% in the 1950s.[78] Although the party ratios in Congress are changeable (the Democratic share of seats usually ranges from 55% to 66%), the changes occur in only a relatively small portion of the districts. By contrast, the rate of

[78] Charles O. Jones, "Inter-Party Competition for Congressional Seats," *Western Political Quarterly* 17 (September 1964), p. 465, as reported and updated in William J. Keefe and Morris S. Ogul, *The American Legislative Process: Congress and the States*, 4th ed. (Englewood Cliffs, Prentice-Hall, 1977), p. 98.

Table 2.15 COMPETITION IN U.S. CONGRESSIONAL AND SENATORIAL ELECTIONS, 1966–1976

CHAMBER AND COMPETITIVE[a] CATEGORIES	ELECTION YEAR					
	1966 (%)	1968 (%)	1970 (%)	1972 (%)	1974 (%)	1976 (%)
HOUSE						
Competitive	17.0	16.6	12.5	14.9	22.3	14.5
Safe	72.2	73.3	76.3	75.2	67.4	78.4
Uncontested	10.8	10.1	11.2	9.9	10.3	7.1
Total	100.0	100.0	100.0	100.0	100.0	100.0
SENATE						
Competitive	29.4	48.5	42.4	47.1	39.9	24.2
Safe	61.8	45.4	57.5	52.9	57.1	69.7
Uncontested	8.8	6.1	0.0	0.0	3.0	6.1
Total	100.0	100.0	99.9	100.0	100.0	100.0

SOURCE: Adapted from William J. Keefe and Morris S. Ogul, *The American Legislative Process*, 4th ed. (Englewood Cliffs, N.J.: Prentice-Hall, 1977), p. 98. Separate calculations for 1976 are based upon *Congressional Quarterly Weekly Report*, March 19, 1977, pp. 491–498.
[a] Competitive districts are those won by margins of less than 10% between winner and next highest candidate.

party turnover in congressional seats was close to 50% in the 1850s. But by the 1890s the party turnover rate had dropped to a little over 20%.[79]

DISTRICT RESULTS

The election returns in each election and each district provide a more direct measure of competition. In about 10% of the U.S. House districts over the recent past, the seat has not been contested; only one party has had a candidate. These uncontested districts are usually Democratic. Most are southern, though some are located in northern cities. The contested districts can in turn be divided into "competitive" and "safe" districts. In a two-party system, we usually regard an election as competitive if the two major candidates are less than 10% apart from one another in their votes. If the difference between them is greater than 10%, the election is viewed as safe. By this definition, about 15% of the House seats were competitive (Table 2.15), while 78% were safe in 1976. By the same definitions, competition to the Senate is somewhat greater each year than to the House.

Party competition is more evenly spread geographically through-

[79] Samuel Kernell, "Toward Understanding 19th Century Congressional Careers: Ambition, Competition and Rotation," *American Journal of Political Science* 21 (November 1977), p. 681, table 1.

Table 2.16 PARTY OF CONGRESSMAN BY REGION, 1972

	REGION			
PARTY	NORTHEAST (%)	MIDWEST (%)	WEST (%)	SOUTH (%)
Dem	55.6	42.1	56.6	69.4
Rep	44.4	57.9	43.4	30.6
Total	100	100	100	100
N =	117	121	76	121

SOURCE: Calculated from U.S. Bureau of Census, *Congressional District Data Book, 93rd Congress,* Washington, D.C.: Government Printing Office, 1973.

out the United States now than at any time since the 1890s, as measured by presidential and gubernatorial elections.[80] The same trends have occurred in congressional elections as well (Table 2.16). Democrats and Republicans held approximately similar proportions of the seats in all the regions of the country except the South in the 1972 election; even in the so-called "solid South," Republicans had gained over 30% of the congressional seats.

Compared to statewide offices, elections to the U.S. House are by far the least competitive, while the U.S. Senate, along with the governorships, have been the most competitive.[81]

No similar tabulation of election data has been reported for state legislatures. We think that legislative elections are even less competitive than are congressional: more districts are uncontested, fewer are competitive, and fewer change party control than in the U.S. House. Paradoxically, the rate of personnel turnover is higher in most state legislatures than in the U.S. Congress. Members serve fewer years in office and more frequently either retire from public office or run for other offices. The greater rate of personal mobility in and out of the state legislature is not as much a function of two-party competition as it is of personal choice. In the 1917–1972 period, for example, the rate of membership turnover in state senates was 43%, and in the lower houses, 38%.[82]

COMPETITION ABROAD

We have little information on the extent of competition in foreign parliamentary elections. Data are available for Canada and Great Britain—the electoral systems most similar to our own. Using the

[80] Jewell and Olson, *American State Political Parties and Elections,* pp. 23–37.

[81] Joseph A. Schlesinger, *Ambition and Politics: Political Careers in the United States* (Chicago: Rand McNally, 1966), pp. 60–62.

[82] Murray S. Stedman, Jr., *State and Local Governments* (Cambridge, Mass.: Winthrop, 1976), pp. 110–111.

definition of 12% difference in the votes between the two highest candidates, 24% of British parliamentary districts were "competitive" in October, 1974, while 76% were "safe." These figures are quite similar to the American Congress. The number of uncontested districts, however, is much lower in Britain.[83]

A different measurement standard has been applied to Canada, because four parties are major competitors in their election. A 3% difference has been used to define competition, coupled with party turnover in a span of four elections. By these standards, 44% of Canadian parliamentary districts in the 1950s were competitive—a much higher rate than in either Britain or the United States. At the other extreme, none were uncontested, perhaps as a result of having four parties rather than only two, each of which has a different regional basis of strength.[84]

The West German Bundestag is also characterized by reelection of incumbents and safe elections. Within single-member districts, 16% of the elections were competitive, defined as having a margin between the two top competitors of less than 10% of the vote.[85]

Measurement of competition in proportional representation systems is much different, and more difficult, than in plurality systems. For those parties which are likely to obtain more than 20% of the vote in any given multimember district, the candidates at the top of their party list are assured of election. With equal assurance, unless their party obtains at least 90% of the votes, the candidates toward the bottom of the list will lose. Only two or three candidates in the middle of the party list are likely to have their electoral fate decided in any given election. Furthermore, the party share of the vote is ordinarily quite stable between any two elections. Thus, party leaders and candidates alike make their nomination decisions with a fair degree of certainty about which ones are likely to be elected.[86]

INCUMBENCY

In these systems the rate of defeats of candidates—especially incumbents—is perhaps the best available measure of competition. Fortunately for our purposes, data are available for West Germany—the one country that uses both proportional representation (for half the

---

[83] Butler and Kavanagh, *The British General Election of October 1974*, p. 334, table 3. These data apply only to England and Wales.

[84] Allan Kornberg, *Canadian Legislative Behavior: A Study of the 25th Parliament* (New York: Holt, Rinehart and Winston, 1967), p. 62, footnote 49.

[85] Loewenberg, *Parliament in the German Political System*, pp. 74, 78.

[86] Jeffrey Obler, "Intraparty Democracy and the Selection of Parliamentary Candidates: The Belgian Case," *British Journal of Political Science* 4 (April, 1974), p. 170.

parliament) and single-member plurality systems (for the other half). Of the members serving in the 1957 Bundestag, 67% of those on party lists in multimember districts were reelected; the corresponding rate for incumbents in single-member districts was 77%.[87] The difference of 10% in the German reelection rates between the two types of district systems indicates that the larger district and multicandidate system, coupled with proportional representation, yields a greater degree of competition than does the single-member plurality system.

Incumbency is also about the only available measure of competition in one-party systems. It is the one-party systems that achieve fairly high rates of personnel turnover, by not renominating incumbents. And in those one-party systems with two or more candidates, incumbents appear to be more liable to defeat than in the competitive systems. In Kenya, for example, 54% of the incumbents seeking reelection in 1969 were defeated, and in 1974, 58% lost their seats. In neighboring Tanzania, in 1970, 34% of the incumbents were defeated and another 34% were denied renomination by the ruling party.[88] As these two examples indicate, a one-party system can produce considerable personnel turnover.[89]

Correlates of Competition

INCUMBENCY

Several factors seem to affect the extent of competition in congressional elections. Incumbency is one, for incumbents win a much higher proportion of their elections than do nonincumbents; the wide difference in the proportions of incumbents winning over nonincumbents is reduced only slightly by the result of the presidential election (Table 2.17).[90]

The congressman's second election is, for him, the critical one. His risk of defeat is greatest the first time he comes up for reelection. But if he wins that one, then the frequency of defeats declines markedly. In the 1956–1974 period, about 6% of the incumbent House members

[87] Loewenberg, *Parliament in the German Political System*, pp. 74, 82.

[88] Joel Barkan, "Bringing Home the Pork: Legislative Behavior, Rural Development and Political Change in East Africa," in Joel Smith and Lloyd Musolf (eds.), *Legislatures in Development* (Durham, N.C.: Duke University Press, forthcoming), chap. 10.

[89] In Yugoslavia, the incumbency return rates have varied from 34% to a high of 54%. See James H. Seroka, "Legislative Recruitment and Political Change in Yugoslavia," *Legislative Studies Quarterly* 4 (February 1979), pp. 105–119.

[90] Milton C. Cummings, Jr., *Congressmen and the Electorate: Elections for the U.S. House and the President, 1920–1964* (New York: Free Press, 1966), pp. 68–72.

Table 2.17   ELECTION VICTORIES BY INCUMBENTS AND
NONINCUMBENTS CONTROLLING FOR PARTY WINNING
PRESIDENCY, IN PRESIDENTIAL ELECTION YEARS 1920–1964

	PARTY LOSING PRESIDENCY (%)	PARTY WINNING PRESIDENCY (%)
Incumbents win	83	97
Nonincumbents win	11	32
Index of difference	72	65

SOURCE: Adapted from Milton Cummings, *Congressmen and the Electorate*, (New York: Free Press, 1966), pp. 69–71, tables 3.3 and 3.4.

were defeated in general elections; the loss rate for freshmen, in their first reelection attempt, was close to 15%. Of all incumbents losing general elections, one-third were freshmen.[91]

The same finding emerges in a national sample of 36 districts. The congressmen were divided almost evenly between having safe election results (over 10% more than their opponent) and marginal ones in their initial election. By the time of their third election, however, three had been defeated, while all of the others had attained personally safe seats. In their initial election, their own votes largely paralleled the competitive status of their party: 80% of the safe party members won by similarly safe margins, whereas 81% of the members from minority and marginal parties won by a narrow margin. All of the three members who were defeated by the time of their third election came from the marginal district parties. That all the other members from marginal and even minority parties developed personally safe seats is an indication that incumbents gain security through their electoral career if they survive the critical first two reelection attempts. The longer House members are in office, the more they tend to have safe rather than marginal seats.[92]

But incumbency might be a declining asset as the incumbent ages and as the political composition of the electorate changes slowly through the years. Among U.S. Senators, those seeking reelection to their fourth terms (of six years' duration each) were defeated much more frequently than incumbents seeking their second and third terms.[93] Incumbency, however, does seem to be increasing in importance in Senate elections, whereas that of party seems to be declin-

[91] Charles O. Jones, *Every Second Year* (Washington, D.C.: Brookings, 1967), p. 68; Jewell and Patterson, *The Legislative Process in the United States*, p. 91.

[92] Roger Davidson, *The Role of the Congressman* (New York: Pegasus, 1969), p. 157.

[93] Donald R. Matthews, *U.S. Senators and Their World* (New York: Vintage, 1960), p. 241.

Table 2.18 PROPORTION OF NONINCUMBENT CANDIDATES WINNING HOUSE ELECTIONS BY ELECTORAL CIRCUMSTANCES OF THE SEAT AND BY PARTY FATE IN PRESIDENTIAL ELECTIONS 1924–1964

	ELECTORAL CIRCUMSTANCES OF SEAT		
		OPEN SEAT PREVIOUSLY HELD BY	
PARTY FATE IN PRESIDENTIAL ELECTION	INCUMBENT OTHER PARTY	OTHER PARTY	OWN PARTY
Party losing presidential election	4%	14%	74%
Party winning presidential election	20%	29%	87%

SOURCE: Adapted from Milton Cummings, *Congressmen and the Electorate* (New York: Free Press, 1966), p. 128, table 4–4.

ing, at least as judged by the aggregate election returns.[94] Data from national voter surveys indicate that, although party voting in senatorial elections is more important than is voting for the incumbent, incumbency of the senator accounts for almost a full half of the instances in which voters split their votes by party between the president and the senator.[95]

PARTY POSSESSION OF SEAT
A second factor associated with competition in congressional elections is the previous party control of the seat. We have already noted (Table 2.14) that more than 75% of the seats have not changed party control, irrespective of whether the same person was in office or not. This factor may largely account for the tendency of incumbents to be reelected. The importance of the prior party control of the congressional seat may be gauged from Table 2.18, which lists three types of electoral circumstances facing nonincumbent candidates: (1) seats held by incumbents of the other party, (2) open seats previously held by the other party, and (3) open seats previously held by one's own party. The percentages of victories by the nonincumbent candidates increase from the first through the third of these electoral circumstances. The same table distinguishes the candidates by the result of their own party's concurrent presidential election: Within each electoral circumstance, the proportion of nonincumbents winning is higher for those whose party was simultaneously winning the presidential election than losing it. But the differences by this last factor are much less than by the electoral circumstances concerning each district's own House seat.[96]

[94] Kostroski, "Party and Incumbency in Postwar Senate Elections," pp. 1213–1234.

[95] Andrew T. Cowart, "Electoral Choice in the American States: Incumbency Effects, Partisan Forces, and Divergent Partisan Majorities," *American Political Science Review* 67 (September 1973), pp. 835–853.

[96] Cummings, *Congressmen and the Electorate,* pp. 76–77.

Table 2.19 PROPORTION OF NONINCUMBENT CANDIDATES WINNING HOUSE ELECTIONS BY ELECTORAL CIRCUMSTANCES OF THE SEAT, 1974 MIDTERM ELECTIONS

ELECTORAL CIRCUMSTANCE AND ELECTION RESULT	PARTY OF NONINCUMBENT CANDIDATE			
	DEMOCRATIC		REPUBLICAN	
	N	%	N	%
1. Incumbent of other party:				
Win	36	22.2	4	2.5
Loss	126	77.8	157	97.5
Total	162	100	161	100
2. Open seat previously held by other party:				
Win	13	56.5	2	7.4
Loss	10	43.5	25	92.6
Total	23	100	27	100
3. Open seat previously held by own party:				
Win	25	92.6	10	43.5
Loss	2	7.4	13	56.5
Total	27	100	23	100

SOURCE: *Congressional Quarterly Weekly Report,* November 9, 1974, pp. 3084–3091.

While these data report presidential-year elections, we would hypothesize that the same results would be obtained for the midterm years as well. This hypothesis is confirmed, at least for the 1974 midterm election. Even though 1974 was a Democratic sweep (the Watergate episode had culminated in Nixon's resignation only two months earlier), the proportions of each party's nonincumbent candidates winning varied by the same three district electoral circumstances as in presidential years (Table 2.19).

NORMAL PARTY STATUS

A third factor that may be associated with the election fate of congressional candidates is the normal party status of their district. Congressmen normally come from the dominant party of their respective districts, it is hypothesized; that is, they come from the party that usually wins elections to most other offices within the district.[97] If so, the tendency of incumbents to be reelected and for nonincumbents to win open seats previously held by their own party largely would be

[97] Keefe and Ogul, *The American Legislative Process,* pp. 109–110; Lewis A. Froman, Jr., "A Realistic Approach to Campaign Strategies and Tactics," in M. Kent Jennings and L. Harmon Zeigler (eds.), *The Electoral Process* (Englewood Cliffs, N.J.: Prentice-Hall, 1966), p. 12.

explained. Indeed, one study has estimated that incumbency, by itself, added only about 2% over the party's normal share of the vote in the 1952–1960 period in House elections.[98] On the evidence of the 36-district sample, however, we would have to judge that the hypothesis is accurate for most congressmen in their initial election. But even this small sample found examples of the very improbable type—the member who was elected even though his own party was minority in its competitive status. Furthermore, the hypothesis does not accommodate those members who build personally safe seats through their incumbency, even though the marginal and even minority status of their district parties does not change.

This hypothesis may be recast in terms of local elections. The congressional office is suspended between the nationwide presidential office and those elected at purely local levels. Perhaps voting for congressional candidates reflects a surge for a party from below as well as a pull from above. To test this interpretation adequately we would need election statistics for a variety of local offices cast within a congressional district, but such data are not reported in any national source. As a result, the only tests of the broader hypothesis are based upon the votes cast for the offices of president, U.S. senator, and governor.[99]

PRESIDENTIAL ELECTION

The presidential election, as the fourth factor, also has an impact on congressional elections, and we have discussed this influence simultaneously with the factors of incumbency and previous party control of the seat.

The votes for the House of Representatives and for president tend to vary together, but not completely. This relationship is shown in Table 2.20 and Figure 2.1 for the postwar presidential election years. Although the graph lines in Figure 2.1 vary together, the presidential line swings up and down more than the House vote. Over a long period, 1896–1964, the congressional vote for the party of the winning presidential candidate has changed only at about 30% of the rate of change (whether gain or loss) of the presidential candidate.[100] But, if anything, the difference in party vote between the two offices has

[98] Robert S. Erikson, "The Advantage of Incumbency in Congressional Elections," *Polity* 3 (Spring 1971), pp. 395–405.

[99] These three offices are the only ones for which the votes are tabulated and reported nationally by congressional district. The data are published in an irregular series by Congressional Quarterly. The presidential-local convergence theory is also expressed in Cummings, *Congressmen and the Electorate*, p. 206.

[100] Cummings, *Congressmen and the Electorate*, pp. 6–7, 25, 58–59; Gerald H. Kramer, "Short-Term Fluctuations in U.S. Voting Behavior, 1896–1964," *American Political Science Review* 65 (March 1971), p. 140.

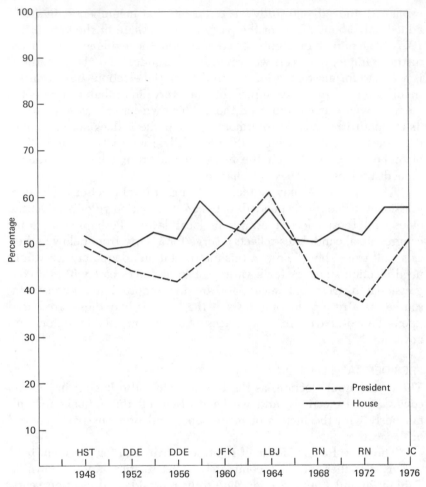

Figure 2.1   National vote for Democratic presidential and U.S. House candidates, 1948–1976. (Source: Table 2.20.)

been increasing. In the five presidential elections since 1948 (Table 2.20), the Democratic share of the national vote for the House has exceeded their presidential vote by over 5%.

The result is that the party of the winning presidential candidate usually (but not always) gains seats in the House in the same election. Tables 2.17 and 2.18, shown earlier, indicate that somewhat higher proportions of congressional candidates of the president's party usually win, under any given district electoral circumstances, than do candidates of the other party. When congressional seat gains are made by the president's party, that gain is interpreted as a "coattail" effect, in which the popular (because he won) presidential candidate pulls in, or attracts votes to, the congressional candidates of his party. Whatever the merits of such an interpretation, we must also consider what

Table 2.20 NATIONAL VOTE FOR DEMOCRATIC PRESIDENTIAL AND HOUSE CANDIDATES, 1948–1976

| YEAR | PARTY OF PRESIDENTIAL WINNER | OFFICE AND DEMOCRATIC VOTE | | DIFFERENCE IN PERCENT OF HOUSE OVER PRESIDENTIAL |
		PRESIDENT (%)	HOUSE (%)	
1948	D	49.6	51.9	+ 2.3
1950			49.0	
1952	R	44.4	49.7	+ 5.3
1954			52.5	
1956	R	42.0	51.1	+ 9.1
1958			59.2	
1960	D	49.7	54.2	+ 4.5
1962			52.3	
1964	D	61.1	57.4	− 3.7
1966			50.9	
1968	R	42.7	50.2	+ 7.5
1970			53.4	
1972	R	37.5	51.7	+14.2
1974			57.6	
1976	D	50.1	56.2	+ 6.1

SOURCES: U.S. Bureau of the Census, *Historical Statistics of the U.S.: Colonial Times to 1970,* Bicentennial ed., part I (Washington, D.C.: Government Printing Office, 1975), p. 1084; U.S. Bureau of the Census, *Statistical Abstract of the United States: 1977,* 98th ed. (Washington, D.C.: Government Printing Office, 1977), p. 496, table 794.

happens in the next succeeding congressional election, which occurs only two years later. In midterm elections, the president's party usually loses seats.

MIDTERM ELECTIONS AND "BOUNCE-BACK"

The rate of the midterm loss is related to the extent of the presidential-year gain. That is, a presidential-year gain in the House seats carries with it a built-in "bounce back" factor. Such presidential year gains and off-year losses are concentrated in marginal districts in which the presidential winner obtained between 40% and 60% of the vote.[101] Furthermore, the off-year losses are also concentrated in the switched-seat districts, that is, the very seats that were shifted to the president's party in the presidential election year. In 1954 and 1958, for example, of those Republican seats that were both switched and marginal, 95% and 100% of those seats were lost in the midterm elections, respectively.[102]

There is one other regularity in the midterm phenomenon: the

[101] Cummings, *Congressmen and the Electorate,* p. 51.

[102] Barbara Hinckley, "Interpreting House Midterm Elections: Toward a Measurement of the In-Party's 'Expected' Loss of Seats," *American Political Science Review* 61 (September 1967), pp. 696–697, footnote 15.

loss of congressional seats by the presidential party is greater in the second presidential term than in the first. The big Democratic gain during the Eisenhower presidency occurred in 1958, not 1954, and during the Nixon-Ford presidential sequence of two terms, in 1974 not 1970. Likewise, the big Republican gains during the Kennedy-Johnson sequence occurred in 1966, not 1962.[103]

There seems to be a bounce-back effect in House seats whenever one party gains an unusually high proportion of the seats. Democrats, for example, gained 49 seats in the midterm election of 1958. Although that Republican loss can be understood in terms of the previous discussion of midterm elections, we can look at the same event from the perspective of the Democrats. In that year, their proportion of the House seats rose from their usual 55–60% share to 66%. In the following presidential election, however, Democrats lost seats, reverting to their normal 60% share, even though Kennedy won in the same election (1960). But Democrats did manage to escape the bounce-back effect in 1976 in the Carter election. In the previous midterm election of 1974, Democrats again won 66% of the House seats. The result two years later was most unusual in that for the first time since World War II, the congressional landslide party (of 1974) did not lose their new seats, but held onto them in a second election (of 1976).

ELECTION BALLOT

A related factor concerns the type of election ballot. The states vary in their form of ballot: Some require the voter to vote separately for each office (an office block ballot), whereas others permit the voter to cast a single vote for a whole party slate (the party column ballot). The latter encourages a consistent party vote among the offices, whereas the latter discourages it.[104]

Competition in Nominations

Competition in American primaries usually is related inversely to competition in general elections. Safe parties are more likely to have contested primaries, while the minority parties in the same districts do not. In competitive districts, by contrast, both parties are likely to have contested primaries.[105]

---

[103] *Congressional Quarterly Weekly Report,* March 25, 1978, pp. 754–756.

[104] Angus Campbell and Warren E. Miller, "The Motivational Basis of Straight and Split Ticket Voting," *American Political Science Review* 51 (June 1957), pp. 293–312.

[105] V. O. Key, *American State Politics: An Introduction* (New York: Knopf, 1956), p. 173. A similar inverse relationship has been found in Belgium; see Obler, "Intraparty Democracy and the Selection of Parliamentary Candidates: The Belgian Case," p. 169, footnote 11.

EXTENT OF COMPETITION

American primary elections for Congress and the Senate are much less competitive than are general elections. Competition in primaries tends to occur in the congressman's initial election. Especially in an open seat—in which the incumbent is not running—several (even over a dozen) candidates may run. Once a candidate has won the nomination, however, and if he then wins the general election, he is likely to not be seriously challenged in the primary for the remainder of his congressional career. In the sample of 36 congressmen discussed earlier, for example, 50% had a contested initial primary. But only 39% had a seriously contested primary any time during their rather long, subsequent congressional careers.[106]

Even in parties lacking a congressional incumbent, 46% of the nominations were uncontested in the 1962 election. The lack of contests at least in part reflected the undesirability of the seat and the minority status of the party. In those districts in which the candidate did reasonably well in the general election (though they still lost), only 21% of the nominations were uncontested.[107]

In the three elections of 1972, 1974, and 1976, 84 incumbent House members were defeated, of whom 22% were defeated in primaries, while the remaining 78% were defeated in general elections. The bulk of the primary defeats occurred among Democrats, whereas Republicans suffered general-election defeats. And although general-election defeats tended to be concentrated among the freshmen members, the opposite was true for primary-election defeats: only two of the 18 nomination defeats occurred among members in their first or second term (refer to Table 2.21).

INCUMBENCY

In most countries incumbency is strongly related to the nomination process. Incumbents are generally entitled to renomination. Since it is not uncommon for an incumbent to serve a decade or more, the nomination decision is made rather infrequently. In American primaries —the nomination method most emphasizing the possibility of open competition—incumbents are frequently not challenged for renomination. When they are, they usually win by sizable margins. The same observation applies to other countries as well.

We may illustrate the tendency of incumbents to be renominated by examining the West German parliament. Of the 228 members

[106] The definition of competitiveness in primary elections is 75%. Any incumbent who obtained less than 75% of the primary vote is classified as having a competitive primary.

[107] Huckshorn and Spencer, *The Politics of Defeat*, pp. 52–53.

Table 2.21 CIRCUMSTANCES OF LEAVING U.S. HOUSE BY SENIORITY:
1972, 1974, AND 1976

	TERMS SERVED							
CIRCUMSTANCES OF LEAVING	1–2		3–5		6+		TOTAL	
	N	%	N	%	N	%	N	%
INVOLUNTARY								
Retirement	5	11.9	12	18.2	60	56.6	77	36.0
Defeat in general election	23	54.8	23	34.8	20	18.9	66	30.8
Defeat in primary election	2	4.7	6	9.1	10	9.4	18	8.4
Death	1	2.3	—		2	1.9	3	1.4
Other	—		2	3.0	3	2.8	5	2.3
UPWARD MOBILITY								
Run for senate	8	19.0	19	28.8	6	5.7	33	15.4
Run for governor	3	7.1	3	4.5	3	2.8	9	4.2
Judiciary	—		1	1.5	1	0.9	2	0.9
Appointive office	—		—		1	0.9	1	0.5
TOTAL	42	99.8	66	99.9	106	99.9	214	99.9

SOURCES: *Congressional Quarterly Weekly Report,* November 11, 1972, pp. 2955–2957; November 9, 1974, pp. 3065–3076; November 6, 1976, pp. 3119–3122. Commerce Clearing House, *Congressional Index,* 92nd Congress, 1971–1972, pp. 3001–3127; 93rd Congress, 1973–1974, vol. II, pp. 3001–3127; 94th Congress, 1975–1976, vol. II, pp. 3001–3120.

elected in single-member districts in 1953, only 43 were not renominated in the next election in 1957. Of them, only about 20 (close to 10%) had sought renomination but were refused by their constituency party. In the following 1965 election, 42 constituency members were not renominated (or about 20%). From the multimember proportional representation districts, also about 10% of the incumbents were refused renomination. In the West German case—unique because it combines both single- and multimember district systems—differences in those systems did not lead to different rates at which incumbents were renominated by their parties.[108]

As the German example indicates, incumbency is an important consideration in multimember proportional representation systems. Precisely where a candidate appears on a party list of several candidates, relative to that party's share of the vote, determines whether that candidate is elected or not. Incumbents, and especially party leaders, are placed at the top of their respective party lists, thus giving them greatest protection. The result is that incumbents are at least as well protected in multiparty and proportional systems as in the U.S. model.

[108] Loewenberg, *Parliament in the German Political System,* pp. 73–74.

A related result is that European parliaments have as much a seniority system (although an informal one) as does the U.S. Congress. The protection of incumbents is achieved, however, by very different methods. In the United States the nomination decision is subject to challenge in an electorate-wide primary, whereas in most other countries the choice is exclusively intraparty. In both systems, however, the result is approximately the same.

By and large, incumbents who choose to run again can expect to gain renomination. Yet British constituency parties have, on occasion, not "readopted" their incumbent member. In the 1948–1974 period, there were only 35 examples. The reasons for the refusal of constituency parties to renominate their own sitting member (whom they had previously "adopted," and for whom they had previously campaigned) were varied, with about half relating to personal characteristics of the members or personal relationships between the member and the party association. But a full half (though only 18 cases in a 26-year period) centered on the political views of the member.[109]

A lively controversy began in the mid-1970s on precisely this point of "readoptions" by constituency parties of their incumbent M.P.s. The argument was that the incumbent should be questioned by the local party and his actions in office scrutinized so that neither he nor the local party could assume an automatic renomination. As of 1978, this argument was advanced by the "left wing" of the British Labour party against what they perceived to be control by the moderates of the parliamentary Labour party and of the party's national headquarters.[110]

As we noted earlier, in one-party systems the proportions of new members in the legislature is much higher usually than in competitive systems. That result is accomplished at the nomination stage, at which time the dominant party does not renominate high proportions of the incumbents.

Exit and Personnel Turnover

Competition in either primary or general elections is only one reason for members leaving parliamentary office. If competition were the only reason, the rates of personnel turnover would be much lower than they are. In the U.S. Congress approximately 40% of the members who left the House in the 1970s were defeated in either primary or general elections (Table 2.21); the corresponding rate in the Senate

[109] A. D. R. Dickson, "MP's Readoption Conflicts: Their Causes and Consequences," *Political Studies* 23 (March 1975), pp. 62–70.
[110] *London Times*, May 25, 1978, p. 16 (Commentary by Ronald Butt, "This Dangerous New Party Game"), and October 4, 1978, p. 4.

Table 2.22 CIRCUMSTANCES OF LEAVING THE SENATE BY SENIORITY: 1972, 1974, AND 1976

CIRCUMSTANCES OF LEAVING	TERMS SERVED				TOTAL	
	1	2	3	4+	N	%
Retirement	3	3	4	11	21	50.0
Defeat in general election	6	3	5	2	16	38.1
Defeat in primary election	2	—	1	1	4	9.5
Death	—	—	—	1	1	2.4
Total	11	6	10	15	42	
Percent of total	(26)	(14)	(24)	(36)		100

SOURCES: *Congressional Quarterly Weekly Report,* November 11, 1972, p. 2951; November 9, 1974, p. 3061; November 6, 1976, p. 3128. Commerce Clearing House, *Congressional Index,* 92nd Congress, 1971–1972, pp. 1851–1893; 93rd Congress, 1973–1974, vol. 1, pp. 1851–1893; 94th Congress, 1975–1976, vol. 1, pp. 1851–1888.

was more than 45% (Table 2.22). Another 20% left the House to seek other political positions, most of them becoming candidates for the U.S. Senate, thus indicating that the House can be a stepping-stone to other, presumably higher offices. The Senate, by contrast, is a final office for most of its members; for them, only the presidency remains as a higher office.

The greater the rate at which members leave, the greater the rate at which new members enter. This rate—called *turnover*—varies among the world's parliaments, with the American Congress and the British Commons having one of the lowest, varying between 10% and 20% since the 1950s.

The turnover rate is related to the industrialization of nations (Table 2.23), with the parliaments having high rates of turnover being in the least industrialized countries.[111] By these standards, the average American state legislature—with turnover rates of about 30% to 40% —would be placed in about the same category as the national parliaments of Switzerland, Israel, and Lebanon.

In addition to the industrialization of the nation, there seems also to be the factor of age of the parliament itself. The longer a parliament has existed, the lower its rate of membership turnover. Although (again) systematic and comprehensive data are lacking, Table 2.24 contrasts the turnover rates for five countries at about the turn of the twentieth century with the rates at about 1960. In each case, the turn-over rate had dropped about 20% to 25% in the intervening half-century. Turnover in the early years of the U.S. Congress was close to 50%, which places the United States, at its early stage of political

[111] Jean Blondel, *Comparative Legislatures* (Englewood Cliffs, N.J.: Prentice-Hall, 1973), pp. 85–87, 160–161.

Table 2.23 MEMBERSHIP TURNOVER RATE BY INDUSTRIAL DEVELOPMENT OF NATION[a]

TURNOVER RATE	I (HIGH)	II	III	IV (LOW)
High			Costa Rica (100) Colombia (77)	Guatemala (100)
		USSR (67)		
			India (60)	Kenya (63) Chad (60)
Medium		Rumania (48) Afghanistan (45)		
	Finland (44)		Chile (41) Lebanon (35)	
		Israel (33)		
Low				
	Switzerland (28) France (26) Austria (24) Australia (24) Canada (18) U.K. (16) U.S. (15)			

SOURCE: Jean Blondel, *Comparative Legislatures* (Englewood Cliffs, N.J.: Prentice-Hall, 1973), pp. 160–161, appendix C.
[a] Figures in parentheses represent the turnover rate.

Table 2.24 MEMBERSHIP TURNOVER RATE IN FIVE NATIONS AT DIFFERENT TIMES

TIME	U.S. (%)	CANADA (%)	SWITZERLAND (%)	CHILE (%)	COLOMBIA (%)
1800	50	—	—	—	—
1890–1920	35	50	44	67	86
1950–1960	15	25	28	41	66

SOURCE: Jean Blondel, *Comparative Legislatures* (Englewood Cliffs, N.J.: Prentice-Hall, 1973), p. 87, table 7–3.

and industrial development, fairly close to contemporary Rumania, India, and Chad in the previous table.[112]

The cumulative turnover, however, is higher in the late 1970s than even a decade or two earlier. By 1979 close to half the House member-

[112] Ibid., pp. 86–87.

ship had served only one or two terms, whereas the equivalent proportion in 1959 was about 30%.

A number of consequences follow for parliaments that have a high turnover in their membership. On one hand, new members are more responsive to new policy preferences in the electorate than the older ones. But new members also have less experience and presumably less competence than the older ones. Furthermore, an institution such as the U.S. Congress, having a much more stable and experienced membership than does the political level of the executive branch, is thereby advantaged in its relationship with the executive.[113] Yet it is also possible that the influx of new and inexperienced members contributed to the difficulties the Carter administration experienced in its first term with Congress.

The fact that over half of those who left the House in the 1970s were not defeated, but left voluntarily, is perhaps a symptom of the discomfort congressmen experience. They retire more frequently, and sooner, in the 1970s than in previous decades, and they complain more —or at least we think they do—about the difficulties and unpleasant features of congressional life. One major source of their complaints is the way the public treats them—demanding certain kinds of votes on selected issues and demanding simple solutions to complex problems.[114]

Voter Turnout

Voter participation, or *turnout*, varies by office and election sequence. In presidential years, turnout in congressional elections is about 10% higher than in midterm congressional elections. Even in presidential years, the number voting for the congressional office is about 4% lower than voting for the presidential office (Table 2.25 and Fig. 2.2). This relationship seems to hold true for every region and in all districts considered separately as well as in the national totals.

We note and generally lament that our voter turnout rates are lower than in other western democracies. The United States usually ranks lower than the European democracies in our voter participation in parliamentary elections. Unfortunately for purposes of comparison, however, the conditions of voting are not the same in the United States as in most other countries.

The difference between the United States and other western democracies lies in the conditions of voter eligibility. In most other countries the voter becomes legally eligible to vote because a govern-

[113] Robert D. Putnam, *The Comparative Study of Political Elites* (Englewood Cliffs, N.J.: Prentice-Hall, 1976), pp. 66–67.
[114] Stephen E. Frantzich, "De-Recruitment: The Other Side of the Congressional Career Equation," *Western Political Quarterly* 31 (April 1978), pp. 105–126.

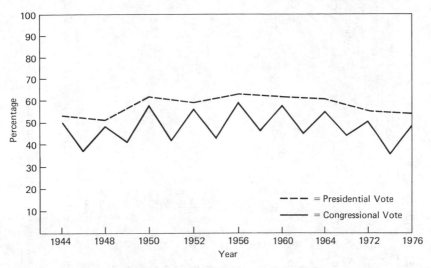

Figure 2.2   Voter turnout in presidential and congressional elections, 1944–1976. (Source: Table 2.25.)

ment agency has the responsibility of finding and listing each adult within any given area (such as a city or county) within one year prior to an election. In the United States, by contrast, no governmental agency has that responsibility. Instead, each person who wishes to vote must find and go to the appropriate office at least one month prior to any given election. While most other western democracies have a single administrative system for their election practices, we have 50 sets of state laws, and as many different administrative arrangements as counties (more than 3000) to implement the various state laws. The difference of who has the responsibility of legally qualifying persons to vote means that a much lower proportion of adults in the United States are actually registered on election day than in other nations.[115] The result is a much lower rate of voter participation.

Although voter participation may be lower in the United States than abroad in general elections, the reverse is true at the nomination stage. Our primaries are designed to attract sizable proportions of the electorate, which creates some of the problems for both parties and candidates that we have discussed earlier. But one result is that a much larger proportion of our population does participate in the making of nomination decisions than in other countries. This statement is accurate,

[115] William J. Crotty, *Political Reform and the American Experiment* (New York: Crowell, 1977), pp. 72–77. Some of the state practices are described on pp. 79–87. See also Steven J. Rosenstone, Raymond E. Wolfinger, and Richard A. McIntosh, "Voter Turnout in Midterm Elections," paper presented at American Political Science Association, New York, 1978, especially pp. 27–29.

Table 2.25 VOTER TURNOUT FOR PRESIDENTIAL AND CONGRESSIONAL ELECTIONS, 1944–1976

| YEAR | ESTIMATED POPULATION OF VOTING AGE | VOTE CAST FOR PRESIDENTIAL ELECTORS | | VOTE CAST FOR U.S. REPRESENTATIVES | | INDEX OF DIFFERENCES | |
| | | | | | | HOUSE DECLINE FROM PRESIDENT (%) | OFF-YEAR DECLINE FROM PREVIOUS HOUSE VOTE (%) |
		NUMBER	%	NUMBER	%		
1944[a]	89,517,000	47,977,000	53.6	45,103,000	50.4	3.2	—
1946	91,497,000	—	—	34,398,000	37.6	—	12.8
1948	94,470,000	48,794,000	51.7	45,933,000	48.6	3.1	—
1950	96,992,000	—	—	40,342,000	41.6	—	7.0
1952	99,016,000	61,551,000	62.2	57,571,000	58.1	4.1	—
1954	101,097,000	—	—	42,580,000	42.1	—	16.0
1956	103,625,000	62,027,000	59.9	58,426,000	56.4	3.5	—
1958[b]	105,727,000	—	—	45,655,000	43.2	—	13.2
1960	107,949,000	68,838,000	63.8	64,133,000	59.4	4.4	—
1962	110,266,000	—	—	51,304,000	46.5	—	12.9
1964	113,931,000	70,645,000	62.0	66,044,000	58.0	4.0	—
1966	115,882,000	—	—	52,874,000	45.6	—	12.4
1968	120,006,000	73,211,562	61.0	66,109,209	55.1	5.9	—
1970	120,456,000	—	—	54,168,913	44.9	—	10.2
1972	140,068,000	77,719,000	55.5	71,270,000	50.9	4.6	—
1974	145,035,000	—	—	52,391,000	36.1	—	14.8
1976	150,041,000	81,551,000	54.4	74,262,000	49.5	4.9	—

SOURCES: Congressional Quarterly, *Politics in America*, 4th ed., 1971, p. 74; U.S. Bureau of the Census, *Statistical Abstract of the United States: 1977*, 98th ed. (Washington, D.C.: Government Printing Office, 1977), p. 508, table 813.

[a] Includes 4,342,000 members of armed forces serving oversees.

[b] Includes Alaska, which voted for a Representative in November 1958, although statehood was not achieved until January 1959.

even though participation in our primaries is much lower than in general elections. In the 1976 congressional elections, for example, the average voter turnout, by district, was about 56,000 in Democratic and about 30,000 in Republican primaries, whereas the average number of persons voting in general elections was about 173,000 per district.[116]

Summary

We have discussed various ways to measure competition and the variations in voter turnout. By almost any measure, not all elections and offices, and certainly not all candidates and districts, are "competitive." In two-party systems, a sizable proportion of districts are likely to be safe for one party or the other. In multiparty systems employing multimember districts, most candidates have reasonably assured chances of election, varying with their placement on the party list. In either two-party or multiparty systems, incumbents are likely to be renominated and reelected. Although one-party systems lack the potential competition from a rival party, some single parties have experimented with multiple candidacies, and most have succeeded in having relatively high rates of personnel turnover in their parliaments.

Voter registration is a little-studied topic, but it is basic to the measurement of voter turnout. It may be that the real rate of voter participation in the United States is lower than elsewhere, but the conditions are so different between this and other countries that we lack the evidence with which to assess the statement.

The election system and the accompanying competition and turnout are expressions, within any given nation, of the relationship between the chief executive and the legislative body. A dual governmental structure, as in the United States, creates a dual election system. The different district systems for the two offices creates different electorates. There is a different rate of voter participation between the two offices, and the degree of competition and voter volatility differs as well. Within unitary parliamentary systems, all of these elements are fused into a single election process.

CONCLUSIONS

Elections are the main means by which members of representative and legislative institutions are now selected. Elections in which a large

---

[116] These figures are calculated from successive issues of *Congressional Quarterly Weekly Report* for 1976. Unfortunately, *CQ* does not report voter turnout in uncontested nominations, but neither do some states. We will never know the "real" number of persons who cast votes in primaries for Congress and thus can report turnout figures only for that minority of instances in which the nomination was contested.

proportion of the adult population is legally free to participate are usually regarded as an important component of democratic systems.

Elections, however, are complex phenomena. They are a kind of social invention, with which we tinker endlessly. Elections have three major components—the district system, the vote-counting method, and the party system—and each of these occurs in many variations. Their most typical combinations are exemplified by the election systems of the United States Congress, the Soviet Union, and of continental Europe.

We ordinarily think of political parties as mainly existing for the purpose of conducting campaigns in general elections. Yet, we have found that, at least for American congressional candidates, the working relationship between the candidates and the district parties varies from virtually complete cooperation and support to none. One of the main factors associated with that variation in campaign performance is the variation in the extent to which political parties are actually organized and functioning entities in various parts of the United States.

We would guess that most election campaigns abroad, compared to those in the United States, would be more centralized nationally and the political parties more active. The greater organizational vitality and activity of foreign parties, compared to American, is also demonstrated in the means by which candidates are nominated. In the United States, most nominations are made by a preliminary election, called *primaries,* whereas in most European nations, the nominations are made within the party organization. But in most countries the nominations are decided locally rather than by a national and centralized authority. The importance of the nomination process increases as a party increases the safety with which it holds a parliamentary seat. Within single-party nations, the nomination process appears to be the stage to which the major competition is displaced from the general election itself.

The recruitment of persons to become candidates for parliament is one of the more common activities by American party leaders. But the likelihood of party leader activity in candidate recruitment increases if the party is well organized and is able to control its nomination process. As a result we would expect, but do not have the evidence to show, that parties abroad are the most active candidate recruitment agents in their parliamentary elections.

Our knowledge of campaign finance practices is even more sketchy than of our previous topics in this chapter on elections. Spending does not always translate into votes. But the opportunities to raise funds are not, at least as judged by data from American senatorial elections, equally or randomly distributed. Incumbents raise and spend more funds than do their challengers, even though the challengers would appear to need the funds more. Campaigns abroad are often financed publicly. Yet the parties—or factions—are more clearly and overtly associated with fund raising and distribution abroad than is usually the case in the United States.

Personnel turnover and competition are both highly variable among the world's parliaments. More turnover is found within single-party systems than within the competitive ones, reflecting the control the dominant party exercises over the entire selection process. Within competitive party systems, incumbents tend to be reelected and also to be renominated. This election result is similar in the United States and in other democracies, even though their parties are organized very differently and use very different nomination methods.

Most elections are not competitive, even though the party systems themselves are competitive. That is, within any given single-member district the election result usually heavily favors one party or the other. Within multimember districts, the placement of candidates on the party lists is the main determinant of their election fates.

There is an implicit trade-off between competition (or at least personnel turnover) and expertise. If government is a complex task and if the administrative and interest group lobbyists are full-time and skilled professionals, how effective can a parliament be if it mainly consists of new and temporary amateurs?

This chapter has mainly considered the means by which citizens become members of parliaments, which in most countries means through some type of elective process. But what types of persons do become members of parliaments, and what views do they hold of their activities as members? The next chapter turns to such questions.

Chapter 3
The Dynamics of Representation

Representation is a complex and continuous process. It is not so much a single and discrete topic as it is a pervasive function that underlies and is expressed through everything else members of parliaments do. So is the function of interacting with the chief executive: In everything the members do, including running for election, their relationship to the chief executive is an omnipresent element. The members as individuals and parliaments as collective institutions, through their specific actions, simultaneously represent their electorates in the districts and interact with the executive power of the nation.

The previous chapter has considered the events through which members are selected by their electorates. Elections are one main means by which citizens are represented. Now we shall look at the other side of the representation relationship—what types of persons are elected as members of parliaments and what they do and think about their responsibilities while in office. This chapter, like the previous one, concentrates on the relationship between the parliament and its electorate.

CHARACTERISTICS OF MEMBERS AND CANDIDATES

Members of national parliaments tend to have more education than does the general population whom they represent. Their occupations are more business and professional than is true for the society as a whole, and their income is higher than the average. Although some women are elected, men are far more numerous both as candidates and as members. While members of parliaments are from relatively higher income and status groups of their society, they are not, however, from the highest of income or status groups.

Demographic Characteristics

The occupational composition of the U.S. Congress from the 1976 election is found in Table 3.1. Lawyers are the single largest occupational category, with business and banking in second place. The category of "other professional" is a disparate grouping of such specific occupations as journalism, medicine, the clergy, and so on. Missing completely from the membership are the blue-collar and middle-class occupations of factory worker, sales clerk, and the like.[1]

In American politics, lawyers are the most frequently found occupational group among legislators and congressmen. This has been the case, at least in Congress, since our beginnings. The proportion of lawyers is about the same for both parties. Republican congressmen, however, tend to come from higher-status law firms than do Democrats. The proportion of lawyers has been higher in the region of the country that, at any given time, was either relatively new or economically undeveloped, especially the South. From 70% to 90% of all southern Democrats in Congress have been lawyers, while 50% to 60% is the usual proportion in other regions.[2]

Many explanations have been suggested for the preponderance of lawyers in American politics. Legislative bodies do enact "laws" and thus handle a subject matter in which lawyers presumably have relevant training and skills. Another explanation is that the legal profession is a "broker" type of occupation, one that mediates between different segments of a society and emphasizes skills in interpersonal relations, the use of words, and in bargaining and negotiation. Although these traits are also useful to a politician, they are by no means confined to the legal profession.

A third explanation is more career oriented: Activity in partisan politics and holding elective office is a recognized means for lawyers

[1] *Congressional Quarterly Weekly Report,* January 1, 1977, p. 20.

[2] Roger Davidson, *The Role of the Congressman* (New York: Pegasus, 1969), pp. 37–49; Donald R. Matthews, *U.S. Senators and Their World* (New York: Vintage, 1960), pp. 35, 40–42.

Table 3.1 OCCUPATIONS OF MEMBERS OF U.S. CONGRESS BY CHAMBER AND PARTY, 1977–1978

	HOUSE						SENATE					
	DEM		REP		TOTAL		DEM		REP		TOTAL	
OCCUPATION	N	%	N	%	N	%	N	%	N	%	N	% (N = %)
Law	155	53.1	68	47.6	223	51.3	46	74.2	22	57.9	68	
Business/banking	69	23.6	49	34.3	118	27.1	14	22.6	10	26.3	24	
Education	57	19.5	15	10.5	72	16.6	8	12.9	4	10.5	12	
Public service politics	34	11.6	26	18.2	60	13.8	12	19.4	14	36.8	26	
Agriculture	6	2.1	10	7.0	16	3.7	3	4.8	6	15.8	9	
Other professional	16	5.5	9	6.3	26	6.0	4	6.5	3	7.9	7	
Labor leader	6	2.1	0	0.0	6	1.4	0	0.0	0	0.0	0	
N =	(292)	—	(143)	—	(435)	—	(62)	—	(38)	—	(100)	

SOURCE: *Congressional Quarterly Weekly Report*, January 1, 1977, p. 20.
NOTE: Members sometimes list two or more occupations. Thus, all percents are calculated on the number of members within each party and chamber.

to obtain judicial positions. In at least four state legislatures lawyers left the legislature at greater rates than did nonlawyers—and did so because they moved (advanced?) to judicial positions. The postlegislative career pattern could attract lawyers to the legislature in the first place. We do not have any information directly on this point, however, for lawyers in the U.S. Congress. By contrast, however, lawyers are almost completely absent from the Danish parliament. In that country, lawyers rise to a judicial position within the Ministry of Justice. Participation in politics in Denmark is itself a full-time career and would detract from a lawyer's full-time service within the Ministry. From this contrast between two countries, we can hazard the guess that the means of advancement to what lawyers most seek—judgeships—is a critical factor that leads lawyers to run for elective office or not.[3]

U.S. Senators were similar to the presidents of America's 100 largest corporations in that both sets of elites had university educations, came from families of long residence in the United States, and were mainly Protestant. They differed, however, in some respects, and on each point of difference the senators were less geographically mobile than were the corporation presidents. The latter tended more to attend Ivy League colleges, whereas the former were more likely to have gone to their home state public universities. Senators came from rural areas and small towns (64%), whereas corporation presidents more often grew up in metropolitan areas (52%). Although both groups were mainly Protestant, corporation presidents more often belonged to the high-status denominations than did the senators. Although the differences are not great between the two sets of elites, the political elite are more typical of the general population than are the economic elite.[4]

Somewhat the same conclusion can be drawn from a comparison of Iowa legislators with other elites in that state. In occupation and education, members of the state legislature were much more like their "attentive constituents" than the general public. To the extent there were differences between legislators and the other political elites, legislators were more like the general public than were the other political elites. But both the legislators and other political elites were disportionately lawyers and in other professional and managerial

[3] The data on state legislatures are reported in Paul L. Hain and James E. Piereson, "Lawyers and Politics Revisited: Structural Advantages of Lawyers-Politicians," *American Journal of Political Science* 19 (February 1975), pp. 41–51. The material on Danish lawyers is found in Mogens N. Pederson, "Lawyers in Politics: The Danish Folketing and United States Legislatures," in Samuel C. Patterson and John C. Wahlke (eds.), *Comparative Legislative Behavior: Frontiers of Research* (New York: Wiley-Interscience, 1972), pp. 25–63.

[4] Andrew Hacker, "The Elected and the Anointed: Two American Elites," *American Political Science Review* 55 (September 1961), pp. 539–549.

Table 3.2   SOCIAL ATTRIBUTES OF LEGISLATORS: ATTENTIVE
CONSTITUENTS AND THE PUBLIC (IOWA)

ATTRIBUTES	LEGISLATORS (%)	ATTENTIVE CONSTITUENTS (%)	PUBLIC (%)
OCCUPATION			
Lawyer	14	15	0
Managerial and other professional	44	57	14
Farmers	33	15	9
Blue-collar workers	5	3	15
Housewives	2	4	35
All other	2	6	27
Total	100	100	100
EDUCATION			
Some grade, high school	9	7	40
High school graduate	14	21	39
Some, graduate college	50	37	17
Postgraduate college	27	35	4
Total	100	100	100
RELIGION			
Protestant	77	81	76
Catholic	15	17	20
Other, No Response	9	3	4
Total	101	101	100
N =	181	484	1001

SOURCE: G. Robert Boynton, Samuel C. Patterson, and Ronald D. Hedlund, "The
Missing Links in Legislative Politics: Attentive Constituents," *Journal of Politics*
31 (August 1969), p. 704, table 1.

occupations (Table 3.2). Likewise, most of the legislators and other
political elites had attended college, whereas the opposite was true
for the general public. The profiles of both the legislators and other
political elites were most similar to that of the general public in their
religion.[5]

In religious affiliations, Roman Catholics were the largest single
group, with close to 25% of the 1977–1978 House membership, and the
Jewish membership was at 6%. Of the Protestant denominations,
Methodists (16%) and Episcopalians (12%) were the two largest in
the U.S. Congress.

The major discrepancies between the demographic composition of
Congress compared to the population as a whole concern social class,
race, and sex. Absent from Congress are blue-collar and wage employees. The black membership of Congress in the 1978 election was

[5] G. Robert Boynton, Samuel C. Patterson, and Ronald D. Hedlund, "The Missing
Links in Legislative Politics: Attentive Constituents," *Journal of Politics* 31
(August 1969), pp. 3–5, 700–721.

Table 3.3 SOCIOECONOMIC ATTRIBUTES OF MEMBERS OF
PARLIAMENT AND CIVIL SERVANTS: THREE EUROPEAN COUNTRIES[a]

	MEMBERS OF PARLIAMENT (%)	CIVIL SERVANTS (%)
FATHER'S OCCUPATION		
Managerial/professional	52	72
Manual	29	8
EDUCATION		
University degree	67	95
SIZE OF COMMUNITY WHERE RAISED		
Over 500,000	27	39
Under 25,000	48	26
N =	253	358

SOURCE: Robert D. Putnam, "Bureaucrats and Politicians: Contending Elites in the Policy Process," in William B. Gwyn and G. C. Edwards (eds.), *Perspectives on Public Policy-Making* (New Orleans: Tulane Studies in Political Science, vol. 15, 1975), p. 186, table 1.
[a] The three European countries included are Italy, Germany, and Great Britain. The figures do not add up to 100% within each attribute.

17, amounting to about 4% of the House membership compared to about 12% of the population; the Senate had one black member. Although women represent slightly over half of the U.S. population, the Senate had no women members from the 1976 election; in the House there were 17 women, or 4% of its membership.[6]

Members of parliament may also be compared to and contrasted with civil servants. In three European nations, members of parliament were more diverse in their socioeconomic characteristics than were the senior civil servants (Table 3.3).[7] Members of parliament and the civil servants both were predominantly from families of business and professional occupations and had obtained university educations, but less so in the case of the parliamentary members. A smaller proportion of parliamentary members also grew up in large cities than did the civil servants. In these respects at least, the elected members of parliament were more similar to their national populations than were the appointed civil servants.

The occupational composition of several of the world's parliaments is listed in Table 3.4 to show variations, not only among specific coun-

[6] *Congressional Quarterly Weekly Report*, January 1, 1977, pp. 19–21.

[7] Robert D. Putnam, "Bureaucrats and Politicians: Contending Elites in the Policy Process," in William B. Gwyn and George C. Edwards, III (eds.), *Perspectives on Public Policy-Making* (New Orleans: Tulane Studies in Political Studies, vol. 15, 1975), p. 186. For additional data on civil servants in a variety of countries, refer to B. Guy Peters, *The Politics of Bureaucracy: A Comparative Perspective* (New York: Longman, 1978), pp. 92–102.

Table 3.4 OCCUPATIONAL COMPOSITION OF PARLIAMENTS IN COUNTRIES BY THREE GEOGRAPHIC GROUPS

| | ATLANTIC | | EASTERN EUROPE | | THIRD WORLD | | |
| | U.S. (%) | U.K. (%) | POLAND (%) | USSR (%) | CHILE (%) | KENYA % | PAKIS- TAN (%) |
OCCUPATION							
Lawyers	56	18	1	1	19	3	18
Professional	23	28	21	31	36	33	—
Business	32	28	—	—	11	23	19
Landowner	9	7	—	—	11	—	58
Government officials	—	2	45	17	—	19	—
Worker, union repre- sentative	1	14	32	50	15	8	—

SOURCE: The figures for specific countries and years taken from Michael Mezey, *Comparative Legislatures* (Durham, N.C.: Duke University Press, 1979), table 11.1, pp. 240–242.
NOTE: Because residual occupations have been removed, columns do not total 100%.

tries but among different categories of countries. The selected nations are arranged by their geographic location, which in general is also associated with different degrees of industrialization. The Atlantic nations are highly industrialized, with the agricultural sector accounting for no more than 10% of the population. In the third-world nations, by contrast, anywhere from half to over 90% of the population are engaged in agriculture, with the Communist party nations of Eastern Europe occupying an intermediate category of economic development. Defined broadly, persons in professional occupations are a sizable component of most national parliaments. Lawyers are not as sizable a group elsewhere as in the United States and are virtually absent from communist nation parliaments. Businessmen are found in most parliaments outside of Eastern Europe, while landowners can be a sizable element in the third-world parliaments. Representatives of organized labor and/or workers loom large only in the Communist party states, while government officials are also a sizable element.[8]

The large proportion of members in high-education occupations in most of the parliaments indicates the complicated tasks of national legislative bodies. They place a premium upon the use and under-

[8] Jean Blondel, *Comparative Legislatures* (Englewood Cliffs, N.J.: Prentice-Hall, 1973), pp. 79–84; Michael L. Mezey, *Comparative Legislatures* (Durham, N.C.: Duke University Press, 1979), chap. 3.

standing of words and of research data. Persons in this type of occupation also have a more flexible work schedule than do factory workers and are more able to arrange their time to attend community meetings and to mobilize voter support.

The absence of workers in many parliaments perhaps reflects a social bias in their political systems or at least the absence of an organized worker's political movement. The presence of landowners perhaps even more indicates the direction of social and economic bias in the whole political system, while the presence of government (and party) officials increases the possibilities for government control over the agenda and results of parliamentary activity.

The marked changes in the composition of the Turkish parliament perhaps is a precursor of changes that might occur in other underdeveloped and traditional nations as they gain independence and attempt to develop economically and politically. In the early Turkish parliaments, around the time of World War I, government officials constituted half of the membership, and the military were almost half of them. The professions constituted about 20% of the membership, while members from the economic sector were under 20%. By the mid-1960s government officials declined to about 20% of the membership (military were at 5%), while the professions increased to over 50% and the economic sector to over 30%. Landowners were never as large a proportion of the Turkish parliament as they have been in Pakistan. Over the same period of time, lawyers have doubled, from 13% in the first parliament to 26% in the mid-1960s. These changes show both a diminution of the overt role of the governmental sector in parliament and a broadening of the socioeconomic base of parliament itself. These twin developments have accompanied the growth first, of an electoral system, and second, of a competitive two-party system.[9]

A similar change had occurred, though much earlier, in the composition of the membership of the British House of Commons. In the 1774–1840 period, landowners were about 80% of the membership of the House. Considerably after agriculture's share of the national income had begun to decline and manufacturing had begun to rise, the proportion of landholders declined to 30% of the members of Commons by 1900, whereas that of manufacturers and mine owners climbed to 35% in 1900 from about 8% in 1840. By 1900, workers constituted about 3% of the membership and rose to about 20% in the 1920s. These changes accompanied the broadening of the suffrage and the growth of party organization and competition. As a rule,

[9] Frederick W. Frey, *The Turkish Political Elite* (Cambridge, Mass.: MIT Press, 1965), p. 210; Dankwart A. Rustow, "The Development of Parties in Turkey," in Joseph LaPalombara and Myron Weiner (eds.), *Political Parties and Political Development* (Princeton: Princeton University Press), pp. 119–125.

Table 3.5 OCCUPATIONAL COMPOSITION OF
PARLIAMENTS IN USSR AND HUNGARY[a]

OCCUPATION	USSR 1966 (%)	HUNGARY 1975 (%)
Government, party, organizations	34.0	28.1
Factory workers	26.6	14.2
Agriculture	19.4	17.3
Professional, managerial, clerical	16.2	25.6
Others	3.7	14.8
Total	99.9	100.0

SOURCES: David Lane, *Politics and Society in the USSR* (New
York: Random House, 1971), pp. 154–156; Peter A. Toma and
Ivan Volgyes, *Politics in Hungary* (San Francisco: Freeman,
1977), pp. 59–62.
[a] The Hungarian data have been rearranged to match the categories
of the USSR data. The categories employed for this comparison are
different from those used in Table 3.4; thus the percentages are
also different.

changes in the socioeconomic composition of political elites in most
societies lag behind the changes occurring in the wider society, perhaps
irrespective of the electoral and party systems.[10]

Whether the presence of lawyers in the American Congress and
the absence of lower-status representatives is itself an indication of
social and ideological bias in the resulting government policy is not
directly answerable from that one datum alone. Lawyers themselves
are a relatively affluent and well-educated group; however, the more
relevant question concerns their clients. If an attorney has clientele of
companies and business, he may develop one set of political views and
friends; if he engages in labor law and workmen's compensation on
behalf of unions and workers, he may develop a different set of political
views and a different set of political friends. In the U.S. Senate,
attorneys who were Republicans came from larger law firms than did
the Democrats.[11]

Communist nations pride themselves on containing a higher proportion of workers and "toilers" in their parliaments than do those of
bourgeois nations. The proportions of the membership of two such
parliaments listed as factory workers (Table 3.5) is certainly much
higher than is found in other countries, whereas the proportions in
professional and managerial positions are perhaps lower. At the same
time, Communist nations' parliaments also contain a large category of
persons usually absent from parliaments—the employees of the gov-

[10] Robert D. Putnam, *The Comparative Study of Political Elites* (Englewood
Cliffs: Prentice-Hall, 1976), pp. 173–179.
[11] Matthews, *U.S. Senators*, p. 35, footnote 32.

Table 3.6   SELECTED DEMOGRAPHIC CHARACTERISTICS OF MEMBERS OF YUGOSLAVIAN FEDERAL ASSEMBLY, 1965–1974

CHARACTERISTIC	YEAR OF ASSEMBLY			
	1965 (%)	1967 (%)	1969 (%)	1974 (%)
Youth	2.2	1.4	1.3	6.5
Male	82.7	82.1	92.1	86.4
Higher education	70.6	75.1	82.4	65.3
Worker/peasant	3.9	1.9	0.6	15.6
Incumbent	36.1	39.0	53.4	34.0
N =	670	670	620	308

SOURCE: James H. Seroka, "Legislative Recruitment and Political Change in Yugoslavia," *Legislative Studies Quarterly* 4 (February 1979), p. 107.

ernment and of the government associated ruling party and the several "mass" organizations such as the trade unions. In the two countries included in Table 3.5 this category, which consists mainly of white-collar and professional employment, is the largest.[12]

The Czechoslovakian parliament, elected in 1971, similarly had a much higher proportion of its members in managerial, clerical and professional occupations (64%) than in the unskilled (17%) and skilled (13%) worker categories combined.[13]

Yugoslavia has attempted to recruit into its federal assembly suitable proportions of youth, women, and workers and peasants. But during the 1960s the proportions of each of those categories decreased, until the ruling party made strenuous efforts to reverse those trends (Table 3.6). The largest change occurred in the worker/peasant category, rising to more than 15%, which was much higher than previously. Changes in the other categories were, by comparison, much smaller.[14]

Taken together, these data from several Communist party nations indicate that their parliaments also tend to attract the better educated

[12] David Lane, *Politics and Society in the USSR* (New York: Random House, 1971), pp. 154–156; Peter A. Toma and Ivan Volgyes, *Politics in Hungary* (San Francisco: Freeman, 1977), pp. 59–62. Each author presents a different set of occupational categories for Eastern European parliaments. For a different list, see D. Richard Little, "Soviet Parliamentary Committees After Khrushchev: Obstacles and Opportunities," *Soviet Studies* 24 (July 1972), p. 46 and footnote 5.

[13] Frank Dinka and Max J. Skidmore, "The Functions of Communist One-Party Elections: The Case of Czechoslovakia, 1971," *Political Science Quarterly* 88 (September 1973), pp. 416–417.

[14] James H. Seroka, "Legislative Recruitment and Political Change in Yugoslavia." *Legislative Studies Quarterly* 4 (February 1979), pp. 106–108.

and the more professional and managerial categories of their societies. Such an imbalance is almost inevitable if their parliaments also contain a sizable proportion of members who are already full-time employees of the government and of the party with its associated organizations.

Another consideration is that the proportion of workers among the parliamentary members serving several terms is much lower than among the entire membership, most of whom serve only a single term. Among the continuing members of the Supreme Soviet, for example, workers and peasants constituted 20%, but they amounted to 38% of the entire membership. The proportion of the continuing members who were party and government officials was 56%, but they represented only 33% of the full membership.[15]

Most of the world's parliaments are part-time. They meet for limited periods of time during the year, and often only for part of the day when they do meet. The result is to permit—indeed, require— members of parliaments to engage in other occupations to earn a living. Only recently has the U.S. Congress become a full-time institution, organizing its activities through the whole year and paying its members accordingly. Of the state legislatures, only California and New York have become full-time institutions.

As Congress has become a full-time institution, it has simultaneously become an arena for a career. Once elected and if reelected, members can expect to stay there, rise in the committee system, and develop active and personally satisfying careers. One result is that congressmen tend to be severed from their prior occupations. They can neither work part-time during the sessions nor during long recesses, for the latter have disappeared. And the longer congressmen stay in office, the less likely it is that they would have a business or a prior job to return to.

There are potential disadvantages either way. If a parliament meets only part-time, members can be accused of having a conflict of personal economic interest. They certainly lack time for extended floor sessions or intensive committee work. If full-time, however, members can be likened to a new class of bureaucrats, cut off from, different from, and thus less "representative" of the people who elected them in the first place.

The question of limitations on outside income is possible only in an institution that is full-time and attempts to pay its members a high enough salary to support themselves. But if members also have outside incomes, at least two questions are raised: (1) What potential conflicts of interest are created for members in acting in the public interest? (2) Are some members to be more limited (or advantaged)

[15] Little, "Soviet Parliamentary Committees," p. 46.

than others because the sources and types of their outside incomes differ?[16]

There is another consequence from having part-time legislators: those who hold other jobs are not able to participate in the full scope of the parliaments' activities. A complaint in Britain, for example, is that the business and professional members work at their occupations in the morning and early afternoon, and thus they are not available to participate in the detailed work of committees, which ordinarily meet in the morning. In the Supreme Soviet, to take another example, the worker and peasant category constituted only 10% of the membership of four major committees (1966–1970), although they comprise close to 40% of all members of the full chamber. A problem facing the full-time worker who is also a member of a part-time legislative body is to obtain permission to leave the job. Although the formal rules protect his right to do so, managers are reluctant to release their key workers—who are more likely to be elected than other types of workers —from their jobs.[17]

Prior Political Experience

Most members of national parliaments have had extensive experience in government and politics. At least this statement appears accurate for parliaments that are fairly stable and show some signs of independent activity.

UNITED STATES

At least 80% of the members of the U.S. House of Representatives, and 90% of those in the Senate, have held prior governmental offices (Table 3.7). By contrast, however, the proportion of governmentally experienced members is much lower in the state legislatures (right-hand columns of same table). Challenging and losing candidates to the U.S. House were more similar to the state legislators, in contrast to the successful candidates, in that relatively low proportions of them had prior governmental experience.

No single office leads to the U.S. House. About a third of the House members in the 1960s had served in state legislatures. A third had served previously in law enforcement positions, including the judiciary. Some members have also had prior experience in locally elective office and some have served in appointed administrative positions. Challenging candidates seem to have about the same profile,

[16] *Congressional Quarterly Weekly Report,* March 5, 1977, p. 388, and April 2, 1977, pp. 591–597.
[17] D. Richard Little, "Soviet Parliamentary Committees," p. 47, and "Legislative Authority in the Soviet Political System," *Slavic Review* 30 (March 1971), p. 69.

Table 3.7 PRIOR PUBLIC OFFICE EXPERIENCE OF U.S. SENATORS AND REPRESENTATIVES, U.S. HOUSE CANDIDATES, AND STATE LEGISLATORS

PRIOR OFFICE EXPERIENCE	U.S. SENATE		U.S. HOUSE			U.S. HOUSE CANDIDATES				STATE LEGISLATORS[g]			
				1965[d]		CHALLENGERS[e]		LOSERS[f]					
	1947–1957[a] (%)	1918–1958[b] (%)	1962[c] (%)	EL[h] (%)	AP[i] (%)	DEM (%)	REP (%)	DEM (%)	REP (%)	N.J. (%)	OHIO (%)	CALIF. (%)	TENN. (%)
Yes	91	92	94	58	72	52	41	40	55	46	57	49	49
No	9	8	6	42	28	48	59	60	45	34	43	51	51
N =	179	450	87	36	36	148	155	110	128	79	162	113	120

[a] Data from Donald Matthews, *U.S. Senators and Their World* (New York: Vintage, 1960), p. 51, table 22. Includes elective and appointive offices.

[b] Data from Joseph Schlesinger, *Ambition and Politics* (Chicago: Rand McNally, 1966), p. 93, table VI-1. Includes only elective offices.

[c] Data from Roger Davidson, *The Role of the Congressman* (New York: Pegasus, 1969), p. 50, table 2–2. Includes elective and appointed governmental and party offices.

[d] Original data. If the elective and appointive categories were combined, 100% of this sample had held some prior governmental office. Party offices are excluded.

[e] Data from Jeff Fishel, *Party and Opposition* (New York: McKay, 1973), p. 49, table 3.8.

[f] Data from Robert J. Huckshorn and Robert C. Spencer, *The Politics of Defeat* (Amherst: University of Massachusetts, 1971), p. 39.

[g] Data from John Wahlke, et al., *The Legislative System* (New York: Wiley, 1962), p. 95, table 5.1. Interviewing done in 1957. Includes elective and appointive office.

[h] Elective.

[i] Appointive.

Table 3.8   FIRST AND LAST GOVERNMENTAL OFFICES
PRIOR TO ENTERING U.S. SENATE

OFFICE	FIRST OFFICE (%)	LAST PRIOR OFFICE (%)
1. U.S. senator	9	—
2. U.S. congressman	6	28
3. Statewide elected	4	24
4. Administration	21	17
5. Law enforcement	14	15
6. State legislature	28	0
7. Local elected	14	6
8. Congressional staff	3	1
Total	100	100
N =	(180)	(164)

SOURCE: Donald R. Matthews, *U.S. Senators and Their World*
(New York: Vintage, 1960), p. 51, table 22, and p. 55, table 27.

except those from decidedly minority parties: Their prior experience
in elective office is much less, probably reflecting the inability of their
party to win local or legislative elections.[18]

Just as the state legislature is part of the experience of congressmen, service in the U.S. House is an important base from which persons
enter the U.S. Senate. Of all persons entering the Senate in the 1947–
1957 period (180 senators), by far the largest proportion (28%)
entered directly from the House; the second largest group entered
from statewide elective office, mainly governorships (Table 3.8). The
pattern of initial public offices of senators resembles that of House
members, with law enforcement, the state legislature, and locally elective offices being predominant. The last office held prior to entering
the Senate was related to the occupation: Lawyers tended to enter
directly from the House, whereas businessmen were more diverse in
their pattern of office. Likewise, the states' party systems were related
to the pattern of the last prior offices, in that governorship and the
U.S. House were the major offices in one-party states, whereas the
two-party states had a more diverse pattern.[19]

PARLIAMENTS ABROAD

Prior office experience in the United States can be compared to that
in other democracies in Table 3.9. Among the United States and five
other nations the rate of prior office-holding experience is considerably

[18] Davidson, *The Role of the Congressman*, p. 50; Robert J. Huckshorn and
Robert C. Spencer, *The Politics of Defeat: Campaigning for Congress* (Amherst:
University of Massachusetts Press, 1971), pp. 39–41; and original data.
[19] Matthews, *U.S. Senators*, pp. 55–57.

Table 3.9 PRIOR OFFICE EXPERIENCE: SIX COUNTRIES, 1950s

OFFICE EXPERIENCE AND SELECTED OFFICES	NATIONAL PARLIAMENTS					
	UNITED STATES (%)	GERMANY (%)	AUSTRALIA (%)	FRANCE (%)	CANADA (%)	GREAT BRITAIN (%)
Prior office experience	72.2	61.6	49.3	49.1	47.8	34.5
Local elective	12.3	32.2	17.7	28.9	27.0	27.8
State legislature	36.5	11.9	21.0	23.8	10.6	—
Law enforcement	31.2	—	3.0	—	6.1	—
No prior office experience	27.8	38.4	50.7	50.9	52.2	65.5
Total	100.0	100.0	100.0	100.0	100.0	100.0
N =	429	519	124	595	263	630

SOURCES: Joseph A. Schlesinger, "Political Careers and Party Leadership," in Lewis J. Edinger (ed.), *Political Leadership in Industrialized Societies* (New York: Wiley, 1967), p. 279, table 9.4; Gerhard Loewenberg, *Parliament in the German Political System* (Ithaca: Cornell University Press, 1967), p. 125, table 23.
NOTE: The selected offices are only the major ones, and thus do not add to the percent for all prior office experience. The data for each nation are for a parliament elected in the mid-1950s.

higher in the United States and Germany and lowest in Great Britain. In all of the five countries with state or provincial governing bodies that intermediate level of office has been part of the prior experience of varying proportions of parliamentary members. Perhaps in partial compensation for the lack of similar intermediate governmental level in Great Britain, the proportion of members of Parliament having previously served in local-level elective positions is higher than in either the United States or Australia, but is fairly similar to the rates shown for France, Germany, and Canada.[20]

One result of these career paths is that the members bring with them an extensive background of practical experience, not only in the substance of public policy but also (and perhaps more important) in the means by which divergent views are expressed and resolved in deliberative assemblies. They also are experienced in the fine art of representation in that they have run for and won election; they have had to contend with constituents, interest groups, and executive branch officials; and they have had to justify themselves to each other, to their constituents, and to the mass media. Whatever the representative

[20] Joseph A. Schlesinger, "Political Careers and Party Leadership," in Lewis J. Edinger (ed.), *Political Leadership in Industrialized Societies* (New York: Wiley, 1967), pp. 278–279; Gerhard Loewenberg, *Parliament in the German Political System* (Ithaca: Cornell University Press, 1967), p. 125.

Table 3.10 SIMULTANEOUS PARTICIPATION BY MEMBERS OF SWEDISH PARLIAMENT IN MUNICIPAL AND PROVINCIAL POLITICS BY CHAMBER (1965)

	CHAMBER OF PARLIAMENT	
	LOWER	UPPER
TYPE OF PARTICIPATION	(%)	(%)
Member of municipal council	57.9	55.6
Member of provincial legislature	42.9	44.4
"Active" in local politics	71.7	68.2

SOURCE: M. Donald Hancock, *Sweden: The Politics of Postindustrial Change* (Hinsdale, Ill.: Dryden, 1972), p. 95, table 7.
NOTE: Because of multiple entries, columns add to more than 100%.

process might entail, the members have had extensive prior experience of that process before coming to the nation's parliament. They also bring with them the points of view of local levels of government. Municipalities and states, as distinct units of government, have a built-in set of spokesmen in national parliaments simply through the apprenticeships served in them by the members themselves.

Perhaps the extreme example of the potentially close relationship between lower levels of government and the national parliament is provided by Sweden, in which most members of parliament are simultaneously also members of either municipal councils or provincial legislatures (Table 3.10). Apparently persons are first elected to the lower-level assemblies and from there are nominated to the national Riksdag.[21] Close to 30% of the German Bundestag members also simultaneously held state and local elective offices, and some 26% of the members of the French Assembly ran for and were elected to local offices while they remained in the Assembly.[22] More recently, 71% of the members of the French Assembly simultaneously held local and provincial elective offices.

For those members who hold simultaneous membership in both a national parliament and a local or provincial legislature, there may be the disadvantage of a severe drain on their time. If members hold such offices sequentially, they gain the experience without needing to handle several positions at once. One indication of the disadvantages of simultaneous membership is the practice in France, beginning in 1978, that no mayors and no chairmen of regional legislative assemblies would be made members of the new government cabinet. The fear has been expressed that the dual (or more) office holding members

[21] M. Donald Hancock, *Sweden: The Politics of Postindustrial Change* (Hinsdale, Ill.: Dryden, 1972), pp. 94–95.
[22] Loewenberg, *Parliament in the German Political System*, p. 125, table 23; Schlesinger, "Political Careers and Party Leadership," pp. 278–279.

Table 3.11   TYPES OF U.S. SENATORS: FREQUENCY AND CHARACTERISTICS

TYPE	%	SOCIOECONOMIC STATUS	POLITICAL EXPERIENCE	AGE AT ENTRY
Professional	55	Not high status	10 years or more	Begin political career at young age in legislature
Amateur	34	Prosperous in own occupation	Less than 10 years	Older
Patrician	7	High-status family	10 years or more	Young
Agitators	4	Not high status	Less than 10 years	Young
	100			
N =	179			

SOURCE: Donald R. Matthews, *U.S. Senators and Their World* (New York: Vintage, 1960), pp. 58–67, 284–285.

would neglect their national responsibilities in favor of their local ones.[23]

At the other extreme are those countries that, like Greece, have few elective offices at lower levels of government. The national parliament is, itself, the major source of elective office. Another example is India, which has a larger number of elective positions at local and state levels, but these positions are not used as lower rungs on a career ladder leading into the national parliament.[24] In these circumstances, not only do lower governmental levels lack a means of access to the national body, but the members themselves lack the previous training in electoral politics and in the dynamics of representation to which we have earlier pointed.

Types of Members

The interplay among the factors we have discussed in this section —education, occupation, socioeconomic status, religion, and prior political experience—has led to some speculation about different "types" of legislators based mainly on these background characteristics. A study of the U.S. Senate in the 1947–1957 period suggested four major types of senators, largely based upon such personal and social background attributes (Table 3.11). The "professional poli-

[23] The more recent French data come from the *London Times,* April 11, 1978, p. 6.
[24] Keith R. Legg, *Politics in Modern Greece* (Stanford: Stanford University Press, 1969), pp. 288–290; Shriram Maheshwari, "Constituency Linkage of National Legislators in India," *Legislative Studies Quarterly* 1 (August 1976), pp. 350–351.

Table 3.12   ATTRIBUTES OF FOUR TYPES OF MEMBERS OF THE
TANZANIAN PARLIAMENT

CHARACTERISTICS	TYPES OF MEMBERS			
	GOVERN-MENT MEMBER (%)	POTENTIAL LEADER (%)	LOCAL (%)	SILENT SUPPORTER (%)
Members of government of the day	100	0	0	50
Began political career prior to 1958	100	44	20	50
Elected by constituency	60	67	100	0
College education or more	33	44	0	17
"High" rate of newspaper reading	100	100	20	50
N =	(18)	(9)	(25)	(6)

SOURCE: Raymond F. Hopkins, "The Role of the M.P. in Tanzania," *American Political Science Review* 64 (September 1970), p. 760, table 1.

ticians" accounted for some 55% of the senators. They had been active in politics for most of their adult lives, beginning service in either the state legislature or in law enforcement positions at an early age. They had steadily, though slowly, risen through governmental levels until finally entering the Senate. They were not wealthy, nor were they of high social status either in their family origins or in their own private occupations. For them, holding public office was a full-time, lifelong career. The second largest category of senators, by these criteria, were the "amateur politicians," those who entered the Senate relatively late in life and had little prior governmental experience. The bulk of their adult life had been spent in private occupations, in which they had become relatively wealthy. The "patrician" type came from high-status families with inherited wealth. They had entered the Senate at a relatively young age, and had made a career out of both extensive prior governmental services and their several terms in the Senate. Finally, the "agitators," 4% of the senators, had neither much prior experience in government nor personal or familial wealth. This small group tended to be the deviant set of senators, both in their backgrounds and in their subsequent behavior within the Senate itself.[25]

In a very different country with a different political system we would expect to find different types of parliamentary members. Four types of members of the Tanzanian parliament have been identified, varying in their education, their previous careers, and their means of selection (Table 3.12). They are also differentiated by their role in the

[25] Matthews, *U.S. Senators*, pp. 58–67.

government of the day, for Tanzania has a parliamentary rather than a separation-of-powers system.[26]

The first type of Tanzanian parliamentarian is a member of the government, either in the cabinet or serving as a junior minister of the government. This type of member is completely absent from the U.S. Congress. The government members tend to have been active leaders of the independence party and to have all been active in politics prior to 1958. They tend to have been elected, rather than appointed, to membership in parliament, and they are among the best-educated group, with one-third having been to college. They all rate high in their reading of newspapers, as an indication of their attention to governmental and political affairs.

The potential leaders are potential rivals to those who hold government office. Within four years of the time of the study (1966), half of this group had been expelled from the ruling party and the other half had been appointed to a government office. This set of rival or aspiring leaders was equipped for political activism through their superior education (they were the most highly educated group), their attention to the daily press, and by their relatively long period of prior political participation. They also had a potential base of independent power because more of them were directly elected in constituencies than were the government leaders themselves.

The locals represented a more numerous category of membership. They were elected in constituencies but had little education (64% had not completed high school), had little previous political experience, and did not follow political news in the press.

The silent supporters were all appointed to parliament and either held governmental office or at least supported the government. They were silent in that they seldom participated in floor debate. They were intermediate between the governmental members and the locals in the extent of the experience, education, and use of newspapers.

A somewhat different, but consistent, way to think of types of members is to link their prior office experience to the activity (or its absence) of the political party in recruiting them to run for office (as discussed in the previous chapter). The agents of candidate recruitment have been dichotomized between the party on the one hand and the candidate himself on the other (Table 3.13). The prior experience of the legislators can be described as either a long and active involvement in governmental and political affairs or as a short and inactive one. Candidates with long experience in government and politics will have developed a set of friends and contacts who themselves are active

[26] Raymond F. Hopkins, "The Role of the M.P. in Tanzania," *American Political Science Review* 64 (September 1970), pp. 754–771.

Table 3.13   FOUR TYPES OF LEGISLATORS

POLITICAL ACTIVITY	AGENT OF RECRUITMENT	
	PARTY	SELF
Active (careerist)	I. Party careerist	III. Office careerist
Inactive (lateral entry)	II. Party coopted	IV. Private occupation entre-preneur

SOURCE: Chong Lim Kim, Justin Green and Samuel C. Patterson, "Partisanship in the Recruitment and Performance of American State Legislatures," in Heinz Eulau and Moishe M. Czudnowski (eds.), *Elite Recruitment in Democratic Politics* (New York: Halsted Press, 1976), p. 83, table 4.1.

in politics and will be following the major political career paths within their district and state. The candidates lacking that prior involvement are "lateral entry" candidates, having gained experience (and perhaps visibility) from private occupations and/or civic activity. The resulting four types of legislators are: (1) the party careerists, who have a long record of political activity and who are recruited to office by the political party; (2) the coopted candidates, who are drafted by the party either to "fill the ticket" or to bring visibility and respectability to the ticket, but who have not been active previously in politics; (3) the office careerists, who have been active in government and politics, but who decide by themselves to seek legislative office; and (4) the private occupation entrepreneurs, who seek office as an incident to, or to actively further, their private occupations.[27]

The four types of legislators, defined by the two criteria, do vary on several background characteristics (Table 3.14), thus linking our concern in this section with recruitment agents to the earlier discussion of attributes of candidates. The party careerists are the oldest in age among the four types, indicating a long career prior to entering the legislature. They are among the least ambitious to run for other office but have the highest rate of incumbency within the legislature. The party-coopted candidates also rank low in ambition for other offices and high in incumbency in this one office. They have the lowest proportion among the four types in the occupations traditionally linked to politics—law and "brokerage" occupations, such as insurance and real estate. The office careerists are distinctive mainly in their ambition to seek offices beyond the state legislature and rank second highest in the proportion who were incumbents in the legislature itself. The entrepreneurs on behalf of their private occupations have a medium

[27] Chong Lim Kim, Justin Green, and Samuel C. Patterson, "Partisanship in the Recruitment and Performance of American State Legislators," in Heinz Eulau and Moishe M. Czudnowski (eds.), *Elite Recruitment in Democratic Politics* (New York: Halsted Press, 1976), pp. 81–86. The labels for some of the candidate types have been changed from the original.

Table 3.14 ATTRIBUTES OF FOUR TYPES OF LEGISLATORS

	LEGISLATOR TYPES			
	I	II	III	IV
				PRIVATE OCCUPATION
	PARTY	PARTY	OFFICE	ENTRE-
CHARACTERISTICS	CAREERIST	COOPTED	CAREERIST	PRENEUR
Age: over 40	78	66	67	68
Occupation:				
Law	54	38	57	52
Brokerage jobs	59	38	57	51
Ambition:				
Aspiring to higher				
office	35	34	53	43
Length of residence:				
Spending half of				
life in district	77	76	75	85
Incumbents	78	78	69	56
Partisanship score	.506	.460	.429	.427

SOURCE: Adapted from C. L. Kim, J. Green, and S. C. Patterson, "Partisanship in the Recruitment and Performance of American State Legislators," in Heinz Eulau and M. M. Czudnowski (eds.), *Elite Recruitment in Democratic Politics* (New York: Halsted Press, 1976), p. 84, table 4.2.
NOTE: Data from legislators in 5 states: New Jersey, Ohio, Tennessee, California and Iowa. Iowa sample excluded from length of residence item.

ranking in the extent of their ambition to higher office but rank lowest in their incumbency in the state legislature. They also, as a group, have the longest period of residence in their local area.

Presumably, the several types of candidates (or incumbents) defined on the basis of their experiences before they entered office might also differ in how they act in office. Although this question mainly will be left for later chapters to explore, we shall indicate one such in-office result among the four types of legislators we are now discussing. Their attitudes toward the importance of the political party in the legislature have been summarized in a "partisanship score," in which the higher the numerical score, the more strongly favorable they are to political parties (last line of Table 3.14). The party careerists had the highest partisanship score, followed by the party-coopted legislators. The other two types of legislators, who had not been recruited by the political party, held the least favorable attitudes toward the role of political parties in the legislature.

This typology concerns the members of five state legislatures. We do not know how the political party was organized or the extent to which it was active in the five states and in the legislative districts. Neither do we know the competitiveness of the district parties. That is, we lack information about those political characteristics of the districts that were found among congressmen to be most directly related to the presence or absence of party recruitment activity. Yet using information only about the legislators themselves, the suggested fourfold typology summarizes a considerable amount of information and results in types entirely consistent with a wide range of background variables.

Summary

In large collective bodies, such as parliaments, we are likely to find a wide range of background characteristics of the members. Their own numbers, plus the complexity and diversity of most nations, would lead to that result. But still we do not find that parliamentary members have the same statistical profile as does the population as a whole. They rank higher than does the general population on income, education, and occupational status.

Furthermore, as the examples of the U.S. Senate and the Tanzanian parliament indicate, patterns of background attributes lead to the definition of several different types of members. Types of members may also be developed from the patterns of their candidate recruitment and the extent of their prior office experience. The resulting types of members also differed among themselves in their demographic characteristics. These typologies help summarize a wide range of otherwise disparate pieces of information about individual members.

Perhaps most institutions in modern society select specially qualified personnel—and thereby persons with more education and higher income than held by the average member of the society. Not only parliaments and civil services, as we have discussed, but also political parties (perhaps especially ruling Communist parties), churches, and labor unions, for example, also have in the upper levels of their staff and on their governing boards, distinctively trained and thus high-status personnel. But on the other hand, the political elites appear to be less distinctive—or more similar to the whole population—than are the elites of other sectors of society.[28]

ACTIVITIES AND ROLES

Once elected, what do members do as representatives? How do they spend their time, and in what ways do they think of their official duties? Succeeding chapters of this book will examine political parties and committees and the relationship between parliament and the chief executive. In this section we shall look at individual members—how they spend their time and how they think of themselves within the parliamentary body.

[28] Lewis J. Edinger, *Politics in West Germany*, 2d ed. (Boston: Little, Brown, 1977), pp. 151–153.

Table 3.15   MAJOR ACTIVITIES OF U.S. HOUSE
MEMBERS

	MEMBERS LISTING ACTIVITY	
ACTIVITY	PRIMARY (%)	SECONDARY (%)
Legislation	77	21
Constituency service	16	59
Communication	2	33
Campaigning	2	14
Other	2	17
Total	99	154ᵃ
N = 87		

SOURCE: Roger Davidson, *The Role of the Congressman* (New
York: Pegasus, 1969), p. 99, table 3–10.
ᵃ Some members listed more than one activity in secondary
category.

Activities

Members of the U.S. House worked, on the average, 11 hours per day
on congressional activities, as did members of the Senate. House
members spent about three hours on the House floor (twice as long
as Senators), with about 1.5 hours spent in committees and subcommittees (less than senators) and another half hour in meetings with
other members and with party groups and party leaders. Time in
individual offices took about 3.5 hours daily; another 2.5 hours were
spent in events and meetings with constituents, either in the Capitol
building itself or elsewhere in Washington. This audit of how members
spend their time was compiled in the early months of 1977 from time
logs kept by members' secretaries. Although individual members vary
from one another and from day to day, these averages do indicate
both the long hours required of full-time members of a full-time
legislative body and also the diversity of their activity.[29]

Two activities absorbed the bulk of the working time of a sample
of House members in the early 1960s: legislation and constituent
service (Table 3.15).[30] Over three-quarters of the sample indicated that
legislative activity—most of which was within their committees—was
their primary activity, and another 20% listed it as their secondary
activity. Only three congressmen failed to list legislation as either their

[29] The audit of House members' time is reported in: U.S. Congress. House.
Commission on Administrative Review, *Administrative Reorganization and Legislative Management*, Vol. 2: *Work Management* (Washington, D.C.: House Doc.
95-232, 1977), pp. 16–19. The audit of Senators' time is reported in: U.S.
Congress. Senate. Commission on the Operation of the Senate, *Toward a Modern
Senate: Final Report* (Washington, D.C., December 1976), p. 28.
[30] Davidson, *The Role of the Congressman*, pp. 98–104.

primary or secondary activity. Constituency service was the second most frequently listed activity: attending to problems of individual constituents with federal agencies, attempting to obtain federal contracts for local industries, and the like. We shall discuss this activity in the next section of this chapter. An important distinction between the two activities of legislation and constituent service is that whereas the latter is mainly handled by staff personnel in the congressman's office, the member mainly does his own work on legislation. In the Senate, however, those at the staff level carry a much larger share of the members' legislative load than in the House.

The next most frequent activities of congressmen were public communication and campaigning. As communicators to the public, members send newsletters, prepare news releases and TV interviews for the district media, and make public appearances. The substance of their communication concerns governmental activity. They usually justify and explain their own actions to their constituents and audiences. They comment upon the actions of Congress as a whole and on events in the wider government. One observer has noted that congressmen tend to justify their own actions to their constituents by criticizing the larger institution of which they are a member.[31] One of the long-run consequences of this behavior is that Congress, as an institution, will lose public confidence relative to the presidency.

Campaigning was listed as their fourth most frequent activity. Although campaigning did not loom as a primary task, it received close to 15% of mentions as a secondary activity. The communications activity we have just discussed is probably related to campaigning; the former is one way by which a legislator may continually campaign in his district without appearing to do so.

We might suppose that how a member spends his time would vary with his length of service. A newly elected member's main concern may be to gain reelection since, as we noted in the previous section, it is those in their first term who are most vulnerable to defeat. Furthermore, newcomers have much to learn about how the House functions and also about the substance of issues. There may be something of an apprenticeship norm, in which new members are expected by their more senior colleagues to keep quiet, work hard, and learn.[32] Finally, legislative leadership is largely a function of committee leadership, which in turn is still largely a function of seniority.

There are several distinctions in how members spend their time depending upon their seniority, especially between the first-termers and all others (Table 3.16). The proportion of members beyond their first

[31] Richard F. Fenno, Jr., *Home Style: House Members in Their Districts* (Boston: Little, Brown, 1978), p. 168.
[32] Matthews, *U.S. Senators,* pp. 92–94.

Table 3.16 ACTIVITIES OF U.S. HOUSE MEMBERS BY
SENIORITY

| | MEMBERS LISTING PRIMARY ACTIVITY BY SENIORITY | | |
| | TERMS | | |
PRIMARY ACTIVITY	ONE (%)	2–5 (%)	6+ (%)
Legislation	59	83	79
Constituency service	24	11	18
Communication	6	3	—
Campaigning	6	3	—
Other	6	0	3
Total	101	100	100
N =	(17)	(36)	(34)

SOURCE: Roger Davidson, *The Role of the Congressman* (New
York: Pegasus, 1969), p. 103, table 3–11.

term stating legislation was their primary activity was more than 20%
greater than that of the first-termers. The constituent service activity
was more variable, although the more senior incumbents mentioned it
less than did the first-termers. Likewise, the senior members made
fewer references to campaigning and external communication than
did the first-term members. These changes are all consistent with our
original expectation: that congressmen with longer service (in this
case beginning with the second term) spend more time on legislative
activity and less on external and district-related activity than do the
newly elected members.[33]

Role Orientations

How do legislators understand themselves in their varied activities?
How do they perceive what they should be doing in their capacity as
elected members of a legislative body? Such understandings and perceptions are termed "role orientations." Because of his membership, the
parliamentary member presumably does—or can do—some things that
others do not. That is, he occupies a certain position (member) within
a certain institution (parliament). What that person does within his
position is termed "role." How he understands and perceives what he
ought to do and what he can do is termed "orientation."[34] We obtain
information about how members perceive themselves through interviews. Whereas their activities as such can be observed overtly and

[33] Davidson, *The Role of the Congressman*, p. 102.
[34] Malcolm E. Jewell and Samuel C. Patterson, *The Legislative Process in the
United States*, 3d ed. (New York, Random House, 1977), pp. 347–348.

Table 3.17 PURPOSIVE ROLES IN CONGRESS AND TWO STATE LEGISLATURES

| | CONGRESS[a] | | STATE LEGISLATURES[b] | |
	PRIMARY (%)	TOTAL[c] (%)	NEW JERSEY[d] (%)	OHIO[d] (%)
PURPOSIVE ROLES				
Tribune	47	82	63	40
Legislative participant	41	67	70	67
Inventor	7	31	49	33
Broker	4	17	33	48
Campaigner	1	8	—	—
Total	100	—	—	—
N =	87	87	79	162

[a] Data are from Roger Davidson, *The Role of the Congressman* (New York: Pegasus, 1969), p. 80, table 3–1.
[b] Data are from John Wahlke et al., *The Legislative System* (New York: Wiley, 1962), p. 259, table 11.1.
[c] Percent of whole sample who referred to each role, whether or not it was their primary one. Thus members made multiple mentions, and percents do not add to 100.
[d] Multiple mentions, so percents do not add to 100.

also measured through documentary sources, how members perceive themselves is obtainable only by asking them.

Purposive Roles

One of the most general role orientations concerns purpose: Members have been asked to describe the job of being a legislator and to note "the most important things you should do here."[35] The intent of this question is to probe the members' understanding of the ultimate aims of their activities in the legislative body. Congressmen tend to be quite eclectic in their views of their major tasks. Most tend to emphasize three rather general views; however, two other tasks are also mentioned by some members.

The tribune role receives the largest number of mentions among congressmen (Table 3.17). In this role, congressmen view themselves as spokesmen for the needs and opinions of the general public. They view themselves as "representatives" in a direct and immediate sense. Over 80% of the congressmen made some mention of this dimension of their job, and close to half indicated that it was the major component of their job. Among state legislators, however, the tribune role received the second highest number of mentions.

[35] Davidson, *The Role of the Congressman*, p. 78. This section on purposive role orientations is based on pp. 78–97, although some of the role labels have been revised from the original.

The legislative participant role received the second highest number of mentions among congressmen. In this role, congressmen view themselves as active participants in the work of committees on legislation, both at the committee stage and on the floor. Whereas the tribune role emphasizes the external aspects of a congressman's job, this role stresses the internal part of his job.

In the inventor role, receiving a distant proportion of mentions, congressmen view themselves as creators or discoverers of policy—of legislative solutions to problems in the wider society. Where the legislative participant role more stresses the negotiation and facilitation of legislative work, this role more emphasizes the substance and content of legislation.

The broker role emphasizes the balancing of competing interests and considerations. Although such a balancing takes place in the furtherance of the foregoing roles, it was seldom discussed by congressmen as a separable and major component of their activity. Likewise, the campaigner role was seldom emphasized in isolation from other roles and activities. All congressmen are elected and most seek reelection (and successfully, too), but few indicate that to seek election and reelection is, by itself, the major component of their job as congressmen.

Seniority and region are more associated with variations in purposive role orientations than are other background characteristics of congressmen. The first-term congressmen place greater emphasis on the tribune role of presenting popular needs and desires to the governmental forum, whereas senior members concentrate more on participation in the legislative work of Congress (Table 3.18). The same table shows the two regions of greatest contrast. Southerners emphasize the legislative participation role and eastern members the tribune role.

Table 3.18 PURPOSIVE ROLES AMONG CONGRESSMEN BY SENIORITY AND REGION

| | SENIORITY | | REGION | |
| | ONE TERM (%) | 2–5 TERMS (%) | EAST (%) | SOUTH (%) |
PURPOSIVE ROLE				
Tribune	53	42	57	35
Legislative participant	23	47	27	58
Inventor	12	6	5	8
Broker	6	6	5	—
Campaigner	6	—	5	—
Total	100	100	99	101
N =	(17)	(36)	(21)	(26)

SOURCE: Roger Davidson, *The Role of the Congressman* (New York: Pegasus, 1969), p. 92, table 3–5, and p. 95, table 3–8.

Other background factors were not as sizably or consistently related to purposive role orientations as were region and seniority.

There was an important in-House difference associated with different purposive orientations: committee and party leaders, especially among Republicans, were more legislative participants (52%) than were nonleaders (31%), although the differences between Democratic leaders and nonleaders was not nearly as great. We might speculate that Democrats, being the long-term majority party in Congress, both felt the responsibilities (or burden) of legislative work and anticipated that their own personal chances were quite good of gaining leadership positions through increasing seniority. Republicans, on the other hand, see little opportunity to become leaders and hence do not take "leadership" roles.

Representative Roles

How congressmen expect they should act as representatives has been probed through two additional types of role orientations: representational style and representational area. The first asks whether congressmen see themselves bound by instructions from a constituency (the delegate role) or as free to make their own judgments in the public interest (trustee). The second asks about which sets of people the congressmen see themselves representing—their specific district or the nation as a whole.

REPRESENTATIONAL STYLE ROLES

About half the congressmen viewed themselves in either the trustee or delegate role; the remainder (46%) viewed themselves as doing some of both—the politico role (Table 3.19). The distributions of members of several state legislatures, and also of the Canadian parliament, are shown with that of congressmen in the same table, arrayed in descending order of the proportion in the trustee role.[36]

We can indicate how members view themselves in the representational style role through their own words. Congressmen who see themselves as trustees in their representative function:[37]

> The Founding Fathers intended us to exericse our own judgement, not to weigh mail.

[36] Malcolm E. Jewell, "Attitudinal Determinants of Legislative Behavior: The Utility of Role Analysis," in Allan Kornberg and Lloyd D. Musolf (eds.), *Legislatures in Developmental Perspective* (Durham, N.C.: Duke University Press, 1970), pp. 499–500. Since these data have been generated by different studies employing quite different questions and methods, it is hard to deduce what factors might be associated with the extensive variations among legislative bodies in the distribution of representational style roles.

[37] The quotes are taken from Davidson, *The Role of the Congressman*, pp. 117–119.

Table 3.19 REPRESENTATIONAL STYLE ROLE ORIENTATIONS AMONG PARLIAMENTS AND LEGISLATURES, RANKED BY PERCENT IN TRUSTEE ROLE

PARLIAMENT OR LEGISLATURE	REPRESENTATIONAL STYLE ROLES		
	TRUSTEE (%)	POLITICO (%)	DELEGATE (%)
HIGH			
Tennessee	81	13	6
New Jersey	61	22	17
Ohio	56	29	15
California	55	25	20
MEDIUM			
Michigan	37	31	33
Iowa	36	—	64
Pennsylvania	33	27	39
U.S. Congress	29	46	23
LOW			
Wisconsin	23	5	72
Indiana	20	61	19
Canadian Parliament	15	36	49

SOURCE: Malcolm Jewell, "Attitudinal Determinants of Legislative Behavior: The Utility of Role Analysis," in Allan Kornberg and Lloyd D. Musolf (eds.), *Legislatures in Developmental Perspective* (Durham, N.C.: Duke University Press, 1970), p. 499, table 4.

> I am not here to reflect the wishes of any one individual or group, but rather to make the right decisions and then to explain them to my constituents.

Congressmen who viewed themselves as delegates:

> The most important thing I do is to represent my people. Ideally, they should have a voice in the government.

By far the largest proportion of congressmen expressed the politico role—they attempted to combine the two alternative and perhaps conflicting considerations of representation:

> I have to vote the way I think right. I like to think the constituency thinks the same way.

> I would mix the roles of representation, especially in areas where I am knowledgeable. . . . On broad issues, I try to reflect the attitude of the constituency—not necessarily that of pressure groups, but of the average person.

Nearly half the congressmen did not clearly hold either of the extreme views about their proper representational style. Rather, they saw merit in both views and like to think that they were able to both "reflect" the views of their constituents and to vote "right." In Chapter 7, on voting decisions, we shall observe that congressmen often vote

Table 3.20 REPRESENTATIONAL AREA ROLE ORIENTATIONS IN LEGISLATIVE BODIES

REPRESENTATIONAL AREA ROLES	U.S. CONGRESS[a] (%)	CANADIAN PARLIAMENT[b] (%)	FOUR STATE LEGISLATURES[c] (%)
District	42	34	45
Nation-District	23	19	30
Nation	28	47	25
Other	8	—	—
Total	101	100	100
N =	(87)	(165)	(283)

[a] Data are from Roger Davidson, *The Role of the Congressman* (New York: Pegasus, 1969), p. 122, table 4.2.
[b] Data are from Allan Kornberg, *Canadian Legislative Behavior* (New York: Holt, Rinehart and Winston, 1967), p. 108, table 6.1.
[c] Reported in Kornberg. For state legislators, the "state" replaces "nation" as the appropriate widest unit, and correspondingly, the intermediate category becomes "state-district."

on legislation in accordance with both their party affiliation and with the population characteristics of their districts.

REPRESENTATIONAL AREA ROLES

The second type of representational role concerns the members' definition of the constituents whom they represent. More than 40% of the congressmen indicated that they voted and acted mainly on behalf of their own congressional districts (Table 3.20). One such member observed:

> A representative is interested primarily with his own little piece of land. A combination of the actions of all Congressmen creates, in effect, House policy.

Members who gave at least equal weight to national considerations as they did to their districts are illustrated by this comment:

> There is a heavy responsibility to represent the people of the district and the country at large . . .

In addition, several members spoke of categories of persons whom they viewed themselves as representing irrespective of where they lived in the country. One member spoke of representing pro–civil-rights advocates, wherever they lived. Another member, chairman of a committee, spoke of representing those segments of the population and economy who were directly affected by the work of his committee.[38]

---

[38] This section on representational area roles comes from ibid., pp. 121–125. The two quotes are from pp. 123 and 120, respectively.

Table 3.21 REPRESENTATIONAL AREA ROLES BY
REPRESENTATIONAL STYLE ROLES: U.S. HOUSE

	STYLE ROLES		
AREA ROLES	TRUSTEE (%)	POLITICO (%)	DELEGATE (%)
National	73	33	—
National-district	18	33	10
District	9	33	90
Total	100	99	100
$N =$	(22)	(39)	(20)

SOURCE: Roger Davidson, *The Role of the Congressman* (New York: Pegasus, 1969), p. 126, table 4–3.

In an electoral system employing single-member districts, as we do in the U.S. Congress, we might expect that most members who define themselves as delegates (as their representational style role) would also see themselves as representing their own specific districts. We might also expect that trustees who see themselves as exercising their own judgments on issues would also define themselves as acting on behalf of a national interest rather than only a specific district. These hypotheses are confirmed: Table 3.21 shows that 73% of congressmen who express themselves as trustees have a national perspective, while 90% of the members in the delegate role view themselves as directly representing their specific districts.

THE CORRELATES OF REPRESENTATIONAL ROLES

The relationship between the two components of representational role orientation, however, is quite different in Canada, even though it employs the single-member district with plurality elections. The two components of role orientation among Canadian members show almost no relationship; delegates are no more likely than trustees to have either a national or district focus. That the Canadian Parliament might function differently than the U.S. Congress is indicated by Tables 3.19 and 3.20, in which we find the proportions of members in the role orientation categories are quite different and, from an American perspective, puzzling. That is, Canada has a lower proportion (by half) of trustees but a very similar distribution as in the U.S. Congress in representational area orientations. At least part of the puzzle is the difference in political parties. Although the contrasting parties will be discussed more fully in Chapter 4, we should note here that Canadian members view themselves as delegates, not of a local district, but of their national political party. They campaign with the national party and work in Parliament to support their national party. Thus, while the delegate role orientation has been found in both parliaments, the source of their

Table 3.22 REPRESENTATIONAL STYLE AND AREA ROLES BY COMPETITIVE STATUS

REPRESENTATIONAL ROLES	COMPETITIVE STATUS OF MEMBERS	
	MARGINAL (%)	SAFE (%)
STYLE		
Trustee	19	35
Politico	37	54
Delegate	44	11
Total	100	100
AREA		
National	19	34
National-district	28	29
District	53	38
Total	100	101
N =	(32)	(52)

SOURCE: Roger Davidson, *The Role of the Congressman* (New York: Pegasus, 1969), p. 128, table 4–4.

representation (or focus) is quite different between the two parliamentary bodies.[39]

Several characteristics of American congressmen are related to how they perceive themselves in their representational roles, particularly their competitive status, their seniority, and their party. The members who were marginal in their competitive status—that is, who were elected with less than 60% of the vote in their previous election— were more delegates and district oriented, while their safe-district colleagues were more trustees and nationally oriented (Table 3.22).[40] This relationship is entirely consistent with the rationale of having an electoral process in the first place: an election is a means of increasing the likelihood that the officials so elected will pay attention to the preferences of their voters.

Competition was related to the role orientations of Canadian M.P.s in the same way as for American congressmen, but this relationship has not been found consistently among the state legislatures.[41] In Indiana, legislators who perceived their primary elections as competitive tended to have a delegate role orientation; this finding is consistent with the other studies of competition but suggests that the

[39] Allan Kornberg, *Canadian Legislative Behavior: A Study of the 25th Parliament* (New York: Holt, Rinehart and Winston, 1967), pp. 107–108.
[40] Davidson, *The Role of the Congressman*, p. 128.
[41] Jewell, "Attitudinal Determinants," p. 481.

Table 3.23   REPRESENTATIONAL STYLE AND AREA ROLES BY SENIORITY

REPRESENTATIONAL ROLE ORIENTATIONS	SENIORITY IN NUMBER OF TERMS			CHANGE (LEAST TO MOST SENIORITY)
	ONE (%)	2–5 (%)	6 PLUS (%)	
STYLE				
Trustee	13	26	38	+25
Politico	31	59	44	+13
Delegate	56	15	18	−38
Total	100	100	100	
AREA				
National	12	33	30	+18
National-district	38	24	27	−11
District	50	42	42	− 8
Total	100	100	100	
N =	(16)	(36)	(33)	

SOURCE: Roger Davidson, *The Role of the Congressman* (New York: Pegasus, 1969), p. 134, table 4–7.
NOTE: The N values vary slightly for the two categories of role orientations.

primary election is perhaps more critical in this respect than the general election.[42]

Seniority is likewise related to how congressmen perceive their representational roles, with the major changes occurring between the first-term members and all others with two or more terms of service (Table 3.23). The freshmen members were disproportionately delegates and district oriented, and the more senior members were more politicos and nationally oriented. But in all seniority categories, the plurality of members remained district oriented. Yet the proportion expressing a national orientation grew to 30% among the senior members from only 12% among the freshmen. These shifts are consistent with the electoral competitiveness variable above, for the senior members have safer elections than do the freshmen members.[43]

Most of the studies of role orientations show us how legislators understand their roles at one time. California freshman legislators, however, have been interviewed at three different times, to ascertain the stability (or change) in their role orientations. Among the three representational style roles, the trustee role grew from 10% of the entering freshmen to over a third after their second year of service in the legislature (Table 3.24). Each of the other two roles decreased,

[42] James A. Thurber, "The Impact of Party Recruitment Activity upon Legislative Role Orientations: A Path Analysis," *Legislative Studies Quarterly* 1 (November 1976), pp. 544–545.

[43] Davidson, *The Role of the Congressman*, p. 134.

Table 3.24 REPRESENTATIONAL STYLE ROLES OVER TIME: CALIFORNIA LEGISLATIVE FRESHMEN

| | TIME PERIODS | | | |
ROLES	PRIOR TO LEGISLATIVE SERVICE	AFTER ONE YEAR	AFTER TWO YEARS	CHANGE IN TWO YEARS
Trustee	10	24	35	+15
Politico	62	62	55	− 7
Delegate	28	14	10	−18
Total	100	100	100	
(N = 29)				

SOURCE: Charles G. Bell and Charles M. Price, *The First Term* (Beverly Hills: Sage Publications, 1975), p. 94, table 5.4.

with the delegate role decreasing the most. These changes, among the same set of legislators as they gain experience, are partly consistent with the seniority variable among congressmen. In both sets of members, the delegate role decreased while the trustees role increased. While the politico role showed contradictory trends between the two sets of members, the least amount of change occurred in this role compared to the other two roles.[44]

Roles in French National Assembly

Members of the French National Assembly have been placed into four types, depending upon their orientations to the Assembly which, in turn, reflect their broader purposes of being in politics in the first place. One type of member is termed the "mission participant," who is in politics to advance the cause of his party and its ideological goals for society. A Communist deputy, for example, explained his initial entry into politics in broad and societal terms:

> In 1935 I . . . was without work and without hope of finding work. There were unemployed people everywhere. I felt strongly that people simply could not allow such a situation to exist. It was not right, it could not be accepted. The society that allows such things to happen is rotten to the core.

A member of a Gaullist party commented that Gaullism meant:

> first of all, the independence of France. And then . . . the search for a new social humanism. Everything that centers on man's dignity—It is a philosophy: against Fascism, for a worship of man.

Apparently, most of the deputies expressing an ideological purpose in politics initially became active in politics through a political party, or

[44] Charles Bell and Charles Price, *The First Term: A Study of Legislative Socialization* (Beverly Hills: Sage Publications, 1975), pp. 94–98.

through their wartime participation in the underground resistance, or through the magnetism of one leader, General de Gaulle himself.[45]

The "program participants," as the second type of French deputy, are immersed in the practical solution to specific problems. They were concerned with obtaining a water system for a community, or about developing a better system of social security for the nation. But they did not express these specific goals in broad ideological terms. Their outlook was more pragmatic. Neither did they place much value in the importance of their political parties. One commented:[46]

> We are all very individualistic. . . . Luckily, we do not try to impose voting discipline on ourselves. We have a *cameraderie*, but not a very good organization.

Another referred to the unimportance of parties in his election:

> Parties . . . (are) not important at all. All that's important is to have local support. I have never run under a party label.

The third type of French deputy, the "obligation participants," entered politics from a strong sense of moral duty. They either perceived a major crisis (e.g., the Algerian crisis that brought de Gaulle to power) and felt they had to become active, or they were asked to run for office and felt they had to accept because it was their duty to serve. This category of deputy had not previously been active in politics, had few ideological goals and little concern with specific policies, and tended to not enjoy being members of the Assembly. Although most members of this type were Gaullists, they placed little value in their political party. They saw their purpose as one of supporting the Gaullist government in the Assembly, to avert the possibility of another governmental crisis. Many of these strands were expressed in this comment.[47]

> In 1967 I knew nothing about politics and I must admit that I have not had any satisfactions since then. . . . Unless it is a certain idea to which I am attached: fulfilling my responsibilities to the people of my district and to my country.

Another observed:

> I have no taste for politics. I never have. I prefer to fish or climb mountains. . . . I am not sure I will stay in the Assembly . . .

The "status participant," as the fourth and final type of French deputy, is in politics to attempt to advance to offices that he highly

---

[45] Oliver H. Woshinsky, *The French Deputy: Incentives and Behavior in the National Assembly* (Lexington, Mass.: Lexington Books, 1973), pp. 61–62, 65.

[46] Ibid., p. 85.

[47] Ibid., p. 108.

values because they are highly valued by others. This type of member often began politics, not with local offices and activity, but on the personal staff of the ministers of national governmental agencies:[48]

> [A] Minister I knew asked me to join his staff, and I accepted right away. . . . Accepting this job could not hurt me and would probably help me rise faster in my career. I was still young, only twenty-three, and it would be a good thing for me.

Deputies of this type are not caught up in ideological movements, have little interest in solving specific issues, and are not burdened with a nagging sense of disagreeable civic duty. Neither do they have much concern for the political party:

> I had to become a Gaullist, since I held a position on a Minister's staff. If you want to get into the Government, you have to be Gaullist, since we have a Gaullist Government. Since I wished to remain in power and later become a Deputy, there was no question about what party I would join.

They saw the Assembly as a place in which ambitious persons strive against one another to gain and hold power. They used public speaking on the Assembly floor as a means of gaining attention. They also very much enjoyed campaigning for election by speaking at public meetings, even though they were somewhat disdainful of the voters' intelligence.[49]

The four types of French Assembly deputies (as of the late 1960s) have had different career paths into the Assembly and may be differentiated on the basis of some of the same variables we have earlier discussed for members of other parliaments. They differ in the extent to which they have been active in political parties. Close to 80% of the mission participants have been active in their party over 15 years, while only 14% of the obligation participants had (Table 3.25). This variable seems to be linked to the proportions of deputies who had been recruited to candidacy through their political party. They differed in the age at which they began political activity and in the age at which they entered the Assembly. The mission deputy began political activity the earliest (at age 24), but took the longest to enter the Assembly. The status and obligation deputies took the shortest time to enter the Assembly from the beginning of their political activity, but the former began politics at a younger age. The obligation deputies had the least seniority in the Assembly and seemed the least satisfied with either politics generally or the Assembly specifically. The mission participant had taken the longest time to reach the Assembly, but once

[48] Ibid., p. 115.
[49] Ibid., pp. 61–126.

Table 3.25   RECRUITMENT CHARACTERISTICS OF FOUR TYPES OF DEPUTIES IN THE FRENCH NATIONAL ASSEMBLY

RECRUITMENT CHARACTERISTICS	TYPES OF DEPUTIES			
	MISSION	PROGRAM	STATUS	OBLIGATION
Party activity: percent over 15 years	79	36	40	14
Age of entry into politics	24.2	32.4	26.0	32.4
Average number years in politics	25.5	21.3	17.0	15.2
Age of entry into Assembly	41.7	47.7	37.0	43.6
Career time to Assembly: years	17.5	15.3	11.0	11.2
Average number years in Assembly	8.0	6.1	6.0	4.0

SOURCE: Oliver H. Woshinsky, *The French Deputy* (Lexington, Mass.: Lexington Books, 1973), pp. 143–150, tables 8.1–8.4.

there, tended to stay the longest. The program and status participants each had, on the average, 6 years of experience, but probably for different reasons. The program deputy was immersed in the detailed work of his committees, whereas the status deputy remained in the Assembly as the means by which he could become appointed as a government minister. Thus, the four types of French deputies, initially defined on the basis of their purpose in politics and in the Assembly, display distinctive career paths into the Assembly.[50] We shall note in the later chapter on floor participation (Chapter 7) that once in the Assembly, the four types behaved differently as well.

Summary

We have explored how congressmen have understood their proper tasks and functions in rather broad and generic senses. Role orientations also exist with respect to each of the other political actors with whom legislators interact. The available data on role orientations toward the chief executive and toward political parties will be examined in succeeding chapters. Here we have asked about members' understanding of their purpose—what they believe they should be doing in the job— and about their perceptions of whom they represent and how. We have found quite a variety of role orientations, both within the U.S. Congress and across several legislative bodies. Within the congressional sample the electoral circumstances and the seniority of members were usually related to their role orientations. Differences in leadership position, in region, and between the parties were less frequently related to role orientations.

[50] Ibid., pp. 143–150.

The dynamic of what happens—and how it happens—within legislative bodies is related, at least in part, to the different understandings members have of their purpose and of their representational tasks. No one role orientation is "proper" or "better"; each is a valid approach to the complex and perhaps frustrating job of being an elected representative in a large and diverse parliament which itself is just part of a larger governmental structure. To the extent that differing electoral circumstances condition members' role orientations, perhaps those differing elections also contribute to the diversity, and maybe the balance, among members with diverse role orientations. We tend to value "competition" and to lament its absence, but perhaps the safe members are able to make a contribution to the activity of a parliamentary body that marginal members cannot afford to make.

THE REPRESENTATIVE AS INTERMEDIARY

The elected representative is an intermediary between his constituency and the central government. His selection occurs within a defined locality, a district, whereas the duties of his office are located at the government's capital. He is thus in a position to express to the central government the views and desires of his electorate; he is also in a position to express to them the policies and purposes of the central government. As an intermediary, he is a communicator—frequently a two-way communicator.

Expression of District Views to the Government

We shall explore the constituency-representative relationship on policy questions more fully in a later chapter. Here we shall concentrate on the representative's intermediary role on casework services and on obtaining projects for the district. The term *casework* refers to the requests and problems of individual persons and companies. The term *projects* refers more to collective matters, such as post office construction, which have an impact upon a sizable number of persons in the area.

CASEWORK SERVICES
The wider and more extensive the services and activities of a government, the greater the degree to which individuals are directly affected. And the more they are affected by government the more they seem to turn to their elected representative as a source of help in dealing with the government. The Social Security Administration, the Veterans Administration, and the Department of Agriculture provide direct services to millions of persons; these agencies probably generate the largest volume of requests by individuals to congressmen for aid and

assistance.[51] Business generates another large volume of similar requests: the more government spends, the more do commercial firms seek government contracts, and the more they turn to their congressmen for assistance of obtaining such contracts. This type of activity is often belittled as the "errand boy" function, and congressmen regard it with mixed feelings: "We have more errand work than before, and less time to do legislative work."

But on the other hand, contacts from aggrieved constituents are one way congressmen have of learning the practical impact of the government agencies they supervise and of the policies they adopt:[52]

> You have to represent your district in contacts with federal agencies. This is often criticized as "errand running," but letters from the district instruct you as to how a program is operating. I do not object to that.

But like it or not, as we noted in a previous section, constituency service was listed as one of the two most important and frequent activities by congressmen.

In multilayered governmental systems, citizens do not always know which services are provided by which governmental units. Cities, states, and national governments provide services in a pattern that is often confusing to the individual citizen. As a result, legislators at one level of government often find themselves requested to aid in the provision of a service over which they have no formal jurisdiction.

One Republican congressman in a competitive central city district, for example, observed that most of the requests he received concerned state and especially city agencies. He deliberately accepted all such requests and attempted to intercede with city and state agencies as a means of building a voter base of support for himself in his competitive district.

This problem is particularly acute in India, in which most direct services to individuals are provided by the state governments rather than at the national level. Yet the ability of the national legislator to work effectively with lower levels of government depends upon the partisan and factional alliances between them. The Republican congressman cited above could largely deal with Republican city and state agencies, which considerably aided him in helping his constituents. In India, opposition party members did not receive cooperation from the state governments controlled by the then-dominant Congress party. But within that dominant (and also large) party, factionalism was

[51] Somewhat similar sources of individual requests have been found in Canada and Chile; see Mezey, *Comparative Legislatures,* p. 162.

[52] The two quotes are from Davidson, *The Role of the Congressman,* pp. 101 and 102, respectively.

rife, and national legislators could not cooperate with their fellow party members at state levels if they were in different factions within the party.[53]

Activity by members of parliament with administrative agencies on behalf of individuals within their districts is "increasingly a major task" in Communist party states as well. Agencies in the Soviet Union are required to "reply to a deputy's inquiry within one month" to state what action, if any, had been taken "to remedy the alleged grievance."[54] The logic of the system in Rumania was indicated in this statement:[55]

Simply put, to get any service done, and done right, one needs to "know someone" . . . A Deputy is for many citizens a means of avoiding bureaucratic tangles, and he therefore becomes a dispenser of favors . . .

Members of parliament are also approached for a variety of services in their district that are not governmental. They may be asked for personal financial contributions (to either organizations or by needy persons), or they may be called upon to intercede in local disputes. Particularly in underdeveloped nations, members of parliaments are highly visible and prestigious persons. As such, they are often called upon to act in a more personal manner than their official duties would prescribe.[56]

We might expect that not all members act the same way, or spend the same amount of time, on any of their tasks, including constituency service. Our most detailed evidence on this point comes from a study of the members of Canadian provincial legislatures: About 60% of them spent up to half of their time on constituency services, and another third spent up to 75% of their time on such activity. Only 9%, however, spent more than 75% of their time on constituency service.[57]

[53] Maheshwari, "Constituency Linkage," p. 342. For a report on a similar circumstance in Great Britain, see L. H. Cohen, "Local Government Complaints: The MP's Viewpoint," Public Administration (London) 51 (Summer 1973), pp. 175–183.

[54] Peter Vanneman, The Supreme Soviet: Politics and the Legislative Process in the Soviet System (Durham, N.C.: Duke University Press, 1977), pp. 166–167.

[55] Daniel N. Nelson, "Citizen Participation in Romania: The People's Council Deputy." Paper read at American Political Science Association, 1975, p. 29 (mimeo).

[56] Maheshwari, "Constituency Linkage," pp. 338–339; Michael Ong, "The Member of Parliament and His Constituency: The Malaysian Case," Legislative Studies Quarterly 1 (August 1976), pp. 441, 418.

[57] This and following paragraph come from Harold D. Clarke, Richard G. Price, and Robert Krause, "Constituency Service Among Canadian Provincial Legislators: Basic Findings and a Test of Three Hypotheses," Canadian Journal of Political Science 8 (December 1975), pp. 520–542.

The amount of time the members spent on constituency service was related both to their role orientations and to some of their personal and constituency attributes. Those whose representational-area roles were oriented to their constituency, for example, spent more time on constituency service than those oriented to province-wide concerns. Likewise, the "delegate" in representational-style orientations, spent more time on constituency-related activities than did the "trustee." The rural and small-town members spent more time in constituency service than did those from urban constituencies and larger cities. Furthermore, the members with less education spent more time on constituency service, as did those who had lived most of their life within their particular constituencies. But one factor was not related to casework: the members' competitive status. That one exception aside, the more locally oriented the member in his role orientations and in his life experiences, the more emphasis he tended to place on constituency "case work."

COLLECTIVE PROJECTS

Members of parliaments are called upon to aid local governments in obtaining desired expenditures by the national government for collective projects such as schools, roads, post offices, dams, housing projects, and the like. Particularly in newly independent and developing nations, the government is likely to be the planner and financer of most economic activity. To local governments, the national government is the only available supplier of funds. Education, the provision of irrigation projects, the building of roads, the construction of housing, and the financing of manufacturing plants are among the major elements in the economic development of localities and provinces. From the point of view of the localities, the national government needs to be persuaded of where to locate such activities, and the locally elected representative is in the best position to attempt that persuasion.

This type of activity is no less important (at least to the localities) in developed nations than in underdeveloped ones. The threat by newly elected President Carter to eliminate water dam projects around the country in early 1977 and the actual veto in 1978 were met with varying degrees of dismay and hostility in the affected areas. Projects provide not only a long-term service, but also short-term jobs. As a result, the construction industry and the construction labor unions are always interested in the provision and distribution of projects.

Within the U.S. Congress, the distribution of projects around the country seems to be one result of dividing the electorate into geographically defined districts, each electing its own representative. But in addition, the distribution of projects is affected by the committee position of particular members, and by the united support which state delegations of congressmen give to the project requests from the individual members from within the state.[58]

DISTRICT-MEMBER INTERACTION

On the whole, members of parliament receive a much higher volume of personal requests than they do collective ones. For example, most members of the India's *Lok Sabha*—that country's national parliament —said that requests from individuals constituted 80% or more of the total volume of requests they had received, whereas the collective category was usually under 10%. Approximately the same proportions were found in the Philippines and in a study of one U.S. Congressman's casework load.[59] The proportions, however, were reversed among members of the Indian state level legislatures; to work for the acquisition of local development projects was by far their most important activity.[60]

Local governments are active participants in the effort to bring national funds and projects into their localities. On such matters the elected national parliamentary representative and the local governments within his district work together as active collaborators in the pursuit of common objectives.

Local officials frequently turn to their elected national representatives, and often they are encouraged to do so by them. Discussion among them about obtaining grants and programs of the national government are frequently the main topic on which they have occasion to see each other.

Having a similar party identity is an aid in their cooperation and interaction. Local governmental officials are frequently the leaders of their local units of their political parties. Thus, when the congressman interacts with his local party on political matters, he is dealing with governmental officials, and vice versa. One congressman, for example, regularly met with the mayors within his district, all of whom shared his same party label. In Malaysia, the local officials similarly were heads of the local party units, and parliamentary members of the ruling party were expected to meet with the local governmental officials on at least a monthly basis. The heads of state governments in India have been reported to consciously organize the M.P.s from their respective

---

[58] John A. Ferejohn, *Pork Barrel Politics: Rivers and Harbor Legislation, 1947–1968* (Stanford: Stanford Press, 1974), pp. 231, 244–252.

[59] Maheshwari, "Constituency Linkage," pp. 337–338; Mezey, *Comparative Legislatures,* chap. 10, p. 4.

[60] Iqbal Narain and Shashi Lata Puri, "Legislators in an Indian State: A Study of Role Images and the Pattern of Constituency Linkages," *Legislative Studies Quarterly* 1 (August 1976), pp. 320–321.

states as a means of obtaining desired programs for the states from the national government.[61]

While the attempt to intercede for the locality in obtaining governmental expenditures for collective projects is a valued activity, it is also a potentially dangerous one. The beginning of the danger is that a whole legislature may attempt to shape the pattern of governmental expenditures to suit the (usually contradictory) purposes of individual districts. The accomplishment of the danger is that the executive officials of that government may, in sheer frustration and despair over the fate of their centrally planned economic development proposals, dissolve the parliament. The coup in Thailand, the elimination of Congress in the Philippines, and the gradual limitation of the powers of the Chilean Congress, are illustrative examples.[62]

We might expect that the volume of requests to legislators both for case work services and the acquisition of projects would vary with the responsiveness of the agencies themselves. The more accessible and open the agencies to local and individual requests, the less such requests would be channeled indirectly through the elected representatives.[63] But the more resistant the agencies to direct approaches by citizens and local governments, perhaps also the more resentful they would be at intermediary activities by legislators. Thus the greater the need for legislator activity in this respect, the greater the dangers that an unresponsive government would abolish the legislature.

Grants, projects, and contracts involve sizable sums of money and are vitally important to the persons or companies concerned. Thus there is the possibility of corruption within the agencies that make the allocations, and there is also the possibility of corruption by the congressman. Recent allegations against several congressmen have concerned their efforts to gain favorable decisions from administrative agencies. In each case the allegation was not that congressmen were bribing agency personnel, but that congressmen were being paid sums of money to obtain the desired agency decisions.[64]

ELECTORAL BENEFITS

Congressmen view casework services and projects as a means of building their own electoral base. One congressman kept a list of the persons

---

[61] Ong, "The Member of Parliament and His Constituency," pp. 408–410; Maheshwari, "Constituency Linkage," p. 343.

[62] Arturo Valenzuela and Alexander Wilde, "Presidential Politics and the Decline of the Chilean Congress," and David Morrell, "Thailand's Legislature and Economic Development Decisions," both in Joel Smith and Lloyd Musolf (eds.), *Legislatures in Development,* chaps. 7 and 13, respectively.

[63] Mezey, *Comparative Legislatures,* chap. 10.

[64] *Congressional Quarterly Weekly Report,* February 18, 1978, p. 283–285.

whom he had helped through the years. At election time he wrote to the persons on his "sweetheart list," and since he has been reelected over a number of terms, he felt that such persons did in fact vote for him. Another congressman made a point of aiding his opponents, "And some of them vote for me after that."[65] Legislators in both the Philippines and in an Indian state have indicated that their personal associations in the district and their provision of personal favors have been more important in their elections and reelections than has their party.[66]

In the United States the allocation of grants and projects presumably rebounds to the credit of the party in power. Congressmen and senators of the president's party are informed first that a given project has been awarded, and thus they have the first opportunity to announce the award in the press to the accompaniment of their name as the source of the information. The agencies, the White House, and the congressmen go to great lengths to ensure that this procedure is followed. Whether the voters either know or care, however, is another matter.

The provision of casework services is also a means by which congressmen bypass policy disagreements from within their districts. Even if a voter disagrees with a congressman on policy questions, but receives casework services from that congressman, the voter might then moderate his opposition or even vote for the congressman. In one district, a leader of an ideological group in strong policy opposition to the congressman lamented about the congressman's success:[67]

> He keeps his fences mended and attends to constituent requests. . . . He thinks that appropriations were invented for his district. . . . He quickly does favors for me, and does it gladly. But he will vote against me on the next bill, too, just as gladly.

U.S. senators, too, have felt that casework and project services brought them a freedom to vote on policy questions.[68]

The ability to provide casework services has been suggested as an important reason for—maybe even the major cause of—the ability of incumbent congressmen to be reelected. As the activities of the national government increase, and as their actions affect a larger number of persons directly, citizens have an increasing need to relate directly to agencies and their civil servants. Correspondingly, citizens have increasing need for congressional mediation with the agencies.

---

[65] John W. Kingdon, *Candidates for Office: Beliefs and Strategies* (New York: Random House, 1966), p. 75.

[66] Narain and Lata Puri, "Legislators in an Indian State," pp. 324–325; Mezey, *Comparative Legislatures,* chap. 10, p. 25.

[67] Personal interview.

[68] Donald Matthews, *U.S. Senators,* p. 226.

To provide such personal and nonissue type of service is a means for the congressman to make friends within the district.[69]

Justify the Central Government to the District

Some governments require their legislators to spend time in the district and to explain and justify the policies of the central government to their constituents. They are viewed more as agents of the regime than as spokesmen for their districts.

Members of the Tanzanian parliament, for example, have been instructed to carry the government's message to the countryside. The function of explaining government policy to the constituency was mentioned more often by Tanzanian members than was any other task (77%), and the function of stating constituency needs to the government received the second highest number of mentions. Members are expected, while parliament is not in session, to spend two or three weeks monthly in their districts meeting with constituents. One member estimated he met 10,000 constituents per month. Another observed, "People most often come to me because they think of me as their man in the government." An important element in the constituency-government linkage function is that the Tanzanian parliamentary member is forbidden to criticize government policies or actions to his constituents. He is, rather, expected to justify and defend.[70]

Communist nations take pride in the number of constituency meetings their parliamentary members have held. In the early 1960s, for example, members of the Polish Sejm held about 32,000 such constituency meetings.[71] That the member, at least in the Soviet Union, is expected to carry the government's message to the hinterland is expressed in this statement by a deputy in the Supreme Soviet:[72]

> I try to use any opportunity I have to inform my electors of the Supreme Soviet's decisions and to mobilize them for their implementation. My official reports to the constituency apart, I pursue this line at the sittings of the District and Village Soviets, at the different meetings and conferences and at my meetings with electors in collective and state farms and in factory shops.

[69] Morris P. Fiorina, *Congress: Keystone of the Washington Establishment* (New Haven: Yale University Press, 1977), chap. 5.

[70] Hopkins, "The Role of the MP in Tanzania," pp. 764, 770. See also Chan Heng Chee, "The Role of Parliamentary Politicians in Singapore," *Legislative Studies Quarterly* 1 (August 1976), p. 436.

[71] Andrzej Burda (ed.), *Sejm Polskiej Rzeczypospolitej Ludowej* (Warsaw: Ossolineum, 1975), p. 523, table 10.

[72] Quoted in Lane, *Politics and Society in the USSR*, p. 157.

Official expectations about the representative's performance in this respect, however, are not always met. The president of Kenya, for example, said that members of his parliament "have a most important duty in the rural areas to urge the people to follow the advice of technicians." Yet, the parliamentary members apparently spend the bulk of their time performing services on behalf of their constituents, and spend relatively little time in explaining government politics to their constituents.[73]

Summary

The representative faces an inherent dualism. As an intermediary and communications link, he can communicate both ways between district and central government. This dualism leads to ambiguity and stress to the extent that the central government expects him to act as their agent of downward communication.

The intermediary role involves the representative in questions of "details," as discussed in the first chapter. The avoidance of large questions of public policy in many countries is precisely what permits representatives in all systems to engage in this type of activity. It would appear that casework services and the procurement of collective propects is the most widespread of all parliamentary activities. In any given society, if a parliament is permitted to exist, its members at least engage in this type of intermediary activity. It is an activity they can perform individually and privately, with no need for either committee meetings or formal sessions of the whole parliament.

CONGRESSMEN IN THEIR DISTRICTS

Congressmen not only live in their districts (though that practice varies around the world) and are elected from their districts, but they also work in their districts. That is, their work world is a divided one, with a portion located at the nation's capital, and the other located in the constituencies they represent.[74]

Just as we shall find that a parliamentary body is a large and complex institution, so congressmen discover, if they did not already know, their constituencies are large, complex, and often heterogeneous. From the congressman's perspective, a constituency has four components— of which the geographic area and its total population is merely the first and most obvious. Within that large population, some smaller number

---

[73] Mezey, *Comparative Legislatures,* pp. 268–269.

[74] This section is based upon Richard F. Fenno, Jr., *Home Style: House Members in Their Districts* (Boston: Little, Brown, 1968).

of persons actually vote for the congressman in general elections, or at least he thinks they do. By subtraction, the member also estimates who his opponents are. A third grouping within the geographic district, smaller than the other two, consists of the congressman's strongest supporters—those who actively supported him in his initial election and perhaps were even active in recruiting him to run for office in the first place. Finally, the smallest set of persons within the constituency are personal friends, the persons whom he intimately trusts—his own "core group," with whom he charts his personal political strategy.

Which of these components of the constituency congressmen have in mind when they indicate a "delegate" role orientation is not known. Perhaps they would vary in that definition, and perhaps the definition would also vary with the type of issue. We shall cite evidence from roll call voting studies (Chapter 8) to indicate that representatives' voting on legislation is more strongly associated with the characteristics of their voter supporters than with those of the district as a whole. We shall also cite evidence to indicate that representatives of different parties who follow one another in representing the same district have very different voting records. They would appear to represent different portions of the same districts.

Congressmen vary in how they conduct themselves in their districts. They even vary in the amount of time they spend in their districts and in the allocation of staff between their Washington and district offices. Although the average number of trips taken from Washington to the district was 35 in 1973, for example, individual members varied from 4 to 365 trips home in that same year.

What a congressman does in the district, whom he sees, whom he talks to, and what he talks about, are all matters that vary from district to district. They also vary with the skills and aptitudes of the human being who holds the congressional office. At one extreme, some members emphasize interpersonal relationships and personal friendships with their voters, while others stress their widespread casework and project procurement services. At the other extreme, some members stress their concern with public issues and emphasize to all audiences —especially those who may not agree—their specific positions on a wide range of issues. We do not know how many representatives would be in each category, and we are not even sure about which types of districts would be associated with the varying approaches.

But each individual representative, in fashioning an approach to the district, seems to be attempting to build a relationship of trust with the electorate. In their very different ways, each representative wants the people of the district to know enough about that representative so that they will give him their personal trust. With trust, the representative can then act in Washington—even though most people will have little specific knowledge—with considerable freedom of choice in the expectation that most people in the district will be inclined to accept the representative's action and his explanations of his actions.

These comments concern American congressmen, elected from single-member districts of approximately 500,000 population each. We do not know how U.S. senators relate to their districts—whole states. In Britain, with much smaller single-member districts than in the United States, members often do not live within their districts and have few personal associations within the district beyond those provided by their political party. We have no idea of how representatives from multimember districts, which are usually rather large, would relate to the people within such districts. Their interactions might proceed mainly through local and partisan affiliations.

CONCLUSIONS

This chapter has had a dual focus: representation and the individual legislator. We have examined characteristics of the individual member of legislative bodies as a means of exploring the larger collective question of representation.

We have found that members are invariably higher in socioeconomic status and in education than is the general population, but we also find they are more typical of their populations than are economic or other governmental elites. We have noted that the socioeconomic characteristics of legislative members shift slowly through time and are related to, but lag behind, the general economic development of the nation.

Members also vary in the extent of their prior political experience —either in lower levels of public office or in political party activity, or both. The opportunity for prior political participation varies among countries, at least in part with the extent to which local and regional offices are elective in the first place. But within nations, members vary in this respect, and in both selected national parliaments and in American state legislatures, form distinct "types" of members.

Individual members also differ in their role orientations—in how they define their major activities and tasks within their legislative bodies. The differences among them are not random. Within any one legislature their differences seem to be related to their seniority and to their electoral security. Among nations, the differences in role orientations reflect institutional and system-wide attributes: the legislature's relationship to the chief executive and the organization of the political parties.

The legislative member is a representative—usually elected and from a district smaller than the whole nation. (We have noted some exceptions in the previous chapter). The legislator is an intermediary between the central government and his geographic portion of the nation. How he views himself in that relationship has been explored under the rubric of role orientation. We have also noted how U.S. congressmen spend their time and have commented upon the apparently universal activities of casework and projects. Although these types of activities can have consequences for the development of legislation, they more immediately require the member to seek tangible goals from the national government for either individuals or businesses or more collective projects for the whole districts. This type of activity appears to be a constant in all nations having parliaments and can become an important way in which legislators review agency activity and establish for themselves a sphere of permitted and not inconsequential activity.

This and the previous chapter have concentrated on the process by which members of parliaments are selected. Chapter 2 concentrated on the electoral process, whereas the present chapter has concentrated on the characteristics of individual members in office and their district-related activities. We have found that the conditions of entry into office—through elections and candidate recruitment—have an impact upon how the members see themselves and conduct themselves in office as representatives.

To this point we have concentrated upon one of the critical components of the environment of legislative bodies—the electorate. We turn next to the chief executive as the other major component in the external environment of parliaments—one that accordingly shapes the very structure of the institution and defines its major tasks.

Chapter 4
Relationships with the Executive and Administrative Agencies

The previous two chapters have described the relationships of parliaments with one of the critical actors in their environment—the electorate. We now turn to the other critical actor in the environment of parliaments—the executive. We shall also include the administrative agencies of the government. Although agencies are often considered to be apart from and different from the political chief executive and his cabinet, the two are closely related, and parliaments tend to regard the cabinet as responsible for whatever the agencies do.

Presidential and parliamentary systems use different words to describe their political chief executives and their main appointees. In parliamentary systems, of which the British are our example, the prime minister and the cabinet members ("secretaries" or "ministers") are "the government of the day." The equivalent American term is "the administration," consisting of the president, the cabinet members, and their aides. Just as the Carter administration succeeded the Ford administration, so the British Conservative government succeeded the Labour government. The permanent set of administrative agencies, which continue from one British government to the next and from one American administration to the next, are not included within the terminology discussed here. Presumably the agencies and their civil service personnel are responsive to political leadership at the top of the governmental structure and hence are included within this chapter. But the terms "government of the day" and "administration" refer specifically to the source of political and policy leadership at the top of the nation's governmental structure.

One major set of questions in the relationship between parliament and the executive branch concerns the selection of the chief executive and the cabinet. These questions involve the architecture of the constitution: whether the chief executive and parliament are considered as two separate branches, as in the American presidential system, or are considered as parts of the same body, as in the British parliamentary system. We shall elaborate this distinction in the first section of this chapter, and then we will discuss the American experience with separation of powers, the circumstances of cabinet and government formation within parliamentary systems, and the impact this distinction has upon the legislative bodies within the two types of systems.

A second major set of questions goes beyond their structural relationship and selection and concerns their activities. We shall look at their mutual involvement in legislation and budget and at the various means by which parliaments and their members attempt to supervise and affect the activities of administrative agencies.

THE FORMAL RELATIONSHIP

Parliamentary and Presidential Systems

In Western democratic nations the two prototypical ways of structuring the relationships between the parliament and the chief executive are termed the "parliamentary" system and the "presidential" or "separation" system. The British case illustrates the first; the American, the second. In the first, the chief executive—the prime minister—is selected by Parliament, and rises to that position through and as a member of Parliament. In the latter, the chief executive—the president—is selected by a process outside of Congress and cannot be a member of Congress while he holds that office. In one, he becomes the prime minister because he is a leader in parliament of the party having a majority in parliament, while in the other, his membership in and leadership of the congressional party is prohibited. In the former case he remains the leader of his party in Parliament and sits on the "front bench" in that body. In the latter he leaves Congress, if he was a member, and governs from the White House.

The British and American systems, for all of their differences, have both evolved from a common root. The American constitution created

a presidential-congressional relationship on the pattern of the writers'
understanding of how the British system then worked. That period
preceded the development of what we now know as the British cabinet
system. At that time, the crown was independent of parliament. The
crown's assent was required for legislation to become law. In a similar
vein, the new American president was given a veto. The king's
ministers were appointed by him, and were answerable to him; impeachment was the only weapon by which parliament could retaliate
against the king's appointed officers. Ironically, the last of the British
impeachment trials was under way as the American constitution was
written. Just as that practice was dying out in the British system, it was
given new life in the American.[1]

The two systems have evolved in different directions since their
common origins two centuries ago. The British prime minister and the
cabinet are now responsible to parliament. They are selected through
and are answerable to parliament—in effect, to the majority party.
The powers of government have shifted from crown to parliament and
from parliament to those party leaders who could control it.

The presidency, as the American analog to the British crown, however, has grown in leadership and has prospered as an independent
political power. Perhaps this office has developed an independence and
power that the constitutional authors could not have visualized, for a
party system and both a wide suffrage and a direct election of the
president did not then exist. Each is a complicated sociopolitical invention, not understood or intended at the time each element began to
develop. The result, however, has been to make the presidency more
independent of Congress than probably was originally intended. The
constitutional convention gave serious thought to making the president
elected by Congress (some of the state legislatures then elected their
governor). When the electoral college was substituted as the selection
means for the president, the original expectation was that no majority
would emerge from the electoral colleges meeting separately in their
respective states and thus Congress would ultimately select the president. That intention in a way presaged the British development of
selecting the prime minister through Parliament. But the American
presidential election evolved to become organized through the party
system, one effect of which has been to remove the presidential selection process from congressional participation.

As a nation, we have reacted adversely whenever the presidential
selection was thrown into the House. The first constitutional amend-

---

[1] Michael P. Riccards, "The Presidency and the Ratification Controversy," *Presidential Studies Quarterly* 7 (Winter 1977), pp. 37–46; Samuel P. Huntington,
Political Order in Changing Societies (New Haven: Yale University Press, 1968),
pp. 106–119.

ment after the Bill of Rights was to remedy a defect made visible in the efforts of the House to resolve the election between Jefferson and Burr. Only a few years later participation by congressmen in the nomination process (King Caucus) was repudiated as undemocratic, and was replaced by the party convention system. In the post–World War II period, many different reforms have been proposed for the presidential election system, most of which would replace congressional selection of the president in the event of deadlock with a popular run-off election. Thus the American system has evolved toward greater independence of the president from Congress, whereas the British system has evolved toward greater dependence of the prime minister upon Parliament.

Variations

The variants among the world's nations on these two basic systems are almost endless. Each country improvises a government-parliament relationship, based partly upon its traditions and partly upon more immediate considerations of either necessity or advantage. West Germany illustrates both the impact of tradition and the reaction against adverse experience. In Germany's original parliaments, the government cabinets were appointed by the kaiser. They met with parliaments, but were not members of that body. The cabinet's physical location was in front of the parliament, raised above it, and turned to face it. The arrangements suggested separation, higher status, and confrontation. To this day, the West German cabinet sits elevated and facing the chamber, even though the bulk of its membership retains simultaneous membership in the Bundestag, and is selected by the Bundestag leaders in response to the results of Bundestag elections. In reacting against their adverse experience in the hectic Weimar Republic (between World War I and the rise of Hitler), West Germany has placed important limits on the extent to which parliament may dismiss the governing cabinet. Although the Bundestag votes the chancellor into office, he may be dismissed only if parliament simultaneously votes into office his replacement. This "constructive vote of no confidence" means that parliament may not unseat a government simply by defeating a government bill, as is possible in Britain. It must first select the successor as well. Not once has such an event occurred since the creation of the West German government after World War II.[2]

France represents something of a hybrid, in that it combines a strong president with the appearance of a parliamentary system. The president, in the Fifth Republic created by de Gaulle, is independently

[2] Gerhard Loewenberg, *Parliament in the German Political System* (Ithaca: Cornell University Press, 1967), pp. 33–36, pp. 221, 390–391.

and directly elected, as in the American system. In addition, the president selects a prime minister who must deal with the Assembly. The Assembly can dismiss the prime minister, thus creating the possibility of stalemate between the Assembly and the president. The president can dissolve the assembly and call for new elections in an effort to resolve the stalemate. But after the election, should the assembly and president continue to disagree over the prime minister and cabinet, there is no readily available means to resolve the dispute within the constitution. As of the mid-1970s, such an irreconcilable dispute has not arisen, for the Assembly's majority has coincided with the president's party.[3] But France could experience in the future the same type of dramatic political conflict faced in Europe in the late nineteenth and early twentieth centuries: Shall the prime minister be selected by and removable by parliament or by an external chief executive?

In World Perspective

Among the world's nations, the presidential and parliamentary systems occupy a middle position, for each balances the status of the chief executive against that of parliament. These systems are flanked on one side by nations that give preponderance to the chief executive and on the other by those in which the parliament dominates. The nations in which their chief executives are preponderant circumscribe the powers of parliament and limit its autonomy in setting meeting times and agenda. Indeed, coups and revolutions around the world regularly abolish parliaments. Whatever the nation, if it is to have a government at all, it must have some effectively controlling entity—and that is termed the executive power. To have a parliament is, for these nations, a luxury. We know, however, of no nation featuring a parliament that has completely dispensed with the equivalent of an executive body.[4]

Not that theorists have not attempted to construct such a system. Their legacy is found in a number of countries that allocate greater discretion and authority to their parliaments than to their executives. Most countries in this category are Soviet-area nations in which the Communist party is the source of leadership and direction for the formal government in both the executive agencies and parliament. Not all chief executives govern through a political party (military juntas and bureaucracies, for example), but in the modern world, parties are the means by which those nations are governed that formally allocate dominance to their parliaments.

[3] John E. Schwarz and L. Earl Shaw, *The United States Congress in Comparative Perspective* (Hinsdale, Ill.: Dryden, 1976), p. 59.
[4] Jean Blondel, *Comparative Legislatures* (Englewood Cliffs, N.J.: Prentice-Hall, 1973), pp. 39–42.

Table 4.1   RELATIVE FORMAL POWERS OF
PARLIAMENTS AND EXECUTIVES: NUMBER OF
COUNTRIES

		COUNTRIES	
FORMAL POWERS	N		%
Strong executives		17	16
Equilibrium		55	51
Parliamentary	27		25
Other	7		6
Presidential	21		19
Strong legislatures		20	19
Not known		16	15
		108	101

SOURCE: Jean Blondel, *Comparative Legislatures* (Englewood
Cliffs, N.J.: Prentice-Hall, 1973), pp. 39–42

Table 4.1 shows the distribution of the world's nations along a
continuum of formal authority between the parliament and chief
executive as of 1971. Half the nations are found in the equilibrium or
middle portion of the scale, having either parliamentary or presidential
systems. The other half, however, are found at either extreme position.
This tabulation is based upon the constitutional powers of the two
political branches to dismiss and dissolve one another. In the strong
executive nations the executive can dismiss the legislature, but that
body cannot remove the executive from office. At the other extreme,
parliament can dismiss the executive, while the executive cannot dissolve parliament. In the middle portion of the scale, these two
capacities are balanced: In parliamentary systems the legislature can
remove the cabinet from office through a vote of "no confidence" and
the cabinet can also dismiss parliament; in presidential systems neither
can dismiss the other from office.

The power to dismiss is related to the power to elect. When the
prime minister is selected by parliament, it usually has the power to
dismiss him and the cabinet from office, and he usually has the power
to dissolve it (in many parliamentary systems, the head of state
formally dissolves parliament upon request by the prime minister). In
presidential systems, neither the president nor the parliament selects
each other; neither can dismiss each other. In the "strong executive"
nations, the executive is not selected by or through parliament; that
official can dismiss parliament, but it cannot affect his tenure in office.
In the "strong legislature" nations, mainly in the Soviet bloc, the formal
power of the prime minister to dissolve parliament is greatly limited,
but its formal powers to dismiss the prime minister and his cabinet
(council of ministers) is unlimited. The formal powers, however, are
unused in the absence of political conflict between parliament and the

executive, for both are subject to prior decisions made through the ruling party.

The power of the chief executive and parliament to dismiss each other from office is also related to the powers and selection of the "head of state." Parliamentary systems tend to be found in nations retaining a constitutional monarchy as the ceremonial head of state, while parliament itself selects the political executive. In some parliamentary nations (West Germany and Israel, for example), the head of state, termed "president," is elected either by parliament or by a larger electoral college that includes parliament. Presidential systems usually lack a monarch, and combine the dual functions of head and chief of state into one office, the occupant of which is selected by a popular election occurring outside of parliament. The "strong executive" nations in Table 4.1 select their executive through popular elections, or have traditional monarchies or military rulers. The "strong legislature" nations typically select both their head of state and their prime minister through parliament.[5]

Limitations on Parliaments

In addition to selecting and dismissing each other from office, which is probably the critical power, each branch has a variety of formal powers allocated to it in making the governmental system work.

EMERGENCY POWERS

Usually the executive is allocated extraordinary and residual authority to act, thereby diminishing the scope of parliamentary autonomy. Constitutions allocate "emergency" powers to governments, and especially to chief executives, in at least half of the world's nations. While some form of parliamentary assent or modification is usually required after the fact, the grants of emergency power to the executive are often vague and ill-defined. The Gaullist constitution of France is an example. Similar powers were invoked by Prime Minister Indira Gandhi in the mid-1970s, and were used not only to curb the press and rival parties, but also to jail opposition members of her own parliament and from her own party.

FOREIGN POLICY

Foreign policy is another sector of activity in which the executive ordinarily has greater powers of action than does the legislature. The ability of chief executives to act independently in foreign policy is illustrated by the invention by American presidents of the "executive

[5] Ibid., pp. 40–42; see also Valentine Herman and Francoise Mendel, *Parliaments of the World* (Berlin: De Gruyter, 1976), pp. 803–804.

agreement" as a device to circumvent the Senate's role in the ratification of treaties. One of the post Johnson-Nixon reforms imposed upon succeeding presidents by a resentful (and fearful) Congress has been a procedure by which executive agreements are subject to congressional review and potential rejection. The Swedish parliament is active in foreign affairs through its long-standing special commission to which the foreign minister has reported and with which he has consulted, presumably in far greater detail and candor than would be done in open meetings of either the parliament as a whole or even in a meeting of a regularly constituted committee.

DOMESTIC LEGISLATION

Even in domestic legislation, and even in nonemergency situations, the executive in many countries shares at least some authority with parliament. In almost two-thirds of the nations, the executive can veto and return a bill to parliament; in most of those, however, parliament can then readopt the bill over the executive's objections.

Quite beyond all of these limitations, however, in about a third of the nations (for which we have information) the executive still has authority in domestic legislation limiting that of parliament (Table 4.2).

REFERENDA

Another important set of restrictions upon parliament's authority over domestic legislation stems from the possibility of referenda. Under a variety of circumstances, referenda may be used in about a third of the nations (for which we have information), in which the citizenry votes on the equivalent of a legislative bill (Table 4.2).

Taking both sets of restrictions together, in about half the nations the authority of parliament over nonemergency domestic legislation is

Table 4.2 RESTRICTIONS ON PARLIAMENTS: NUMBER OF COUNTRIES BY DOMESTIC LAWMAKING POWERS OF EXECUTIVES AND REFERENDA

| | EXECUTIVE LAWMAKING POWERS | | | | | |
| | NONE | | SOME | | TOTAL | |
REFERENDA	N	%	N	%	N	%
No	39	49	12	15	51	65
Yes	12	15	16	20	28	35
Total	51	(64)	28	(35)	79	100

SOURCE: Jean Blondel, *Comparative Legislatures* (Englewood Cliffs, N.J.: Prentice-Hall, 1973), pp. 39–42. (Of 108 nations tabulated, both items were known or measurable for only 79.)
NOTE: Each cell states the proportion (%) each is of the total of 79 cases.

wide.[6] At the other extreme, parliament is limited both by executive powers and by the existence of popular referenda in 20% of the nations. The referendum not infrequently is used by chief executives as a weapon against parliament, as did de Gaulle with his Assembly. In other instances the referendum is resorted to by government officials when they do not feel prepared themselves to make a highly controversial decision. In other cases, opponents of a given bill may force a referendum in an effort to reverse a parliamentary decision likely to displease them, of which the Italian divorce and abortion referenda in the 1970s are examples. Even Great Britain resorted to a referendum on joining the European Common Market. Although it is only advisory by law, the British government pledged to abide by its results. Similar referenda in Norway and Denmark made the legally binding decision on the same question in the early 1970s. Switzerland and many of the American states make extensive and regular use of referenda; justified in the name of "direct democracy," one result is to limit the powers of their respective legislative bodies. In the American states, at any rate, legislatures have been widely distrusted and unrespected; state governors have similarly been circumscribed by referenda and by the device of having many separately elected "executive" branch officials.

THE AMERICAN EXPERIENCE

Although the American constitutional prescriptions about the relationships between the president and Congress largely have been unchanged, we have varied radically in our practice of that relationship. We have gone through wide swings, ranging from congressional dominance over the president to the reverse. Very early, Jefferson selected the officials of Congress, and his agents met with the party caucus to consult with and even instruct them on how to act on legislation. Although Jefferson was the exponent of limited government, and is cited today as an agrarian decentralist, his action in office created important precedents for both an activist national government and for an activist president.[7]

Strong presidents usually have been succeeded by strong Congresses, which have reacted adversely against their immediately prior experience. Jefferson was followed by the assertiveness of Congress during the Monroe presidency. Lincoln was followed by assertive Con-

[6] Blondel, *Comparative Legislatures*, pp. 36–38.
[7] Wilfred E. Binkley, *President and Congress* (New York: Knopf, 1947), pp. 49–60; George Galloway, *History of the United States House of Representatives* (Washington, D.C.: House Committee on House Administration, House Doc. No. 250, 89th Congress, 1965), pp. 89–90.

gresses during the Johnson and Grant presidencies. More recently, the perceived excesses of the Johnson and Nixon administrations have been reacted to by Congress in attempting to develop institutional restraints against Ford and Carter.

Separated Institutions Sharing Power

The terms *separation of powers* and *checks and balances* are ordinarily used to describe the relationship between president and congress. These terms apply to politics an eighteenth-century imagery of a mechanistic universe and as such have little practical meaning today.

A better phrase might be *separated institutions sharing functions.*[8] The powers, or the functions, are shared. Rather, the institutions— and more important, the people within them—are separated from and different from one another. The differences in the elections between president and Congress build into them different policy preferences. Merely by holding elections at different intervals and by using different district sizes, political differences are projected into the two institutions.

But why would not a president, needing congressional assent to his policies, seek to coopt into his own administration the leaders of Congress? A president could appoint as his secretary of state, for example, the chairman of the Senate's Foreign Relations Committee. The same person could then act for the president in both offices and thereby could secure a greater measure of congressional consent to presidential policies. Precisely this result is achieved through a parliamentary system, in which the executive officers are members of parliament.

One little phrase in the U.S. Constitution—and only one—prevents such a maneuver:

> No senator or representative shall, during the time for which he was elected, be appointed to any civil office under the authority of the United States . . . and no person holding any office under the United States, shall be a member of either House during his continuance in office. (Art. I, Sec. 6b)

We would guess that the architecture of the Constitution—each branch of government is authorized in separate articles—would not be sufficient to prevent presidents from attempting to coopt powerful congressmen into their own administrations. This single "incompatibility clause," however, is sufficiently precise and specific to have served as the lynch pin of the separated institutions. Congressmen, indeed, are

---

[8] The imagery is discussed in J. Bronowski, *The Ascent of Man* (Boston: Little, Brown, 1973), chap. 7. The phrase comes from Richard E. Neustadt, *Presidential Power: The Politics of Leadership* (New York: Wiley, 1960), pp. 33–37.

appointed to governmental office, and members are sometimes elected president or vice president while in Congress. Yet their appointment or election takes effect only upon their resignation from their congressional seat.

Such appointments frequently relate to the congressman's committees and their legislative competence. In the Carter Administration, for example, the congressmen appointed as secretaries of agriculture (Bergland, D-Minn) and transportation (Adams, D-Wash) had both served on the congressional committees having jurisdiction over those departments, and both had been active in developing legislation affecting them.

Parliamentary systems of the British tradition usually require that cabinet members also be members of Parliament, whereas presidential systems based on the American model specifically prohibit dual membership (as does Sweden, based upon neither tradition). But most countries with parliaments do not specify either condition. As a matter of practice, however, almost all cabinet members in such countries are also members of parliament.[9] The diverse traditions and systems of such countries (e.g., Belgium, Canada, Czechoslovakia, and Japan) indicate that dual membership is an effective method of governance for the prevailing party. The widespread practice of dual membership also indicates that membership in parliament is an effective means of, if not an absolute precondition for, obtaining executive office. It is entirely possible that the United States would have developed the same practice—dual membership—except for the brief but explicit prohibition in the constitution.

Recent "Parliamentary" Events

Even so, several events during the Nixon presidency brought us closer to the practices of a parliamentary system.

The constitution had just been revised to accommodate our recent experiences of presidential assassination (Kennedy) and incapacitating illness (Eisenhower). In the event of a vacancy in the vice presidency the president was to nominate, but Congress to confirm, a new vice president. Within a year of the first vice presidential succession under these new provisions (Ford replaced Agnew), Ford became president upon Nixon's resignation. Through that unexpected chain of events, Congress had, in effect, selected a president. Furthermore, Congress then held additional confirmation hearings on the second vice president to be selected by the new procedure (Rockefeller).

There was looming in the coming 1976 presidential election another possibility that would have increased Congress' activity in the

[9] Herman and Mendel, *Parliaments of the World*, pp. 807–808.

selection of the president—the possibility of a deadlock in the electoral college. Although such a deadlock had not materialized in several other close recent elections, and neither did it in 1976, a deadlock seemed a real possibility. It was possible that either party would split. The Reagan wing of the Republican party and the Wallace wing of the Democratic party could conceivably have split from their parties' nominees and have conducted third-party independent campaigns. A very possible result, in that event, would have been to cast Congress again in the role of president selector. We have not seen this development in more than 150 years, but when and if it occurred we would have experienced an important alteration in the relationship between president and Congress.[10]

Differences over Policy and Jurisdiction

Within the American system, the very separation of institutions and officials creates political differences between the president and Congress. The system tends to encourage, even if it does not create, such differences. Perhaps we may best illustrate this phenomenon with the first American Congress in its first encounter with President Washington. The Senate, according to the constitution, shall "advise and consent" to presidentially suggested treaties. But what does that phrase mean in practice? Before it was done the first time, no one knew. Washington's solution was to come to the Senate chamber personally. Washington brought with him his leading adviser on the proposed treaty with Indians. He had written a series of questions for the Senate to answer, each of which was stated, "Do you advise and consent" to a specified provision, to which the senators could presumably reply with a simple yes or no. The senators did not know how to respond. As one of them wrote in his journal, "There was a dead pause." One senator then asked that the papers be read to the Senate, thus causing the first delay. The senator noted that President Washington "wore an aspect of stern displeasure."[11]

The possibilities of delay are endless in a collective deliberation. Parliaments—even the first Congress—have complicated procedures. The president, apparently, wanted to spend a few hours with the Senate and to be able to leave with its advice but also its consent to his own proposals. The first Senate had only 26 members, for only 13

---

[10] The selection by the Georgia Legislature in 1966 of Lester Maddox as governor is widely credited in that state as ending the previous dominance of the legislature by the governor.

[11] William Maclay, "Journal of William Maclay," in Allen Johnson (ed.), *Readings in American Constitutional History, 1776–1876* (Boston: Houghton Mifflin, 1912), pp. 162–165.

states were then in the Union. But the Senate postponed the questions until the following week, and then resorted to another device for delay (as the President would see it) but also for thorough and free discussion (as the senators would see it):

> I had, at an early stage of the business, whispered to Mr. Morris that I thought the best way to conduct the business was to have all the papers committed. My reasons were that I saw no chance of a fair investigation of subjects while the President of the United States sat there, with his Secretary of War to support his opinions, and overawe the timid and neutral part of the Senate. Mr. Morris hastily rose, and moved that the papers communicated to the Senate by the President of the United States should be referred to a committee of five, to report as soon as might be on them.

The Senate, after debating this proposal in Washington's presence, finally agreed to create the committee and agreed that nothing further could be done until the next week. President Washington then reacted, as reported by the same participant:

> . . . the President of the United States started up in a violent fret. "This defeats every purpose of my coming here," were the first words that he said. He then went on that he had brought his Secretary at War with him to give every necessary information; that the Secretary knew all about the business, and yet he was delayed. . . . A pause for sometime ensued. We waited for him to withdraw. He did so, with a discontented air.

The same senator even suggested that Washington left in "sullen dignity." Washington never returned. Thus, the precedent had been set, though not planned: The Senate would meet and vote separately from the president, even on those matters on which it shared jurisdiction with him.

In a system of separated institutions—which must come to some minimal agreement for government policy to be decided—the procedures to be used between the two, the proper jurisdiction of each, and the question of which one is "right," are all matters which arise as they interact with each other. Whether they cooperate or dispute with one another varies through time and with circumstance. But they are free to disagree because their separateness means that neither possesses the ultimate sanction over the other—threat to their continuance in office.

The logic of the system of separated institutions was expressed during debates over ratification of the constitution through the Federalist Papers:[12]

[12] Alexander Hamilton, John Jay, and James Madison, *The Federalist: A Commentary on the Constitution of the United States* (New York: Modern Library, n.d.), "The Federalist No. 51," p. 337.

But the great security against a gradual concentration of the several powers in the same department, consists in giving to those who administer each department the necessary constitutional means and personal motives to resist encroachments of the others . . . ambition must be made to counteract ambition. The interest of the man must be connected with the constitutional rights of the place.

Perhaps conflict and disagreement are more to be expected than is cooperation between the president and Congress in a system of separated institutions sharing powers. Their separate elections and different constituencies increase the likelihood that they will support different policies. The same separateness of their election procedures means that neither, under ordinary circumstances at least, participates in either the selection or the removal of the other from office.

The separateness of institutions, through having them occupied by different people, provides each with the capacity to actively oppose the other. That they share functions provides the opportunity for such opposition. Their "powers" or functions are shared. There is no clear dividing line between them, but rather a vague blending of their powers. What the respective duties shall be of each branch is not rigidly defined in the constitution, but rather, remains to be worked out through the ongoing interaction between the executive and the Congress. At the very least, each branch requires the passive acquiescence of the other to their proposals, but each branch is well equipped to oppose the other actively.

CABINET FORMATION AND DISSOLUTION

In previous sections of this chapter we have discussed formation of "the government" and selection of "the cabinet." To an American reader these terms are perhaps unfamiliar; to a reader from any country the events designated by these terms are at least complex if not also confusing.

In parliamentary systems, selection of the prime minister and the cabinet depends directly on the composition of parliament resulting from the latest election. In presidential systems, the selection of the president and his cabinet depends directly on the presidential election; the composition of congress is irrelevant.

The Party System

How the decisions are made of who becomes prime minister and of who enters the cabinet within parliamentary systems varies with the party systems. In a two-party system the relative size of the two parties clearly separates the majority party from the minority. The majority party forms the new "government of the day." The majority's leader becomes the prime minister, and he selects his cabinet from among the leading, or at least promising, members of his party; the minority party becomes "the opposition."

In a three (or more) party system, the relationships among the parties become more complicated. If one party has a majority, it forms the cabinet. But if, as is much more likely, no party has a majority, the largest party usually attempts to form the government. In West Germany, for example, the chancellor has always come from the largest party. For most of the time, the smallest of the three German parties (Free Democrats) has held the balance of votes (and hence power) between the two much larger parties. In Sweden the former Agrarian party was usually included in the government with the much larger Social Democrats. In both countries the largest party was usually a bit short of a majority; the much smaller party held the needed margin of votes to make a majority. Hence in both countries the smaller party joined with the larger to form a coalition government. In multiparty systems the major question in an election is frequently one of "which party will have the plurality" rather than "which party will be the majority."

There are occasions when the largest party, however, does not join the "government of the day." The 1975 Swedish elections, for example, resulted in major losses for the governing plurality party (Social Democrats), which, however, remained the largest single party in parliament. Its loss of seats resulted in its resignation from power. A coalition of previously opposition parties then formed the new government. The prime minister was the leader of the largest party within the coalition, though not of the largest single party in parliament.

Governments in a parliamentary system need not be formed by a majority. Governments can be formed by a minority party or coalition. It does receive a majority vote when it takes office, or at least a majority does not vote in opposition to its formation or vote against it on major bills. That is, some parties, having the balance of power, refuse to join the cabinet but nevertheless will make is possible for the cabinet to govern. In some instances such as in Sweden, the Social Democrats, though by far the largest party, lacked an absolute majority. The Communist party, holding the balance of seats, always voted in support of the Social Democratic minority government, even though the Social Democrats would not permit the communists to enter the government. In other instances, such as in Belgium, the parties that supported the government by their votes refused to join the cabinet, though they were invited to do so.[13] Perhaps the most startling instance in the 1970s has occurred in Italy, where the large Communist and

[13] *Keesing's Contemporary Archive* (London), May 27–June 2, 1974, pp. 26533–26535.

several smaller parties abstained on votes affecting the Christian Democratic cabinet, thereby giving the latter party a clear majority of all votes cast.

The more heterogeneous the nation and the larger the number of parties, the less likely a nation is to have a majority or even a sizable plurality party. For the same reasons, the parties are likely to view their differences as sizable, important, and difficult to reconcile. The instability of some nation's cabinets (e.g., France prior to de Gaulle, and Italy) are major examples.

As of late 1978, the governments of Great Britain, Sweden, and Italy all were in office as minority governments. In each country, a sufficient number of nongoverning party votes supported the governing party (or coalition) to maintain the current government of the day in office. In both Britain and Sweden, the form of support was the act of abstention, but it worked differently in the two countries. In Britain, enough members abstained to give the government a majority of the votes actually cast. In Sweden, by contrast, a proposed government assumes power if an absolute majority of votes are not cast against it. The minority government of 1978–1979 came to power in exactly that way. The vote cast was 39 votes in favor (all from its one minority party) to 66 votes against (from an unusual combination of Conservatives and Communists). This low vote total (105 votes cast of a membership of 349) resulted from the decision of the two largest parties to abstain. Because an absolute majority of all the members did not vote against the proposed government, it was approved. In parliamentary systems, acquiescence is a form of power.

Factors in Cabinet Formation

By and large, the representation of parties within governing cabinets is proportional to their share of seats in parliament. The share of parliamentary seats and inclusion in the cabinet are among the major decisions made by the previous election.[14]

Size alone, as the above discussion indicates, is not the only factor. A number of others may be identified: minimum winning size, ideological and policy similarities, and the presence of the Communist party. How large should a governing coalition become? If it included all of the parties in parliament, it would simultaneously maximize its proportion of the vote and its internal heterogeneity. It would also, presumably, have to distribute the available offices among all parties.

[14] Eric C. Browne and Mark N. Franklin, "Aspects of Coalition Payoffs in European Parliamentary Democracies," *American Political Science Review* 67 (June 1973), pp. 453–469; Gerhard Loewenberg, "The Influence of Parliamentary Behavior on Regime Stability," *Comparative Politics* 3 (January 1971), pp. 185–186.

To provide some degree of internal stability and also to limit the number of participants to which offices must be allocated, cabinets are usually formed from some but not all parties within any given parliament. One leading theory of coalition formation argues that a coalition will tend to be formed of the "minimum winning size"; that is, within the existing distribution of parliamentary seats, governing coalitions tend to be formed among that combination of parties containing the smallest possible number of seats over the needed 50% threshold. The available studies of coalition formation in parliaments indicate that governing coalitions do tend to be formed in accordance with the "minimum winning size" principle.[15]

Ideological consistency and policy agreement modify and limit both the proportionality and minimum-size principles. Governments have to govern; they will propose bills for which they will need a majority vote. To increase the likelihood of obtaining the needed majority of votes on the floor, cabinets have been formed of parties that together exceed that minimum number. They attempt to develop a common policy. To include more than the minimum-size coalition in the cabinet gives the participating parties an assured opportunity to help shape the government's policy. In return, they are expected to provide the vote of their members in support of that policy when it arrives on the floor in the form of legislation.[16]

The presence and size of the Communist party have had a major influence on the formation of parliamentary coalitions. Seldom since the late 1940s has it been included in any Western European governing cabinet. In some countries (Scandinavian) it has been too small, usually, to have made much of a difference.

In other nations, where it has been the second or third largest party (Italy, France), it has been viewed by most of the other parties as a major threat, not only to their own power but also to the maintenance of the entire governing system. The Communist party has been viewed as "antisystem," against which all of the other many and diverse "prosystem" parties tend to unite.[17]

Within the western democracies, the Communist party has made

[15] James Q. Wilson, *Political Organizations* (New York: Basic Books, 1973), pp. 269–270.

[16] Peter H. Merkl, "Coalition Politics in West Germany," pp. 30, 39 and 41–42, and Wayne L. Francis, "Coalitions in American State Legislatures," p. 410; both in Sven Groennings, E. W. Kelley, and Michael Leiserson (eds.), *The Study of Coalition Behavior* (New York: Holt, Rinehart and Winston, 1970).

[17] George W. Rice, "The Electoral Prospects for Non-Ruling Communist Parties," *Midwest Journal of Political Science* 17 (August 1973), pp. 597–610; Giovanni Sartori, "European Political Parties: The Case of Polarized Pluralism," in Joseph LaPalombara and Myron Weiner (eds.), *Political Parties and Political Development* (Princeton, N.J.: Princeton University Press, 1966), pp. 137–176.

its most notable gains in Italy. It is the second largest party in parliament and governs more regions and municipalities than does any other single party. Thus it has developed a larger corps of experienced local administrators than has any other single party. In attempting to become Italy's largest parliamentary party in the 1976 election, it promised that it would not alter Italy's foreign policy (membership in NATO) and that it would respect and continue Italy's competitive democratic and parliamentary system. Its important gains, though short of its goal, required the plurality Christian Democrats to openly negotiate with the Communist party on the formation of the next Italian cabinet. That the Communist party would engage in such negotiations was itself a notable change, but brought it much criticism from militant and more leftist partisans. The result was that the Communist party agreed to support the cabinet formed by the Chrisitan Democrats (by abstaining from voting), the two parties agreed to consult in advance of the government's announcement of economic and social policy, and the Communist party was permitted to name the Speaker of the Chamber of Deputies and several committee chairmen and vice-chairmen.

An Italian governmental crisis was created in early 1978 by the refusal of the Communist party (since it was only slightly smaller than the ruling Christian Democrats) to continue its acquiescence in the latter's government. The crisis was resolved by the agreement of the latter to admit the Communist party (and the several smaller parties) to the status of voting supporters on the floor, even though no Communist deputy was admitted to the cabinet itself. This agreement was a holding action until it was feasible to call for new elections. The Communist party continued to insist upon its desire and right to enter the governing cabinet, while at least a substantial portion of the Christian Democrats remained adamantly opposed.[18]

Cabinet Stability

Governments may fall. In most systems, elections must be called within a stated interval (usually 3 to 5 years), but governing cabinets may fall within shorter periods of time. They may lose a critical vote, which may or may not have been a surprise to them, or the cabinet may perhaps have resigned over internal disagreements. Either way, cabinet governments, particularly in multiparty systems, have failed and been

---

[18] *New York Times,* June 24, 1976, p. A1; *Wall Street Journal,* January 17, 1978, p. 18 and March 6, 1978, p. 6. Presumably one of the political purposes of the militant Red Brigades through acts of terrorism has been to upset the agreements between the Christian Democrats and the Community party.

recreated in rapid succession. To give some idea of the numbers involved, one study found 196 different cabinets in 19 parliamentary democracies from the end of World War II through the 1960s.[19]

By and large, the stability of cabinets is related to the same factors previously discussed in their formation. The greater the number of coalition parties (and thus the smaller the size of each of them), the more frequently cabinets fall. The larger the size of the cabinet (above the minimum-size principle), the shorter the duration of the cabinet.[20] The number and size of opposition parties, however, had no statistical relationship to the durability of cabinets, except for the Communist and fascist parties. The larger these "antisystem" parties in parliament, the greater the instability of the governing "prosystem" coalitions.[21]

The circumstances under which cabinets fall are quite varied. In some cases, cabinets decide to resign and to call for new elections. They are not so much threatened with defeat on a parliamentary vote as they are aware that within a relatively short time their term in office will come to an automatic end, and they must call for elections anyway. In another circumstance, an election may have produced a very narrow margin for the governing party or parties; the cabinet fairly quickly calls for a new election in an attempt to increase their number of seats in parliament. The British Labour government did precisely that, and successfully, in the early 1950s.

A more recent British example, however, illustrates a more critical and dangerous situation for the government. In 1976 and 1977, the Labour government gradually lost its majority through special (or "bye") elections, and also had lost minor votes in parliament. In those circumstances, the Conservative leader called a vote of "no confidence" in early 1977. If all non-Labour parties voted together, Labour would have lost, as indicated in the "Anti-Labour Coalition" column of Table 4.3. The Liberal party, however, voted with Labour, producing the vote configuration in the right-hand column of the same table. The Labour prime minister and the Liberal party leader negotiated for several days in advance of the vote. Labour continued in office and avoided having to resign and call a new election at the price of agreeing to modify some of its economic program and to consult in the future with the Liberal party. The Liberals agreed, according to

---

[19] Michael Taylor and V. M. Herman, "Party Systems and Government Stability," *American Political Science Review* 65 (March 1971), pp. 28–37.

[20] Lawrence C. Dodd, "Party Coalitions in Multiparty Parliaments: A Game-Theoretic Analysis," *American Political Science Review* 68 (September 1974), pp. 1093–1118. This study is based upon a somewhat different sample of countries and especially of time periods than the Taylor study.

[21] Taylor and Herman, "Party Systems and Government Stability," pp. 35–36.

Table 4.3 BALANCE OF POWER IN THE BRITISH HOUSE OF COMMONS, 1977

PARTIES	SEATS	ANTI-LABOUR COALITION	LABOUR-LIBERAL COALITION
Labour	309 }	309 ⎱	322
Liberal	13 ⎫		
Conservative	278		
Ulster Union	10	315	302
Scottish Nationalists	11		
Welsh Nationalists	3 ⎭		
Total	624	624	624

SOURCE: *Wall Street Journal,* March 21, 1977, p. 7.

speculation in the press, because they, along with Labour, feared election losses.[22] The anti-Labour coalition did win in 1979.

Communist Systems

The Communist party nations have adopted the parliamentary system of selecting their chief executives and cabinets. The Supreme Soviet elects the chairman of the Council of Ministers, who is the equivalent of the prime minister. He, in turn, nominates the cabinet, or the Council of Ministers, which is then voted upon by the Supreme Soviet. As in democratic parliamentary systems, the nominations are made by the largest party (or coalition), which in the Soviet Union is the single party. Within the Eastern European nations, there is a variation in that they have several parties. In each country, however, the Communist party (variously named) has a majority by itself and retains careful control over the other recognized and much smaller parties. In each instance about which we have information, parliaments of the Communist party nations have unanimously voted for the Communist party nominees for chairman and all other members of the Council of Ministers. The ruling party is a "hegemonic" party in such systems, and the other permitted parties do not seek to contest or obtain governmental control. They neither oppose the formation by the ruling party of the governing cabinet nor do they seek to win larger shares of the votes or nominate more candidates than the ruling party now permits.[23]

[22] *Wall Street Journal,* March 23, 1977, p. 10, and September 29, 1977, p. 14; *New York Times,* September 29, 1977, p. A9. The debate and division list may be found in: United Kingdom, House of Commons, *Parliamentary Debates (Hansard),* March 23, 1977, cols. 1285–1418.

[23] Jerzy J. Wiatr, "The Hegemonic Party System in Poland," in Jerzy J. Wiatr and Jacek Tarkowski (eds.), *Studies in Polish Political System* (Warsaw: Polish Academy of Sciences Press, 1967), pp. 108–123.

Presidential Systems

Within presidential systems, the congress can also participate in the selection of the president, in either of two usual ways. In the first, as in the United States, the congress can resolve a deadlock in the popular election system. Chile was another illustration, but in that country selection of the president by congress was typical, whereas in the United States it has happened only twice (1800 and 1824). If no presidential candidate in Chile received an absolute majority of the popular vote, the congress would select the plurality candidate, even though his own party usually lacked its own majority within the congress. Chile's last elected president, Salvatore Allende, was selected through this procedure.

The other way in which congresses participate in the selection of a president is as part of a much larger electoral body. For an early period of the French Fifth Republic, the president was elected by an electoral college consisting of local officials and the members of the Assembly. This system was soon supplanted by a direct popular election system, eliminating the role of the Assembly altogether. We would guess that in presidential systems, the more usual function of a parliament in selecting the president is to act as in the first method.

Contrasting Systems

Parliaments within "parliamentary systems" have a very different task from that of congresses within "presidential systems." In the latter, the president is usually elected separately from the parliament, and that official is responsible for forming the cabinet or "the administration." In the former, the cabinet and prime minister are selected by parliament. Whether the cabinet members themselves are also members of parliament or not—though usually they are—is less critical than the requirement that they are ultimately answerable to and dismissable by parliament. How the cabinet selection system works depends to a considerable extent upon the party system: parliaments without a single majority party or at least a single sizable plurality party tend to generate cabinets with less stability than do parliaments with a single sizable party. Presumably presidential systems produce governments of greater stability than do parliamentary systems, for the terms of office tend to be fixed by the election calendar, and the composition of the cabinet does not hinge upon continued congressional approval or even support.

PRESIDENTIAL-PARLIAMENTARY SYSTEM DIFFERENCES

As a result of the emphasis in parliamentary systems upon the formation and dismissal of the government and the absence of this emphasis in a presidential system, the act of "voting" can have an entirely different meaning in the two legislative bodies. There is also a second difference in government stemming from this contrast in function between the parliamentary and presidential systems: The persons nominated for the office of chief executive have very different political and governmental backgrounds. We shall discuss each difference in turn.

Meaning of the Vote

In a parliamentary system any vote on a bill or on even a procedural motion is potentially a vote on the tenure of the government. In a presidential system a vote in congress affects only the bill or motion itself. The vote may help or hinder the president, and it may be in support or opposition to his policies, but it does not—save impeachment—affect his tenure in office.

The voting act also has different meanings for the political parties in the two systems. In a parliamentary system a member who votes against his party on a critical vote either is declaring a change in his own party affiliation or risks expulsion from his party. In a presidential system a congressman may vote either with or against his party on a bill, but that vote does not affect his party affiliation. Indeed, some congressmen consistently vote against their party but neither leave it nor are expelled.

But parliamentary systems are not necessarily or always as stringent as the above paragraphs indicate. Indeed, lacking an absolute majority 1977–1979, the British Labour government lost several votes in the House of Commons. Neither had the Labour government regarded its loss as a vote of "no confidence," nor had the opposition Conservative Party called for a vote of censure against the government. Both major parties recognized that neither would gain by a resignation of the government and hence by elections. Both were content to skirmish on amendments and issues without regarding the government's loss as a mandate to dissolve the government.[24]

But given the refusal of both leading parties to regard the votes on legislation as involving the continued life of the governing cabinet, maverick members of the Labour Party voted against their own party's governmental position on issues, and the minor parties voted as they pleased. When the Labour government did convert an opposition motion technically, that the salary of the chancellor of the exchequer be cut in half) on the tax bill into a vote of no confidence, the maverick Labour members voted solidly with their party's government, and the Liberal party members abstained. The result was that

[24] *Wall Street Journal,* May 11, 1978, p. 8. *London Times,* May 9, 1978, p. 1–2; May 11, 1978, p. 1–2; May 12, 1978, pp. 1, 2, 16.

the Labour government narrowly won, thanks to the support of several minor party members.

There are some votes in the American Congress which begin to approach the significance of voting in the parliamentary system. The first vote cast in the life of a two-year Congress is to elect the Speaker (in the House) and the president pro tem (in the Senate). The vote is entirely by party. Each of the two parties in the House nominates its respective leader for Speaker, and each party votes solidly for its nominee. In the Senate the equivalent vote, between the senior member of each of the two parties, is also solidly by party. This vote selects people to occupy office and thus approximates the parliamentary task of selecting a prime minister and cabinet. The congressional vote selects the presiding officer and also simultaneously affects the chairmanship of every committee. The individual member, by the same vote, officially declares his or her party affiliation. Though elected a Democrat, if he voted for the Republican candidate for Speaker, he would automatically change parties in Congress. We recently have had two senators elected as independents; one has voted with the Democrats on organizing the Senate (Byrd, Va.) and the other with the Republicans (Buckley, N.Y.), and by that means, each entered his respective congressional party.

Members of the American Congress would not understand, nor would they agree with, a statement made by a former British prime minister about the duties of a member of parliament:[25]

> The most obvious duty (I do not say the only duty) of any individual member of a parliamentary majority is . . . to assist Government business . . . and in particular to be found in the Government lobby whenever the House divides. He may further these ends by his eloquence. He may do so even more effectually perhaps by his silence.

Although American congressmen would not agree, perhaps American presidents would (however secretly and silently). Party cohesion is usually much stronger in parliamentary than in presidential systems, for much more depends on the outcome of the vote in the former than in the latter system.

The Chief Executive

The second difference between presidential and parliamentary systems lies in the experience and background of the persons nominated in their respective systems for the position of chief executive. We can best

[25] A. J. Balfour, *Chapters of Autobiography*, p. 134, as quoted in Ivor Jennings, *Parliaments*, 2d ed. (New York: Cambridge, 1957), pp. 359–360.

illustrate these differences by comparing the British prime minister with the American president.

One important contrast between the two nations' chief executives is in their prior governmental experience. Britain features a single route of advancement to the position of prime minister—through Parliament, from back-bench member to junior minister to minister, and then to a major position within the cabinet. The United States, by contrast, has a wide variety of prior experiences among those nominated for president. Of the presidential nominees in this century, two-thirds had experience in state or local government, and more than half served in appointive governmental positions. Less than half had served in Congress at all, and their average length of service was 9.9 years. In contrast, all of the British party leaders (thus, nominated for prime minister) were members of Parliament, having served an average of 20.2 years in that body.

While most cabinet members in other parliamentary systems are also members of parliament at the time they become cabinet members, they vary extensively in the length of their prior service in parliament. Of the several countries for which we have evidence, the British Parliament is atypical. While over half of the British cabinet ministers had served 10 or more years in Parliament, only 8% of the members of the Australian cabinet had parliamentary service of that length, while almost 30% of the Canadian cabinet members had been in their Parliament for a year or less.[26]

The British selection system might be termed an "apprenticeship system," in which politically ambitious persons first enter Parliament and then gradually advance into responsible positions under constant evaluation by, and through constant interaction with, their parliamentary peers and leaders. By contrast, the American presidential selection system is more "entrepreneurial" in that each aspirant puts together his own resources and sources of support in varied combinations. The outsider image, with which President Carter could convert his lack of Washington experience into an asset that permitted him to arrive there at the top, is fully consistent with a "separation" system but incompatible with a parliamentary system. In the latter system the sole route to the nation's chief political prize is through parliament itself.[27]

[26] Joseph A. Schlesinger, "Political Careers and Party Leadership" in Lewis J. Edinger (ed.), *Political Leadership in Industrialized Societies* (New York: Wiley, 1967), pp. 286–287.

[27] Hugh Heclo, "Presidential and Prime Ministerial Selection," in Donald R. Matthews (ed.), *Perspectives on Presidential Selection* (Washington, D.C.: Brookings, 1973), pp. 19–48.

LEGISLATION

One of the major activities of a parliament is to consider "bills" or "acts." Together, they are termed "legislation." A bill is a proposal; if adopted, it becomes an act, which in turn becomes a "law" or a "statute." Whether all "major" decisions in government are made by parliament, whether all major decisions of parliament are made by legislation, and whether all legislation is "major" are questions we shall raise, but not answer, at this point. Furthermore, the definition of a bill is probably not the same among all nations, and within any one country a single bill may range in size from a half-page to several hundred pages. Nevertheless, "legislation" constitutes one major (if only vaguely defined and measured) category of parliamentary activity.

Legislation is also shaped by cabinets, prime ministers, and presidents. In nations having parliaments, chief executives require the consent of parliament before they can engage in certain actions. Chief executives at least require adoption of a budget and permission to levy taxes. Beyond those minimal requirements, and varying extensively among nations, executives must have, or at least seek, the consent of parliament to a wide range of proposed governmental activity.

The Executive and the Legislative Agenda

The sheer number of bills introduced into parliaments, as discussed in Chapter 1, varies greatly among nations. The proportion of all bills introduced that are "government bills" likewise varies among nations. In almost half of the parliaments (e.g., Australia, Czechoslovakia), the government introduces 90% or more of all bills, while in some others (e.g., Canada, Costa Rica) government bills account for less than 60% of all bills introduced (Table 4.4).[28]

Not all bills are equal. Government bills are adopted by parliaments at a much higher rate than are non–government-sponsored bills. In more than half of the countries (e.g., Australia, Denmark), almost all government bills are enacted by parliament. In other countries (e.g., France, Rumania) under 90% of government bills are adopted (Table 4.4). Of the 40 countries for which data are available, almost half concentrate in the upper left-hand cell of Table 4.4. In these countries the government introduces at least 90% of all legislation, and more than 90% of that is adopted. In only three countries, at the other extreme in the lower right-hand cell, does the government introduce less than 60% of all bills—and less than 60% of those are enacted.

---

[28] Herman and Mendel, *Parliaments of the World,* pp. 631–637.

Table 4.4 PROPORTION OF GOVERNMENT BILLS PASSED AND PROPORTION OF BILLS INTRODUCED BY THE GOVERNMENT

PERCENTAGE OF GOVERNMENT BILLS PASSED	PERCENTAGE OF BILLS INTRODUCED BY THE GOVERNMENT				
	90–100 (N)	60–89 (N)	59 OR LESS (N)	TOTAL (N)	TOTAL (%)
90–100	18	3	3	24	60
60–89	1	7	5	13	33
59 or less	0	0	3	3	7
	19	10	11	40	
Percentage of total	48	25	28		100

SOURCE: Valentine Herman and Francoise Mendel, *Parliaments of the World* (Berlin: De Gruyter, 1976), pp. 631–637.
NOTE: Annual average of a five-year period. N = number of parliaments.

The extent to which the government dominates the parliament's legislative agenda varies somewhat with the total number of bills introduced. The government has tended to introduce more than 90% of all bills in those parliaments in which 99 or fewer bills have, on the average, been introduced annually (Table 4.5). At the other extreme, of those parliaments in which 200 or more bills are introduced annually, in only two out of the 11 countries has the government introduced 90% or more of those bills. In the middle category, of 100–199 bills introduced annually, the countries are evenly divided between those in which the government has introduced 90% or more and those in which 90% or less were introduced by the government.

The countries of the world do not fit into neat patterns on these measures. Countries that we usually group together, such as the British-derived countries, the Eastern European nations, or the newly independent countries, are scattered through all categories, as shown in Table 4.6, which lists the countries in each cell of Table 4.5. While some Eastern European nations (East Germany, Czechoslovakia) are

Table 4.5 GOVERNMENT BILLS INTRODUCED AND TOTAL NUMBER OF BILLS INTRODUCED

PERCENT OF BILLS INTRODUCED BY GOVERNMENT	TOTAL NUMBER OF BILLS INTRODUCED			
	1–99 (N)	100–199 (N)	200+ (N)	TOTAL (N)
90–100	12	5	2	19
89 or less	7	5	9	21
Total	19	10	11	40

SOURCE: Valentine Herman and Francoise Mendel, *Parliaments of the World* (Berlin: De Gruyter, 1976), pp. 631–637.
NOTE: N = number of parliaments.

Table 4.6 GOVERNMENT BILLS AND TOTAL NUMBER OF BILLS FOR VARIOUS NATIONS

PERCENT OF BILLS INTRODUCED BY GOVERNMENT	TOTAL NUMBER OF BILLS INTRODUCED		
	1–99	100–199	200 OR MORE
90–100	Bangladesh	Australia	Malaysia
	Czechoslovakia	Ireland	Netherlands
	East Germany	South Africa	
	Fiji	Spain	
	Ivory Coast	Sri Lanka	
	Jordan		
	Malta		
	Monaco		
	Pakistan		
	Senegal		
	Tunisia		
	Zambia		
89 or less	Hungary	India	Austria
	Kuwait	Israel	Belgium
	Poland	Japan	Canada
	Rumania	South Korea	Costa Rica
	South Vietnam	West Germany	Denmark
	Switzerland		Finland
	USSR		France
			New Zealand
			United Kingdom

SOURCE: Valentine Herman and Francoise Mendel, *Parliaments of the World* (Berlin: De Gruyter, 1976), pp. 631–637.

in the upper left-hand cell of Table 4.6, having a small number of bills most of which are introduced by the government, the USSR is located in the lower left-hand cell; that is, a small proportion of its few bills are sponsored by the government. A number of entities can initiate legislation in the Supreme Soviet, of which the government (or Council of Ministers) is only one. Of a total of 141 proposed laws sent to the Supreme Soviet in the 1938–1960 period, only 49 of them (35%) had been initiated by the Council of Ministers. The Council of Elders, an internal management group, had initiated 29 bills and the Presidium of the Supreme Soviet 27 (about 20% each); committees of the Supreme Soviet were the sources of 15 proposed bills (11%).[29]

For four democratic countries (Table 4.7), we can directly compare the adoption rates of government bills and of non-government bills. Well over 80% of all government-sponsored bills were enacted by the parliaments of all four countries, while the success rate of non-

[29] Peter Vanneman, *The Supreme Soviet: Politics and the Legislative Process in the Soviet System* (Durham, N.C.: Duke University Press), pp. 52–57, 132.

Table 4.7 ADOPTION RATES OF GOVERNMENT BILLS IN BRITAIN, WEST GERMANY, FRANCE, AND CANADA

COUNTRIES	PERCENT OF GOVERNMENT BILLS ADOPTED	PERCENT OF NON-GOVERNMENT BILLS ADOPTED	PERCENT OF ALL ADOPTED BILLS SUPPORTED BY GOVERNMENT
Great Britain (1957–1969)	96	27	77
West Germany (1949–1969)	89	39	76
France (1961–1966)	81	04	93
Canada (1968–1972)	90	10	90

SOURCES: John E. Schwarz and L. Earl Shaw, *The United States Congress in Comparative Perspective* (Hinsdale, Ill.: Dryden, 1976), p. 199, for Great Britain, West Germany, and France; R. V. Stewart Hyson, "The Role of the Backbencher: An Analysis of Private Members' Bills in the Canadian House of Commons," *Parliamentary Affairs* 27 (Summer 1974), pp. 265–266, for Canada.

government bills ranged from 4% up to almost 40%. An additional measure of the use of parliament's time by the government is provided in the far right-hand column in the same table: government bills accounted for over three-fourths of all bills adopted by the four parliaments.[30]

One difficulty with these numbers is that bills vary greatly in their scope, complexity, and sheer number of pages. A "bill" in the U.S. Congress, for example, can be either a half-page or can approximate the length and bulk of a city phone directory. Our impression of Communist party parliaments is that their bills—usually few in number —are complex and lengthy. They tend to be general-purpose enabling acts or recodifications of whole sections of the statute books. But regardless of what a "bill" is in any given parliament, the government of the day tends to dominate the legislative agenda.

In most systems, the choice of how many bills a parliament will consider is made by the government. The chief executive can decide whether any given matter will be submitted to parliament or would be better accomplished internally through executive decrees or agency regulations. A government will use the parliament for those matters that it considers of major importance and wishes to symbolize to the whole population. Matters of lesser importance would be handled internally by the executive branch. We can illustrate a bit of this

[30] Schwarz and Shaw, *The United States Congress in Comparative Perspective*, pp. 198–199; R. V. Stewart Hyson, "The Role of the Backbencher: An Analysis of Private Members' Bills in the Canadian House of Commons," *Parliamentary Affairs* 27 (Summer 1974), pp. 262–272.

reasoning by citing a meeting of the Polish Council of Ministers, as reported in the Polish press. The Finance Ministry had proposed an administrative decree that would greatly revise the system of buying and selling of food products, with the purpose of increasing the amount of food available to consumers. The proposed administrative decree was itself in the form of an amendment to a previous decree issued in 1951. The discussion at the Council of Ministers meeting centered, not on the merits of the proposal, but upon its form— whether it should be issued as an administrative decree or submitted to the Sejm as a new law.

The Vice Premier stated that this "important event" merited a "special law." The Premier commented, "We are making important political and economic history, but it is drowned in the text of an old decree . . ."

Outsiders are invited to attend these meetings for appropriate portions of the agenda. On this occasion, a member of the Sejm's relevant committee was present, and stated "It would be desirable that a new law appear, the contents have already been agreed upon" in the parliamentary committee. In the face of these comments by the government's leaders, and by a member of the Sejm committee, the Finance Minister agreed—perhaps reluctantly—that his agency could prepare a new proposed law in two weeks.[31]

Governments ordinarily control the time and agenda of parliaments in all governmental systems. That control is usually accomplished through the majority party (or coalition), which in parliamentary systems is also the government. From the government's perspective they have work to do. Part of their work is to obtain parliamentary consent, which usually is officially delivered through the vote. A government will have a certain number of measures it wishes parliament to adopt; a government may very well have more programs than can possibly be scheduled for consideration in a single year of parliamentary meetings. Thus it is faced with the twin problem of deciding upon its own legislative priorities and of managing the time and members of parliament to accomplish its legislative agenda for the year.

Formulation of Government Proposals

Not much is known publicly about how governments decide their legislative priorities, although we do have a description of the procedure followed by Britain's first Labour government after World War II. The cabinet created a Future Legislation Committee to develop a legislative agenda in advance of a parliamentary year. Each

---

[31] *Polityka,* January 1, 1972, as translated in Radio Free Europe, *Polish Press Survey,* no. 2355, February 7, 1972.

minister had to decide which bill proposals, out of a large potential, he would advance for his particular agency. He then had to seek the approval of a relevant cabinet policy committee and consult with the Treasury on the financial aspects of the proposal. Finally, the "clamant" ministers came before the Future Legislation Committee, as described by its chairman:[32]

> . . . the Future Legislation Committee met a roomful of clamant Min-isters persuasively arguing the case for the inclusion of their Bill or Bills in the next sessional programme. These were interesting though some-times trying meetings . . . always more legislation was sought than there was parliamentary time available. . . . The argument and the questioning would proceed between the members of the Committee and the other Ministers and, indeed, between the other Ministers themselves.

Once a cabinet minister obtained approval of this committee to develop a bill, he was faced with the task of having it written, and then he had to win its approval from yet another committee of the cabinet. Each bill was to be presented in the name of the cabinet as a whole and thus had to have the cabinet's approval. On the floor, how-ever, and in committee stage, the initiating minister had the major responsibility for guiding and defending his particular bill.

A common pattern in the preparation of proposed legislation, at least within industrialized democracies, is that extensive negotiations occur among affected agencies and interest groups. In a complex and interdependent society, almost no government action affects only one agency or one segment of society. Even if only one industry is affected, it is likely to be divided into competing subunits, and labor and con-sumers may (or may not) also have views in conflict with manage-ment. To consult widely with all affected groups and entities is the usual practice in a twin effort to obtain proposals that are workable and also acceptable. Within legislative bodies the act of voting is an institutionalization of the consultation process. Committee hearings in the U.S. Congress are another example. This same practice is also found within government agencies as they prepare bills to submit to their legislative body. The consultative process does not begin with parliament; it is more a generic process that occurs within the gov-ernment itself.

We may illustrate the widespread consultative process with the development of proposed legislation in West Germany on transportation in the early 1950s.[33] Two bills were prepared, each by a different

[32] Herbert Morrison, *Government and Parliament: A Survey from the Inside* (New York: Oxford, 1954), pp. 223–228. The quote is on p. 234.

[33] This section on the West German bills is taken from Gerard Braunthal, *The West German Legislative Process: A Case Study of Two Transportation Bills* (Ithaca: Cornell University Press, 1972), pp. 31–80.

agency, with the main purpose of shifting freight traffic to the railroads from highways. Because tax revenues and government expenditures were important further purposes of the bills, the one bill that specifically concerned finance was prepared in the Finance Ministry. The other, the Highway Relief Bill, was prepared in the Transportation Ministry. The two government agencies were vitally interested in, and affected by, each other's bills, and yet they disagreed on critical provisions. In addition, a host of other government agencies were also affected, especially the Economic Affairs Ministry, which tended to speak for industrial and business management. The Finance Ministry proposed, for example, a series of taxes on automobiles, heavy trucks, and gasoline. The taxes were opposed by the Economic Affairs Ministry and not especially supported by the Transportation Ministry either. The latter, in turn, wished to prohibit certain categories of heavy goods from the highways, to which both the Finance and Economic Affairs ministries objected. In addition, many other agencies, for example Agriculture and the Post Office, objected to specific provisions that they feared would adversely affect their interests.

Basic to the disagreements among the government agencies were the disagreements among the industries. Trucking firms, automobile manufacturers, the petroleum industry, railroads (the biggest of which was itself a government agency), and the steel industry were major protagonists. The housing industry, for example, was concerned over the prohibition of housing construction materials—because of their weight—from the highways, and agriculture was concerned both with the transportation of food and with taxes on farming tractors. These disagreements within the economic sector led to a round of conferences within industrial business groups, which failed, however, to result in any agreement. The government agencies themselves wished to develop a consensus among the outside-interest groups, or at least to obtain support from the groups for their own particular views of what should be in the proposed legislation. To achieve these contradictory objectives, the better part of two months was used in formal conferences with interest group representatives.

The two lead agencies were authorized in March of 1953 to begin preparation of their two main bills. The Cabinet finally approved of two proposed bills—considerably altered by now through the ensuing consultations—a year later in March 1954. The Cabinet's approval of the bills to be submitted to parliament did not, however, mean that all disagreements had been eliminated, or that the agencies either agreed among themselves or with the outside interest groups. Rather, this approval merely signified that enough progress had been made to shift the needed further negotiations into the parliamentary forum. In our subsequent chapters on parties and committees (Chapters 5 and 6, respectively), we shall trace the troubled fate of these two bills within the Bundestag.

But the parliament was not an inactive bystander during the intra-executive branch negotiations. Earlier versions of the bills had been debated in the Bundestag, but had not been approved, indicating the high degree of controversy associated with them, and thus setting the stage for the agency-group negotiations we have just discussed. Furthermore, the main opposition party, the Social Democrats, forced a parliamentary debate, urging the government (led by Chancellor Adenauer of the Christian Democrats) not to delay further but to submit promptly a legislative proposal for the Bundestag to consider. The opposition party did not itself develop its own proposal but assumed that a proper activity a parliament can expect of the government is the preparation of policy proposals.

The executive-legislative relationship in the United States is quite different from that in parliamentary systems. The president and his officials are excluded from membership in Congress, and from even being present on the floor (Fig. 1.2). The distinction between administration bills and all others is not always a clear one, and the procedure by which "the administration" decides its legislative priorities are not as clearly defined as in the preceding British and German examples.

President and Congress

ENACTMENT RATE

By whatever measures and definitions one uses, however, the president and his program are not as dominant or as successful with Congress as prime ministers are in their parliaments. One measure is a "presidential enactment rate," a compilation of presidential legislative requests to Congress, of which the number adopted can be calculated as a percentage. From the Eisenhower presidency through Carter's first two years, the proportion of presidential legislation that has been adopted by Congress has in a two-year period ranged from a low of 31.5% for Ford to a high of 52.6% for Eisenhower (Table 4.8). The enactment rate of executive-sponsored legislation by the U.S. Congress is probably the lowest in the world.[34]

---

[34] The data, compiled and reported by Congressional Quarterly, understate the adoption rate for each president by an unknown amount. The data are reported annually, and exclude those bills introduced in the first year but adopted in the second year of a two-year congressional term. Table 4.8 thus tabulates the total of one-year successes within a presidential term rather than the total of two-year successes. Furthermore, the two-year period is an average, and thus is lower than some single-year percentages as shown in Table 7.2. *Congressional Quarterly Almanacs*, 1962–1974; *Congressional Quarterly Weekly Report*, March 20, 1976; and Schwarz and Shaw, *The United States Congress in Comparative Perspective*, p. 223, table 6.5.

Table 4.8   PRESIDENTIAL LEGISLATION ENACTMENT: NUMBER OF BILLS INTRODUCED, NUMBER PASSED, AND ENACTMENT RATE, BY PRESIDENT, TERM, AND PARTY

PARTY, PRESIDENT, AND TERM		INTRODUCED (NUMBER)	ADOPTED (NUMBER)	(%)
REPUBLICANS				
Eisenhower	1954–1956	664	349	52.6
	1957–1960	851	335	39.4
Nixon	1969–1972	669	243	34.8
	1973–1974	280	90	32.1
Ford	1974–1975	?	?	31.5
DEMOCRATS				
Kennedy	1961–1963	1049	414	39.5
Johnson	1964	217	125	57.6
	1965–1968	1685	675	40.1

SOURCES: *Congressional Quarterly Almanacs* 1962–1974; John E. Schwarz and L. Earl Shaw, *The United States Congress in Comparative Perspective* (Hinsdale, Ill.: Dryden, 1976), p. 223, table 6.5; *Congressional Quarterly Weekly Report*, March 20, 1976, pp. 649–656.
NOTES: With some exceptions, this table includes the whole term of a president. The exceptions include Eisenhower (no comparable data available for 1953), Kennedy (assassination), Nixon (resignation), and Ford (missing data).

ROLL CALL APPROVAL RATE

A second measure of presidential fate on legislation is based upon roll call votes rather than upon bills. Of all roll call votes cast in Congress, the president has taken a position on some number of them. The proportion of those roll calls on which his position was upheld by Congress is measured by the "roll call approval rate." This rate has ranged from a low of 57% for Ford to a high of 84% for Kennedy, of those presidents filling more than a two-year term (Table 4.9). The lowest score, compiled by Nixon as Watergate and impeachment loomed, and the highest score, compiled by Johnson in the aftermath of an assassination, both illustrate the distorting effect of dramatic and unusual circumstances. We cannot directly compare these success rates with other countries, however, for in no other country is it necessary to keep such meticulous scores to know how successful the chief executive is with parliament.[35]

The two measures of presidential success with Congress on legislation are quite different. The approval rates on roll calls are much higher than on the enactment rates of legislation.

One difference is that the president can take a position on a roll call that is defensive; that is, the purpose is to defeat a bill or an amendment initiated within the Congress in addition to seeking positive support for his own bills.

[35] *Congressional Quarterly Almanac*, 1977, pp. 21B–27B.

Table 4.9   PRESIDENTIAL ROLL CALL APPROVAL
RATES BY PRESIDENT, TERM, AND PARTY

PARTY AND PRESIDENT	TERM	ROLL CALL APPROVAL RATE (%)
REPUBLICANS		
Eisenhower	1953–1956	79.2
	1957–1960	62.2
Nixon	1969–1972	73.0
	1973–1974	55.1
Ford	1974–1976	57.6
DEMOCRATS		
Kennedy	1961–1963	84.5
Johnson	1963–1964	88.0
	1965–1968	81.5
Carter	1977	75.4
	1978	78.3

SOURCE: *Congressional Quarterly Almanac,* 1977, p. 21B; and
Congressional Quarterly Weekly Report, December 9, 1978,
p. 3407.

Another difference, as Table 7.2 will illustrate, is that most presidential bills are adopted if they get to the floor. But a sizable proportion are stopped in committee stage, and smaller proportions either pass one house but not the other, or are passed in both houses but in different form and are not reconciled by a conference committee.[36]

PARTY AND PARTY SIZE

American presidents—particularly since World War II—often lack what most prime ministers have: a party majority in the legislature. Although presidents serve irrespective of the party majority in Congress and irrespective of the fate of their own legislation, the party composition of Congress does affect their legislative success. The presidential bill enactment and roll call approval rates discussed immediately above are presented in Tables 4.10 and 4.11 by the party majority—and its size—in Congress, using the House of Representatives as our example. The identity and size of the congressional majority are markedly related to both measures of presidential success. The one Republican president (Eisenhower) to have had a Republican majority (but for only two out of his eight years), and the Democratic presidents (Johnson in 1964, Carter in 1976) who had an overwhelming Democratic majority of two-thirds, have had the most success with Congress. Nixon and Ford, who faced Democratic Congresses during the entirety of their presidencies, were least successful.

[36] Schwarz and Shaw, *The United States Congress in Comparative Perspective,* pp. 223–225.

Table 4.10 PRESIDENTIAL LEGISLATION ENACTMENT
RATES BY PARTY MAJORITY AND SIZE, FOR CONGRESS
AND PRESIDENTIAL TERMS

	PARTY MAJORITY AND PARTY SIZE IN HOUSE OF REPRESENTATIVES		
		DEMOCRATIC	
PARTY AND PRESIDENT[a]	REPUBLICAN (%)	50–60% (%)	66% (%)
REPUBLICANS			
Eisenhower	64.7	45.3	36.5
		42.5	
Nixon		39.6	
		32.1	
		29.5	
Ford[b]		36.0	27.0
DEMOCRATS			
Kennedy		49.8	
		27.5	
Johnson		57.6	62.9
		51.5	

SOURCES: *Congressional Quarterly Almanacs*, 1962–1974; John E.
Schwarz and L. Earl Shaw, *The United States Congress in Comparative Perspective* (Hinsdale, Ill.: Dryden, 1976), p. 223, table
6.5; *Congressional Quarterly Weekly Report*, March 20, 1976, pp.
649–656.
[a] This table measures the congressional two-year term, whereas
Table 4.9 measures the presidential four-year term. The truncated
congressional term for Kennedy (1963–1964) and Nixon's truncated congressional term (1973–1974) are reported separately. In
both cases, Johnson's and Ford's portions of the remaining congressional terms are reported separately.
[b] Only 1974–1975.

PARTY SUPPORT

The measure of presidential legislative interaction we have discussed
to this point has concerned Congress as a whole entity. Individual
congressmen vary greatly in the extent to which they support the
president; one of the factors associated with variations in their presidential support is their own political party (Table 4.12). Republican
congressmen, regardless of the party composition of any particular
Congress, have voted in support of Republican presidents and in
opposition to Democratic presidents. Most northern Democrats vote
even more strongly in support of Democratic presidents and in opposition to the programs of Republican presidents. Southern Democrats
are in between the two other party groups. Although they do not support Democratic presidents as much as do northern Democrats, neither
do they support Republican presidents as much as do Republicans.
The different presidential support voting patterns by party affiliation
underlie the different presidential success rates in Tables 4.10 and

Table 4.11 PRESIDENTIAL ROLL CALL APPROVAL RATES BY PARTY MAJORITY AND PARTY SIZE, BY PRESIDENT AND CONGRESSIONAL TERMS

		PARTY MAJORITY AND PARTY SIZE IN HOUSE OF REPRESENTATIVES		
			DEMOCRATIC	
PARTY AND PRESIDENT[a]	REPUBLICAN (%)	50–60% (%)	66% (%)
REPUBLICANS			
Eisenhower	85.9	72.5	58.5
		72.0	
Nixon		75.5	
		70.5	
		55.1	
Ford		58.2	57.4
DEMOCRATS			
Kennedy		84.5	
Johnson		88.0	86.0
		77.0	
Carter			76.9

SOURCE: Calculated from *Congressional Quarterly Almanac*, 1977, pp. 21B–24B.

[a] This table measures the congressional two-year term, whereas Table 4.9 measures the presidential four-year term. The truncated congressional term for Kennedy (1963–1964) is included with his full congressional term in a single figure, whereas Nixon's truncated congressional term (1973–1974) is reported separately. In both cases, Johnson's and Ford's portions of the remaining congressional terms are reported separately.

Table 4.12 PRESIDENTIAL SUPPORT SCORES BY PARTY AND FACTION OF CONGRESSMEN, BY PRESIDENT

		PARTY AND FACTION OF CONGRESSMEN			
			DEMOCRATIC		
PRESIDENT, PARTY, AND TERM	REPUB-LICAN (%)	SOUTH (%)	NORTH (%)	ALL DEMOCRATS (%)
Eisenhower (R) 1953–1956	69.5	45.8	50.5	47.5
Eisenhower (R) 1957–1960	62.5	41.7	51.0	46.0
Kennedy (D) 1961–1963	38.2	55.0	76.4	68.0
Johnson (D) 1964	41.5	57.0	74.1	67.5
Johnson (D) 1965–1968	45.7	50.4	68.2	60.0
Nixon (R) 1969–1972	64.7	52.2	43.0	46.5
Nixon (R) 1973–1974	61.5	48.0	33.5	37.5
Ford (R) 1974–1976	60.3	48.8	36.2	40.0
Carter[a] (D) 1977–1978	42	53	67	63

SOURCE: *Congressional Quarterly Almanac*, 1953–1976, and *Congressional Quarterly Weekly Report*, January 7, 1978, pp. 11–12.

[a] The Carter figure is for 1977 only.

4.11. Just as the party composition of parliament affects the party composition of the ensuing cabinet, so does the party composition of Congress affect the legislative success of the president.

Figures 4.1 and 4.2 show in greater detail how U.S. senators have voted on presidential legislation by political party. The two figures show Republican and Democratic senators separately. The upward sweep of dots from left to right for Republican senators shows that the more they vote with their political party on legislation, the more they tend to vote in support of the Republican president's (Ford) legislative proposals. The opposite downward sweep from left to right for Democratic senators shows that the more they vote with their party, the less they tend to support the Republican president. The inverse relationship between Democratic party unity and Republican presidential support is the same for both northern and southern Democrats,

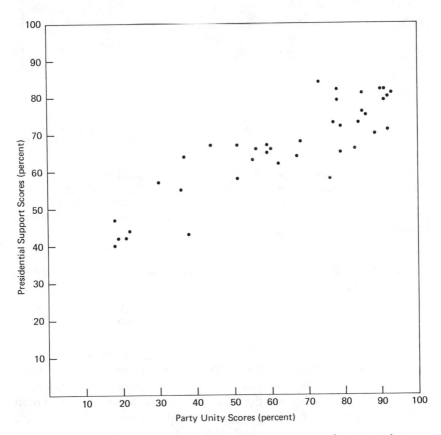

Figure 4.1   Republican presidential support scores and party unity scores for Republican senators, 94th Congress. Note: A Republican (Ford) was president. (Source: Congressional Quarterly, *Roll Call, 94th Congress,* pp. 26, 29.)

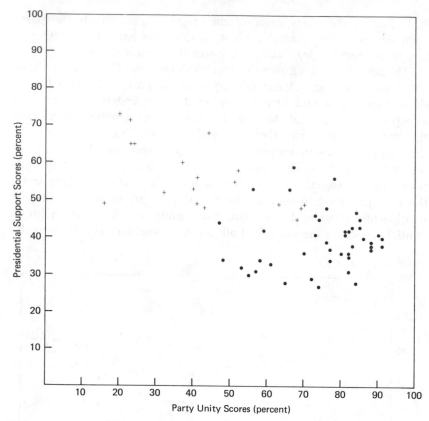

Figure 4.2   Republican presidential support scores and party unity scores for Democratic senators, 94th Congress. (Dots: northern senators. Crosses: southern senators.) Note: A Republican (Ford) was president. (Source: Congressional Quarterly, *Roll Call, 94th Congress,* pp. 26, 29.)

though southern Democrats begin and end much higher on the presidential support scale, and lower on the party unity scale, than northern Democrats. The contrast between the two groups of Democrats again illustrates, this time in the Senate, the regional factionalism among Democrats.

When Carter became president, the voting patterns shifted (Figs. 4.3 and 4.4). But the shift was entirely consistent in that Democratic senators' voting support of Carter legislation increased as did their party unity score, whereas the more the Republican senators voted with their party, the less they supported Carter's legislative proposals.

POLICY RELATIONSHIPS
The preceding paragraphs and tables suggest several patterns in the relationship between president and Congress, which vary with the major political characteristics of each branch. Presidents can be

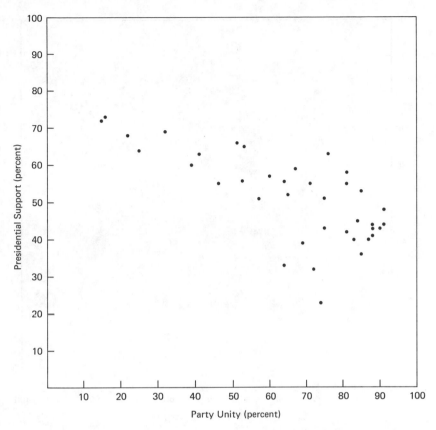

Figure 4.3   Democratic presidential support scores and party unity
scores for Republican senators, 1977. Note: A Democrat (Carter) was
president. (Source: *Congressional Quarterly Weekly Report,* January 7
and January 14, 1978, pp. 13, 81.

characterized by their party, as either Democrat or Republican,
whereas Congresses can be placed in three categories of Republican,
nominal Democratic in which Democrats have 55% to 60%, and
policy Democratic in which Democrats have 66% of the seats. The
distinction between the two types of Democratic congresses is in the
size of the Democratic majority, which in turn alters the potential
"swing" role of southern Democrats. In a nominal Democratic congress,
southern Democrats are sufficiently numerous to constitute a working
majority when they combine with Republicans. In a policy Democratic
congress, however, northern Democrats come close to having a majority
by themselves, thus reducing the ability of the conservative coalition
to form a majority. The resulting six categories in Table 4.13 characterize the relationships between presidents and Congresses from the
Eisenhower election of 1952 through the Carter election of 1976.

In cells A and F in Table 4.13, the party of the president matches

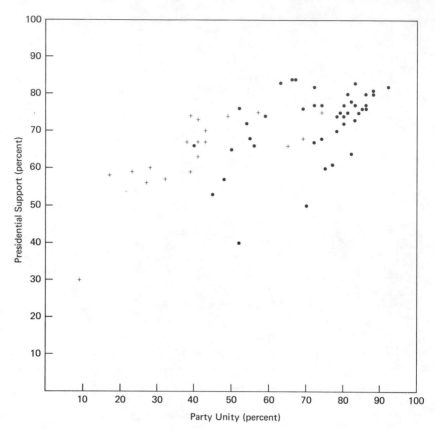

Figure 4.4   Democratic presidential support scores and party unity scores for Democratic senators, 1977. (Dots: northern senators. Crosses: southern senators.) Note: A Democrat (Carter) was president. (Source: *Congressional Quarterly Weekly Report*, January 7 and January 14, 1978, pp. 13, 81.)

the party and policy majority of congress. These two circumstances may be designated the "policy enactment" relationship for Republicans and Democrats, respectively. At the opposite extreme, the party of presidents and the policy majorities in congress are diametrically mismatched. In 1958 and 1974, Republican presidents were faced with Democratic policy majorities, while in 1946, a Republican Congress served with President Truman, a Democrat. These circumstances lead to a "veto" relationship in which the controlling congressional majority attempts to enact legislation which the president opposes, and against which he wields the veto as his weapon of last resort.

The middle column of the same table presents the intermediate but frequent circumstance of a congress with a nominal Democratic majority, but in which the conservative coalition between southern Democrats and Republicans can form a majority on any given vote. For Democratic presidents, who ordinarily propose legislation to ex-

Table 4.13 POLICY RELATIONSHIPS BETWEEN PRESIDENT AND CONGRESS BY POLITICAL CHARACTERISTICS, 1952–1976

PARTY OF PRESIDENT	CONGRESS: PARTY MAJORITY AND SIZE		
	REPUBLICAN	NOMINAL DEMOCRATIC: 55–60%	POLICY DEMOCRATIC: 66%
Republican	A. Policy enactment Eisenhower, 1952	B. Avoidance Eisenhower, 1954, 1956 Nixon, 1968, 1970, 1972	C. Veto Eisenhower, 1958 Ford, 1974
Democratic	D. Veto (Truman 1946)	E. Stalemate Kennedy, 1960, 1962 Johnson, 1966	F. Policy enactment Johnson, 1964 Carter, 1976

pand the activities of the federal government, the result is "stalemate" (cell E). For Republican presidents, who ordinarily exercise less legislative initiative, the absence of a supporting majority is less important. (Since 1952, Republican presidents have proposed a yearly average of 189.5 bills and Democratic presidents have proposed an average of 368.9 bills annually.) A more aggressive Republican, President Nixon, took independent action within the executive branch (such as impoundment of funds), in effect an "avoidance" behavior toward Congress (cell B).

Since the 1952 election (but before that, too) the most common relationship between president and Congress has been one of opposition. Only three elections (cells A and F) have produced policy enactment relationships. Two of those instances, however, lasted for only a two-year period; in the next congressional election, the president lost his needed margin of policy support. Of the three presidents in this circumstance, Johnson was best equipped to take advantage of a policy majority in congress. Unlike the others (Eisenhower and Carter), he had long experience in Congress and was intimately familiar with legislation and with the details of federal agency activity. Furthermore, he was not newly taking office; he had assumed office in midterm (because of the Kennedy assassination) and had been serving as vice president. The others were in their first term and spent considerable time in their first year just in formulating their legislative program.

Each of the policy enactment relationships occurred as the result of presidential elections, whereas each of the veto relationships occurred as the result of midterm congressional elections.[37] Those midterm elections that produce a Congress exactly mismatched with the

[37] Patricia Hurley, David Brady, and Joseph Cooper, "Measuring Legislative Potential for Policy Change," *Legislative Studies Quarterly* 2 (November 1977), pp. 393–395.

political and policy characteristics of the president have, since the end of the Civil War, been associated with a high frequency of vetoes and especially with congressional attempts to override those vetoes.[38] At least part of the impact of landslide presidential elections, and of the reversed-landslide midterm elections, is that a higher proportion of new members than usual is brought into Congress. It is the newly elected members who provide the policy changes, for, as we shall note in more detail in Chapter 7 (Floor Procedures and Voting), congressmen are quite stable in their voting patterns on legislation. It is not that incumbents change their policy preferences in response to election swings, but that newly elected members vote differently from the members whom they have replaced.

The size of a party majority needed to enact policy varies with that party's own cohesion. Likewise, its ability to enact policy is related to the size and cohesion of the other party.[39] Although party cohesion has varied over the years in the American Congress, it has been fairly constant, in the post–World War II period, as we shall demonstrate by means of party unity scores in the next chapter. Given the propensity of sizable numbers of southern Democrats to vote against the president of their party, coupled with the inclination of a few Republicans to provide some support, Democratic presidents have required the 66% party margin in Congress as a prerequisite to the extensive adoption of their policy proposals.[40]

The policy enactment relationship between Johnson and the Congress elected in 1964 did produce a rich harvest of legislation, although the Eisenhower Congress elected in 1952 did not. In part, the contrasting legislative results stem from the two presidents' very different views of their proper activity. Eisenhower purposively deferred to congressional leadership, while Johnson modeled himself on the legislative activism of Franklin Roosevelt.[41] The opposite set of circumstances, in which the president of one party faces a Congress controlled by the other, has been termed the "truncated majority." The dynamics and extent of hostility, however, between president and Congress would

---

[38] Jong R. Lee, "Presidential Vetoes from Washington to Nixon," *Journal of Politics* 37 (May 1975), pp. 532–544.

[39] Patricia Hurley, David Brady, and Joseph Cooper, "Measuring Legislative Potential for Policy Change," *Legislative Studies Quarterly* 2 (November 1977), pp. 387–393.

[40] David R. Mayhew, *Party Loyalty Among Congressmen* (Cambridge: Harvard University Press, 1966), pp. 165–168. See also Robert E. Goodin, "The Importance of Winning Big," *Legislative Studies Quarterly* 2 (November 1977), pp. 399–407.

[41] For Eisenhower, see Randall B. Ripley, *Majority Party Leadership in Congress* (Boston: Little, Brown, 1969), pp. 117–135. For Johnson, see James Sundquist, *Politics and Policy: The Eisenhower, Kennedy, and Johnson Years* (Washington, D.C.: Brookings, 1968).

appear to vary with the size of the opposition party, thus distinguishing between the veto and avoidance relationships.[42]

FOREIGN AND DOMESTIC POLICY

The executives of most countries are likely to have more success with the legislative body on foreign policy than on domestic issues. According to the American expression, "politics stops at the water's edge." Although that statement is not literally true, it does symbolize the usual expectation that the conduct of foreign policy is more the prerogative of the executive than of the legislative body. The typical deference Congress has shown the president on foreign-policy matters has come under attack recently, largely as a reaction against our experience in Vietnam. But as President Carter's initiative in the Middle East has shown, the President has far greater latitude of action than he usually possesses on domestic issues. Perhaps because of this factor, presidents usually spend much more of their personal time and energies on foreign-policy matters than on domestic issues.[43]

When the executive brings a foreign-policy matter to the parliament, the usual result is that the executive obtains more support from his own party than on domestic policy. But foreign policy also presents the executive an opportunity to appeal to the other parties in the name of overreaching national goals. The Truman era of "bipartisan" foreign policy is an example. A more recent example is provided by Israel, in which Premier Begin pledged that a Knesset vote in 1978 on the issue of settlements on Israeli-occupied lands would be free of party discipline.

CONGRESSIONAL LIAISON STAFF

The Congress is, for the president, one of his constituencies, for which a specialized staff office has developed. Just as a president appoints a press secretary to deal with the media, so a president also now appoints a congressional liaison staff to deal with Congress. While presidents have always interacted with (and worried about) Congresses, a specialized staff was first appointed during the Eisenhower administration. Eisenhower brought to the White House the congressional liaison staff idea developed years earlier within the Pentagon.[44]

The congressional liaison staff has a nebulous task—"to pass the

[42] Three examples of truncated majorities are discussed in Ripley, *Majority Party Leadership in Congress,* pp. 136–167.

[43] The experience abroad is summarized in Schwarz and Shaw, *The United States Congress in Comparative Perspective,* pp. 306–313. For the American experience see Robert J. Sickels, *Presidential Transactions* (Englewood Cliffs, N.J.: Prentice-Hall, 1974), pp. 72–80, 112–144.

[44] Personal interviews, and Stephen H. Wayne, *The Legislative Presidency* (New York: Harper & Row, 1978), p. 142.

president's program" is how the staff usually state it. They are communicators and thus coordinators. They chart the progress of presidential legislation through the congressional maze. They talk with the agencies, with committee leaders, and especially with the party and chamber leaders. Collectively, the staff attempts to know and talk with all members of the Congress. The members have usually been allocated among the liaison staff by geographic region, but the Carter administration introduced a new organizing principle—to allocate the liaison staff among congressional members on the basis of the member's committee assignments. This method takes advantage of how congressmen spend the bulk of their legislative effort and parallels the agency relationships to members that are also largely structured by committee. Thus, the White House liaison staff is able to monitor and coordinate legislative activity between the agencies and the members on the basis of a subject matter and functional specialization.

The concerted use of the agency-member relationship on behalf of the president's legislative program began with the Kennedy administration. The agencies' own congressional liaison staffs met weekly with the White House staff to report on congressional developments. This information was summarized for the president to help prepare him for his weekly meetings with the party leadership from the House and Senate.

The legislative liaison staff originated mainly to provide services to individual congressmen. They would want to know what an agency was doing about a situation within the district, or they might want to clear a patronage appointment, or they might want to arrange a tour of the White House for a visiting constituent. The sheer volume of such requests would, alone, create the need for a specialized staff. But the same staff could, and now does, also lobby Congress on behalf of the president's legislative program.

At committee stage of legislation, the White House liaison staff mainly attempts to monitor developments. The main expertise on the bills at that stage rests with the agencies, which in turn have developed a working relationship over a period of years with the committee members and their staff. But as bills near the floor, the White House staff becomes more active, paralleling within the executive branch the increased activity of the party leaders in comparison to the committee leaders.

As bills near the floor, concern centers on the extent of support and opposition in the chamber as a whole and on the tactics with which to handle anticipated opposition. This set of circumstances calls for close cooperation and coordination among all supporting partners of a given bill: the committee and party leaders in Congress, the agency and White House staff, perhaps the president himself, and the outside interest groups.

Apart from a constant flow of phone calls and personal visits, there are at least two occasions on which coordination occurs among the supporting partners. One is through the biweekly breakfast meetings at the White House between the president and the chamber and party leaders. The floor leaders of the president's party (whether majority or minority), the Speaker (if of the president's party), the party whips, and (perhaps) committee leaders attend, along with the president and some of his ranking aides, to discuss recent and coming legislative events. Although the agenda is partly set in advance, participants report that anyone is free to raise any matter at the meetings. The discussion may center on recent world events, or on anything else, and is not necessarily narrowly confined to the immediate legislative situation (Fig. 4.5).

The second occasion for formal coordination has occurred in meetings in the Speaker's office, at least when the president has been of the same party. These meetings concentrate on the floor stage of a given bill, likely to occur within the week, if not within days. This type of coordination meeting occurs only on the most important and controversial legislation. The Speaker and other party leaders, the committee leaders, the presidential liaison staff, the agency secretary

Figure 4.5   Congressional leadership breakfast with President Carter. President Carter flanked by Speaker Tip O'Neill (left) and Senate Majority Leader Byrd (right). (White House photograph)

and his liaison staff, and perhaps also interest group leaders are present at any one meeting. The committee leaders and agency personnel attending vary with the topic of the bill. The meeting assesses the relative balance of votes, on either critical amendments or on the bill as a whole, and ascertains what might be done to obtain the needed votes if the strategists felt they were in danger of losing.

FORMULATION OF THE PRESIDENT'S PROGRAM

The origins and formation of the president's legislative program are not as clearly defined in the United States as in Britain. The president's legislative program is coordinated through the Office of Management and Budget, which in turn is one of the agencies directly serving the president within the executive office of the president. The director of the Office of Management and Budget is one of the major appointments the president makes to his personal staff.[45] One of the responsibilities of this office is to prepare the president's legislative program and to review all legislative requests by agencies for their conformity to the president's own program.

One of the persistent problems facing the president has been to gain control over "his" executive branch. It was not until the 1920s (a reform from World War I) that the president had any role to play at all in shaping the budget; each agency had made its own budget requests directly to the appropriate congressional committee. It was not until the Truman administration (a reform from World War II) that the president began centralizing the legislative requests of agencies in accordance with his own legislative goals.[46]

One important source of a president's legislative program is his own campaign for the office. Particularly in the early years of a presidency, the president will attempt to implement his campaign themes. Candidate John Kennedy stressed economic recovery in his campaign, and thus much of his early legislation as president concerned minimum wages, tax stimulation of the economy, and aid to economically depressed areas. Although his campaign also stressed civil rights, legislation on that topic was considerably delayed.

Candidate Jimmy Carter stressed numerous themes and promised sweeping reforms. Upon taking office, however, he and his staff postponed making specific proposals on some topics, finding that they

[45] Until the Nixon administration, this appointment was a personal one, not requiring senatorial confirmation. That requirement was imposed by Congress in reaction against Nixon's budgetary and impoundment tactics. President Carter, however, became the first victim of that new requirement: The senatorial committee that had initially considered the Bert Lance appointment held further hearings within Carter's first year on allegations concerning Mr. Lance. Within a week of those hearings, Lance had resigned.

[46] Wayne, *The Legislative Presidency*, pp. 73–93.

were more complicated than had been thought during the campaign. The energy crisis did prompt the Carter administration to issue a set of proposals within three months of the inauguration. An aide (James Schlesinger, who then became the new energy secretary) was appointed to prepare an energy proposal within the three-month deadline. He and his small staff worked hurriedly (because of the short deadline) and also secretly. Not only did congressmen not know of the content of the prospective energy proposals, but affected officials within the Carter administration did not know either. Several of the economic advisers—any energy program will have an important impact on the economy—heard rumors about the economic and tax implications of the thinking of the energy group and in effect got themselves included in some of the discussions. Yet a complaint at the Treasury Department among the Administration's own appointees was that the energy group would not provide them with enough information so that the Treasury experts could in turn provide the energy group with realistic estimates of the likely tax consequences of their own proposals. As another illustration of the relatively small and closed group decision process within the administration, the secretary of transportation did not learn about the transportation-related portion of the proposal until the day before Carter's address to Congress. He apparently did not approve that portion, but his only recourse was to submit a memo to the president.[47]

Welfare reform was another major issue in the campaign, one about which Carter promised an early proposal. An administration study group was immediately formed to prepare recommendations to the president. This task force was more broadly based than the energy group. Directed by an assistant secretary in HEW, it included persons from other government agencies and from congressional committees and state and local officials. Its original intention was to develop and agree upon a single comprehensive proposal. By early April of the first year, however, the group abandoned that goal, finding that the totality of welfare and income maintenance programs was too complicated for a single rapid solution. Rather, they opted to outline four different alternative strategies. That report was made public within the month.

President Carter then announced that his administration would continue to develop a set of proposals, and that his program would be presented to congress within another six to eight months. In the meantime, major agencies had severe disagreements with one another over portions of the future proposals. At one publicized meeting, the secretaries of HEW and labor met in the White House to discuss their differences over employment incentives and job training programs.

[47] *New York Times*, April 24, 1977, pp. A1, A28.

Their meeting adjourned with an announcement of their new agreement. What was atypical about that meeting was not the fact of disagreements between officials within an administration, but that the disagreement was handled at the top levels of the agencies and was given extensive newspaper publicity.[48]

Ample time—frequently years—is required for all interested officials, legislators, and interest groups to arrive at a common understanding of a complicated problem, much less to arrive at an agreement among their frequently divergent and opposed views. Energy and welfare issues certainly belong in this category. A different approach —when time has permitted—from that taken by the Carter administration may be illustrated by the use of royal commissions in Britain and Sweden.

A royal commission is appointed by the government to investigate and report on an issue. The political parties are represented, as are the major affected interest groups. Ideally, the diversity of their membership and the reputation of its chairman, together with its status as a "royal" body, will lead its members to find common agreement among themselves, and to thereby incline their respective parties and groups to support the recommendations. Presumably the government (of the day) and parliament will find the recommendations acceptable and will enact the government's bill based upon the report. Britain's health insurance system, for example, was developed in this fashion by the "Beveridge" Commission during World War II to prepare for the postwar period. Sweden makes more extensive use of royal commissions: in the 1955–1967 period, for example, more than 900 such commissions had been formed, having a combined total of more than 3600 members. A particularly controversial issue in Swedish politics, concerning the financing and benefits of a social security system, engaged two different commissions over an eight-year period.[49]

Role of Legislators in Executive Formulation

As the British, German, American, and Swedish examples indicate, the process by which the chief executive decides what legislation to propose is complicated. It is a process in which legislators may and sometimes do participate, although the opportunities are reduced in a presidential system. In a parliamentary system the governing cabinet is in parliament; its members are frequently members of parliament. To say the government formulates its legislative program is to say that

[48] *New York Times,* April 3, 1977, pp. A1, A40.
[49] Christopher Wheeler, *White-Collar Power: Changing Patterns of Interest Group Behavior in Sweden* (Urbana: University of Illinois Press, 1975), pp. 42, 71.

those members of parliament who lead the governing party or coalition formulate a legislative program for the other members of parliament to receive and deliberate. In a presidential system, consultation with members of congress is not an automatic by-product of the structure of government; rather, if consultation is to occur, members of the administration and members of congress must deliberately plan and strive for it. In the rush of events, in a process that is already complicated, the administration is apt to pay little attention to congress in the short run, even though its legislative program might thereby be advantaged in the long run.

But in the perspective of a decade or more, rather than of a few years, parliaments can play a major role in the shaping of government's legislative programs. In competitive democracies, at least, the opposition and governing parties (or coalitions) are apt to change places. The new government, after an election, is likely to have shaped its policies while in opposition.

The American Democratic party, in particular, has been able to shape its policies through Congress when Republicans have held the presidency. The Democrats, during 14 of the 16 years of Republican administrations after World War II, have themselves been the congressional majority. Thus, they have controlled all congressional committees, along with the bulk of the committee budget and staff. The economic legislation of the Kennedy administration and the environmental and energy legislation of the Carter administration, for example, have been shaped largely by the preceding Democratic congresses while in opposition to Republican presidents.[50]

Summary

Parliaments vary greatly in the number of bills each considers. In most, however, a sizable proportion of all bills introduced is sponsored by the government of the day, and an even higher proportion is adopted. In most legislative bodies, the executive largely sets the agenda of the bills they will consider. Perhaps prime ministers within a parliament can more easily control it than can presidents outside a congress, but a large measure of executive influence seems a constant factor in all governmental systems.

In the American system, the party composition of Congress, matched with the president's party, leads to six different types of relationships between the two political branches. In most instances since

[50] Sundquist, *Politics and Policy*, and David E. Price, "Policy Making in Congressional Committees: The Impact of 'Environmental' Factors," *American Political Science Review* 72 (June 1978), p. 573, table 3.

1952 their relationship has been one of either stalemate or avoidance. In only three congressional terms has the party of the president matched the policy majority of Congress.

In all systems, the process by which the government decides its legislative program is complicated and often extends over a period of months if not years. There is, in effect, a "legislative process" within the executive. Over a span of years, the reactions of parliaments to executive-proposed legislation, and the flow of events in election campaigns, have helped shape the legislation that in any given year the chief executive will propose.

THE BUDGET

Parliaments have one power all executives need—the power to authorize expenditures and to levy taxes. But the very importance of the financial function has led executives to limit these parliamentary powers. In Britain and France, for example, parliament may not increase appropriations over the government's request, although parliament may decrease them. If the government is to be responsible for the conduct of the nation's business, it must be able to manage the relationship between expenditures and income. In parliamentary democracies the result is that parliament will use the budget as an occasion for an extended debate on the policies and purposes of the government, but the budget will survive as presented.

In some countries the government is authorized to implement its proposed budget if parliament has not acted on it within a specified time span. If parliament cannot amend, neither can it defeat a proposed budget. If parliament actually voted against the government's budget, the government would fall. Thus, from both constitutional and political reasons, the government's budget in most political systems is adopted; and if it is not adopted, it is acted upon by the government in the absence of an actual vote to defeat the budget and along with it, the government of the day.[51]

There are two major variations from the main pattern. In the first —and perhaps the United States is the only persistent example— Congress frequently amends proposed expenditures and, even more, the proposed taxes of the administration. The extent of amendments to proposed expenditures is illustrated, for the foreign-aid program, in Table 6.15. Amendments to taxation proposals may be illustrated by the Carter energy program. Its proposed steep increase in the gasoline tax was eliminated in one of the first congressional actions on the entire energy proposal. The centerpiece, as Carter called it, of his energy program was another tax—the proposed tax upon the price of oil as it

---

[51] Loewenberg, *Parliament in the German Political System*, pp. 274, 373–377.

came out of the ground. This proposal was the most controversial of all the disputes embodied in the energy program. It was never resolved by the House-Senate conference committee, for the two houses had diametrically disagreed in their versions. The 1977–1978 Carter tax bill is another example. Although the Congress completely changed it from a "reform" bill to a "reduction" bill, President Carter signed it anyway. The more important of the defeats suffered by the British Labour government, referred to earlier, have been on taxation bills. Although the government did not resign, it was forced to modify other portions of the tax schedules to compensate for the changes forced upon it by the votes in the House of Commons.

The other main variation is that members of parliament attempt to increase those expenditures that would benefit the individual member's districts. This variation seems to occur in a wide variety of countries: U.S. congressmen seek increased appropriations for public works, water reclamation projects and airplane contracts in their districts and states; members of the Supreme Soviet seek increased governmental expenditures in the five-year plan in their provinces; members of the Thailand parliament and of the Chilean congress (both abolished in the 1970s) sought increased expenditures for projects within their respective provinces. In most countries the effect of these district-oriented revisions is not to increase but to reallocate expenditures within a set amount. The effect in the United States, however, is also to increase the budget. As a result, presidents Nixon and Carter have both criticized Congress for "wasteful" spending. One of Carter's first acts in office was to try to stop expenditures on a number of water dam projects that were not merely planned, but even in mid-construction. Some of Carter's congressional allies suggested that he could find more adept ways of winning friends "on the Hill" than by threatening a highly cherished (at least by them) power to bring federal funds into their states and districts. The result after a year was, first, that the new administration had not been able to decide upon a comprehensive water project policy and, second, that senators on the relevant committees had saved their states' projects from deletion.[52]

Budgets are far more complicated than the question of expenditures for specific programs and tax rates for one year. In the first place, costs for government programs are likely to grow more rapidly than anyone had anticipated at the beginning. Perhaps two types of programs are particularly vulnerable to unanticipated escalating costs. The first are high-technology programs, best symbolized by the "cost overruns" in armaments production. The second are the human services, in which costs are dependent upon the need in society for the service.

[52] *Congressional Quarterly Weekly Report* (March 4, 1978), pp. 565–574; *Washington Post*, March 12, 1978, p. A14.

Examples are food stamps for low-income persons and revenue sharing for cities. As a result, both the executive branch and Congress now develop five-year projections of anticipated costs of existing and new programs.

The second complication in the budgetary process stems from the first: bargaining and compromise to cut costs. Most nations find that their need for government programs exceeds their current tax revenues. One way to bring the two into an acceptable balance is to limit costs, which in turn is mainly a matter of limiting programs (rather than of reorganizing agencies). Most such decisions are made within the executive branch, which usually takes a full year to shape the budget it will present to its legislative body. The agencies bargain and negotiate with each other, with the central budget agency, and with the chief executive over the content of the budget prior to its being reviewed by the legislature.[53]

Within the U.S. government, the Office of Management and Budget centrally coordinates the formulation of the budget for the president. This office, however, was made part of the presidency only in 1939 and was not even created until after World War I. Until that time each agency prepared its own budget and sent it directly to the Congress, completely bypassing the President.[54]

The third source of complication is that the government's budget has become a major instrument of achieving goals for the whole economy, particularly in achieving desirable rates of economic growth and in balancing, if not avoiding, the evils of inflation and unemployment. The rate of spending and the size of the deficit almost become more important than the specific objects for which the funds are spent.

A fourth complication is found in countries with centrally planned economies. In both Communist party nations and in newly developing nations, the government is the major source of economic activity. Thus its budget is a national economic plan. In these countries the budget is the gross national product rather than only one component. As a result, the Committee on the Economic Plan in the Supreme Soviet, for example, is also the budgetary committee.

Within the U.S. Congress the appropriations committees and the tax-writing committees are among the most powerful and prestigious committees in each chamber. The House Ways and Means Committee, for example, because it has jurisdiction over the tax system, also has jurisdiction over international trade and most portions of the public welfare system, for both sets of policies rest upon the use of the tax

[53] Aaron Wildavsky, *Budgeting: A Comparative Theory of Budgetary Processes* (Boston: Little, Brown, 1975), pp. 203–231.
[54] Louis Fisher, *Presidential Spending Power* (Princeton, N.J.: Princeton University Press, 1975), pp. 9–58.

power. In both chambers, the appropriations committees are the largest (see Tables 6.8 and 6.9), and in both they function through semi-autonomous subcommittees. Most spending decisions by Congress are made within the subcommittees, over which the full committee and floor sessions exercise limited review and revision. As a result, agencies are concerned with at least two committees within each chamber: the committees holding jurisdiction over its program and that subcommittee within Appropriations handling its budget.[55]

Until World War I, appropriations requests were handled by separate committees; to combine them into a single committee was intended as a step toward coordination. Yet the decentralized subcommittee system did not achieve much more coordination than previously, and the separation between appropriations and taxation committees was a further source of noncoordination of budgetary decisions within Congress.

A new coordination procedure has been developed by Congress, largely under the stresses of the Nixon presidency. Each house created a budget committee that was responsible for preparing a statement of annual income targets and of spending limits. Once adopted by the two houses, this statement would be binding upon all the other committees. In addition, a new budget staff was created, to provide Congress with its equivalent to the president's Office of Management and Budget. The twin purpose of this change is, first, to increase the capacity of Congress to deal with the president on budgetary matters and second, to increase the capacity of Congress to make considered and single decisions about the whole budget rather than many decisions about only portions of the budget. The second purpose was the means by which the first purpose could be achieved. These changes rank among the most significant in the Congress since the end of World War II.[56]

The immediately precipitating actions by the Nixon administration were its consistent and large-scale use of an esoteric procedure termed "impoundment." In effect, presidents have often not spent a small portion of funds appropriated by Congress. Under Nixon, however, this minor practice was escalated to a major tactic by which the administration attempted to terminate programs which the Democratic Congress wished to continue. Thus, the struggle to set policy on spend-

[55] Richard F. Fenno, Jr., *Power of the Purse: Appropriations Politics in Congress* (Boston: Little, Brown, 1966), pp. 264–349.

[56] John W. Ellwood and James A. Thurber, "The New Congressional Budget Process: The Hows and Whys of House-Senate Differences," in Lawrence C. Dodd and Bruce I. Oppenheimer (eds.), *Congress Reconsidered* (New York: Praeger, 1977), pp. 163–173. See the later discussion in Chapter 7 of this volume.

ing was extended beyond the Congress to a postcongressional stage. Congress reacted by creating a set of procedures by which the president was required to request Congress' permission to withhold expenditures. Should Congress not approve, then the request was denied. Although this procedure is a separate one from the process by which coordinated budget decisions are made, both were created at the same time and in response to the same tactics of the Nixon administration.[57]

Within the states the legislatures adopt budgets very close, in total amounts, to those proposed by their governors. Some 592 agencies within 19 states were found to have requested an average increase of 24% over their current budgets. The governors cut those requests by an average of 14%, which was the major change made in the entire budgetary cycle. The legislatures' actions varied from a cut of 8% below to an increase of 19% over the governors' recommendations.[58]

Some state legislatures have developed, as has the U.S. Congress in the 1970s, a central budget staff to provide the same expertise about the budget to the legislators that is available to the chief executives through their budget bureaus. The development of this type of fiscal staff in the Wisconsin legislature did lead to an increase in the number of changes, and in the amounts of dollars involved, by the legislature in the governor's recommended budget over previous years. But perhaps a more important and long-run change stems from the existence of a set of staff persons in the legislature with whom executive branch budget officers must, and can, talk. Agency personnel check with the legislative staff in the early stages of the preparation of agency budget requests to the governor, and it would appear that both the agencies and the governor's staff are more careful than previously to scrutinize and justify their own proposals before sending them to the legislature in the first place.[59]

Although in most countries the powers of legislative bodies over executive proposed budgets has declined over a long period of time, in the United States both Congress and the state legislatures have been making concerted efforts to reverse that process. The state effort has been slow and halting, but one of steady progress. The congressional effort, by contrast, was greatly stimulated by the Nixon administration's provocative tactics, which in turn had been preceded by a long struggle between Congress and the Johnson administration over the conduct of the war in Vietnam.

[57] Fisher, *Presidential Spending Power,* pp. 147–201.

[58] Ira Sharkansky, "Agency Requests, Gubernatorial Support and Budget Success in State Legislatures," *American Political Science Review* 62 (December 1968), pp. 1220–1231.

[59] Alan Rosenthal, *Legislative Performance in the States: Explorations of Committee Behavior* (New York: Free Press, 1974), pp. 158–160.

AGENCY REVIEW AND SUPERVISION

Once legislation has been proposed, deliberated, amended, and voted, what happens? Presumably the agencies, under the direction of the political executive, administer or "execute" the adopted law. But the potential activity of parliament does not cease. Indeed, its activity on any given matter or agency may increase. Parliaments can review how agencies have administered adopted policies, how agencies spend the budget, and how agencies treat individual citizens. In addition, parliaments may review rules and regulations issued by executive branch agencies, and can require, as has the U.S. Congress, that certain of them are subject to congressional veto.

The average congressman will have far more contact with the executive branch at the agency level than with the White House. Presidential contact will be infrequent, and most legislation a congressman works on would probably not be affected by the president's program. But the concerns of his constituency and the work of his committees will bring him into contact with numerous agencies, and through a committee he might develop a specialized knowledge of an agency and its programs. The reverse may also be true; for most agencies, their more frequent interaction may be with congressmen on related committees than with staff in the White House, much less with the president himself.

In politics, knowledge is power; one kind of knowledge congressmen seek is knowledge about agency activity. Presidents and their staffs, too, seek knowledge about agency activity. Both congressmen and presidents seek such knowledge as a means of making better policy decisions—as each might separately and differently define the term "better." It may be that congressmen are more able than are presidents to obtain such information and to exercise review and supervision over agencies.[60]

Floor

Some parliaments have developed specific procedures to permit agency review on the floor. The British question time is perhaps the best example. In the first hour of each day's meeting, members may raise questions with the government ministers. Questions are now stated in writing, with most of the responses also made in writing. But a number of responses are made orally on the floor, and the questioning member —or others—may raise "supplementary" questions following the minister's initial answer. Figure 4.6 reproduces from *Hansard*, the official record of Parliament, a list of questions for one day. The first

[60] Wayne, *The Legislative Presidency*, p. 180.

No. 28   **THURSDAY 6TH DECEMBER 1973**   1529

ORDER PAPER

QUESTIONS FOR ORAL ANSWER

Questions to the Prime Minister (see pp. 1531-32) will begin at 3.15 p.m.

*   1 **Mr S. Clinton Davis** (Hackney, Central):   To ask the Secretary of State for the Home Department, if he will make a statement on the Government's policy with regard to the Report of the Criminal Law Revision Committee concerning evidence and procedure in criminal trials.

*   2 **Miss Janet Fookes** (Merton and Morden) :   To ask the Secretary of State for the Home Department, if he will change his method of collecting statistics relating to fireworks accidents, so that they become available sooner than at present.

* 36 **Mr Maurice Edelman** (Coventry, North):   To ask the Secretary of State for Social Services, what inspection he has made within the last three months of imported Japanese mackerel, in the light of the occurrence of Minamata disease transmitted by mercury-polluted fish.

* 37 **Dame Irene Ward** (Tynemouth):   To ask the Secretary of State for Trade and Industry, whether, in the future interests of the taxi drivers and of the public due to the irregularity of public transport, he will consider declaring taxis 'public transport' and eligible for fuel for their unrestricted use.   [*Transferred*]

Questions to the Prime Minister will begin at 3.15 p.m.

*Q 1 **Mr Michael Meacher** (Oldham, West):   To ask the Prime Minister, what further meetings he has planned with the TUC and CBI.

5 S 2

1532   **Order Paper ; 6th December 1973**   No. 28

QUESTIONS FOR ORAL ANSWER—*continued*

*Q 2 **Mr Dennis Skinner** (Bolsover) :   To ask the Prime Minister, if he has plans for holding future talks with the leaders of the NUM ; and if he will make a statement.

*Q 3 **Mr Grimond** (Orkney and Shetland):   To ask the Prime Minister, if recording machines are used to record any of his or other Ministers' meetings or conversations ; and on what conditions.

*Q16 **Mr Wyn Roberts** (Conway):   To ask the Prime Minister, if the public speech of the Secretary of State for Trade and Industry at Liverpool on 17th November on British industry represents Government policy.

*Q17 **Mr Arthur Lewis** (West Ham, North) :   To ask the Prime Minister, whether he has received the communication dated 1st December from the honourable Member for West Ham, North, regarding the miners' pay dispute ; when he intends to reply ; and whether he will make a statement.

Figure 4.6   Questions listed for oral answer in the British House of Commons.

set of questions was directed to the minister in charge of the Home Department; the second set was directed to the prime minister.

The beginning portion of the question time for the prime minister is reproduced from *Hansard* in Figure 4.7. In that portion, the chancellor of the exchequer substituted for the prime minister. Once the reply had been made to the stated question, the debate record shows

HOUSE OF COMMONS

Thursday 6th December 1973

The House met at half-past Two o'clock

PRAYERS

[Mr. SPEAKER *in the Chair*]

ORAL ANSWERS TO QUESTIONS

1445   *Oral Answers*

CBI AND TUC (MEETINGS)

Q1. **Mr. Meacher** asked the Prime Minister what further meetings he has planned with the TUC and CBI.

The Chancellor of the Exchequer (Mr. Anthony Barber: I must inform the House that since my right hon. Friend ·the Prime Minister it taking the chair at the tripartite discussions on Ireland, I have been asked to reply.

I have nothing to add to what my right hon. Friend told my hon. Friend the Member for Kingston-upon-Thames (Mr. Norman Lamont) on 8th November. —[Vol. 863, c. 231.]

Mr. Meacher: When the right hon. Gentleman does meet those bodies, will he explain how he justifies the fact that over and above the two of three billion pounds which the Government will now have to borrow to cover next year's deficit they are encouraging the nationalised industries and local authorities to borrow from abroad at a rate of a further two billion pounds per year, so that by this time next year we can expect to be in "hock" to the tune of from five to six billion pounds? Since, in the present world economic situation, one-eighth of our national income is committed to foreign debts, does this not show reckless housekeeping?

Mr. Barber: The alternative is to pursue the sort of policies that were pursued by the Labour Government.....

6 ч 19

Mr. Healey: Is the Chancellor of the Exchequer aware that there will be disappointment on both sides of the House that reports to the effect that he courageously admitted yesterday that the assumptions on which he based his Budget strategy had been undermined by the energy crisis now appear to be untrue and that he is still showing the same complacency that he and his right hon. Friend the Secretary of State for Trade and Industry have been showing for so many weeks?

Will the right hon. Gentleman comment on the trade figures published yesterday which show, contrary to Government claims over the last few weeks, that the volume of imports has not increased since January whereas the volume of exports has increased by 9·6 per cent.?—I am sorry. Obviously I was overcome by the

Government propaganda to which I referred. I meant to say that the volume of exports had not increased since January, whereas the volume of imports had increased by 9·6 per cent.

Mr. Barber: I am sure that the right hon. Gentleman, in the national interest, will agree with everyone else in the country that the efforts being made by our export industries at present are first-class. No one would seek to deny that who has the national interest at heart. The simple fact is that when the right hon. Gentleman speaks in the way he does, he does this country no service whatsoever. If I may say so, he would do well to heed the words of Mr. Len Murray, who said that people who exaggerate temporary problems do Britain no service at all.

Mr. Healey *rose*——

Mr. Speaker: Order. We have spent seven minutes on this Question, but I shall call the right hon. Member for Leeds, East (Mr. Healey).

Mr. Healey: I rise on a point of order, Mr. Speaker. Is it in order for the Chancellor of the Exchequer to impugn my patriotism for quoting figures published yesterday by the Department of Trade and Industry?

Mr. Speaker: That is not a matter for the Chair.

Figure 4.7   Prime minister's question time in the British House of Commons.

that others continued to raise related questions. The question, about the economic policies of the Conservative government, was soon entered into by a former (and also succeeding) member of the Labour cabinet (Mr. Healey), thus illustrating how question time can both raise major policy questions and generate partisan exchange between the leading spokesmen of the major parties in the House.

That particular round of questioning was terminated by the Speaker because of its length, and they then went on to the next question. Although 17 questions had been listed that day to the prime minister for oral reply, only three were discussed on the floor. Although most of the 37 questions listed that same day for the Home Department (and a few for other departments) were in fact discussed on the floor, another 116 questions had also been listed for written answer. Approximately 20,000 such questions are stated and answered in a year's time.[61]

Committees

Committees, however, are the most commonly used forum for agency review. Committees of the American congress, for example, regularly hold hearings reviewing agency programs. In addition, many programs require authorizing legislation at periodic intervals of one to five years, and each requires an annual budget. Both requirements present the committees with scheduled opportunities to inquire into both the adequacy of the policy and the means by which the agency or agencies administer the program.

Reviews of specific agencies and programs by committees are encouraged in those parliaments whose committees parallel the structure of administrative agencies. That principle is used in approximately half of the world's parliaments and in turn is associated with the number of committees. Since agencies are numerous, committees ordinarily will also be numerous if their jurisdiction parallels agencies. The relationship between the principle of committee organization and the number of committees is expressed in Table 4.14. For those 17 parliaments having 16 or more committees, 15 organize them to correspond to administrative departments (e.g., West Germany, United States). For the 37 parliaments having 15 or fewer committees, only

---

[61] United Kingdom, House of Commons, *Parliamentary Debates (Hansard)*, December 6, 1973, cols. 1425–1451, and *Order Paper*, December 6, 1973, pp. 1529–1543; United Kingdom, British Information Service, *The British Parliament* (London: HMSO, 1973), pp. 30–31. See also G. W. Jones, "The Prime Minister and Parliamentary Questions," *Parliamentary Affairs* 26 (Summer 1973), pp. 260–273; D. Judge, "Backbench Specialization—A Study in Parliamentary Questions," *Parliamentary Affairs* 27 (Spring 1974), pp. 171–186.

Table 4.14 NUMBER OF PARLIAMENTS ACCORDING TO COMMITTEE STRUCTURE AND NUMBER OF COMMITTEES

COMMITTEES PARALLEL DEPARTMENTS	NUMBER OF COMMITTEES				
	1–9	10–15	16–19	20+	TOTAL
Yes	7	4	9	6	26
No	19	7	1	1	28
Total	26	11	10	7	54

SOURCE: Valentine Herman and Francoise Mendel, *Parliaments of the World* (Berlin: De Gruyter, 1976), pp. 471, 474–486.

11 form their committees on the same basis, of which Australia and East Germany are examples.[62]

Those more numerous countries that have a relatively small number of committees and are not organized by departmental jurisdiction create a special type of committee to review agency performance. To cite the British example, four supervisory committees have been created by Parliament to provide a financial audit (the Public Accounts Committee), to seek economies in government spending (the Expenditures Committee), to supervise the industries managed by public corporations (the Select Committee on Nationalized Industries), and to review administrative orders that have the effect of law (Committee on Statutory Instruments).[63]

In the first chapter we indicated that review of administrative activity, particularly through parliamentary committees, seems to be increasingly important within Communist party nations. The numerous committees of the Polish Sejm, for example, exercise administrative review on those matters within its legislative jurisdiction. In this respect, the Polish committees approximate the American. Over a three-year period in the mid-1960s the 19 committees held over 700 meetings. In addition, they have formed subcommittees and ad hoc "working groups" to inquire into specific problems and also to take field trips throughout the country. The committees and their subgroups can raise questions with administrative agencies through the device of "requests," of which some 1400 had been adopted over a three-year period. Although such requests initially mainly concerned local matters, they have assumed a "more general character and are by now one of the generally applied methods of work in the committees." Their number and their reach apparently attracted concern from the higher levels of Polish government, for the Sejm's presidium ruled, in

[62] Herman and Mendel, *Parliaments of the World,* pp. 471, 474–486.
[63] Schwarz and Shaw, *The United States Congress in Comparative Perspective,* pp. 278–281.

1963, that the agencies "to which the committees direct their requests are not bound to carry out the recommendations contained therein; they have only the duty to respond to them."[64]

Committees of the Supreme Soviet have been re-formed to exercise a supervisory and review function over administrative agencies, especially over those agencies that engage in economic production and distribution activities. By the early 1970s some 13 standing committees in each chamber had such review functions. Their creation and activity was apparently a response to the Communist party's effort to reform the economy. The committees may address inquiries to the government (Council of Ministers) and while the ministers must consider such inquiries and recommendations, there is no legal means by which they could be forced to implement the committee's recommendations.[65]

Variations in Agency Supervision

Supervision and review of administrative agency activity is no less important in state legislatures than in national parliaments. Although we lack a survey of all 50 of the state legislatures, we can examine the performance of the review function by the committees in the Connecticut legislature. Of its 13 committees, three were judged to be very active in reviewing agencies: the committees on State and Urban Development, Education, and Environment. Another four were judged to be relatively inactive: Public Personnel, Public Health, Government Administration, and Liquor Control. Six committees were moderately active in reviewing agencies, including the committees on Labor, Insurance, and Human Rights.

Given the uneven performance of agency review and supervision by committees of the same legislature (in 1971–1972), we can ask what factors were associated with variations in committee performance of this function? The most important characteristic seems to be the frequency of committee meetings. If committees do not meet, they cannot function. The more frequently they do meet, the more active and apparently also effective they have been in reviewing agencies. Whether or not the committee functions through a subcommittee structure is also related to reviewing agencies, in that subcommittees permit a greater frequency of the committee meetings to which we

[64] Remigiusz Bierzanek and Andrzej Gwizdz, "Parliamentary Control over the Administration in Poland," *Polish Round Table* (Warsaw: Yearbook of the Polish Association of Political Sciences, 1967), pp. 167–168.

[65] Vanneman, *The Supreme Soviet*, pp. 145–148. The new constitution of the USSR, adopted in 1977, specifically provided that committees could investigate agencies, but that the latter were required only to inform the committees what actions had been taken as a result (Articles 117 and 125).

have just referred. Attitudes of the committee members were also related to committee activity: committees whose members thought committees should exercise agency review and who themselves wished to participate in that task were more active in agency review than committees whose members did not share that outlook. Seniority was, finally, inversely related to agency review. Committees with junior members—but only if the committees had an active subcommittee system—were more active in agency review than were committees with more senior members.[66]

Somewhat similar circumstances seem to operate within the U.S. Congress as well. Members are not at all sure that intensive scrutiny of agency activity is worth their time. It is a detailed and time-consuming task. Their inquiries are often prompted by complaints they hear from their constituents, which makes the casework function—discussed earlier in the chapter on representation—an important dynamic in the congressional-executive relationship. Congressmen pursue casework requests on an individual basis with the concerned agencies and tend to feel that such contacts are more effective than formal inquiries in obtaining information about the agencies.

Systematic review by congressmen, and especially by committees, would appear to be encouraged under several conditions: (1) congressmen disagree with an agency activity; (2) congressmen's constituents disagree with an agency activity; (3) the congressional majority party faces a president of the opposition party; (4) congressmen perceive an actively hostile or evasive president; and (5) congressmen believe that accountability and supervision are valued by the general public. The first three conditions are fairly continuous, while the fourth was made more obvious during the Johnson and Nixon presidencies. The fifth seems to characterize a popular mood capitalized upon by the Carter presidential campaign in 1976.[67]

Another factor concerns the organization of Congress and the recognition given within Congress to the importance of the agency supervision and review function. In 1974 the House of Representatives strengthened the capacity of its committees to review administrative actions consistently. It authorized each standing committee to undertake oversight functions by stipulating that either each subcommittee would exercise oversight on matters within its jurisdiction or a special oversight subcommittee would be created. In addition, the major investigative committee, the Government Operations Committee, was

[66] Rosenthal, *Legislative Performance in the States*, pp. 88, 104–108.

[67] Morris S. Ogul, "Congressional Oversight: Structures and Incentives," in Lawrence C. Dodd and Bruce I. Oppenheimer (eds.), *Congress Reconsidered* (New York: Praeger, 1977), pp. 207–221; Seymour Scher, "Conditions for Legislative Control," *Journal of Politics* 25 (August 1963), pp. 526–551.

authorized to conduct hearings and investigations on matters otherwise within the jurisdiction of other standing committees. The purpose of these changes has been to provide for a continuing and regular, rather than episodic and haphazard, review by Congress of executive branch agency activity.[68]

Specialized Procedures

The U.S. Congress has developed two specialized means to increase its capacity to monitor and to review agency activity and has discussed two additional procedures suggested by the Carter administration.

REPORT REQUIREMENT

Not infrequently agencies and perhaps the president himself are required by Congress to report either on an annual basis or upon taking certain kinds of actions. This reporting requirement is now sufficiently frequent that an annual congressional publication is issued simply to provide a bibliographic guide to the reports.[69] One example of this type of requirement is found in the Foreign Military and Security Assistance Act of 1977, in which the president was required to notify relevant committees of intended projects and arms sales.

CONGRESSIONAL VETO

Just as the president can veto a congressional act, so Congress has found a means of vetoing an executive branch action. As of 1976, close to 200 pieces of legislation had such a provision, almost half of which had been enacted since 1970—another example of congressional reaction against the Nixon administration. The congressional veto procedure can take several forms: A proposed action would be considered approved if Congress did not adopt a resolution of disapproval; a proposed action would not be approved unless Congress did adopt such a resolution; the resolution could become effective upon adoption in one house, or in both; Congress would have 30, 60, or 90 days in which to act. But what all such provisions have in common is the twin requirements that, first, Congress be informed of a pending action, and, second, Congress has a specified period of time in which to take (or refuse to take) action upon the agency notification.[70]

The resolution of disapproval in 1978 of the contentious arms

[68] Roger H. Davidson and Walter J. Oleszek, "Adaptation and Consolidation: Structural Innovation in the U.S. House of Representatives," *Legislative Studies Quarterly* 1 (February 1976), pp. 56–60.

[69] U.S. Congress. General Accounting Office, *Requirements for Recurring Reports to the Congress* (Washington, D.C.: Government Printing Office, 1978).

[70] *Congressional Quarterly 1976 Almanac,* pp. 508–510.

sale "package" to the three Middle Eastern countries of Israel, Egypt, and Saudi Arabia is an example (Fig. 4.8). The resolution of disapproval was defeated in the Senate, 44-54, thus permitting the president to proceed with the intended sale of military planes.

Some congressmen, including Democrats, have argued that Congress should enact a general-purpose provision, applying the legislative veto as a standard practice against a wide range of executive branch actions. This proposal is perhaps another example of how later presidents (Carter) inherit the consequences of the actions of earlier ones (Johnson and Nixon). President Carter, as we would expect of any president, condemned the proposal and threatened his own veto against any such legislation.[71]

ZERO-BASE BUDGET

In addition to the two congressional procedures discussed above, several different budgeting approaches have been tried to permit higher level executive branch officials to better understand and control agency activity. The Carter administration has attempted to use a method termed zero-base budgeting, which in effect asks budget planners to assume that the given agency and its program were not in existence so that planning and budgeting could be done from a fresh start. Congress may itself adopt such an approach to the president's budget requests, and if so a considerable amount of new staff and new committee procedures would probably be needed.

SUNSET LAWS

A second Carter administration proposal, which the Congress may adopt for itself, is the notion that all government programs should expire on a periodic basis, and that no programs will be continued unless Congress explicitly legislates to the contrary. The objective would be to permit both the president and the legislative body to re-examine the need and rationale for each government agency and program on a periodic basis. If implemented, this proposal too would require the development of an additional staff and new committee procedures in Congress.

Audit and Review Staff

Numerous parliaments and state legislatures have specialized units to audit government agency expenditures to ascertain whether or not the expenditures have conformed to legal and parliamentary stipulations. In Britain this function is handled by one of the specialized committees, whereas in the United States the General Accounting Office (GAO)

[71] *Congressional Quarterly Weekly Report,* June 24, 1978, pp. 1623–1624.

Calendar No. 737

95TH CONGRESS
2D SESSION

S. CON. RES. 86

[Report No. 95–806]

IN THE SENATE OF THE UNITED STATES

MAY 11 (legislative day, APRIL 24), 1978

Mr. SPARKMAN (from the Committee on Foreign Relations) reported the following concurrent resolution; which was ordered to be placed on the calendar

---

CONCURRENT RESOLUTION

Relating to action by the Congress on certain sales of armaments to Egypt, Israel, and Saudi Arabia.

1 *Resolved by the Senate (the House of Representatives*

2 *concurring),* That the Congress objects to the proposed sale

3 to Egypt of fifty F–5 aircraft and related defense articles and

4 services as described in the statement submitted by the

5 President, pursuant to section 36 (b) of the Arms Export

6 Control Act, to the Speaker of the House of Representatives

7 and to the chairman of the Committee on Foreign Relations

8 of the Senate on April 28, 1978 (transmittal numbered

9 78–32).

VII—O

Figure 4.8 Congressional veto: resolution of disapproval of arms sales to Middle East, 1978.

performs the same function for Congress. Although such units begin with a narrow concentration on fiscal accounts and legalisms, they develop an expertise that makes them much more useful to legislators. Simply to expand their concern from law to efficiency, for example, permits them to raise many more and broader questions about agency activity and organization. That expertise, in turn, then becomes useful to legislators in assessing the utility of executive branch proposals for new legislation. The reaction of the Congress against the Johnson and Nixon presidencies, and the generally heightened concern with "accountability," has increased the scope and extent of GAO's reports and investigations beyond the narrow concern for technical auditing.[72]

Summary

Review, or at least questioning, of agency activity would appear a more widespread and frequent activity by parliaments than is their participation on policy deliberation. Agency supervision fits within the two categories described in the first chapter of detailed questions and issues of intermediate importance. Whether a parliamentary member is concerned with agency activity throughout the country or just within his own district, to raise and probe such matters seems to be the one common activity in which most parliaments engage.

Agency review activity can occur on the floor, best illustrated by the British question time. Those parliaments with a sizable committee structure tend to conduct the bulk of such activity through the committees. The individual members' activity on behalf of constituents is, however, a continuing and we think persistent means by which members raise questions about agencies and their conduct. Numerous parliaments have created specialized audit committees or staff offices, while in the United States several new ventures are being attempted to increase and regularize the review of administrative activity by congressional committees and members.

CONCLUSIONS

The relationship between the executive and legislative entities within a governmental system range from the broad issues of the very architectural structure of government to the detailed questions of a constituent's complaint about one action by one administrative agency. The same consideration, stated differently, is that the relationship be-

---

[72] Joseph Pois, "Trends in General Accounting Office Audits," pp. 245–277, and Ira Sharkansky, "The Politics of Auditing," pp. 278–318, both in Bruce L. R. Smith (ed.), *The New Political Economy: The Public Use of the Private Sector* (New York: Halsted Press, 1975).

tween the two entities pervades all other actions taken by the legislative body.

The two dominant ways in which democratic nations structure the relationship between executive and legislative entities, termed parliamentary and separation-of-powers systems, respectively, are midpoints on a continuum of relationships between the executive and legislative bodies. A good many nations give a preponderance of power and prerogative to executive officials, and even within democratic systems nations reserve to their chief executive extraordinary powers to act either in foreign policy or in domestic crisis. Referenda are another means by which parliaments are limited—and in ways that frequently work to the advantage of the executive branch.

Systems that form the government of the day from parliament ask of their legislative bodies a large and important task that is usually removed from congresses within presidential systems. How such cabinets are formed is mainly a function of the party system within each parliament. While most cabinets do comprise a majority, minority governments are by no means uncommon, as even the British are finding in the midst of their two-party system.

Legislation is at least one major activity of legislative bodies, but it is an activity in which executives are highly interested participants. In most countries the bulk of the legislative agenda is suggested by the executive, and usually most government bills are adopted—but not invariably. Even in parliamentary systems, parliament does defeat government legislation. In the U.S. Congress, the president ordinarily faces a difficult task in obtaining approval of most of his legislation, with the major circumstances being defined by the parties of the two branches, and by the size of the president's party within Congress.

The budget and administrative review are two additional matters on which executive and legislative entities interact. The U.S. Congress appears to be a most atypical body in that most parliaments approve executive budgets largely as submitted. Within the United States, appropriations and taxation have become major battlegrounds between the two branches and have led to major recent reforms through the creation of a new budget procedure and committee.

Administrative review, in various forms, would appear to be one of the basic or at least generic activities of legislators. This type of activity is found in all legislative bodies. How such activity is conducted, however, seems to vary by the committee structure of the parliament.

The relationship between the president and Congress in the United States has become more combative and hostile during the Johnson and Nixon administrations than it seemed to be previously. The congressional view that both presidents attempted to circumvent congressional preferences on Vietnam was only strengthened by Nixon's practices of impoundment, veto, and secrecy. The culmination of that struggle came with Nixon's resignation in the face of a most likely impeachment by the House and even conviction by the Senate. But Nixon's successors continue to pay the price of congressional reaction. The devices of congressional veto, the requirement of executive branch reporting to congress, the strengthening of committee supervision of agencies, and the reluctance of a policy Democratic Congress to accept President Carter's most important legislation on energy are all examples of how Congress has prepared itself to resist any president.

This chapter on the executive branch completes our examination of the major actors in a parliament's environment. The other major component of the external environment is the electorate, or constituency, represented by the members. These outside actors define the critical environment within which a parliament functions and define its major tasks.

We shall next turn to the parliament's internal organization to examine how a parliament organizes itself to accomplish its external tasks. We have not, however, been able to avoid discussing in these chapters both political parties and parliamentary committees. Parties and committees are important in parliaments because they are the major means by which a parliament organizes itself to cope with its external environment.

Chapter 5
Internal Organization: Political Parties in the Legislative Process

Parliaments are usually large institutions. Their memberships can reach up into the 400 to 700 range. In a formal and legal sense the members are all equal, for each has been elected by a specified set of voters in accordance with the election system of that particular society.[1] Yet most groups develop an internal division of labor, in which the various tasks to be performed by the collective group are subdivided into manageable portions and allocated among the membership. Persons within groups develop specialized patterns of activity, and in so doing they also create patterns of leadership and followership. That is, large groups develop positions of leadership and management within them. Legislative bodies are no exception. Political parties and committees are the two main means by which parliamentary bodies organize themselves internally to permit the parliament to perform its work—that is, to interact with its external environment.

[1] Appointed members could be either more or less equal than the elected members, but we do not know of any relevant study on this point.

TWO INTERNAL ORGANIZATIONAL STRUCTURES

The two main means of organizing the members and the work of legislative bodies are quite different. Indeed, they are essentially antithetical and opposite ways of organization. Ultimately the two forms of internal organization compete for power and influence; where one is strong and vigorous the other tends to be weak and ineffective.

Committee organization presupposes a division of labor by subject matter, whereas party organization presupposes a grouping of members by generalized preferences. These preferences—relating to who should occupy office if not also to policy outcomes—may take the form of factions in the absence of a party, as in some American state legislatures. But in most national parliaments the political party is the expression of organization on this generalized basis.

Most national parliaments are organized principally by party rather than by committee. The dominance of committees has been found only when the parties are either weakly organized or many in number so that no one party or coalition can strongly organize the cabinet. The American Congress illustrates the first condition; the French Assembly in the 1950s and the Swedish Riksdag in the 1920s illustrate the second.

Some parliaments do have effective and partially autonomous committee systems, even though they have majority cabinets and well organized parties. The German Bundestag since the 1950s and the Swedish Riksdag since the 1930s illustrate this circumstance. The efforts to strengthen the political parties in the U.S. Congress in the 1970s has moved that body toward this category as well.

Parties tend to be centralizing in effect; committees, decentralizing. That is, parties are usually fewer in number than are committees. The fewer parties tend to be larger in size and thus more diverse in their membership than are committees. Parties potentially deal with the whole range of governmental issues; committees usually handle a more limited range. As a result, parties tend to bring parliamentary members (and voters) together to find common ways of working together in spite of their differences and to merge members into a few number of groups. Committees, by contrast, tending to be organized on the basis of limited jurisdiction, tend to split the parliamentary membership into numerous groups. The different tendencies of party and committee as organizing devices within parliamentary bodies are charted in Table 5.1.

The political party is the more important of the two internal organizational methods. That is, what committees are and what they might become is a result of what parties are and what they become. In effect, committees have the scope and importance that parties and party leaders permit them to have. In parliamentary systems, commit-

Table 5.1 INTERNAL ORGANIZATION OF
PARLIAMENTS: PARTY VS. COMMITTEE

CRITERION	PARTY	COMMITTEE
Number	Few	Many
Size	Large	Small
Jurisdiction	Broad	Narrow
Member diversity	Broad	Narrow
Organizational consequence	Centralizing	Decentralizing

tees become what the government of the day permits. We shall look at parties in this chapter and at committees in the next.

CABINET FORMATION

The first task of a party is to form the government. In parliamentary systems the government of the day is selected through the parties in parliament, whereas in presidential systems that task usually is removed from the congressional party.

Joining the Cabinet

The major decision of parties within parliamentary systems is whether to enter the government or to go into opposition. As indicated in the preceding chapter, the difficulty and complexity of this decision are much greater in a multiparty system than in a two-party or single-party system. In multiparty parliaments each party has to decide whether or not it wishes to be associated with the other potential coalition partners. Part of their considerations concern which offices shall be allocated to which parties. Presumably, the most "important" offices will be allocated to the largest parties in the coalition—such as the foreign, defense, and economic ministries and perhaps also justice and the treasury. The complexity of these decisions is indicated by the Dutch experience after their 1976 elections: more than seven months were required to form a five-party coalition out of the 11 parties represented in parliament.

The 1977 Israeli election further illustrates the potential difficulties of forming a government in a multiparty system. The largest of the previously opposition parties—the Likud—became the largest party in parliament (though short of a majority) and hence was expected to be the dominant partner in a coalition government. Its leader and prospective prime minister, Menachem Begin, personally offered the foreign ministry to Moshe Dayan, the leader of a faction within the previously governing Labor party. That personal offer, though accepted, was something less than universally applauded. In the first place, Dayan was immediately called a "traitor" by his own party, whereupon he resigned from that party, though he retained his parliamentary seat. In the second place, one of the other potential coalition parties was highly offended by the offer to Dayan, claiming that it had not been consulted and that the decision of which party receives which office is to be decided through interparty negotiation. Finally, the Likud party threatened to split over the Dayan offer. Likud itself (the name means "unity") is a "bloc" of several parties and thus had its own internal problems. Its several leaders claimed that their dominant leader had the responsibility of first consulting with them, rather than acting independently. The Likud bloc had not faced these problems for the 20 years it had been in the opposition; governance subjects a party to more stresses and strains than does opposition.

The 1976 Swedish election provides another example of opposition parties forming a governing coalition. Compared to Israel, the Swedish circumstances were much simpler. In the first place, Sweden had five parties in parliament; Israel, 11. In the second place, the governing coalition had three parties; the Israeli, five. In the third place, the three Swedish parties had negotiated with each other over the previous ten years to arrive at a common understanding of policy. As a result they campaigned together in the election, pledging to form the new government if together they obtained a majority of the seats.

The government also changed, and dramatically so, in the Indian election of 1977. The Congress party, the major independence organization, had governed India, ever since it won independence, under the leadership of Nehru and later of his daughter, Mrs. Indira Gandhi. She had in 1975 imposed martial law and press censorship and had jailed many of the leaders of opposition parties and of opposition factions within her own party. While India had many parties, the Congress party was by far the largest, and had won two-thirds of the parliamentary seats in the preceding 1971 election. When Mrs. Gandhi suddenly and unexpectedly called for parliamentary elections, the opposition leaders immediately formed a single party, the Janata— People's—party, an amalgamation of four previously separate and antagonistic parties. Their common front was later joined by former Congress party members, called the Congress for Democracy. The newly united parties won an impressive victory but then were faced with immediate disunity over the question of who of the leaders from which of the parties would become the new prime minister. After several days of tense negotiation, the parties agreed to permit two elder and respected statesmen to decide among the two leading contenders. Their choice was not accepted without further recrimination, but that choice did lead to a multiparty cabinet in which the electoral partners consented to serve.[2]

[2] *Facts on File* (January 22, 1977), p. 45.

Selection of Party Nominee

Interparty negotiation presupposes that parties have an internal structure of decision making and that it has created some kind of a governing committee empowered to at least talk with similarly constituted committees of other parties. If a party expects, or hopes, to be the party to name the prime minister, then it must designate the person as its leader and hence nominee. In general terms, there are two ways for a party's nominee for prime minister to be selected: first, within and by the parliamentary party; and second, by party units located outside of parliament.

INTERNAL SELECTION

The British and Swedish parties illustrate the first, or parliamentary party, method. That is, all members of parliament of a given party select their leader. A new prime minister may be selected in between elections, especially if a majority party has formed the cabinet. When an incumbent prime minister resigns, the majority party can select a new prime minister without calling new elections. When Harold Wilson resigned the British prime ministership, for example, in 1977, the Labour party elected a new leader, James Callaghan, who then became the new prime minister (see Table 5.5). Similarly, the Christian Democrats in West Germany continued in power by replacing the resigned Adenauer with Erhardt as chancellor, as the Socialist party replaced the resigned Brandt with Schmitt as chancellor.

EXTERNAL SELECTION

The second, or extraparliamentary party, method of selecting the prime minister nominee is in turn found in two varieties. In the first, the party holds a convention; in the second the party decision is more confined to a small governing elite. The convention method is illustrated by Canada, Israel, and India. The party conventions of these countries resemble the American presidential convention system. The parties select delegates from around the nation, the convention adopts a platform and, most importantly, votes upon the candidate who will lead the party's election campaign as the nominee for prime minister. In some cases, such as the renomination of the incumbent Mrs. Gandhi by the Congress party in India in 1977, the nomination is a foregone conclusion. But in other cases, the choice is narrowly contested until the final vote on the convention floor. The Israeli Labor party, for example, almost replaced the incumbent prime minister, Y. Rabin, in its 1977 convention, by a vote of 1445 to 1404.

The closed elite method of selecting party nominees for governing positions is illustrated by the Soviet Union. While the premier is officially selected by the Supreme Soviet, that act ratifies prior decisions taken within the highest councils of the Communist party. For example, the resignation in 1964 of Khrushchev from his multiple posts, including premier, was announced to and accepted by the party's Central Committee. He first resigned as first secretary of the Communist party, as a member of its Presidium, and also as chairman (premier) of the governmental Council of Ministers. The following day, the Presidium of the Supreme Soviet also met, and accepted his resignation as premier. His resignation, and replacement as premier by Kosygin, was unanimously accepted at the next regularly scheduled meeting of the Supreme Soviet.[3]

In both varieties of the extraparliamentary party selection method, the decision of which party enters and forms the government is made, in the first instance, by the result of the parliamentary election. Furthermore, the resulting government must be acceptable to a majority of the parliament. Nevertheless, the decision of which person shall lead the party in parliament is made by the party outside of parliament. The national convention method is an effort to at least broaden, if not to "democratize," the leadership decision from the confines of parliament itself to some wider and perhaps more representative and diverse party forum.

SELECTION BY HEAD OF STATE

There is a third major method of selecting a prospective prime minister —by the head of state. In a formal sense, the crown or the ceremonial president has the responsibility in most parliamentary countries to officially request a member of parliament to attempt to form the government. In most countries that request is made to the leader of the largest, whether majority or plurality, party.

But until the 1960s, the Conservative party prime minister was selected by the British crown. That party did not adopt an internal leadership election method until the selection of Edward Heath in 1965. Prior to then, when the Conservatives won a majority, the crown exercised a personal choice among the leading contenders. The crown consulted with advisers from within the party, as illustrated by these remarks by a retiring prime minister, Harold MacMillan, about his efforts to select his preferred replacement:

> I proposed that Ministers outside the Cabinet and Under-Secretaries; regular Conservative supporters in the House of Lords; and all Conservative Members of the House of Commons should be consulted.

These wide consultations within the Conservative party were themselves an innovation, a deliberate effort by MacMillan to broaden the

---

[3] L. G. Churchward, *Contemporary Soviet Government* (New York: Elsevier, 1968), pp. 137–138.

previous practice which he thought "too restricted." A few days later, after the consultations had occurred, the queen met with MacMillan:[4]

> She then asked for my advice as to what she should do . . . and said that she did not need and did not intend to seek any other advice but mine. . . . She agreed that Lord Hume (who did become the next Prime Minister) was the most likely choice to get general support, as well as really the best and strongest character.

Selection of the President by Congress?

We earlier said that selection of the chief executive is not a task of the congressional parties in presidential systems, but this statement needs qualification. For, as we indicated in the previous chapter, the Chilean congress regularly selected their president because, in a multiparty system, seldom could any candidate obtain a majority of the popular vote.

In the United States we have come very close to having a deadlock in the electoral college—which does require a majority of those votes—and thus of having the presidential selection made in the House of Representatives. In the 1968 election, with George Wallace the candidate of a sizable third party vote, that possibility was a very real one. In at least some House campaigns, candidates pledged themselves in the general election to cast their vote for president, should that circumstance arise in the House, for the candidate who obtained the most votes in their particular district. Most of these instances were in the South, and thus the House candidates (especially Democrats) were pledging themselves to vote against the official nominee of their own party. Had these possibilities developed, we might have seen the beginning of a multiparty system in American politics.

CHAMBER OFFICERS

Every parliament has a set of officers who officially conduct its affairs. Every parliament has a presiding officer, termed *Speaker* in the British-derived parliaments and termed *President* in the French-derived parliaments. Many parliaments have a governing or at least advisory council representing the parties within them. In addition, a set of officers is designated to keep order (sergeants at arms) and to manage the large volume of paper work (clerks). In this section we shall be concerned mainly with the political and decision-making offices of the presiding officer and of the advisory councils rather than with the more routine and supportive offices of sergeant at arms and clerk. We shall also discuss the Rules Committee in the U.S. House of Representatives,

[4] Harold MacMillan, *At the End of the Day, 1961–1963* (New York: Harper & Row, 1973), pp. 509, 515.

for it has played a major role in the development of the powers of the House Speaker and hence of the majority party.

The British Speaker

The United States and Great Britain strongly contrast in their speakership. Ours, of course, derives from theirs. Both are selected by their parties, but their relationship to their party and hence to the chamber is very different. In the British House of Commons, the Speaker is nominated by the majority party, with the agreement of the opposition party. He has not, however, been an active partisan in the House, and has rarely served in either the cabinet or the shadow cabinet. Once elected, he becomes nonpartisan. He resigns from his party and the other party rarely runs a candidate against him in this district. When the previous minority becomes the new majority, the Speaker continues to serve. In effect, he has a lifetime tenure in the office.[5]

The British Speaker is more challenged by floor proceedings than is his American counterpart. More of the important legislative activity occurs while the Speaker is presiding in the British Commons than in the U.S. House (refer to Chapter 7). In addition, British M.P.s are more boisterous and interrupt one another more than do American congressmen. Not infrequently the ingenuity, if not also the rectitude, of the Speaker is challenged by direct appeals from the benches as illustrated in the debate on the motion of no confidence in the House of Commons in March 1977 (Fig. 5.1).

The U.S. Speaker

In the U.S. House of Representatives, by contrast, each party nominates its leader for speaker. In a parliamentary system the party leaders would become the prime minister; in a presidential system the party leaders become Speaker. While the U.S. Speaker has responsibilities toward the House as a whole, and particularly toward the minority, he remains the active leader of his party in the House. He becomes one of the most important officeholders of his party nationally and is active on legislation in the president's program. Furthermore, he remains Speaker only as long as his party remains the majority. Should the other party obtain the majority, that party would nominate its floor leader as Speaker, who then would be elected on a party-line vote. The previous speaker would step down, becoming the floor leader of the new minority party. The Democrats' Sam Rayburn and the Republicans' Joe Martin exchanged places in this fashion when the Republicans won the majority in the House elections of 1946 and 1952.

[5] Ivor Jennings, *Parliament,* 2d ed. (New York: Cambridge, 1975), pp. 63–71.

1305 *Her Majesty's Government*   23 MARCH 1977   *(Opposition Motion)*   1306

[The Prime Minister.]
mind my saying that at no time in our discussions did any questions of this sort come up and that the hon. Gentleman and myself would have regarded it as insulting if we had endeavoured to bargain on that basis.

Mr. James Molyneaux (Antrim, South): I am grateful to the Prime Minister for giving me this opportunity for denying that any such point was raised at any time. I think that we would both view any such report with contempt. May I also say in fairness to the Prime Minister that all our discussions were conducted on the basis that there could be no concession or sacrifice of interest on the part of either of us?

The Prime Minister : I was saying that my right hon. Friend the Lord President and I had discussions with the Leader of the Liberal Party and with the hon. Member for Cornwall, North (Mr. Pardoe). It is our view that there is a sufficient identity of interest between us at present to establish some machinery that will enable us to consult each other about future developments in this Parliament—[Hon. Members: "Oh."] We therefore—[An Hon. Member: "Sing it again."]

Mr. William Molloy (Ealing, North): Chuck him out.

Mr. Speaker : Order. The House knows that I cannot see behind me, but I can hear. I hope that whoever has been shouting at my left ear will stop doing it and go away.

The Prime Minister : You have no idea how much you have relieved my mind Mr. Speaker. I thought that it was you shouting at me.

We have therefore agreed to establish some machinery to keep our positions under review and we intend to try an experiment that will last until the end of the present parliamentary Session, when both the Liberal Party and ourselves can consider whether it has been of sufficient benefit to the country to be continued - - [*Interruption.*] I am very happy to see the Opposition applaud this new-found stability in Parliament. It will give this Administration the stability it needs to carry on with the task of regenerating British industry and of securing our programme.

16 N 2

We therefore intend to set up a joint consultative committee under the chairmanship of my right hon. Friend the Leader of the House. This committee will examine policy and other issues that arise before they come to the House, and of course, we shall examine the Liberal Party's proposals. [*Interruption.*] I think that Conservative Members should listen to this, because their fate may depend upon it.

The existence of this committee will not commit the Government to accepting the views of the Liberal Party, nor the Liberal Party to supporting the Government on any issue. There will, however, be regular meetings between Ministers and spokesmen of the Liberal Party including meetings, for example—which have already begun—between the Chancellor of the Exchequer and the Liberal Party's economic spokesman.

Mr. Cranley Onslow (Woking): On a point of order, Mr. Speaker. Is it not a well-established practice that Budget proposals are not divulged to anybody in advance? May we be assured that that practice will not be set aside in this relationship between the Government and the Liberal Party?

Mr. Speaker : That is not a point of order. I suggest to the House that we shall not know more unless we listen.

Mr. Kenneth Lewis (Rutland and Stamford): On a point of order, Mr. Speaker. In view of what the Prime Minister has just said, may we take it that the next Liberal Party spokesman will be speaking from the other side of the House?

Mr. Speaker : Order.

Mr. Kenneth Lewis *rose——*

Mr. Speaker : Order.

Mr Kenneth Lewis *rose——*

Mr. Speaker : Order. I warn the hon. Gentleman that he has been extremely discourteous to me. I warn hon. Members that unless they resume their seats when I stand up and call for order, I shall order them out of the Chamber. I know the importance of the vote tonight to both sides, but the House must treat its Speaker with courtesy.

Mr. Timothy Raison (Aylesbury): Will the Prime Minister give way?

Figure 5.1   The Speaker in the British House of Commons. (Source: United Kingdom, House of Commons, *Parliamentary Debates (Hansard)*, March 23, 1977, cols. 1305–1306.

The powers of the Speaker of the U.S. House of Representatives have varied through the years. Their powers were at their height in the 1890–1912 period under "czars" Cannon and Reed. Their powers essentially joined their leadership of the majority party with those of the presiding officer. They appointed, through the Rules Committee, all committee members and chairmen; they controlled the flow of legislation to the floor by controlling the Rules Committee; and they controlled the opportunities for debate and amendments by the minority on the floor by their exercise of the powers of the chair. Some of the epic struggles within the House have concerned the growth of and limitations on these powers of the Speaker over the members of the House.

The solutions adopted in the U.S. House in the 1910–1912 period to the powerful speakership broke the power of both the Speaker and the majority party. The House Rules Committee retained its considerable powers (see Chapter 7) intact, although it did lose its power to make committee assignments. Furthermore, the Speaker was removed from the Rules Committee and ultimately lost his control over it. As a result, the standing committees retained and even increased their powers over legislation (see Chapter 6). The Speaker lost control over them; his power to name both members and chairmen was lost to the "seniority" rule. Both of these "progressive" and "democratic" reforms of the 1910–1912 era became the very targets of reforms in the 1960s and 1970s.[6]

By the mid-1970s the powers of both the Speaker and majority party had increased somewhat. The Speaker's powers were most directly increased by the Democratic party's new provision that all Democratic members of the House Rules Committee were to be nominated directly by him. No longer would southern Democrats be able to forge an alliance on that committee with Republicans to block Democratic legislation. The second change provided that Democratic seats on the House legislative committees would be filled by nominations by a representative party committee, in which the Democratic Speaker could exercise considerable influence, if not control. Finally, although the position of Democratic chairmen of committees is filled through nominations made by the party's Steering and Policy Committee, that body normally follows seniority. Although such nominations are subject to a direct caucus vote, again the result normally follows seniority. (The latter two changes, which directly concern committees, will be discussed more fully in the next chapter).

All three changes have been instituted mainly by northern Democrats to limit the power of the more conservative but minority southern

---

[6] Randall B. Ripley, *Party Leaders in the House of Representatives* (Washington, D.C.: Brookings, 1967), pp. 12–22.

Democrats who, in combination with Republicans, could stymie the legislative program of Democratic presidents and thwart the legislative goals of the more moderate and liberal Democrats in the House. That is, these changes have largely resulted from the intra–Democratic party factionalism.

We would guess that speakers in most state legislatures exercise the same controls over their committees and floor deliberations as did the former "czars" of the U.S. House. Ordinarily, state legislative speakers create committees, appoint their members and their chairmen, refer bills to committees as they see fit, and control the flow of bills to the floor.

Speakers in state legislatures are—as in all parliaments—officially chosen by an election among the members. Yet the dynamics behind this vote varies among the states. In some (e.g., Connecticut) the speaker is chosen on a party vote, as in the U.S. House. In others (e.g., Arizona) he is selected by cross-party factional alliances. In still others (e.g., Texas) the speaker is selected by factional voting within the single, or least dominant, party. In still other instances (e.g., Alabama) the speaker essentially has been selected by the governor. Unfortunately, we have few studies of the state speakerships; we do not know in any systematic or comprehensive way about their powers or their selection.

The American state legislatures vary widely in the tenure and selection of their presiding officers. The most common pattern is that presiding officers serve from one to five terms (23 lower houses; 20 upper houses). In another set of states, the invariable practice, at least since the end of World War II, has been service of one or two terms, having in effect a rotation system into but also out of office (14 lower houses and 14 senates). At the other extreme, presiding officers have served six or more terms (six lower houses; eight senates). One result of the usual practice of short, if not limited, terms is that in few states are incumbent presiding officers either challenged or defeated.[7]

The Senates

The American national and state senates present yet another set of varying circumstances. Their presiding officer (vice president, lieutenant governor) is directly elected and is not selected by the senate from among its own membership. This officer is externally selected.

[7] Eugene R. Declercq, "Inter-House Differences in American State Legislatures," *Journal of Politics* 39 (August 1977), pp. 774–785; Malcolm E. Jewell and Samuel C. Patterson, *The Legislative Process in the United States*, 3d ed. (New York: Random House, 1977), pp. 135–141.

About half the states follow the U.S. Senate in excluding that officer from a direct leadership role. The U.S. Senate elects a president pro tem, who is the senior member of the majority party. Although the vice president has been Republican for 16 years during the 1948–1976 period, for 14 of those years the Senate's majority has been Democratic. But it is the majority leader (now Robert Byrd, W.Va.) who sets the legislative schedule and manages the affairs of the Senate, whereas the vice president's powers in the Senate are limited and his duties are almost perfunctory.

Even in the U.S. Senate, however, the vice president has an occasionally important task. He can break a tie vote. During the Nixon administration, Vice President Agnew twice cast such votes. In the Carter administration's first year, Vice President Mondale cast one tie-breaking vote, supporting the Administration's position against a Republican amendment on the social security bill. Mondale's vote was the 216th recorded vote cast by vice presidents since the first year of the first Congress.[8]

The vice president, as presiding officer of the Senate, also can issue rulings from the chair and recognize members to speak. Mondale demonstrated the latent importance of these actions during the filibuster on the 1977 natural gas bill, a vital portion of the Carter administration's energy package. This episode will be explored at greater length in Chapter 7, on floor proceedings, but we may note here that the filibuster was broken only because the vice president exercised his powers as presiding officer. He issued the parliamentary rulings sought by the majority leader (they were of the same party and both supported the Carter administration), and proceeded to recognize only the majority leader, ignoring the many opponents also seeking recognition on the floor (refer to Figure 7.6).

In about half the states (again, we do not know exactly how many), the lieutenant governor, though externally elected, is the real leader of the senate. He forges an alliance with a majority, and with their support he manages the internal affairs of the state senate in the same way the speaker does in the state's lower chamber; that is, he appoints committee members and chairmen after having created the committees in the first place, and through them controls the fate of legislation. In one such senate, a senator opposed to the lieutenant governor offered this assessment:

> I would say that the committee chairmen are appointed by the Lieutenant Governor for one purpose—that is to think like the Lieutenant Governor.

[8] *Congressional Quarterly Weekly Report,* November 12, 1977, pp. 2408–2409.

A supporting senator of the same lieutenant governor was more explicit, in his discussion of a bill opposed by the lieutenant governor, which did not get a hearing in committee and was not reported to the floor:

> Well, there was not any point in hearing it. . . . Of course, the chairman gets his orders. If the Lieutenant Governor has said, " I want it out (of committee)," then it would have come out.

The same senator went on to say, "I have been here under several Lieutenant Governors, and they were all the same."

Multiparty Parliaments

In multiparty parliaments the office of speaker is filled by agreement among the parties in the governing coalition. In addition to the one office of speaker, at least some parliaments have a number of assistant speakers who are also selected by interparty agreement. In some instances each party places one of its members in the assistant speaker office, although the Communist party has usually been excluded from this office in Western European parliaments. One measure of the success of the Italian Communist party in the 1970s was that it sought, and was awarded, the speakership as part of its price for its tacit agreement to support the government of the Christian Democrats.

Evolution

The office of the speaker, like the institution of parliament, has had a long period of evolution. One of the most critical stages in its development involved determining to whom the office was responsible —to the crown or to the parliament itself. Upon that definition rode the larger question of the independence of parliament from the crown. In the seventeenth and eighteenth centuries, dramatic conflicts arose in Britain between the crown and Parliament. In one celebrated instance, the king and his troops stormed into a meeting of Parliament, intending to arrest several members who had opposed him. The king demanded to know whether the several members were present. After a period of silence from the members, the Speaker replied:[9]

> May it please your majesty, I have neither eyes to see nor tongue to speak in this place, but as the House doth direct me, whose servant I am.

Out of such experience arose the practice of the House of Commons giving formal permission before an emissary of the crown can even

[9] As quoted in Sydney D. Bailey, *British Parliamentary Democracy,* 3d ed. (Boston: Houghton Mifflin, 1971), p. 62.

be admitted into the chamber. Our previous mention of the selection of some state legislative speakers by the governor is an illustration of the larger question of how the relationships between a legislative body and the chief executive develop in practice.

The British House developed, and the American House has continued, another practice out of the same conflict: the Committee of the Whole House. When the British Speaker was under suspicion as a spokesman for the king, and as one who reported to the king what happened in parliament, the Committee of the Whole House was invented to exclude the Speaker. A committee is not the parliament; it is unofficial and informal. It can make no official decisions. Since it is not the parliament, the speaker does not preside. Rather, committees are usually chaired by chairmen. To this day, when either House proceeds by Committee of the Whole House, the Speaker steps down, and his place is taken by a presiding officer addressed as "Mr. Chairman," rather than as "Mr. Speaker." In the American House the chairmen for this proceeding are appointed from the majority party by the Speaker, whereas in the British House the chairmen are appointed from both parties by the Speaker. That British practice is made possible by the nonpartisan role of the Chair, whether occupied by either Speaker or Chairman.[10]

The speakership in Sweden has recently added an additional function. In addition to the usual duties of presiding at plenary sessions, the Speaker has been substituted for the Crown in the selection of new governments of the day. When the Prime Minister and his three-party coalition resigned in 1978, for example, the Speaker, not the King, conducted talks among the several party leaders. The Speaker, not the King, proposed the new prime ministerial candidate, who was then accepted by the Riksdag as a whole.

The House Rules Committee

The powers of the Speaker of the U.S. House of Representatives intertwine with those of the Rules Committee. That Committee occupies —or at least has occupied—a unique place in the management of legislative activity. It straddles the flow of legislation from the substantive legislative committees (discussed in the following chapter) to the floor. This committee, in effect, defines the rules under which each bill will be brought to and considered on the floor of the House. If it does not act to recommend a set of rules for a given bill, that bill ordinarily would be blocked from floor action. Thus the committee wields a potential veto over most legislation.

That potential was exercised selectively but effectively by an

[10] Ivor Jennings, *Parliament*, pp. 71–73.

alliance of Republicans and southern Democrats from the mid–New Deal to the Kennedy administration. The majority party named ten members; the minority, five. When Republicans were in the majority, they and their Speaker were clearly in control of the committee's decisions. When Democrats were in the majority, however, three southern Democrats often could, and did, vote with the five Republicans to effectively block the bills supported by a majority of the House Democrats and by the Democratic Speaker. When a Democrat was president, his bills suffered the same fate. Under the prevailing practices of the House, the Democratic Speaker was powerless to remove the deviating members from that committee. As we noted above, the power of the Speaker over this critical management committee was removed during the reforms of the 1910–1912 period. Those changes were in the name of liberal reform and of increased democratization; precisely the same goals were being thwarted by the way in which the reforms had come to work in practice.

Throughout this chapter and the next we shall detail a long period of party reform in the 1960s and 1970s, which has had the effect of increasing the power of the party majority over deviating members —especially the power of the party's northern and propresidential wing over the southern contingent. That reform began with efforts to change the Rules Committee.

The first and major move was made in the first months of the Kennedy administration in early 1961. Kennedy's supporters feared that his legislation would be blocked by the then-existing Rules Committee, the chairman of which, Representative Howard Smith (D-Va.), was also leader of the conservative coalition. Of the variety of proposals considered to limit the Rules Committee, the then-Speaker, Sam Rayburn (D-Tex.), chose the least ambitious: the Rules Committee would be enlarged by an additional five members, divided three for Democrats and two for Republicans. That move would permit the Speaker to appoint three loyalist Democrats which would give the Democratic leadership a slim (and also fragile) one-vote majority on the committee. This modest change became the focal point for intensive lobbying by the administration and its opponents. It was adopted by a slender five-vote margin in a dramatic and tense floor vote.[11]

In retrospect, this slight dent in the power of the conservative coalition had a major consequence. Not only did Kennedy legislation

[11] Robert L. Peabody, "The Enlarged Rules Committee," pp. 129–164, and Milton C. Cummings and Robert L. Peabody, "The Decision to Enlarge the Committee on Rules: An Analysis of the 1961 Vote," pp. 167–194, both in Robert L. Peabody and Nelson W. Polsby (eds.), *New Perspectives on the House of Representatives* (Chicago: Rand McNally, 1963).

flow to the floor (with the dramatic exception of aid to education), but this move became the first in a series of internal party reforms that have had the effect of strengthening the party and also the powers of the Speaker. The Rules Committee became, as of the early 1970s, a loyal arm of the Speaker's leadership.

A number of foreign parliaments have various types of steering or executive committees, which appear to have analogous tasks as the U.S. House Rules Committee. Parliaments of Communist party states, for example, usually have a "presidium," while the German Bundestag has a Council of Elders. Although the German Council appears mainly to be a forum within which party leaders agree on agendas and on the party division of chamber offices, the Presidium of the Supreme Soviet also functions year round in place of the Supreme Soviet, which meets infrequently.[12]

INTERNAL PARTY ORGANIZATION

The third major task of a parliamentary party is to organize itself. We have made many references in preceding sections about party leaders and intraparty factions. The management of the members of a party is every bit as complicated as is the management of parliament as a whole.

Party Leaders

In the U.S. House, each party has the offices of floor leader and whip. The majority, in addition, fills the speakership.

ACTIVITIES

The floor leader is responsible for the scheduling of floor activity. Every Thursday in the House, the minority leader will ask of his majority counterpart if he could inform the House of the likely schedule for the coming week (Fig. 5.2). The majority leader then formally announces the major bills he expects to bring to the floor and how time will be allocated. A similar practice is used in the British House of Commons (Fig. 5.3).

Scheduling is no minor or routine task. The floor leaders follow developments in the committee and attempt to sequence their activities to produce a steady flow of bills to the floor. They need also to antici-

[12] Gerhard Loewenberg, *Parliament in the German Political System* (Ithaca: Cornell University Press, 1967), pp. 202–206; D. Richard Little, "Legislative Authority in the Soviet Political System," *Slavic Review* 30 (March 1971), pp. 57–73.

LEGISLATIVE PROGRAM

(Mr. MICHEL asked and was given permission to address the House for 1 minute and to revise and extend his remarks.)

Mr. MICHEL. Mr. Speaker, I take this time for the purpose of inquiring of the distinguished majority whip, the gentleman from Indiana (Mr. BRADEMAS), as to the program for next week.

Mr. BRADEMAS. Mr. Speaker, will my distinguished colleague, the minority whip, yield?

Mr. MICHEL. I will be happy to yield to the gentleman.

Mr. BRADEMAS. I thank the gentleman for yielding.

The program for the House of Representatives for the week of May 15, 1978, is a follows:

On Monday, the House meets at noon for the Consent Calendar and one bill under suspension, which is:

H.R. 11209, maritime satellite telecommunications services, followed by H.R. 12222, to complete consideration of the International Development and Food Assistance Act of 1978.

Then there is a conference report on Senate Concurrent Resolution 80, the budget for the U. S. Government for fiscal year 1979.

Then there is H.R. 12641, temporary debt limit increase, under a modified open rule, with 1 hour of debate.

On Tuesday, the House meets at noon for the Private Calendar and seven bills which will be considered under suspension. Votes on suspensions will be postponed until the end of all suspensions. We will consider:

H.R. 4030, holdings of private foundations in public utilities;

H.R. 5551, duty suspension on 2-methyl, 4-chlorophenol;

H.R. 11005, international trade commission authorization;

H.R. 1337, Constructive sale price for excise tax on trucks, buses, and so forth;

S. 2093, Exchange Stabilization Fund provisions; and

H.R. 12467, Rehabiliation Act amendments.

H.R. 12255, Older Americans Act amendments.

Following these suspensions, we shall consider H.R. 10392, to establish a Hubert H. Humphrey Fellowship at Woodrow Wilson Center, under an open rule, with 1 hour of debate.

We then have a conference report on H.R. 9005, District of Columbia appropriations, fiscal year 1978, and H.R. 11686, the Department of Energy National Security authorizations, fiscal year 1979, under an open rule, with 1 hour of debate.

On Wednesday, the House will meet at 10 o'clock in the morning on H.R. 39, the Alaska National Interest Lands Conservation Act, subject to a rule being granted.

On Thursday, the House will meet at 10 o'clock a.m. to consider H.R. 10929, Department of Defense Authorization Act, fiscal year 1979, subject to a rule being granted, and H.R. 7814, flexible and compressed work schedules for Federal employees, under an open ru e, with 1 hour of debate.

On Friday, the House will meet at 10 o'clock a.m. to consider the following bills: H.R. 8099, Water Rights for Ak-Chin Indians, subject to a rule being granted.

H.R. 10729, Commerce Department authorizations, fiscal year 1979, subject to a rule being granted; and

H.R. 11291, Fire Prevention and Control Act, under an open rule, with 1 hour of debate.

The House will adjourn by 3 p.m. on Fridays and by 5:30 p.m. on all other days except Wednesday. Conference reports may be brought up at any time, and any further program will be announced later.

Mr. Speaker, might I ask the distinguished gentleman a question with respect to Wednesday? The bill, H.R. 39, is highly controversial. I understand the Committee on Rules probably will not meet until Tuesday. In the event there is no rule on that piece of legislation, and that is the only one scheduled for that day, is there any conjecture on what might take its place.

Mr. BRADEMAS. Mr. Speaker, if the gentleman will yield further, I would not want to speak with complete authority on that. Other legislation is available and will be rescheduled and announced to the Members in the event the Alaska bill does not come up.

Mr. MICHEL. Now once we have passed May 15 and the 3 o'clock p.m. convening time for Wednesdays is over, I note we will be coming in at 10 o'clock a.m. on Wednesdays, Thursdays, and Fridays. Does that suggest there would be some limitation on when we would adjourn on Wednesdays, so far as time is concerned?

Mr. BRADEMAS. Mr. Speaker, if the gentleman will yield further, a reasonable hour is the answer to the question. Did the gentleman ask about a reasonable adjournment on Wednesday?

Mr. MICHEL. Is it 6 p.m. on Wednesday or does it run to midnight?

Mr. BRADEMAS. I think the gentleman would want to be reasonable with respect to assigning what is a reasonable hour.

Figure 5.2   The schedule for next week: U.S. House of Representatives. (Source: U.S. Congress, *Congressional Record,* May 12, 1978, pp. H3858–H3859.)

BUSINESS OF THE HOUSE

Mrs. Thatcher: May I ask the Lord President to state the business for next week?

The Lord President of the Council, and Leader of the House of Commons (Mr. Michael Foot): The business for next week will be as follows:

MONDAY 28TH MARCH—Conclusion of the debate on the Statement on the Defence Estimates.

Remaining stages of the General Rate (Public Utilities) Bill [*Lords*], and of the Marriage (Scotland) Bill [*Lords*].

Motion on EEC Documents Com.(76)660, S/102/77, R/616/77, S/232/77 and R/388/77 on fishery resources.

TUESDAY, 29TH MARCH—My right hon. Friend the Chancellor of the Exchequer will open his Budget.

EEC Documents R/566/77 and R/567/77 on economic policy guidelines will be relevant.

At 7 o'clock the Chairman of Ways and Means has named opposed Private Business for consideration.

Proceedings on the Agricultural Holdings (Notices to Quit) Bill [*Lords*], and on the British Airways Board Bill [*Lords*], which are consolidation measures.

WEDNESDAY, 30TH MARCH and THURSDAY, 31ST MARCH—Continuation of the Budget debate.

At the end on Wednesday, debate on the Chairman of Ways and Means' ruling of 10th February.

FRIDAY, 1ST APRIL—Private Members' motions.

MONDAY, 4TH APRIL—Conclusion of the Debate on the Budget Statement.

Mrs. Thatcher: Will the Leader of the House tell us when the White Paper on direct elections will be published? As he knows, there is a debate on this subject tomorrow, and it would be helpful if we could have it by then. Is the White Paper already in print, and will it come through unchanged?

Mr. Foot: I am glad to assure the right hon. Lady on the second point—no alterations are required to the White Paper. It will be published next week, and I am sorry that it cannot be published in time for tomorrow's debate.

. . .

Mr. Brocklebank-Fowler: Has the Lord President noted the continued progress of Early-Day Motion No. 222 which stands in my name and which has now received the support of 335 right hon. and hon. Gentlemen in all parts of the House? In those circumstances, noting the considerable support for a debate on the establishment of a Select Committee for Foreign Affairs, will the right hon. Gentleman now reverse his decision of a few weeks ago and give the House an early opportunity to debate this subject?

[*That this House, dissatisfied with the infrequency and nature of debates on Foreign Affairs, urges the Government to set up a Standing Foreign Affairs Select Committee whose Reports should be debated in the House within 30 days of publication.*]

Mr. Foot: I cannot promise a debate in the near future, because up to Easter the time of the House is pretty full. I cannot see any chance before Easter of having such a debate. I cannot promise that it will be debated at an early stage afterwards because we have some important business at that time, too. However, I do not rule out such a debate altogether. This proposal has been put forward on a number of occasions over many years. The Opposition might wish to raise the subject at some time. However, I know that they also would have some difficulty in fitting in this matter before Easter.

Figure 5.3 The schedule for next week: British House of Commons. (Source: United Kingdom, House of Commons, *Parliamentary Debates (Hansard),* March 24, 1977, cols. 1463–1470.)

pate likely developments on the floor and to be aware of prospective time-consuming amendments.

The whip, or assistant leader, handles communications between the party leadership and the members. The whip is particularly responsible for the attendance of members on the floor to vote. His staff checks on the attendance plans of members and arranges "pairs" for absent members. In the U.S. House, the whip, on major bills, takes a "whip check" by polling the members on how they intend to vote. Members who may not vote in the desired manner, but may also be open to persuasion, may be talked to by the speaker, by other congressmen, or perhaps by the White House staff or interest group lobbyists.[13]

In the British House of Commons, the whip's office, like the American derivative, sends a weekly "whip notice" to party members, a schedule of forthcoming bills and votes. The British whip notice, unlike the American (Fig. 5.4) is underlined to indicate the increasing degree of importance attached to a vote by the party leadership. A "three-line whip" designates that the vote is deemed by the party leadership as of highest importance; in their parlance, "the whips are on." In a later section, we shall examine the voting records of members on such major issues.

In the U.S. Senate, each party has a leader and an assistant leader. The majority leader combines the leadership functions, which, in the House, are split between the Speaker and floor leader, although he does not preside over floor sessions. The assistant-leader position is much less defined as a formal whip than in the House. The task of polling members on coming votes is more informally and voluntarily assumed by individual senators.

The vote polling and scheduling functions are closely linked, for party leaders are also legislative strategists. They attempt to pass, or block, legislation. In this respect the majority party has an advantage, for it is mainly responsible for scheduling decisions. If the party leaders expect to lose a vote, they will postpone the bill until they do have the votes. On President Carter's bill for election day voter registration, for example, the bill cleared the legislative committee in April 1977. But it never was brought to the floor because the party leadership and the committee sponsors feared they did not have the votes in the House to pass it. Earlier in the same year, a crippling amendment was adopted to another Carter bill, much to the surprise and embarrassment of the Democratic leadership and committee sponsors in the House. Their response was simply to suspend further floor consideration of that bill.

Scheduling decisions require the party leaders to talk with one another. Although the opposition has at least the right to be informed, in practice the majority and opposition leaders try to arrive at an agreement about the schedule. In British practice, segments of time are officially allocated to the opposition party to use at their discretion. When that time shall occur, for example, is negotiated between the

---

[13] Walter J. Oleszek, "Party Whips in the United States Senate," *Journal of Politics* 33 (November 1971), pp. 955–979; Randall B. Ripley, "The Party Whip Organizations in the United States House of Representatives," *American Political Science Review* 58 (September 1964), pp. 561–576; *Congressional Quarterly Weekly Report,* May 27, 1978, pp. 1301–1306.

JOHN BRADEMAS
INDIANA
MAJORITY WHIP

Congress of the United States
House of Representatives
Office of the Majority Whip
Washington, D.C.   20515

225-5604

CHIEF DEPUTY WHIP
DAN ROSTENKOWSKI
ILLINOIS

DEPUTY WHIPS
BENJAMIN S. ROSENTHAL
NEW YORK
BILL ALEXANDER
ARKANSAS
GEORGE E. DANIELSON

May 12, 1978

WHIP NOTICE INFORMATION
Legislative Program   —   51600
Floor Information   —   57400
Whip Information   —   55606

My dear Colleague:
The program for the House of Representatives for the Week of May 15, 1978 is as follows:

MONDAY

HOUSE MEETS AT NOON
Consent Calendar
Suspensions (One Bill)

1. H.R. 11998   —   Insulation Safety Standards

H.R. 12222   —   International Development and Food Assistance Act of 1978, Authorizations
(COMPLETE CONSIDERATION)

CONFERENCE REPORT ON S Con. Res. 80 — Budget for the United States Government, FY'79

H.R. 12641   —   Temporary Debt Limit Increase
(MODIFIED OPEN RULE, ONE HOUR)

TUESDAY

HOUSE MEETS AT NOON
Private Calendar
Suspensions (7 Bills)

VOTES ON SUSPENSIONS WILL BE POSTPONED UNTIL END OF ALL SUSPENSIONS
1. H.R. 4030   —   Holdings of Private Foundations in Public Utilities
2. H.R. 5551   —   Duty Suspension on 2-methyl, 4-chlorophenol
3. H.R. 11005   —   International Trade Commission Authorization
4. H.R. 1337   —   Constructive Sale Price for Excise Tax on Trucks, Buses, etc.
5. S. 2093   —   Exchange Stabilization Fund Provisions
6. H.R. 12467   —   Rehabilitation Act Amendments
7. H.R. 12255   —   Older Americans Act Amendments

H.R. 10392   —   Establish Hubert H. Humphrey Fellowship at Woodrow Wilson Center
(OPEN RULE, ONE HOUR)

CONFERENCE REPORT ON H.R. 9005 — District of Columbia Appropriations, FY'78

H.R. 11686   —   Department of Energy National Security Authorizations, FY'79
(OPEN RULE, ONE HOUR)

WEDNESDAY

HOUSE MEETS AT 10 a.m.

H.R. 39   —   Alaska National Interest Lands Conservation Act
(SUBJECT TO A RULE BEING GRANTED)

THURSDAY

HOUSE MEETS AT 10 a.m.

H.R. 10929   —   Department of Defense Authorization Act, FY'79
(SUBJECT TO A RULE BEING GRANTED)

H.R. 7814   —   Flexible and Compressed Work Schedules for Federal Employees
(OPEN RULE, ONE HOUR)

FRIDAY

HOUSE MEETS AT 10 a.m.

H.R. 8099   —   Water Rights for Ak-Chin Indians
(SUBJECT TO A RULE BEING GRANTED)

H.R. 10729   —   Commerce Department Authorizations, FY'79
(SUBJECT TO A RULE BEING GRANTED)

H.R. 11291   —   Fire Prevention and Control Act
(OPEN RULE, ONE HOUR)

THE HOUSE WILL ADJOURN BY 3 p.m. ON FRIDAYS AND BY 5:30 p.m. ON
ALL OTHER DAYS EXCEPT WEDNESDAYS

•••••••••• CONFERENCE REPORTS MAY BE BROUGHT UP AT ANY TIME ••••••••••
ANY FURTHER PROGRAM WILL BE ANNOUNCED LATER

Sincerely,

John Brademas

John Brademas
Majority Whip

Figure 5.4   Whip notice: U.S. House of Representatives.

Table 5.2 MAJORITY PARTY FLOOR LEADER ELECTION: U.S. HOUSE DEMOCRATS, 1977

CANDIDATES AND STATES	FIRST VOTE	SECOND VOTE	GAIN	THIRD VOTE	GAIN
Burton (California)	106	107	(1)	147	(40)
Wright (Texas)	77	95	(18)	148	(53)
Bolling (Missouri)	81	93	(12)	—	
McFall (California)	31	—		—	
Total	295	295		295	

SOURCE: *Congressional Quarterly Weekly Report,* December 11, 1976, p. 3295.

party leaders, especially by the whips. In multiparty parliaments, formal or at least fairly regular meetings occur among the party leaders. The Council of Elders, for example, in the German Bundestag arranges the legislative schedule and advises the presiding officer on rules and procedures. In the Swedish Riksdag, the party leaders confer informally but frequently on matters of common concern to them. In the USSR's Supreme Soviet, a Council of Elders recommends the chairmen and members of the committees and arranges the agenda.[14]

SELECTION

The major party leadership positions are elective within each party, with the exception that House Democrats appoint their party whip. Elections of party leaders are held by secret ballot. Thus, it is not possible, at least with certainty, to describe each aspirant's supporters and to thereby designate factional patterns within the parties. The 1977 House Democratic election of their new majority leader illustrates the confusing mix of ideology, region, House internal considerations, and personal proclivities that probably led members to choose among the four candidates. Two candidates held other and lower party offices, including the whip (McFall) and Burton, while a third was a leading party strategist on the Rules Committee (Bolling), and the fourth, the eventual winner, was widely liked but thought to have the least chance (Wright). No candidate won the needed majority on the first ballot, with the whip (McFall) dropping out with the fewest votes. On the second ballot, Bolling dropped out, by only two votes less than Wright. Again on the third and final ballot, Wright won by only one vote. The pattern of the votes (Table 5.2) suggests that most of

[14] Loewenberg, *Parliament in the German Political System,* pp. 202–208; Ingvar Amilon, "Party Leadership Conferences: A Study in Swedish Parliamentary Practice," in Herbert Hirsch and M. Donald Hancock (eds.), *Comparative Legislative Systems* (New York: Free Press, 1971), pp. 323–329; Peter Vanneman, *The Supreme Soviet: Politics and the Legislative Process in the Soviet System* (Durham, N.C.: Duke University Press, 1977), p. 220.

the losers' votes shifted to the eventual winner. Although the two finalists differed in region (north-south) and in voting patterns, the victor was, by southern standards, a party loyalist. In addition, each candidate attracted a following—and opposition—formed as much on personal and almost accidental grounds as on questions of public policy.

The 1977 Senate Republican election for minority leader also illustrates the complex factors in the selection for party leadership. The two candidates were the assistant leader and a former aspirant for the same position, who had gained fame and reputation as the ranking minority member on the Watergate Committee. One was northern; the other southern. One had served longer in the Senate than the other. But they differed little in the major outlines of their voting records. This election, as among House Democrats, was a narrow one, with Baker (Tennessee) winning 19–18 over Griffin (Michigan).[15]

SELECTION PATTERNS

Five major patterns characterize the circumstances under which party leaders have been selected in the U.S. Congress (Table 5.3).

Table 5.3 SELECTION PATTERNS OF PARTY LEADERS SERVING 1977–1978: U.S. CONGRESS

SELECTION METHOD	STATUS OF OFFICE	
	INCUMBENT	OPEN
ELECTIVE		
Uncontested House	I. Status Quo Rhodes, minority leader Michael, minority whip	II. Consensus O'Neill, Speaker
Senate		Byrd, majority leader
Contested House	IV. Revolt	III. Competition Wright, majority leader
Senate		Baker, minority leader
	V. Appointment	
APPOINTIVE House		Brademas, majority whip

SOURCE: Nelson Garrison, "Partisan Patterns of House Leadership Change, 1789–1977," *American Political Science Review* 71 (September 1977), pp. 935–936.

[15] *Congressional Quarterly Weekly Report*, December 11, 1976, pp. 3293–3295, January 8, 1977, pp. 18–19, 35, 42–43.

Four of the patterns are elective, while the fifth is by appointment. The elective patterns vary by whether or not there is an incumbent in the office and whether or not the election is overtly contested. The selection of the House Republican floor leader and whip in 1977 illustrates the "status quo" type of election, in which the incumbent officers are reelected without opposition. The opposite type of selection, the revolt in which an incumbent is challenged, did not occur in either party or in either chamber in 1977. Although an office is open, a "consensus" choice can be made, in which the winner is not contested. The selection of Tip O'Neill as Speaker in 1977 was an example. His advancement to that office from the position of majority leader illustrates the career pattern developed among their offices by House Democrats. Competition, in which an open office is contested by two or more candidates, was illustrated in 1977 by House Democrats and also by Senate Republicans for the position of floor leader.

The occupants of major party offices for both parties in the House since the mid-1950s are listed in Table 5.4, which also indicates the

Table 5.4 U.S. HOUSE PARTY OFFICERS AND SELECTION METHOD,[a] BY PARTY AND YEARS, 1955–1978

OFFICE	PARTIES AND YEARS				
	DEMOCRATS				
	1955–61	1962–70	1971–72	1973–76	1977–78
Speaker	(1) Ray-burn[b]	(2) McCor-mack	(2) Albert	(1) Albert	(2) O'Neill
Leader	(1) McCor-mack[c]	(3) Albert	(3) Boggs[d]	(3) O'Neill	(3) Wright
Whip	(5) Albert	(5) Boggs	(5) O'Neill	(5) McFall	(5) Brade-mas

	REPUBLICANS			
	1955–58	1959–64	1965–73	1973–78
Leader	(2) Martin[e]	(4) Halleck	(4) Ford	(3) Rhodes
Whip	(2) Arends[f]	(2) Arends	(4) Arends	(1) Michael
Conference Chairman	(2) Hope	(2) Hoeven[g]	(3) Laird	(3) Anderson[h]

SOURCE: Robert L. Peabody, *Leadership in Congress* (Boston: Little, Brown, 1976), pp. 269–294.

[a] Selection methods indicated by number in parentheses, as follows: (1) status quo; (2) consensus; (3) competition; (4) revolt; (5) appointive.

[b] Initially elected 1940 to this party office. Died in office.

[c] Initially elected 1940 to this party office.

[d] Died in office.

[e] Held this office since 1939.

[f] Held this office since 1943.

[g] Elected 1957 by consensus. Defeated in revolt by Ford, 1962.

[h] Elected 1969. Survived revolt in 1971.

selection method used for filling each of the offices. During this period of two decades, Republicans have more selected their party leaders by competition, and even revolt, than have Democrats. The incidence of open competition among Democrats, however, has increased since the early 1970s. One important factor limiting competition in both parties has been the longevity (in both seniority and age) of established party leaders. Speaker Rayburn, Majority Leader McCormack, Minority Leader Martin, and Minority Whip Arends each served longer in those offices than have any others in our history.

What other factors are related to the extent to which competition and even revolt occur within the American congressional parties? One factor, hard to establish with any precision, concerns the personal skills and abilities (and also weaknesses) of the incumbent leaders. Perhaps because of his long service and advancing age, Minority Leader Martin was perceived by his party colleagues as failing in personal ability and, more important, as increasingly isolated from the bulk of new members within the party. Implication in personal scandal would be another liability. (Drunkenness for one leader and involvement in Korean bribery charges for another have been associated with their subsequent defeats.)

The immediately previous selection experience within a party seems to have an impact upon how that party handles its next succession. The pattern among House Democrats of promoting its party officers up the career ladder has the effect of lessening overt challenges to both that practice and to the persons seeking election to the next highest office. The same logic, only in reverse, applies to previous revolts and to bitter competition. The hard feelings and animosities engendered in one fight may lead to another in an attempt to either consolidate or revenge the previous one.

A third factor concerns the majority-minority status of the party. The status of the party, by itself, has little relationship to the methods of party leadership selection but whether the party is gaining or losing seats is more immediately important. The majority party does, however, function in a more benign environment than does the minority: its leaders have more committee assignments, more staff, and more resources to allocate to their members than do the minority leaders. But if the minority party has been losing seats or has failed to make anticipated gains, the resulting disappointment and sense of party failure can lead to challenges to established incumbents. Both of the House Republican revolts occurred in such circumstances: Halleck defeated Martin after major Republican losses in 1958, and Ford defeated Halleck after a similar experience in 1964.

It is not only a sense of resentment against a failed leadership that results from an election loss, but the internal balance of power within the party can be shifted. Republican defeats in 1958, 1964, and 1974 eliminated a good many senior members, and the party's recovery in following years brought in an equivalent number of junior members. Thus the supporters of the previous leadership were weakened in strength within their congressional party and the senior leadership had placed upon it an arduous and time-consuming, but critical, task— to become acquainted with and work with the new members. It is in this respect that the previous consideration of personal skill becomes important in incumbent leaders.

Finally, there is an important difference between the two parties, especially in the House. Democrats are less united in their voting patterns than are Republicans. Their response to their lack of issue agreement has been the development of intraparty bargaining over the selection of party leaders, whereas among Republicans the clearly dominant conservatives simply outvote and defeat the much smaller moderate segment of the party. As a result, Democratic party leaders tend to be ideological middlemen and to come from geographic border and mountain states, from larger cities, and from the moderate South; Republican leaders more commonly come from the party heartland of the Midwest and are usually within the conservative wing of their parties.[16]

BRITISH SELECTION

In parliamentary systems, the equivalent elections—for the top positions of their party—nominate the prime minister. The vote patterns in the British parliamentary Labour party election in 1976, to which we have previously referred, were somewhat similar to that among American House Democrats. In the British Labour parliamentary party, four candidates ran to replace the resigned prime minister: one each was designated, by the press at least, as candidates of the left and right wings. Two others were compromise candidates, to be supported if the more strongly, but narrowly, supported candidates should lose. As in the American party election, a majority was required to win. In the first ballot, the lowest vote was obtained by one of the two compromise candidates (though the other was the eventual winner). On the second ballot, the low man was the "left wing's" preferred candidate, while on the third and final ballot, Callaghan won by a healthy margin. Again, we can only guess about the vote shifts; the eventual winner appeared to have inherited the votes of the losers (Table 5.5).[17]

---

[16] This section is largely based upon Robert L. Peabody, *Leadership in Congress: Stability, Succession and Change* (Boston: Little, Brown, 1976), pp. 266–315, 465–508. See also Barbara Hinckley, "Congressional Leadership Selection and Support: A Comparative Analysis," *Journal of Politics* 32 (May 1970), pp. 268–287, and Garrison Nelson, "Partisan Patterns of House Leadership Change, 1789–1977," *American Political Science Review* 71 (September 1977), 918–939.

[17] *Keesing's Contemporary Archive,* May 14, 1976, p. 27719.

Table 5.5 INTRAPARTY ELECTION OF LEADER AND PRIME MINISTER: BRITISH PARLIAMENTARY LABOUR PARTY, 1976

		BALLOTS			
	FIRST	SECOND		THIRD	
CANDIDATES		(VOTE)	(GAIN)	(VOTE)	(GAIN)
James Callaghan	84	141	(57)	176	(35)
Michael Foot	90	133	(37)	137	(4)
Roy Jenkins	56	—		—	
Anthony Benn	37	—		—	
Dennis Healey	30	38	(8)	—	
Anthony Crosland	17	—		—	
Not voting	3	5		4	
Total	317	317		317	

SOURCE: *Keesing's Contemporary Archive*, May 14, 1976, p. 27719.

Executive Committees

Most parliamentary parties have, in addition to designated individual officers, an executive or governing committee that acts as an intermediary between the party members and the officers and also acts in lieu of and between meetings of the full membership. In parliaments on the British model the governing party's cabinet is the executive committee for its party, whereas the opposition party's executive committee is a "shadow cabinet," which presumably would become the governing cabinet when its party gained a majority of the seats.

There is little uniformity among parliamentary parties in either the composition or functions of their executive committees. Some members are directly elected, others serve ex officio, and still others are appointed. Not uncommonly, the chairmen of the party's several internal committees are included on the executive committee. In other instances, geographic areas and designated factions are also represented.

U.S. CONGRESS

The American congressional parties have only recently begun to use an executive committee system. For most of the modern period, party leaders have turned to informal groups and personal consultations within the parties instead of using formal meetings and committees. But this situation is slowly changing.

House Republicans led the way. They have created a Policy Committee that attempts to find (not impose) a common party point of view on major legislation. It became active while Democrats held the presidency under Kennedy and Johnson in the 1960s. American parties typically rely upon their members on the legislative committees to take the lead in thinking about and suggesting party positions on legislation within their committees' jurisdiction. Thus Republicans on a relevant legislative committee would make a presentation of issues to the Policy Committee, and the Policy Committee would, if it thought a common party viewpoint was possible, attempt to state a party position that, in turn, would guide the party leaders on the floor.

But it is the House Democrats who, in the early 1970s, have most developed a party executive committee system. Like the Republicans, their reforms have occurred while they were in the opposition to the president (Republican Nixon). House Democrats restructured their Steering and Policy Committee, and expanded its functions. The membership, as of 1977, is listed in Table 5.6 to indicate its composi-

Table 5.6 HOUSE DEMOCRATIC STEERING AND POLICY COMMITTEE, 1977–1978

CATEGORY		NUMBER
PARTY OFFICERS		3
Speaker, Thomas O'Neill (Mass.)		
Majority Leader, Jim Wright (Tex.)		
Caucus Chairman, Thomas Foley (Wash.)		
ELECTED BY REGIONAL CAUCUSES		12
West		
Lloyd Meeds (Wash.)		
Henry Waxman (Calif.)		
Midwest		
David Obey (Wis.)		
Morgan Murphy (Ill.)		
Richard Bolling (Mo.)		
South		
Kika de la Garza (Tex.)		
Walter Flowers (Ala.)		
Dawson Mathis (Ga.)		
Northeast		
Jonathan Bingham (N.Y.)		
John Dent (Pa.)		
Norman D'Amours (N.H.)		
Robert Roe (N.J.)		
APPOINTED BY SPEAKER		9
Whip	John Brademas (Ind.)	
Chief deputy whip	Dan Rostenkowski (Ill.)	
Deputy whip	Bill Alexander (Ark.)	
Deputy whip	George Danielson (Calif.)	
Deputy whip	Benjamin Rosenthal (N.Y.)	
Black caucus	Ralph Metcalfe (Ill.)	
Women members	Barbara Jordan (Tex.)	
Second- and third-term members	Charlie Rose (N.C.)	
First-term members	Peter Kostmayer (Pa.)	
TOTAL		24

SOURCE: *Congressional Quarterly,* "Committees and Subcommittees, 95th Congress," Supplement to *Weekly Report,* April 30, 1977, pp. 45–46.

Table 5.7 SENATE PARTY POLICY COMMITTEES, 1977, BY
REGION, LEADERSHIP STATUS, AND PARTY

	REGION	
PARTY	NORTH	SOUTH
DEMOCRATIC POLICY COMMITTEE		
Chariman	Robert Byrd (W.Va.)	
Leadership	Alan Cranston (Calif.)	James Eastland (Miss.)
	Hubert Humphrey (Minn.)	
Members	Quentin Burdick (N.Dak.)	Ernest Hollings (S.C.)
	Daniel Inouye (Hawaii)	
	Warren Magnuson (Wash.)	
	Edmund Muskie (Maine)	
	Adlai Stevenson (Ill.)	
REPUBLICAN POLICY COMMITTEE		
Chairman		John Tower (Tex.)
Leadership	Carl Curtis (Neb.)	Howard Baker (Tenn.)
	Robert Dole (Kans.)	
	Clifford Hansen (Wyo.)	
	Bob Packwood (Ore.)	
	Ted Stevens (Alaska)	
Members	Orrin Hatch (Utah)	Dewey Bartlett (Okla.)
	S. I. Hayakawa (Calif.)	Strom Thurmond (S.C.)
	John Danforth (Mo.)	
	Pete Domenici (N.Mex.)	
	Robert Griffin (Mich.)	
	Jacob Javits (N.Y.)	
	James McClure (Idaho)	
	Charles Percy (Ill.)	

SOURCE: *Congressional Quarterly,* "Committees and Subcommittees, 95th Congress," Supplement to *Weekly Report,* April 30, 1977, pp. 17–18.

tion and basis of election: Three elected party leaders serve ex officio; 12 are elected by regional groups of members; and an additional nine are appointed by the Speaker (who was a Democrat during this time) to include the party's whip and several of his deputies, and also to include representatives of the newer members and of the black and women members as well. The major activity of this committee, as of 1978, is to nominate the chairman of the House legislative committees and also to name the party's members to those committees. Thus, this party committee became the essential means by which party selection of committee chairmen was substituted for the seniority rule as recounted earlier in this chapter.

Both parties in the Senate have governing committees, but they have not been as active as their House counterparts. Again, in the 1970s, Democrats have attempted to revive their governing committees, and particularly to increase the activities of the Steering Committee in the selection of party members as chairmen and members of legislative committees (Table 5.7). The periodic demands among Senate

Democrats to revitalize their party committees are more expressed by junior members and nonleaders, than by those senators who are either party leaders or committee chairmen. The existing leadership has tended to function individually and personally and has not attempted to institutionalize party leadership through the party committees.

GERMANY

Executive committees are far more active and important in many of the world's parliamentary parties than they are in the United States. In Germany, for example, the Bundestag party executive committees play a central part in deciding the party's policy on legislation both in the legislative committees and on the floor. The members of the executive committee for all three parliamentary parties, including the party officers, are elected. Among the Christian Democrats, the election of members to the executive committee results in representation of that party's major factions approximately proportional to their size in the parliamentary party membership as a whole.[18]

FRANCE

In the French parliamentary parties the "bureau" supervises their party members on legislative committees and controls the parties' positions on legislation on the floor. Within the government party, for example, no individual Gaullist member may suggest legislation or ask oral questions without the agreement of the party bureau. Although elections to the bureau and to party offices are frequently contested, the result generally has been the selection of persons acceptable to the prime minister and to the Gaullist presidents.[19]

Party Caucus

Meetings of the full membership of the parliamentary party are likewise variable in their frequency and importance. In some parliamentary parties, such as in West Germany and France, the parliamentary parties meet weekly and consider the coming legislative agenda, both in committees and on the floor. The full party meeting is presumably the most authoritative source of party policy. When such meetings adopt a party view on a proposed bill, then all of the party's members are expected to vote with the party's position. The exact scope of a party membership meeting, however, varies among the parliaments. In the French Gaullist party group, for example, the membership meeting may not

[18] John E. Schwarz and L. Earl Shaw, *The United States Congress in Comparative Perspective* (Hinsdale, Ill.: Dryden, 1976), pp. 80–81.
[19] Ibid., pp. 84–85.

consider a proposal until it has first been approved by its executive committee (*bureau*).[20]

GERMANY

The German party meetings consider legislation as it progresses to the floor through introduction and committee stages. Since first reading and introduction (see Chapter 7) are, in West Germany, an occasion for a general debate in which party spokesmen state their respective party's positions on the bill in question, each party must come to some understanding of what its position shall be. The parties also have membership meetings to consider the position their spokesmen should take at critical moments in committee stage. Finally, they also meet prior to floor stages to adopt party views on major amendments and upon the bill itself.[21]

Party meetings often lead to decisions binding upon individual members of how they shall vote, either on the floor or in committees. In the instance of the German highway bills we discussed earlier (in Chapter 4) the governing party, the Christian Democrats, were badly split. Their splits reflected continuing and unresolved disagreements among several government agencies, which in turn reflected the opposing views of railroads, truckers, and various industries, all of whom were supporters of the governing party. As a result the party caucus could not resolve the issues, and members of the government's own party opposed the government both at committee stage and on the floor.[22]

UNITED STATES

Party meetings (variously called caucuses or conferences) are frequent and important in some of the American state legislatures. In Connecticut and New Jersey, for example, the parties caucus weekly and, during the rush of the end of the session, set daily party policy on coming legislation. Few state parties, however, much less any in the Congress, are able to enforce a tight discipline over its members who do not vote on the floor as the party meeting directs.[23]

In the U.S. Congress, party membership meetings were infrequent during the 1940–1970 period. The Democratic party leaders (Rayburn

[20] Ibid.

[21] Gerard Braunthal, *The West German Legislative Process: A Case Study of Two Transportation Bills* (Ithaca: Cornell University Press, 1972), pp. 107–112, 144–145, 190.

[22] Ibid., pp. 193–194.

[23] Jewell and Patterson, *The Legislative Process in the United States,* pp. 159–161.

in the House, Johnson in the Senate) both had a highly personalist style of leadership and both believed that party meetings would only serve to exacerbate intraparty differences. If party meetings were held, the members would perhaps be more acutely aware of their contradictions and act accordingly. The party caucuses met at the beginning of a two-year congressional term to select their party leaders and to organize the chamber. Then they would not meet until two years later. The parties, in effect, had no forum within which collective deliberation and decision could occur.

Beginning with the Nixon presidency, however, House Democrats began to meet more frequently. They could use the caucus to oppose the Republican president. An influx of new members and the determined and continuing efforts of the liberal faction among House Democrats combined to develop procedures by which the party caucus could be called into session, raise issues, and take decisions by voting. One result has been that the caucus has instructed the Democratic members on relevant House committees to report legislation terminating our military role in Indochina and in permitting an amendment to a tax bill on the oil depletion allowance.[24]

The Democratic Steering and Policy Committee was revived and, for the first time since World War I, the caucus voted upon and rejected committee chairmen. After the 1974 Democratic sweep, three Democratic committee chairmen were challenged and removed by votes in the caucus. The revived Steering and Policy Committee now nominates committee chairmen to the caucus, which then votes whether or not to accept the nominations. In the 1975 vote, the choices of the chairmen of both the Agriculture and Armed Services committees were made by that procedure, and hence are listed in Table 5.8 with yes-no votes. The initial nominations for the other two listed committees, however, were defeated in the caucus. Thus, those chairmanships were voted upon a second time using a different procedure in which the two incumbents each faced an opponent. The result was the defeat of one of the two incumbent chairmen (Table 5.8).[25] Through these procedures House Democrats have considerably modified the "seniority rule," illustrating the more general point that the status and importance of committees is ultimately a decision made by the political parties.

---

[24] Ibid., pp. 161–165; Norman J. Ornstein, "Congress: The Democrats Reform Power in the House of Representatives, 1969–1975," in Allan P. Sindler (ed.), *America in the Seventies: Problems, Policies and Politics* (Boston: Little, Brown, 1977), pp. 2–48.

[25] *Congressional Quarterly Weekly Report*, January 25, 1975, pp. 210–212. See also Barbara Hinckley, "Seniority, 1975: Old Theories Confront New Facts," *British Journal of Political Science* 6 (October 1976), pp. 383–399.

Table 5.8 HOUSE DEMOCRATIC CAUCUS VOTES ON COMMITTEE CHAIRMEN, 1975

| COMMITTEE | INCUMBENT CHAIRMAN | VOTES ON RETENTION OF INCUMBENT CHAIRMEN | | | |
| | | VOTE | | | |
		YES	NO	CHALLENGER	VOTE
Agriculture	William Poage (Tex.)	141	146		
Armed Services	F. Edward Hebert (La.)	133	152		
Banking and Currency	Wright Patman (Tex.)	117		Henry Reuss (Wis.)	152
Administration	Wayne Hayes (Ohio)	161		Frank Thompson (N.J.)	111

SOURCE: *Congressional Quarterly Weekly Report*, January 18, 1975, pp. 114–116 and January 25, 1975, pp. 210–212.

ACTIVITY

What happens in party caucuses? Most are held privately, and thus cannot be reported directly, although House Democrats, beginning in 1975, have begun to hold open meetings. For other systems, we do have statements from Canadian M.P.s about their party caucuses. They indicated a rather wide range of activities:[26]

> We decide what our stand will be on pending legislation—which of us will speak on what bills and in what order . . .

Discussion of strategy on current legislation was mentioned by well over a majority of the Canadian sample. By contrast, very few of the American party caucuses considered pending bills.

Another category of response pointed to the development of party consensus, on both policies and internal matters:

> Long range major party policies. We try to hammer out some consensus on future programs and organization.

Party meetings can also ventilate grievances; one result can be the maintenance of party consensus:

> Gripes! It's . . . an opportunity to air our complaints, to get off our chest anything that is bothering us.

Not all members are pleased with their party caucuses. Only three percent of a large sample gave this type of reply:

> We do not *discuss* anything. We sit and are told.

[26] Allan Kornberg, "Caucus and Cohesion in Canadian Parliamentary Parties," *American Political Science Review* 60 (March 1966), pp. 84–85.

Internal Party Committees

To this point, we have discussed the hierarchical structure of parliamentary party organization: elected officers, executive committees, and full membership meetings. In many, if not most, parliamentary parties, the internal structure is much more complicated, for they tend to have many committees. Generally speaking, parties tend to have three types of internal committees: organizational, generalist, and specialist.

ORGANIZATIONAL AND GENERALIST COMMITTEES

Organizational committees, like the executive committee, are concerned with the internal management and decision-making process of the party. House Republicans, for example, and both parties in the Senate, have separate committees to make assignments of their party members to the chamber committees.

A generalist committee is a party unit to which all nonleaders belong. In British terms it is a "back-bencher" committee, of which the first and best known is the Conservatives' 1922 committee. A large influx of new members, as among American congressional parties, brings in reform ideas. The British Conservative nonleaders wanted some means of comunicating among themselves and of communicating with the party leadership, which sometimes meant with the government itself. When in opposition, the party leadership attends the weekly meetings; when in the government, the cabinet ministers attend only upon invitation.[27]

SPECIALIST COMMITTEES

The third type of party committee is the specialist committee, which concentrates upon a limited subject matter. Parliamentary parties tend to duplicate within themselves the same complicated systems of committees found in the full chamber. Indeed, the party committees tend to consist of those party members who serve on the equivalent chamber committee. In this way, members who become experts in the chamber on legislation also become their party's experts. The party contingents on chamber committees both formulate the party's position on a bill, and negotiate with their opposite numbers in the other parties on that committee. Thus, they become both the means of developing intra- and inter-party positions on those bills within the jurisdiction of their chamber committees. Generally, the party membership will look to their fellow members on the chamber committee, and in the party committee, for leadership in formulating the party's position on the bill. The frequent meetings of the membership and of the executive

[27] Schwarz and Shaw, *The United States Congress in Comparative Perspective,* p. 73.

committee are means by which the party committees are informed of, and kept within, general party sentiment. The party committees, especially of the governing party, are also a means by which the government ministers may consult with their parliamentary party in advance of proposing legislation.[28]

The two West German highway bills, for example, were considered by two of the six specialist committees of the ruling Christian Democratic Party. The party groups on Food and Economic Affairs and on Transportation each met on the bills prior to consideration by the Bundestag committees. One of the party committees called in outside experts and met with the officials of one of the sponsoring government agencies. To prepare for that meeting the agency itself held a conference among its officials who would appear before the party's committee. In addition to the two existing specialist committees of the party an informal group, consisting of the party's transportation experts and of its leaders on the chamber committee, also met. Following the meetings of the specialist and informal committees within the Christian Democratic party was a meeting of the party's executive committee, which voted to support one of the government's bills (the Transportation Finance bill) but to oppose the government's other bill (the Highway Relief bill). Here we have an example of the government's own party in the Bundestag taking an official position against one of its own bills. This formal decision by the ruling party's executive committee in the Bundestag effectively sealed the fate of the government bill it opposed; that bill never got out of the chamber committee.[29]

The British parliamentary parties have developed systems both of specialist committees and of "spokesmen." Both are defined by issue specialization. The spokesmen are appointed by the opposition party to present its case to Parliament on a given issue. Each spokesman, in effect, monitors the activities of his ministerial counterpart. The party spokesmen are, in turn, related to the party's specialist committees. Among the Conservatives when in opposition, for example, the chairmen of the party's 19 specialist committees were all the party's frontbench spokesmen. When Labour was in opposition, however, the correspondence between the two statuses was not as marked.[30]

American congressional parties usually do not have a set of specialist committees, although the same result is achieved as in other

[28] Ibid., pp. 81–82, 85; Braunthal, *The West German Legislative Process,* pp. 105, 145.

[29] Braunthal, Ibid., pp. 126–128.

[30] Robert M. Punnett, *Front Bench Opposition: The Role of the Leader of the Opposition, the Shadow Cabinet and Shadow Government in British Politics* (New York: St. Martin's, 1973), pp. 304–311.

parliaments through the practice of deference being paid by other members to those party members who are on a relevant chamber committee. Congressional Democrats did form temporary task forces in the early 1970s to attempt to develop party-wide plans on energy and on the economy. The energy task force combined party members from both the House and the Senate, whereas the task force on the economy was confined to House Democrats. In each instance the task forces included members of relevant legislative committees. Their respective reports, however, were rather general and did not resolve the problem of multiple and competing jurisdictions among the several legislative committees. As a result, little has been enacted that directly reflects the reports of either task force.[31] Here again the American congressional parties are distinctive from those of other democratic parliaments in that they have, by comparison, a rudimentary structure of internal committees, either for their own governance or for the development of party policy positions.

FACTIONS

In our earlier discussions of the selection of party leaders and of the relationships between American presidents and congresses, we have referred to internal differences within political parties. The term *faction* is applied to such intraparty differences. The very word itself can be used as a term of opprobrium; among Communist parties, factionalism is akin to heresy and schism. But we shall use the term as a neutral designation of differences of opinion, and action based upon such differences, within political parties.

Parties as Coalitions

Few parties are monolithic in organization or homogeneous in composition. They tend to be coalitions of subgroups, the unity of which cannot be taken for granted by the party leaders. One of the party leaders' main tasks is to nurture and maintain the existence of their party. A description, originally applied to the leadership of the German Christian Democratic Union, applies to all parties and their leaders: the party needs a leader[32]

> . . . who is basically uncommitted to any one group (within the party) and who, once installed, derives his power from his ability to moderate

[31] The Democratic energy task forces are reported in *Congressional Quarterly Weekly Report,* March 1, 1975, p. 426, and the economy task force in *Congressional Quarterly Weekly Report,* July 27, 1974, p. 1971.

[32] Peter Merkl, "Coalition Politics in West Germany," in Sven Groennings, E. W. Kelley, and Michael Leiserson (eds.), *The Study of Coalition Behavior* (New York: Holt, Rinehart and Winston, 1970), p. 27.

and mediate among the groups while they in turn trust his fairness in generating a consensus on specific policies.

West Germany's Christian Democratic Union clearly illustrates the subgroup basis of party organization. It is a coalition of factions, some of which have their own formal organizations and have their own staff and offices.

The organized groups within the CDU include: (1) a Bavarian (regional) separate party formally affiliated with the CDU parliamentary party; (2) the labor group, consisting of labor union members within the CDU parliamentary party; (3) the middle-class and small business affairs discussion group; and (4) the study group on food and agriculture. In addition, less formally organized groups meet on an irregular basis on large business affairs and on problems of the family. One other and important basis of group formation cutting across all of the above is religion, for the Christian Democratic Union originated as a deliberate effort to unite the previously separate religious parties.

It is out of this multigroup mosaic that the above-cited leadership characteristic arises. A party leader is a manager of intraparty conflict. As a result, while all of the factions are represented in the party's executive committee and on its internal party committees, the party-wide leaders ordinarily do not belong to any of the organized factional groups.[33]

The Japanese Liberal Democratic Party illustrates a different form of factionalism—though no less pervasive or important than in the German case. Like the German CDU, the Japanese LDP is the more conservative of the several parties in its country. Both were also formed after World War II as a merger of several previously separate parties. The Japanese LDP factionalism is more personal, however, than the German, both in organizational form and in basis of voter support. The Japanese factions are designated by the name of their leader, who in turn is the faction's candidate for party leader and hence for prime minister, since the party has held a majority ever since the end of the U.S. occupation. The factions apparently do not differ appreciably on policy, for all rest upon business support and financing. They are mainly leader support groups that have formed on the basis of personal preferences and the ability of the leader to raise campaign funds for their respective sets of parliamentary supporters (see Chapter 2). Because of the personal basis of the factions, they have combined and re-formed at various times. They lack the group basis and hence the stability of the German factions.[34]

[33] Loewenberg, *Parliament in the German Political System*, pp. 161–163; Schwarz and Shaw, *The United States Congress in Comparative Perspective*, p. 81.

[34] Michael Leiserson, "Coalition Government in Japan," in Sven Groennings, E. W. Kelley, and Michael Leiserson (eds.), *The Study of Coalition Behavior*, pp. 80–102.

The British Labour party illustrates yet another factional system. That party has a number of "sponsored" candidates, as discussed in Chapter 2 on elections. Although most are sponsored by labor unions, a number are also sponsored by cooperative societies and professional associations. Furthermore, both the unions and the cooperative societies have group membership in the external party at both local and national levels. Nevertheless, factionalism within the parliamentary Labour party is only partly related to the pattern of candidate sponsorship by interest groups. Rather, the important splits within the Parliamentary Labour party are among various labor unions; the coal miners —with a heavy concentration in Wales—are in the "left wing," whereas other unions, such as steel and trucking, are in the "right wing." The unaffiliated Labour M.P.s are likewise distributed among the divergent wings of the party. Factionalism within the Labour party does appear in voting patterns and also on attitudes toward selected issues, while the intraparty differences among Conservatives appear much less.[35]

Factionalism in the German CDU is group and voter based; in the Japanese LDP, factionalism is personality and campaign finance based; in the British Labour party, factionalism has more of a generalized policy or ideological cast, with admixtures of group support and personal loyalties.

Ethnic-based factionalism is particularly divisive within a party. In at least some nations that are ethnically divided, the political parties form within, rather than across, ethnic divisions. But in other multiethnic nations, such as Belgium, the major and "traditional" parties have been nationwide, based upon class and economic issues, and each contains within them both the French- and Dutch-speaking regions. Under the stress, however, of ethnic separatism, not only did new ethnic parties emerge, but each of the major parties divided into ethnic-based wings in the 1968 election, with each one conducting separate campaigns within its respective region of the country. The resulting cabinets were more a balance among ethnic groups than among political parties.[36]

U.S. Congress

Factionalism within the American congressional parties is more amorphous and thus more difficult to describe. The most pervasive and

[35] Allan Kornberg and Robert C. Frasure, "Policy Differences in British Parliamentary Parties," *American Political Science Review* 65 (September 1971), pp. 701–703; Philip Norton, "Intra-Party Dissent in the House of Commons: The Parliament of 1974," *The Parliamentarian* 58 (October 1977), pp. 240–245.

[36] Alvin Rabushka and Kenneth Shepsle, *Politics in Plural Societies: A Theory of Democratic Instability* (Columbus, Ohio: 1972), pp. 117–118.

stable factional split is among Democrats and is usually characterized
—as we have earlier—by region and ideology. Liberal Democrats—
mostly northern—are organized through the Democratic Study Group
(DSG), which was formed in the late 1950s as the Eisenhower administration was nearing its end and the Democrats were preparing for an
anticipated new Democratic presidency. At that time, southern Democrats were disproportionately represented in committee chairmanships,
while the Texan leadership of Rayburn (House) and Johnson (Senate)
deemphasized party meetings or party committees. Liberal Democrats,
to increase their own organization, cohesion, and power, formed the
DSG. It developed its own factional study committees to form party
positions on policy and created its own whip system to maximize its
voting strength on the House floor. It has been an active and vital
organization in support of liberal Democratic presidential programs
and in opposition to those of Republicans. It also has attempted to
raise campaign funds and to provide other forms of campaign support
to promising Democratic challengers to Republican incumbents. It has
cooperated with such outside organizations as the Democratic National
Committee, the AFL–CIO, Americans for Democratic Action, and the
Committee for an Effective Congress.[37]

Conservative Democratic congressmen—mainly southern—have
had less need for formal organization because of their senior positions
on the House legislative committees (until the mid-1970s) and their
smaller numbers. Yet they have developed leaders, and ad hoc meetings
among them do occur. Their original leader in the 1930s was Eugene
Cox (Georgia), who, on the critical Rules Committee, formed an
alliance with the Republican leadership.[38]

Representative Howard Smith (Virginia) later also led the conservative contingent from his position on the Rules Committee. In
the 1960s and 1970s southern congressmen have lost their secure hold
on many of the House committees. Their factional leaders have become
more dispersed, tending to vary with the issue, and hence tend to be
senior southern Democratic members on appropriate House committees,
especially on Ways and Means.[39]

Among Republicans, the splits are less pervasive and vary considerably by issue. Yet, the few moderate to liberal Republicans have
met in the Wednesday Club, named for its day of meeting, in both the

[37] Arthur J. Stevens, Jr., Arthur H. Miller, and Thomas E. Mann, "Mobilization
of Liberal Strength in the House: 1950–1970: The Democratic Study Group,"
American Political Science Review 68 (June, 1974), pp. 667–671.

[38] Joe Martin, *My First Fifty Years in Politics* (New York: McGraw-Hill, 1960),
pp. 84–85.

[39] John F. Manley ,"The Conservative Coalition in Congress," *American Behavioral
Scientist* 17 (November/December 1973), pp. 223–247.

House and Senate. The House Republican Wednesday Club has a membership of about 35.[40] The more conservative Republicans in the House have organized the Republican Study Committee, with about 70 members.

Splits frequently emerge in party leadership elections among Republicans. In the House, for example, moderate John Anderson (Illinois) has been challenged for the post of conference chairman by the more conservative Samuel Devine (Ohio). In the Senate the more conservative Carl Curtis (Nebraska) has been challenged by the more moderate Jacob Javits (New York) for their conference chairmanship.[41]

In both parties of both houses the factions are only tenuously defined. Although some organizations do exist, many congressmen are only peripherally involved, and the alignments among them vary by time and issue. A good illustration of shifting and tenuous factional alignments is provided by energy and environmental issues. Ordinarily, Michigan Democrats and the dominant labor union in their state, the United Auto Workers, are in the vanguard of the liberal Democratic wing and in support of the programs of Democratic presidents. But on automobile pollution and on gasoline taxes as an energy conservation measure the Michigan Democrats and the UAW combine with auto managements specifically and with business organizations and conservative congressmen generally to actively protect the auto industry from the controls sought by their usual allies—the environmentalists and the Democratic administration.

Democrats and Southern Democrats

The recent increase in the activity and functions of the House Democratic caucus and steering committee results from a long-term effort by moderate and liberal Democrats to counter the ability of southern conservative Democrats to thwart the programs of Democratic presidents and to also thwart the programs of the moderate and liberal Democrats in Congress, Within the party caucus, southern Democrats are greatly outnumbered by northerners. Within the typical House, however, southern Democrats can form a working majority in combina-

---

[40] U.S. Congress. House. Commission on Administrative Review, *Background Information on Administrative Units, Members' Offices, and Committees and Leadership Offices* (Washington, D.C., June 30, 1977), p. 97. *Congressional Quarterly Weekly Report,* January 18, 1976, p. 112, lists the Senate members of the Wednesday Club.

[41] *Congressional Quarterly Weekly Report,* December 23, 1972, p. 3205, and January 18, 1975, p. 112. Republican factions are discussed in *Congressional Quarterly Weekly Report,* August 19, 1972, pp. 2051–2054.

tion with Republicans. Thus the argument over where decisions should be made—in party or on the floor—is largely a dispute over which faction shall be advantaged.

NUMBERS

The number of southern Democrats has been decreasing within the congressional Democratic party. Population shifts nationally have, with the exception of Florida and Texas, drawn population out of the South. In addition, although they have been losing seats, though slowly, to Republicans, the reverse party trend has occurred outside that region. And when Democrats have gained a 66% share of the House seats, that growth has been mainly in the North. The relative regional strength among House Democrats is indicated in Table 5.9, which shows the number and proportion of seats by region for a nominal Democratic congress of 1973–1974 and the policy Democratic congress of 1977–1978. Although Democrats gained seats in both regions, the gains disproportionately were outside the South.

In deliberative assemblies, votes are power; thus, moderate and liberal Democrats have made their greatest advances in strengthening the party caucus when their votes within the party have been greatest —during the policy Democratic congresses elected in 1964 and 1974. The 1964 election was a watershed in American politics. It marked the rapid growth of Republicans in the deep and rural South on the one hand, and the growth of liberal and presidentially supportive Democratic northern seats in Congress on the other. The presidentially oriented Democrats had the bitter experience of seeing Kennedy legislation effectively blocked by the conservative coalition. Their method of attempting to counteract Republican-inclined southern Democratic congressmen was to serve notice that any Democratic congressmen who openly supported Goldwater for president in 1964 would lose their privileges as Democrats within the House. That major privilege was continued seniority on the Democratic side of the committees. Here we see the first attempt to modify the hallowed seniority rule.

Table 5.9 REGIONAL DISTRIBUTION OF SEATS AMONG HOUSE DEMOCRATS IN NOMINAL AND POLICY DEMOCRATIC CONGRESSES

| | TYPE OF DEMOCRATIC CONGRESSES[a] | | | | | |
| | NOMINAL | | POLICY | | GAINS | |
REGION	(N)	(%)	(N)	(%)	(N)	(%)
North	155	65	199	69	44	86
South	84	35	91	31	7	14
Total	239	100	290	100	51	100

[a] The "nominal" Democratic congress example was elected in 1972. The "policy" Democratic congress was elected in 1976.

PARTY SANCTIONS

In 1964 two House Democrats openly supported Goldwater's election over Johnson, and in 1968 one other House Democrat supported Wallace as the third-party presidential nominee. All three members were disciplined by the House Democratic caucus. Two of the three ultimately left the House to run for governor of their respective states. The third promptly switched parties and was reelected to the House as a Republican.

We can trace the regional basis of Democratic party factionalism after the 1968 election, for the caucus vote was public, while the earlier sanction votes had been secret. Northern Democrats overwhelmingly voted for the seniority sanction, while southerners were even more strongly opposed (Table 5.10). The party leaders of that time voted against discipline. Perhaps as a harbinger of later developments, those who subsequently became party leaders either voted to impose sanctions, or at the very least they abstained.

The precedent had been set—that congressmen of a given congressional party owe some degree of loyalty to that party and that the congressional party has some means of sanctioning disloyal behavior. That this sanction was directed at election behavior, rather than at legislative activity, perhaps indicates that the political party is above all else a means of selecting persons to fill office. Since that time, no congressman has openly campaigned for the presidential nominee of the other party, however much he may have disagreed with the selection and policies of his own party's candidate. Dissenting Democratic congressmen have since chosen silence.

Summary

Factionalism seems to coexist with political parties. Parties differ, however, in the extent, basis, and depth of their factionalism and in the

Table 5.10 HOUSE DEMOCRATIC CAUCUS VOTES ON SENIORITY SANCTIONS AGAINST MEMBERS SUPPORTING NON-DEMOCRATIC PRESIDENTIAL CANDIDATES, BY REGION, 1965 AND 1969

	REGION			
	NORTH	SOUTH	TOTAL	
ISSUE	(%)	(%)	(N)	(%)
Vote to Discipline				
Rep. Rarick (La.), 1969				
Yes	87	5	101	58
No	13	95	73	42
Total	100	100		100
N =	113	61	174	

SOURCES: 1969 vote: Rep. John Rarick, "Extension of Remarks," *Congressional Record* (Daily ed.), January 30, 1969, p. E670–E671.

means by which they attempt to mold a party-wide cohesion from their internal diversity. A good many parliamentary parties abroad have a far more complex internal organization than do the American congressional parties, and in at least some instances the organization of their factions approaches that of their parties.

Within the American congressional parties factionalism has been most apparent among Democrats. It has been the House Democrats who have attempted to revive their party caucus and have taken important steps to define the minimal conditions of party loyalty. Among Republicans the growth of the "New Right" and of a self-conscious conservatism may bring to that party in the future the same experience of factionalism that has marked Democrats ever since the New Deal period of the 1930s.

PARTY COHESION

To what extent do legislators vote together by political party? In general, the American Congress votes by party much less than do most other parliaments. Party cohesion in Congress is said to be "low," whereas party cohesion in other parliaments is "high."

Differences in Voting Circumstances

This general observation, though accurate, is also misleading because it is incomplete and oversimplified. The major oversimplification stems from the very different circumstances of floor voting among legislative bodies. In the previous chapter, on chief executives, we indicated that in parliamentary systems any vote could become a vote on the continuance in office of the cabinet, whereas in presidential systems few votes ever achieve that degree of importance. Thus, to compare party voting in the American Congress with that in the British Parliament is to confuse two very different types of voting.

A second source of simplification is that the rules and options for voting also vary among parliaments. For example, in the French National Assembly the government decides which, if any, amendments shall be voted upon. The government also decides which version of the bill shall be brought to the floor—but, in effect, so does the cabinet in the British parliament. Finally, the French government can require a "package" or "blocked" vote, in which the vote occurs on the entire bill and the amendments accepted by the government, rather than on separate portions of the bill.[42]

---

[42] William G. Andrews, "The Constitutional Prescription of Parliamentary Procedure in Gaullist France," *Legislative Studies Quarterly* 3 (August 1978), pp. 488–493.

Third, the physical act of voting is also quite different among parliaments. In some parliaments, of which the Supreme Soviet is an example, voting occurs only by a show of hands (see Figure 7.10). In Tanzania only a few votes have ever been taken. The question of how members vote can be answered only for those votes in which the names of members are listed—a record or roll call vote. A number of parliaments use voting machines, as does the U.S. House. Others orally call the roll of names, to which the individual member responds, as in the U.S. Senate. In Britain, members vote by "division," in which they walk into different rooms (lobbies), and their names are recorded by clerks. In those parliaments in which few votes are taken, in which voting is not recorded, or in which voting is secret (as in Italy), we can hardly answer the basic question. In most others, however, we can answer the question only for those votes on which names are recorded, for such parliaments also have other and less formal methods of voting, such as by voice and by standing.

Party cohesion is related to factionalism; one is usually the reverse of the other. But the extent to which factionalism is expressed in voting patterns varies with the circumstances of the vote. The opportunities for factional voting are greatest in the American Congress, while they are much reduced in most other parliaments. The many variations in voting procedures, conditions, and rules make it very difficult to obtain comparable evidence from a variety of parliaments; we are limited in the trends we can identify and in the degree of confidence we can place in our own observations.

Although we shall explore floor procedure and voting methods more fully in Chapter 7 (Procedures and decision making on the floor), at this point we raise the question of the extent to which parliamentary parties are cohesive in their voting on the floor.

Extent of Cohesion

Parliamentary parties from four countries are ranked in Table 5.11 by the extent of their party cohesion in roll call voting. Both British parties and three of the five French parties rank in the most cohesive category, in which 95% or more of their members vote together with their parties.[43] The West German parties are found both in the most cohesive category (Social Democrats) and in the middle category (Christian Democrats and the Free Democrats) along with a French party (Catholic). Ranking as the least cohesive parties among the four countries are the American parties and a French party (Radicals).

[43] Although there is a difference between the two main British parties, the Conservative party is more cohesive than the Labour party. See Robert E. Goodin, "The Importance of Winning Big," *Legislative Studies Quarterly* 2 (November 1977), p. 406, footnote 3.

Table 5.11 EXTENT OF VOTING COHESION IN PARLIAMENTARY
PARTIES IN FOUR COUNTRIES

VOTING COHESION			
CATEGORY	PERCENT	COUNTRY	PARLIAMENTARY PARTY
Highest	95–100%	France	Communists
			Gaullists
			Socialists
		Great Britain	Conservatives
			Labour
		West Germany	Social Democrats
Medium	70–95%	France	Catholics
		West Germany	Christian Democrats
			Free Democrats
Low	Below 70%	United States	Republicans
			Democrats
		France	Radicals

SOURCE: Adapted from John E. Schwarz and L. Earl Shaw, *The United States Congress in Comparative Perspective* (Hinsdale, Ill.: Dryden, 1976), pp. 119, 153. Mainly covers 1948–1968 period.

Party cohesion—even high cohesion—does not mean a complete absence of voting against one's party. In the West German Bundestag in the 1953–1957 period, for example, 20% of the Christian Democratic members voted eight or more times against the position of their party. In the 1959–1964 period the British Conservative Party experienced seven occasions in which a sizable number of its members voted against the party whip, and in an earlier two year period, 1945–1947, more than 30% of the Labour members voted against their party at least once.

More recently, British M.P.s have increasingly voted against their own party, and members of the government party have increasingly voted against their own government. In over half of the instances in which government policy was defeated, members of the governing party had voted against the government in the 1974–1978 period. We are perhaps witnessing the beginnings of a sizable and important shift in the practices of the British House of Commons.[44]

Factors Associated with Cohesion

Although we shall consider some of the factors associated with roll call voting by individual members in Chapter 7, let us now raise an equivalent question for parliamentary parties as a whole: What factors are associated with the different degree of party cohesion? Again we

---

[44] Schwarz and Shaw, *The United States Congress in Comparative Perspective,* pp. 124, 136; and John E. Schwarz, "The Quiet Revolution: The Awakening of the British House of Commons in the 1970's" (unpublished paper, University of Arizona, 1978), p. 15.

find that we do not have sufficient evidence with which to answer this question systematically for most of the world's parliaments. Rather, we can more concentrate on several Western European parliaments and draw inferences from them.

GOVERNMENTAL STRUCTURE

The first factor, we might speculate, associated with party cohesion is the structure of government: Those parliaments in which the fate of the cabinet's continuance in office rests upon the outcome of a vote have cohesive voting by party. Although this explanation does seem suitable to Great Britain, it does not completely account for either the French or the German parties. In both countries, parliament may vote the government out of office but only under highly restricted circumstances. Up to the time of this writing (1979) neither country had experienced a government removal by that means since the beginning of their current constitutions. Furthermore, this factor does not account for the low and moderate cohesion of other French parties which existed during the prior Republic and which could, in that period, vote a government out of office. This factor might even be losing some validity in Britain, for on several occasions in the mid-1970s, the government party lost a vote on a three-line whip, and yet did not choose to consider that loss a vote on its continuance in office.[45]

ELECTION STRUCTURE

A second factor that can be considered as related to the extent of party cohesion concerns the election—that is, whether the chief executive is chosen through parliaments or whether the elections of parliament and president are conducted separately. Great Britain and West Germany, having either high or at least moderately cohesive parties, contrasted with the United States, do fit the pattern. France is the exception; its three major parties during the Fifth Republic vote cohesively, even though the president is directly elected as in the United States.

NOMINATIONS

A third factor concerns the nomination process: the extent to which party leaders consider voting loyalty in parliament in deciding whom to nominate for parliamentary elections. This factor does seem to operate in Great Britain and France; in both countries, parties in the electoral districts reward party loyalty and have refused renomination to dissenters from the parliamentary party. In Britain such action has been taken mainly by the local parties, while in France the national leadership of the party has been involved in such actions. Bundestag members, at least within the CDU, are less often renominated than in

[45] Norton, "Intra-Party Dissent in the House of Commons: The Parliament of 1974," p. 245, footnote 18.

Britain or France, but voting dissent from the parliamentary party does not seem to be an important factor in the renomination decision. The more important considerations seem to be local ones of electoral appeal.[46]

Among the least cohesive parties, nomination decisions in the United States can hardly be said to have been made by party "leaders" at all. Rather, most states nominate through the direct primary, in which candidates can be and are criticized precisely because they supported their national party too much rather than too little. Thus, of the three factors we have discussed to this point, the renomination considerations seem to most completely fit the ranking of the several parliamentary parties by degree of cohesion.

PARTY-CONGRUENT BACKGROUNDS

The fourth factor, "party-congruent" backgrounds, is also related to the extent of party cohesion. That is, parties in which the parliamentary members share a common background (of social class, education, experience, etc.) and which contrasts with that of the other party or parties are likely to be more cohesive in their voting patterns than are parties in which the parliamentary members do not share a common background. The parliamentary parties of high cohesion, both British parties and the French Gaullist party, all do share common background traits. The British Conservative M.P.s mainly come from middle- and upper-class families, are in business and professional occupations, and have attended the prestige preparatory schools and universities. Labour M.P.s, by contrast, come from working-class families and disproportionately have been associated with labor unions. The same contrasts mark the French Gaullist members from the Socialist and Communist parties.[47]

By contrast, the parliamentary members of the German CDU and of both American parties are more diverse. American congressmen of both parties tend to resemble one another in their occupation and social origins—relatively middle class in background, and business and professional in occupation. The German CDU more resembles the other European parties in its class composition and in its social contrasts with the Socialist party; it is, however, more diverse than the other European ones in that it consciously embraces both religious groups and bridges occupational and class divisions. Its elaborate factional organization, discussed in an earlier section, both expresses and attempts to accommodate its diverse composition.

The Soviet Union and Eastern European nations have quite diversely constituted memberships of their parliaments. Their diverse

---

[46] Schwarz and Shaw, *The United States Congress in Comparative Perspective,* pp. 137–140.

[47] Ibid., pp. 131–132.

social backgrounds are a source of pride to them, and social diversity seems to be an objective to be achieved by the Communist party through the nomination and election process. This social diversity, however, is not accompanied by political diversity, for approximately 75% of the members of the Supreme Soviet are members of the Communist party. Few proposals are submitted to a vote, and the voting that does occur is by a show of hands. Thus, even if social diversity might lead to a difference of opinion, the voting methods or procedures discourage both the means of expressing a difference and the means by which an outside observer could perceive that expression.

CAREERS

The fifth and final factor we shall consider for its relationship to party cohesion is the members' career possibilities: Those parties that affect the members' career advancement are more cohesive than those parties that either do not, or cannot, affect their members' career advancement. This factor reflects the governmental structure factor discussed above, but adds to it the consideration of party organization and discipline. The British parties are perhaps the best example. In the British system the parliamentary party is the usual means by which an aspiring politician enters the government. Although the British cabinet is ordinarily a small body (usually about 15–20 members) and thus constitutes a small proportion of all the members of the governing party, about 75 members are appointed to a variety of lesser and supporting governmental and party positions. The lesser positions presumably are the means by which a member then becomes eligible to be considered for prime minister some years hence. As a result, the parliamentary majority party has appointed about 20% of its members to offices available within the government. The appointed members could be expected to, and do, vote with the party; in addition, however, those other members who might wish themselves to receive a party appointment would also vote in accordance with the party leadership.

The West German CDU represents an intermediate condition between that of the British and that of the American. Although West Germany has a parliamentary system, the number of government appointments is quite small—only about a dozen. It has a much larger number of positions within the parliamentary party (about 50), but these positions are defined, unlike the British case, as separate from the government. As a result, the parliamentary party leaders of the CDU had about the same rates of party-loyal voting as did the ordinary member; it was only the few cabinet ministers who more consistently supported the party and government position.[48]

48 Ibid., p. 139.

The American congressional parties make no appointments to government offices. They control, potentially, only those offices internal to a House as a whole and internal to itself. As noted previously, the party fills only two or three major party offices. The persons selected as leaders tend to be moderates and brokers; although they are not extremely disloyal in their voting records, neither are they closely identified with the majority faction of their respective parties. The congressional parties have available a much larger number of committee chairmanships than chamber or party offices. Yet until 1974 no party had filled those positions over the past half-century except through the automatic seniority rule, which had the effect of rewarding party deviance rather than support.

SUMMARY

We have reviewed five factors that could be associated with the extent to which parliamentary parties vote cohesively on the floor. Although we can hardly prove generalizations for the world's parliaments from a review of the parties of four atypical countries, this review suggests that each of the five factors has a plausible association with party cohesion, particularly when these factors are taken in combination. The last three factors—nomination practices, party-congruent backgrounds, and career possibilities—are linked to party cohesion in the four countries we have considered. Two factors associated with the distinction between a parliamentary and presidential system, however, are not consistently related to party cohesion. Britain and the United States are the extreme cases; in Britain each factor leads to party cohesion, whereas in the United States each factor leads to the lack of party cohesion. Germany and France represent intermediate circumstances in these respects.

Party Cohesion in the States

The state legislatures vary extensively in the extent to which their parties vote cohesively. In one-party states the dominant party ordinarily has many splits. It is the two-party legislatures in which each party has an opportunity to vote cohesively and against the other party. But not all of them do vote by party on legislative roll calls. The most important factor appears to be the characteristics of the constituencies: Parties in which legislative constituencies are more homogeneous tend to vote more cohesively on legislation than do parties with more diverse constituencies. In the urbanized and industrialized northern states, Democratic legislators tend to be elected from urban districts and especially from districts with concentrations of labor unions and ethnic and racial minorities, whereas Republicans tend to be elected from high income urban areas and the smaller towns. Within the less urbanized states, by contrast, both of the parties draw from a more diverse set of districts, thus reducing the internal consistency of their represented constituents.[49]

PARTY ATTITUDES

Another factor is also related to the extent of party cohesion—the attitudes held by parliamentary members toward their parties. Whether such attitudes are regarded as cause or effect is perhaps an arbitrary distinction. What must be noted, however, is that members of parliament hold pronounced views toward themselves in relationship to their political party. Furthermore, party attitudes vary extensively, both within a single parliament and between parliaments.

Attitudes are best measured through interviews with the members themselves. The prior section, on voting, measures an act; this section measures a thought, or even emotion. Voting is measured by what a member does; attitudes are measured by what a member says, especially in interviews asking the same question(s) of all the members interviewed. The available interview evidence, unfortunately for our world-wide purposes, comes only from the United States and from Canada.

Canadian Parliament

Though located on the same continent as the United States and sharing many of the same population characteristics, Canada has a government that is modeled upon the British parliamentary system. Canadian M.P.s think very differently about their party than do American Congressmen. They were asked, "What are the advantages of going along with your party?" Their responses may be grouped into five categories, ranging from those who saw no advantages to those who saw party cohesion as the means by which the parliamentary system functions (Table 5.12).[50]

The no-advantage and the self-interest responses were the least often mentioned. Those who saw no advantage to Canadian party cohesion seemed either to be opposed to parties ("It can be a positive disadvantage") or to be too new to have understood their own system ("I have not been here long enough . . ."). Those who reported the advantage of party cohesion as a matter of self-interest did so in terms of career advancement considerations, which we discussed in the prior section for other parties:

> You do not want to risk your personal future by becoming known as a malcontent and disturber of the peace.

[49] Jewell and Patterson, *The Legislative Process,* pp. 382–388.
[50] Kornberg, "Caucus and Cohesion in Canadian Parliamentary Parties," p. 84.

Table 5.12 ADVANTAGES OF PARTY COHESION
AMONG CANADIAN M.P.s

ADVANTAGES	PERCENT
1. None	11
2. Self-interest	13
3. Self and party interests	14
4. Party oriented	48
5. Parliamentary system oriented	14
Total	100
$(N = 165)$	

SOURCE: Allan Kornberg, "Caucus and Cohesion in
Canadian Parliamentary Parties," *American Political Science Review* 60 (March 1966), p. 84.

The largest set of answers was in terms of the party itself:

> In our party it is not a question of there being any personal advantages.
> You do it for the sake of the party. In the Government, it is a question
> of keeping themselves in power. It is a matter of efficiency and survival.
> It is like fighting a war, you cannot function as a party in this system
> without being united.

The fifth category of answers was in terms of the parliamentary
system, although many of the party-oriented replies were spoken in
the context of the Canadian system:

> It comes down to the whole system of party government in Canada.
> There are none of the personal advantages your question implies. The
> system, being a party system, simply does not tolerate M.P.s who disagree publicly with their party.

U.S. Congress

Several different studies have been done of U.S. congressmen, each
asking different questions, none of which exactly matched the
Canadian question. Perhaps the most similar question asked of U.S.
House members was, "Do you want to act in accord with party positions?"[51] The responses ranged from a "strong yes" to a "no." Almost
three-fourths of the congressmen were in the "strong yes" category,
with the distribution between the two parties almost the same. Southern Democrats gave the lowest percentage of "strong yes" responses
among Democrats (57%), and northeasterners among Republicans
(56%).

Northern Democrats could easily vote with their party: "I have a
general conviction that my party is right," or "I find that the party is
right 99% of the time." "My policy is to accept everything Democratic
unless it is terrible."

[51] Ripley, *Party Leaders in the House of Representatives*, pp. 140–145.

Southern Democrats—a majority of whom fell in the same category—expressed their strong support of the party with a greater sense of difficulty than did the northerners:

> I go through great throes when I cannot go along with my party. It is not an easy choice to vote against your party.

Strongly supportive Republicans from the Northeast, as their least-loyal region, expressed similar difficulties in supporting the party:

> I will vote against the party if it does not mean much. But I will go with them if the vote is close. I will also go along if I do not know much about the bill.

Republicans from the other regions had, like northern Democrats, little hesitation in expressing party support. Some of their comments reflect their minority status in Congress and, at the time of the interviews (early 1960s), their lack of the presidency:

> Sure I want to go along. It is easier to go with the party when in the minority. Ike was not conservative enough and I kicked over the traces a few times. But in the minority you are just looking for reasons to oppose what the majority supports. This is easier.

The fear that perhaps party loyalty is not a local and electoral asset is expressed by those congressmen in the "weak yes" response to the party support question:

> Personally, I am a loyal Democrat. . . . I would like to vote with the leadership on more things but I just cannot. My constituency won't permit it. (southern Democrat)

In the least supportive, but rare, response categories, congressmen expressed considerable alienation from their parties:

> I am a maverick. . . . I do not want to feel coerced. But even we mavericks can show our responsibility and identity as Republicans on a few issues like debt limit and tax recommittal, although even on these I would change my vote to save the bill if necessary. (Republican)

The question asked of U.S. House members probed their personal preferences. The responses expressed what the members wanted to do and what they preferred to do. There is a strong association between their responses, preferences, and their voting record: The congressmen's party loyalty voting scores varied with the extent of their party-supportive answers to the question.

Another question probed the party obligations which members felt they incurred as elected officials: "To what extent do you feel you have an obligation to vote with your party on legislation?" The prior question asked for personal preferences, while this one probed for a sense of duty or responsibility. The positive response was much lower to this normative question than to the preference question: Only about a third indicated they had any degree of obligation to vote with their party, while the majority denied that party obligation. The responses were fairly similar for the two parties.

One of the more emphatic statements assenting to a party obligation was made by a Republican who has been the majority leader in his state legislature before coming to Congress:

> Yes! I am a straight party man! To these mavericks I say go to hell. They vote against the party even when their own districts do not require it— they come from safe Republican districts. Voting every which way is no good. You cannot build a party that way; you need party discipline.

While many congressmen have earlier served in their state legislature, not many have well-organized and disciplined parties; perhaps this member expressed a lonely view in the Congress because of his own rather unique earlier experience.

The more common denial of any party obligation or responsibility was expressed by another Republican:

> I go along with the party on minor matters. But I disagree on issues affecting my district and state, and on the national welfare.

A number of congressmen were consistently loyal in their legislative voting, but nevertheless, denied any obligation to do so:

> The congressman has no obligation to vote with the party. This is not an English parliamentary system. He is free to vote as he interprets the situation in and light of his convictions and circumstances in his district.

Several other members also expressed the view that circumstances in the American Congress were different from those in parliamentary systems; thus, these responses compliment those of Canadian M.P.s who responded that they supported their parties for reasons of party advantage and because of the requirements of the parliamentary system.

Congressmen—at least most of them—do value their party. But this attachment to party is not so much a result of party leadership or organizational constraint as it is a result of the prior commitments of district and personal views on legislation.

To congressmen the congressional party is not so much a source of attitude on issues as it is an instrument, or a vehicle, through which they attempt to gain allies. A moderate and urban Republican commented, "Yes, I want to be with my party, but more importantly, I want my party to be with me!"

There is one source of agreement between the American and

Canadian interviews: both refer to the chief executive as the source of "party" legislation, with the Canadians using the term "the government," and the Americans the terms, "president" or "administration." The American interviews were done during the Johnson administration, and Democrats, whether they supported the administration or not, acknowledged it as the source of Democratic bills. One Democrat said, "The president is the operative party here." Republicans turned to their congressional party policy committee for issue leadership, but acknowledged the president as the source of party policy, either by referring to their earlier experience under Eisenhower or to Democratic presidents as providing negative definitions of Republican policies. They were in the circumstance during the Kennedy-Johnson years as a conservative southern Democrat described his situation under Eisenhower: "It is easier to vote 'no' than to vote 'yes.'"

Summary

Congressmen are not in agreement on what their party should be or could become. Their differing views are compounded of their personal stands on issues, their agreements and disagreements with the president, and the policies preferred by their district electorates. Many of the same liberal northern Democrats, cited above, themselves strongly opposed Johnson's Vietnam policies toward the end of his administration.

The complexity and confusion of American congressional attitudes toward their political parties offer a strong contrast with those of Canadian M.P.s. This contrast, in turn, reflects the very different characteristics of their respective political parties and also reflects the differences between a parliamentary and a presidential governmental structure. Unfortunately, we lack comparative sets of interviews with parliamentary members in other countries.

NONPARTY GROUPS

Members of legislative bodies can also organize themselves by characteristics other than their political party. The strategy of such groups is to concentrate upon an issue or a set of issues, attempting to gain support for their position within and across all political parties. They attempt to avoid becoming involved in interparty strife.

Within the U.S. House, the black and women's congressional caucuses are examples of groups of members formed on the basis of a demographic attribute, to which members would be attracted across party lines. The rural caucus appeals to members on the basis of constituency characteristics, while the New England caucus unites members across party lines from a single region. Some groups are more broadly defined by issue interests: The Environmental Study Conference and the Members of Congress for Peace through Law are examples. An even more broadly defined congressional group is the Congressional Clearinghouse on the Future. These nonparty groups range in size from a dozen to almost 200 members. Some include members from both chambers, while others do not. Most prepare briefing and information services for their members on coming legislation, while others also attempt to mold and coordinate strategy among their members on bills and amendments.[52]

CONCLUSIONS

Political parties are complex organizations. They are also highly variable from one country to another. In some countries the parliamentary party is a highly organized and cohesive entity. In some countries the parliamentary party is the critical link between parliament and the chief executive. In Communist party states and in some newly independent nations the single party is the dominant element within government; in others the single party is only a creation of the dominant leader.

American congressional parties are, compared to most parliamentary parties, uncohesive and not strongly organized. They are today the product of a concerted and elaborate attempt to break the power of strong leadership at about the turn of the century, which was perceived as overly strong and symbolized by the term "Czar" applied to the House Speakers.

One trend within the American Congress—especially among House Democrats—over the past decade has been to increase the power of the political party. Sanctions have been applied against House Democrats who openly supported presidential candidates of other parties, and incumbent committee chairmen have been removed from their chairmanships. This trend is consistent with the reform efforts in the national Democratic conventions, which have broadened popular participation by enforcement of national party control over state and local parties.

There are contrary trends, however, in that simultaneous concurrent growth of subcommittee power and autonomy has considerably decentralized policy and party leadership within the House. Furthermore, it is too early to tell whether the party changes are only a product

[52] U.S. Congress. House. Commission on Administrative Review, *Background Information on Administrative Units, Members' Offices, and Committees and Leadership Offices: Communication from the Chairman,* pp. 95–96.

of intraparty factionalism or will survive as genuine party-wide developments.

In a way the efforts to reform our parties by increasing their national organizational power and sanctions is to move in the direction of the British model of a parliamentary party. In countries with strongly developed and cohesive parties it is perhaps ironic that their reform efforts are in our direction—to loosen the organizational centralization of their parliamentary parties.

Chapter 6
Internal Organization: Committees in the Legislative Process

If parties are one means by which the members and work of a parliament are organized, committees are the other major device for internal organization. Although most parliaments use both methods, the importance and activities of committees are far more variable among nations than are those of parties.

Parties and committees are alternative ways of organizing a parliamentary body; they are also ultimately contradictory and even mutually exclusive means of internal organization. The importance of each is inversely proportional to the other. The more important the committees, the less important the parties, and vice versa.[1] The mutual antagonism between these two means of internal organization may be illustrated by the contrast between the British House of Commons and the American Congress. British committees are relatively few and unimportant, with the major legislative decisions being made inside each party. American committees are far better organized, more numerous, and make critical decisions on bills, with the party leadership being

[1] Malcolm Shaw and John D. Lees, *Committees* (Durham, N.C.: Duke University Press, forthcoming), chap. 10, p. 44.

relatively less important in most legislative decisions. In Commons, proposals to strengthen the committee system have been rejected by party leaders; in Congress, a recent effort has been made to strengthen the parties by reducing the autonomous organization and powers of committees.

Probably the most important distinction to be made among parliamentary committee systems is between those in which committees have original jurisdiction over legislation and those in which committees only consider legislation in an advisory and amendatory capacity. From this distinction flow many other differences in the ways in which parliaments organize and utilize their committees. These distinctions will be discussed in the first section of this chapter. We shall then describe the activities of committees as working groups and examine them in relationship to the chief executive and to political parties. Finally, we shall consider several problems of coordination that a complicated committee system creates for itself.

Most of the material to be discussed in this chapter concerns the American Congress, because its committees are better organized, better staffed, produce a larger volume of printed documentation, and are more powerful than the committees in most other of the world's parliaments.

COMMITTEE SYSTEMS AND COMMITTEE TYPES

Committee Systems

In some parliaments (of which the U.S. Congress is the best example), legislative committees have complete powers over the bills assigned to them, whereas in other systems (of which the British House of Commons is the best example) committees consider only the details of bills (Table 6.1). Congressional committees receive bills upon introduction, can refuse to report a bill, or can extensively amend it if they do send the bill to the floor. That is, congressional committees have complete discretion over all aspects of the proposed bill. By contrast, a bill in the British Commons is not sent "upstairs" to a committee until after that bill has been debated on the floor, and the House has accepted the bill in principle. Only after that decision by the House does a committee work on a bill, but its competence is restricted to details and specifics. It cannot reject the bill, or change any provisions regarded by the majority party (i.e., the cabinet) as matters of principle and general policy.

A further constraint upon committees in the British House of Commons is that until recently financial matters were not referred to committees. The principles of both spending and taxation bills are mainly handled by the whole membership in an informal procedure

Table 6.1 CONTRASTING LEGISLATIVE COMMITTEE SYSTEMS:
U.S. CONGRESS AND BRITISH HOUSE OF COMMONS

CRITERIA	U.S. CONGRESS	BRITISH COMMONS
Place in stage of legislative procedure	Initial; prior to floor	Secondary; after approval on floor
Discretion over bill	Complete	Details only
Version of bill on floor	Committee	Cabinet
Floor leaders in charge of a bill	Committee leaders	Cabinet and opposition party leaders
Number	Many	Few
Size	Small	Large
Jurisdiction	Fixed	Changing
Membership permanence	Yes	No
Chairmanship selection	Seniority rule; internal to committee	By Speaker
Chairmanship allocation among parties	Majority party only	Mostly majority party
Power to investigate	Yes	By few select committees
Staff	Yes	No

termed "Committee of the Whole House," which will be discussed more fully in the following chapter on floor proceedings. The effect of this procedure is to deny the possibility that some small portion of the membership might assume control over the essentials of finance and spending. Rather, the cabinet, the responsible minister (chancellor of the exchequer), and the majority party retain firm control at all stages of consideration of these measures.

Those committees that receive bills before they are considered on the floor have the opportunity to be in charge of the following floor debate. In the U.S. system the ranking members of both parties on a committee will be in charge of a bill from the time it is introduced (usually by them) to the final step of presidential signature. The ranking committee members will be in charge of committee hearings and decisions and will be in charge of floor debate and voting in the full chamber. If a conference committee will be needed to reconcile interchamber differences, the same ranking committee members will be appointed to the conference committee. When the conference committee report returns to each chamber, the same members will be in charge, again, of floor consideration. Finally, when the president signs the bill in a public ceremony, the same committee leaders will be there, standing behind the president in the picture (see Fig. 6.1) and receiving the pens used to sign the bill.

A number of other differences accompany the differences in legislative activity. U.S. committees are more numerous, are smaller, and, accompanying their fixed jurisdiction, have a relatively fixed member-

Figure 6.1   Signing an act of Congress; President Carter signs the
Energy Bill, November 9, 1978, flanked by congressional party and
committee leaders. (White House photograph)

ship. That is, once a member goes on a committee, he ordinarily has
the right to remain on that committee. From membership permanence
stems the seniority rule, through which the member who has been on
the committee's majority party side the longest becomes chairman. As
we have already seen in the previous chapter, this aspect of the
American congressional system has recently been modified.

The British system, in contrast to the American, has fewer but
larger legislative committees. The committees have neither fixed jurisdictions nor memberships. All of these characteristics preclude the
members as individuals, and the committees as collective entities, from
developing either expertise in a given subject matter or any sense of
status or importance from their committee activity. The committee

chairmen are selected by the Speaker and are expected to preside at committee stage in the same impartial way the Speaker does at floor stage. They come from the two largest parties, and are assigned in rotation to the various committee meetings.

The two countries also differ in the selection method and powers of the chairmen. The British committee chairmen are, in the main, selected by the Speaker to form a "panel," who then chair the legislative committees on a rotating basis as bills are referred to the committees. Until recently, chairmen of American congressional committees have been selected through the "seniority" rule, which effectively removed that choice from both the Speaker and from the congressional party.

Quite in addition to the consideration of legislation, American congressional committees have the twin powers of investigation and agency supervision. As we noted in Chapter 4, committees are a major means by which parliaments may scrutinize the activities of administrative agencies. Those countries that structure their parliamentary committees to parallel the organization of government agencies are better equipped to review agency activities than those that do not (refer to Table 4.14). The United States and Poland are examples of parliaments in which committees regularly, as part of their continuing duties, review and investigate agency administration of programs entrusted to them.

About half the countries follow the British model, in which the legislative committees do not have the authority to investigate administrative agencies. Instead they typically create specially defined committees to investigate selected aspects of administration, which cut across numerous agencies and have no specific subject matter content. The British Public Accounts Committee is a case in point. Its charge is to ascertain whether or not agencies have expended funds legally and properly. It does not have jurisdiction over the content or propriety of the policies themselves. It does have an important postaudit function, and its potential importance is indicated by the requirement that its chairman be from the opposition party—a major exception to the usual British practice.

Committees are far more than meetings of some members of parliament. They can also consist of staff to obtain evidence and to analyze issues and problems, quite in addition to the clerical tasks of record keeping and bill drafting. The American congressional committees are a clear exception to the rest of the world in that the committees all have a permanent and professional staff assigned to them. In other parliaments, and in most of the American state legislatures as well, the staff for committees are few, largely clerical, and mostly "borrowed" from administrative agencies.

In the early sessions of the American Congress, standing committees were not used. Rather, bills were referred to ad hoc committees. Each committee was created for, and dissolved with the conclusion of its work upon, a single bill. This procedure is used currently in some parliaments (e.g., Denmark's Folketing). From these beginnings, the current American system of strong standing committees slowly evolved. Although the early U.S. Congress was modeled upon the British House of Commons in its procedure and organization, the two parliaments have, from that common origin, evolved very different committee systems.

Most parliaments have relatively few committees. For the 54 countries for which we have information, almost half have nine or fewer committees (Table 4.14), of which Australia, Zambia, Czechoslovakia, India, and South Africa are examples. A number of former British colonies are in this group, following Britain's lead. Among the seven countries having 20 or more committees are Argentina, Austria, Belgium, Denmark, Netherlands, Poland, and the United States. Countries such as West Germany, Japan, Switzerland and the Soviet Union are in the middle group, having from 10 to 19 committees.[2]

With the exception of the clustering of former British colonies, there does not seem to be much of a pattern among nations or political systems in the number of committees. The one pattern that does appear has already been indicated in Table 4.14: the larger the number of committees, the more they tend to parallel the organization of administrative agencies. A fairly large number of committees permit—though do not require—a subject-matter specialization among them. To the extent that committee specialization corresponds to the jurisdiction and activities of government agencies and thus to the major cabinet offices, the possibilities are increased for parliamentary knowledge about and supervision over the conduct of agency activities and executive initiated legislation.

The size of committees also varies among parliaments and within any one parliament. One limiting consideration is the size of parliament itself. A large parliament may, with few committees, either have very large ones or have only some of its members serving on committees. At the other extreme, a small parliament with many committees may have both small ones and its members serving on many such committees. (Tables 6.8 and 6.9 list the U.S. congressional committees and their sizes.)

Another limiting consideration more concerns the tasks of the committees themselves. A large committee having a broad subject

[2] Valentine Herman and Francoise Mendel, *Parliaments of the World* (Berlin: De Gruyter, 1976), pp. 631–637. For an alternative list, see Jean Blondel, *Comparative Legislatures* (Englewood Cliffs, N.J.: Prentice-Hall, 1973), pp. 156–157, col. 7.

matter may divide into specialized subcommittees, whereas a small committee could be overwhelmed by too large a subject matter and too extensive a workload. But if one task of a committee is to work upon a portion of the parliament's business, another task is to represent the membership of parliament. The requirements of representation may lead to a rather large committee, depending upon the diversity of parliament's members. In the U.S. Congress, the Appropriations Committees are the largest committees in their respective chambers, reflecting the importance of their activities and the desire by all interested segments of members to be represented in the work of those committees. At the other extreme, the House Rules Committee, one of the three most important committees in the House, is fairly small. Its major task, though covering most legislation from other committees, is limited to clearing bills for action on the floor. Its centralized leadership function and the desire of party leaders to control it lead to a fairly small size. As we indicated in the prior chapter, the House Rules Committee is more a chamber management committee of the parties than a committee with a typical limited jurisdiction.

Within the Supreme Soviet the largest committees handle the budget and the basic economic enterprises. The Planning and Budget Committee has 51 members for each of the two chambers, while the Industry Committees have 41 members each. The other committees have 31 to 35 members each.[3]

Although in most parliaments all members are assigned to committees, in some they are not. In the British Parliament, for example, committee participation is limited by the practice of at least some members of holding full-time jobs. In the Supreme Soviet, as another example, the total number of committee memberships amounted to about 60% of the full size of the Supreme Soviet (1966–1970), while the number of committee memberships in the Polish Sejm has now exceeded the total membership, amounting to 140% of the total.[4]

But the Supreme Soviet has yet another practice, which complicates our understanding of the term "member." The committees apparently attach to themselves a number of experts on a given bill, those experts in effect becoming voting as well as deliberating members of the committee whenever the committee works on the relevant bill.[5]

Although we have stressed the inverse relationship between party and committee strength, some parliaments do combine both a strong party system with a strong committee system. Both Germany and

[3] Peter Vanneman, *The Supreme Soviet: Politics and the Legislative Process in the Soviet System* (Durham, N.C.: Duke University Press, 1977), p. 123.

[4] D. Richard Little, "Soviet Parliamentary Committees After Khrushchev: Obstacles and Opportunities," *Soviet Studies* 24 (July 1972), pp. 43–44; and Poland, *Rocznik Polityczny i Gospodarczy*, 1974 (Warsaw: GUS), pp. 101–102.

[5] Vanneman, *The Supreme Soviet*, p. 132.

Sweden, as examples, have standing legislative committees, possessing broad jurisdiction over legislation. Both also have relatively few and strongly organized parties. The legislative committees, in these instances, become the locale within which the parties' experts negotiate with one another. Assuming that the majority party (or coalition of parties) members on the committee remain united in support of the government's bill, the majority members will attempt to compromise on minor points to reduce the intensity of opposition to the bill if not to develop a compromise that most parties would be able to support on the floor. Even if a party (or coalition) has a majority, the leaders would ordinarily rather have a noncontentious debate and solid vote margin than a bitter and divisive debate with a narrow vote margin.

There is one important difference, however, between the German and Swedish committees: West German legislative committees have defeated government bills, but Swedish committees have not. This difference is critical in principle, though it is infrequent in practice. Although West German governments are created by a vote of parliament, that government cannot be dismissed from office by a rejection of one of its bills. Furthermore, the government ministers, once selected, are no longer leaders of their party, though they continue as members of the Bundestag. The Swedish Riksdag is more similar to the British Commons in these respects: the cabinet ministers remain the leaders of the parliamentary party. They could, if they chose, make a vote on any given bill a test vote on the continuance of the current cabinet. Although we lack interview evidence on these points, it would appear that the partial removal of the German cabinet from parliament frees parliament to create its own parliamentary party leadership and creates the conditions under which a Bundestag committee can even defeat a government proposal.[6] It would, by contrast, appear that in Sweden the committee members, remaining under the active leadership of their cabinet members, do not have the same freedom of maneuver.

Committees not only facilitate negotiation among party leaders but also provide an important locale within which the leaders of a party confront the views of their own members. In addition to the network of groups within a party, the British "back-benchers" use parliamentary committees as a forum within which they can raise questions with the minister and suggest changes for his consideration. If a minister cannot secure support from his own party at committee stage, his bill would encounter the prospect of defeat on the floor—in face of which he

[6] John E. Schwarz and L. Earl Shaw, *The United States Congress in Comparative Perspective* (Hinsdale, Ill.: Dryden, 1976), pp. 77, 207–210; Gerard Braunthal, *The West German Legislative Process: A Case Study of Two Transportation Bills* (Ithaca: Cornell University Press, 1972), pp. 153–156.

might withdraw or at least postpone his own bill. This reaction has been observed in the British, French, and German parliaments.[7]

France has experienced both extremes of committee autonomy and importance. Since the end of World War II, its Assembly committees alternatively have had plenary jurisdiction over legislation and have had their powers considerably reduced. During the Fourth Republic, the Assembly committees held powers of amendment and defeat over legislation, even though the Assembly parties created the cabinets. The difficulty lay in the number and size of parties: no party had a majority, so that several parties formed a coalition to form a government. The cabinets were unstable and frequently dissolved. Under these circumstances the members most concerned about, and expert in, a given subject matter gravitated to the committee with jurisdiction over that subject. They agreed among themselves on a bill, quite independently of the wishes of their own party leaders or cabinet, and it was their bill that then reached the floor and could be adopted. This circumstance represented the height of committee power.

Charles de Gaulle, reacting against the fragmentation of parties and the relative instability and powerlessness of cabinet government in the preceding Fourth Republic, created in the Fifth Republic a very different committee system. Assembly committees were reduced in number, increased in size, and restricted in powers. Committees may debate a government bill and propose amendments. But the version that reaches the floor for debate and voting is decided by the cabinet, not the committee. Furthermore, the Assembly may vote on only those amendments the government approves. Thus, Assembly committees have lost to the cabinet not only policy jurisdiction but even control over details. Finally ad hoc investigatory committees of the French Assembly are limited in duration to four months, after which they are disbanded and cannot be reconstituted during the following year. These changes, along with the greatly increased constitutional powers of the cabinet over the Assembly, have resulted in a major diminution of the powers of French legislative committees.[8]

In single-party parliaments members apparently have greater freedom to work in committees than on the floor. Although in most one-party parliaments any bill proposed by the government will pass, committees do have varying latitude to examine and even modify the details of legislation. Some parliaments include members of the non-ruling party (e.g., Poland), and others (even in the USSR) have independent members not affiliated with any party. Although we know little of how such members are placed on parliamentary committees, it is within the committees that such members are able to speak, to raise

[7] Schwarz and Shaw, ibid., pp. 201–209; Braunthal, ibid., pp. 142–155.
[8] Philip Williams, *The French Parliament* (New York: Praeger, 1968), pp. 50–64.

questions, and even to suggest revisions. Committees also provide an opportunity for the ordinary member of the ruling party to speak and to act. Few Eastern European parliaments meet for long periods of time; thus few members are able to speak in floor debate. If members are to speak and act legislatively, the committee system can better provide the locale and opportunity than can sessions on the floor.[9]

Parliaments vary in the extent to which they refer bills to committees. Even in one-party parliaments with strong central party leadership, important bills can be referred to committees. In the Russian parliament, for example, 14 of 27 statutes adopted in the 1958–1962 period were referred to committees. In the 1962–1966 period, of the 241 proposals introduced to the Supreme Soviet, only 53 were referred to any of the standing committees. In addition, the most important annual bills—the budget and economic plan—are usually examined by the standing Planning-Budget Committee of the Supreme Soviet.[10]

In addition to the major functions of committees we have already discussed, some parliaments allocated other tasks to their committees. The Italian parliament, for example, permits its committees to enact legislation without reporting it to the floor. Usually committees formally act in an advisory capacity to the whole chamber, but in Italy the final authoritative act of adopting (or not) legislation can be handled by the committees themselves. Committees are given this authorization for legislation considered of minor importance and little controversy.[11]

American committees have also, on occasion, taken on an additional function—of investigating persons and private groups for alleged infractions of the law. The hearings conducted in the 1950s by Senator Kefauver (D-Tenn.) on organized crime and by Senator McCarthy (R-Wis.) on disloyalty raised many questions about infringement by congressional committees upon the civil liberties of the targets of their investigations.

Types of Committees

The many committees in the world's parliaments defy any simple classification into a few types, but we will suggest ten different types of

[9] Hansjakob Stehle, *The Independent Satellite: Society and Politics in Poland Since 1945* (New York: Praeger, 1965), pp. 178–179; Vanneman, *The Supreme Soviet,* pp. 140–146.

[10] L. G. Churchward, *Contemporary Soviet Government* (New York: Elsevier, 1968), p. 127, reports the 1958–1962 datum; Little, "Soviet Parliamentary Committees," p. 55, reports the 1962–1966 figure.

[11] Giuseppe Di Palma, "Institutional Rules and Legislative Outcomes in the Italian Parliament," *Legislative Studies Quarterly* (May 1976), p. 151.

Table 6.2   A TYPOLOGY OF COMMITTEES, WITH EXAMPLES

	PERMANENCE OF JURISDICTION AND MEMBERSHIP	
FUNCTION	SHIFTING	PERMANENT
Legislation	Britain, Denmark	U.S., West Germany, Poland, Canada
Budget	—	U.S., West Germany, USSR
Government review	—	Britain, U.S.
Investigative	U.S., Britain	—
Internal leadership	U.S.	U.S., West Germany, USSR

parliamentary committees based upon the two criteria of, first, whether their membership and jurisdiction is permanent or shifting and, second, its major task (Table 6.2). Of the ten possible types, we have found examples of only seven; three of the logical possibilities in the table are vacant.

Most committees probably have a legislative function; that is, they review proposed bills. Most committees of this type probably more resemble the American than the British pattern in that they have a permanent existence rather than a shifting membership and jurisdiction.[12] Most parliaments also resemble the American model in that their budget and tax-writing tasks are assigned to specific and permanent committees, whereas the British Parliament handles those matters mainly on the floor. The government review function can either be allocated among the existing legislative committees as in the U.S. model, or be assigned to a few permanent committees expressly created for that purpose. The British committees on Expenditure and on Nationalized Industries are examples of the latter circumstance, as are the Governmental Affairs Committees in the U.S. Senate and the Government Operations Committee in the House. Investigatory committees can also be created. They are usually ad hoc, formed for a specific investigation and dissolved once that task has been completed. The U.S. Senate's Watergate Committee is an example.

Another type of committee has an internal management or leadership task. The U.S. House Rules Committee is an example of such a committee of considerable importance to the fate of most legislation. Other internal management committees are more routine in their tasks, such as the House Administration Committee's jurisdiction over the allocation of office space and staff. Most parliaments have an internal leadership committee, called the Council of Elders in both West Germany and the Soviet Union, which frequently consists of the leaders of the several parliamentary parties. It is more of a negotiating locale for the party leaders than a committee of the chamber itself. Neverthe-

---

[12] The German and British practices are discussed in Schwarz and Shaw, *The United States Congress in Comparative Perspective*, pp. 278–283.

less, like the House Rules Committee, it handles the scheduling of legislation. Although most of the internal management committees appear to be permanent, the U.S. Congress has occasionally appointed ad hoc committees to review committee organization and internal procedures.

A very different type is the joint committee, formed by members from two (or more) houses of parliament, which is possible only in parliaments having two or more chambers. The joint committee frequently could be placed in any of the previous categories. That is, this type of committee is more defined by its structure than by its function. Conference committees in the United States are examples of ad hoc committees formed between the two houses for a legislative and/or budgetary purpose, to work out a compromise between two different versions of the same bills passed in each house. The U.S. Congress also has four permanent joint committees; none of these, however, reviews legislation. Until Sweden abolished its upper house in the early 1970s, all of its permanent legislative committees were joint between the two houses. Apparently the committees of the Supreme Soviet, though formed separately in the two chambers, frequently meet together as a matter of practice.

Prestige Ranking

Another way to classify committees is in terms of their relative desirability to members. Such a prestige ranking occurs only inside any given legislative body, and is hard to extend across national boundaries to include more than a single parliament. We can cite two studies of prestige rankings, one in the American Congress, the other for the Canadian Parliament.

U.S. CONGRESS

Six committees in the U.S. House of Representatives are listed in Table 6.3 in descending order of importance and desirability. One way to measure the relative rankings of committees is to examine the transfers of the members among them. The Ways and Means, Appropriations, and Foreign Affairs committees have almost no one leaving them to join another committee, whereas the transfers out of the other three committees are much higher. The second column shows one of the consequences of such transfers for each committee as a whole: close to 40% of the members of the Interior and Post Offices committees have not had prior experience on those committees. Although membership stability is one major distinguishing feature of the American committee system contrasted with the British, such membership stability is not found equally on all the congressional committees. That freshmen become members of the lower-ranked committees is

Table 6.3 COMMITTEE RANKINGS IN THE U.S. HOUSE BY FIVE CRITERIA, 1955–1956

COMMITTEES	MOVEMENT FROM	TO	NEW MEM-BERS (%)	MEM-BERS SEEKING COMMIT-TEES (%)	AVER-AGE YEARS OF HOUSE SERVICE	FRESH-MAN MEM-BERS (%)
Ways and Means	0	12	21	71	6.6	4
Appropriations	1	27	20	65	3.7	14
Foreign Affairs	2	12	23	93	3.1	30
Education and Labor	10	4	27	58	1.2	69
Interior	23	1	36	61	.80	73
Post Office	20	0	41	29	.78	74

SOURCE: Adapted from Richard F. Fenno, Jr., *Congressmen in Committees* (Boston: Little, Brown, 1973), tables 2.2 and 2.4, pp. 17 and 19–20, and table 4.4, p. 112.

indicated in the last two columns. Freshmen tend to be placed on Education and Labor, on Interior, and on the Committee on Post Office and Civil Service.[13]

A third criterion by which to judge committees is the method of obtaining membership. The second column of the same table shows the proportion of members who actively sought to be placed on each committee: Ways and Means and Foreign Affairs have the highest rate of self-selection, whereas the Post Office and Civil Service Committee the least. To make up for the lack of member interest in the unchosen committees, some members are assigned to committees. This method has been used only with the bottom three committees, accounting from 18% to 53% of their memberships.

The interest and activity of the party leaders in placing members on committees is another indication of the relative importance of the committees, but on this criterion we have less precise evidence. Party leaders have selected 30% to 40% of the members of the Ways and Means and the Appropriations Committees, but no more than 15% of any of the others. For both of the budget-related committees, party leaders seek members who have earned the reputation of being conscientious in their work habits, approachable and cooperative in their interpersonal relationships, and moderate in their policy attitudes. But party leaders have also used a policy-acceptability criterion, especially for Ways and Means. That committee, because of its tax jurisdiction, handles some of the major contentious issues between the parties, such as foreign trade and Medicare, and now tax reform. Because these

[13] Richard F. Fenno, Jr., *Congressmen in Committees* (Boston: Little, Brown, 1973), pp. 17–20.

issues are involved in presidential campaigns, an important component of the party leaders' choice is the attitude of the prospective member toward the presidential administration of their respective parties. Though the party leaders have shown relatively less interest in the Education and Labor Committee, they have selected members who would support (or oppose) the policies of Democratic presidents on minimum wages, the "war on poverty," and aid to education.[14]

CANADIAN PARLIAMENT

Several different measures, though necessarily different from those used for the Congress, have been combined to form a prestige index for the committees of the Canadian House of Commons. One measure was based upon the members' own observations about the importance to them of their committees. A second measure was the membership turnover rate, which is quite similar to the American measure. A third measure was based upon the extent to which party whips acted to ensure a full attendance at committee meetings. And the fourth measure was the volume of committee activity—the number of meetings and reports.

The top five ranking committees, by this composite measurement, were those on Finance, Transport and Communications, External (Foreign) Affairs and Defense, Justice, and Agriculture. At the other end of the scale, the committees on Privileges and Elections, Broadcasting, and Fisheries and Forestry ranked the lowest.

We would guess that committees involved with finances, foreign affairs, and national defense would rank as highly valued and important committees in most parliaments. Justice, because it involves the penal and often the police systems, would also be important in many countries. The relatively high importance in Canada of transport and agriculture perhaps more reflects the unique circumstances of that nation (or perhaps of then-current issues).[15]

Party and Chamber Committees Compared

The party committees discussed in the previous chapter may be compared with the chamber committees discussed here on the basis of their specialization. We have just noted that chamber committees, as in the United States and West Germany, are specialized by topic, in contrast to the nonspecialized committees of British-type parliaments. But consider the contrast with the party committees: They are highly specialized, by topic, in both West Germany and Britain. The party

[14] Ibid., pp. 25, 33–34.
[15] Allan Kornberg and William Mishler, *Influence in Parliament: Canada* (Durham, N.C.: Duke University Press, 1976), pp. 162–167.

committees in the United States, however, are unspecialized. As we will see in a coming section, there is a close interplay in the West German Bundestag between the chamber committees and the party committees: Their parallel structures permit, if not encourage, the members to function simultaneously as members of the two sets of related committees in working upon the same bills. In the British system, by contrast, the party committees seem to function mainly for the opposition party as a means of reacting to the government.[16] In the United States, the congressional parties have made only feeble efforts to form party policy positions: by default, a party's position is defined by the president (if of that party) or by the party members on the chamber committees.

Committee System Strength

We may compare the importance and strength of committee systems in eight countries and attempt to assess some of the characteristics of those nations that would be associated with variations in committee importance. Although our judgments are only in general terms, the committee systems of the United States, Italy, West Germany, and the Philippines (until its congress was abolished) appear more active and more important in their parliaments than in the other four countries of Canada, Great Britain, India, and Japan (Table 6.4). The four latter countries are all modeled upon the British parliamentary system; with the exception of Japan, their committees have all of the characteristics ascribed earlier to the British system. By contrast, the four countries with more important committee systems are either presidential in governmental structure or are examples of the parliamentary system found on the European continent.

The two sets of countries are also differentiated by the presence or absence of control by a single party. Committee systems are more important in the countries in which either no party has a majority (e.g., Italy), or in which the two parties, as in the United States, frequently split control of the Congress and the presidency. In the British type of parliamentary system, one party usually controls both the executive and the legislative body (although Britain began to depart from this pattern in the mid-1970s).

As we indicated earlier, committees tend to be more important if they have jurisdiction over legislation prior to its consideration at floor stage. The one exception is Japan.

We have referred to a legislative process within the executive branch in Chapter 4. In all systems, legislation is written, researched,

16 Anthony King, "Modes of Executive-Legislative Relations: Great Britain, France and West Germany," *Legislative Studies Quarterly* 1 (February 1976), p. 18.

Table 6.4 COMMITTEE SYSTEMS IN EIGHT PARLIAMENTS IN RANK
ORDER OF IMPORTANCE WITH SELECTED CHARACTERISTICS

ORDER OF IMPOR- TANCE	COUNTRIES	CONSTITU- TIONAL STRUCTURE	SINGLE- PARTY CON- TROL[a]	SEQUENCE: PRIOR TO FLOOR	PRIOR PREPA- RATION[b]
High	United States	Presidential	no	yes	low
Moderate	Italy	Cont. parlm.[c]	no	yes	low
	West Germany	Cont. parlm.	no	yes	high
	Philippines	Presidential	no	yes	?
Low	Canada	Br. parlm.[d]	yes	no	high
	Britain	Br. parlm.	yes	no	high
	India	Br. parlm.	yes	no	high
	Japan	Br. parlm.	yes	yes	high

SOURCE: Malcolm Shaw and John Lees, *Committees* (Durham, N.C.: Duke University Press, forthcoming), chap. 10.
[a] Of chief executive and legislature.
[b] Prior preparation of legislation by the executive and/or party before the proposed bill is sent to parliament.
[c] Continental parliamentary refers to systems modeled upon the French pattern.
[d] British parliamentary refers to systems modeled upon the British pattern.

and modified within the executive branch prior to its submission to the legislature. But nations vary in the thoroughness with which the executive attempts to consult with outside interest groups and to obtain agreement from all interested participants prior to its submission to parliament. Systems also vary in the extent to which the political parties consider and compromise legislation prior to its consideration by the committees. The process we have earlier described for Britain and West Germany illustrate countries ranking "high" in this respect, while the process by which the Carter administration prepared its energy proposal would place the United States in the "low" category. All of the four countries in which committees are relatively unimportant feature extensive prior executive and party preparation of legislation.

These judgments are as tentative as they are general. It would appear, however, that the constitutional structure provides the basic context within which committees are formed, whereas the pattern of dominance among the systems' parties defines the more immediate condition under which they function. Within those circumstances the sequencing of the committee jurisdiction and the extent of prior bargaining within the executive and major parties also help define the importance and strength of committee systems within parliaments.[17]

[17] This section is based upon Shaw and Lees, *Committees,* chap. 10.

Summary

We have considered the U.S. and the British committee systems as contrasting types, developing their distinctions on a series of criteria and indicating where other countries' parliamentary committees would fit. The basic distinction concerns the scope of jurisdiction committees possess over legislation.

We have also considered different ways of thinking about types of committees, both between legislative bodies and within any single one. We developed a two-dimensional way of classifying committees across legislative bodies and discussed a prestige ranking of committees within the U.S. and Canadian Houses. Finally we have attempted to compare committee systems in eight nations and have suggested several factors that seem to be associated with the degree of importance and strength of their committees.

COMMITTEES AT WORK

Hearings held by congressional committees are probably their one activity best known to the general public, for hearings are sometimes given extensive publicity. But the activity of committee members on legislation begins far in advance of the hearings, and continues far beyond them as well.

Bill Formulation

In the U.S. Congress, committees—especially their ranking members—are closely involved with a bill from its very beginning to the final steps. The stability of committee jurisdictions and the continuity of membership and of staff permit all participants to know in advance to which committee any given bill will be referred. As a result, major bills, especially those sponsored by the administration, will be introduced by a member of the relevant committee—often by a ranking member. The bill may be introduced by the committee chairman or by the chairman of the subcommittee to which the bill will be sent within the full committee. Indeed, such ranking members may have been consulted as the bill was being formulated. The long-term stability of committees and their memberships is paralleled by the stability of agencies and the civil service status of their employees, and also by the long-term existence of major interest groups and the fairly continuous service of their lobbying staffs. Thus all major participants in the legislative process on any given topic will know one another, will have worked together previously, and can consult with one another in the development of new legislation.

A new administration is a potential exception. To the extent that a new president brings with him a new staff and set of appointees, the new administration will lack the backlog of prior experience. Even though new officials will know neither the persons, the politics, nor the issues, the Carter campaign converted this situation into an electoral advantage. But the result was, in the rushed preparation of its energy proposals, that congressmen were not consulted in advance, and that the committee chairmen learned of the Carter proposals very little in advance of the general public.

The Sifting Function

Before hearings begin, however, another step must occur after the bill has been referred to a committee; that is, the committee must decide to hold hearings on a particular bill. It is at this point that committees make one of their major contributions to legislation: the sifting function. Here is the place at which the roughly 20,000 bills introduced in each two-year Congress are winnowed down to the roughly 1000 that pass. It is not so much that a committee decides not to consider a bill; rather, in the absence of a positive decision that a bill will be considered, nothing further happens to it. Although hearings will be held on the major administration bills, it is at this point where many of them are stopped, too. In 1960, for example, the last year of the Eisenhower administration, 23% of the president's legislative proposals received no action at all at committee stage. The corresponding percentages dropped to the range of 10% during several years of the Johnson administration (1965–1967).[18] Likewise, in the Italian parliament 20% of the government sponsored bills received no attention in the committees; for private-member bills, however, the proportion not receiving any action within the committees was nearly 80%.[19] Another indication of the sifting function of American congressional committees is found in Table 6.5, listing the number of bills received by and reported from five committees in the House. At the maximum, one committee reported 12% of the bills referred to it. On the average, only 6% of the referred bills were reported by the committees.[20]

In one session of the New Jersey legislature (1970–1971), the assembly committees received over 1700 bills, of which they reported out 590 (34%). Of the governor's bills, however, 100% were reported to the floor by the committees. This legislature illustrates yet another variation in systems: Not all bills are referred to committees in the

[18] Schwarz and Shaw, *U.S. Congress in Comparative Perspective*, p. 224. See also table 7.2 in the next chapter for more recent administrations and years.

[19] Di Palma, "Institutional Rules and Legislative Outcomes in the Italian Parliament," p. 163, table 5.

[20] Fenno, *Congressmen in Committees*, p. 257, table 6.20.

Table 6.5 BILLS RECEIVED AND REPORTED BY FIVE HOUSE
COMMITTEES, 89TH CONGRESS

| | | BILLS REPORTED | |
COMMITTEE	BILLS RECEIVED (N)	(N)	(PERCENT OF BILLS RECEIVED)
Ways and Means	3161	109	3
Interior	1057	130	12
Education/Labor	950	51	5
Post Office	870	48	6
Foreign Affairs	364	34	9
Total	6402	372	6

SOURCE: Adapted from Richard F. Fenno, Jr., *Congressmen in Committees* (Boston: Little, Brown, 1973), p. 257, table 6.20.

first place. The assembly committees were bypassed on 9% of the bills introduced in the assembly, and were bypassed on a much higher proportion (33%) of bills referred from the senate. Of the governor's bills, 27% were sent directly to the floor, thus bypassing the assembly's committees. Committees in the New Jersey legislature were less completely involved in the screening and sifting function than are committees in the U.S. Congress: They receive a lower proportion of all bills, and report out a higher proportion of the bills they do receive.[21]

The sifting function is not possible in British-type parliaments, for their committees receive bills only after they have been debated and adopted in principle on the floor by the full House. It is those committees, such as in the American Congress and the German Bundestag, receiving bills prior to floor consideration that can delay and stop legislation.

Hearings

Hearings will be held promptly on most major administration bills and on other bills of major interest to the ranking members. The hearings are the first major forum within which a bill will receive public visibility and, more important to its enactment, its first sustained scrutiny by Congress' experts—the members of the committee and their staff. If a bill in the hearings appears unreasonable, unworkable, undesirable, or unacceptable to major portions of Congress and the public, that bill will have suffered fatally.

The hearings may be reported in the newspapers and perhaps shown on television; the transcripts of the hearings will be published, and made available to the public and to all members of Congress. As a

[21] Alan Rosenthal, *Legislative Performance in the States: Explorations of Committee Behavior* (New York: The Free Press, 1974), pp. 127–128.

result, the hearings are carefully prepared. Government and other witnesses will present written testimony and supporting documents. They will prepare for the real hearings and its questioning by holding mock hearings during which they will practice receiving and responding to questions. The committee members themselves and their staff will develop a series of questions that will often indicate the member's basic support of or opposition to the bill's intent.

Government witnesses, especially on administration bills, will be the first persons to testify at the committee hearings. Major interest groups will also state their positions. They may support the bill, in whole or in part. They may, like the AFL-CIO often does on economic legislation, believe that the administration's bill is not strong enough. The groups may seek exemptions from the bill for themselves, as do the automobile industry and unions from stringent pollution controls, or they may oppose the bill in its entirety. Their opposition may be expressed through the presentation of alternative bills to better achieve —as they see it—the purpose of the original bill, as the AMA has suggested alternative health financing plans to the Carter administration's proposed publicly financed health insurance.

Hearings may take a couple of hours or several months. The published transcripts may be a thin pamphlet in size or contain several volumes of hundreds of pages each. The Senate's Watergate investigation hearings, for example, occupied 22 volumes, amounting to a total of 5858 pages.

Questioning of witnesses usually proceeds in a set pattern. After the witness has made the presentation (the written statements must be submitted in advance and distributed to the committee members), the chairman begins the questioning. In some committees, especially at investigative hearings, the committee's counsel will be the first questioner. Once the members begin their questions, they usually take turns, alternating between the party sides in descending order of seniority, which is the same order in which they are seated. First the chairman and then the ranking minority member, then the next ranked majority member, followed by his minority-side counterpart, and so on to the most junior members of the committee. Frequently the members will be limited in time (e.g., ten minutes) so that all members may have an opportunity to raise questions. The failure of some chairmen to distribute time equally to the junior members, even on the majority side, has led to bitterness among the members on those committees.

Markup

The *markup* stage follows the hearings. This term refers to the process of revising a bill, in which some words (or whole sections) are scratched out and others written in; the bill's copy is physically written or marked upon. It is at this point, which may take months, that the committee officially decides the provisions of the bill. A controversial bill may be debated and voted upon section by section, or line by line. The votes may be perilously close, and the outcome may be in doubt until the official vote is finally taken. Critical portions of the Carter administration's energy proposal, for example, were decided by one- and two-vote margins: The proposed pricing and tax provisions for natural gas were defeated and seriously revised by a two-vote margin in the House Subcommittee on Energy and Power. That decision was then reversed in the full Commerce Committee by only a one-vote margin. In the Senate, the Energy Committee was evenly split, 9–9, on the same issue and thus brought the bill to the floor without a recommendation. The same narrow split was continued in the Conference Committee, on which the Senate conferees remained evenly divided on the question of federal regulation of natural gas prices.[22]

Members usually sit arranged by party, and in descending order of seniority on each party side. During hearings in the formal and large hearing rooms the members sit at the front on a raised platform behind a curved table. At the markup stage, the members of small committees use a conference table to encourage direct discussion among the members, although the larger ones have no other place to work than in the hearing room on their raised platform. The members' deportment toward one another mixes the formalities of floor procedure (will the senator yield?) with the informalities of first-name joking banter. One example of the informality of committee proceedings is shown in Figure 6.2, even though it concerns a conference committee rather than a committee at work on a bill within its own chamber.

Only since the mid-1970s has this decision-making stage of committee proceedings been open to the public. Until then, the public's only view of that process occurred during the Nixon impeachment meetings of the House Judiciary Committee, in which each article of the impeachment resolution was read, debated, amended, and voted on live television.

Even before the public was admitted, however, agency personnel frequently attended the committee meetings. This practice was typical for the House Ways and Means Committee in preparing tax bills. Each amendment required an estimate of its tax consequences, which only the Department of the Treasury was able to provide. Now that the public is admitted, the faithful attenders are usually from the agencies, joined by interest-group lobbyists and the press.

[22] *Congressional Quarterly Weekly Report,* June 11, 1977, pp. 1137–1138; July 2, 1977, pp. 1335–1337; September 17, 1977, p. 1958.

Figure 6.2   Negotiation in Committee: Conference Committee on Energy.

Issue: The penalty on "gas guzzlers." How much of a penalty fee should an automobile manufacturer be charged for cars not meeting the standard of 18 miles per gallon, and under what conditions could the energy secretary impose the penalty?

Rep. Rogers: What about $7.50?

The House bill had stated $5.00 penalty for each tenth of a mile in excess of the standard; the Senate had adopted $10.00.

Sen. Metzenbaum: I'll take that.

Rep. Rogers: $7.50.

Rep. Dingel: This is not an auction.

He grumbled. From Michigan, he wanted stringent conditions under which the penalty could be assessed. The others wanted to bypass such conditions.

Rep. Staggers (chairman): Let's talk it out here, John.

Rep. Dingel: I'll make the same offer I did with the $7.50.

He insists that the secretary must make a "substantial" finding.

Rep. Eckhardt: What about "will result in or tend to compel" substantial energy conservation?

Rep. Rogers: Let's take "tend to compel." That's all right.

Rogers looked over to Dingel.

Rep. Dingel: That's your judgment, not mine.

Sen. Metzenbaum: I'll take "tend to compel."

Rep. Dingel: Let me just put a little paragraph on the end.

Still not willing to give in. Impatience in the room seemed to swell.

Later the same day:

Rep. Rogers: Significantly encourage?

Another wording suggested.

Someone: How about "affect"?

Rep. Dingel: Will result in or affect.

He agreed.

Sen. Jackson: Howard?

As chairman of the Senate conferees, Jackson seeks and gains agreement from his colleagues.

Sen. Metzenbaum: That's not bad.

SOURCE: *Congressional Quarterly Weekly Report*, September 30, 1978, p. 2715, supplied the verbatim dialogue in the left column of this figure, and is the basis for the commentary and interpretation in the right column.

Report

The final product of the committee stage of a bill is the revised version of the bill adopted by a committee vote, accompanied by a printed report. The committee report contains the text of the bill as originally introduced and as revised, and also contains the reasoning and justification for the committee's thinking. If the committee is not unanimous, the report will contain the majority view together with one or more dissenting statements. It may also contain several supplemental views. The report, thus, is the committee members' official public statement of their thinking about the bill in question. The printed report, as is the printed transcript of the hearings, is distributed to all members of Congress and are made available to the public upon request. See Figure 6.3 for a copy of the cover page of the report of the House Ad Hoc Committee on Energy on the Carter's administration's energy bill. It is the report upon the same bills in the hearings, shown in Figure 6.4, conducted by the Subcommittee on Energy and Power of the House Committee on Interstate and Foreign Commerce.

The Energy Bill, as reported to the House by the Ad Hoc Committee on Energy, is shown in Figure 6.5. This reproduction of the first page (of a 580-page bill) briefly states the bill's legislative history within the House and, just below the bill number, also states the number of the accompanying committee report shown in Figure 6.3.

One of the amended pages of this bill is shown in Figure 6.6. The original section 9 is printed in the bill with lines drawn through to show that those words had been stricken, and a new section 9, printed in italics, written in. Thus members can see both the original text and the committee's revised text as an amendment. The amendment shown here, concerning the definition of "old" and thus also of "new" oil and gas, was a critical source of dispute through the entire bill's laborious course through both houses and the ensuing conference committee as well.

Subsequent Stages

Although we shall discuss floor stage in greater detail in Chapter 7, we should note here that completion of the committee stage of a bill does not terminate the committee members' involvement with the bill. Instead, they turn their attention to floor stage, for they will be in charge of debate and voting on the floor. Should the two houses disagree in their versions of the bill, each chamber will send representatives to a conference committee on that bill. It is the ranking members of the original committees who are appointed to the conference committee, and it is they who will then have to bring the conference committee's

95TH CONGRESS *1st Session*	HOUSE OF REPRESENTATIVES	REPT. No. 95–543 VOLUME I

NATIONAL ENERGY ACT

REPORT

OF THE

AD HOC COMMITTEE ON ENERGY
U.S. HOUSE OF REPRESENTATIVES

TOGETHER WITH SUPPLEMENTAL, MINORITY, AND ADDITIONAL VIEWS

[Including Cost Estimate of the Congressional Budget Office]

ON

H.R. 8444

JULY 27, 1977.—Committed to the Committee of the Whole House on the
State of the Union and ordered to be printed

U.S. GOVERNMENT PRINTING OFFICE

93–621 O   WASHINGTON : 1977

Figure 6.3   Report of the House Ad Hoc Energy Committee: front cover.

PART 1
NATIONAL ENERGY ACT

HEARINGS

BEFORE THE

SUBCOMMITTEE ON ENERGY AND POWER

OF THE

COMMITTEE ON
INTERSTATE AND FOREIGN COMMERCE
HOUSE OF REPRESENTATIVES

NINETY-FIFTH CONGRESS

FIRST SESSION

ON

H.R. 6831, H.R. 687, H.R. 1562, H.R. 2088, H.R. 2818, H.R. 3317, H.R. 3664, H.R. 6660, and all similar and identical bills

BILLS TO ESTABLISH A COMPREHENSIVE NATIONAL
ENERGY POLICY

MAY 9, 10, 11, AND 16, 1977

Serial No. 95–22

Printed for the use of the
Committee on Interstate and Foreign Commerce

U.S. GOVERNMENT PRINTING OFFICE

WASHINGTON : 1977

91–931 O

Figure 6.4   Hearings on Carter Energy Bill by House Subcommittee on Energy and Power: front cover.

Union Calendar No. 283

95TH CONGRESS
1ST SESSION

H. R. 8444

[Report No. 95–543]

IN THE HOUSE OF REPRESENTATIVES

JULY 20, 1977

Mr. ASHLEY introduced the following bill; which was referred to the Ad Hoc Committee on Energy for a period ending not later than July 27, 1977

JULY 27, 1977

Reported with amendments, committed to the Committee of the Whole House on the State of the Union, and ordered to be printed

[Omit the part struck through and insert the part printed in italic]

A BILL

To establish a comprehensive national energy policy.

1   *Be it enacted by the Senate and House of Representa-*

2   *tives of the United States of America in Congress assembled,*

3   **SECTION 1. SHORT TITLE; TABLE OF CONTENTS.**

4   (a) SHORT TITLE.—This Act may be cited as the

5   "National Energy Act".

6   (b) TABLE OF CONTENTS.—

Sec. 1. Short title; table of contents.
Sec. 2. Findings and statement of purposes.
Sec. 3. National energy goals.
Sec. 4. References to Federal Power Commission and Federal Energy Administration.

I—O

Figure 6.5   The Energy Bill as reported to the House floor: first page.

185

1	(A) which was not leased before April 20,
2	1977; or
3	(B) which was leased before such date, under
4	a lease which terminated or was abandoned before
5	such date and was not in effect on such date.
6	(8) The term "new well" means a well the surface
7	drilling of which was begun after April 20, 1977.
8	~~(9) The term "old well" means any well other~~
9	~~than a new well.~~
10	*(9) The term "old well" means any well which—*
11	*(A) produced crude oil, natural gas, or both,*
12	*on or before April 20, 1977; or*
13	*(B) was capable of producing crude oil,*
14	*natural gas, or both, on April 20, 1977.*
15	(10) The term "completion location" means the
16	subsurface location from which crude oil or natural gas
17	is or has been produced from a reservoir.

Figure 6.6 The Energy Bill (H.R. 8444) as reported with an amendment by the Ad Hoc Committee on Energy. (Note: The original language removed by the committee has lines through the wording. The new language inserted by the committee is printed in italics. The original wording left unchanged is in ordinary (roman) type.)

report back to the floors of their respective houses to win adoption of the report.

If the president signs the bill, the committee members' only remaining immediate task is to attend the bill signing ceremony. If, however, the president vetoes the bill, then the ranking committee

Table 6.6   COMMITTEES BY NUMBER OF COMMITTEE MEETINGS
AND SUBCOMMITTEE MEETINGS, U.S. HOUSE[a]

SUBCOM-MITTEE MEETINGS	FULL COMMITTEE MEETINGS		
	1–9	10–24	25 OR MORE
200+			Appropriations
100–199	Judiciary	Science	Armed Services
		Education, Labor	International Relations
		Commerce	
51–99	Government	Banking	Agriculture
	Operations	Interior	Ways and Means
	Post Office	Merchant Marine	
	Public Works		
1–50	District of		House Administration
	Columbia		
	Small Business		
	Veterans		
None	Standards of	Budget	Rules
	Conduct		

SOURCE: U.S. Congress. House. Commission on Administrative Review, *Administrative Reorganization and Legislative Management*, Vol. 2: *Work Management*, p. 32, table 12.
[a] This table includes the first five months of 1977.

members, in consultation with the party leaders, decide whether or not to attempt to override the veto. If they decide to make the attempt, it is, once again, the committee members who lead floor debate and voting.

Meeting Frequency

Not all committees are equally active. Table 6.5, to which we have already referred, shows differences among committees not only in the proportion of bills they report to the floor, but also in the number of bills they receive in the first place. Another measure of activity is the frequency of meetings, whether for legislative or investigatory purposes. Table 6.6 shows the House committees by the frequency of their meetings both as whole committees and by subcommittees. Those committees located near the lower left-hand corner have relatively few meetings, whether of the whole or of subcommittees, whereas those in the upper right-hand corner have relatively many meetings, both as a whole and in subcommittees. Some committees function mainly through subcommittees, having relatively few meetings of the full committee but many of the subcommittees, of which the Judiciary Committee is an example. A few committees do not use subcommittees, but they are usually active as whole units, especially the Budget and Rules Com-

Table 6.7 SPEAKING IN COMMITTEE AND ON THE
FLOOR BY CATEGORY OF MEMBERS: CANADIAN
HOUSE OF COMMONS, 1969[a]

MEMBER CATEGORY	COMMITTEE: AVERAGE NUMBER OF SPEECHES	RATIO OF COMMITTEE TO FLOOR SPEECHES
All	664	43:1
Government party	1046	149:1
Opposition parties	454	22:1
Party leaders	933	154:1
Back-bencher	580	39:1

SOURCE: Allan Kornberg and William Mishler, *Influence in Parliament: Canada* (Durham, N.C.: Duke University Press, 1976), pp. 156 and 158, tables 4.11 and 4.12.
[a] Based upon sample of 34 members.

mittees.[23] This information covers the first five months of the first year of a two-year term, and hence the relative frequencies between subcommittee and full committee meetings may shift as bills are processed through the subcommittees and are then considered by the full committees on their way to the floor.

Committees in European Parliaments

This pattern of intensive involvement with each piece of legislation by the committee is precluded in the British system. The government and its majority party control and handle all stages of the bill. Even if the bill is amended in its details in the committee, it is the government that decides which amendments to accept and which version of the bill to bring back to the floor for final action.

The Canadian Parliament has, within the past decade, grafted an American-type committee system onto its British-derived parliament. One result, at least, has been to greatly increase the opportunities for members to speak. The average member, during a recent one-year session, spoke in committees over 660 times. Members of the government party spoke much more frequently than did the members of the opposition parties, and leaders of all parties, as might be expected, spoke more frequently than did the back-benchers of all parties (Table 6.7).

For all categories of members of the Canadian House of Commons,

[23] U.S. Congress. House. Commission on Administrative Review, *Background Information on Administrative Units, Members' Offices and Committees and Leadership Offices* (Washington, D.C.: House Doc. 95-178, 1977), p. 32, table 12.

the committee provided many more opportunities to speak than did the floor, thereby benefiting back-benchers and the opposite parties. But it was the party leaders and the government party members who most increased their speaking frequencies in committee over their use of the floor. Although committees expand the opportunity for participation, the patterns of speaking frequencies on the floor were not altered —but perhaps magnified—in the committees.[24]

The German and Swedish committees are more like the American ones. Their committees assume control of a bill, and it is their version that comes to the floor, whether or not the government approves. In the German Bundestag, for example, the two highway bills to which we have earlier referred each went to a different committee in the Bundestag. The Highway Relief bill, prepared by the Transportation Ministry, was mainly within the jurisdiction of the Bundestag's Transportation Committee. The Transportation Finance bill, prepared in the Ministry of Finance, mainly belonged to the jurisdiction of the Finance Committee. Yet because the two bills were closely related to each other, the two agencies had closely cooperated at each step in their preparation; likewise, the two bills were considered simultaneously by, though split among, the legislative committees. In addition, two other Bundestag committees considered the bills in an advisory capacity, the committees on Local Government and on Economic Affairs. The former, containing many members who were simultaneously officials of city and local governments, and the latter, with members closely related to business and industrial management, each sought exemptions from the two bills which favored the segments of society whom they represented. The latter committee, closely corresponding in jurisdiction to the governmental Ministry of Economic Affairs, flatly opposed one of the bills, as had its counterpart agency earlier.

The Finance Committee was the main decision-making committee, for it had jurisdiction over the main bill on Transportation Finance. The other bill was never reported out of the Transportation Committee and was thus killed. The Finance Committee, to coordinate its work with the three other committees, invited the members of those committees to meet with it when it made the final decisions the Transportation Finance bill. As we earlier indicated, the party caucuses and specialized party committees had also considered and acted upon each of the two bills. The final sessions of the Finance Committee became the locale of the last attempts at both interparty and intercommittee negotiation prior to the bill's appearance on the floor. The committee supported the government's provisions in some respects while rejecting others. In some instances the government's position was saved only by the supportive votes of the opposition Social Democrats, in the face

[24] Kornberg and Mishler, *Influence in Parliament,* pp. 156–159.

of extensive disaffection among its own party members of the Christian Democrats.[25]

Although the French General Assembly also has standing committees, their powers over legislation are much less than in the German parliament. As part of the effort to reduce the powers of the Assembly as a whole in relationship to the government, the committees have also been curbed. The French committees can adopt amendments to a government bill and bring them to the floor only with the government's permission. In addition, the government can control the time and agenda of the floor, so that committee amendments may be avoided or not even presented to the Assembly.[26]

The Supreme Soviet

The main work of committees of the Supreme Soviet of the USSR is done through their subcommittees, which are apparently formed specially for each bill. Most legislation, as opposed to budgetary matters, is handled by the standing Committee on Legislative Proposals of each of the two chambers, which often meet jointly and form an ad hoc joint subcommittee for each bill. The subcommittee, however, contains outside persons in its membership for the consideration of any specific bill. The subcommittee formed to consider the proposed law on the fundamental principles of criminal procedure, for example, had only six members of the Supreme Soviet among its 28 members. The other members were from the concerned administrative agencies and from university faculties and institutes of law. The first draft of the proposed code was prepared by a juridical commission, which in turn was created jointly by the Council of Ministers and the Communist party. Its draft was then sent to the specially created subcommittee of the Supreme Soviet. The subcommittee developed and considered three additional drafts during the following year (1958). The first subcommittee draft was distributed to all members of the parent Committees on Legislative Proposals, at least seven of whom held conferences in their home districts among jurists to consider the draft. The second draft was published in all the national law journals to encourage comments. This second draft contained important changes over the first, which in turn had been modified from the originally received document. One observer commented, ". . . it is clear from my conversations with subcommittee members that they regarded the Judicial Commission's draft as little more than a set of working

[25] Braunthal, *The West German Legislative Process*, pp. 142–155.

[26] William G. Andrews, "The Constitutional Prescription of Parliamentary Procedures in Gaullist France," *Legislative Studies Quarterly* 3 (August, 1978), pp. 488–493.

papers . . ." There was still a third draft within the subcommittee which was largely the version finally adopted by the Supreme Soviet. But the third draft, too, was distributed to the full Committees on Legislative Proposals and was considered both in district conferences and by the concerned administrative and legal agencies of the government.

The changes made in successive drafts were both numerous and substantive. The issue was not unimportant, for criminal law can be used to curb the expression of political or other dissent. Apparently the Communist party took no overt role in these discussions and expressed no clear preference. As a result, the disputes were open and spirited, though the participants were largely confined to that specialized sector of society that professionally worked with criminal law in the universities, the judiciary, and the prosecutorial offices. The subcommittee sessions themselves,

> by all accounts . . . had been marked by frequent and spirited debates. One informant emphasized . . . that . . . members of the subcommittee understood that their professional obligations included the duty to allow the joint Committee on Legislative Proposals to hear all sides of every issue.

The subcommittee apparently attempted to achieve consensus among its divided members. In the absence of such consensus, issues were decided by a majority vote. Those who lost in the subcommittee could present their case to the full committee, and on at least four issues the full committee reversed the recommendation of the subcommittee's majority. That the Supreme Soviet approved the final text without dissent does not disguise the debate and disputes that led to the proposal placed before them, nor did it prevent a continuance of the same debate among the same specialized sectors of society afterward. The result seems to have been a compromise among the contending sides.[27]

We do not know whether this case study is typical or not of the way in which committees and subcommittees of the USSR Supreme Soviet work on legislation. But in general outline, the procedures for initiating and considering legislation in the USSR had, by the early 1970s, developed into the following pattern:

1. The decision to legislate belonged to the party organization.

2. Drafting the legislation was largely handled by the subcommittees of the Supreme Soviet, constituted on an ad hoc basis for each proposed bill, and including in their memberships outside experts and consultants.

---

[27] John Gorgone, "Soviet Jurists in the Legislative Arena: The Reform of Criminal Procedures, 1956–58," *Soviet Union* 3 (Part 1, 1976), pp. 9–33. The two quotes are from p. 12, footnote 37, and p. 25, respectively.

3. Deliberation on and amendment of the initial draft by an interplay between discussions in private subcommittee meetings and solicitation of public and outside reaction. The final version would be considered and approved by the standing committee of each chamber, usually meeting in joint session.

4. Ratification by a floor session of the Supreme Soviet, usually in joint session.

The major change this pattern has made from the Stalinist period has occurred in the second step of drafting and the third step of deliberation. In the previous system, the Council of Ministers—the government agencies—would draft the legislation and also handle the amendments and deliberation stages, so that the only role for the Supreme Soviet was the perfunctory one of ratification. Although subcommittees under the current system meet in private, the evidence available to us indicates that their meetings are frequent, lively, and not always harmonious.[28]

Consideration of the budget and economic plan occasions extensive committee activity. The Committee on Planning and Budget begins its meetings several months in advance of the session to adopt the annual budget and economic plan. It apparently meets with government ministers and is entitled to ask for and receive supporting documents. Its committee chairman speaks on the floor of the Supreme Soviet to offer his committee's results, along with the government officials. In examining the budget for 1969 and the five-year economic plan, the two houses of the Supreme Soviet formed 32 subcommittees, with over 200 deputies as members. The subcommittees held over 100 meetings, and the full Planning and Budget Committees met 27 times.[29] To the extent that the Supreme Soviet has assumed a more active part in Soviet government, it is largely attained through an expanded system of committees and subcommittees.

There is yet another clue to the importance—or at least the potential importance—of committees in the Supreme Soviet: the occupational and institutional affiliations of the committee members. Whereas party officials constituted 21% of the entire membership of the Supreme Soviet, that same category constituted 53% of the continuing membership (over several terms) on the four most important committees, while the proportion of workers and peasants declined to 5% from their chamber-wide proportion of 38%. Furthermore, while party members constituted 75% of the total membership, they held 97% of the continuing memberships (and 92% of all memberships) on the same four major committees.[30]

[28] Vanneman, *The Supreme Soviet*, pp. 132–134, 139–143.

[29] Ibid., pp. 12–14.

[30] Little, "Soviet Parliamentary Committees," pp. 48–49.

This brief review of committee practices in selected parliaments indicates a very broad range in the status and powers of committees. The American committee system is unique in its powers and autonomy within the legislative chamber. The greatly circumscribed status of committees in the British Parliament represents the other extreme, with the committees of other parliaments falling between the American and British systems.

COMMITTEES AND THEIR ENVIRONMENTS

Committees are created to accomplish certain tasks. Those tasks are usually not internal to the committee itself but are externally directed. The committees exist within a legislative chamber, and thus the chamber itself may be the most important part of the committee's environment. But in addition, those actors external to the legislative body may also be significant features of the political environment to which the committee responds, be they the chief executive, interest groups, or constituencies. In the following sections we shall discuss chief executives and political parties as significant portions of committees' external environment; in this section we shall discuss six U.S. House committees in some detail and categorize them by the ways in which they define and relate to portions of their external political and governmental environment. Although they are each different in many respects, they tend to cluster into two types: the purposive committee and the permeable committee.[31]

Purposive Committees

The purposive committees, as the first of two general types, has a strong sense of group identity and high internal morale. The members take pride in their work as collectivities. They view themselves, and are seen by others, as making a distinctive contribution to the work of the House. That is, their work has a recognized and well-defined purpose—to further some distinctive task of the House as a whole.

The purposes of the three committees in this general type are indicated by their jurisdiction. Both the Ways and Means Committee and the Appropriations Committee have jurisdiction over one of the House's constitutionally mandated functions—the initiation of money bills. The third committee, the Interior Committee, had (at the time of the study) a very different kind of task—processing constituency oriented projects for all members of the House.

[31] Fenno, *Congressmen in Committees,* is the basis for this entire section. His term for the first type of committee is "corporate."

The three purposive committees strive to be successful on the floor of the House. To the outsider, it may seem strange that not all committees seem to share this objective, but it is precisely this distinction that is one of the most important between the two general types of House committees. Suitable synonyms for our names of the committee types could be House-oriented and external-oriented.

All three committees take pride in bringing bills to the floor that will be adopted and will avoid either major crippling amendments or outright rejection. The Ways and Means Committee handles some of the most controversial legislation in contemporary American politics but attempts to avoid partisan controversy on the floor by a careful, and slow, search for internal consensus. It is a diverse committee in its composition; its agreements and disagreements are likely to be reflected in the pattern of floor debate and voting. The Appropriations Committee similarly seeks compromise among its diverse membership, and its leaders on both party sides actively work to avoid minority reports. The Interior Committee, though not as diverse in its membership as the other two, also seeks internal compromise, especially between the western and nonwestern members and between the conflicting purposes of conservationists and commercial users of dams and parks. All three committees, presenting a united (or fairly so) report to the House, ordinarily win approval for their bills on the floor.

As one indication of the particular importance of these three committees to the House, all three bring their bills to the floor under specially protected circumstances. Although the details of their special circumstances in floor proceedings will be deferred to the next chapter, the prospect of floor events following committee stage is an important consideration in the working procedures and substantive decisions of these committees.

Two of the three purposive committees take a distinctive posture toward the executive branch. The Appropriations Committee usually cuts budget requests, but by a moderate amount.[32] The Ways and Means Committee similarly receives its major proposals from the executive branch, which are important items in the president's program, but shapes them to meet the (usually) more cautious and conservative views of the House as a whole.

The third purposive committee, Interior, shares an orientation to success on the House floor, but faces a very different external environment. Rather than mainly working on executive-branch proposals, it deals more with House members themselves and their requests for

[32] Of bureau budgets submitted in the 1947–1962 period, the House Appropriations Committee made cuts in 74% but in only 20% of the cases were the cuts more than 10% of the requested budget. Ibid., pp. 194–195.

reclamation projects, national parks, and so on. The Department of Interior is an active collaborator with congressmen in seeking approval of the projects rather than acting as an outside proposer, stimulator, and supplicant.

Something of the internal procedures and sense of the effort to construct a consensus among diverse members is indicated by a member of the Appropriations Committee:

> There's no two-party system on Appropriations. In full committee, the chairman of the subcommittee gets up and then the ranking minority member of the subcommittee. And they say what a good job the other has done. . . . There's never any dissent.

Similarly, a member of the Interior Committee observed about its bipartisan cooperation:

> There's a kind of cohesiveness in the Committee that overrides partisan considerations. The key here is that there are not any ideological issues. You do not hear the Republicans saying we cannot afford this or that. And the reason is that everyone has a project in his district that he wants or will want.

All three sets of committee members take pride in their committees and are satisfied with their committee assignment and with their work on the committees. An Appropriations Committee member spoke of power within the House:

> The process here is one where consent must be obtained before anythings gets done. If you are one of those from whom consent must be obtained, then you are a more important person in the House. When you are on the Appropriations Committee you are that kind of person.

Other members have described their sense of in-group identity on the Appropriations Committee: "I think it's more closely knit than any other Committee." Another spoke of "an *esprit de corps*, a comradeship." As we shall see in discussing the other general type of committee, members do not see themselves in this prideful and satisfied way.

The perceptions of the purposive committee by other congressmen reflect and support the self-image held by the committee members. One party leader observed:[33]

> They're a dedicated committee, a powerful committee, and a tireless committee. They are the hardest workers in the Congress.

One measure of the satisfaction of members with their assignments to Appropriations and Ways and Means is the few transfers from those committees to join others, as we noted earlier (Table 6.3). The Interior Committee is a clear exception to this standard. If members leave they

[33] The items quoted are from ibid., pp. 88, 92, 93, 201, and 198, respectively.

seek a more powerful committee, not because of dissatisfaction with its internal procedures or from a sense of low morale or lack of House relevance. They look back upon Interior as having been a good initial assignment, a good training ground for later service in the House.

Permeable Committees

The second general type of committee, the permeable committee, contrasts with the purposive type on most characteristics. The permeable committees are much less concerned than the first type with winning approval of their bills on the House floor. Rather, their orientation is more toward external participants. The Civil Service and Post Office Committee mainly supports the pay raise requests of the postal worker unions. The Foreign Affairs Committee mainly supports the foreign aid requests of the executive branch. The Education and Labor Committee is internally divided, with each member individually seeking to write his own version of desirable public policy. What these three unlike committees have in common is a lack of interest in winning House approval on the floor. Paradoxically, one committee is relatively successful—the Post Office Committee. Its success, however, stems not so much from the activities or skills of its members as from the constituency-based lobbying of the postal workers.

The external actors in each committee's environment are far more important to the permeable committees than is the House itself. The composition of their environments, however, is quite different. The Post Office Committee mainly interacts with the postal employee unions and secondarily with associations of government employees. The Foreign Affairs Committee's one major bill is on foreign aid, which is an executive-branch proposal. That bill, however, is usually the target of cuts and restricting amendments on the floor. That the committee overwhelmingly supports the administration's bill (irrespective of party) makes it unrepresentative of the House and reduces its capacity to successfully anticipate or deal with House hostility.

The Education and Labor Committee works within a much more complex and pluralistic environment. Its jurisdiction includes labor-management relations, education, and the war on poverty. Thus, the major interest groups of American society and the national parties and their presidential candidates are interested in this committee's work. The activity of this volatile-issue committee is much more affected by the partisan context (see Chapter 4) of the president's party and the size of the Democratic majority than any other committee in the House. Members wish to join this committee to shape public policy. But they pursue this goal individually. They battle more than they compromise with each other. Furthermore, they continue their intracommittee disputes on the floor itself. At least the other two committees in this group are fairly united—if unsuccessful—on the floor. Because all three committees are more responsive toward external elements in their environment, this category is termed *permeable*, in contrast to the first type, which has a House-directed purpose.

The three committees in the latter group lack the high morale and satisfactions of the first. Either the members in this category do not value their committees or their committees are not respected and valued by other congressmen. They are thought to be unrepresentative of the House and ineffectual on the floor. The members of both the Post Office and Foreign Affairs committees acknowledge and regret their lowly status but have found no satisfactory remedy. Education and Labor is an anomaly in this respect: Although it is widely disdained in the House as unrepresentative and ineffectual, its members are very pleased. It is not that the members are pleased with the committee itself or have any strong sense of group morale, but rather, the committee is a forum within which each member happily pursues his own policy objectives.

Something of the interest that outside participants show in the permeable committee may be illustrated by comments from two outside interest group spokesmen. Concerning the Education and Labor Committee, and AFL-CIO official commented:

> We watch the Education and Labor Committee very carefully. . . . We have to control the labor committee. It's our lifeblood.

A postal worker federation leader expressed a bipartisan view toward the executive branch with the Post Office Committee:

> The Administration is our chief stumbling block and always has been, under the Republicans as well as the Democrats. Our rapport with the Congress, especially with the committee, is excellent.

An executive-branch official had a similarly approving comment about the Foreign Affairs Committee:

> I cannot think of any trouble we have with the . . . Committee in getting our bills passed. Most of them support the Administration on foreign aid.

While the members acknowledge and appreciate the supportive and collaborative relationships they have with their outside clientele groups, they are, nevertheless, unhappy with their own committees and their place in the House. Members of the Foreign Affairs Committee want to help shape the nation's foreign policy, but they have found no suitable way and are unhappy at their relative inactivity. One member said, "The subject matter, foreign affairs, is important but not the committee." Another observed, "We do not have anywhere near the power we should have."

The very different internal working style of Education and Labor is indicated by this observation by a committee member about one of his amendments:

> I tried . . . in the Committee . . . and I will try it again on the floor. . . . They (the party leadership) tried to talk me out of it before. . . . I just believe in it, that's all.

Another Education and Labor Committee member compared his committee with the Interior Committee, another in our first or purposive category:[34]

> The overall quality of the Education and Labor members is higher than Interior. Its intellectual level is a cut above Interior. Even so . . . there's a greater tendency to trust Interior on the floor. The guys on the floor do not have the confidence in Education and Labor.

Senate Committees

The House committees (at least the six that have been compared above) contrast as a group with the Senate committees. Although we have pointed to the differences among House committees, they do share characteristics from the House that set them apart from those in the Senate. The two chambers are quite different in several respects, and these chamber differences are reflected in their respective sets of committees.

The Senate committees seem to combine the characteristics of the House Interior and the Education and Labor Committees. On one hand, the committees are sensitive to and accommodating toward the wishes of all members of the Senate. Senate committees commonly accept amendments and additions offered by most any member so long as the issue is not a vital one to the purposes of the bill. On the other hand, the committee members function as individualists both on committees and on the floor. As a group, the Senate committees are not purposive; they are not oriented toward the achievement of highly valued tasks that are distinctive to the Senate as an institution. Neither are any of their committees highly valued as a source of group pride and identification or as a distinctive group with an identifiable working style. Rather, committees are locales within which each member pursues his own goals and willingly accommodates the preferences of most other senators as well.

These characteristics of Senate committees derive from the Senate as a whole. Senators have several committee assignments and, on most, several subcommittee assignments. House members on the highly valued committees have only one major committee assignment, to

34 The items quoted are from ibid., pp. 31, 39, 221, 222, and 238–239, respectively.

which they devote most of their time and effort. House committees can, for their members, become work groups. Senate committees are, for their members, another locale in which members can pursue their own policy goals. Senate committees are not so much a source of personal pride and group identity as a source of additional staff, a means of personally conducting hearings, and a source of personal publicity. Although senators take great pride in the Senate as a whole, within it they tend to function as constituency and policy entrepreneurs—as individualists—and accord to all other senators the same freedom of personal accommodation that they seek for themselves. Senate committees are much more permeable than purposive.[35]

The research leading to the purposive-permeable distinction among House committees was done in the 1960s. Since then, numerous changes have occurred in the structure of House committees generally and in several of the specific committees themselves. Both the Ways and Means and the Appropriations Committees have been limited in their autonomy by the House. The Post Office Committee's tasks were reduced by conversion of the Post Office from an executive-branch agency to a semiindependent corporation. Foreign Affairs was changed in name to International Relations. Yet we would expect that the essential characteristics of the House committees, and the points of comparison with the Senate, would remain unchanged. Although specific committees may change in certain attributes or might even change from one basic type to another, we suspect that the two generic types of committees would remain accurate descriptions of the kinds of committees found at any one time in the House and that House committees would, as a group, contrast with those in the Senate.

Variations in the House Commerce Committee

As the preceding discussion suggests, the definition of "environment" relevant to any one congressional committee can extend way beyond the confines of Capitol Hill to include the executive branch. That relevant environment also includes those segments of the public active and interested in the policy matters handled by each committee. There is no precise way to measure such public awareness, but issues can at least roughly be categorized by the degree of general public awareness —ranging from those narrow issues that involve specific industries or groups to those that not only affect wide segments of the public but also arouse their attention. Communications regulation is an example of an issue with a "narrow" public, whereas environmental protection is one with a high degree of public salience.

[35] Ibid., chap. 5.

Another dimension along which issues vary in how they involve the public lies in their degree of conflict. Some issues, such as medical research, raise little conflict, but health care delivery (and public health insurance) arouse widespread and intense conflict in the general public and also among affected interest groups.

All of these issues are handled by a single committee, the House Commerce Committee, which deals with a wide range of issues and a correspondingly wide range of outside clientele groups. It is perhaps more diverse in both respects than most of the committees discussed in the preceding section.

Most of the issues considered by the Commerce Committee do not raise a strong degree of executive-branch concern, and thus this committee is less directly involved consistently with the executive than were the preceding committees. But executive-branch involvement does occur, especially on those issues that attract considerable public attention and also require a considerable amount of expertise—such as environmental protection. On that type of issue, the committee and the executive-branch agencies support one another, thus paralleling the State Department and Foreign Relations Committee relationship discussed previously.

This example of a single committee indicates that external conditions may vary among the issues considered by that committee. Perhaps we have here a clue to yet another distinction among committees: While some face a relatively constant set of outside actors and thus a relatively homogeneous environment across their issues, others interact with very different outside participants depending upon the specific issue and thus face a relatively heterogeneous policymaking environment.[36]

Committees Abroad

We can only speculate about the committees in foreign parliaments, for we lack the needed research. Parliaments with standing committees could develop similarities to the American congressional ones. On the whole, parliaments on the British model would be precluded from such developments. Within the German Bundestag, the Appropriations Committee seems to have the most intensive work schedule and to remain at work through most of the year. More than other committees it also retains a stable membership. From what we know of the Bundestag, their Appropriations Committee might approximate the "pur-

[36] This section is based upon David E. Price, "Policy Making in Congressional Committees: The Impact of 'Environmental' Factors," *American Political Science Review* 72 (June 1978), pp. 548–574.

posive" committee of the U.S. House. So might the standing committees of the Swedish Riksdag for, like the American committees, they have permanent jurisdictions and a stable membership.

The Italian standing committees resemble the American House Interior Committee, in that they handle a large volume of small bills, and seem to do so on a basis of mutual accommodation among the membership of the entire parliament and also among the several parties.[37]

Most parliaments lack a sense of membership loyalty to and identification with their committees. Their loyalties are elsewhere, especially toward their political party. In part, members do not believe their committees to be important arenas of decision making, and therefore they do not seek or value membership on the committees. Their perception is largely accurate, and the whole process becomes circular.[38]

We do have some interview evidence from the French and Italian parliaments indicating that members vary in the importance they attach to their respective committees. In the Italian case, large majorities of both the Communist and Christian Democratic deputies thought that their participation in committees was "very important" (98% and 88%, respectively). By contrast, only 67% of the Christian Democrats rated their participation in their party affairs as "very important."[39]

The importance French deputies give to participation in their committees varies among the four types of deputies we earlier identified in Chapter 3. Of the four types, the status deputy most consistently avoided participation in the committees, whereas deputies of the program type—those who liked detail work on legislation—stressed the importance of their committee activities.[40]

Summary

We have identified two major types of committees, based upon case studies of six American committees, and have speculated about their counterparts in foreign parliaments. The two major types of committees are mainly differentiated by their external orientation: the purposive type seeks success within its chamber, whereas the per-

[37] Di Palma, "Institutional Rules and Legislative Outcomes in the Italian Parliament," pp. 151–160. The German Appropriations Committees is described in Loewenberg, *Parliament in the German Political System,* pp. 374–377.

[38] Hans Baerwald, *Japan's Parliament* (New York: Cambridge, 1974), pp. 93–94.

[39] Robert Leonardi, Raffaella Nanetti, and Gianfranco Pasquino, "Institutionalization of Parliament and Parliamentarization of Parties in Italy," *Legislative Studies Quarterly* 3 (February 1978), pp. 175–176.

[40] Oliver H. Woshinsky, *The French Deputy: Incentives and Behavior in the National Assembly* (Lexington, Mass.: Lexington Books, 1973), pp. 91–93, 136.

meable type of committee is more responsive to its external clientele. Members of the former type of committee have a strong sense of internal identity and morale and feel themselves to be highly valued and respected by their fellow congressmen; those on the latter lack both internal morale and colleague respect.

These distinctions are suitable to a complex and permanent committee system as found in the United States, Germany, and Italy. In the British tradition, the impermanent legislative committees would hardly fit either type, although their more continuous investigative committees might. We have also noted that at least one American congressional committee faces different policymaking environments varying markedly by the specific issues within its diverse jurisdiction.

The distinction between two general types of committees rests upon the committees' orientation to their environments. We now turn to a more specific examination of two critical aspects of committee environments—the chief executive and the parties.

COMMITTEES IN RELATIONSHIP TO THE EXECUTIVE

Most important legislation is government sponsored. With relatively few exceptions, the major and controversial bills in any given session will be written in government agencies and proposed by, or at least in the name of, the chief executive and the cabinet. As a result, much committee activity will be directed toward the executive—either in receiving and revising its legislation or in supervising and reviewing its administration of policies already adopted by parliament.

Independence from the Executive

Committees can be a source of parliamentary independence from the government; they can also be a source of close cooperation and even dependence. Their potential for independence of the executive stems from their unofficial status and their relatively small size. If a chief executive wishes to dominate a parliament, some of its members may meet outside of a formal session of the whole body. Indeed, they need not even meet within the parliamentary assembly building at all. They may meet unobtrusively, if not privately. Records need not be kept, and yet legislation may be discussed and strategy formulated. Committees could select their own chairmen and use informal procedures to permit open discussion. Committees were used in this fashion in the British Parliament in the early seventeenth century against King Charles, who resentfully noted:[41]

[41] Antonia Fraser, *Cromwell: The Lord Protector* (New York: Knopf, 1973), p. 34.

> We are not ignorant, how much the House hath of late years endeavored
> to extend their privileges, by setting up general Committees for Religion,
> for Courts of Justice, for Trade, and the like . . .

The absence of committees increases the dependence of parliament upon administrative agencies. If bills are written by the agencies, and if all of the research work for the parliament is also done by the same administrative agencies, the parliament becomes dependent upon the information the agencies are willing to provide. This situation arose in our first Congress. The Ways and Means Committee was established to write tax legislation, but was disbanded within a few months in favor of reliance upon Alexander Hamilton as secretary of the Treasury. The early Congresses only used ad hoc committees to review each bill. They did not create standing or permanent committees, for they depended upon the department secretaries to prepare reports as requested by the Congress. This system was displaced after Andrew Johnson's administration by a system of standing committees, which accompanied a reduction of Congress' dependence upon the executive-branch agencies.[42]

We have seen more recent examples of Congress' distrust of material furnished by executive-branch agencies. At least some leading supporters of the Vietnam "Gulf of Tonkin" resolution later came to believe they had been deceived by the administration. Within the past decade, Congress has taken steps to require the administration to report to it and to its committees information on use of troops overseas and on the use of executive agreements. Likewise, the Congress has created a specialized Committee on the Budget, with a sizable staff, to provide the same information and coordination for itself which the Office of Management and Budget does for the president.

Committees—the specialized committees—are the legislative equivalent of executive-branch agencies. If they obtain their own staff, the committees become a "counterbureaucracy" that can attempt to provide for parliaments the expertise and staff support that agencies provide the executive.[43] If, however, the committees are dependent upon staff support provided by the agencies, then the parliamentary committees, as in Japan, are not able to define and defend alternative points of view.[44]

---

[42] George Galloway, *History of the United States House of Representatives* (Washington, D.C.: House Committee on House Administration, House Doc. No. 250, 1965), pp. 59–72, 89–90.

[43] Shaw and Lees, *Committees*, p. 10.58.

[44] Baerwald, *Japan's Parliament*, p. 101.

Committee Cooperation with Agencies

Committees, however, can also become a source of cooperation with and even dependence upon administrative agencies. Committees that parallel the functional specializations of administrative agencies interact continuously with those agencies. The permanent civil service is matched by fairly permanent committee memberships, and they in turn are matched by fairly permanent lobbying staffs of the major interest groups. The result is often a long-term accommodation among those three elements: agency, committee, and group.

Their accommodation and mutual support—sometimes termed a functional "subsystem"—creates problems for both Congress and the president. For the president, the problem is that the agency's program and budget may not agree with those of the president's administration. His task is to interrupt the cooperative communications between agency and committee and to interject his own program concerning the agency into the legislative process. For Congress, its problem is that its advice on an agency's program comes from those members who are most supportive of the agency. And for the congressional parties, the same problem is created for them that is created for the president; they may not obtain support of a party position from their own members on that particular committee.

For both the president and Congress, part of the problem rests with the very composition of the committees, compared to the agencies. A congressman will want to join committees for several reasons—one of which is the committee's relevance to his district. The committee will have jurisdiction over certain agencies that have a particular importance in the district. Most of the members of the Environment and Interior Committee, for example, come from western states in which national forests and parks are located, whereas many of the members of the Merchant Marine and Fisheries Committee come from districts with ports for ocean shipping. Thus the local ties developed by agencies because of their programs are reinforced in the congressional committees. The Departments of Interior and Agriculture and the Army Corps of Engineers are examples.

Committees can also be a source of access to those persons and groups that do not obtain what they want from the agencies. The Bureau of Indian Affairs, for example, within the Department of the Interior, has shifted its policy several times since the end of World War II. In part, its changing policies have reflected the changing party of the president. The congressional subcommittees on Indian affairs have then held hearings inquiring into the workability and consequences of the current bureau policy. The hearings have been a major forum within which those who disagreed with the current policy have been able to express their views, obtain publicity, and win support among at least some congressmen.[45]

Another example is provided by the complex set of issues affecting pollution, safety, and health. In 1976 the Food and Drug Administration proposed a ban on the use of saccharin because it was suspected as a cancer-inducing agent. Not only was the production and use of saccharin a major commercial venture (diet colas, for example), but saccharin was used by diabetics as a safe substitute for sugar in their own diets. Within weeks, after FDA had indicated it would go ahead with its proposed ban, the relevant House unit—the Subcommittee on Health of the Commerce Committee—announced it would hold hearings on the whole issue. In this case the subcommittee chairman was attempting both to modify the FDA position and to reverse an earlier decision taken in the House on the same issue. The result was a suspension of FDA's intended ban.[46]

One of the problems, for both the administration and for Congress itself, is that committee jurisdictions do not exactly match those of the administrative agencies. The Department of Health, Education, and Welfare, for example, has a heterogeneous collection of subject matters as indicated by its cumbersome name. No one committee in Congress has that particular set of subjects within its jurisdiction. Welfare—because it is tied to the Social Security system, which in turn is financed through taxes—is in the House Ways and Means Committee and in the Senate Finance Committee, which have jurisdiction over taxes. Education is handled in the House by the Education and Labor Committee and in the Senate by the Human Resources Committee (formerly termed the Labor and Public Welfare Committee). Health itself is split among congressional committees: the tax-financed portions belong to the tax committees, whereas the issue of the quality and distribution of health care mainly rests within the jurisdiction of the Commerce Committee in the House, but the Human Resources Committee in the Senate. The fact that most congressional committees function through a series of subcommittees only intensifies administrators' problems in that time-consuming coordination of effort is required.

Congressional committees wish to deal with the decision makers within agencies. They want the cabinet department secretary himself to appear before them on any matter within his agency. These appearances by cabinet secretaries and by operating agency heads is vitally important in winning congressional knowledge and approval of them and their policies. It is the American functional substitute for the "questions" directed in the British Parliament toward the cabinet

[45] J. Leiper Freeman, *The Political Process* (New York: Doubleday, 1955).
[46] *Congressional Quarterly Weekly Report*, June 25, 1977, p. 1299; March 26, 1977, pp. 539–541.

ministers. Yet the agency heads may very well spend more than half of their working time on the Hill, especially in appearances before congressional committees and the many subcommittees.

Executive Liaison with Committees

Just as the White House has a "congressional liaison" office (see Chapter 4), so do the agencies. The agency congressional liaison staff tends to concentrate their work with the members of the relevant congressional committees: the Department of Agriculture with the Agriculture Committees, the Department of Defense with the Armed Services Committees, and so on. They also concentrate on the subcommittees which, within the Appropriations Committees, handle their budgets.

Beginning with the Kennedy administration, the White House has attempted to coordinate the agency lobbying efforts on behalf of the president's legislative goals. The White House staff in general and its own specific congressional liaison staff cannot know all members of Congress personally. Their own efforts are concentrated on the party leadership. But any given agency staff will come to know, on both a personal and working basis, the members of the committees relevant to the agency. Although they too will concentrate on the committee and subcommittee chairman and ranking members of both parties, the agency staff must and will become acquainted with even the most junior of committee members and their staff.

The White House attempts to use for its own purposes these agency-committee working relationships, which collectively cover the entire Congress and span the entire executive branch. Agencies are expected by the White House congressional liaison staff to be responsible at committee stage for the development of legislation in the president's program. The White House staff has neither the time nor knowledge to work intensively with all the bills, particularly at the committee stage.

As legislation nears the floor, the interest and activity of the White House staff and of the congressional party leaders increase. It is in the markup stage that the critical decisions will be made affecting the fate of administration legislation. The agency staff and perhaps also an assistant secretary (if not the cabinet member himself) will be active at this stage; moreover, the White House staff will become better informed, follow events on a daily basis, and will perhaps also involve the president. President Carter, for example, met with members of the House Ways and Means Committee at the White House several times during its consideration of his energy proposal. He has also met with committee members of both parties to explain and present to them new proposals on energy, taxes, and the economy. On one close vote within the Commerce Committee on a vital portion of the Carter energy proposal (regulation of natural gas prices), the president personally phoned two wavering Democratic members to gain their votes.[47]

The agency liaison staff and major officials remain active at floor stage on bills affecting them. Ordinarily it is their decision to accept, or not, proposed amendments. But the main strategy of managing the floor stage expands from the agency and committee personnel to include the party leaders and the White House staff. They may hold several coordination meetings in the course of floor action on an important bill, depending upon the amount of opposition the bill is encountering.

The constitutional structure of a nation has an important effect at this point. In British-type parliaments, the government minister is not only a member of a legislative committee, but also the leader of the majority side on that committee. In an American-type system, cabinet officials are neither. They may be present at committee hearings and at the markup stage, and they may intensively and informally consult at all stages of committee procedure; however, they are in the position of attempting to exercise suasion and influence as outsiders rather than power as insiders.

Bill Formulation

One consequence of the stability of committee jurisdictions and continuity of memberships, paralleling that of the agencies, is that they are able to consult with one another as a bill is being written. Interest groups are also consulted early in the bill-drafting process. Many bills take several years to be considered and finally adopted and thus go through several versions. In effect, the basic research and thinking behind a bill in one year will have been done through committee hearings and debates in previous years.

When a new administration takes office, its own legislative ideas may have come from the prior legislative work done by the committee members of its party. Much of the economic legislation of the Kennedy and Carter administrations had been developed by the Democratic-controlled committees during the preceding Republican administrations. The Kennedy administration, for example, adopted Senator Paul Douglas' (D-Ill.) depressed-areas bill as its own, and President Carter adopted Senator Edmund Muskie's (D-Maine) public-works bill in his program. President Kennedy's first major piece of economic legislation was the same bill he had worked on when, as Senator Kennedy, he was chairman of the relevant subcommittee on the Senate's Labor

[47] Ibid., July 2, 1977, p. 1337.

and Public Welfare Committee. Here we see a major advantage Democrats have reaped from their continuous majority in Congress. They have controlled the staff and activities of the committees, using them as resources either against the incumbent Republican president or as a workshop in which to develop legislation for the next time the Democrats gained the White House.[48]

We have earlier indicated that nations vary in the thoroughness with which the executive prepares legislation prior to submitting it to the legislative body. As one example we have referred to the hearings conducted by German ministries in preparing the transportation bills. The royal commissions in Britain and Sweden, as other examples, often conduct public hearings and assiduously seek the views of all interested participants. The commissions in effect become an arena for the formulation of compromises in an effort to build majority support for their recommendations. If an extensive consultation and compromise process occurs prior to consideration by the parliament, there is less need for committees to assume those functions. In the United States, however, in which the administration seems to be less thorough in these respects, the scope of congressional committee activity is increased.[49]

Party Ratios on Committees

In Chapter 4 we noted the difficulties facing a government when it lacked a majority in parliament or congress. Those problems are also faced, and perhaps accentuated, at the committee level. The more important the committees in the legislative process, the more critical the problem. Republican presidents, ever since the 1954 election, have faced congressional committees on which the majority of members and all chairmen have been Democratic. Still the president must propose legislation, and the Congress and its committees must react. Moreover, the agencies continue, as does their need for appropriations and for authorizing legislation. Thus agencies become adept at dealing with committee chairmen irrespective of their party and that of the president.

In parliamentary systems, if the government has a large enough majority, it will have a majority on each committee. The Japanese cabinet formed after the 1976 elections, for example, obtained only a very small majority. Although the Liberal Democratic Party was able to form the government on a majority vote, it lost a working majority in some of the committees. In multiparty parliaments the usual prac-

[48] James L. Sundquist, *Politics and Policy: The Eisenhower, Kennedy, and Johnson Years* (Washington, D.C.: Brookings, 1968).
[49] Preparation of the presidents' legislative programs is discussed in Stephen J. Wayne, *The Legislative Presidency* (New York: Harper & Row, 1978), chaps. 3, 4.

tice is to allocate committee chairmanships and vice-chairmanships among the parties proportional to their numbers in the parliament. Thus the government faces committees at least partly controlled by opposition party members.

The situation is even more perilous for minority governments. It is a minority not only on the floor but in every committee. The cabinet can govern only with the acquiescence of the "swing" members on the committees who are willing to vote with the government even though they have not joined it.

Committees can, however, become the locale of extensive cooperation among parties. If the parties are in opposition to one another on the floor over the major and grand contentious issues of their time, and perhaps with a heavy ideological emphasis, committees can more attend to the practical and working details of policy. The experts from the several parties may have a common outlook on the practicalities of their particular subject matters. The opposition in Italy, for example, between the Christian Democrats and the Communists, expressed through elections and on the floor, was accompanied by their extensive cooperation in committees. Their cooperation at the working-committee level preceded and perhaps helped pave the way for their 1976 agreement of cooperation and tacit support on the floor in forming the government and adopting its policies.[50]

Summary

The dilemmas in the relationship between the chief executive and legislative committees seem to appear in every country. Committees can be a source of autonomous action against the government. At the same time, committees are also controllable by the government. In the debates over the development of a system of standing committees in the Canadian Parliament, for example, one of the fears expressed was that the capacity of opposition parties to question and to debate against government proposals, especially on the budget, would be limited if such matters were referred to a committee rather than handled directly on the floor.[51] On the other hand, the government, especially in a parliamentary system, holds ultimate control over the committees and, if need be, will simply not permit its vital bills to be referred to a committee in the first place. The more important and active certain committees become, the more the government will have reason to attempt to control and limit them.

[50] Di Palma, "Institutional Rules and Legislative Outcomes in the Italian Parliament," p. 151.
[51] Michael Rush, "The Development of the Committee System in the Canadian House of Commons, II," *Parliamentarian* 55 (July 1974), pp. 151, 157.

Our attention in this section has concentrated on the legislative relationship between committees and the government; however, review and supervision of the agencies is perhaps a more constant and widespread function of committees. Although we have stressed the ephemeral and limited functions of legislative committees in the British Parliament, for example, their several permanent committees for agency review are their most active and vital committees. The increased activity of committees in Communist party states is likewise mainly in agency review and supervision. This task, perhaps more generic among parliaments of the world than the legislative task, has been discussed mainly in Chapter 4 on chief executives.

COMMITTEES AND PARTIES

Neither political parties nor governments trust parliamentary committees. As the preceding discussion indicates, the committees can be a source of opposition on any particular bill or to any particular government. In addition, however, committees develop an autonomy from the party system. They can become valued objects in their own right. Their very existence can create precedents and loyalties that greatly complicate the adoption of a government or party policy. Although restive members have persistently argued for a greater use of committees in the British Parliament, the governments of both parties have steadfastly refused. For the same reasons, the French Fifth Republic has greatly limited the powers and functions of their Assembly committees. The relatively increased activity and importance of committees in the Canadian Parliament, though, and in some of the Communist party parliaments, indicate opposite trends.

For the past 50 years, the American Congress was the leading example of committee autonomy. The presumptive right of committees to have bills referred to them, and their practice of not reporting bills they opposed, made it very difficult for either the president, the party leaders, or a clear majority of the Congress, to pry a desired bill loose from its committee. The classic example of this problem has concerned civil-rights legislation.

U.S. House

One of the difficulties faced by the majority party leaders in the U.S. Congress has been their inability to change the membership or chairmanships of the committees. Traditionally, the political parties selected only the new members of committees. Once a member went on a committee, he would expect to remain on that committee without interference or complaint from his party, irrespective of how he voted or what he did. There were only two circumstances under which an existing member would leave a committee: by his own choice or by the loss of seats by his party in the chamber and hence on the committees. In the latter instance, if he were a junior member of the committee, his seat might be eliminated. But neither instance involved the exercise of choice or powers by the political party or its leaders.

The irony of this situation was perhaps best captured in early 1961, when congressional allies of the Kennedy administration attempted to add five seats to the House Rules Committee (and barely succeeded). The purpose of that change, as everyone acknowledged, was to give the new administration a working majority on that committee. The chairman of the Rules Committee, Representative Howard Smith (D-Va.), was the leader of the southern Democrats opposed to Kennedy legislation and led the fight against the motion to add the new seats to his own committee. He argued that the addition would simply permit the party leaders to "pack" the committee in favor of the Kennedy administration. The Speaker, Sam Rayburn (D-Tex.), took the floor to make this retort to Smith's charge:

> And, talk about packing. Way back in 1933 we had a tremendous contest in this House. One side won. They put up a man for membership on the Committee on Rules; our side put up their man, and we at that time packed the Committee on Rules with the gentleman from Virginia (Mr. Smith).

"Our side," in that first year of the New Deal, supported both by Smith and Rayburn, consisted of the Democratic allies of the new Roosevelt administration.[52] But once on the committee, Smith had opposed the Democratic House leadership and every Democratic president since Roosevelt with impunity. Furthermore, he rose through the seniority system to become the committee's chairman.

As we indicated in Chapter 5, on political parties, this situation is now considerably changed, at least for House Democrats. All committee assignments for House Democrats are proposed by the Policy and Steering Committee, which is the leadership committee of the House Democrats. Although its choices for committee memberships can be challenged in the caucus, they have not. But their nominations for committee chairmen have been challenged and even reversed (Table 5.8).

Until 1975, when this system was first used, House Democrats had a "committee on committees," that is, a party committee to select its members for the House committees. The members of that party committee were the Democratic members of the House Ways and Means Committee. One result of that combination was that the members of the party committee were just as immune from the party leadership as were

[52] U.S. Congress, *Congressional Record* (Daily Ed.), January 31, 1961, p. 1508.

the members of the House committee. That is, the party leaders could not control the members of their own party's committee once a member joined that combined party-House committee. The party leaders, under that system, usually exercised a choice over who went on the Ways and Means Committee and on the Rules Committee as new members. But otherwise, the autonomous committee on committees largely made their own choices, further removing control over House committees from the majority party leadership. The one exception was the House Education and Labor Committee, in which the conservative coalition killed legislation advanced by nationally oriented Democrats and which became their themes against the Republican administration in the 1960 election: minimum-wage expansion and aid to elementary and secondary schools. Speaker Rayburn, beginning in 1954, began placing northern and liberal Democrats on that committee as seats became available, with the result that the committee had a solid liberal majority when Kennedy was elected president in 1960. The Republican leadership replied by placing several conservatives on the same committee.[53]

The new party procedure by which House Democrats select committee chairmen has not, however, reduced the seniority standings of committee chairmen. In two of the three committee chairmanship changes discussed in the preceding chapter, the party-elected chairman was next in the seniority line to the deposed chairman. In the third committee, the newly elected chairman was fourth highest in seniority. The deposed chairmen had, on the average, 39 years of service in the House, whereas the new chairmen averaged 20 years. Thus the change in years of service was more extensive than were the modifications of the seniority principle within committees. The seniority principle restrains the new selection system as well as the old: Once a member goes on a committee, he is virtually unremovable against his will, and most chairmen continue to be selected in accordance with seniority.

Perhaps the most important development, however, was the procedural change itself, which has increased the potential powers of the political party (at least among House Democrats) over the committee system. The 1975 precedent was confirmed by the removal in 1977 of a sitting chairman of an Appropriations subcommittee.[54] It may be that one of the most important results of the new procedure is that existing chairmen modify their behavior within their committees, either as a result of, or in anticipation of, a close vote within the caucus upon their chairmanship.

House Republicans have a "committee on committees," which is separate from their other party committees. Its sole task is to select

[53] Fenno, *Congressmen in Committees*, pp. 33–34.
[54] *Congressional Quarterly Weekly Report*, January 29, 1977, p. 159.

Republicans for their side of the House committees. Each state's Republican delegation has one member on that committee. States lacking Republican congressmen thus cannot be represented, whereas states with only one Republican can be. The Republican committee, however, functions through an executive committee that includes representatives from the largest state party delegations. Furthermore, in the full committee the members cast a vote weighted by the number of party seats each has in his particular state. Given the absence of as extensive a regionally and ideologically based factionalism among Republicans as among Democrats, the Republican committee on committees has funtioned more harmoniously with its party leaders than has been the case among Democrats.

But even under the House Democrats' former system, and still under the House Republicans' continuing system, congressmen would indicate that committee appointments were one not-inconsiderable source of power held and exercised by the party leaderships. As a Republican observed in the mid-1960s:

> They can use committee assignments against you. Select committees count too. I have a whole folder of requests to Halleck (then the party leader) for the last six years. I never got anywhere.

A Democrat was more successful in getting on a high-prestige committee.[55]

> Committee assignments are a terrifically important stick in the hands of the leadership. A member can make two choices if he wants some independence—fight the leaders from the beginning of his career or fight them after getting the committee of his choice. I made the second choice. I am on Appropriations . . .

Members typically are asked to indicate their committee preferences. In the U.S. Congress they make their requests known to the representative of their state delegation on the Republican committee on committees, and to their regional or group representative on the House Democratic Steering and Policy Committee. They are advised to talk with their state delegation chairman, with the party leaders, and with the chairman or ranking minority member of the committees on which they seek membership. In the German Bundestag, members are requested by their party leaders to fill out rather comprehensive questionnaires, including personal background information.[56]

As we have already noted, members seek committees with particular relevance to their districts. Another consideration for the in-

[55] Both quotes are from Randall Ripley, *Party Leaders in the House of Representatives* (Washington, D.C.: Brookings, 1967), pp. 152–153.
[56] Loewenberg, *Parliament in the German Political System,* pp. 191–196.

dividual congressman is his own personal interests. One greatly interested in foreign policy, for example, might seek that committee in the House, even though it is not particularly important to his voters. Other committees attract members because they are considered important and prestigious.

The same considerations seem to apply to other parliaments as well. In the West German Bundestag, for example, the party leaders tend to reserve for themselves its most prestigious committee—the Foreign Affairs Committee. Members with close ties to labor gravitate toward the Social Policy Committee, members with ties to large business toward the Economic Committee, and those with ties to agriculture toward the Agriculture Committee.

We see in both the American and the German cases the tendency for members from certain kinds of districts, with certain kinds of group support, and with interest in certain kinds of government policy, to concentrate in relevant committees. These characteristics make of such members the experts of their respective parties. The parties must depend upon their members within the committees for the basic development of party policy. Yet the relevant characteristics of the members may be shared among the parties, and indeed they may form a common point of view toward government policy irrespective of the preferences of their party leaders or the government.

Reinforcing the constituency-relevant character of committee assignments in the U.S. Congress is the state delegation in the House. Some state delegations seem to have continuous representation on at least some of the committees; a retiring member from a certain state will ordinarily be replaced by another from the same state's party delegation.[57]

In some instances, at least, party leaders attempt to place a member on a committee to emphasize the importance to their party of the category of new political developments represented by that member. When the first Republican House member was elected from Texas, for example, he was placed on the Ways and Means Committee, even though freshmen were rarely assigned to that prestigious committee. The purpose of the Republican leaders was to indicate to the South generally the value they placed upon the region and thereby increase their chances of winning more Republican seats there. A closely related reason for members to seek certain committees is to protect or increase their desire to be reelected. However that purpose may work for the individual member, there is little reason to think that

[57] Fenno, *Congressmen in Committees*, p. 20; Charles Bullock, "The Influence of State Party Delegations on House Committee Assignments," *Midwest Journal of Political Science* 15 (August 1971), pp. 525–546.

any particular committee or set of committees increases the reelection chances of freshman congressmen as a whole.[58]

Members who seek to change committees usually shift from committees of low power or prestige to more powerful and prestigious ones. The typical pattern is to move from the Veterans' Affairs Committee, for example, to Foreign Relations or Finance in the Senate, or to Rules or Ways and Means in the House, rather than the reverse (refer to Table 6.3).[59]

U.S. Senate

In the Senate both parties select their committee members through party committees, subject to confirmation in their respective party caucuses, but neither party has yet attempted to modify the seniority rule. Yet the Senate Democrats are moving toward a new system in emulation of the House Democrats. Through the middle 1970s, however, fights over committee assignments within the Senate Democratic Caucus have occurred on new assignments, particularly to the Judiciary Committee. This committee has taken on a marked ideological and factional cast, for its jurisdiction includes civil rights (and thus was a major battleground in the 1950s and 1960s), antitrust, and constitutional amendments. Senators Kennedy (D-Mass.) and Allen (D-Ala.) have been among the major protagonists in that fight. As members of the Judiciary Committee, both have attempted to place like-minded colleagues on that committee.[60] With the death of Senator Allen in 1978 and the retirement of Senator Eastland (D-Miss.) from the Judiciary Committee chairmanship at the end of the same year, the ideological balance of that committee was again in question, for Eastland's successor as chairman in 1979 was Kennedy (D-Mass.).

Although Senate Republicans are as badly divided as are their Democratic counterparts, their conservative majority has not been challenged in their party conferences in the same open manner as with the Democrats. In neither chamber are Republicans as inclined to modify their committee selection system as are the Democrats. Reform, however, more often occurs in the party lacking the White House. Many

[58] Charles S. Bullock, "Freshman Committee Assignments and Reelection in the United States House of Representatives," *American Political Science Review* 66 (September 1972), pp. 1004–1006.

[59] Malcolm E. Jewell and Chu Chi-hung, "Membership Movement and Committee Attractiveness in the U.S. House of Representatives, 1963–1971," *American Journal of Political Science* 18 (May 1974), p. 436.

[60] For an unflattering and hostile view of the Judiciary Committee in both houses, see Peter H. Schuck, *The Judiciary Committees* (New York: Grossman, The Ralph Nader Congress Project, 1975).

of the Democratic reforms occurred during the Nixon-Ford presidencies; perhaps Republicans will initiate more internal changes during the Carter administration (as they did during the Kennedy-Johnson years).

State Legislatures

The states vary widely in their practices in appointing members and chairmen of committees. As a result, they also vary extensively in the stability of memberships and chairmanships of their committees. Among six states for example, the proportion of new members on their appropriations committees ranged from a low of none in Virginia (both houses) to a high of 75% in the Wisconsin House and 76% in the New Jersey Senate. Another four chambers had over 50% of new members on this most important of committees. Another indication of turnover within state legislatures is provided by examining the proportions of new chairmen in all the states of the three important committees on appropriations and taxes: In the 1966–1971 period, the average proportion of new chairman in both legislative chambers was close to 40%. The lowest turnover rates (that is, the most stability) of chairmen were found in New York, Virginia, and South Carolina. The highest turnover rates in committee chairmen (over 40%) were in California, Connecticut, Delaware, and North Carolina.

Although the relatively high rates of turnover in committee chairmanships is partly related to the high rates of membership turnover in the legislatures themselves (refer to Chapter 2), the frequent change in committee chairmanships—particularly of the major committees— reflects prevailing leadership practices in their respective chambers. The Virginia and South Carolina legislatures, for example, have a seniority rule that, in turn, reflects stable party and factional control of the whole chamber. On the other hand, in Wisconsin, California, and Arizona, as different parties and factions gain control of the speakership, the new speaker appoints his supporters to the major committees. In the New Jersey Senate, to cite yet a different type of practice, committee chairmanships rotate in an elaborate career pattern: chairmen of major committees ascend an office ladder culminating in the position of presiding officer of the state senate.

But there seems to be at least one other factor leading to instability in both memberships and chairmanships of committees in the state legislatures: On the whole, committees are not very important. As a result, legislators do not wish to hold onto a committee seat or to gain either seniority or experience on it.[61] While the state legislatures

[61] Alan Rosenthal, *Legislative Performance in the States,* pp. 176–184 and state sources cited therein.

are organized on the same formal pattern as the U.S. Congress, the reality of their committee systems seems to be quite different, and in this respect they more resemble foreign parliaments.

Parliaments Abroad

Those many other parliaments that, like the American Congress, maintain standing committees also do not escape the circumstances and problems we have just outlined for the congressional and state legislative parties. Most parliaments select committee members through their political parties. Although they seldom have formalized seniority rules, in practice the choice by party leaders of committee members and chairman is restricted. In the West German Bundestag, for example, close to 80% of the committee members in any one session were also members of the same committee in the previous session. Likewise, chairmen are usually selected on the basis of their expertise, which in turn is a function of their experience on the committee. Once selected, the chairman is rarely removed by his party. Once appointed, party members may—or may not—closely coordinate their work with the party leaders and may—or may not—support party policy on the committees. In at least some of the Bundestag committees, members have formed cross-party alliances that are counter to the positions of their party leaders and thwart the policies of the government of their own party.[62]

Party Share of Chairmanships

In multiparty parliaments, chairmanships are shared among the parties in proportion to their numbers in the chamber. The precise allocation is itself a subject of negotiation among the parties. In all parliaments (about which we have evidence) party leaders negotiate on the entire structure of the committee system: how many committees there shall be, and their jurisdiction; the size of each committee and the number of seats on each allocated to each party; and, in multiparty parliaments, the allocation of chairmanships and vice-chairmanships among the parties.[63]

We may illustrate the party allocation of seats and chairmanships with three examples. The first, the American Congress, allocates a majority of seats on all committees and all chairmanships to the majority party. The size of each committee and the number of party

[62] Loewenberg, *Parliament in the German Political System*, pp. 191–202; M. Donald Hancock, *Sweden: The Politics of Postindustrial Change* (Hinsdale, Ill.: Dryden, 1972), p. 174.
[63] Loewenberg, ibid., pp. 150–151; Hancock, ibid., p. 174.

Table 6.8   SIZE AND PARTY RATIOS ON COMMITTEES,
U.S. SENATE, 1977–1978

COMMITTEE	DEMOCRATS		REPUBLICANS		TOTAL
	(N)	$(\%)$	(N)	$(\%)$	(N)
Agriculture, Nutrition and Forestry	11	61	7	39	18
Appropriations	16	64	9	36	25
Armed Services	11	61	7	39	18
Banking, Housing and Urban Affairs	9	60	6	40	15
Budget	10	63	6	37	16
Commerce, Science and Transportation	11	61	7	39	18
Energy and Natural Resources	11	61	7	39	18
Environment and Public Works	9	60	6	40	15
Finance	11	61	7	39	18
Foreign Relations	10	63	6	37	16
Governmental Affairs	10	59	7	41	17
Human Resources	9	60	6	40	15
Judiciary	11	65	6	35	17
Rules and Administration	6	67	3	33	9
Veterans' Affairs	6	67	3	33	9

SOURCE: *Congressional Quarterly Weekly Report,* April 30, 1977, pp. 4–17.

seats on each is shown in Tables 6.8 and 6.9 for the Senate and House in 1977–1978.

Our second example is Poland, which, though a communist state, has two parties in addition to the ruling United Polish Workers Party. Its parliament contains all three parties, plus a group of unaffiliated members. The three parties, but not the independents, are represented among the committee chairmen as shown in Table 6.10, which lists the parties by their size in the chamber and the number of their committee chairmanships. The important committees—concerning the budget and the economic plan, heavy industry, and rules—are, as befits any governing party, chaired by that party. All three parties are also represented on the committees roughly in proportion to their size in the full chamber. But apparently strict proportionality is discarded for those committees of particular relevance to each party. In the Heavy Machine Industry Committee, for example, the United Polish Workers Party is disproportionately represented, the Peasant Party similarly in the Agriculture and Light Industry Committee, and the Democratic Party in the Committee on Private Commerce.[64]

Our third example is the Bundestag of West Germany in the early 1950s. The Christian Democratic Party, with 45% of the vote and

[64] Andrzej Burda (ed.), *Sejm Polskiej Rzeczypospolitej Ludowej* (Warsaw: Ossolineum, 1975), pp. 305, 504, 516–518.

Table 6.9   SIZE AND PARTY RATIOS ON COMMITTEES, U.S. HOUSE OF REPRESENTATIVES, 1977–1978

COMMITTEE	DEMOCRATS (N)	DEMOCRATS $(\%)$	REPUBLICANS (N)	REPUBLICANS $(\%)$	TOTAL (N)
Agriculture	31	67	15	33	46
Appropriations	37	67	18	33	55
Armed Services	25	65	13	33	40
Banking, Finance and Urban Affairs	31	66	15	32	47
Budget	17	68	8	32	25
District of Columbia	13	65	6	30	20
Education and Labor	24	65	12	32	37
Government Operations	29	67	14	33	43
House Administration	17	68	8	32	25
Interior and Insular Affairs	29	63	14	30	46
International Relations	25	68	12	32	37
Interstate and Foreign Commerce	29	67	14	33	43
Judiciary	23	68	11	32	34
Merchant Marine and Fisheries	27	66	13	32	41
Post Office and Civil Service	17	68	8	32	25
Public Works and Transportation	29	67	14	33	43
Rules	11	69	5	31	16
Science and Technology	27	68	13	32	40
Small Business	25	68	12	32	37
Standards of Official Conduct	6	50	6	50	12
Veterans' Affairs	19	68	9	32	28
Ways and Means	25	68	12	32	37

SOURCE: *Congressional Quarterly Weekly Report,* April 30, 1977, pp. 19–44.

nearly half of the seats, formed the government in coalition with three minor parties. The Christian Democrats obtained 18 (a full half) of the 36 committee chairmanships, with the second largest party, the Social Democrats, obtaining 13 committee chairmanships. This party, the sole opposition party, was nevertheless allocated chairmanships in accordance with the proportionality principle. The remaining five

Table 6.10   MEMBERS AND COMMITTEE CHAIRMANSHIPS BY PARTY, POLISH SEJM, 1972–1976

PARTY	MEMBERS OF SEJM (N)	MEMBERS OF SEJM $(\%)$	CHAIRMANSHIPS OF COMMITTEES (N)	CHAIRMANSHIPS OF COMMITTEES $(\%)$
Polish United Workers Party	255	55.5	15	67
United Peasant Party	117	25.4	5	23
Democratic Party	39	8.5	2	9
Unaffiliated	49	10.6	0	0
Total	460	100.0	22	99

SOURCE: Andrzej Burda (ed.), *Sejm Polskiej Rzeczypospolitej Ludowej* (Warsaw: Ossolineum, 1975), pp. 504, 516–518.

Table 6.11 STATE LEGISLATURES RANKED BY
EFFECTIVENESS OF COMMITTEES

GREATER EFFECTIVENESS	MEDIUM EFFECTIVENESS	LESSER EFFECTIVENESS
Arizona	Alaska	Alabama
California	Colorado	Arkansas
Florida	Idaho	Connecticut
Hawaii	Kansas	Delaware
Iowa	Louisiana	Georgia
Kentucky	Maine	Illinois
Minnesota	Maryland	Indiana
Nevada	Mississippi	Massachusetts
North Dakota	Nebraska	Michigan
Ohio	New Mexico	Missouri
Oklahoma	North Carolina	Montana
Washington	Oregon	New Hampshire
West Virginia	South Carolina	New Jersey
Wisconsin	South Dakota	New York
	Tennessee	Pennsylvania
	Virginia	Rhode Island
		Texas
		Utah
		Vermont
		Wyoming
$N = (14)$	(16)	(20)

SOURCE: Alan Rosenthal, *Legislative Performance in the States* (New York: Free Press, 1974), p. 42.

chairmanships were apportioned among two of the remaining three small parties. On individual committees, the seats were also allocated proportionately. On the Transportation Committee, for example, the Christian Democrats held 15 (over half) of the 29 seats, with the Social Democrats holding nine. The remaining five seats were divided among the three smaller parties.[65]

Party vs. Committee

The 50 state legislatures help illustrate the general theme of the inverse relationship in power and importance between parties and committees. The committee systems of the state legislatures have been ranked by the degree of their effectiveness in receiving and processing legislation (Table 6.11). Those legislatures having committees that receive most of the introduced bills, that can and do amend them, and that prepare reports that are accepted on the floor are considered effective. Those committee systems that can be and are bypassed and whose bill reports are severely amended or rejected on the floor are judged ineffective.

[65] Braunthal, *The West German Legislative Process*, p. 123.

Table 6.12   CHARACTERISTICS RELATED TO EFFECTIVENESS OF
COMMITTEES IN STATE LEGISLATURES

FACTOR	CHARACTERISTIC	RELATIONSHIP (GAMMA)
Appointment of members	Decentralized	0.40
Party organization and cohesion	Low	0.53
Gubernatorial governors' compared to legislature's power over agencies	Legislature stronger	0.23
Factors combined: distribution of power	Dispersed	0.58
$N = 50$		

SOURCE: Alan Rosenthal, "Legislative Committee Systems: An Exploratory Analysis," *Western Political Quarterly* 26 (June 1973), pp. 258–261.

The characteristics of the legislature that are most directly related to the effectiveness of their committee systems mainly concern the power and organization of the party, the speaker, and the governor (Table 6.12). If the appointment of members is relatively decentralized and not concentrated in the hands of the speaker or the party leadership, the committees tend to be more effective. If the legislative party itself is not well organized and is not cohesive in roll call voting on the floor, committees tend to be more effective. If the legislature is judged more powerful over the administrative agencies than is the governor, there is a small tendency for committee systems to be more effective. When all three of these factors are combined, the more dispersed or decentralized the distribution of power within the legislature, the more are committees likely to be effective in the processing of legislation.[66] Both abroad and within the United States we find that the importance and power of committees and parties are inverse to one another as competing and even rival ways of organizing the members and the work of legislative bodies.

Committees and Consensus

Committees are not only the work locale of parliaments; they are also small groups within which members become acquainted with one another across party lines. Particularly in committees with a stable membership, the members come to know one another as human beings. They even become friends. Christian Democrats and Communists in Italy, and Gaullists and Communists in France, for example, have developed amicable and cooperative working and personal relation-

[66] Alan Rosenthal, "Legislative Committee Systems: An Exploratory Analysis," *Western Political Quarterly* 26 (June 1973), pp. 258–261.

ships across and in spite of the ideological and social-class divisions between their parties.

Committees are more likely to produce unanimous decisions, whereas proceedings on the floor are more likely to lead to partisan strife. Several circumstances seem to contribute to this result: (1) Conflict is painful among friends, whereas agreement facilitates a comfortable working relationship over a long time span. (2) Committees work on details and practical matters, whereas floor debate is more concerned with principles. (3) Committees in most parliaments work in private, thus permitting a more open and frank discussion than if the members were in public. (4) The small size of committees permits more informal and flexible procedures than does the larger membership in formal floor sessions.

The foregoing points will be elaborated at greater length in the next chapter, on floor stage: Their end result, however, is to reduce partisan conflict in committees. Yet because committees are creatures of the whole parliament, which in most nations means creatures of the government and the parties, the reduction of partisanship within committees is usually a varied and only partial result.[67]

One of the continuing tensions in parliaments concerns the relationship of the committees to the government; a closely associated tension concerns the committees' relationships to the political parties. The relative autonomy of American congressional committees from both marks them apart from those in most other parliaments. Yet we have noted similar tendencies in at least some other parliaments (especially West Germany), and the party-committee relationship has undergone significant modification in the American Congress, especially among House Democrats.

COORDINATION, RULES, AND POWER

A committee system is created to solve certain problems within a legislative body. At the very least, committees divide the work of parliament into smaller units and allocate those units to some number of members less than the whole. At the most, they make many of the decisions affecting the fate of legislation. But the more active and important the committees, the greater the likelihood that their very existence will create other problems within the parliament, especially problems of coordination. These problems concern not only organiza-

[67] Shaw and Lees, *Committees*, pp. 10.87–10.91; Robert Dahl, *After the Revolution?* (New Haven: Yale University Press, 1970), pp. 74–75; Giovanni Sartori, "Will Democracy Kill Democracy? Decision Making by Majorities and by Committees," *Government and Opposition* 10 (Spring 1975), pp. 131–158.

tional rationality and efficiency but also the acquisition and use of power with which to advance preferred concepts of public policy.

The most generic problems of coordination inhere in the relationships of committees to the parties and to the government. These we have already discussed and shall continue to discuss both here and in later chapters as well. In this section, however, we shall turn to four problems that are internal to the committee system itself.

Jurisdiction

The first such committee-related problem concerns their jurisdiction. Although a fixed and stable jurisdiction has been pointed to as one of the strengths of standing committees in the United States and Sweden, as two examples, and as a source of continuity of leadership and of expertise, it is perhaps impossible to define jurisdictions that unambiguously apply to all of the thousands of bills introduced annually. Some bills will apparently belong to no committee, and some will apparently belong to two or more committees. It is the latter circumstance that leads to the greater difficulties.

In systems lacking permanent committee jurisdictions, the problem hardly arises. Typified by many legislatures in the American states, the Speaker simply refers bills at his discretion to the committees he prefers.

In the American Congress, the most common way to resolve such issues is through discussion. The bill's sponsor(s), the chairmen of the several committees, the party leaders, and the parliamentarian arrive at a common understanding of how the bill shall be referred. In some instances the bill's referral depends upon how it is written, and the authors and sponsors will be careful to write the bill so that it will go to the committee they prefer rather than to the one(s) they fear. A 1977 example was a bill providing that users of river transportation would, for the first time, pay for the use of federally constructed dams and locks on the rivers. If this payment were written as a tax, the bill would be referred, in the Senate, to the Finance Committee. The authors wanted to avoid this committee, for it and its chairman would oppose the payment. But if the payment were written as a user "charge," rather than as a "tax," the bill would go to the Commerce Committee. Its sponsors selected the latter course.[68]

The same bill illustrates another way of resolving jurisdictional disputes—the double referral. The bill in question was referred to two committees, the Environment and Public Works Committee and the Commerce, Science and Transportation Committee. The bill nicely

[68] *Congressional Quarterly Weekly Report,* June 25, 1977, p. 1279, and June 4, 1977, pp. 1117–1119.

illustrates the interconnected and complex characteristic of modern life in a large industrial nation: Everything tends to affect everything else; as a result, neither committee jurisdictions nor agency functions are likely to be neatly defined. The bill provided for a public-works project, the construction of a new set of locks on the Mississippi River, which was also an interstate commerce question affecting transportation. Thus, the two committees had jurisdiction over the same bill. Both committees shared the leadership of floor debate, and both were represented on the subsequent conference committee. The rules of the House now authorize the Speaker to make double referrals, and also sequential ones. In the former the bill is referred to two committees simultaneously, whereas in the latter the bill goes to one committee after it has been processed by the first. During the first five months of 1977, close to 2000 bills had been referred to two or more committees.[69] The Speaker may also divide a bill, splitting it between two or more committees, as he did with Carter's 1977 energy bill.

Carter's energy program also illustrates the multifaceted and multi-committee character of legislation. What we have termed *the energy program* consisted of well over 100 specific items, which collectively lay in the jurisdiction of five committees in the House of Representatives. The energy proposals were divided into their component parts and referred to the appropriate committees. But the Speaker created a new ad hoc committee to receive the energy bills from the original and standing committees. Its task was to fashion a single coordinated package out of the various parts from the original committees. Each of the original committees was represented on the new energy committee (Table 6.13) to gain both their knowledge of, and presumably their consent to, the final version of the bill. The Speaker gave the original committees a deadline (mid-July) to report their bills to the new Energy Committee. The Carter program was announced mid-April, but the specific proposals took another several weeks to be sent to Congress. In effect, the committees had about three months to hold hearings and to mark up their bills. During this time, the new Energy Committee held several organizational meetings, arranged its own schedule, and met at the White House with the president. More quietly, the Energy Committee, along with the party leaders, monitored progress within the several original committees and attempted to coordinate their activities.[70]

The same coordination problem was handled differently in the Senate. The energy package was divided into two parts and sent to

69 U.S. Congress. House. Commission on Administrative Review, *Administrative Reorganization and Legislative Management*, vol. 2: *Work Management* (Washington, D.C.: House Doc. 95-232, 1977), p. 34.

70 *Congressional Quarterly Weekly Report*, May 21, 1977, pp. 957–959; July 16, 1977, pp. 1435–1438.

Table 6.13 HOUSE AD HOC SELECT COMMITTEE
ON ENERGY, 1977: OVERLAPPING MEMBERSHIPS
WITH STANDING COMMITTEES

	MEMBERS ON ENERGY COMMITTEE	
STANDING COMMITTEE	(N)	(%)
Commerce	11	28
Ways and Means	10	25
Interior	7	18
Government Operations	6	15
Banking	5	13
Science and Technology	4	10
Merchant Marine	4	10
Joint Economic	4	10
All other committees	24	60
N =	(40)	

SOURCE: *Congressional Quarterly Weekly Report*, April 30,
1977, pp. 41, 51–57.

only two committees: All tax-related matters went to the Finance
Committee, and all other components went to the Energy and Natural
Resources Committee. Coordination between the two committees would
occur on the floor. The difference between the two chambers in
handling the same problem on the same bill illustrates the guiding
role of the party leaders. Apparently, each different method of achieving coordination was the choice of the Democratic majority party
leadership—the Speaker in the House (O'Neill, Mass.) and the
Majority Leader in the Senate (Robert Byrd, W. Va.).

To illustrate the difficulties of matching committee jurisdictions
with contemporary, but shifting, policy problems, we may examine
both energy- and health-related bills. Within the first five months of
1977, more than 600 bills had been introduced in the House relating
to energy, and more than 1800 bills concerning health. The energy bills
were referred to a total of 19 committees; health bills were referred
to 18. The Commerce Committee received more bills than did any other
committee, amounting to nearly half of the health bills but less than
30% of the energy bills (Table 6.14). Committees on Interior, Science,
Public Works and Transportation, and Banking and Urban Affairs,
received 10% or 9% of the energy bills each. Of the health bills, close
to 30% were referred to Ways and Means, and the next highest proportion, 10%, was in the jurisdiction of the Committee on Education
and Labor.[71]

The budget is another example of the difficulties of coordination
among committees. At various times in our past, one committee has ˜

[71] Commission on Administrative Review, *Work Management*, pp. 32–33.

Table 6.14 MULTIPLE COMMITTEE JURISDICTION: BILLS
ON ENERGY AND HEALTH REFERRALS TO COMMITTEES,
U.S. HOUSE[a]

COMMITTEES TO WHICH BILLS REFERRED	BILLS BY POLICY TOPIC	
	ENERGY (%)	HEALTH (%)
Commerce	27	45
Ways and Means	2	28
Interior	10	1
Science and Technology	9	—
Public Works and Transportation	9	1
Banking and Urban Affairs	9	1
Education and Labor	3	10
Judiciary	4	3
All others	27	11
Total	100	100
N =	617	1806

SOURCE: U.S. Congress. House. Commission on Administrative Review,
Administrative Reorganization and Legislative Management, vol. 2:
Work Management, p. 30, tables 13 and 14.
[a] Includes first five months of 1977.

handled both taxation and expenditures. But ever since 1921, when we
reformed our budget process in the aftermath of World War I and its
attendant economic crises, the two tasks have been allocated to two
different committees: Ways and Means in the House and Finance in
the Senate have written tax legislation, whereas Appropriations in both
chambers have handled expenditures.

The most recent effort at budgetary coordination has been the
creation of "Budget Committees" in each chamber, which first took
effect in the early 1970s. A single committee was empowered, in each
chamber, to develop a statement of income and expenditures, which,
when adopted by both houses, would become binding upon the committees and also upon Congress itself. These virtually unprecedented
powers were designed in response to President Nixon's attack upon the
"spending" proclivities of Democratic Congresses and also by his
attempt to evade their preferences through the extensive use of
impoundment.

To better arm itself against the president, Congress centralized
power within itself by creating a new committee that could coordinate
the financial decisions of two of the most powerful and important committees in each chamber. Yet the very effort created conflict between
the new Budget Committees and the others. Not only were the tax-
writing and Appropriations committees subject to potential restraint,
but likewise the authorization committees were expected to report
legislation that did not authorize expenditures in excess of the limits
reported by the Budget Committees and accepted on the floor. The

House Budget Committee leadership has attempted to handle these potential conflicts through negotiation and discussion off the floor, whereas the Senate Budget Committee leadership has directly challenged bills from other committees on the floor.[72]

Still another way to limit the autonomy of committees has been used occasionally in the Senate: to send a bill to a committee with a deadline, by which time the committee is required to report the bill back to the floor. Assuming the conditional referral is ordered and sustained by a majority vote, the committee must comply. This device has been used in the Senate on civil rights legislation on the 1960s. Although a majority (and certainly the chairman) of the Judiciary Committee opposed such legislation, a solid bipartisan majority of the Senate supported it. The equivalent procedure in the House, called a discharge petition, has been used only sporadically and usually unsuccessfully.

Our previous example of the German highway bills indicates that coordination among committees is a generic rather than only an American problem in legislative systems with permanent committees having fixed jurisdictions. The two bills were sent to four committees, each of which had a different set of constituency ties and a different set of cooperative relationships with the agencies. Three of the committees were advisory to the Finance Committee. Each committee proceeded separately, but in the end they met together when the Finance Committee made the final decisions. The result was defeat for one of the two government bills, and extensive amendment of the other.[73]

Subcommittees

The second problem of committees is created by the existence of subcommittees. Subcommittees are formed for the same considerations as are full committees: They permit an allocation of lesser tasks to a smaller set of members within committees that are perhaps rather large and have a sizable and complex workload. A small number of committees is more easily coordinated than a large number, but the small number would each have an imposingly diverse jurisdiction. If jurisdictions are made more manageable, the number of committees increases, thereby compounding the coordination problem.

One solution to this conundrum is to create subcommittees, but they in turn replicate all of the problems of the relationships between

[72] John W. Ellwood and James A. Thurber, "The New Congressional Budget Process: The Hows and Whys of House-Senate Differences," in Lawrence C. Dodd and Bruce I. Oppenheimer (eds.), *Congress Reconsidered* (New York: Praeger, 1977), pp. 176–182.

[73] Braunthal, *The West German Legislative Process*, pp. 142–155.

the full committees and the parent chamber. Shall their jurisdiction be relatively fixed and permanent? Shall their memberships be relatively stable? How shall their chairmen be selected? How much authority shall the subcommittees have over legislation; shall the full committee accept, or amend, the reports to them from their subcommittees? How shall the party ratios be calculated? What rules of procedure and debate shall be used? To what extent shall they have staff? Since the U.S. Congress uses subcommittees more extensively than do other parliaments, this set of problems is (so far) mainly American.[74]

The importance to the House of the existence of subcommittees is indicated by the attention reformers have given them within the Democratic party caucus. To help define the answers to the questions posed in the previous paragraph, the Democratic caucus adopted a "subcommittee bill of rights." Subcommittees were given fixed jurisdictions and staff; subcommittee chairmen were selected through the party caucus on each committee; and each Democratic member of a committee could become chairman of a subcommittee.[75]

Active subcommittees can indicate a relatively decentralized committee structure, in which the committee has allocated most decision-making powers to its subcommittees. The House Appropriations Committee is an illustration. The full committee reviews, but mainly accepts, the decisions of its several subcommittees. The subcommittee chairman and ranking minority member instead of the full committee's chairman and minority counterpart, then regularly handle their particular bills on the floor.[76]

The number and use of subcommittees has greatly increased since the early 1950s.[77] There has been a considerable decentralization of legislative power from, but also within, the full committees. In part, at least, the increased use of subcommittees reflected the rise to middle seniority of a northern and liberal Democratic political generation (elected in the 1950s) to challenge and begin to displace an older, high-seniority generation of southern conservative Democrats (elected in the 1940s and earlier). In effect, a two-pronged attack has been waged upon the senior southern conservative committee chairmen by the majority of northern liberals within the Democratic party: One

---

[74] Norman J. Ornstein, "Causes and Consequences of Congressional Change: Subcommittee Reforms in the House of Representatives, 1970–73," in Norman J. Ornstein (ed.), *Congress in Change: Evolution and Reform* (New York: Praeger, 1975), pp. 88–114.

[75] Ibid., pp. 105–107.

[76] Richard Fenno, *Power of the Purse: Appropriations Politics in Congress* (Boston: Little, Brown, 1966), pp. 438–447.

[77] The number of meetings and committees and subcommittees in the House combined has doubled from 3210 in the 84th Congress to 6975 in the 94th Congress. Commission on Administrative Review, *Work Management*, p. 2.

prong of the strategy, previously discussed, has been to use the political party to centralize power and to curb the independence of committees and their chairmen; the other has been to decentralize power to sub-committees within the full committees. The beneficiaries of both parts of the strategy have been northern liberal Democrats and the policies they prefer.

Authorizing vs. Appropriations Committees

The third problem presented by committees in the U.S. Congress is that of coordination between the Appropriations Committee and all the other committees that write legislation. The committees we have discussed earlier, such as Education and Labor, Banking and Currency, Interior, and so on, are *authorizing* committees. They examine pro-posed programs and policies, and authorize the expenditure of a certain amount of funds to accomplish the approved policies and programs. They are commonly termed *authorization* or *program* committees. But it is only the Appropriations Committee which can "appropriate" the funds to be spent. Thus, most programs and agencies go through Congress twice—first, for the initial program authorization (which may last from one to several years) and, second, for the annual appropriation.

There is usually antagonism between the program committees and the Appropriations Committee and now also the Budget Committee. The program or authorization committees usually approve and protect the programs within their jurisdiction. An interest in making public policy in a given program is one attraction that a committee has to its members. By contrast, the Appropriations Committee is more con-cerned with limiting the expenditure of funds. Whereas the program committees often wish to expand the agencies and programs within their legislative jurisdiction, the Appropriations Committee wishes to cut their expenditures. The differing perspectives, and actions, of the two types of committees may be illustrated by comparing the foreign-aid funds authorized by the Foreign Affairs Committee and those appropriated by the Appropriations Committee, in both houses (Table 6.15). Although Congress usually cuts funds for this purpose, the amount of the reductions is much greater at all stages of the appro-priations bill than of the original authorization bill. The appropriate contrast that highlights the difference between the two committees is the first line, showing the two committees in the House. There is also a chamber difference, in which the Senate is more favorable to foreign-aid appropriations at all stages than is the House. But even in the Senate, the Foreign Relations Committee is somewhat more favorable toward the foreign-aid program than is its counterpart Appropriations Committee.

Table 6.15 AUTHORIZATION AND APPROPRIATIONS: PROGRAM
SUPPORT AND REDUCTION IN FOREIGN-AID BILLS, 1955–1960

CHAMBER AND STAGE	AUTHORIZATION BILL (%)	APPROPRIATIONS BILL (%)
HOUSE OF REPRESENTATIVES		
Committee	− 7.7	−22.3
Floor	−10.0	−22.2
SENATE		
Committee	− 8.0	−11.7
Floor	−10.5	−13.7
Conference	−10.3	−18.7

SOURCE: Adapted from Richard F. Fenno, Jr., *Congressmen in Committees* (Boston: Little, Brown, 1973), p. 219, table 6.9.

A congressman who had gone on the Appropriations Committee from one of the program committees expressed his own change of outlooks as a result of making the committee change:[78]

> I suppose I came here a flaming liberal; but as the years go by I get more conservative. You just hate like hell to spend all this money. It's an awful lot of money. I used to look more at the program, but now I look at it in terms of money . . .

The Senate has attempted to cope with this conflict between committees by a policy of overlapping membership. Designated members of program committees become members of the Appropriations Committee when the latter considers the appropriations for agencies within the jurisdiction of the relevant program committees. This device, together with the Senate's practice of usually accepting the appropriations requests of all its members, considerably lessens tensions between Appropriations and the other committees.

The previously discussed new Budget Committees may reduce tensions between Appropriations and the program committees by erecting financial limits that apply equally to both types of committees. Not infrequently, the Budget Committee chairmen have, on the floor, warned their colleagues that their enthusiasm for a given program would violate the previously voted and binding financial limits on a given type of expenditure. More often than not, these warnings have been delivered against the program committees rather than the Appropriations Committee.

The House, which experiences the tension more acutely, has also adopted another method of committee limitation: party caucus approval of committee chairmen. Although we have already discussed this reform, we should note here that the same reform was simul-

[78] Fenno, *Congressmen in Committees*, pp. 126–127.

taneously applied against the chairmen of the subcommittees of the Appropriations Committee. Only one has been rejected by the Democratic caucus, but several have compiled sizable negative votes. Resignation from the House has probably saved one or two from eventual ouster from their subcommittee chairmanships.

Internal Rules and Power

The fourth and final committee system problem we shall discuss concerns power and procedure. By what rules shall the committees (and subcommittees, too) proceed? Rules channel the expression of conflict. Rules are frequently adopted by committees to limit the powers of chairmen who disagree with a majority of their own committee. Such a chairman may avoid calling committee meetings, may stall the hearings, may refuse to ask the Rules Committee (if in the House) for clearance to the floor, or may refuse to call up a bill on the floor. Such a chairman may create or abolish subcommittees, and appoint or demote their chairmen. In two of the House committees we have designated as "permeable," the Education and Labor Committee and the Civil Service and Post Office Committee, the chairmen alienated a sizable majority of their members, including many of their own Democrats. The result was adoption by each committee of new rules that gave to the majority the right to call committee meetings and to take bills from their committee to the floor.[79] Another House committee with considerable internal strife has been the Banking and Currency Committee, on which a conservative coalition had a policy majority under a liberal chairman. When members of a committee are in disagreement, the rules then become an issue, for each side will attempt to use the rules to defend its own view of proper public policy within the committee.

Each House can, and does, prescribe rules for its committees. These rules make the committees responsible to the full chamber and also channel the expression of conflict within the committees. One example concerns the quorum: Senate rules stipulate that 50% of a committee's membership must be present for the committee to transact business legally. This requirement was violated by the Senate Committee on Foreign Relations when, under the press of time, it brought a measure to the floor without a majority of members having been present and voting. The bill's manager had contacted the absent members, so he had their knowledge and consent. Nevertheless, a point of order was raised against the committee report, and the ruling of the chair was that the report could not be considered on the floor because it had never officially left the committee. In this instance there was no

[79] Ibid., pp. 130–133, 135–137.

question of intracommittee conflict, but still the chamber enforced one of the rules by which it protects itself against improper procedures within its own committees.[80]

A more general problem of power is created by the division of a large body into smaller units: maintenance of the same strength of parties (and factions) on each smaller unit as in the larger body. Party strength in most committees is proportional to their seats in the whole chamber; and in the U.S. Congress, this is also true in subcommittees. This general rule, however, has not been followed in the House's three most important committees: Ways and Means, Appropriations, and Rules. On those three major committees, the majority party usually holds 66% of the seats, irrespective of having a smaller proportion in the House itself. Yet, the working relationship of southern Democrats with Republicans has often deprived the House Democratic leadership of working control even within those committees.

The problem is compounded when committees divide into even smaller subcommittees. A large party ratio often becomes just one or two persons more than the other party on any given subcommittee. The problems (or opportunities, depending upon your point of view) this narrow margin creates may be illustrated by the Senate Judiciary Committee and the proposed constitutional amendment to abolish the electoral college. Senator Birch Bayh (D-Ind.) was chairman in 1977 of the Constitutional Amendments Subcommittee. His party had four members to the Republican's two on the subcommittee since Democrats held 62% of the seats in the Senate, and 11 seats to the Republican's six on the full Judiciary Committee. Opponents of the proposed amendment, sponsored by Senator Bayh, attempted to send the amendment back to Bayh's own subcommittee rather than report it to the floor. Bayh opposed the move, for with the new membership of his subcommittee the amendment would be killed there. If only one Democrat (James Allen, Ala.) would vote with the Republicans against it, the committee would thereby be tied. A motion to report the amendment to the full committee would fail on a 3-3 tie vote within the subcommittee. For that reason, the bill's author opposed sending the bill back to his own subcommittee, but his motion succeeded in the full Judiciary Committee by only a one-vote margin. The immediate aftermath was, in the full committee, a stalemate, for the bill's many opponents began a series of delay tactics. They threatened to delay consideration (and perhaps to stop any action at all) on another bill unless the proposed constitutional amendment was dropped.[81] The issue was finally resolved when the proponents threatened to hold up action on bills the other side wanted. Both sides resolved their mutual stale-

[80] *Congressional Quarterly Weekly Report,* October 8, 1977, p. 2178.
[81] Ibid., June 25, 1977, p. 1295.

mate by agreeing to send the bills in question to the floor. This episode illustrates that a large party majority can dissolve into an almost even balance when that majority is subdivided into relatively small committees. The large percentage advantage turns out to be just two or three persons over the other party.

CONCLUSIONS

Committees are one organizational device available to parliaments to divide the workload among their members. The extent to which committees are used, however, varies among the world's nations. The main contrast is between systems in which committees possess original and full jurisdiction over legislation and those in which committees are restricted to advisory consideration of detailed amendments. From that contrast follows a number of other differences concerning the permanence of members, the selection of chairmen, and the powers of investigation.

The extent to which committees exist, the scope of their authority, and the autonomy of their memberships are essentially decided by the government of the day in parliamentary systems and by the political parties in all systems. Governments both feel threatened by committees and can act to control and use them. Parties are a competing alternative mode of internal organization, and party leaders may seek to limit committee autonomy as a means of protecting the party's ability to manage the affairs of parliament and to control their own members.

Once created, committee systems create their own sets of management problems. Allocation of jurisdiction among them, scheduling meetings and development of a flow of legislation to the floor, the creation of subcommittees, and the channeling of internal conflict (either party or factional) are among the major problems facing committees.

The potential of committee systems to develop expertise, and hence power, in their relationships with chief executives may be illustrated by the observation made by one of Washington's best-known newcomers:[82]

> I have never had any experience with the Congress. I have been surprised at the quality of their knowledge of subjects, particularly in view of the fact that individual members of the House and Senate specialize or concentrate on a particular aspect of domestic or international affairs and almost invariably they know more about the subject than I do, at least those members of a subcommittee who have long years of dealing with a single subject.

[82] Jimmy Carter interview, *New York Times,* December 5, 1977, p. 42.

Chapter 7
Procedures and
Decision Making
on the Floor

A parliamentary body is best symbolized to the general public when all of its members meet at one time "on the floor." The floor is both a location and a step in the legislative process. As a location, it is a large room in which the whole membership meets. As a step in the legislative process, it is an arena for certain types of actions and certain types of decisions.

But "the floor"—or more elegantly put, the "plenary meeting"—is only one location and only one stage of decision making. The committees and the parties, especially, are also arenas within which members meet and make decisions.

Each arena is different from the others. Size is the most obvious physical difference. Committees (or subcommittees) are usually the smallest operating unit of a parliament, whereas most parties are intermediate in size. The plenary meeting includes all the members; it is the largest gathering of the whole parliament.

Diversity is another point of difference among the several legislative arenas. Committees are often specialized by subject-matter jurisdiction, by type of district, and by type of member. Although parties are usually much broader and more inclusive than committees, they

343

too eliminate much diversity by excluding nonparty members and including only those who either were elected, or have later affiliated, with the parliamentary party. Parties vary widely in their size and heterogeneity, but are usually something smaller than, and something less heterogeneous than, the full membership. Even the Communist party does not occupy all the seats in the Supreme Soviet. The whole membership presumably portrays the diversity of the nation's population.

Publicity is another respect in which the arenas differ. Plenary meetings are usually open to the public; the press and even television are often present. In part, the meetings are ceremonial in form. The opening meeting of a year's session often includes a "Speech from the Throne" or the president's "State of the Union" Address, while governors present "State of the State" addresses. These meetings are great occasions of state, with the visitor galleries full, and often carried live on TV to the general public. Even though most floor sessions are perhaps dull and technical to the general public and even though attendance of the members may be quite low at any one moment, it is the plenary meeting of the whole membership that most draws the attention of the media and of the public.

As a result the members, the parties, and the government calculate their activities and their words on the floor. Most legislative behavior at any stage is purposive, but on the floor, the general public becomes one of the audiences toward which legislators act purposefully. Because it is public, whatever is done and said on the floor commits the actors to positions that they will have to live with in the future.

Party meetings are usually private, and committee meetings in many countries are also closed. But even when they are open to the public and to the press as in the United States, most committee meetings receive little media attention except for the more dramatic investigatory hearings.

The relative privacy of the party and committee arenas permits the members to speak more frankly with one another. Parties can form agreements, and governmental officials may be questioned and may respond without staking out public positions. The private arenas can be less ideological, and less electoral, than the public arenas of the floor. They can also be more specific, whereas floor debate is often addressed to more general questions. Thus the same parties that contest each other in elections and both wage ideological debate and attempt to defeat one another on the floor may cooperate and find agreement in the committees.

A final difference among the arenas of legislation concerns their authority. Unless specific authority has been allocated to committees (as in Italy), the final and authoritative decisions of a parliament are made on the floor. In parliaments with a developed committee system, most bills will be stopped in the committees. In parliaments with functioning party caucuses, how the party members will vote and debate on the floor will be decided in the caucus. But the plenary meeting retains potential jurisdiction over all bills, and could order a committee to report a bill back to the floor. And the party caucus' effectiveness is known only as the individual member casts his vote on the floor. It is on the floor, and especially in the act of voting, that the parliament as a whole makes decisions. Although parties and committees make decisions for themselves, technically their decisions are at best recommendations and advisory to the full body. It is the officiality and final character of decision making on the floor that attracts the publicity and compels the prior calculations of words and votes by members and the government.[1]

STEPS IN THE LEGISLATIVE PROCEDURE

Floor and Committee Alternation

The most common pattern among parliaments in handling legislation is to alternate between floor and committee stages. As shown in Table 7.1, the introduction and referral of a bill to committee is the bill's first appearance on the floor in the U.S. Congress. In the Senate the bill is introduced orally from the floor by its sponsor, whereas in the House a member simply drops the bill's text in the "hopper," which is a box at the side of the clerks' desk, and a written notice appears in the next day's *Congressional Record* (Fig. 7.1). A bill is brought to the floor a second time after the committee has worked on it and has reported the bill to the floor. Most of the floor activity on a bill will occur at this point. The chamber debates the bill and considers and votes upon amendments. When the amending stage is complete, the bill is ready for final passage, or third reading. Final passage usually takes no more than a half hour, whereas the amendment stage can take anywhere from one or two hours in the House to a month in the Senate. But final passage mainly consists of one or two votes on whether the bill, as amended to that point, should be passed or not. A very skeletal outline of Senate procedures is shown in Figure 7.2 for a noncontroversial bill.

The West German procedure largely follows the American pattern, although in the former there is a general debate at first reading, and

---

[1] Michael Mezey, *Comparative Legislatures* (Durham, N.C.: Duke University Press, 1979), pp. 54–56; Malcolm Shaw and John D. Lees, *Committees* (Durham, N.C.: Duke University Press, forthcoming), pp. 10.85–10.91.

Table 7.1   STEPS IN LEGISLATIVE PROCEDURE IN SELECTED COUNTRIES

	FLOOR	COMMITTEE		FLOOR	
U.S. House	Introduction, refer to committee	Filter, hearings, report	Rules Committee	Committee of Whole: Debate, amendments. Readings 1 and 2	Final passage. Reading 3
U.S. Senate	Introduction, refer to committee. Readings 1 and 2	Filter, hearings, report		Debate, amendments	Final passage. Reading 3
British Commons	Introduction, debate, vote. Readings 1 and 2	Amendments		Report stage: Debate, amendments	Final passage. Reading 3
West Germany	Introduction, debate, refer to committee. Reading 1	Filter, report		Debate, amendments. Reading 2	Debate, amendments, final passage. Reading 3
Poland	Introduction, debate, refer to committee. Reading 1	Amendments		Debate, amendments, final passage. Reading 2	

additional debate and amendments are permitted at third reading (as is the case in some U.S. state legislatures).[2] Poland has a simplified procedure, in which our second and third readings are collapsed into a single stage. But both are similar to the American Congress in that the major floor activity on a bill occurs after a bill has been reported out of a committee.

The British procedure, though ours grows from it, is quite different. A major debate at second reading, unlike ours, occurs prior to committee stage. It is at this point that the British House of Commons votes whether or not to accept the bill on principle. Only after that prior and major decision is made is a bill sent to committee. At that

[2] Gerard Braunthal, *The West German Legislative Process: A Case Study of Two Transportation Bills* (Ithaca: Cornell University Press, 1972), pp. 112–121, 188–198.

July 21, 1977   CONGRESSIONAL RECORD — SENATE

INTRODUCTION OF BILLS AND JOINT RESOLUTIONS

The following bills and joint resolutions were introduced, read the first time and, by unanimous consent, the second time, and referred as indicated:

By Mr. NELSON:

S. 1902. A bill to amend the Social Security Act and the Internal Revenue Code of 1954 to strengthen the financing of the social security system, to reduce the effect of wage and price fluctuation on the system's benefit structure, and to eliminate from that system gender-based distinctions; to the Committee on Finance.

By Mr. JACKSON (for himself, Mr. ANDERSON, Mr. KENNEDY, Mr. METZENBAUM, Mr. HART, and Mr. SCHWEIKER):

S. 1903. A bill to amend chapter 55 of title 10, United States Code, to authorize the use of health maintenance organizations in providing health care under such chapter, and for other purposes; to the Committee on Armed Services.

By Mr. BARTLETT:

S. 1904. A bill to amend the Customs Administrative Act of 1938 to prohibit the Secretary of the Treasury from extending the privilege of admission free of duty without entry of their baggage and effects to high officials of the United States Government; to the Committee on Finance.

By Mr. DOLE (for himself, Mr. JAVITS, and Mr. STAFFORD):

S. 1905. A bill to authorize Federal assistance to private, profitmaking agencies and organizations under title II of the Rehabilitation Act of 1973; to the Committee on Human Resources.

By Mr. CRANSTON:

S. 1906. A bill to establish the Channel Islands and Santa Monica Mountains National Park and Seashore in the State of California, and for other purposes; to the Committee on Energy and Natural Resources.

By Mr. WILLIAMS:

S. 1907. A bill to amend the Social Security Act to provide medicare benefits for individuals who require total parenteral nutrition (TPN) as a result of intestinal surgery; to the Committee on Finance.

By Mr. WALLOP (for himself and Mr. HANSEN):

S. 1908. A bill to provide for the transfer and conveyance of the silver service of the United States Ship *Wyoming* to the Wyoming State Museum, and for other purposes; to the Committee on Armed Services.

By Mr. ROTH:

S.J. Res. 76. A joint resolution proposing an amendment to the Constitution of the United States with respect to the reconfirmation of Federal judges after a term of ten years; to the Committee on the Judiciary.

Figure 7.1 Notice of bill Introduction: U.S. Senate.

point the Commons has an option. "Committee stage" can occur either "upstairs" in a standing committee as described in Chapter 6, or on the floor in "committee of the whole," meaning the whole membership acts as a committee. This latter option has been used mainly for appropriation and taxation bills and sometimes for other important legislation. Decreasing use of committee of the whole procedure is now being made to save floor time. Even detailed provisions of the finance bill are now considered in a standing committee. This fairly recent change in the British Commons illustrates the shortness of time relative to the amount of legislative business brought to Parliament. Even though the British Parliament is virtually a year-long body, there is a shortage of floor time to consider legislation and to accommodate the desires of members to speak on the floor.[3]

[3] M. T. Ryle, "Developments in the Parliamentary System," in William Thornhill (ed.), *The Modernization of British Government* (Totowa, N.J.: Rowman and Littlefield, 1975), pp. 7–30. The most complete discussion of British procedure is found in Lord Gilbert Campion, *Introduction to the Procedure of the House of Commons,* 3d ed. (London: Macmillan, 1958).

PROHIBITION OF RATE DISCRIMI-
NATION

Mr. ROBERT C. BYRD. Mr. President, I ask unanimous consent that the Senate proceed to the consideration of calendar order No. 723, S. 2249.

The PRESIDING OFFICER. The bill will be stated by title.

The legislative clerk read as follows:

A bill (S. 2249) to prohibit discrimination in rates charged by the Southwestern Power Administration and to require due process in the confirmation of such rates by the Federal Energy Regulatory Commission.

The PRESIDING OFFICER. Is there objection to the present consideration of the bill?

There being no objection, the Senate proceeded to consider the bill, which had been reported from the Committee on Energy and Natural Resources with an amendment on page 2, beginning with line 6, strike through and including line 11, so as to make the bill read:

Be it enacted by the Senate and House of Representatives of the United States of America in Congress assembled,

SECTION 1. Power and energy marketed by the Southwestern Power Administration pursuant to section 825s of title 16, United States Code (1970), shall be sold at uniform systemwide rates, without discrimination between customers to whom the Southwestern Power Administration delivers such power and energy by means of transmission lines or facilities constructed with appropriated funds, and customers to whom the Southwestern Power Administration delivers such power and energy by means of transmission lines or facilities, the use of which is acquired by lease, wheeling, or other contractual arrangements. Agreed points of delivery shall not be changed unilaterally.

The amendment was agreed to.

The bill was ordered to be engrossed for a third reading, read the third time, and passed.

The PRESIDING OFFICER (Mr. HARRY F. BYRD, Jr.). Without objection a motion to reconsider the vote is tabled.

Figure 7.2 Floor procedure in the U.S. Senate. (Source: U.S. Congress, *Congressional Record* (Daily Ed.), May 15, 1978, p. S7510.)

Committee stage in the British Parliament is very different from the American or German examples. As discussed in the last chapter, it is confined to the details of a bill, the main principles having already been approved at second reading on the floor. Furthermore, the government minister, not the committee chairman, is in charge of the bill at the following floor stages.

The bill from the committee is presented to the House at "report stage," which is a separate step in legislative procedure on the floor. Although it is not considered part of third reading, it is a necessary preliminary. The debate at report stage occurs on the bill as a whole (as amended by what the government will accept from the committee), and separate votes can be taken on specific amendments. In this respect, the British are quite similar to the American and German procedure. At third reading, the question is whether or not to pass the whole bill.

There are endless variations among the world's parliaments in the details of their procedures. But in the main, they all feature an interplay between committee and the floor. In the American and German pattern, the committees do the preliminary work and thereby greatly affect the final shape of a bill, while in the British pattern, committees are secondary both in impact and in the sequence in which they receive and work upon the bill.

Parliaments also vary in their use of the terminology of "readings." The British Commons and some American state legislatures describe their procedures in terms of "first reading" and so on, but this terminology has largely disappeared from usage in the U.S. Congress.

Procedures of Bicameralism

Bicameral parliaments have an additional set of procedures to handle disagreements between the two chambers, of which there are two major types. The U.S. Congress illustrates one procedure, in which a "conference committee" is appointed to reconcile differences between the houses. The conference committee report can occasion a major debate in either or both houses and can be the subject of close votes. In the second procedural type, or "shuttle" system, illustrated by Belgium and Italy, the bill is sent from one chamber to the other until they both agree to the same wording.[4]

A third procedure is used for those parliaments in which the two houses are not equal in legislative powers: the "upper" house can only delay legislation. The British House of Lords, for example, can refuse to accept a bill adopted by Commons and can also amend it. If the House of Commons votes for the bill a second time in its original form, the bill becomes law after a year's delay, with the Lords' version being eliminated. But even in this system, floor time of the House of

[4] Inter-Parliamentary Union, *Parliaments: A Comparative Study on the Structure and Functioning of Representative Institutions in Forty-One Countries* (New York: Praeger, 1961), p. 187.

Commons is required to debate and vote upon the bill a second time in its amended form.

Still another segment of floor time on a bill is required in those systems, such as the American, that permit an executive veto. If the party and committee leaders decide to attempt to override a veto, that step can only be taken on the floor.

Legislative Obstacle Course

Each step in legislative procedure is a potential obstacle at which a bill may be defeated. The various stages are like a steeplechase (or obstacle course) in which each stage is a separate challenge and a potential disaster. The bill's supporters must calculate how to obtain a majority at each stage, whereas its opponents strive for a majority for their side, thereby killing the bill. Proponents must guide the bill successfully through each stage, but opponents need win only once. A negative vote at any one stage will effectively kill the bill. But opponents have another weapon—delay. A bill delayed up to final adjournment has been killed, even without a vote. Nothing happens in the absence of a positive action on the bill. For opponents, the absence of positive activity is just as good as (and perhaps much less trouble than) a negative vote.

We can chart the successive elimination of bills in Table 7.2, which shows the fate of presidential legislation in the U.S. Congress for several years and presidents. Almost half of the presidential bills are adopted each year, although Johnson in 1965 was more successful.

Table 7.2   ACTION ON PRESIDENTIAL LEGISLATION BY STAGE OF LEGISLATIVE PROCESS BY PRESIDENTS AND SELECTED YEARS

| | PRESIDENT AND YEAR | | |
| | JOHNSON | NIXON | |
STAGE	1965 (%)	1970 (%)	1972 (%)
No action	8.5	21	24
Committee hearings but not reported	4.3	17	6
Reported by committee but not taken to floor	.6	1	2
Passed in one chamber only	4.3	9	10
In conference committee	1.7	1	7
Negative vote: committee or floor	8.5	5	7
Approved	69.0	46	45
Total	100.0	100	100
Number of proposals	469	210	116

SOURCES: John E. Schwarz and L. Earl Shaw, *The United States Congress in Comparative Perspective* (Hinsdale, Ill.: Dryden, 1976), p. 224, table 6.6; *Congressional Quarterly Almanacs*, 1970, pp. 106–115; 1972, pp. 76–83.

Table 7.3 NUMBER OF BILLS AT SUCCESSIVE STAGES OF
LEGISLATIVE PROCEDURE: U.S. CONGRESS, 1973–1974

| STAGE OF PROCEDURE | SESSION AND CHAMBER ORIGINATING BILLS | | | | | | |
| | FIRST SESSION | | SECOND SESSION | | TOTALS | | |
	HOUSE	SENATE	HOUSE	SENATE	HOUSE	SENATE	TOTAL
ORIGINATING CHAMBER							
Introduced	12,150	2,860	5,540	1,400	17,690	4,260	21,950
Reported by Committee	347	326	394	307	741	633	1,374
Passed	260	280	288	246	548	526	1,074
SECOND CHAMBER							
Reported by Committee	152	36	232	91	384	127	511
Passed	177	105	292	176	469	281	750
Enacted	145	100	236	168	381	268	649

SOURCE: "Résumé of Congressional Activity of Ninety-Third Congress," *Congressional Record* (Daily ed.), January 10, 1975, p. D1427.

What happened to the other half? Only 5% to 8% of the presidential bills were defeated by a negative vote. All the others were delayed. By far the largest group (20–24%) received no action at all in the Nixon years, showing again the sifting function of committees. Another group (8–17%) were passed in at least one house, but had not completed all steps in the other, or had been delayed in conference committee. Another group (5–18%) had received committee hearings at least but had not gotten to the floor. Thus about 55% of the bills had either been adopted or had received a negative vote. All the others were defeated by the passage of time. The legislative process is not only an obstacle course and endurance contest; it is also a race against time.[5]

The same point can be illustrated for all legislation, not only those bills proposed by the president. For the 1973–1974 Congress, Table 7.3 shows the number of bills introduced in each chamber, by session, and traces their progression through successive stages of legislative procedure.[6] The big drop in the survivability rate of bills comes at committee stage of the chamber in which the bills are originally introduced. In the first session, for example, of the 12,000 bills introduced in the House less than 350 were reported by House committees; of them, 260 reached the floor and were passed. The numbers are

[5] John E. Schwarz and L. Earl Shaw, *The United States Congress in Comparative Perspective* (Hinsdale, Ill.: Dryden, 1976), p. 224; *Congressional Quarterly Almanac(s)*, 1970, pp. 106–115, and 1972, pp. 76–83.
[6] U.S. Congress, *Congressional Record* (Daily ed.), "Resume of Congressional Activity of Ninety-Third Congress," January 10, 1975, p. D1427.

fairly constant across the originating chambers and for the two sessions: 300 to 400 bills were reported by the committees and 240 to 280 bills were considered and adopted on the floor of the originating chambers. These figures demonstrate the sifting power of congressional committees.

The numbers again decrease as bills go through the second chamber of their journey through the legislative process. House bills survive more in the Senate than do Senate bills in the House, with the result that over the two-year period 120 more House bills were enacted than were Senate-originated bills. In part, this difference reflects the constitutional requirement that money bills originate in the House.[7] Table 7.3 also considers only those public bills that require the action of both chambers. It underestimates the activity of the Senate, for its exclusive role in treaty ratification and nomination confirmation is excluded from these figures.

The major point from Table 7.3 is the much smaller number of bills enacted than originally introduced. Over the two-year period a total of 21,950 bills were introduced in both chambers together; 649 were enacted. The point of greatest reduction in the number of bills is in the committees of the originating chamber. Once bills have cleared that hurdle, their numbers are not cut greatly at successive stages of congressional procedure. The initial sifting decision, the major obstacle in getting to the floor, rests with the committees in the originating chamber.

The massive energy bill of the Carter administration's first year (1977) illustrates the need for careful timing of successive stages of the legislative sequence. The sense of urgency was communicated by President Carter in imposing a short three-month deadline for the development of his own plan to submit to Congress. When his proposal was released in mid-March, the Speaker and party leaders had developed a schedule for House consideration of that large and complicated bill. As we indicated in Chapter 6, it was divided and referred to five standing House committees under a deadline. Their portions of the bill, as amended by them, were then referred to the Ad Hoc Energy Committee to reconcile difference among the original committees. This added reconciling committee itself had only one week in which to do its work. The next week its bill and report were before the Rules Committee to obtain a "rule" governing floor debate and procedures on the House floor. The whole bill was then debated, amended, and

---

[7] Of 136 bills sent to conference committees in the 92nd Congress, 72% originated in the House. Of course, all of the 41 tax and appropriations bills did. Of the 95 nonmoney bills, however, 60% of them also originated in the House; see Gerald S. Strom and Barry S. Rundquist, "A Revised Theory of Winning in House-Senate Conferences," *American Political Science Review* 77 (June 1977), p. 451, table 2.

passed in one week on the House floor, and House action was completed the last day prior to the August recess the same year. Senate committees began their initial scrutiny of the bill almost immediately, with the Senate majority leader serving notice that most other bills would be kept off the Senate floor to make room in a busy schedule for floor consideration of the energy bill.

In spite of this concerted and sustained effort, the energy package stalled in the Senate, and then spent close to a year in conference committee. Carter's "moral equivalent of war," as he termed his energy package, was frontally attacked both in Senate committees and on the Senate floor, was subjected to guerrilla warfare in conference committee, and barely survived conference committee, though not without some severe amputations.

The energy bill does illustrate, though, how the chief executive can command the attention of Congress. When Congress is controlled by sizable majorities of his own party, and when the congressional party leaders take an active role in scheduling and managing legislation, a major presidential bill will receive full and also expeditious consideration. Note the contrast in the enactment rates between presidential bills in Table 7.2 and all bills in Table 7.3: Close to half the presidential bills were successful, contrasted with less than 3% for the latter (649 bills passed out of 21,950 introduced).

GETTING TO THE FLOOR

Bills do not flow automatically to the floor. Someone has to decide whether a bill will be taken to the floor, and when and how. Someone also has to decide who will do it. Although these decisions are important in any parliament, they have been particularly critical in the U.S. Congress. It is at this point that the filibuster in the Senate and the Rules Committee in the House exercise their power.

The Senate

In the Senate, when a bill is ready for the floor, the majority leader will address the presiding officer, asking unanimous consent that the Senate proceed to the consideration of Senate Bill such and so, citing its number. In most cases no one objects, and the bill is on the floor (Fig. 7.2). But someone might object, for this point is the critical place at which a filibuster may occur. If there is objection, the majority leader states his request in the form of a motion. Motions are debatable. Thus a filibuster occurs more on the motion to debate the bill than on the bill itself. The object of a typical filibuster is to prevent consideration of the bill and is an effort to force the majority leader to withdraw the bill from the floor in the interest of being able to consider other legislation.

The House

The House handles this problem much differently and more expeditiously. The House Rules Committee reports a special "rule" for each bill, which in effect suspends the standing rules of the House and authorizes consideration of the bill under new provisions. The report of the Rules Committee is debatable—but for only one hour. Then a vote must occur on adoption of the special rule. It is adoptable by a majority vote.

Upon adoption of the rule, a motion is in order that the House resolve itself into the Committee of the Whole for the consideration of the bill in question. Although this motion can be subject to a vote, it is not debatable or subject to dilatory tactics. The Senate has unlimited debate (we shall discuss below the cloture petition as a means of cutting off a filibuster), but there is no such practice in the House. Instead, time is carefully controlled and limited. Debate on the special rule is limited to one hour, and then the rule itself, as we shall also discuss below, limits time for debate on the bill to a few hours.

Adoption of the rule is ordinarily a noncontroversial matter, as will be noted in a later section. Upon occasion, however, opponents of a bill will attempt to defeat the rule, thereby preventing consideration of the bill itself. That attempt was successful in early 1978 on a campaign finance bill. The bill would have affected Republican fund raising much more adversely than that of Democrats; as a result, Republicans caucused on the bill and obtained a united party vote against adoption of the rule. Enough southern Democrats joined them to defeat the rule, thereby keeping the bill off the floor. The coalition was successful in this parliamentary tactic even though the Democratic House leadership strongly supported the bill and urged adoption of the rule itself.[8]

Party and Committee Leadership

The decision to take a bill to the floor is made in the U.S. Congress by a combination of the party leaders and the ranking members of the committee. They jointly decide when and how to bring the bill to the floor in the Senate. In the House they jointly decide when to bring the bill to the Rules Committee. When the rule is granted, they then jointly decide when and how to bring the bill and accompanying rule to the floor.

[8] *Congressional Quarterly Weekly Report,* March 25, 1978, pp. 752–753.

They also decide whether or not to keep the bill on the floor in the event of an unexpected defeat. In 1977, for example, a damaging amendment to a civil service bill was adopted unexpectedly in the House. That bill, which would permit civil service employees to engage in certain forms of partisan politics, was strongly supported by organized labor and the Carter administration. The amendment, however, would have prohibited unions of federal employees from spending funds for any political purpose. When this amendment was adopted, the floor manager for the bill and the majority party leaders suspended House consideration of the bill. It was brought back to the House three weeks later when the party and committee leaders decided they could pass the bill without the damaging amendment, as they did.[9] In the Senate, the power of the majority leader to withdraw a bill from the floor was vividly shown by Senator Byrd's (D-W.Va.) refusal to withdraw a major portion of the president's energy bill in the face of a filibuster on the issue of government regulation of the price of natural gas. In the middle of that 1977 filibuster, Byrd flatly stated:[10]

> I think that the Senate is under duty to pass a bill. . . . The President has stated that we have that responsibility. . . . We have spent, now, 11 days on this bill. I am of the firm determination to proceed with the bill. . . . I do not know what the Senate will do with it. They may vote it up or down. But for us to spend 11 days and then for me to turn around and take it down, I could not justify that.

In the States

In about half of the American state legislatures, bills reported by committees are required to receive floor consideration. In the other half of the states, however, some combination of chamber leadership and party leaders decide which bills actually are taken to the floor. This intermediate step has been particularly important in Arizona, Colorado, Connecticut, Pennsylvania, and New Jersey. In the New York Assembly, the Rules Committee takes charge of legislation in the latter third of a legislative session. In most of these states the legislative party is well organized and strongly led, and in the New York Assembly the Rules Committee is an arm of the chamber and party leadership. Here again we find evidence for the proposition advanced in earlier chapters that parties and committees are alternative and rival means of internal organization.[11]

9 *Congressional Quarterly Weekly Report,* May 21, 1977, p. 1016; June 11, 1977, p. 1145.

10 U.S. Congress, *Congressional Record* (Daily ed.), September 30, 1977, p. S16021.

11 Alan Rosenthal, *Legislative Performance in the States: Explorations of Committee Behavior* (New York: Free Press, 1974), p. 29.

ON THE FLOOR

House procedure is more structured than in the Senate. It is more predictable, more uniform, and takes less time, for it is more subject to rules and time limitations. We shall outline the House procedure used for major bills contrasting it with procedure in the Senate.

In the House

House procedure takes this outline form:

    I. Full House: Adoption of the Rule
   II. Committee of the Whole
      A. General Debate
      B. Amendments
  III. Full House: Authoritative Decisions
      A. Amendments
      B. Motion to Recommit (optional)
      C. Final Passage

RULE ADOPTION
We have already discussed the first step, adoption of the rule. The special rule, in effect, suspends the standing rules to permit the House to consider the bill under expedited procedures in the Committee of the Whole. The Committee of the Whole is the entire membership using relatively informal and flexible procedures defined in the rule.

GENERAL DEBATE
First, the rule limits the time for general debate, usually from two to four hours. The more important or controversial the bill, the longer the time for general debate. The longest time given a bill since 1961 has been 10 hours, allocated to the Civil Rights Act of 1965. An indication of the unique importance of the prospective Nixon impeachment was that the House leadership was considering a 20-hour rule. The time limitation for general debate on the 1977 energy bill was quite unusual in this respect: It provided that one day, rather than a specific number of hours, should be allocated to general debate. But it also provided that time for general debate would be divided equally between the two parties.

AMENDMENTS
Second, the rule defines the number and scope of amendments. An "open" rule permits an unlimited number of amendments to all portions of the bill, whereas a "closed" rule prohibits amendments. Tax bills have often been brought to the House floor under a closed rule. A "modified closed" rule permits a few amendments, which are clearly

specified and limited in the terms of the rule, as in the case of the energy bill in Figure 7.3.

Third, the rule states that amendments are considered under the five-minute rule, meaning that each speaker on an amendment has five minutes to debate. Although several hours can be taken on a controversial amendment, this rule has the effect of considerably shortening time on most amendments in the House compared to the Senate. Amendments in the Senate, by marked contrast to the House, are subject to unlimited debate. The 1977 filibuster on the natural gas bill, for example, was against an amendment, not the whole bill itself. The Senate spent the better part of two weeks (and several whole nights) on that one amendment because of the filibuster, whereas the same amendment in the House was debated and voted upon in one day.

THE OFFICIAL HOUSE

The Committee—even of the Whole—is advisory to the House. It formally can only advise the full and official House. The membership meeting as the full House handles the bill on its third reading, and it is at that point that the House makes its official and legal decisions on the bill. It, in effect, reviews the decisions made by the Committee of the Whole, and although it usually accepts those decisions, it can also reverse them. Consequently, the rule specifies, fourth, that upon completion of amendment stage in Committee of the Whole (which completes second reading), the full House shall proceed to vote upon the bill on final passage. One preliminary step is always taken: either acceptance or revoting on any amendments adopted in the Committee of the Whole.

The rule also specifies whether or not a motion to recommit is in order. It usually is. A motion to recommit sends the bill back to the originating committee; this motion is reserved to the minority to make. It is, in effect, a last-ditch attempt by the minority to appeal to the better instincts of the majority. The motion comes in two forms, with very different effects. In one form, without instructions, the bill is killed. If a bill is returned to committee, the committee will not resurrect it. The House would have voted against the bill, and the committee would be wasting its time to bring the bill back. The simple motion to recommit is a drastic one, which is not often offered, and almost never is accepted. Thus a second form, with instructions, is used more often. The instruction is a type of amendment that changes the bill in certain respects. If it were adopted, which it usually is not, the committee chairman would immediately report the amended version of the bill to the floor, and it would be that version that would be on the floor for final passage. But a motion to recommit is not in order on the floor in the full House unless the special rule provides for it.

95TH CONGRESS
1ST SESSION

H. RES. 727

[Report No. 95-546]

IN THE HOUSE OF REPRESENTATIVES

JULY 28, 1977

Mr. BOLLING, from the Committee on Rules, reported the following resolution;
which was referred to the House Calendar and ordered to be printed

JULY 29, 1977

Considered, amended, and agreed to

RESOLUTION

1   *Resolved,* That upon the adoption of this resolution it

2   shall be in order to move, clause 2 (1) (5) and (6) of rule

3   XI and sections 303 (a) and 402 (a) of the Congressional

4   Budget Act of 1974 (Public Law 93-344) to the contrary

5   notwithstanding, that the House resolve itself into the Com-

6   mittee of the Whole House on the State of the Union for the

7   consideration of the bill (H.R. 8444) to establish a com-

8   prehensive national energy policy, and all points of order

9   against sections 771, 2022, and 2033 of said bill for failure

10   to comply with the provisions of clause 5, rule XXI, are

11   hereby waived. The first reading of the bill shall be dispensed

12   with. After general debate, which shall be confined to the

Figure 7.3   Resolution for House floor consideration of the Energy Bill.

2

1 bill and shall continue not to exceed one legislative day, to

2 be equally divided and controlled by the chairman and rank-

3 ing minority member of the Ad Hoc Committee on Energy,

4 the bill shall be considered for amendment under the five-

5 minute rule by parts instead of by sections, and each part

6 shall be considered as having been read for amendment. No

7 amendment to the bill shall be in order except pro forma

8 amendments for the purpose of debate and except the follow-

9 ing amendments, which shall be in order...

(p. 3)

16   (9) An amendment numbered 1 printed in the Con-

17   gressional Record of July 28, 1977, by Representative

18   Waggonner;

19   (10) An amendment printed in the Congressional

20   Record of July 28, 1977, by Representative Conable...

(p. 4)

13 At the conclusion of the consideration of the bill for amend-

14 ment, the Committee shall rise and report the bill to the

15 House with such amendments as may have been adopted,

16 and the previous question shall be considered as ordered on

17 the bill and amendments thereto to final passage without

18 intervening motion except one motion to recommit with or

19 without instructions.

COMMITTEE OF THE WHOLE

To resort to a Committee of the Whole membership on the floor in lieu of the House's official status permits the use of special rules in place of the standing rules. The informality and flexibility saves considerable time in several respects. First, under the standing rules, each member may speak for one hour. If all 435 members availed themselves of that rule, many weeks would be required even to debate the bill, much less work on amendments. But under Committee of the Whole procedures, general debate of two to four hours will occupy one afternoon, and amendments can be handled in one or two additional afternoons. Second, the quorum for the official House is 216, or half the membership, whereas the quorum in Committee of the Whole is 100 members. It is much easier to keep 100 members on the floor than twice that number to maintain the quorum. In practice, many fewer members than that may be on the floor at any one time, and as long as no one challenges the presence of a quorum, the chamber may proceed without interruption.

Symbolism mixes with substance in floor sessions. The mace, a traditional symbol of authority, is placed on a stand to the right of the Speaker when the House is in session. But when the House resolves itself into the Committee of the Whole, the mace is removed from its pedestal, for the House is no longer in session. Likewise, the presiding officer of the official House is the Speaker, but a chairman is appointed to preside during floor sessions of Committee of the Whole House. Both acts of symbolism are carried over into the U.S. practice from the British House of Commons.

The Committee of the Whole procedure is used only for those bills that the House is working on for the first time in any given two-year period. If the same bill returns from conference committee, or if the bill has been vetoed and thus returns to the House again, the House proceeds in its official capacity, with the Speaker in the chair.

THE ENERGY BILL IN COMMITTEE OF THE WHOLE

Debate and consideration of amendments, under the modified closed rule, took only one week on the very complex administration's Energy Bill (Fig. 7.4). In the Senate the bill was divided into five separate bills and took the better part of two months on the floor. That difference in floor time reflected the major differences in the organization of the two chambers: Although general debate in the House was restricted to one day by the Rules Committee, and only nine amendments were permitted, the Senate leadership had to struggle with the cumbersome unanimous-consent agreement system and ran into a filibuster. The Senate then discovered that not even adoption of a cloture petition could stop obstructionist tactics and bring a motion to a vote.

NATIONAL ENERGY ACT

Mr. ASHLEY. Mr. Speaker, pursuant to the provisions of House Resolution 727, I move that the House resolve itself into the Committee of the Whole House on the State of the Union for the consideration of the bill (H.R. 8444) to establish a comprehensive national energy policy.

> Chairman of the Ad Hoc Energy Committee brings bill to the floor.

The SPEAKER. The question is on the motion offered by the gentleman from Ohio (Mr. ASHLEY).

The question was taken; and the Speaker announced that the ayes appeared to have it.

Mr. CHARLES H. WILSON of California. Mr. Speaker, I object to the vote on the ground that a quorum is not present and make the point of order that a quorum is not present.

> Absence of a quorum noted by a Republican.

The SPEAKER. Evidently a quorum is not present.

The Sergeant at Arms will notify absent Members.

The vote was taken by electronic device, and there were— yeas 365, nays 12, answered "present" 1, not voting 55, as follows:

> All members are notified of impending debate; vote by electronic machine on question of moving into Committee of the Whole. A quorum is present.

[Roll No. 487]

YEAS—365

Abdnor	Brodhead	Delanev
Addabbo	Brooks	Dell⸱·
Akaka	Broomfield	D⸱
Alexander	Brown, Calif.	
Ambro	Brown, Mic⸱	
Ammerman	Brown. ⸱	
Anderson,	Buc⸱	
Calif.	ₚ⸱	
Anderson, Ill.		
Andrews,		
N. D⸱⸱		
An⸱⸱ . . .		

So the motion was agreed to.

The result of the vote was announced as above recorded.

IN THE COMMITTEE OF THE WHOLE

Accordingly the House resolved itself into the Committee of the Whole House on the State of the Union for the consideration of the bill (H.R. 8444) to establish a comprehensive national energy policy, with Mr. BOLAND in the chair.

The Clerk read the title of the bill.

By unanimous consent, the first reading of the bill was dispensed with.

> The House becomes the Committee of the Whole to consider the Energy Bill. The presiding officer is a chairman, not the Speaker.

The CHAIRMAN. Under the rule, the gentleman from Ohio (Mr. ASHLEY) will be recognized for one-half of the debate on this legislative day and the gentleman from Illinois (Mr. ANDERSON) will be recognized for one-half of the debate on this legislative day.

> General debate under the rule.

The Chair recognizes the gentleman from Ohio (Mr. ASHLEY).

Mr. ASHLEY. Mr. Chairman, this is a momentous occasion for the House of Representatives. Today we begin consideration of an omnibus energy bill, which for the first time in our country's history will establish a rational, comprehensive national energy policy. Never before in the annals of this House has there been considered in one bill subject mat-

> General debate opened by Chairman of the Ad Hoc Energy Committee as floor manager for the proponents.

Figure 7.4 Debate and voting in the U.S. House: the Energy Bill, 1977. (Source: U.S. Congress. *Congressional Record,* (Daily Ed.), August 1–5, 1977, pp. H8172–H8827.)

ter which encompasses 113 separate legislative initiatives involving the jurisdiction of five major standing committees of the House. Never before has this body considered legislation of more direct a⌐ vital interest to the future of our N⌐

Today the energy future of ⌐ is very uncertain and ver⌐ is uncertain because of ⌐ between energy sur⌐ the United Stat⌐ insecure bec⌐ on foreig⌐ cans— . . .

Mr. ANDERSON of Illinois. Mr. Chairman, I yield myself 1 minutes.

(Mr. ANDERSON of Illinois asked and was given permission to revise and extend his remarks.)

Mr. ANDERSON of Illinois. Mr. Chairman, as I am sure those who were present for the debate on the rule on this legislation observed last Friday, we are considering it under rules of procedure that are unusual, if not unprecedented, in the history of this House. One of the interesting features of the rule is that it makes H.R. 8444 in order under a rule whereby we will consider it in terms of general debate for a legislative day.

. . .

Let me say at the very outset, Mr. Chairman, as I proceed to consider and discuss the legislation before us, that I am going to take a position that is quite different from that which has just been enunciated by the able and distinguished chairman of the Ad Hoc Energy Committee, the gentleman from Ohio (Mr. ASHLEY). That does not mean in any way that I want to detract from the idea that the gentleman from Ohio (Mr. ASHLEY) has presided with great dignity and, I think, with essential fairness during the 3 long days of markup that were spent on H.R. 8444. My differences with the gentleman—and they are many, both procedural and substantive—certainly do not in any way detract from my admiration—yes, even my affection—for the gentleman from Ohio as one who is sincerely dedicated to his cause.

The energy bill that we proceed to debate today, Mr. Chairman, can perha⌐ most accurately be described as a ⌐ loaf. Unfortunately, we canno⌐ complete that old proverb o⌐ goes on to say that "a ⌐ ter than none." In ⌐ a half a loaf, if ⌐ it was report⌐ would no⌐ coun⌐ . . .

Mr. ANDERSON of Illinois. Mr. Chairman, I yield 10 minutes to the gentleman from New York (Mr. CONABLE).

(Mr. CONABLE asked and was given permission to revise and extend his remarks.)

The ranking Republican member of the Ad Hoc Energy Committee, and floor manager for his side, opens general debate for his side of the aisle.

Praise for chairman coupled with opening attack on the bill.

Mr. CONABLE. Mr. Chairman, I rise in opposition to this bill. I opposed it in the Committee on Ways and Means, with the hope that the ad hoc committee would make appropriate changes that would allow me to vote for it. Unfortunately, they have not only not made those changes that I felt were necessary but, worse, they have made changes which make the bill even less attractive than it was.

I cannot in conscience support what is a punitive measure, negative in approach, designed to impose burdensome costs and regulation on the American people when there are alternatives available which would help solve the energy crisis without punitive action.

In the light of what I have said, it is interesting to note that I think we all sense widespread public approval of ~ energy program and also a ~ʷᵗ ̎ public disinterest in tʰ ̖ there's the rub. T̎ ̖ ̖ energy prᵒᶜ̎ conᵉ̎ . . .

A major Republican spokesman against the bill.

Mr. ASHLEY. Mr. Chairman, I have no additional requests for time.

Mr. Chairman, I move that the Committee do now rise.

The motion was agreed to.

Accordingly the Committee rose; and the Speaker having resumed the chair, Mr. BOLAND, Chairman of the Committee of the Whole House on the State of the Union, reported that that Committee, having had under consideration the bill (H.R. 8444) to establish a comprehensive national energy policy, had come to no resolution thereon.

End of general debate on Monday.

. . .

NATIONAL ENERGY ACT

Mr. ASHLEY. Mr. Speaker, I move that the House resolve itself into the Committee of the Whole House on the State of the Union for the further consideration of the bill (H.R. 8444) to establish a comprehensive national energy policy.

The SPEAKER pro tempore. The question is on the motion offered by the gentleman from Ohio (Mr. ASHLEY).

The motion was agreed to.

IN THE COMMITTEE OF THE WHOLE

Accordingly the House resolved itself into the Committee of the Whole House on the State of the Union for the further consideration of the bill H.R. 8444, with Mr. BOLAND in the chair.

The Clerk read the title of the bill.

The CHAIRMAN. When the Committee rose on Monday, August 1, 1977, all time for general debate had expired.

Pursuant to the rule, the bill is considered by parts and each part is considered as having been read for amendment. No amendment shall be in order except pro forma amendments and

Beginning of amendment stage on Tuesday.

The chair states the amendment procedure permitted under the rule.

amendments made in order pursuant to
House Resolution 727, which will not be
subject to amendment, except amendments recommended by the ad hoc Committee on Energy and amendments made
in order under House Resolution 727.

Mr. ASHLEY. Mr. Chairman, I ask
unanimous consent that the Committee
amendments to the table of contents and
the table of contents be passed over and
considered after all other amendments
have been considered, in order that they
can be correctly disposed of.

The CHAIRMAN. Is there objection
to the request of the gentleman from
Ohio?

There was no objection.

The CHAIRMAN. The Clerk will designate the part of the bill now pending *f*
consideration.

The Clerk read as follows:

Page 9, line 1, section 2. (Se⁻
follows:)

Sᴇᴄ. 2. Fɪɴᴅɪɴɢs ᴀɴᴅ ᶠ⁻

(a) Fɪɴᴅɪɴɢs.— ⁻
(1) the U⁻⁻
shortage a⁻⁻
energⱴ . . .

The CHAIRMAN (during the reading). Does the gentleman from Ohio re-
new his request that the amendment be
considered as read and printed in the
Rᴇᴄᴏʀᴅ?

Mr. BROWN of Ohio. I do, Mr. Chairman.

The CHAIRMAN. Is there objection to
the request of the gentleman from Ohio?

There was no objection.

(Mr. BROWN of Ohio asked and was
given permission to revise and extend
his remarks.)

Mr. BROWN of Ohio. Mr. Chairman,
this is the amendment which was made
in order by the Rules Committee, to be
offered by the gentleman from Ohio, and
is the amendment which has been known
generally as the Krueger-Brown-Wirth
amendment, which was narrowly defeated in the Commerce Committee and
is the amendment which seeks to terminate on a gradual basis the price controls of the Federal Government in the
area of natural gas.

Now, as we begin the debate on ⁻
of the most important and contr⁻
portions of H.R. 8444, my a⁻
to the natural gas pricin⁻
would like to take eac⁻
back to late Janua⁻
of this year. At ⁺⁻
ural gas use⁻
west an⁻
onlⱴ⁻ . . .

On the third day (Wednesday), one
of the major amendments is offered to
reduce government control of the
price of natural gas.

consider the amendment with the same
generosity they have considered other
amendments to this bill, and pass the
amendment.

Mr. ASHLEY. Mr. Chairman, I rise in
opposition to the amendment.

(Mr. ASHLEY asked and was given

The chairman of the Ad Hoc Energy
Committee opens debate against the
amendment.

permission to revise and extend his remarks.)

Mr. ASHLEY. Mr. Chairman, it strikes me that there are five major policy defects in the Brown-Krueger amendment.

First of all, deregulation as proposed will result in demand-driven prices $5 or more per thousand cubic fe··

Second, deregulation will res··· $56 billion to $88 billion in v·· to natural gas produce·

Third, deregulatic· or no increase in · to the incen··· of H.R. 8·· . . .

Mr. BROWN of Ohio. Mr. Chairman, will the gentleman yield?

Mr. ASHLEY. I yield to the gentleman from Ohio.

Mr. BROWN of Ohio. I appreciate the gentleman's yielding.

I would just like to observe that the gentleman is predicting natural gas prices to go through the roof. I think the gentleman from Ohio is familiar with

. . .

Mr. ASHLEY. Mr. Chairman, I ask unanimous consent that all debate on this amendment conclude at 3:30 o'clock p.m.

The CHAIRMAN. Is there objection to the request of the gentleman from Ohio?

Mr. ASHBROOK. Mr. Chairman, reserving the right to object, could we get an indication as to how much time that would mean for Members who have not spoken?

Most of us have been sitting here while certain Members have been allowed to speak for 10, 12, and 15 minutes. Are we now to be denied the opportunity to speak for even 5 minutes?

The CHAIRMAN. The Chair observes about 30 Members standing. That would mean that about 2½ minutes would be alloted to those who have requested time.

Mr. ASHBROOK. Then, Mr. Chairman, I must object.

The CHAIRMAN. Objection is heard.

Mr. ASHLEY. Mr. Chairman, I move that all debate on this amendment conclude at 3:30 o'clock p.m.

The CHAIRMAN. The question is on the motion offered by the gentleman from Ohio (Mr. ASHLEY).

The question was taken; and on a division (demanded by Mr. ASHBROOK) there were—ayes 45, noes 11.

So the motion was agreed to.

. . .

The CHAIRMAN. The Chair recognizes the distinguished Speaker of the House, the gentleman from Massachusetts (Mr. O'NEILL).

Mr. O'NEILL. Now, we come to the

Direct and quick questioning of each other begins.

Time limitation is a problem even in Committee of the Whole.

However, it can be settled by a majority vote.

After more debate, the Speaker closes debate against the amendment by speaking from the floor.

Brown-Krueger amendment. Let us consider the consequences of the deregulation of natural gas. Let us consider the added cost to the consumer. The cost to the consumer over and above the a⌐ ⌐ committee amendment would ⌐⌐ lion to $79 billion betwee⌐ year 1985. The Libr⌐⌐ that the figure ⌐⌐ consumer w⌐⌐⌐ under t⌐ . . .

I believe this bill will go down, if the Krueger-Brown amendment is adopted. I think it would be wrong. I think it would be an injustice to this country.

I say to you, look at your conscience. Do you want to go home on Saturday of this week and say that the Congress has failed? As between the people and the independent gas producers working together on one side and big oil on the other. Where do you core down?

Believe me, the future of America in 1985, the economy of this country, the defense of this Nation, are at stake. This is at the heart of this bill.

I ask you to vote down the Krueger-Brown amendment.

The CHAIRMAN. All time has expired.

The question is on the amendment offered by the gentleman from Ohio (Mr. BROWN).

The question was taken; and the Chairman announced that he was in doubt.

Voice vote on the amendment.

RECORDED VOTE

Mr. BROWN of Ohio. Mr. Chairman, I demand a recorded vote.

A recorded vote was ordered.

Record vote.

The vote was taken by electronic device, and there were—ayes 199, noes 227, not voting 7, as follows:

[Roll No. 499]

AYES—199

Listing of members' names by their vote.

Abdnor	Evans, Del.	Mahon
Anderson, Ill.	Evans, Ind.	Mann
Andrews,	Findley	Marlenee
N. Dak.	Fish	Marriott
Archer	Flowers	Martin
Armstrong	Flynt	Mattox
Ashbrook	Forsythe	Metcalfe
AuCoin	Frenzel	Michel
Badham	Frey	Milford
Bafalis	Fuqua	Mill⌐⌐
Barnard	Gammage	
Bauman	Gia⌐⌐	
Beard, Ten⌐		
Bo⌐⌐ . . .		

NOES—227

Addabbo	Foley	Nichols
Akaka	Ford, Mich.	Nix
Alexander	Ford, Tenn.	Nolan
Allen	Fountain	Nowak
Ambro	Fowler	Oakar
Ammerman	Fraser	Oberstar
Anderson,	Gaydos	Obey
Calif.	Gephardt	Ottinger
Andrews, N.C.	Gibbons	Panetta
Annunzio	Gilman	Patten
Applegate	Ginn	Patterson
Ashley	Gonzalez	Pe⌐⌐⌐
Aspin	Gore	
Baldus	⌐	
Baucu⌐ . . .		

So the amendment was rejected.

...

The CHAIRMAN. The question is on the amendment of the ad hoc committee to part I, title II.

The ad hoc committee amendment was agreed to.

AMENDMENT OFFERED BY MR. CUNNINGHAM

Mr. CUNNINGHAM. Mr. Chairman, I offer an amendment.

The CHAIRMAN. The Chair will inquire of the gentleman from Washington (Mr. CUNNINGHAM) whether or not this amendment is permitted under the rule.

Mr. CUNNINGHAM. Mr. Chairman, it is my understanding that at present it is not. It is also my understanding, in talking with the gentleman from Ohio (Mr. ASHLEY), that should the House be allowed to totally exert its rules, the amendment could be made in order.

The CHAIRMAN. Does the gentleman from Washington (Mr. CUNNINGHAM) seek unanimous consent to consider the amendment?

Mr. CUNNINGHAM. Mr. Chairman, what I would prefer would be first to explain the amendment.

At the Chair's suggestion, I do ask unanimous consent that the amendment be considered.

The CHAIRMAN. Is there objection to the request of the gentleman from Washington?

Mr. BOLLING. Mr. Chairman, I reserve the right to object.

The CHAIRMAN. The gentleman from Missouri (Mr. BOLLING) reserves the right to object.

Mr. ALLEN. Mr. Chairman, I object.

The CHAIRMAN. The Clerk will report the amendment.

Mr. ALLEN. Mr. Chairman, I object.

...

Mr. ROSTENKOWSKI. Mr. Chairman, I rise in support of the ad hoc committee amendment.

Mr. Chairman, those of us who consider ourselves realists understand that a gasoline tax is a highly emotional and politicized issue. Regardless of the outcome of this vote it is good that the ad hoc committee has given us the oppor-

...

Mr. STEIGER. Mr. Chairman, I move to strike the requisite number of words. I rise in opposition to the amendment.

Mr. Chairman, I listened with great interest to the statesmanlike position taken by the gentleman from Illinois.

I commend the gentleman for his courage, but I think he is wrong. The gentleman from Ohio, the distinguished man of the ad hoc committ~ understood him c~ wants us to g~ used to ~ . . .

The result.

On Thursday, the fourth day, amendment stage continues.

A committee amendment is accepted by voice vote.

An effort to offer an amendment not authorized by the rule.

The effort is blocked by a single objection.

An amendment to tax gasoline is offered for the administration by the Energy Committee.

A leading Republican opponent speaks against the amendment.

Mr. ASHLEY. Mr. Chairman, will the gentleman yield?

Mr. STEIGER. I yield to the gentleman from Ohio.

Mr. ASHLEY. Did the gentleman think that the goal that the President articulated, and that I referred to, is a justifiable goal?

Mr. STEIGER. A reduction in the rate of gasoline consumption by 10 percent?

Mr. ASHLEY. By 1985.

Mr. STEIGER. The goal by 1985 is embodied even within the Republican substitute that we will be debating a little later. Yes, I do think that goal is a worthy objective.

. . .

The CHAIRMAN. All time has expired. The question is on the amendment offered by the gentleman from New Jersey (Mr. HOWARD) as a substitute for the ad hoc committee amendment to part II, title II.

The question was taken.

RECORDED VOTE

Mr. MARTIN. Mr. Chairman, I demand a recorded vote.

A recorded vote was ordered.

The vote was taken by electronic device, and there were—ayes 82. noes 339, not voting 12, as follows:

[Roll No. 503]

AYES—82

Alexander	Evans, Colo.	Ottinger
Anderson,	Pascell	Pickle
Calif.	Flowers	Pritchard
Andrews,	Fowler	Rangel
N. Dak.	Fraser	Reuss
Ashley	Gephardt	Richmond
Aspin	Giaimo	Roberts
Badillo	Gibbons	‒
Baldus	Ginn	
Beilenson		
Bennett . . .		

NOES—339

Abdnor	Chappell	Fary
Addabbo	Chisholm	Fenwick
Akaka	Clausen,	Findley
Allen	Don H.	Fish
Ambro	Clawson, Del	Fisher
Ammerman	Clay	Fithian
Andrews, N.C.	Cleveland	Flood
Annunzio	Cochran	Florio
Applegate	Cohen	Flynt
Archer	Coleman	Foley
Armstrong	Collins, Ill.	Ford ‒ ‒
Ashbrook	Collins, Tex.	‒
AuCoin	Conable	
Badham	C‒	
Bafalis . . .		

So the amendment offered as a substitute for the ad hoc committee amendment was rejected.

The result of the vote was announced as above recorded.

The CHAIRMAN. The question is on the ad hoc committee amendment to

RECORDED VOTE

part III, title II.

Mr. STEIGER. Mr. Chairman, I demand a recorded vote.

A recorded vote was ordered.

An example of quick exchanges on the floor.

Advance notice of a Republican substitute bill to be offered the next day.

A substitute amendment is voted on before the original amendment.

The first vote is by voice.

It is badly defeated on a record vote.

The original amendment is then immediately and equally badly defeated (list of names omitted).

The vote was taken by electronic device, and there were—ayes 52, noes 370, not voting 11, as follows:

...

AMENDMENT IN THE NATURE OF A SUBSTITUTE OFFERED BY MR. ANDERSON OF ILLINOIS

Mr. ANDERSON of Illinois. Mr. Chairman, I offer an amendment in the nature of a substitute.

The Clerk proceeded to read the amendment in the nature of a substitute.

Mr. ANDERSON of Illinois (during the reading). Mr. Chairman, I ask unanimous consent that further reading of the substitute be dispensed with and, Mr. Chairman, further due to the size and the fact that H.R. 8555 is printed and has been available in bill form. I ask unanimous consent that printing of the bill in the RECORD at this point be dispensed with beeause of the cost that would be involved.

The CHAIRMAN. Is there objection to the request of the gentleman from Illinois?

...

Without objection, the unanimous-consent request of the gentleman from Illinois is agreed to .

There was no objection.

(Mr. ANDERSON of Illinois asked and was given permission to revise and extend his remarks.)

Mr. ANDERSON of Illinois. Mr. Chairman; we are now at the most crucial point in consideration of this bill. The House has tried to perfect the bill H.R. 8444 and has failed. The bill is still defective. The close votes on all substantive amendments is ample evidence.

The substitute energy plan which I am offering to the House today is the only energy policy which is truly an energy policy and not a tax or welfare reform measure in disguise. The substitute is a far superior plan for several reasons. It is the only program that sets goals which can be reached. It is the only program which provides mode~'
effective means for stimulati~
duction of oil, gas, an~
only program whi~'
break on ou~
It is t~...

On the fifth and final day (Friday), the Republican manager for the bill offers a substitute bill.

Mr. DINGELL. Mr. Chairman, I rise in opposition to the Republican substitute.

...

Let us talk about what the substitute (H.R. 8555) does.

First of all it decontrols crude; it deregulates natural gas. It contains a plowback of the crude oil equalization tax.

There is only one person that is going to get stung by this substitute—that is the American consumer. It will divert billions—not millions, but billions—of dollars to oil and gas producers and it

A Democratic speaker against the Republican substitute.

will drain billions—not millions, but billions—from the American consumers.

This substitute will reduce consumer purchasing power. It will increase inflation. It will reduce consumer spending. It will increase recessionary pressures enormously. It will reduce real gross national product. It will reduce real growth. And it will increase unemployment.

Mr. Chairman, there are other aspects of this substitute which are high¹ satisfactory to me. Howeve⸗ tions to those other ⸗⸗ ondary to my ⸗⸗⸗ economi⸗ no⸗⸗ . . .

Mr. ASHLEY. Mr. Chairman, I move to strike the last word.

Mr. Chairman, I fully understand that the membership wants to vote, and I will be sensitive to that wish. I simply want to make one or two points, if I might.

First of all, with respect to the Republican substitute that is before us, I will say that the proposals contained in the substitute, H.R. 8555, are no more compelling when considered together, th⸗⸗ they were when we considered th⸗⸗ arately yesterday and earli⸗

Mr. Chairman, we ⸗ ing—we in th⸗ ⸗ tives—th⸗ ⸗ the . . .

The majority floor manager for the bill speaks against the Republican substitute.

In conclusion, Mr. Chairman, I would like to say that I have great pride in the way that the House of Representatives, the majority and minority alike, have addressed this difficult subject area. I particularly would like to comment on the cooperation of the minority. Yes, they take different views than we in the majority. That is to be expected. But it seems to me that it might be well, Mr. Chairman, for those of us on the majority to understand the kind of frustration that must beset the minority, who are outnumbered by some 2 to 1 in this body. I think it is well for all of us to understand that there has not been any effort at dilatory tactics. There has not been any effort to delay proceedings. It can well be said, Mr. Chairman, that if the minority had wanted it, we would not be completing action on this massive bill before us today.

Mr. ANDERSON of Illinois. Mr. Chairman, will the gentleman yield?

Mr. ASHLEY. I yield to the gentleman from Illinois (Mr. ANDERSON).

Mr. ANDERSON of Illinois. I thank the gentleman for yielding.

Mr. Chairman, I am not sure that the gracious remarks of the gentleman will make the pill go down any easier, but I have not heretofore commented on the performance of the chairman, as others have done, and I would not want the record of this debate to close without adding for myself, as ranking minority

Closing remarks complimenting the opposition.

The sentiments are reciprocated even though he knows his substitute bill will lose on the coming vote.

member, that, despite all of the fundamental and frequent disagreement on substantial issues, I have appreciated at all times the demeanor and the conduct and the fairness and the dignity with which the chairman has presided over the ad hoc committee. I want to thank the gentleman.

Mr. ASHLEY. I thank the gentleman for his remarks.

So, Mr. Chairman, I would simply say in conclusion that we in this body, on this committee, and in this House, to which we will soon be returning, can, I think, take a considerable measure of pride in the fact that we have addressed, as best we can, a matter of vital national importance, and that we have acted collectively in the best interests of the people of the United States as we see them.

The CHAIRMAN. The question is on the amendment in the nature of a substitute offered by the gentleman from Illinois (Mr. ANDERSON).

The question was taken; and the Chairman announced that the noes appeared to have it.

First a voice vote.

RECORDED VOTE

Mr. ANDERSON of Illinois. Mr. Chairman, I demand a recorded vote.

A recorded vote was ordered.

The vote was taken by electronic device, and there were—ayes 147, noes 273, not voting 13, as follows:

Then a recorded vote (names omitted).

. . .

The CHAIRMAN. There being no further amendments, under the rule, the Committee rises.

End of Committee of the Whole.

Accordingly the Committee rose; and the Speaker having resumed the chair (Mr. BOLAND) Chairman of the Committee of the Whole House on the State of the Union, reported that that Committee, having had under consideration the bill (H.R. 8444) to establish a comprehensive national energy policy, pursuant to House Resolution 727, he reported the bill back to the House with sundry amendments adopted by the Committee of the Whole.

The Speaker presides again in the full and official House.

The SPEAKER. Under the rule, the previous question is ordered.

Is a separate vote demanded on any amendment?

Mr. EDGAR. Mr. Speaker, I demand a vote on the so-called Horton amendment.

Revote officially on an amendment.

The SPEAKER. Is a separate vote demanded on any other amendment? If not, the Chair will put them en gros.

The amendments were agreed to.

The SPEAKER. The Clerk will report the amendment on which a separate vote has been demanded.

The Clerk read as follows:

Amendment: Strike line 5 on page 377 and all that follows, up to and including line 25 on page 386; reletter succeeding subparts accordingly.

The SPEAKER. The question is on the amendment.

The question was taken; and the Speaker announced that the noes appeared to have it.

. . .

So the amendment was agreed to.
The result of the vote was announced as above recorded.

The SPEAKER. The question is on the engrossment and third reading of the bill.

The bill was ordered to be engrossed and read a third time, and was read the third time.

MOTION TO RECOMMIT OFFERED BY MR. STEIGER

Mr. STEIGER. Mr. Speaker, I offer a motion to recommit.

The SPEAKER. Is the gentleman opposed to the bill?

Mr. STEIGER. After thorough consideration, Mr. Speaker, I am opposed to the bill.

The SPEAKER. The Clerk will report the motion to recommit.

The Clerk read as follows:

Mr. STEIGER moves to recommit the bill H.R. 8444 to the Ad Hoc Committee on Energy with instructions to report back the same to the House forthwith with the following amendment. Strike out line 12 on page 469 and all that follows through page 512, and renumber subsequent parts accordingly.

The SPEAKER. The gentleman from Wisconsin (Mr. STEIGER) is recognized for 5 minutes.

(Mr. STEIGER asked and was given permission to revise and extend his remarks.)

Mr. STEIGER. Mr. Speaker, it is somewhat easier to explain this since there have been others who have given the speech for me. Therefore, Mr. Spea⸢
I can be relatively brief althou⸢⸢
say to the distinguished ⸢⸢
ad hoc committee ⸢⸢
tioned by m⸢
use ⸢⸢ . . .

Mr. LATTA. Mr. Speaker, will the gentleman yield?

Mr. STEIGER. I yield to the gentleman from Ohio.

Mr. LATTA. I thank the gentleman for yielding.

What the gentleman has just said is if one votes against this motion to recommit, he is voting for a 7 cent additional tax on gasoline; is that correct?

Mr. STEIGER. That is correct.

Mr. LATTA. Secondly, the way this provision now stands, there is no exception for agricultural purposes; is that correct?

Mr. STEIGER. That is also correct.

Mr. ULLMAN. Mr. Speaker, I rise in opposition to the motion to recommit.

Mr. Speaker, I am not going to take my full time, but let me start by expressing my appreciation—and I th⸢

Voice vote indicates one result.

A record vote reverses the voice vote.

Bill is ready for final passage.

Republican motion to recommit.

Democratic speaker against motion to recommit.

for all of us—to the Speaker for putting together this package, and to the gentleman from Ohio (Mr. Ashī⌐‾⌐ chairman of the ad hoc ⌐‾ did a magnificen⌐‾ from Ṃ⌐‾ tⁱ⌐ . . .

The SPEAKER. The question is on the motion to recommit.

The question was taken; and the Speaker announced that the noes appeared to have it.

Mr. STEIGER. Mr. Speaker, on that I demand the yeas and nays.

The yeas and nays were ordered.

The question was taken by electronic device, and there were—yeas 203, nays 219, not voting 11, as follows:

Voice vote on motion to recommit.

Record vote.

[Roll No. 512]

YEAS—203

Abdnor	Flynt	Moss
Allen	Forsythe	Mottl
Anderson, Ill.	Fountain	Myers, Gary
Andrews,	Frenzel	Myers, John
N. Dak.	Frey	Nichols
Applegate	Fuqua	O'Brien
Archer	Gammage	Pettis
Armstrong	Gilman	Pickle
Ashbrook	Goldwater	Poage
Badham	Goodling	Pre⌐‾
Bafalis	Gradison	
Bauman	Grassleʸ	
Beard, Tenn.	Gⁱⁱ‾ ˙	
Benjamin		
Bevilⁱ . . .		

NAYS—219

Addabbo	Beard, R.I.	Burlison, Mo.
Akaka	Bedell	Burton, Johᴎ
Alexander	Beilenson	Burton, Phillip
Ambro	Bennett	Byron
Ammerman	Biaggi	Carney
Anderson,	Bingham	Carr
Calif.	Blanchard	Cavanaugh
Andrews, N.C.	Blouin	Chisholm
Annunzio	Boland	Clay
Ashley	Bolling	Collins, Ill
Aspin	Bonior	Conve⌐‾
AuCoin	Bonker	⌐
Badillo	Brademas	
Baldus	Bro⌐ⁱ	
Barnard		
Baucuв . . .		

So the motion to recommit was rejected.

The result of the vote was announced as above recorded.

The SPEAKER. The question is on the passage of the bill.

Mr. STEIGER. Mr. Speaker, on that I demand the yeas and nays.

The yeas and nays were ordered.

The vote was taken by electronic device, and there were—yeas 244, nays 177, not voting 12, as follows:

Ready for vote on final passage of whole bill as amended.

Record vote.

[Roll No. 513]

YEAS—244

Addabbo	Ammerman	Annunzio
Akaka	Anderson,	Ashley
Alexander	Calif.	Aspin
Ambro	Andrews, N.C.	AuCoin

. . .

NAYS—177

Abdnor	Burleson, Tex.	Dellums
Allen	Burton, John	Derwinski
Anderson, Ill.	Butler	Devine
Andrews,	Caputo	Dickinson
N. Dak.	Carter	Dornan
Applegate	Cederberg	Drinan
Archer	Chappell	Duncan, Tenn.
Armstrong	Clausen,	Early
Ashbrook	Don H.	Edwards, Ala.
Badham	Clawson, Del	Edwards, Okla.
Bafalis	Cleveland	English
Bauman	Cochran	
Beard, Tenn.	Col--	
Benjam¹⁻ . . .		

So the bill was passed.
The result of the vote was announced as above recorded,
A motion to reconsider was laid on the table.

The result. Bill is now ready for the Senate.

In the House, both the Rules Committee and floor stage were conducted in accordance with the Speaker's preferences. The Speaker had promised that the House would complete floor action on the entire bill within one week. The Rules Committee, which had two members on the Ad Hoc Energy Committee, provided one day of general debate on the floor and authorized nine specific amendments to be offered by designated members. No other amendments would be in order. As a result, the House disposed of the entire bill with 47 votes, counting all forms of voting on all procedural and preliminary steps, whereas the Senate had 128 roll calls alone during the two-week filibuster.

Both the administration and the opponents wanted authorization from the Rules Committee to offer certain amendments on the House floor, but both sides agreed that a stringent limitation on the number of amendments was needed to handle the bill expeditiously. The opposition's major amendment concerned the deregulation of the prices of natural gas, which we first discussed in the earlier chapter on committees. The administration proponents had lost the gas tax in committee stage and wanted to recoup their losses on the floor. In addition, Republicans wished to offer a comprehensive substitute and also a motion to recommit. Although many of the amendment votes were closely contested, we shall concentrate on the two amendments concerning natural gas prices and the gasoline tax.

Debate on the bill itself was held on a Monday, the first day of a week-long floor stage in the House. General debate was opened, and time was controlled, by the chairman and the ranking minority member of the Ad Hoc Energy Committee for their respective party sides of the aisle. Amendments were considered on the remaining four days of the same week. But the Committee of the Whole could consider only those amendments specifically designated by the rule. The chair stated the ground rules for amendments as the Tuesday session began, and the debate excerpt (Fig. 7.4) from Thursday shows how a member was prevented from offering an unauthorized amendment.

The opposition amendment on deregulation of natural gas prices, was offered on Wednesday, the third day of floor proceedings. This issue, narrowly fought in subcommittee and in full committee, was likewise narrowly decided on the floor. The close vote was a classic example of the conservative coalition, in which Republicans and northern Democrats voted almost solidly against each other, with southern Democrats occupying the middle and swing position. Although a majority of the latter voted with Republicans, they themselves were badly split, reflecting the twin pulls of the administration and of their divergent constituency interests. Although some of the major oil and gas producing states are southern (Texas and Louisiana, for example), other southern states are consumers (North Carolina and Georgia, for example) and are no different in that respect from Massachusetts or Connecticut.

The importance to the administration of defeating this amendment was symbolized by the appeal made on the floor by the Speaker. That the Speaker would make any comment at all, even from the floor as a member rather than as the presiding officer, illustrates the very different definitions we and the British have of the proper role of the occupant of the same office.

The gasoline tax amendments—these amendments were favorable to the administration—were offered the next day (Thursday). The administration's original proposal on the gasoline tax was a request for a maximum of 50 cents tax per gallon, depending upon the amount of oil consumption in the next few years. A measure of how far the administration had retreated was in the amendments offered on the floor—to tax gasoline at either 4 or 5 cents. Both lost, and lost badly.

The administration's position was not aided by confusion and lack of coordination among their own supporters, who were themselves divided over how the proceeds of the tax were to be used. One motion provided that the proceeds were to be allocated to highways and some energy research purposes, whereas another would have allocated the funds to both mass transit and highways. These divergent purposes also reflected a conflict between two of the standing committees. That not even a single and coordinated strategy would have won an affirmative vote, however, is indicated by the vote pattern on the two motions: not only did Republicans and southern Democrats vote "no," but northern Democrats were themselves badly split.

After the specific amendments were considered, the Republican minority had two options to prevent adoption of the energy bill, in addition to simply voting "no." The first Republican option was to offer a substitute for the whole bill, which was considered as the final amendment (on the last day). The vote on the substitute bill was the last order of business within the Committee of the Whole. It was defeated on a party-line vote.

When the Committee then dissolved and the membership became the full and official House, the second Republican option was to offer a motion to recommit. This motion eliminated the tax on "crude oil," but the Republican substitute was more comprehensive. The motion to recommit gave the minority a second opportunity to appeal to their colleagues. This motion lost, as did the substitute, but by a very narrow margin. Having defeated the motion to recommit, the one remaining vote in the House was on final passage.

The energy bill was unusually complex and the House took five days on it, whereas most bills are handled in no more than three days on the House floor. This bill illustrates most of the parliamentary proceedings and legislative options available in the House—amendments, substitutes, and a motion to recommit—and also illustrates the careful control of time that the leadership can exercise through the Rules Committee and the Committee of the Whole.

ALTERNATIVE PROCEDURES

To handle a large number of less important and controversial bills, there are expedited and simpler procedures. On designated days, the House will take up bills on the "Suspension Calendar" and on "Consent Calendar." Bills on the former are debated for no more than 20 minutes, and must obtain a two-thirds vote (not merely a 50% vote) to pass, for technically the motion is to suspend the rules of the House and pass the bill in question. Bills on the latter calendar are adopted if no one objects. If even a single member objects, the bill is not passed. Thus the greater the agreement on a bill, the easier it is to pass the House. Under both procedures the full House is in operation, with the Speaker in the chair and the mace on its pedestal.

TYPICAL SCHEDULE

Both the House and Senate usually convene at 12 noon, leaving the mornings free for committee work. But once in session, the two chambers organize their time quite differently. The House immediately takes up the major bill of the day. After a few preliminaries and a roll call to establish a quorum, the House is generally working on its major business of the day by 12:30 P.M. Its work on bills is often completed by 6 P.M., although it can and does remain at work on a bill until the late evening. When the major legislative work of the day is completed, most members leave the floor, but the House often remains in session to hear "special orders." Members can reserve time to speak on any matter they wish. Their remarks are faithfully recorded in the *Congressional Record*, which is perhaps the most immediate goal of making the speech to an empty chamber. Few members care how long the House remains on special orders for any given day, for they will not be there and will not be listening, and they will not be summoned by a quorum call or for a vote.

In the Senate

The Senate often does not take up its main bills until mid-afternoon. It begins at 12 noon with "morning hour," during which time senators introduce bills and may speak for a short time on any matter. The morning hour may go on to about 2 P.M. Then the Senate takes up its bills. Its legislative activity is usually over by 6 P.M., but, like the House, it can go into nighttime sessions or begin earlier in the day.

The flow of Senate debate and amendments is much more flexible and leisurely than in the House. As in the House, the ranking committee members on both sides of the aisle are in charge of floor stage on their bill. They will begin with general debate; unlike the House, however, general debate is neither limited in duration nor confined to any single sequence in the consideration of the bill. Amendments may be proposed and voted at various intervals. Each amendment is, like the bill itself, subject to unlimited debate. There is no five-minute rule in the Senate.

How, then, does debate ever end? On most bills the senators interested in them have no wish to prolong debate or delay the vote. The party leaders usually confer among themselves and with the committee leaders on any given bill and announce a tentative schedule.

UNANIMOUS CONSENT AGREEMENT

The "unanimous-consent agreement" is the device used in the Senate to limit debate when more informal understandings are not sufficient. The agreement can apply to the bill as a whole, to a single amendment, or to a group of amendments. The limitations in this procedure are indicated by its name; it must be unanimous. Any single senator, for any reason, can object. The agreements are usually negotiated by the party leaders with the committee leaders and with any other senators active on the bill. When a tentative version has been developed, the whole Senate is informed and the agreement proposed. Not infrequently various senators will raise questions, and the terms can be revised during their discussion on the floor of the proposed agreement. If no one objects, the agreement is officially made, and its terms govern and limit the following debate and voting. If, however, any single senator objects, there is not unanimous consent, and debate goes on as before. What the House can accomplish through a "rule" adopted by a 50% vote can be achieved in the Senate only by a 100% agreement.

A somewhat untypical unanimous-consent agreement in 1977 will illustrate the general procedure in proposing one, and will also illustrate some of our earlier points about stages of legislative procedure. In scheduling the Black Lung Benefits Revenue Act of 1977, the Senate leadership had anticipated that a companion bill would be first acted upon in the House, but House action was delayed. Since revenue bills must constitutionally originate in the House, the Senate could not take final action on its bill. As a result, the party and committee leaders had consulted one another and on the first day of debate proposed a unanimous-consent agreement that the Senate take all steps on the bill up to but not including final passage. Figure 7.5 excerpts the floor discussion from the *Congressional Record.* The majority leader (Byrd, D-W.Va.) proposed the unanimous-consent agreement, with the minority leader (Baker, R-Tenn.) and the bill's floor manager from the originating committee (Randolph. D-W.Va.). The terms of the unanimous-consent agreement, which were accepted, provided as stringent a limitation upon final passage debate and amendments as is achieved in the House. This incident also illustrates that "third reading" is retained in the Senate as a distinct parliamentary step. It also indicates how the House bill would be used by the Senate as the legislative vehicle for the content of its own bill. The Senate committee had worked on a Senate bill, and all floor debate and amendments would also occur on the Senate's originated bill. But upon final passage it would be the House bill's number that would emerge, not the Senate's.

Procedures can be more complicated in the Senate than in the House. The absence of a "rule" and Committee of the Whole procedure, coupled with the tradition that the Senate both makes and interprets its own rules, gives to Senate debate a free-form quality. Any amendment and any issue can become the subject of a long, drawn-out series of maneuvers. One motion often used in the Senate, but rarely in the House, is the motion to table. It is a quick way to dispose of an amendment without voting on it directly. It is, however, then subject to a motion to reconsider. Thus, four or five votes may be required to dispose of the preliminary motions as a way of disposing of the main motion itself.

THE FILIBUSTER

While the Senate attempts to find unanimous consent among its 100 members, that effort sometimes fails. The filibuster can then be resorted to as a weapon of force by the minority against the majority. The leader of one filibuster effort was asked why there was a filibuster on a certain bill: "Because we didn't have the votes," he replied.[12]

The object of a filibuster is to force the majority to yield to the

[12] Personal interview.

UNANIMOUS-CONSENT AGREEMENT

Mr. ROBERT C. BYRD. Mr. President, I have discussed with the distinguished minority leader a proposed unanimous-consent request which I think is absolutely necessary in the light of conversations that have been had with the distinguished manager of the black lung bill, Mr. RANDOLPH; with the distinguished ranking minority member of the committee, Mr. JAVITS; with the distinguished chairman of the committee, Mr. WILLIAMS, and with other Members, in order that we may avoid what otherwise could become a constitutional question. We do not want any constitutional question to endanger the black lung bill. We do not want the Senate to have to do its work twice.

.
:

The minority leader is fully in accord with me that because of these reasons a unnaimous-consent agreement is going to be necessary to avoid the constitutional question and in order to avoid the Senate's having to do its work twice.

So the request is as follows:

I ask unanimous consent that the agreement on S. 1538, the black lung bill be modified so that instead of final passage of the bil before the Senate completes its business today, after third reading of the bill it be returned to the Calendar and the majority leader shall be powered to have the Senate resume its consideration at any time—when I say any time, of course, I am going to consult with the minority leader and the manager of the bill and the ranking member, the latter two of whom will have to manage the bill—without further debate or motions thereon in order.

Mr. President, I further ask unanimous consent that when the Senate receives a black lung bill from the House, it be placed on the Calendar, the majority leader be empowered to have the Senate consider it at any time—with the same consultations—and that no amendment or motion relative thereto be in order other than a motion to strike all after the enacting clause and insert in lieu thereof the text of S. 1538 as amended by the Senate, with no debate in order with respect to the House bill or the substitute therefor.

Mr. BAKER. Mr. President, reserving the right to object—and I will not object—the distinguished majority leader and I discussed this matter, and I have, in turn, discussed it with representatives of the distinguished senior Senator from New York, who is the ranking member of the committee and has a deep interest in this subject.

I think the agreement is satisfactory, and I am prepared in a moment to agree to its being entered.

I think, Mr. President, it is important to proceed with this matter. Notwithstanding this difficulty. We have to try to accommodate this disagreement, because the black lung bill is a matter of such consequence and importance to the people of my area, my State, my region of the country, that I think it is important to proceed as promptly as possible.

So I express my appreciation to the distinguished majority leader and the chairman of the committee, to Senator RANDOLPH and to Senator JAVITS, for putting us in a position to act with promptness on the Senate side even though we have to make extraordinary and unusual arrangements to provide for it.

This agreement has been cleared with the distinguished Senator from New York, and I do not object to it.

Figure 7.5   Unanimous-consent agreement: the Black Lung Bill. (Source: U.S. Congress, *Congressional Record* (Daily Ed.), July 21, 1977, p. S12514.)

preferences of the minority. If a filibuster succeeds, the bill in question is withdrawn from the floor. The filibuster was used in the early part of this century by outnumbered progressives and liberals, but it has been more used since World War II by conservatives on economic matters, and especially by southerners on civil-rights legislation. Now that the major civil-rights bills have been passed, the filibuster has lost its anti-civil-rights character and is used by a variety of senators on a variety of issues.

Its utility, however, has been greatly reduced from the 1960s, for it more easily can be ended through a "cloture" petition, which results in a vote on the question of terminating the filibuster. The needed vote is 60% of the full membership; previously it was 66% of those present and voting. That difference of 6% (six senators) has often meant the difference between ending or continuing the filibuster. Two days after a cloture petition is filed, the vote is held on ending the filibuster. If a minimum of 60% vote is attained, the time of each senator is limited for further debate to one hour. But upon the failure of a cloture vote, the majority leaders in the 1960s and 1970s have promptly filed a second petition, and even a third. If on the third try, they still cannot get a 60% vote, then the bill at issue is withdrawn and the Senate goes on to other bills, as happened on the campaign finance bill in mid-1977.

The 15-year period of 1961–1975 was the crucial time in the use and modification of the filibuster. In the initial period, 1917–1960, 23 cloture petitions were filed to stop filibusters, of which only four (or 17%) were successful (Table 7.4). In the 1961–1975 period the use of cloture petitions, and their success, increased markedly: 80 petitions were filed, of which 20 (25%) were successful. This period ended when the filibuster rule itself (Rule 22) was modified in spite of a filibuster by the opponents to its modification. Using the then-existing rule of 66% votes needed to terminate a filibuster, that filibuster was ended, and the modifications that lowered the number of votes needed to adopt a cloture petition were then accepted. In the succeeding period, beginning with 1975, the number of cloture petitions and their success rate greatly increased. If the first two years of the new, modified vote requirement are an indication of the next decade or two, about half of the filibuster attempts will be successful in achieving their goal of preventing Senate consideration of the bill in question, but that is a much lower rate of success than in any previous Senate era.

The filibuster has been used successfully during the Carter administration. In late 1977, for example, the Senate leadership made three attempts to end a filibuster on sections of a campaign finance bill. That effort failed, and as a result the Democratic floor leaders and the bill's chief sponsor Clark, (D-Iowa) decided to withdraw the dis-

Table 7.4 CLOTURE PETITIONS, U.S. SENATE: NUMBER AND RESULTS OF VOTES IN THREE TIME PERIODS, BY REQUIRED MINIMUM VOTE

	MINIMUM VOTE AND TIME PERIODS					
	66 VOTES				60 VOTES	
RESULT OF VOTE	1917–1960		1961–1975		1975–1976	
	(N)	(%)	(N)	(%)	(N)	(%)
Passed	4	17.4	20	25	14	58.3
Failed	19	82.6	60	75	10	41.7
Total	23	100	80	100	24	100

SOURCES: *Congressional Quarterly Almanac*, 1975, p. 37; 1976, p. 27.

puted portions from the larger bill, thus permitting the remainder of that bill to be considered and (successfully) voted upon.[13]

FILIBUSTER ON NATURAL GAS PRICE DEREGULATION

The 1977 filibuster on the price deregulation of natural gas produced several new developments in the Senate. The filibuster leaders, Senators Abourezk (D-S.Dak.) and Metzenbaum (D-Ohio) were defending President Carter's position that government regulation of natural gas prices should be continued. The opponents of the president's position were supporting an amendment by Senators Pearson (R-Kans.) and Bentsen (D-Tex.). The filibuster was launched in face of the prospective adoption of that amendment. The majority leader organized a successful cloture petition; however, it did not bring the amendment to a prompt vote. The filibuster leaders had taken the precaution of filing almost 500 amendments to the bill prior to the cloture vote, and thus the amendments were in order. The filibuster leaders then began calling up each amendment in turn, often forcing several roll call votes on each, with each roll call itself taking no less than 15 minutes. This continued filibuster substituted endless procedure for endless talk and, as such, was an innovation.

Many of the existing rules in parliamentary bodies to expedite debate have been forged when an active and determined minority, using the weapons of delay, has been countered by new rules to permit the majority to limit debate, to eliminate delaying tactics, and to bring measures to a vote. The expeditious rules of the House of Representatives grew out of such turmoil, as have those of the British House of Commons. In an analogous circumstance the 1977 natural gas filibuster produced new rules and procedures to limit delaying tactics. Senator Byrd, the majority leader, and Vice President Mondale devised a new strategy by which the vice president, in his capacity as presiding officer of the Senate, would declare those amendments out of order that he deemed offered for purposes of delay. The vice president ruled he has that power, and his ruling was sustained by a vote of the Senate. This ruling established new authority in the chair, in conjunction with the majority leader, to limit individual members of the Senate. Thereupon the majority leader began calling up the amendments, which were then rapidly and without either debate or appeal ruled out of order by the vice president. By the end of the same day, the filibuster leaders halted their "filibuster by amendment," claiming that the president, because of the role of the vice president, had deserted his own defenders. The next day, the amendment was adopted, as was the whole bill itself. These votes were anticlimactic; the major decisions had already been made in the launching and then the breaking of the filibuster.

---

[13] *Congressional Quarterly Weekly Report*, August 6, 1977, p. 1643; *Campaign Practices Reports*, August 8, 1977, pp. 1–2.

The flow of reasoning, and also of hard feelings, in the filibuster is illustrated in Figure 7.6. Extracts from debate in the *Congressional Record* are found on the left-hand side of the figure, and press commentary is placed to the right. The press reporting and commentary provide an interpretation of what was happening, while the words spoken on the floor were the events themselves. This figure illustrates how the power of the presiding officer can be used and how the Senate responds. The drama and conflict of these events—all within a single day—are by no means typical of the Senate. But these events do illustrate how the Senate can act under extreme circumstances.

In general, filibusters are most effective toward the end of a session. A large number of bills are waiting action. Everyone is vitally interested in other bills—whatever their commitment to the filibustered bill itself. Time is the weapon of force employed by a filibuster—not only the denial of time to vote on the bill in question, but an erosion to time to work on other bills as well.

ATTENDANCE AND DEBATES

Rarely are most of the members on the floor at any one time. The British House of Commons does not even have space for all the members to stand, much less sit. Most members will be present for a vote, but with the exception of an oral roll call, members can vote quickly and leave the chamber. Large numbers usually do not need to be present at any one time (Fig. 7.7). Members usually do not need to listen to the debates, and for several reasons.

Reasons for Nonattendance

Members are ordinarily familiar with the issues and with the politics of the issues. Not many new issues arise in any one year; a member with a few years of service already will have experienced the issue and its politics. The arguments, for example, on the minimum-wage bill of 1977 in the Carter administration were largely unchanged from the minimum-wage bill of 1961 in the Kennedy administration. The arguments are similar, and so is the alignment of those for and against the bill. Even the "energy crisis" only intensified already existing issues and

---

Figure 7.6 Ending a filibuster: natural-gas pricing, 1977. (Sources: U.S. Congress, *Congressional Record* (Daily Ed.), October 3, 1977, pp. S16154–16212; *Congressional Quarterly Weekly Report,* October 8, 1977, pp. 2122, 2127–2128, 2136–2138; *Washington Post,* October 4, 1977, pp. A1, A4, and October 9, 1977, p. A12; *Wall Street Journal,* October 4, 1977, p. 16, and October 7, 1977, p. 12; Jack Germond and Jules Witcover, "The White House and the U.S. Senate," *Greensboro* (N.C.) *Daily News,* October 7, 1977, p. A4.)

Events and Remarks
on the Floor

Reports and Commentary
in the Press

I. The Formal Ruling

Mr. ROBERT C. BYRD. Mr. President, I will repeat the point of order.

Mr. President, I make the point of order that when the Senate is operating under cloture, the Chair is required to take the initiative under rule XXII to rule out of order all amendments which are dilatory or which on their face are out of order.

After 13 days, one all-night session, and over 120 roll calls on delaying amendments, the Senate was awash with frustration.

The majority leader devised a tactic to rule pending amendments out of order without either vote or appeal. The tactic triggered an eruption.

The VICE PRESIDENT. The requested ruling goes to the meaning of rule XXII which provides that once cloture is invoked no dilatory motion or dilatory amendment or amendment not germane shall be in order. The purpose of the rule is to require action by the Senate on a pending measure following cloture within a period of reasonable dispatch. The Presiding Officer must take judicial notice of the fact that we have now been for some 13 days, I believe, on this measure, well over 100 votes having been taken. Therefore, it is the opinion of the Presiding Officer that the point of order is well taken. The Chair will take the initiative to rule out of order dilatory amendments which, under cloture, are not in order——

Mr. ABOUREZK. I appeal the ruling of the Chair.

The VICE PRESIDENT. The Presiding Officer would like to finish his ruling—which, under cloture, are not in order and which on their face are out of order.

Mr. ABOUREZK. I appeal the ruling of the Chair and ask for the yeas and nays.

The VICE PRESIDENT. Is there a sufficent second?

Mr. ROBERT C. BYRD. Mr. President, I move to lay that motion on the table, and I ask for the yeas and nays.

The VICE PRESIDENT. Is there a sufficent second? There is a sufficient second.

The yeas and nays were ordered.

Mr. HARRY F. BYRD, JR. Will the Chair put the question before the Senate votes?

The VICE PRESIDENT. This is a motion to table an appeal from the decision of the Chair that, under cloture, amendments which are out of order on their face can be ruled out of order by the Chair on its own initiative.

.
.
.

Mr. ABOUREZK. Mr. President, I yield myself 5 minutes, and I ask the attention of my colleagues. If I might try to analyze what just happened for

The administration sent the vice president up to help break the filibuster.

By 79-14, the Senate voted to table the appeal and thus uphold Mondale's ruling.

Abourezk was inflamed. Expressed shock Mondale would cooperate with Byrd.

the Members of the Senate, I would appreciate their attention.

What just happened is that the Vice President of the United States has come up to the Senate for one specific purpose, and that is to make certain rulings upon the parliamentary procedures that had been thought out ahead of time.

.
.

I heard the rumor this morning. Several people came up to me and said the rumor is out on the street the Vice President is coming up to make specific rulings to end the filibuster. I said, "I do not believe it. I just do not believe it would happen because the position we are taking, those of us on this side of the issue, happens to agree identically with the position taken publicly with the administration.

.
.

Now, why did the Vice President come up to make those rulings? Why did that happen? I do not know. I know there are any number of Senators here who could have been put in the Chair, could have been placed in there, and who would have made the very same rulings, and there would have had to have been a decision on it because there are Senators here who feel very strongly one way or the other.

I can only surmise—I do not know because there was a flurry of meetings this morning between the leadership and the members of the administration—I can only surmise that something has happened that I do not know about, Members of the Senate on my side of the issue do not know about, and I do not even care to know about them.

I do not want to know. All I know is I have been told from time beginning, beginning from the time that I went into politics, that all governments lie. For a long time I knew that, and I was aware of it. There is one thing I never thought would happen, and that is that Jimmy Carter would lie.

I reserve the remainder of my time.

.
.

The VICE PRESIDENT. The Chair would ask for 4 minutes indulgence from the Senate.

Mr. ROBERT C. BYRD. Mr. President, I make that request.

The VICE PRESIDENT. Is there objection. The Chair hears none, and it is so ordered.

The Senator from South Dakota indicated he learned this morning that the Vice President was part of some deal. The truth of it is the Vice President arrived at 11 o'clock this morning in the Senate. The majority leader advised him he was planning to propound certain questions relating to the meaning of rule XXII. He wanted the Vice President to be aware of those questions, and it was at that point, and only at that point, that the Vice President was aware at all that these questions would be propounded.

There was one suggestion, since this was a crucial issue dealing with the long-delayed question which has been around this Senate for over 60 years as to the meaning of the word "dilatory"—and there could hardly be a more crucial issue affecting the rules of this body—there was a suggestion that it might be wise if the Vice President absented himself and let someone else rule.

I refused to accept that suggestion because it is the Vice President's only constitutional duty to preside. The Vice President has that duty especially at those moments when crucial questions and profound questions of parliamentary procedure are at issue.

．
．

There is no question about this Vice President's position on the merits of the deregulation issue before this body, and I assume the Senator from South Dakota knows that.

There is nothing more sacred to me or to the President than our integrity, and I am not here to apologize for my integrity.

Mr. ROBERT C. BYRD addressed the Chair.

The VICE PRESIDENT. The Senator from West Virginia.

Mr. ROBERT C. BYRD. Mr. President, I think that almost anything I would say at this point would be repetitious.

But, nonetheless, I feel it my duty to speak briefly on this matter that has been raised by the distinguished Senator from South Dakota.

．
．

Whatever the Senate does in working its will on the bill is up to the Senate. But I do not think that the Vice President should be criticized because he came here at the request of the majority leader for the purpose of establishing some rulings that the leadership considers to be important if we are ever going to get this bill to conference.

．
．

Mr. ABOUREZK. I want to say that it is not the integrity of the Vice President that I am impugning. What I am saying—and I want to make it very clear—is that we have had the rug pulled out from under us by the President of the United States and the Vice President is merely doing what he is supposed to do.

．
．

Mondale's reply to Abourezk's insinuations of duplicity.

The ruling enraged Senate liberals, which is the very group Mondale had been lobbying on behalf of President Carter.

II. Application of the New Rule

Mr. ROBERT C. BYRD. Mr. President, I call up amendment——
The VICE PRESIDENT. The Chair has recognized the Senator from West Virginia.

By midafternoon, the new powers were employed with devastating effectiveness.

AMENDMENT NO. 890

Mr. ROBERT C. BYRD. I call up amendment No. 890.
The VICE PRESIDENT. It is not in order since it seeks to amend the bill in two places.

Byrd yelled, rapid fire.

Mondale answered immediately.

AMENDMENT NO. 898

Mr. ROBERT C. BYRD. Mr. President, I call up amendment No. 898.
The VICE PRESIDENT. It is not in order since it seeks to amend the bill in two places.

Byrd shouted.

Mondale answered back.

AMENDMENT NO. 920

Mr. ROBERT C. BYRD. Mr. President, I call up amendment No. 920.
The VICE PRESIDENT. The amendment is not in order since it seeks to amend the bill in two places.

AMENDMENT NO. 941

Mr. ROBERT C. BYRD. I call up amendment No. 941.
The VICE PRESIDENT. The amendment is not in order for the same reason.

.
.
.

Abourezk tried repeatedly to cut in, but was ignored. Mondale recognized only Byrd, who rattled off each amendment like an auctioneer. The fix, obviously, was in.

Mr. Abourezk. I make the point of order that this is a steamroller.*

.
.
.

Abourezk bellowed; ignored, turned his back to return to his seat.

AMENDMENT NO. 1036

Mr. ROBERT C. BYRD. Mr. President, I call up amendment No. 1036.
The VICE PRESIDENT. The amendment is not in order for the same reason.
Several Senators addressed the Chair.
Mr. SARBANES. Mr. President, is the ruling of the Chair that an appeal does not lie to the rulings of the Chair?
The VICE PRESIDENT. The Senator from Maryland.
Mr. SARBANES. Is the Chair ruling that appeals do not lie to the rulings of the Chair?
The VICE PRESIDENT. The Chair has recognized the leader of the Senate under the customs of the Senate.

.
.
.

Other senators, obviously shocked, were on their feet. Mondale recognized only Byrd. In 10 minutes, 33 amendments were buried.

Sarbanes managed to gain recognition. Clearly upset.

Mr. SARBANES. I yield to the Senator from Maine for a question.
Mr. MUSKIE. A further point, may I say to the Senator, when the majority leader put this point of order earlier, I asked him whether or not it would have the effect of denying the right of appeal which a vote of the Senate established just last Saturday. The majority leader assured me that it would not.

.
.
.

*Not in the Congressional Record, but reported in the press.

You cannot tell me that what is going on now is a simple application of the rule. Over and over again, the Chair is putting the question. There are no precedents, and the Chair wants the Senate to establish this ab initio—from the beginning—a new order of things, a change in the rules. That is what you are talking about, and you are doing it by commanding a majority who is your majority only on this issue. I do not think that is the way to do it.

.
.

Mr. CULVER. Mr. President, a point of order. Is the point of order debatable?

The VICE PRESIDENT. Under the rules of cloture, it is not debatable.

SEVERAL SENATORS. Regular order.

Mr. ROBERT C. BYRD. Mr. President, I ask unanimous consent that I may have 5 minutes in which to discuss the point of order.

The VICE PRESIDENT. Is there objection?

Mr. CULVER. Objection.

The VICE PRESIDENT. Objection is heard.

Several Senators addressed the Chair.

.
.

The VICE PRESIDENT. The Senate will be in order.

Mr. ROBERT C. BYRD. But, Mr. President, we have come to a situation here in which it is not just the accommodation of a Senator that is involved; it is, rather, the accommodation of the Senate itself.

We have heard talk about the abuse by the leadership of its prerogatives. We have heard talk about the abuse of the custom of preferential recognition of the majority leader. What about the abuse of the rules to which every Member of the Senate on both sides of the aisle has been subjected for the last 13 days and 1 night? What about that abuse of the rules? What about the abuse of the Senate itself, when we have stood here hour after hour—and I have done it, I have pleaded, I have tried to get unanimous consent, I have had meetings in my office with Senators on both sides of the question, I have tried in every possible way available to me to get the Senate to come down to a resolution of the issue, and my words and pleadings have fallen upon deaf ears.

.
.

No change in the filibuster rule was devised over the weekend. But there have been some new precedents set here today that had to be set, and they were discussed over the weekend.

My interest here is not in putting at a disadvantage those who stand with Mr. METZENBAUM and Mr. ABOUREZK on the basic question. I have voted with them every time on the basic question. But I

Muskie's voice rose in volume to match his mushrooming outrage.

A chorus of outrage at Byrd and the administration. It was a rare scene of pandemonium in the usually staid Senate.

Drew gasps from the galleries. Palpable tension was in the air.

Byrd was yielded time by other senators.

A tongue as sharp and punishing as those before him. He yelled to the point where his words broke with the strain. . . . a tirade in return. . . . ranted and bellowed.

am trying to put a stop to this filibuster, and that is what the Vice President is trying to do, and that is what the administration is trying to do. That is why the Vice President is here today. He is not here, as someone has said, to—what did Mr. ABOUREZK say about the President?—pull the rug out from under us. The Vice President is here to get the ox out of the ditch. The ox is in the ditch! That is why the Vice President is here!

The administration is for the position that the filibusterers hold. The President has said in no uncertain terms that he intends to veto outright deregulation. What more do you want? You know you are going to win in conference. You know if outright deregulation gets through conference, the President will veto it. What kind of a charade do you think the American people are going to be fooled into thinking this is?

I say it is long past time, Mr. President, to stop this filibuster, and to stop the abuse of the Senate and its rules. It was for that reason that I, in this instance, took extraordinary advantage of my prerogative as leader to be recognized. One has to fight fire with fire when all else fails.

[Applause, Senators rising.]

．
．
．

Mr. JAVITS. Mr. President, I yield myself 2 minutes, and I would like to yield then a minute to Senator SARBANES who started this whole discussion.

Mr. President, I have been here a long time. I am very proud of this body. I am very jealous of what it does. I do not want to see it run down the drain in a moment of exasperation. Thirteen days are but a moment in the life of this body; the precedents and the order and the procedure a century.

There was more.

It was all the more stunning because it was wrenched from a man who normally is a study in self-control.

The first calm voice in almost 30 minutes.

III. The Aftermath

COMPREHENSIVE NATURAL GAS POLICY

The Senate continued with consideration of S. 2104.

Mr. METZENBAUM. I would like to say to Members of the Senate that Senator ABOUREZK and I have just indicated that we do not intend to filibuster by amendment; that as far as we are concerned the Senate may proceed in an orderly manner to dispose of the pending legislation. We feel that in view of the fact that the administration indicated quite clearly that they did not support the filibuster, in spite of the fact that they have indicated a strong opposition to deregulation legislation, that they ought to be given the opportunity to make such efforts as they can make in order to defeat the legislation in the Senate or, if not there, if it be necessary

That same evening.

for the President to veto it. As a consequence, we have publicly indicated and
now indicate to the Senate that we do
not intend to offer any further amendments to the pending legislation, except
if there might be some incidental one,
but not in connection with the large
number that are presently pending.

Comment by Byrd in an interview the
following weekend: Everything else
had failed . . . . I anticipated it would
result in the volatile situation you saw,
but I had no choice.

was responded to by already proposed solutions. One of the major
controversies in the Carter 1977 energy bill concerned the regulation
of the price of natural gas, which we have already discussed. The same
issue was one of the dramatic issues of the Eisenhower administration
in the mid-1950s.

Even if members do not have prior personal experience on any
given issue, they often rely upon selected colleagues for guides to the
issue and its politics. Other members from one's party, from one's
state delegation, or from a similar-type district can all provide cues to
any one member about the likely impact of any given issue upon his
district, and of the likely response of his district to the issue.[14] Congressmen search for such cues in a variety of settings—such as on the
floor. But even there a member may learn more through informal
conversations than by listening to the debate itself. Other settings for
exchange of information among congressmen on legislation include
meetings of state delegations, meetings of informal groups (among
them) sitting with one another at lunch, and at evening social occasions. The extensive network of party committees and working groups,
discussed in Chapter 5, performs the same function in foreign
parliaments.

Furthermore, members lead complex and hectic lives, and are apt
to be attending to other parliamentary business even though they are
not on the floor. Committees often meet while the chamber is in floor
session. Members may be contacting administrative agencies. Members
may be visiting with constituents. Members may be conferring with
one another. All of the other activities and forums of parliamentary
activity discussed in this book compete with floor sessions for the
members' time and energy.

[14] John W. Kingdon, *Congressmen's Voting Decisions* (New York: Harper & Row,
1973).

ORDER OF BUSINESS

Mr. ROBERT C. BYRD. Mr. President, the Senate will now proceed to take up the conference report on the budget resolution, under the leadership of Mr. MUSKIE and Mr. BELLMON.

I ask the distinguished Senator whether or not he expects a rollcall vote.

Mr. MUSKIE. Mr. President, we have inquired of all interested parties—I think we have—and there is no desire for a rollcall vote. So far as we are concerned, there is no need for a rollcall vote, unless some Senator now present wishes it.

Mr. ROBERT C. BYRD. Mr. President, if I may be heard by all Senators——

The PRESIDING OFFICER (Mr. MATSUNAGA). The Senate will come to order. The Senate will be in order.

Mr. ROBERT C. BYRD. Mr. President, unless a Senator now indicates that he intends to ask for the yeas and nays on the adoption of the conference report on the budget resolution, I take it that there will be no rollcall votes, and the matter will be decided by voice vote, and Senators may govern themselves accordingly.

Mr. MUSKIE. Mr. President, will the Senator yield?

Mr. ROBERT C. BYRD. I yield.

Mr. MUSKIE. I suggest that this report is of surpassing interest, and for those who would like to linger for the purpose of hearing it, we would be delighted to have an audience.

Mr. ROBERT C. BYRD. Of course. I thank all Senators.

Figure 7.7 The inverse relationship between attendance and not voting. (Source: U.S. Congress, *Congressional Record* (Daily Ed.), May 15, 1978, p. S7446.)

Purposes of Floor Debate

What then, is the purpose of floor debate? Debate is largely intended for other audiences at other times. In many parliaments a verbatim transcript is published—we have the *Congressional Record*—of floor debate. It is a public record of the reasoning and intent of Congress. Debate permits each side to state its best arguments and to launch its most damaging attacks upon the other side. The resulting rationale will be useful—at least potentially—the next time the issue arises in parliament, or in the next election campaign, or in a potential later court test of the legislation. No political decision maker wants to make erroneous statements or to be proved wrong by later events. Each side makes the best case available to it. Each side hopes that later events will prove it correct. Each side commits to the public record its best estimate and its most telling set of arguments.[15]

In foreign parliaments with a greater degree of party discipline than in the U.S. Congress the ensuing vote will largely follow party lines. The decision of how the party members vote will have been made within the party caucus, not in floor debate of the whole parliament. But party members, too, must build a public record and justify their position, looking toward the next election, if nothing else. One observer has characterized the British parliament, for example, as a continuous election campaign.[16]

Floor debate can be used to reach and mobilize public opinion outside parliament. It thus becomes one effective—if indirect and long-run—way of influencing the policies proposed by the executive. The British cabinet, for example, usually considers the coming week of parliamentary business as the first item on its weekly agenda, and both the government's leader of the house and the chief whip attend Cabinet meetings.[17]

Floor sessions in parliamentary systems also include question time, which we have discussed in Chapter 4. Members of the cabinet and, especially, the prime minister can be questioned on the floor, and they can reply on the floor. The competition among British members for the limited time available has led to restrictions on the number of questions any one member can ask. Still the spontaneity of oral exchange and the diversity of topics considered, make this period the best-attended event in the typical day's meeting of Parliament, in both Britain and Canada.[18] (Refer to Figs. 4.6 and 4.7.)

Apparently there has been at least one similar episode within parliaments of Communist party states, in which a two day debate was held in the Polish Sejm on a particularly potent form of parliamentary question called *interpellation.* An interpellation, commonly used in European parliaments, is a formal and written question that potentially could lead to a no-confidence vote. While that end result was not possible or contemplated in Poland, the interpellation was treated

[15] Mezey, *Comparative Legislatures,* pp. 76–77.

[16] Bernard Crick, *The Reform of Parliament* (London: Weidenfeld and Nicolson, 1964), pp. 25–26.

[17] G. W. Jones, "Development of the Cabinet," in William Thornhill (ed.), *The Modernization of British Government,* p. 58.

[18] Ryle, "Developments in the Parliamentary System," pp. 18–20; Robert J. Jackson and Michael M. Atkinson, *The Canadian Legislative System: Politics and Policy-Making* (Toronto: Macmillan, 1974), pp. 80–81.

seriously. A small group of Sejm members, organized into one of the three Catholic caucuses called *Znak,* sent a written interpellation to the premier, demanding an explanation for police brutality in the government's treatment of students who protested and demonstrated against the action of the government in closing a play. One month later, after the demonstrations had been curbed, the Sejm occupied two days in debating the interpellation. This step in itself was unusual, for interpellations are not usually responded to in formal session. The initiating group's members were, according to one observer, denounced by government speakers. The premier began the series of "insults and charges" against them. The debate was characterized by "viciousness" and "polemics." Yet the debate was held, and the Znak deputies replied to the government's position and defended their own on the floor.[19] Although this event apparently did not lead to a formal vote, this episode and the more common question time discussed above illustrate that parliaments may address themselves to a wide variety of governmental issues without debating a specific bill and without leading to a vote.

Attendance Frequency

Having said that debate changes few votes and that members often have better use of their time than to be on the floor, we do not intend to imply the logical extension that no attendance at all is also useful. All parliaments have a quorum requirement—the minimum number of members who must be present before the body has a legal existence—to prevent a small minority from making decisions in the name of the whole parliament. The most common quorum requirement is half the membership; since most votes are decided by a majority of those present and voting, barely over 25% of the whole membership might be sufficient to carry a vote.

Some parliaments consistently have low attendance, and others even have difficulty in forming a quorum. Both the Italian Assembly and the former Philippine Congress typically have low attendance at floor sessions. The Afghanistan parliament obtained a quorum for only four of 32 scheduled plenary sessions; the other 28 had to be cancelled. The Kenyan National Assembly, too, has often not attained a quorum, and average attendance has been no more than one-third of the membership.[20]

---

[19] Stefania Szlek Miller, "The 'Znak' Group: 'Priests' or 'Jesters'? (1956–1970)," *The Polish Review* 21, no. 4 (1976), pp. 76–77.

[20] Mezey, *Comparative Legislatures,* chaps. 4 and 6; Joel Barkan, "Bringing Home the Pork: Legislative Behavior, Rural Development and Political Change in East Africa," in Joel Smith and Lloyd Musolf (eds.), *Legislatures in Development* (Durham, N.C.: Duke University Press, 1978), chap. 10, footnote 6.

Table 7.5 VOTING PARTICIPATION SCORES, U.S. CONGRESS,
BY CHAMBER, PARTY, AND REGION, 1976

VOTING PARTICI-PATION SCORE	SENATE			HOUSE			
	DEMOCRATS		REPUB-LICANS	DEMOCRATS		REPUBLICANS	
	NORTH (%)	SOUTH[a] (%)	(%)	NORTH (%)	SOUTH[a] (%)	SOUTH[a] (%)	NORTH (%)
96–100	8.7	25.0	7.9	23.1	22.8	33.3	24.8
90–95	23.9	12.5	23.7	36.0	21.5	51.9	29.9
85–89	19.6	25.0	23.7	18.2	22.8	11.1	24.8
80–84	15.2	12.5	21.0	7.4	10.1	.0	7.7
50–79	28.3	25.0	21.0	12.3	21.5	.0	7.7
0–49	4.3	0.0	2.6	3.0	1.3	3.7	5.1
Total	100.0	100.0	99.9	100.0	100.0	100.0	100.0
N =	46	16	38	203	79	27	117

SOURCE: *Congressional Quarterly Almanac,* 1976, pp. 1021–1023.
[a] For purposes of this table, the South is defined as the 11 former Confederate states.

Perhaps the circumstances of low attendance on the floor are more important than the attendance level itself. If members miss not only the debates but also the votes, then by default decisions are made elsewhere. If members are not even in the capitol, or are attending to personal and private affairs, then the parliament suffers and is likely to decline in status and importance. Perhaps very low attendance is an indication that it already has.

U.S. congressmen pride themselves on their attendance record, which is most easily measured by the proportion of all recorded votes on which they have voted. A congressman with a low attendance record is subject to criticism by challengers in the next election. Attendance at floor voting has been quite high in both the House and Senate (Table 7.5).

Attendance in the House runs a bit higher than in the Senate for most of the party and regional groups, with 23–33% of the senators being present for less than 80% of the roll calls; the equivalent House figures have varied between 4% and 23%. Northern Democrats were most absent by this measure in the Senate, whereas southern Democrats were most absent in the House. These data for the House directly contradict the assertion that the "Tuesday-Thursday Club" phenomenon characterizes northern Democrats in contrast to the presumed greater attention to legislative business by southern Democrats. To the extent attendance is a valid measure, the distinction is misplaced, at least within the House.[21]

[21] The Tuesday-Thursday club thesis may be found in Raymond E. Wolfinger and Joan Heifetz, "Safe Seats, Seniority and Power in Congress," *American Political Science Review* 59 (June 1965), pp. 337–349.

The Drama of Debate

Floor debate can be dramatic. For its participants it can be both a time of anxiety and exhilaration. When followed by a major vote, the debate becomes a showcase for each side, and for its leadership and for its arguments. The drama and sense of confrontation is perhaps more emphasized in a British-type parliament, in which two major parties sit facing each other and motions of no confidence can be raised and voted.

DEBATE IN BRITAIN

Former Prime Minister MacMillan's diary, written following his participation in such a debate shows that although he was relieved to know that his own government won the vote, he could also comment on the quality of his own debate and that of his major opponents from the Labour party:[22]

> I decided that it was a time to try to rally the country and the Party. So I both opened and wound up the Polaris debate with vigorous speeches. The first was long but well-argued and impressive—a massive effort, to which the House listened for an hour without interruption. The wind-up was good and (in a noisy House) I was able to deal with Gordon-Walker, Brown and Wilson fairly effectively. Wilson was "thin" and not as good as usual.

The persons named in this diary excerpt were the leaders of the opposition Labour party whom he faced in the debate. Although the results of Parliament's voting are much more predictable in Britain than in the United States Congress, voting is not without its anxieties to the leaders. Prime Minister MacMillan noted that at the conclusion of the debate, "In spite of the fears of the whips, we had a good division with a majority of over a hundred."[23] We have earlier quoted a U.S. Senator in the opposite circumstances, confronting defeat in his filibuster on the 1977 natural gas deregulation amendment (see Figure 7.6).

Although floor votes are more predictable in the British Commons than in the American Congress, the debates preceding the votes are regarded as more important there than here. As illustrated by the above quotation, the memoirs of British political figures comment, much more than do the American, about the importance of making a good speech on the floor and of acquitting themselves well in the floor exchanges.

Debate can often occur even though a bill itself is not on the floor and even though a vote will not occur on a specific piece of legislation. The British Parliament, in particular, has evolved a set of procedures

[22] Harold MacMillan, *At the End of the Day, 1961–1963* (New York: Harper & Row, 1973), p. 372.
[23] Ibid., p. 373.

by which topics of current interest can be scheduled for a full-scale debate, and while legislation may be the ultimate goal, the more immediate task is for the government to explain, and for the opposition leaders and for the back-benchers of all parties to probe, government policy in relationship to the problem under discussion. One such debate, on an "adjournment motion," is excerpted in Figure 7.8, in which the stated topic was immigration and race relations. The government side was led by the minister in charge, the secretary of state for the Home Department, while the Labour opposition was led by its newly designated spokesman on that topic who had formerly himself been in charge of the same department during the previous Labour government. The members are unfailingly polite and complimentary to one another, with frequent use of terms such as "friend," "honorable," and "right honorable." If the one speaking does not yield the floor to another seeking to interject, that refusal is stated apologetically. Although each party seeks to strike points against the other, the members seem happiest when they can agree. Since the debate has been arranged by the party leaders in advance, both major parties had their major spokesmen present to open and close the debate. Since this debate was on the adjournment motion, no vote was either expected or taken.

Participation in Senate Debate

Not all members can speak at once; not all can offer amendments. Time, if nothing else, limits floor participation, and both the rules and common courtesy prevent two members from speaking simultaneously. Yet not all members participate to the same extent.

In the U.S. Senate over a four-year period, the least any one senator spoke was 28 times, while the most was 1953 times. Several informal norms in the Senate in the mid-1950s discouraged excessive use of floor time. One such norm was "apprenticeship," whereby the freshman members were to work hard, listen often, and talk seldom. Another was "specialization," wherein each senator was to become an expert in some set of topics, mostly related to his state and to his committees. If a senator spoke only on those topics in which he was a specialist, he would use the floor less than others who disregarded that norm. Use of the senate floor was inversely related, in turn, to the senators' legislative effectiveness: Senators who spoke most often had the lowest proportion of their own bills adopted.[24] It is perhaps ironic

[24] Donald R. Matthews, *U.S. Senators and Their World* (New York: Vintage, 1960), pp. 115, 274. At the time of this study, in the 1950s, the liberals spoke the most but had little power on the committees. As governmental activists, they also introduced many bills. The combined result was low effectiveness, and thus this finding may be time-bound.

1469   *Immigration and*   6 DECEMBER 1973   *Race Relations*   1470

IMMIGRATION AND RACE RELATIONS

Motion made, and Question proposed,
That this House do now adjourn.—[*Mr. Humphrey Atkins.*]

4.11 p.m.

The Secretary of State for the Home Department (Mr. Robert Carr): May I open the debate by saying how much I welcome the presence of the right hon. Member for Birmingham, Stechford (Mr. Roy Jenkins). I am sure that the House also welcomes him back as the principal Opposition spokesman on home affairs. We are all sad to lose his predecessor, the hon. Member for Hitchin (Mrs. Shirley Williams), from this post.

I am glad to have the opportunity for a full debate on race relations and immigration. We have on the Table three important reports from the Select Committee dealing with some of the most serious problems in race relations. There is the report on housing, the report on police-immigrant relations and the report on education. No doubt many hon. Members will wish to concentrate mainly on one or more of these reports. The Government will welcome, and will take seriously into consideration, the views expressed about the reports. I want the debate to cover immigration as well as to discuss race relations because it is essential to set off discussion of race relations within this context. I say that because the Government believe strongly that the creation of public confidence in respect of the effective limitation of future immigration is an essential pre-condition for a constructive approach to the problems of race relations.

When I last spoke to the House on the subject, when we debated an aspect of illegal immigration at the end of June, I laid down four basic principles on which the Government founded their policy of race relations and immigration. I shall briefly recapitulate those principles.

:

5.0 p.m.

Mr. Roy Jenkins (Birmingham, Stechford): I find myself coming back after a relatively brief interlude of, I think, 20 months to the feel of a Dispatch Box in front of me and to the less tangible return of a departmental subject from which I have been away for a rather longer interval—one of almost exactly six years. I am grateful to the Home Secretary for his kind words of welcome and am glad that my first appearance in this new Shadow rôle should be in a debate on a subject as important, even if also as delicate and in some ways intractable, as that which we are discussing today.

Certainly it was one of the aspects of my work at the Home Office which I and those who were with me between 1965 and 1967 found most worth while. We

:

language. That underlines the importance not only of an early response but an adequate response from the Department of Education and Science to the Select Committee's report.

Mr. Tom Ellis (Wrexham): Is my right hon. Friend aware that the Russell Report on adult education refers specifically to the problem which he has been discussing? Will my right hon. Friend ask the Secretary of State for Education and

1493   *Immigration and*   6 DECE

Science if she will turn her attention to it?

Mr. Jenkins: I am grateful to my hon. Friend the Member for Wrexham (Mr. Ellis) for raising that important and informative matter. I shall be glad to let the point ride off me and on to the right hon. Lady. I hope that she will pay attention to it.

I now turn to the important matter of police relations with minority groups. The

:

Figure 7.8   Debate in the British House of Commons. (Source: United Kingdom. House of Commons, *Parliamentary Debates (Hansard),* Dec. 6, 1973.)

5.44 p.m.

Mr. Sydney Chapman (Birmingham, Handsworth): I am surprised as well as

1499   *Immigration and*   6 DECE

[MR. CHAPMAN.]
diffident to be called immediately after the speeches of my right hon. Friend the Secretary of State and the right hon. Member for Birmingham, Stetchford (Mr. Roy Jenkins). I dare to intervene briefly because I have the privilege of representing an area where, to say the least, there are very real problems concerned with immigration and race relations. I calculate that 25 per cent. of the population in my constituency is made up of coloured immigrants.

There is no doubt that the problems have been accentuated by emotion. There
:
:

7.31 p.m.

Mr. J. Enoch Powell (Wolverhampton, South-West): I hope that the hon. Member for Coventry, South (Mr. William Wilson) will not have got himself into any trouble with the Law Society, for he has performed an important service by what he put on the record this afternoon about the behaviour and standards of the police. I hope that the contents of his speech will be well noted out of doors amongst the public generally and in particular amongst the police forces.

The debate has not lacked a whole series of encomia upon the work of the Select Committee, three of whose reports are before the House. Some of the
:
:

1533   *Immigration and*   6 DECE

Mr. Bidwell *rose*——

Mr. Powell: I am anxious to be as brief as possible.

Mr. Bidwell *rose*——

Mr. Powell: I apologise to the hon. Gentleman. He knows that time and again I have given way to him, and engaged in debate with him; but I am anxious, and have promised, to make my remarks as brief as possible. I ask him on that account to forgive me for not giving way.

9.32 p.m.

The Under-Secretary of State for the Home Department (Mr. David Lane): This has been a very useful debate and, to adopt a word used by a number of hon. Members, a candid debate. On the whole, it has also been encouragingly constructive. Unlike some hon. Members, I am glad that we have had a debate on such a wide canvas covering both the problems of immigration and these great issues of race relations. The two are very closely inter-related.

We are all aware that it is not easy to reconcile tight immigration control with positive work for better race relations. No one going round the country talking to people working in the field can fail to see the difficulties. On the
:
:

Constructive work in race relations needs to be given a higher priority by us all if the hope of harmoney is to be made stronger than the fear of discord.

In home politics at this time there is no greater challenge than the building of a harmonious society for our children as well as for ourselves. It is a task in which we must succeed, because we dare not fail.

The Parliamentary Secretary to the Treasury (Mr. Humphrey Atkins): I beg to ask leave to withdraw the motion.

Motion, by leave, withdrawn.

that, in earlier chapters, we have stressed the limitations upon parliaments as a whole and also upon individual members stemming from short or infrequent meetings. Yet, we find that in the U.S. Senate, which meets the year round, informal norms have discouraged floor use. If all senators used their individual right to unlimited debate, however, the senate would accomplish very little other than obstruction.

The use senators made of the floor varied with the controversy of the legislation being discussed. The closer the votes on the bills and amendments, the longer the debate. Debate does appear to be purposive. If a bill or amendment will be decided by a lopsided vote, there is little point in argument (refer to Fig. 7.2). The number of senators speaking on any one bill (in a sample of ten bills in 1961) ranged from a low of two to a high of 69. On the average, 17 senators spoke on the floor on any one bill.[25]

The frequency with which individual senators used the floor, however, ranged widely. Of 99 senators, 14 spoke extensively on three or more of the ten bills. They were the "generalists." The largest single category, of 45 senators, was the "specialist," who spoke extensively upon one or two issues only. But the "nontalkers," 40 of the senators, were almost as numerous. They spoke on a few issues but not extensively on any of them. The only characteristic of senators that seemed to make any difference in the frequency and extent of their floor speaking on legislation was seniority: The newly elected members spoke less, thus observing the previously mentioned norm af apprenticeship. But other characteristics of senators that one might expect to be related to their use of the floor were not, such as previous political experience, size of state, and personal or party competitive status.[26]

Participation in House Debate

Debate in the House is structured very differently than in the Senate. Use of Committee of the Whole House, with stringent time limitations, means that because of the larger membership of the House (435 compared with 100 in the Senate) the individual members have less time in which to compete with one another for the floor. In a two-year period, the frequency of floor remarks for a sample of members ranged from three to 439, considerably fewer per year than reported for the Senate. In the same two-year period, the number of bills introduced by House members ranged from none to 120, but the maximum number adopted for any one member was only six. Over half the sample

---

[25] Robert G. Lehnen, "Behavior on the Senate Floor: An Analysis of Debate in the U.S. Senate," *Midwest Journal of Political Science* 4 (November 1967), p. 509.

[26] Ibid., pp. 514–521.

Table 7.6 RELATIONSHIPS AMONG NUMBER OF BILLS AND
AMENDMENTS INTRODUCED AND COMPETITIVE STATUS:
U.S. HOUSE, 1965–1966[a]

	NUMBER OF BILLS INTRODUCED		NUMBER OF AMENDMENTS INTRODUCED		COMPETITIVE STATUS OF PARTY	
	r	p	r	p	GAMMA	p
Number of floor remarks	.49	<.001	.75	<.001	.30	<.20
Number of bills introduced			.20	<.70	.37	<.10
Number of amendments introduced					.50	<.01
N = 98						

SOURCE: David M. Olson and Cynthia T. Nonidez, "Measures of Legislative Performance in the U.S. House of Representatives," *Midwest Journal of Political Science* 16 (May 1972), p. 272, table 1, and p. 274, table 2.
[a] The measure of association is either Pearsonian r for intervals data, or gamma for
ordinal rankings. The smaller the p value, the greater the confidence we can place
in the measure of association.

of House members had no bill pass in that two-year period. The
members also varied in the frequency with which they offered amendments to bills on the floor. More than 40% introduced no floor amendments, and the highest number for any one member was 33. The
number of floor amendments was related to the number of bills, and
especially to the frequency of floor speaking (Table 7.6), but none
was related to an effectiveness index—measured, as in the Senate, as
the proportion of bills introduced that were adopted. Neither were
they related to a measure of specialization. As in the Senate, the background characteristics of the members were not related to their legislative activity. Competitive status of the members' district parties, however, was related to their floor activities, especially in offering
amendments.[27]

Participation in the Bundestag

Relatively few members have availed themselves of the floor in the
German Bundestag. In the four-year period from 1957 to 1961, 59%
of the members spoke ten or fewer times on the floor. Unlike in the
U.S. Congress, the use of the floor was related to characteristics of the
members, especially to their occupations. Bundestag members who
were not engaged in politics full time continued to work in private
occupations; they were frequently proposed by their respective interest

[27] David M. Olson and Cynthia T. Nonidez, "Measures of Legislative Performance
in the U.S. House of Representatives," *Midwest Journal of Political Science* 16
(May 1972), pp. 270–275.

Table 7.7 FLOOR SPEECHES OF TYPES OF MEMBERS OF TANZANIAN PARLIAMENT

CHARACTERISTIC OF SPEECHES	TYPE OF LEADER			
	GOVERNMENT MEMBER	POTENTIAL LEADERS	LOCALS	SILENT SUPPORTERS
80% or more nationally oriented	40%	56%	24%	60%
10% or more critical of government	13%	67%	48%	0
N =	15	9	25	15

SOURCE: Raymond Hopkins, "The Role of the M.P. in Tanzania," *American Political Science Review* 64 (September 1970), p. 762, table 3.

groups to the parties for nomination and tended to be active in parliament on the topics of relevance to their occupation. These members tended to use the floor less than the full-time politicians and tended to specialize on the topics related to their occupation. Their speaking on the floor was limited in both frequency and in breadth of topics discussed.[28]

Debate in Tanzania

The content of floor speeches can be an indication of how the members view their role in the legislature and of the policy stances they take toward the government. The content of floor speeches given in the Tanzanian parliament varies with the types of members we had earlier identified on the basis of their background characteristics (Chapter 3). One type of member so identified was the "local," elected by a constituency, with little education, and who infrequently read newspapers. This type of member's speeches were the least nationally oriented in their content (Table 7.7); that is, they usually addressed themselves to matters of direct concern to the member's particular district. Although the government was not often criticized by anyone, it was the potential leaders—also the potential rivals to the existing leaders—who were the most critical of government policy, with the locals being the next most critical group. The silent partners were the least critical. We had already noted that the potential leaders had, within a few years, been either brought into the government or expelled from the parliament. Expulsion was also the fate of the two government members who, in their floor speeches, were most critical of the government.[29]

[28] Gerhard Loewenberg, *Parliament in the German Political System* (Ithaca: Cornell University Press, 1967), pp. 110–112.
[29] Raymond F. Hopkins, "The Role of the M.P. in Tanzania," *American Political Science Review* 64 (September 1970), pp. 761–762.

Debate in the French Assembly

The four types of French Deputies, identified in Chapter 3, made quite different use of the floor. Of the four types of members, the program deputies made the most use of the floor, while the obligation deputies made the least (Table 7.8). The program deputies, mainly interested in the development of specific legislation, closely followed bills in committee and on the floor, while the obligation deputies had little interest in legislation and did not even enjoy being members. Program deputies were most distinctive, furthermore, from the other types in the particular use, not just in the amount of time, they made of the floor. There are two occasions in the French Assembly when bills and amendments are discussed in detail: in the presentation of a committee's report and in debate on the bill by section and clause. It is on these occasions requiring detailed expertise that the program deputies were most active, and the mission type deputies the next most, while the status deputies were the least, active. It was on other occasions that status deputies made the most use of the floor: they more frequently delivered prepared speeches and more frequently asked prepared questions of government ministers. Both forms of floor participation called attention to themselves, both employed prepared rather than spontaneous discourse. and neither required detailed legislative knowledge. The obligation deputies ranked lowest in all forms of floor participation. In the U.S. Senate there was some indication that infrequent use of the floor is associated with influence and legislative success, but in the French Assembly the infrequent use of the floor by

Table 7.8 USE OF THE FLOOR IN THE FRENCH GENERAL ASSEMBLY BY FOUR TYPES OF DEPUTIES

	TYPES OF DEPUTIES			
USE OF THE FLOOR	MISSION	PROGRAM	STATUS	OBLIGATION
All types of speaking on floor: percent above median	42	71	50	29
Speeches in general debate: percent above median	47	43	60	43
Expertise speaking: percent above median	53	64	40	43
Ratio of time on expertise to all comments	30.6	33.6	21.7	22.9
Written questions: percent above median	37	29	50	14
Disruption index: percent above median	68	36	60	14

SOURCE: Oliver H. Woshinsky, *The French Deputy* (Lexington, Mass.: Lexington Books, 1973), pp. 128–139.

obligation deputies seems to be part of their general pattern of non-participation and disinterest in politics and in the Assembly itself.

Some parliaments are characterized by rude, if not disorderly, conduct among the members. The Japanese and Israeli parliaments are examples, as was the American Congress during an earlier period. In the French Assembly there are "numerous instances of rude and provocative behavior." Their debates[30]

> are often characterized by acrimonious bickering, sharp, pungent exchanges across the aisles, and frequent interruptions of a speaker by one or many Deputies.

Of the four types of French deputies, the mission and status deputies most frequently engage in disruptive behavior on the floor. Deputies not only interrupt speakers without their permission, but also, as they themselves speak, seem to invite interruptions from the floor by resorting to "provocative statements, badgering the opposition, demagoguery and publicity-seeking" rhetoric.[31] The mission deputies use these devices to propagate their ideological views in a contest against others, whereas the status deputies apparently engage in disruptive floor behavior to attract attention to themselves.[32]

Debate in Canada

In a British-type parliament, floor time belongs to the opposition. Although the governing cabinet wants—and usually gets—its bills passed, it must hear and respond to the complaints and the arguments of the three opposition parties. In the Canadian Parliament, for example, the members of the three opposition parties made, on the average, many more speeches than did the supporters of the cabinet party (by a factor of 2 or 3, depending upon the party). Of course, the party leaders spoke more frequently than did the back-benchers of all parties: for example, 40% of the party leaders made over 21 speeches in a single year, while only 22% of the back-benchers did.

In the use of question time the leaders of the opposition parties were also more active than were their own back-benchers in that 32% of the former asked over 100 questions in a single year, whereas only 11% of the back-benchers did.[33]

---

[30] Oliver H. Woshinsky, *The French Deputy* (Lexington, Mass.: Lexington Books, 1973), pp. 137–138.

[31] Ibid., p. 186.

[32] This section on use of the floor in the French Assembly is based upon ibid., pp. 127–140.

[33] Allan Kornberg and William Mishler, *Influence in Parliament: Canada* (Durham, N.C.: Duke University Press, 1976), pp. 128–146.

Floor time is limited, and somewhat formal. The committees provide additional time, and in a less structured setting, for participation. As we indicated in Chapter 6, however, the same patterns were found in the Canadian committees of unequal frequency of speaking just as on the floor.

VOTING METHODS

Voting is a physical act, the result of which is a formal decision by the collective body. The act of voting can also be a declaration by the individual members of the position they take on the issue at hand.

Most parliaments use a combination of recorded and unrecorded voting methods. Unrecorded votes do not provide a statement of the members' names and how they voted, whereas recorded ones do. The unrecorded votes are taken fairly quickly—by voice, by a show of hands, or by counting members as they stand. Recorded votes take longer—by calling the roll or by having members walk through designated lobbies and having their names noted by clerks. A number of parliaments record votes by electronic voting machines, with a button at each desk or many consoles at various locations on the floor easily reached by the members. Some parliaments —such as Italy and Japan —also use secret voting.[34]

With the exception of the electronic voting machine, the several voting methods in current use are of great antiquity. Although we do not know precisely how each method first developed, we can trace the methods of voting by voice and of counting the members by physically dividing them to this description of the early sixteenth century in the British Parliament:[35]

> (The Speaker) sayeth, as many as will have this bill goe forwarde, which is concerning such a matter, say yea. Then they which allow the bill crie yea, and as many as will not say no: as the crie of yea or no is bigger, so the bill is allowed or dashed.

But even then, it was not always clear that more persons had shouted one way or the other:

> If it be a doubt which crie is the bigger, they divide the house, the speaker saying, as many as doe allow the bill goe downe with the bill, and as many as do not sit still. So they divide themselves, and being so divided they are numbered who make the more part, and soe the bill doth speede.

[34] Valentine Herman and Francoise Mendel, *Parliaments of the World* (Berlin: De Gruyter, 1976), pp. 405–411.
[35] Sir Thomas Smith, *De Republica Anglorum*, Book II (1583), as quoted in Campion, *An Introduction to the Procedure of the House of Commons*, p. 19.

Congress

In the U.S. Congress, voice and sometimes standing votes are used initially on most motions and bills and most questions are settled by these unrecorded and quick methods. Votes are recorded in the House by electronic voting and in the Senate by a roll call to which members respond orally as their names are called by the clerk. On major questions the party and committee leaders want to put members "on the record," so that they and the supporters of a bill (but also the opponents) can know how every member voted. Although individual members might prefer to avoid a public commitment on any given bill, they too usually want their voting positions known to use in their reelection campaigns.

There is always the possibility that the form of voting itself may affect the result of the vote. A direct reversal of the vote result was seen on the "cargo preference" bill in the House in 1977. The bill would require that a certain percent (9.5%) of imported oil be transported in tankers built and owned by Americans. The maritime industry owners and unions alike lobbied hard for the bill, which had the support of President Carter. The bill passed the House on a voice vote, when the opponents inadvertently did not ask for a recorded vote. The bill's supporters, fearing an ultimate backlash if the bill should again come to the floor for adoption of a conference report, then agreed to permit the bill to be reconsidered the following day by a recorded vote. Thereupon, the bill was defeated by a 90-vote margin.[36]

Public Access

The public has a double problem in ascertaining how any given member of parliament has voted. The first is to have recorded forms of voting in place of unrecorded methods. But the second is to obtain the documentation for that recorded vote. One of the big battles in the "reform" of the British House of Commons in the nineteenth century was to make their voting ("division") lists public and hence available to the press.[37] It is still difficult in many of the American state legislatures to obtain copies of roll call votes cast on the floor, and within the U.S. Congress copies of the roll call votes cast within committees are also difficult to obtain.

Communist Parliaments

Communist party states vote only by a show of hands (Fig. 7.9). Although individual members can abstain fairly safely, any member

[36] *Wall Street Journal*, October 20, 1977, p. 5.
[37] Ronald Butt, *The Power of Parliament* (New York: Walker, 1967), p. 85.

Figure 7.9 Voting in the Supreme Soviet. Leonid I. Brezhnev (right, middle), Communist party chief, is elected president of the Soviet Union during the start of a two-day session of the Supreme Soviet. He is the first Soviet leader to combine both posts. (Source: Associated Press.)

who might vote oppositely would be very visible to the whole assembly and to the party leaders. All legislation and motions, when presented to the Supreme Soviet, are adopted unanimously.[38] We can speculate that the party leaders have chosen a vote method that maximizes their opportunity to obtain unanimous votes in support of their positions. In the brief period of liberalization in Czechoslovakia in 1968 the National Assembly did, however, cast divided votes on several questions.[39]

Divided votes have also been cast in the Polish Sejm. The Catholic caucus called Znak opposed a proposed bill on assemblies, which would require that all groups obtain government authorization prior to holding a meeting. The Znak spokesman in this debate moved to send the bill back to committee to revise it. The Znak deputies were the only ones to vote in favor of the motion, while five other deputies, affiliated with another Catholic group, abstained. All others voted against the motion. The pattern of the vote on passing the bill was precisely the

[38] Peter Vanneman, *The Supreme Soviet: Politics and the Legislative Process in the Soviet System* (Durham, N.C.: Duke University Press, 1977), p. 84.

[39] H. Gordon Skilling, *Czechoslovakia's Interrupted Revolution* (Princeton, N.J.: Princeton University Press, 1976), p. 227.

same, only in reverse. The debate and vote on this bill is one occasion for which we have evidence that members of the Polish Sejm have actually voted against the position of the government and the ruling party.[40]

We may illustrate the voting methods of the Polish Sejm and the formal decorum of debate, by quoting from the transcript:

> Sejm Marshall (the Speaker):
> Having come to the end of the list of speakers, I now close the debate and we will proceed to the vote. I first put Deputy Lubienski's (the Znak speaker) motion to the vote. Deputy Lubienski moves that the draft of the Assembly Law be referred back to the Committee for Internal Affairs for further revision. Those in favor, please raise their hands. Four persons—thank you. Those against? Thank you. Any abstentions? Five. I declare Deputy Lubienski's motion rejected.

The same procedure was used to state the question on the bill itself. The Marshall ended the proceedings: "I therefore declare that the Sejm has passed the Assembly bill."[41]

We have earlier noted the growing activities of committees within the parliaments of Communist party states, and have cited examples of extensive debate upon, and, revisions of, proposed legislation. Apparently, in Russian thinking, it is far better to have extended debate and wide consideration than to decide issues by a majority vote. They would much rather have a degree of consensus forged through compromise than the expression of outright disagreement. The committees are the proper and useful forum in which to obtain such discussion and compromise. This quotation from a Soviet author illustrates their thinking about the value of compromise instead of voting:[42]

> It is wrong to decide arguments and differences of opinion which may arise with respect to a certain provision of a draft by simple voting. The principle or formula in question should be considered again and again, specialists should be invited, supplementary materials should be procured. It is important to achieve a solution on all fundamental questions, and to use voting for the final determination of issues only as an extremely rare exception.

40 S. Miller, "The 'Znak' Group," pp. 74–75; Hansjakob Stehle, *The Independent Satellite: Society and Politics in Poland Since 1945* (New York: Praeger, 1965), pp. 180–181.

41 Poland, Sejm, Kad. III, Sesja III, *Sprawozdanie stenograficzne z 10 posiedzenia*, March 29, 1962, pp. 63–86, as quoted in Stehle, ibid., pp. 304–305.

42 A. S. Pigolkin, *Podgotovka proektov normativnykh aktov* (Moscow, 1958), pp. 40–41, as quoted in John Gorgone, "Soviet Jurists in the Legislative Arena: The Reform of Criminal Procedure, 1956–58," *Soviet Union* 3 (Part 1, 1976), p. 13, footnote 47.

Congressional Changes

The U.S. House of Representatives recently has changed its voting method on amendments in Committee of the Whole. Until 1971, voting at that crucial stage was conducted by unrecorded methods: voice, standing, and tellers. The last type of voting has now been discarded in favor of a recorded vote by electronic voting machine. In the former tellers' vote, the chair would appoint two tellers, or counters, one from each side of a question, who would stand in the center aisle on the House floor. First the members voting affirmatively would walk up the aisle, being counted as they trooped by. Then those voting in the negative would be counted as they walked up the aisle past the tellers. The basic decision on amendments would be made by this unrecorded method. Members could vote against their party with fair safety, for although they voted in public, it was hard for any single party leader or clerk to identify all 435 members as they walked quickly up the aisle. Indeed, some Democratic party leaders feel that the change from unrecorded tellers to recorded voting in Committee of the Whole has been the single most important change in the House in this decade.[43]

Types, Frequency, and Controversy

Voting, at least in Congress, is a frequent activity. In a single week's period, 136 separate votes were cast in the House and 123 in the Senate (Table 7.9). Most of these many votes were cast by voice in both chambers. Although amendments to bills were more often the subject of recorded votes than other types of motions, most of them, too, were decided by the quicker and anonymous voice method. Even the vote on final passage on legislation was more often handled by voice than recorded vote. Several differences stand out between the two chambers: (1) Conference reports were usually adopted by roll calls in the House but by voice in the Senate; (2) the Senate voted on treaty ratifications, whereas the House did not consider such matters; and (3) the Senate handled some amendments through subsidiary procedural motions such as to table an amendment and to reconsider a previous vote.[44]

On a single bill, to illustrate the more general pattern, close to 50 separate votes were taken in the two chambers (Clean Air Act, Table

[43] Personal interview.
[44] These data are for the week of July 14, 1977. We do not know whether this particular week is typical or not. Data are derived from the *Congressional Record*, July 14–21, 1977, and from *Congressional Quarterly Weekly Report*, July 23, 1977, pp. 1544–1555.

Table 7.9 NUMBER OF VOTES BY TYPES OF MOTIONS AND METHODS OF VOTING IN U.S. CONGRESS FOR ONE WEEK, 1977

CHAMBER AND TYPE OF MOTION	VOTE METHOD			
	VOICE	STANDING	RECORD	TOTAL
HOUSE				
Amendments	56	3	6	65
Final passage	24	—	1	25
Conference Committees[a]	4	—	14	18
Suspension of rules	7	—	7	14
Rule adoption	—	—	2	2
Committee of the Whole	—	—	1	1
Procedural	13	—	1	14
Total	104	3	29	136
SENATE				
Amendments				
Substantive	47	—	18	65
Procedural	1	—	4	5
Nominations	14	—	—	14
Final passage	7	—	3	10
Conference reports	8	—	2	10
Unanimous consent	9	—	—	9
Resolutions	8	—	—	8
Treaties	—	—	2	2
Subtotal	94	0	29	123
Total	198	3	58	259

SOURCES: *Congressional Quarterly Weekly Report,* July 23, 1977, pp. 1544–1555; U.S. Congress, *Congressional Record,* July 14–21, 1977.
[a] Including adoption of 12 reports.

7.10). The Senate cast more votes than the House, reflecting the more flexible rules in the former than in the latter. In both chambers, the bulk of the votes were on amendments. The House cast only two votes in bringing the bill to the floor, whereas in the Senate, votes were not taken on the question of bringing the bills to the floor at all. Likewise, the variety of motions possible and the number of separate votes needed are limited at the end of floor consideration of a bill. The motion to recommit in the House and the vote on final passage in both chambers are single motions. It is at amendment stage that the most extensive skirmishing occurs.

Not only do most of the votes occur on amendments, but the most controversy is likely to take place on amendments. Table 7.11 shows, for the more frequent types of motions displayed earlier in Table 7.9, both the number adopted and rejected, and also for the record votes, the average number of votes cast on each side of the question. With the exception of amendments, most of the other types of motions were adopted. And even for amendments, most of those voted upon by voice were also adopted. Of those motions voted upon by roll call,

Table 7.10 NUMBER OF VOTES ON CLEAN AIR ACT (H.R. 6161)
BY TYPES OF MOTIONS AND METHODS OF VOTING IN
U.S. CONGRESS, 1977

CHAMBER AND TYPE OF MOTION	VOTE METHOD			
	VOICE	STANDING	RECORD	TOTAL
HOUSE				
Rule adoption	—	—	1	1
Committee of the Whole	—	—	1	1
Amendments	8	1	5	14
Recommit	1	—	—	1
Final passage	—	—	1	1
Subtotal	9	1	8	18
SENATE				
Amendments				
Substantive	17	—	9	26
Procedural	—	—	3	3
Final passage	—	—	1	1
Subtotal	17	0	13	30
Total	26	1	21	48

SOURCES: U.S. Congress, *Congressional Record,* May 26, 1977 and June 10, 1977; *Congressional Quarterly Weekly Report,* May 28, 1977, pp. 1023–1030, 1086–1091; June 11, 1977, pp. 1135–1137, 1188–1189; and June 18, 1977, p. 1266.

only the amendments were decided by fairly small margins, while most of the other types of motions carried by sizable margins. Furthermore, floor debate more occurs on amendments than upon the bill itself.[45]

Usually (except for a filibuster in the Senate) a bill will be brought to the floor without much controversy. As a rule the bill will finally pass. But what is not so certain is its content, for it is subject to all manner of amendments. But once all amendments have been disposed of, the bill will ordinarily be adopted. If the bill survives to conference committee, and that committee issues a report, it is also likely that the reports will be adopted by a sizable margin. Thus amendments subject to a roll call are likely to be the most controversial of all decisions facing Congress.

The pattern of amendments, contrasted with final passage, may be further illustrated by the House debate and voting on the 1977 minimum-wage bill. Periodically the minimum wage is raised and coverage extended, and that decision is one of the continuing (since the New Deal) legislative fights between labor and management, between liberals and conservatives, and between the president and the opposition party. Nine amendments were narrowly decided by roll call votes in the House on the 1977 bill (Table 7.12). On one

[45] Lehnen, "Behavior on the Senate Floor" makes the same observation for the Senate at pp. 509–510.

Table 7.11 NUMBER OF MOTIONS ADOPTED AND REJECTED, AND VOTE MARGINS, BY TYPES OF MOTION AND METHOD OF VOTING, BY CHAMBER FOR ONE WEEK, 1977

	VOTE METHOD AND RESULT						
	VOICE		RECORDED				
CHAMBER	ADOPT	REJECT	ADOPT		REJECT		
AND MOTION	*N*	*N*	*N*	YES–NO	*N*	YES–NO	TOTAL
HOUSE							
Rule adoption	—	—	2	363–25	—		2
Committee of the Whole	—	—	1	298–3	—		1
Amendments	46	10	—		6	163–210	65
Final passage	24	—	1	244–88	—		25
Conference reports	1	—	11	350–57	—		12
Subtotal	71	10	15		6		102
SENATE							
Amendments							
Substantive	45	2	9	55–37	9	28–63	65
Procedural	1	—	2	63–30	2	28–68	5
Final passage	7	—	3	71–10	—		10
Conference reports	8	—	1	85–8	1	43–53	10
Treaties	—	—	2	93–0	—		2
Subtotal	61	2	17		12		92
Total	132	12	32		18		194

SOURCE: Same as Table 7.9.
[a] This table includes some, but not all, types of motions included in Table 7.9. The yes–no numbers are averages of the votes cast within each category.

amendment the administration's position (and also that of organized labor) was defeated, 223–193. Another amendment, which reduced coverage of small businesses, was also narrowly adopted, 221–183. A third amendment, to reduce the minimum wage for youthful employees, was even more narrowly defeated, thus upholding the administration's position, by 210–211. On final passage, however, the bill was adopted in the House by the lopsided vote of 309–96. The opposition on final passage was mainly Republican, and even they were narrowly split, 61–76. The same pattern was repeated in the Senate, in which the amendments that were forced to a roll call were decided more narrowly than was final passage. This bill provides another example of the contentiousness of amendments. That some type of bill would pass was almost beyond question. What was subject to question, however, was its precise content; the latter issue was settled through the highly contested amendment process on the floor.[46]

[46] *Congressional Quarterly Weekly Report,* September 17, 1977, pp. 1947–1948, 1987–1988.

Table 7.12 NUMBER OF VOTES ON MINIMUM-WAGE BILL BY TYPES OF MOTIONS, METHODS OF VOTING, RESULTS, AND AVERAGE VOTE RESULTS, IN U.S. CONGRESS, 1977

CHAMBER AND MOTION	VOICE ADOPT N	VOICE REJECT N	STANDING ADOPT N YES–NO	STANDING REJECT N	RECORDED ADOPT N YES–NO	RECORDED REJECT N YES–NO	TOTAL
HOUSE							
Rule Adoption					1 331–44		1
Committee of the Whole	2						2
Amendments	7	4	1 52–38		6 255–162	3 172–242	21
Recommit		1					
Final passage					1 309–96		1
Conference report					1 236–187	1 138–266	2
Subtotal	9	5	1	—	9	4	27
SENATE							
Amendments Substantive	11	—	—	—	2 78–11	11 32–59	24
Procedural	1				—	2 41–50	3
Final passage					1 63–24	—	1
Conference report	1				—	—	1
Subtotal	13				3	13	29
Total	21	5	1		12	17	56

SOURCES: U.S. Congress, *Congressional Record,* September 14, 1977, pp. H9377–H9394; September 15, 1977, pp. H9432–H9486; October 6, 1977, pp. S16518–S16553; October 7, 1977, pp. S16624–S16585. *Congressional Quarterly Weekly Report,* September 15, 1977, pp. 1947–1948 and 1985–1988; October 8, 1977, p. 2173; and October 15, 1977, pp. 2195–2196 and 2210–2211.

PATTERNS OF VOTING

Voting on legislation is the most-studied single activity of American congressmen. It is mainly in Congress, and also in many of the state legislatures, that the outcome of the vote is in doubt. In most other parliaments, voting ordinarily is by political party. It is thus more predictable and there is less variation to study. As a result, most American studies implicitly ask: To what extent, and under what circumstances, do members vote with their party? Abroad the question is: To what extent, and under what circumstances, do members vote against their party? In this country the question to be probed is the extent of party loyalty; abroad the question concerns the extent of party "rebellion," to use the British term.[47]

We have already touched upon voting behavior on the floor in our earlier discussions in the chapters on chief executives and on political parties (Chapters 4 and 5 respectively) of how parliamentary bodies respond to chief executives and of the variations among them in their degrees of party cohesion. Those discussions mainly concerned parliaments as whole bodies. In this section we shall consider voting behavior among individual members.

We shall discuss several factors that seem to be related to the extent to which members vote with their party: holding of party-controlled office, issues, region, constituency and state, the position of the president, and the election returns in the members' districts. These six factors are most commonly discussed in the research literature on roll call voting behavior.

1. Offices

In the earlier chapter on political parties we noted that parliaments varied in the number of government positions to which they made appointments and suggested that this factor was related to variations in the extent of party cohesion among parliaments. This same factor also has an impact on how individual members vote within any one parliament. As indicated earlier, the British governing party appoints approximately 70 of its own parliamentary members to various government offices. Those members are expected to, and do, vote with the government.

THE BRITISH PARLIAMENT

This same factor also appears to condition the voting behavior of ordinary members who are perhaps desirous of obtaining such appointment in the future. At least we can define an "eligible" group of members, and examine their voting behavior. Most of the government appointments are made from members who are relatively young and/or who are in their first five years of parliamentary service.[48] This group of "eligibles" has been more loyal in their party voting than have the

---

[47] Robert E. Goodin, "The Importance of Winning Big," *Legislative Studies Quarterly* 2 (November 1977), p. 403.

[48] Schwarz and Shaw, *The United States Congress in Comparative Perspective*, p. 175, table 5.3; Robert J. Jackson, *Rebels and Whips: An Analysis of Dissension,*

"noneligibles." Of the 8 occasions in Commons, 1959–64, on which a
sizable number of Conservative members voted against their party,
72% of those who were eligible for government appointment were
loyal to their party on all votes, while only 53% were consistently
loyal who were no longer eligible for appointment. On one specific
vote, 17% of the noneligibles voted against their party, while only
5% of the eligibles did.[49]

Furthermore, party-loyal voting has changed among the same
members as they, through age and length of service in parliament, have
shifted from the eligible into the noneligible category. Of 70 Conservative party M.P.s who made this change, the rate of their party-
deviant voting rose from 13% to 39%. Their decrease in party loyalty
strongly suggests (but does not prove) that the failure to achieve a
governmental appointment led to their propensity to vote against their
party and its leadership.[50]

Party leaders are fully aware of this dynamic. The chief whip for
the Conservative party during the time period from which the above
figures were calculated, observed that "the hope of office is an incen-
tive" to support the party leadership. Furthermore, party and governmental appointments are made on the criterion—among others—of
party loyalty. The chief whips are consulted on all appointments and
apparently they have been asked mainly about the prospective ap-
pointee's party loyalty. To quote the same Conservative chief whip
again, " 'a regular rebel . . . is by definition not suitable for office. He
can't be. It isn't a sensible attitude.' "[51] As a result, of those Conservative members who had been rebels in their voting, only about
6% were appointed to higher office, whereas the rate of appointment
among all back-bench members was about 20%.[52]

The United States represents the opposite circumstance. Having
a separation-of-powers system, the congressional party cannot make
appointments to governmental office. Rather, the congressional party
controls only offices internal to itself or to the chamber as a whole.

THE GERMAN BUNDESTAG

West Germany represents an intermediate circumstance between the
United States and Britain. Although Germany has a parliamentary

---

Discipline and Cohesion in British Political Parties (London: Macmillan, 1968),
p. 190; Donald Searing and Chris Game, "Horses for Courses: The Recruitment of
Whips in the British House of Commons," *British Journal of Political Science* 7
(July 1977), pp. 368–369.

[49] Schwarz and Shaw, *United States Congress in Comparative Perspective*, p. 178,
table 5.5, and p. 181, table 5.10.

[50] Ibid., p. 180.

[51] Martin Redmayne, quoted in ibid., p. 135, footnote 48, and p. 136.

[52] Ibid., p. 136.

system, the number of government appointments is quite small—only about a dozen. It has a much larger number of positions within the governing parliamentary party (about 50), but these positions are defined as being separate from the government. This distinction parallels a difference in their voting loyalty. Within the 1953–1957 period when the Christian Democrats were the governing party, their members who held cabinet positions had very high rates of party-loyal voting: Only 25% voted against the party position four or more times. The rate of voting against the party four or more times was 46% among all party members. The parliamentary party leaders had an intermediate rate of party defection (36%). Only the few cabinet members had an unusually high rate of party loyalty in their voting.[53]

THE U.S. CONGRESS

In the United States we find the same relationship between party office and party voting as in Germany. Yet in making that comparison we must keep in mind that the German parties are much more cohesive than ours are. The German Christian Democrats have had cohesion scores ranking from a low of 78 up to the low 90s, whereas those of American parties usually range in the low 60s. For Democrats from some southern states, to vote with their party more than half the time is something of an accomplishment.

There are a few consistent differences in party voting loyalty among party leaders and committee leaders, at least as measured for three types of roll call votes in the 1975–1979 Congress (see Table 7.13, with rank orders presented in Table 7.14). The party leaders among House Democrats and Senate Republicans are consistently highest in party loyalty in their roll call voting. Committee leaders in all four chamber-party combinations rank lowest. For most chamber-party combinations the differences among the categories of leaders and members are quite small. It is only among House Democrats that sizable differences appear, mainly in the conservative coalition and party unity scores. The number of persons in the category of party leader

The American Congress has two types of internal leadership positions—the party and the committee. Until recently the latter position of committee chairman was filled entirely by the seniority rule, which had the effect of largely removing that office from the control of party leaders. Although party leaders could place members on a committee initially, their rise to the chairmanship proceeded autonomously and automatically after that initial selection. As a result, committee chairmen came from the usually "safe" districts, which, until recently, largely meant rural Southern districts, at least for Democrats.

[53] Ibid., p. 139, table 4.8.

Table 7.13   AVERAGE VOTING SUPPORT SCORES FOR PARTY LEADERS, COMMITTEE LEADERS, AND ALL MEMBERS IN U.S. CONGRESS, BY CHAMBER, 1975–1976

PARTY AND CATEGORY OF MEMBER	CHAMBER AND ROLL CALL VOTE SUPPORT SCORES					
	HOUSE			SENATE		
	PRES. (FORD)	CON- SERVA- TIVE COALI- TION	PARTY UNITY	PRES. (FORD)	CON- SERVA- TIVE COALI- TION	PARTY UNITY
DEMOCRAT						
Party leader[a]	32.8	13.3	87.3	48.0	36.5	72.0
Auxiliary party leader[b]	40.5	41.9	62.0	38.8	19.4	69.2
Committee leader[c]	38.2	40.1	61.5	49.3	42.5	57.7
All members	36.0	(N)21.0[d] (S)63.0	68.0	44.0	(N)17.0[d] (S)67.0	65.0
REPUBLICAN						
Party leaders[a]	76.7	68.7	67.3	75.6	70.7	67.3
Auxiliary party leader[b]	66.2	77.1	73.2	71.4	76.0	73.2
Committee leader[c]	65.2	68.2	67.8	66.4	63.7	62.0
All members	63.0	73.0	70.0	66.0	64.0	63.0

SOURCE: Congressional Quarterly, *Congressional Roll Call*, 1976, pp. 20–48.
[a] Party leaders are the elected or appointed persons who serve the party as a whole unit: In the House, floor leader, whip, chairman of caucus, and for Democrats only, chief deputy whip. In the Senate, floor leaders, whip and, for Republicans only, chairman of the conference.
[b] Auxiliary party leaders are appointed regional whips.
[c] For Democrats, the committee leaders are the chairmen; for Republicans, the ranking minority member.
[d] For Democrats, conservative coalition support scores are presented separately for northern (N) and southern (S) members.

are quite small, especially in the Senate; thus individual preferences and constituencies can have a major impact on the average scores presented in the table. As we might expect, the party loyalty of leaders of congressional committees is less than that of the party leaders. The party loyalty, however, of the leaders of American congressional parties would appear to be somewhat less than among the party leaders of other national parliaments.

2. Issues

Party voting varies by the issue. Variations between the congressional parties, as well as within each, are illustrated in Table 7.15 on seven

Table 7.14 RANK ORDER OF PARTY LOYALTY IN ROLL CALL SCORES FOR PARTY LEADERS, COMMITTEE LEADERS, AND ALL MEMBERS IN U.S. CONGRESS, BY CHAMBER, 1975–1976

| PARTY AND CATEGORY OF MEMBER | CHAMBER AND RANK ORDER OF SUPPORT SCORES | | | | | |
| | HOUSE | | | SENATE | | |
	PRES.	CONSERVATIVE COALITION	PARTY UNITY	PRES.	CONSERVATIVE COALITION	PARTY UNITY
DEMOCRATS						
Party leader	1	1	1	3	2	1
Auxiliary party leader	4	3	3	1	1	2
Committee leader	3	2	4	4	3	4
All members	2	—	2	2	—	3
REPUBLICANS						
Party leader	1	3	4	1	2	2
Auxiliary party leader	2	1	1	2	1	1
Committee leader	3	4	3	3	4	4
All members	4	2	2	4	3	3

ᵃ This table is based upon Table 7.16. For Democrats high party loyalty was measured as low support for President (Ford), and low support for the conservative coalition; for Republicans the opposite were measures of high party loyalty.

major issue topics.[54] Democrats and Republicans disagree on the role of the national government in the economy and on government price supports for agriculture. On social welfare issues, Democrats tend to vote together, but eastern Republicans begin to emerge as a distinct voting group from their more numerous and more conservative Republican colleagues. On the issues of limiting the amounts of subsidy paid to individual farm holders, on civil liberties, and on international involvement, each party generally oppose one another, but with southern Democrats and eastern Republicans tending to vote against their own parties. On the issue of national security reorientation (limiting the military role abroad; increasing congressional power relative to the president) only northern Democrats tend to vote in favor, whereas the southerners join Republicans in opposition.

Five of the seven issue categories have been present in the Congress during the entire 15-year period of 1957–1972, which spans the last of the Eisenhower period through Nixon's first term. Two of the issue categories, however, are relatively new. The issue of limiting

[54] This section is based upon Aage R. Clausen and Carl E. Van Horn, "The Congressional Response to a Decade of Change: 1963–1972," *Journal of Politics* 39 (August 1977), pp. 624–666, and Aage R. Clausen, *How Congressmen Decide: A Policy Focus* (New York: St. Martin's, 1973).

Table 7.15 PATTERNS OF SUPPORT AND OPPOSITION ON SEVEN
ISSUES BY PARTY, AND REGION, U.S. HOUSE, 1957–1972

| | PARTY AND REGION | | | |
| | REPUBLICANS | | DEMOCRATS | |
ISSUE CATEGORIES	OTHER	EAST	SOUTH	OTHER
Economic	N[a]	N	Y	Y
Agricultural assistance	N	N	Y	Y
Social welfare	N	Y	Y	Y
Agricultural subsidy limit[b]	N	Y	N	Y
Civil liberties	N	Y	N	Y
International involvement	N	Y	N	Y
National security reorientation[b]	N	N	N	Y

SOURCES: Aage Clausen, *How Congressmen Decide* (New York: St. Martin's, 1973),
p. 107; Aage Clausen and Carl E. Van Horn, "The Congressional Response to a
Decade of Change: 1963–1972," *Journal of Politics* 39 (August 1977), pp. 633–
657.
[a] N means "no" on the issue; Y means "yes."
[b] The agricultural subsidy and national security issues were found only in the
1968–1972 period. The other five issues were present in the entire 1957–1972
period.

agricultural subsidy payments and of reorientating national security
commitments are the two new issues to have appeared during the
Nixon administration. Both sets of new issues reflected either new
problems in American politics or at least the new awareness of additional problems. The question of limiting the size of agricultural
subsidies reflected both the growing urbanization of the population
and the growth of "agribusiness" in place of the family farm. The
cluster of votes in the national security issue category reflected both
our disillusionment with the Vietnam War and the reaction by Congress against the policies and the manner of both the Johnson and
Nixon administrations.

Among the seven issue categories the party differences are most
marked on three domestic issues: government role in the economy,
agricultural assistance, and social welfare. These three categories en-
compass the bulk of the domestic issues shaped during the depression
and defined by the New Deal.

Party differences are much less on civil liberties and on agricultural subsidy limits. Until the passage of the Civil Rights Bill of
1965, the civil-rights issue was largely defined in terms of elimination
of legal discrimination in the South. As a result, northern Democrats
and Republicans formed a "northern coalition" in opposition to southern Democrats. Since then, however, the issue has been broadened to
include not only other racial issues, such as school busing, but a
variety of others such as sex discrimination and life-style issues. The
result has been both a move away from strong support by both parties
and a mixture of responses within each party.

The agricultural subsidy limitation issue is a fairly recent one, and the considerable variation within each party and across the parties perhaps reflects the uncertainty with which this issue is defined and understood.

Issues of foreign policy are frequently less partisan than are the domestic issues. On both sets of international issues in the U.S. Congress, the party alignment is unclear, but in different ways. International involvement usually has bipartisan support from Congress, although party cohesion is low; that is, significant groups dissent within both parties. On the new issue of redefining the military extent of our foreign policy and of also redefining the respective prerogatives of the president and Congress in the shaping of foreign policy, Republicans have tended to support the preexisting practices, as have southern Democrats. It has mainly been northern Democrats—and much more in the Senate than in the House—who have defined and supported this new issue in congressional roll call voting.

3. Region

The major deviating regional group from the national party patterns is the southern Democrats. As we have noted in the earlier chapters on chief executives and on parliamentary parties, and now immediately above, southern Democrats occupy an intermediate position between the two northern-based parties. They have, however, been united among themselves only on civil liberties and race relations issues.

The extent to which southern Democrats have voted with Republicans and differently from northern Democrats, thus forming the conservative coalition, has varied through the years, as has the success rate of the coalition. The coalition has been formed on 10% to 30% of all roll call votes in any one term in each chamber, from the beginning of the Kennedy administration into the first year of the Carter administration. The success rate—the proportion of all roll calls which the coalition won—has varied from 5% to 22% in the same time period. On the whole, coalition formation has been growing in both houses, as did its success rate, at least until the middle of the Nixon administration for the House and into the Carter administration for the Senate (Table 7.16 and Fig. 7.10).[55]

This observation about the extent and growth of the conservative coalition has been based upon a certain definition: When more than half of the southern Democrats vote with more than half of the Republicans, and in opposition to more than half of the northern Democrats, the coalition is said to appear. Another study has used a more

[55] *Congressional Quarterly Almanac,* issues 1962–1976; *Congressional Quarterly Weekly Report,* January 7, 1978, pp. 4–5.

Table 7.16 CONSERVATIVE COALITION APPEARANCES AND VICTORIES IN U.S. CONGRESS, 1961–1977, BY CHAMBER AND BY TERM

CHAMBER AND TWO-YEAR TERMS OF CONGRESS	TOTAL NUMBER OF ROLL CALLS	CONSERVATIVE COALITION AS PERCENT OF TOTAL NUMBER OF ROLL CALLS	
		APPEARANCES (%)	VICTORIES (%)
HOUSE			
1961–1962	240	16.2	10.0
1963–1964	232	11.6	7.8
1965–1966	394	22.3	6.3
1967–1968	478	22.0	14.6
1969–1970	443	20.1	14.2
1971–1972	649	27.9	22.0
1973–1974	1078	21.8	14.6
1975–1976	1273	24.6	13.6
1977–1978	1469	21.8	12.7
SENATE			
1961–1962	428	23.1	12.8
1963–1964	534	17.6	8.0
1965–1966	493	26.6	12.2
1967–1968	596	21.1	14.4
1969–1970	663	26.5	17.3
1971–1972	955	28.5	20.8
1973–1974	1138	25.0	13.5
1975–1976	1290	26.6	14.1
1977–1978	1222	25.1	15.8

SOURCE: Compiled from various issues of *Congressional Quarterly Almanac*, 1962–1978.

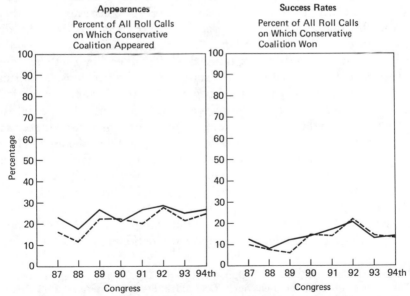

Figure 7.10 Conservative coalition in the U.S. House and Senate 1961–1976: appearances and success rates by two-year terms. (Dashed lines: House. Solid lines: Senate.) (Source: Based upon data in Table 7.16.)

Table 7.17 SOUTHERN DEMOCRATIC VOTING WITH NORTHERN DEMOCRATS AND WITH REPUBLICANS: U.S. HOUSE, 1957–1970[a]

| | | | ROLL CALLS ON WHICH SOUTHERN DEMOCRATS VOTED WITH | |
| | | | NORTHERN DEMOCRATS | REPUBLICANS |
CONGRESS	YEARS	PARTY OF PRESIDENT	(%)	(%)
85–86	1957–1960	R	29.5	7.
87–88	1961–1964	D	39.	3.5
89–90	1965–1968	D	16.5	15.
91	1969–1970	R	12.	21.

SOURCE: Figures are estimated from Barbara Hinckley, " 'Stylized' Opposition in the U.S. House of Representatives: The Effects of Coalition Behavior," *Legislative Studies Quarterly* 2 (February 1977), p. 15, table 3.
[a] This table uses the 75% vote standard in place of Congressional Quarterly's 50% vote standard.

stringent definition of 75% voting strength. This definition considerably reduces the frequency of coalition appearance, but nevertheless the same finding emerges: that its appearance has been growing over the past two decades. Table 7.17 shows the percentage of roll calls in the House on which, by the latter definition, southern Democrats voted with northern Democrats and with Republicans respectively. The frequency of southern Democratic votes with their party allies has decreased, whereas it has increased with the Republicans.[56]

The growth, not merely the maintenance, of conservative coalition voting by southern Democrats perhaps contradicts the thesis of the emergence of the "new" South. The time period covered by the relevant studies perhaps captures the pivotal era in southern, and hence in national, politics. The data cited in the previous section on party voting patterns by issues began with the Eisenhower period. The following Kennedy-Johnson presidencies were the period of national civil-rights legislation and, in the South, of voter registration programs and beginning efforts to integrate public schooling. These events were accompanied by southern Democrats leaving their national party (e.g., Senator Thurmond of South Carolina), by southern third-party movements in national presidential politics (e.g., Governor Wallace of Alabama), and by a "southern strategy" by the Nixon administration.[57] The Carter presidential campaign revitalized those southern Democrats willing to support the national Democratic party:

[56] Barbara Hinckley, " 'Stylized' Opposition in the U.S. House of Representatives: The Effects of Coalition Behavior," *Legislative Studies Quarterly* 2 (February 1977), p. 15.
[57] Reg Murphy and Hal Gulliver, *The Southern Strategy* (New York: Scribner, 1971).

They continued, however, to be the regional group that gave least voting support to Carter on his legislation during that administration's first years.

Southern Democrats continue to support the conservative coalition. Even the newly elected ones do. The coalition was not the remnant of senior and aged southern Democrats, for the newly elected ones supported the coalition to the same extent as did their senior counterparts. In the last two years of the Johnson administration, for example, newly elected southern Democrats voted with the conservative coalition 68% of the time, and their more senior members supported the coalition 69% of the time.[58]

The United States is more varied than can be summarized by dividing it into only two regions. One study has defined eight regions (New England and the Pacific states, for example, are defined as separate regions) and has related those regional variations to roll call voting in the Congress. Region, by itself, however, hardly makes any difference to how congressmen vote on the domestic issues (using the same seven major issue categories defined in the party section above) of government involvement in the economy or of agricultural policy. It is on civil liberties and race relations, again, that region makes a major difference. It also makes some difference on social welfare and on international relations legislation. On both sets of international issues, easterners and those from the Far West provide the most support within both parties. And within both parties, the southerners provide the greatest amount of opposition.[59]

Although regions do differ from one another in their population and economic characteristics, the differences in congressional roll call voting among regions is not reduceable to a difference in their districts. Although the South, for example, is more rural than the North, that difference does not satisfactorily account for the regional voting differences among Democrats, for urban southern Democrats vote more with the conservative coalition than do their northern city counterparts, and the same difference is found among rural Democrats by region as well.[60]

Regional variations among Republicans are more subtle than the massive one among Democrats between northern and southern con-

[58] This statement is based upon the 50% definition. Barbara Hinckley, " 'Stylized' Opposition," p. 17, table 5; Barbara D. Sinclair, "The Policy Consequences of Party Realignment—Social Welfare Legislation in the House of Representatives, 1933–1954," *American Journal of Political Science* 22 (February 1978), pp. 99–100.

[59] Clausen, *How Congressmen Decide*, pp. 161–171; Clausen and Van Horn, "Congressional Response," pp. 653–657.

[60] W. Wayne Shannon, *Party, Constituency and Congressional Voting* (Baton Rouge: Louisiana State University Press, 1968), pp. 134–147, tables 66 and 76.

Table 7.18 REGIONAL VARIATION AMONG REPUBLICANS IN SUPPORT FOR PRESIDENT FORD ON ROLL CALL VOTES, 1976, IN HOUSE AND SENATE

| | REGION OF REPUBLICAN MEMBERS | | | | |
CHAMBER	EAST	MIDWEST	WEST	SOUTH	TOTAL
·Senate	48	69	67	70	62
House	52	68	59	71	63

SOURCE: Congressional Quarterly, *Roll Call, 1976* (Washington, D.C.: Congressional Quarterly, 1977), pp. 22–23.

gressmen. But eastern Republicans, and to a lesser extent, west coast Republicans, differ from their party. The eastern members, particularly, had lower presidential support scores (for Ford) than did Republicans from other regions, while the southern Republican contingent was most loyal (Table 7.18).[61] The defection of eastern members from their party colleagues in the House appears to have grown in a ten-year period: On those roll calls in which northern Democrats voted differently from the noneastern Republicans, the eastern Republicans voted with the Democrats 46% of the time in 1969–1970, but had voted that way only 29% of the time in 1959–1960.[62] This trend reflects Goldwater's quip, while campaigning for the presidency in 1964, that the East Coast should be sawed from the rest of the country and permitted to float to sea. This trend perhaps also reflected Nixon's appeal to "middle" America, coupled with his "southern strategy."

The regional differences in the contemporary Congress took shape in the period of the Great Depression and the response of the New Deal to it. Of the domestic-issue dimensions discussed in the preceding section, two clearly appeared in the roll call voting patterns in the 1930s: the role of the national government in the economy, and agricultural assistance. A third domestic-issue dimension, social welfare, also began to appear then. The correlations between party and roll call voting on the three issue dimensions were quite strong, and on the government role in the economy, party was an important factor even in the 1920s (Table 7.19).

The higher the correlation, the less variation between regions; thus regionalism became relatively more important in the 1937–1938 Congress than in the previous New Deal Congresses (1933–1936) on two of the three issues. But during the entire 1925–1938 period, south-

[61] Congressional Quarterly, *Roll Call, 1976* (Washington, D.C.: Congressional Quarterly, 1977), pp. 22–23.

[62] Barbara D. Sinclair, "Political Upheaval and Congressional Voting: The Effects of the 1960s on Voting Patterns in the House of Representatives," *Journal of Politics* 38 (May 1976), p. 329.

Table 7.19 CORRELATION BETWEEN PARTY AND ROLL CALL VOTING ON ISSUE DIMENSIONS, U.S. HOUSE, 1925–1938[a]

ISSUE DIMENSIONS	CONGRESSES AND YEARS						
	69 1925– 1926	70 1927– 1928	71 1929– 1930	72 1931– 1932	73 1933– 1934	74 1935– 1936	75 1937– 1938
Government role in economy	.95	.94	.90	.94	.96	.90	.94
Agriculture	.09	.13	.93	—	.90	.89	.76
Social welfare	—	—	.89	.89	.90	.92	.83

SOURCE: Barbara D. Sinclair, "Party Realignment and the Transformation of the Political Agenda: The House of Representatives, 1925–1938," *American Political Science Review* 71 (September 1977), pp. 942–948, tables 2, 4, and 6.
[a] Correlations expressed as Pierson *r* coefficients.

ern congressmen tended to be more loyal to their party—not less— than were Democrats from other regions; and among Republicans, the midwesterners, with their heritage of the progressive movement, were more supportive of government activity on all three domestic issue dimensions than were the easterners (Table 7.20). An indication of coming changes, however, was the voting pattern on the minimum-wage bill. We have referred earlier to the 1977 bill; the voting alignments by party and region when it was first debated by Congress (1938) are found in the bottom line of Table 7.20. Southern Democrats supported it much less than did eastern Democrats, and eastern Republicans supported it a little more than did the midwesterners, thus setting the regional alignment on that issue that has persisted into

Table 7.20 SUPPORT SCORES ON THREE ISSUE DIMENSIONS BY PARTY AND REGION, U.S. HOUSE, 1937–1938

ISSUES	PARTY AND REGION						
	DEMOCRATS				REPUBLICANS		
	ALL	EAST	SOUTH	MID-WEST	ALL	EAST	MID-WEST
Government role in the economy	89.4	89.8	94.7	80.7	6.2	3.2	12.1
Agriculture	76.8	76.6	88.6	65.6	9.1	.9	28.9
Social welfare General	83.6	85.0	84.3	—	7.7	3.4	15.8
Minimum wage bill	77.8	99.0	39.2	—	43.5	46.1	39.8

SOURCE: Barbara D. Sinclair, "Party Realignment and the Transformation of the Political Agenda: The House of Representatives, 1925–1938," *American Political Science Review* 71 (September 1977), pp. 942–948, tables 3, 5, and 7.

the 1970s. Although sectionalism has always been an important characteristic of American politics, its contemporary frame did not emerge until the late 1930s.[63]

4. State and Constituency

Characteristics of representatives' districts, or the constituents whom they represent, are usually measured by the census. The census measures can be grouped together by districts, by states, and also by regions.

Ideally, the best measure of the district attitudes on issues would come from a public-opinion poll within each district. It is hard (and expensive) enough to simultaneously sample each of the 50 states, much less the 435 congressional districts. Only one study has been reported in which public opinion surveys have been done—and that was in a sample of districts, not all districts.[64]

Three different ways have been used to estimate the likely constituency attitude on a series of legislative bills. One uses a national public-opinion poll and applies the results to each state, making the assumption that if, for example, 75% of rural persons want to see the federal government provide financial assistance to public education that the same proportion of rural residents in each state would have that opinion. That is, the demographic distribution of opinion in the national sample is projected onto the demographic composition of each state.[65]

Another method to estimate the likely opinion of a state's population has been to calculate the distribution of congressmen's votes on any given issue by the population characteristics of the districts. That distribution is then assumed to be an accurate expression of the opinion of citizens on that issue. How each individual congressman has voted is then measured against the estimated standard.[66]

The third method is to use the results of voting on referenda in

[63] Barbara D. Sinclair, "Party Realignment and the Transformation of the Political Agenda: The House of Representatives, 1925–1938," *American Political Science Review* 71 (September 1977), pp. 940–953.

[64] Warren E. Miller and Donald E. Stokes, "Constituency Influence in Congress," *American Political Science Review* 57 (March 1963), pp. 45–56.

[65] John E. Jackson, *Constituencies and Leaders in Congress: Their Effects on Senate Voting Behavior* (Cambridge: Harvard University Press, 1974), pp. 147–181; John L. Sullivan and Daniel R. Minns, "Ideological Distance Between Candidates: An Empirical Examination," *American Journal of Political Science* 20 (August 1976), pp. 445–446.

[66] This method, perhaps because it is a near tautology, does overestimate the effect of the constituency; see John E. Jackson, *Constituencies and Leaders in Congress*, p. 44.

Table 7.21   PARTY OF CONGRESSMAN BY PERCENT URBAN
POPULATION IN DISTRICT, 1972

| | PERCENT URBAN IN DISTRICT | | | |
PARTY	0–54 (%)	55–74 (%)	75–95 (%)	96–100 (%)
Democratic	46.3	50.5	50.6	72.1
Republican	53.7	49.5	49.4	27.9
Total	100	100	100	100
N =	108	109	89	129

SOURCE: U.S. Bureau of Census, *Congressional District Data Book,
93rd Congress* (Washington, D.C.: Government Printing Office,
1973).

the representatives' districts and then compare how they have voted
on analogous issues in the legislature with how their constituents had
voted in referenda. This method is possible only in states, such as
California, that make extensive use of referenda.[67]

The reader may conclude that the measurement of "the district"
is no simple task. There is certainly no uniformity among the studies
in how "the district" is defined or measured.

Socioeconomic characteristics of representatives' districts affect
the importance of political parties upon the policy votes of individual
representatives in at least two major respects. First, given types of
districts tend to elect candidates of a given party. Districts largely
composed of central cities, the working class, lower educational attainment, and ethnic minorities tend to elect Democratic congressmen, at
least in northern states, whereas suburban districts in both the North
and South tend to elect Republicans (Tables 7.21 to 7.25).[68] Rural
areas are more split between the parties. Thus the type of district
affects government policy in the first instance by conditioning the
party affiliations of officials elected to government.

Second, representatives from districts atypical of their party tend
to vote less with their party colleagues than do representatives from
districts that are typical of their party. This relationship, first noted
in a study of the Massachusetts legislature, also has been found in a
variety of other legislatures and in Congress. When constituencies are

[67] James H. Kuklinski, "District Competitiveness and Legislative Roll-Call Behavior: A Reassessment of the Marginality Hypothesis," *American Journal of Political Science* 21 (August 1977), pp. 627–638.

[68] Original calculations for the 1970s from U.S. Bureau of Census, *Congressional
District Data Book, 1972*. Similar findings are reported for the 1960s in Barbara
D. Sinclair, "Electoral Marginality and Party Loyalty in House Roll Call Voting,"
American Journal of Political Science 20 (August 1976), p. 472.

Table 7.22 PARTY OF CONGRESSMAN BY PROPORTION CENTRAL CITY AND SUBURBAN POPULATION IN DISTRICT, 1972

	CENTRAL CITY		SUBURBAN	
PARTY	61–89 (%)	90–100 (%)	81–98 (%)	99+ (%)
Democratic	64.5	93.0	33.3	31.4
Republican	35.5	7.0	66.7	68.6
Total	100	100	100	100
N =	62	43	24	35

SOURCE: Calculated from U.S. Bureau of Census, *Congressional District Data Book, 93rd Congress* (Washington, D.C.: Government Printing Office, 1973).

Table 7.23 PARTY OF CONGRESSMAN BY PERCENT BLACK POPULATION IN DISTRICT, 1972

	PERCENT BLACK			
PARTY	1–5 (%)	6–13 (%)	14–29 (%)	30+ (%)
Democratic	43.5	59.1	74.2	83.7
Republican	56.5	40.9	25.8	16.3
Total	100	100	100	100
N =	232	88	66	49

SOURCE: Calculated from U.S. Bureau of Census, *Congressional District Data Book, 93rd Congress* (Washington, D.C.: Government Printing Office, 1973).

fairly homogeneous within a political party, party voting cohesion is higher than when constituencies are heterogeneous: The homogeneous condition was apparently more satisfied in the U.S. House of Representatives in the 1890s and early 1900s than now.[69]

There is some support for constituency theories of legislative voting from abroad. Deviations from party voting in the British House of Commons were more common among the atypical rural district Labour M.P.s than among their more typical urban colleagues: The atypicality pattern, however, did not hold for Conservative M.P.s. Studies of

[69] David W. Brady and Phillip Althoff, "Party Voting in the U.S. House of Representatives, 1890–1910: Elements of a Responsible Party System," *Journal of Politics* 36 (August 1974), pp. 753–775; Lewis A. Froman, Jr., "Inter-Party Constituency Differences and Congressional Voting Behavior," *American Political Science Review* 57 (March 1963), pp. 57–61; Duncan MacRae, Jr., "The Relation Between Roll Call Votes and Constituencies in the Massachusetts House of Representatives," *American Political Science Review* 46 (December 1952), pp. 1046–1055.

Table 7.24 PARTY OF CONGRESSMAN BY MEDIAN YEARS
OF SCHOOL OF DISTRICT POPULATION, 1972

	MEDIAN YEARS OF SCHOOL			
PARTY	11.3 OR LESS (%)	11.4–12.0 (%)	12.1–12.2 (%)	12.3 OR MORE (%)
Democratic	79.2	65.0	44.0	41.9
Republican	20.8	35.0	56.0	58.1
Total	100	100	100	100
N =	106	80	125	124

SOURCE: Calculated from U.S. Bureau of Census, *Congressional District
Data Book, 93rd Congress* (Washington, D.C.: Government Printing
Office, 1973).

Table 7.25 PARTY OF CONGRESSMAN BY PERCENT
FAMILIES IN POVERTY IN DISTRICT, 1972

	PERCENT FAMILIES IN POVERTY			
PARTY	1–5 (%)	6–8 (%)	9–13 (%)	14+ (%)
Democratic	33.8	45.9	60.3	77.3
Republican	66.2	54.1	39.7	22.7
Total	100	100	100	100
N =	77	122	126	110

SOURCE: Calculated from U.S. Bureau of Census, *Congressional District
Data Book, 93rd Congress* (Washington, D.C.: Government Printing
Office, 1973).

voting in the French Assembly have also pointed to the intersection
between party and constituency.[70]

Constituencies are much more heterogeneous in the U.S. Senate
than in the House, simply because of size. With the exception of the
five smallest states, which have only one House member each (though
two senators), the other 45 states are larger than the congressional
districts within them. Although in 1970 California, the most urban
state, had an urban population of 90% and Vermont at 32% was the
least urban, most states contain a variety of rural and urban populations combined in metropolitan, suburban, and rural mixtures. Senators
from Illinois are just as likely to be concerned with the problems of

[70] Robert J. Jackson, *Rebels and Whips: An Analysis of Dissension, Discipline and
Cohesion in British Political Parties* (London: Macmillan, 1968), pp. 196–197;
Howard Rosenthal, "The Electoral Politics of Gaullists in the Fourth French Re-
public: Ideology or Constituency Interest?" *American Political Science Review* 63
(June 1969), pp. 476–487.

Table 7.26 ROLL CALL VOTING MODELS, BY PARTY AND REGION, U.S. SENATE, 1961–1963: NUMBER OF SENATORS

| | PARTY AND REGION | | | | | |
| | DEMOCRATS | | | REPUBLICAN | | |
MODELS OF VOTING	EAST	WEST	SOUTH	EAST	WEST	TOTAL
1. Constituency	2	5	10	8	5	30
2. Party leader	5	3	—	—	—	8
3. Committee	3	—	—	—	4	7
4. Constituency + leader and/or committee	9	9	3	8	10	39
5. President + constituency and/or committee	3	5	3	2	—	13
Total	22	22	16	18	19	97

SOURCE: John E. Jackson, *Constituencies and Leaders in Congress* (Cambridge: Harvard University Press, 1974), p. 80, table 4.8.

big farmers as of big cities, for example, because both types of constituents are within their state.

Characteristics of the districts do seem to be closely related to how senators have voted on roll call legislation. Table 7.26 shows the distribution of senators by five different models or statements of the factors that are most highly associated with how they vote. The first three models are "pure" types, in which a single factor accounts for most of the roll call voting. Thirty senators fit the constituency model, by far the largest single group. All of the hybrid groups, too, contain constituency as one of the elements. Not only were 30 senators responsive mainly to their districts, but all were—at least to some extent. The impact of the constituency on senators' voting, however, was not similar in all party and regional groups. It was southern Democrats and eastern Republican senators whose voting was most directly associated with the characteristics of their respective states. Again, we see these two regional groups emerge as the most different segments of their respective parties.[71]

Representatives are responsive to their constituencies in roll call voting because such responsiveness is, presumably, a part of their job. The effective district sanction against violation of that relationship is the threat of electoral defeat. Thus one study has narrowed the concept of district to that of the representatives' electoral coalition. Applied to the U.S. Senate in the 1963–1964 years, estimates were made of the likely contribution of each of four categories of population to the senator's vote total in each state. How senators voted on four

[71] John E. Jackson, *Constituencies and Leaders in Congress*, p. 80, table 4.8. Unfortunately for our purposes, region was included as one of the measures of constituency.

Table 7.27 RELATIONSHIP BETWEEN THREE SETS OF
CHARACTERISTICS OF NORTHERN SENATORS AND VOTING ON
FOUR ROLL CALL INDICES, 1964[a]

	CHARACTERISTICS OF SENATORS		
ROLL CALL INDICES	STATE POPULATION	ELECTORAL COALITION	ELECTORAL COALITION PLUS PARTY
Conservative coalition	.38	.56	.66
Federal role	.20	.41	.61
AFL-CIO	.17	.39	.55
Americans for Democratic Action	.18	.41	.59

SOURCE: Gregory B. Markus, "Electoral Coalitions and Senate Roll Call Behavior:
An Ecological Analysis," *American Journal of Political Science* (August 1974),
p. 604, table 2.
[a] Numbers shown are R^2 values.

different sets of roll call indicators was then compared against the
measures of their respective electoral coalitions. The statistical
measure of association is provided for the electoral coalition in the
middle column of Table 7.27. The figures are, on each of the four roll
call indices, higher than for just the population characteristics of the
state taken as a whole. This difference indicates that there is some
merit in thinking of constituency as those persons in the district who
have voted, or are likely to vote, for the winner. The figures indicate
a fairly high association of roll call voting with this particular measure
of constituency.

The third column of the same table adds the statistical effect of
political party. On all four of the roll call indices, to add the senator's
party increases the degree of statistical association with the voting,
indicating that both party and constituency simultaneously are related
to how senators vote.[72]

This study, however, flatly contradicts the previous one in at least
one respect. Although the former study asserted that constituency was
particularly important for southern Democrats, the present one found
that southern Democrats voted fairly consistently, so there was less
association between either their population or electoral coalition
measures with their roll call votes. Using the same four indices of
roll call voting, the smaller figures in the "South" columns of Table
7.28 indicate that for the selected measures of the composition of the
senators' electoral coalition each measure was less associated with roll

[72] Gregory B. Markus, "Electoral Coalitions and Senate Roll Call Behavior: An
Ecological Analysis," *American Journal of Political Science* (August 1974), p. 604,
table 2.

Table 7.28 RELATIONSHIP BETWEEN ELECTORAL COALITION CHARACTERISTICS AND VOTING ON FOUR ROLL CALL INDICES, U.S. SENATE, 1964, BY REGION[a]

| | ELECTORAL COALITION CHARACTERISTIC AND REGION | | | |
| | MANUFACTURING PERCENT | | AGRICULTURE PERCENT | |
ROLL CALL INDICES	NORTH	SOUTH	NORTH	SOUTH
Conservative coalition	−.43	.44	.73	−.16
Federal role	.36	−.28	−.60	.13
AFL-CIO	.39	−.32	−.56	.23
Americans for Democratic Action	.39	−.36	−.59	.21
N =	58	17	58	17

SOURCE: Gregory B. Markus, "Electoral Coalitions and Senate Roll Call Behavior: An Ecological Analysis," *American Journal of Political Science* (August, 1974), p. 602, table 1.
[a] Numbers shown are *r* values.

call voting for southern than for nonsouthern senators, with only one exception.[73]

One way to solve, or at least to evade, the problem of measuring constituency characteristics is to examine those districts that are represented by different congressmen. Over a given period of time some districts will be represented by the same person, another set will be represented by two or more different persons of the same party, and still another set will be represented by different persons from different parties. In both chambers, the highest amount of party-related change occurred on the same issues previously identified as showing high degrees of party voting: government in the economy, social welfare, and agriculture. On each of the five issues, by contrast, there was minimal change in voting positions when the seat was held by the same person. The amount of voting change remained modest when the person but not the party changed. By far the greatest change occurred when the same districts were represented by members of different parties, in both the House and the Senate.[74]

These findings tend to support our previous ones that party and constituency are interrelated, that party and constituency have independent effects from each other, and that the importance of each factor varies by issue. We are not likely to find any single-factor ex-

[73] Ibid., pp. 602–603. The contradiction among roll call studies is to be expected, given the wide variety of different measures and methods used to attempt to describe and understand essentially the same phenomena and concepts.

[74] Aage Clausen, *How Congressmen Decide*, p. 141. Related data are reported in Morris P. Fiorina, *Representatives, Roll Calls, and Constituencies* (Lexington, Mass.: Lexington Books, 1974), pp. 102–106.

planation for, or even statistical association with, voting on legislation.

Constituencies of different characteristics need not necessarily be opposed to one another on legislation. Urban and rural districts might be expected to have differing points of view on farm-related bills, for example. They also have had opposing views on food stamps, urban mass transit, and some social-welfare issues. Beginning in 1975, however, leaders of urban congressmen (especially from New York and the Boston area) and of rural congressmen (especially from the rural South) began negotiations to form an urban-rural coalition among Democrats. At a meeting of the Democratic caucus, the urban leaders pledged support for agricultural bills. As a result, rural congressmen have voted for federal loans to New York City and for urban mass transit authorization and financing. Urban members in return voted for agricultural appropriations and for inclusion of rural areas in transportation and energy programs. The 1977 agricultural bill was a vivid demonstration of their newly formed alliance: City congressmen voted for price support subsidies on a wide range of crops, whereas the rural members voted for urban-sponsored changes in the food stamp bill. One urban leader was quoted as saying, "We have forged a real, working urban-rural coalition." One term for trading votes is *logrolling*; another term is *coalition building*. In this case, the coalition was built from very different kinds of constituencies. Democrats, more than Republicans, have been able to build such coalitions within their congressional parties in the post–World War II period.[75]

5. The President

The position of the president on a bill or amendment does not, by itself, seem to sway many votes at the roll call stage. The president's position is usually supported by his own party members and may be opposed by the other party. Not infrequently, the president's position is compatible with the constituency interests of at least a sizable minority of Congress. Thus, support for the president's position often appears through the other correlates of roll call voting we have discussed above.

We have shown in Chapters 4 and 5 that the success rate of presidents in getting their legislative proposals adopted by Congress varies with the size of their party's majority in Congress. We have also shown that the presidential support scores for members varies markedly by their party and region. But few members of the president's party vote for all presidential proposals; likewise, few members of

[75] *New York Times,* July 30, 1977, pp. A1, A8; David R. Mayhew, *Party Loyalty Among Congressmen: The Difference Between Democrats and Republicans 1947– 1962* (Cambridge: Harvard University Press, 1966).

the opposition party vote against all such proposals. The presidential support scores, shown in Table 4.12 by party and region, do not vary between 100 for complete support and 0 for complete opposition but rather between 33 and 76, showing partial degrees of each. In Carter's first year, for example, the average presidential support score for northern Democrats in the House was 74%, for southern Democrats it was 64%, and for Republicans it was 42%.[76] That is, the president is likely to inherit a substratum of voting support from the opposition party, in part because a fair number of proposals initiated in the name of the president concern activities of the national government that are fairly routine and will continue without substantial change irrespective of who is president.

Perhaps the most stringent test of the ability of the president to obtain voting support from Congress is in that narrow segment of bills that members of the president's party will support, but will oppose when the same bills are proposed by a president of the other party. Foreign-aid legislation specifically—and foreign-affairs bills more generally—fit these criteria. Presidents of both parties have supported foreign-aid programs and have generally pursued an internationalist foreign policy. The voting patterns of Republican congressmen are the test case, for Democrats have generally supported the foreign-policy programs of the president irrespective of his party. Republicans, however, have been much less supportive than Democrats when the president has been a Democrat. But how have they voted on similar legislation when they have held the White House?

Table 7.29 shows the percentages of several party and regional groups that have voted in favor of international involvement measures. The rate at which Republicans support such issues varies in both houses and, in all three presidencies, by their region, with the coastal group being more supportive. All four sets of Republicans, however, declined in their support of such issues when Kennedy and Johnson replaced Eisenhower, and three of the four Republican groups then increased their voting support when a Republican, Nixon, returned to the White House. Democrats showed the same pattern in reverse. For both parties, House and Senate members alike provided more voting support for their own party's president on international issues than for the other party's.[77]

On the four sets of domestic issues, no such change took place as presidents changed. Voting on domestic issues, both by party-regional groups, and among individual congressmen, was much more stable than their voting patterns on foreign-affairs issues.

---

[76] *Congressional Quarterly Weekly Report*, January 7, 1978, pp. 11–12.

[77] Clausen, *How Congressmen Decide*, pp. 199–206; Clausen and Van Horn, "Congressional Response," p. 653.

Table 7.29 PERCENT OF PARTY AND REGIONAL GROUPS WITH HIGH VOTING SUPPORT FOR INTERNATIONAL INVOLVEMENT ISSUES, U.S. CONGRESS, BY CHAMBER, DURING THREE ADMINISTRATIONS

PARTY, CHAMBER, REGION	PRESIDENT AND PARTY		
	EISENHOWER REPUBLICAN (%)	KENNEDY-JOHNSON DEMOCRATIC (%)	NIXON REPUBLICAN (%)
REPUBLICANS			
Senate:			
Coastal	90	70	70
Interior	50	25	45
House:			
Coastal	85	30	65
Interior	30	5	30
DEMOCRATS			
Senate:			
Northern	60	85	60
Southern	40	60	15
House:			
Northern	70	85	75
Southern	25	35	30

SOURCE: Cell entries are estimated from Aage Clausen, *How Congressmen Decide* (New York: St. Martin's, 1973), pp. 201, 203, figures 15, 16.
NOTE: Each cell entry is the percentage of the party-regional group within each chamber that gave high voting support to international involvement issues during each presidency. Thus the figures do not add to 100%.

That the chief executive has greater impact on parliaments (at least upon the members of his own party) on foreign than on domestic policy has also been found abroad. Voting cohesion has been higher within the governing parties on foreign than on domestic issues in Germany, France, and Great Britain.[78]

While the preeminence of the chief executive in foreign policy seems to be one of the few findings about legislative behavior that have been confirmed in several countries and over a considerable period of time, legislative dissent does occur on foreign-policy matters. Congressional resistance to the Vietnam War began among Democrats during the Johnson presidency. In Great Britain both parties, but especially Labour, split over the issue of joining the Common Market.

6. Electoral Competition

Competitiveness of representatives' elections is a variable that combines with the constituency factor we discussed earlier. Although we have measured competition itself in Chapter 2, in this chapter we are

[78] Schwarz and Shaw, *The United States Congress in Comparative Perspective*, pp. 306–313.

interested in tracing the impact of electoral competition on how members vote on bills and amendments.

ELECTION RETURNS FOR CONGRESS AND PRESIDENT

Most speculation on this question argues that competition will have an impact on party voting in parliament. One argument is that the more competitive the representative's election, the more he needs help from the rest of the party ticket. The latter phrase is always interpreted to mean the top of the ticket (though the logical possibility also exists that it could mean the more local offices). The end term of the argument is that the congressman's election is dependent upon the president's, and will thus tend to support presidential policy in Congress (or gubernatorial policy if a legislator.)[79]

But, perversely, there is an equal and opposite argument. The marginal representative usually comes from districts atypical of his party—which is why, if he wins, he does so narrowly. Thus his election depends upon dissociating himself from the rest of his unpopular (if not minority) party ticket. If elected, he will "vote his district" in preference to either his party or his president (or governor) in the event of conflict between them.

These contradictory arguments both assume that a legislator's roll call voting will vary with the competitiveness of his own election. The evidence for this assumption, however, is ambiguous at best. The tendency for representatives with competitive elections to deviate from the party in roll call voting has been found in several congressional and state legislative studies[80] but not in others.[81] The British findings are likewise ambiguous.[82]

[79] James MacG. Burns, *The Deadlock of Democracy* (Englewood Cliffs, N.J.: Prentice-Hall, 1963).

[80] The congressional studies include W. Wayne Shannon, *Party, Constituency and Congressional Voting*, and Jeanne Martin, "Presidential Elections and Administration Support Among Congressmen," *American Journal of Political Science* 20 (August 1976), pp. 483–489. The state legislative studies include Thomas R. Dye, "A Comparison of Constituency Influences in the Upper and Lower Chambers of a State Legislature," *Western Political Quarterly* 14 (June 1961), pp. 473–480; Duncan MacRae, "The Relation Between Roll Call Votes and Constituencies in the Massachusetts House of Representatives"; and Pertti Pesonen, "Close and Safe Elections in Massachusetts," *Midwest Journal of Political Science* 7 (February 1963), pp. 54–70.

[81] Sinclair, "Electoral Marginality and Party Loyalty in House Roll Call Voting"; Thomas A. Flinn, "Party Responsibility in the States: Some Causal Factors," *American Political Science Review* 58 (March 1964), pp. 60–71; Hugh L. LeBlanc, "Voting in State Senates: Party and Constituency Influence," *Midwest Journal of Political Science* 13 (February 1969), pp. 33–57; Sarah McCally Morehouse, "The State Political Party and The Policy-Making Process," *American Political Science Review* 67 (March 1973), pp. 55–72.

[82] Robert J. Jackson, *Rebels and Whips*, p. 195.

Table 7.30 RELATIONSHIP BETWEEN PRESIDENTAL SUPPORT SCORES
AND DEMOCRATIC VOTE FOR PRESIDENT BY CONGRESSIONAL
DISTRICT, BY PARTY AND REGION OF CONGRESSMEN, 1965–1973[a]

ELEC-TION YEARS	ROLL CALLS	PRESI-DENT, PARTY	PARTY AND REGION				
			REPUB-LICANS	DEMOCRATS			TOTAL
				SOUTH	NORTH	ALL	
1964	1965	Johnson, Dem.	.55	.51	.11	.53	.56
1968	1969	Nixon, Rep.	−.31	−.29	−.24	−.05	−.13
1972	1973	Nixon, Rep.	−.33	−.54	−.30	−.50	−.52

SOURCE: John Schwarz and Barton Fenmore, "Presidential Election Results and Congressional Roll Call Behavior: The Cases of 1964, 1968 and 1972," *Legislative Studies Quarterly* 2 (November 1977), pp. 414–420, tables 2, 3, and 5.
[a] Numbers shown are *r* values.

Both of the contrary arguments about the impact of competitiveness are based upon the presumed relationship of the representative's electoral margins to the votes obtained by other candidates of his party. On this point the evidence is much clearer: The higher the presidential vote in a district, especially relative to that of the representative himself, the more likely he is to support the president's program (if of the same party). This relationship holds irrespective of the representative's own competitive status. Thus the same studies negating the first argument confirm the second.[83]

The proportion of the votes cast in each congressional district for the presidential candidate of any given party seems, by itself, to have a relationship to how the congressman from that district votes on legislation. The association between the proportion of the vote received by Democratic candidates for president in three recent elections (1964, 1968, 1972) and the congressmen's presidential support scores in the years immediately following those elections has been fairly strong for most groups of congressmen (Table 7.30). For the House as a whole, the relationship was strongest after the 1964 and 1972 elections, but almost nonexistent immediately following Nixon's first election in 1968. The strength of the association between roll call voting on presidential proposals and the presidential election result in the dis-

[83] Jeanne Martin, "Presidential Elections and Administration Support Among Congressmen"; George C. Edwards, III, "Presidential Electoral Performance as a Source of Presidential Power," *American Journal of Political Science* 22 (February 1978), pp. 152–168; J. Vincent Buck, "Presidential Coattails and Congressional Loyalty," *Midwest Journal of Political Science* 16 (August 1972), pp. 460–472; Loren Waldman, "Liberalism of Congressmen and the Presidential Vote in Their Districts," *Midwest Journal of Political Science* 11 (February 1967), pp. 73–85.

Table 7.31 RELATIONSHIP BETWEEN LIBERAL SUPPORT SCORES AND DEMOCRATIC VOTE FOR PRESIDENT BY CONGRESSIONAL DISTRICT, BY PARTY AND REGION OF CONGRESSMEN, 1965–1973[a]

ELEC-TION YEARS	ROLL CALLS	PRESI-DENT, PARTY	PARTY AND REGION				
			REPUB-LICANS	DEMOCRATS			TOTAL
				SOUTH	NORTH	ALL	
1964	1965	Johnson, Dem.	.35	.41	.40	.62	.58
1968	1969	Nixon, Rep.	.56	.60	.45	.70	.70
1972	1973	Nixon, Rep.	.47	.69	.49	.67	.66

SOURCE: John Schwarz and Barton Fenmore, "Presidential Election Results and Congressional Roll Call Behavior: The Cases of 1964, 1968 and 1972," *Legislative Studies Quarterly* 2 (November 1977), pp. 414–420, tables 2, 3, and 5.
[a] The Liberal support score is from Americans for Democratic Action. Numbers shown are *r* values.

tricts has been decreasing for Republican congressmen, growing for northern Democrats, and changing for southern Democrats.[84]

On the whole, the impact of presidential elections has been even stronger on congressional voting on ideological issues than on presidential ones. Using the roll call votes compiled by the Americans for Democratic Action as a measure of "liberalism," the correlation coefficients in Table 7.31 are in most cases higher than for the corresponding category of congressmen in the preceding table. For each party and regional category of House member the association has increased over the three presidential elections between the size of the vote cast for Democratic presidential candidates and the extent to which the members cast "liberal" votes on legislation. This growth in the ideological impact of the presidential election results parallels a similar growth of ideology among presidential candidates and in the electorate. We do not now know, however, whether these two developments, occurring together, have a causal relationship or not.

These findings help us understand the ability of safe-seat southern Democrats to vote against legislation proposed by Democratic presidents: Such congressmen ran well ahead of the presidential candidates of their own party. This relationship has a mirror-image effect for the other party: Congressmen coming from districts carried by presidential candidates of the other party tend to support legislation proposed by the victorious president of that other party and thus deviate from their own party. In Table 7.30, for example, the correlations change in the

[84] John E. Schwarz and Barton Fenmore, "Presidential Election Results and Congressional Roll Call Behavior: The Cases of 1964, 1968, and 1972," *Legislative Studies Quarterly* 2 (November 1977), pp. 414–420.

expected direction for the opposition party in each of the three presidential elections. Republican congressional voting on Johnson legislation in 1965 showed a strong correlation with his election results in their districts in the 1964 election. Similarly in 1969 and 1973, voting on Nixon legislation by Democratic congressman—especially southern—was related to how well Nixon had done in their districts in the preceding presidential elections.[85]

This body of research establishes, first, that a legislator tends to support the legislative positions taken by the presidential or gubernatorial candidates who run ahead of him within his own district and, second (but not as firmly), that a legislator whose own electoral margins are narrow tends to reduce his support of his party's legislative positions to vote protectively "with" his district.

Switched-seat congressmen have given extra high support to the policy views of their respective parties after two elections that produced an unusually sizable presidential vote and also a large number of members of the president's party: the elections of 1896, which produced a Republican sweep, and of 1964, which produced a Democratic sweep. In both Congresses—of different parties as well as eras—the newly elected switched-seat members gave far more support to their party than did the continuing members of their same party. In the 1896 Congress, some 54% of all Republican House members voted with their party above the average (mean) support level, whereas 86% of the switched-seat Republicans did. The magnitude of difference in party support between the two sets of Democrats after the 1964 election was about the same.[86]

We established earlier (in Chapter 2) that marginal congressmen who win party-switched seats in a presidential year are the most vulnerable congressmen to defeat in the next succeeding midterm election. Here we have just noted that this type of congressman is also likely to vote with his party and in support of presidential legislation. Paradoxically, the same congressmen who are most likely to vote with the president on bills from electoral considerations are the ones most likely to face defeat in the next election.

VOTER TURNOUT

Turnout is another district-level electoral factor that could affect policy choices by representatives. Two studies asked why southern Democratic congressmen voted more conservatively than did their

[85] Ibid.; see also Milton C. Cummings, Jr., *Congressmen and the Electorate: Elections for the U.S. House and the President, 1920–1964* (New York: Free Press, 1966), pp. 122–123.
[86] David W. Brady and Naomi B. Lynn, "Switched Seat Congressional Districts: The Effect on Party Voting and Public Policy," *American Journal of Political Science* 17 (August 1973), p. 537.

northern colleagues. The answer was that lower turnout rates in southern districts meant that lower-status groups, more favoring liberal policies, did not vote, thus emphasizing the importance of the more conservative segments of the electorate who did vote. Even if this relationship held at the time of the studies (1950s), it needs reexamination to accommodate the larger and more diverse southern electorate of the 1970s; it also needs replication in other regions and to other offices.[87]

PRIMARIES

The above electoral factors all concern general elections. Since most nominations in the United States are made by primary elections, the same type of questions may be asked about their impact upon the policy choices of elected officials. The nonuniformity, and until recently the relative unavailability, of primary election statistics have discouraged studies of primaries for any purpose. Few studies have even touched upon their impact on policy choices of elected representatives. They usually find that representatives' competition in their primaries does not have an effect on how they vote on legislation. One study, though, indicates that when the governor runs ahead of legislators in primaries within the legislators' own districts (for Democrats, but not for Republicans) those legislators do vote in support of gubernatorial legislative programs.[88] The best we can say is that the few probes taken in the political subsoil of the relationship of primary elections to public policy have not yet found very much; neither can we affirm that the few studies until now are at all adequate to sample the underlying strata.

Summary

In this section we have reviewed some of the potential major influences upon how individual legislators vote on bills and amendments. Since voting in the American Congress and in state legislatures is much more variable than in the parliaments of other western democracies, most of the research on this question has been done on American legislative bodies.

[87] V. O. Key, *Southern Politics* (New York: Knopf, 1949), pp. 526–528; G. Robert Boynton, "Southern Conservatism: Constituency Opinion and Congressional Voting," *Public Opinion Quarterly* 29 (Summer 1965), pp. 259–269.

[88] Morehouse, "The State Political Party and the Policy-Making Process"; Robert W. Becker et. al., "Correlates of Legislative Voting: Michigan House of Representatives, 1954–1961," *Midwest Journal of Political Science* 6 (November 1962), pp. 384–396; Julius Turner, "Primary Elections as the Alternative to Party Competition in 'Safe' Districts," *Journal of Politics* 15 (May 1953), pp. 197–210.

A wide number of possible sources of influence have been identified. Rarely do we find that any one factor is preeminent. Rarely do we find that any one characteristic is highly associated (in a statistical sense) with the vote pattern to the exclusion of other characteristics. But neither is voting on legislation random. Voting is purposive, or at least the individual legislator thinks he is acting for a purpose—perhaps for several purposes. We do find among legislators uniformities in how they vote and have discussed the most important of these in this section.

CONCLUSIONS

In this chapter, we have discussed the end point of the legislative process in the consideration of legislation. When a bill reaches the floor from a committee, the parliament is ready to take final and authoritative action on that bill. But the floor stage itself is complicated and multifaceted, with a major distinction occurring between amendments and final passage.

Many events occur on the floor in addition to the consideration of legislation. In parliamentary systems the daily encounter between government and all the other members during the question time is a major event. And in all systems the floor is an arena in which government supporters face, and must respond to, their critics. In such encounters the government spokesmen are the formal equals of their critics: All are elected, and all members are equal in their status. Parliaments are collegial bodies. And as representative bodies, they are likely to contain the government's critics as well as their adherents.

In considerations of legislation on the floor, the affairs of a parliament are conducted by some combination of party and committee leaders. These individuals are responsible for bringing the bill to the floor, for the management of debate and consideration of amendments, and for the votes on final passage. Each step, including getting the bill officially before the chamber, is complicated and is a potential booby trap for the bill. In the U.S. Congress, getting the bill to the floor in the first place has given rise to the power of the Rules Committee in the House and of the filibuster in the Senate.

The act of voting is no less varied and complicated than the step of bringing the bill to the floor. The methods of voting vary among nations, with most using a combination of unrecorded quick procedures and recorded methods that take a longer length of time. The recorded vote is the atypical form of voting, in that most matters are settled by the unrecorded and informal methods. It is on amendments, at least in the U.S. Congress, that roll call votes most often occur. It is also on amendments that the most controversy usually arises on a given bill. Once the amendments have been decided, the bill's final passage is ordinarily assured.

In most parliaments the result of a vote is known in advance. In one-party bodies or in parliaments controlled by the executive there is no question about how the members will vote. But in most parliaments with two or more parties the result of a vote usually is also known in advance, once the respective parties announce their position. That is, members will ordinarily vote in accordance with their party.

It is mainly in the U.S. Congress and in the state legislatures that voting is less predictable. For this reason, most of the studies of how members vote on roll calls have been done in the United States. Although the political party is an important attribute of the votes of many members (especially Republicans and northern Democrats) on a wide range of issues (especially economic and social-welfare issues), members also vote against, or at least differently from, their parties. The extent of such voting is not random but is associated with a variety of factors, among which the constituency, the region, and the issue are the most important.

Chapter 8
Congresses and Parliaments in Their Political Environment

We have attempted to examine the world's parliaments—what is known about them and what is not. We have looked at parliaments and their members as representatives of their electorates and as participants in the governance of their nations. We have more closely viewed parties and committees as the major means by which the members are organized and the work flow allocated and managed. Finally, we have looked at floor sessions, both as a distinct stage in the consideration of legislation and as a distinct arena in which parliamentary activity occurs. We have also attempted to trace the major patterns of legislative voting, especially in the U.S. Congress, in which party alignments are among the least stable of the major national parliaments.

CONTRADICTORY TRENDS

We have observed several different, and perhaps contradictory, trends in the parliaments of Western Europe and North America during the 1970s.

We have seen a tendency toward the development of two large political formations within nations that have had several if not many parties. Germany, for example, now has three parties represented in its Bundestag, compared to the half dozen or more in the 1950s. Of the three parties, two are each close to majority size, with the much smaller third party usually forming a governing coalition with one of the two giant parties. In Italy the many parties, though still surviving in parliament, have been reduced to a small share of the seats, whereas only two parties each almost evenly divide 80% of the seats between them. Sweden and Norway retain multiparty systems, but they have long had a dual coalition system, in which the moderate and conservative parties have coalesced against the socialist parties. Even France has settled into a four-party system, in which two sets, each composed of two parties, face each other in coalitions of approximately even size.

Great Britain, however, has moved in the opposite direction in the 1970s. Instead of having two large parties, each of which usually obtains a clear majority of parliamentary seats if not votes (refer to Chapter 2 on the distortion effect), Britain has seen the development of several small regional parties along with a continuing "third" party. The governing Labour party lost an absolute majority of parliamentary seats and was thus forced into a formal agreement with the Liberal party to ensure a majority in the event of a vote of "no confidence."

The parallel developments in the United States have been differently expressed, in part because of our presidential system. We have had almost as many years of divided government between president and Congress as we have had of same-party composition between the two branches since the end of World War II. Furthermore, we have seen factions in presidential elections split from their parent party to form third-party candidacies as in 1948 (Dixiecrats) and 1968 (Wallace candidacy).

The stability of governments in parliamentary systems and the dynamics of events within legislative bodies result from the party system. Parties—as they form and disintegrate, as they form coalitions, and as they form the government or go into opposition—largely decide the stability and the continuity of their respective nations' governments.

SURVIVABILITY AND EPISODIC EXISTENCE

Most nations of the world are relatively new, and in most nations a parliament and an election system are even newer. The perils of party instability are rarely absent even in the Western European and North American nations, in which parliamentary institutions were originally developed and have had a long period of time to evolve. But in newly formed and often economically undeveloped nations, it is an unresolved question whether or not a system of parliaments and elections can be transplanted and survive.

Most nations have parliaments, although in many their existence is sporadic. They are often abolished for a time and then are reconstituted. In only five of 138 nations, as of 1971, had a parliament never been formed. But in perhaps 30 to 40 nations at any one time, parliaments are abolished. In only a few countries have parliaments survived continuously over a fairly long period.[1]

Parliaments, though episodic, are persistent. They persist, though widely condemned. Why? What accounts for their persistence, and especially for their reemergence, once they have been abolished?

These questions should be viewed in a larger context. Parliaments are a part—not the whole—of a governmental system, and governments themselves are a part—not the whole—of the nation and its society and economy. Instability and precariousness affect whole nations, not just their parliaments. Especially for the new and economically undeveloped nations of the world, their boundaries may be disrupted by their neighbors and populations may be included within those boundaries against their will. Their economies may likewise be fragile, even if the state is of long duration, such as Thailand, Iran, or the Latin American countries. Beset by scarce resources, inflation, and unemployment, perhaps no decision maker and no governmental institution can make decisions that are both acceptable to a broad cross section of the population and are also effective. Nations with undeveloped economies are caught in a worldwide network of trade and finance within which they are each relatively unimportant and helpless participants. Beset from without and divided from within, how are governments to act and to survive?

In these volatile and unstable circumstances, parliaments are potentially useful to governments in obtaining voluntary support for the government from their population.[2] In coping with potential internal divisions, governments strive to gain support from their population. The greater the consensus within a nation that the nation should exist as a nation, that the existing governmental institutions are proper, and that governmental decisions should be obeyed, the more likely the nation will be stable and that socioeconomic conflicts will be compromised without physical disruption. But in many nations this state of affairs is only partially attained. Conflicts occur not only over tangible

---

[1] Jean Blondel, *Comparative Legislatures* (Englewood Cliffs, N.J.: Prentice-Hall, 1973), pp. 7–9.

[2] Allan Kornberg and Kenneth Pittman, "Representative and Military Bodies: Their Roles in the Survival of Political Systems of New States," in Joel Smith and Lloyd Musolf (eds.), *Legislatures in Development* (Durham, N.C.: Duke University Press, forthcoming), chap. 3.

economic issues but over the very existence of the state and over the proper ways in which the governmental system should be organized.

Under these circumstances, either the existing civilian executive may attempt to bypass the parliament and reduce its autonomy or the military may intervene directly. But the military has no magic solution for the nation's predicament in the world economy. Moreover, coercion is less than efficient in securing obedience from the nation's population —and may even be counterproductive. If the population obeys voluntarily, the task of governmental leaders is greatly simplified.

Parliaments can contribute to voluntary obedience and hence become useful even to authoritarian rulers. Parliaments as an institution may enjoy more popular support than do the rulers themselves. The existence of a parliament is permitted in an effort to "translate support for the representative institution into support for the leadership itself." For this very practical reason, if for no other, the leaders of new and unstable nations, even the military leaders, "exhibit an affinity for the *idea* if not the reality of representative bodies."[3]

But parliaments, once created, are partially unpredictable and uncontrollable by other authorities. The complaint of a British king in the seventeenth century is a case in point. The king had attempted to manipulate the elections to the House of Commons and commented about their members: "since they derived all matters of privilege from him and by his grant, he expected they should not be turned against him."[4] From the point of view of the chief executive, and especially of authoritarian executives, parliaments are always in danger of being turned against them.

Even Spain's legislative assembly, during the Franco dictatorship, began to question the actions of his government. Toward the end of his regime a new category of member was introduced—the "family" representatives, who were the only directly elected set of members (though a minority) of that body. They cast half of the negative votes on Franco's selection of Prince Carlos (the current king) as his successor and raised over half of the over 200 questions asked in parliament of the government.[5]

As another example, this time from a Communist party state, the Polish Sejm's committees directed numerous "requests" to government agencies. As noted in Chapter 4, the Sejm's presidium limited the impact of those committee requests by ruling that the agencies need not obey, but only answer, them. It would appear that the creation

---

[3] Ibid. The two separated quotations are on pp. 21 and 22, respectively.

[4] Sydney D. Bailey, *British Parliamentary Democracy*, 3d ed. (Boston: Houghton Mifflin, 1971), pp. 12–13.

[5] Juan Linz, "Legislatures in Organic Statist-Authoritarian Regimes—The Case of Spain," in Smith and Musolf (eds.), *Legislatures in Development*, chap. 4.

of committees to parallel the structure of government agencies, and the encouragement given them to meet through the year and to investigate agencies in the field, resulted in more autonomous and vigorous action than the Communist party leaders, in retrospect, thought useful.

Furthermore it is by no means clear that a parliament is necessarily "representative."[6] It may be so constructed that the claim could be advanced seriously that the president, or even the military, is more representative of and responsive to the whole population than is the parliament. In many nations, for example, rural areas are over-represented by the district system: In Peru, eight times as many voters are found in an urban district as in a rural one. Furthermore, the vote is more easily manipulated, if not simply controlled, among rural peasants than among urban workers and the educated middle class.

If, in addition, the powers of such a legislative body are sharply circumscribed by the chief executive, then the parliamentary members are likely to be no more "responsible" than they are representative. The members may seek to obtain increased governmental funding or outright favoritism for their localities and for the rural aristocracy and neglect, at least in the eyes of the executive, the needs of long-term and nationwide development.

The result of the downward spiral of powerlessness and unrepresentativeness can be this type of commentary on a Latin American parliament:[7]

> Parliament is not the right vehicle for the [socioeconomic] transformation. The plutocratic classes, with their pressure groups, with their safe seats, are there; they control . . . the congressmen who are never there, those who do not know the country's social reality, the opportunists, and the experts in cheating.

A further and logical result is the abolition of parliaments and, along with them, competitive elections.

The proper place of parliaments in the governmental system of their respective nations is, for most countries, an unresolved question. Not infrequently parliaments are simply abolished, only to return again. Once in existence, they are a potential limitation upon the chief executive in achieving immediate goals, but at the same time they can also be useful to the chief executive in the long-run governance of the nation.

[6] Carlos Alberto Astiz, "The Decay of Latin American Legislatures," in Allan Kornberg (ed.), *Legislatures in Comparative Perspective* (New York: McKay, 1973), pp. 118–121.

[7] Eduardo Santa, *Sociologia Politica de Colombia* (Bogota: Ediciones Tercey Mundo, 1964, p. 125), quoted in ibid., pp. 125–126.

ARE PARLIAMENTS IN DECLINE?

That parliaments are in "decline," and suffer "pathologies" is an old theme in discussion and writing about governmental institutions. This seemingly constant theme is a reflection both of the hopes that political thinkers have placed upon representative and deliberative bodies and of the uncertainties and complexities facing the world's nations. Parliaments do not exist in a vacuum; rather, as we indicated in Chapter 1, they exist in a social and political environment.[8]

The most immediate task of a parliament is to interact with the executive. Perhaps the most general, and certainly ever-present, question concerns the balance of power between them. Parliaments are widely perceived to be losing power relative to the executive. Members of parliaments frequently believe that about themselves, and earlier chapters have recounted various ways in which they attempt to reverse that trend. A legislative staff and permanent committees that parallel the structure of agencies are two common institutional devices for achieving this purpose. But as a nation becomes increasingly industrial and complex, the issues become increasingly difficult and technical. The executive, in that situation, is ordinarily better staffed and possesses superior sources of information to the parliament. If, in addition, crises occur (war, oil price increases, and depression, to name a few), the executive has all the more reason to act upon its own preferences and to do so quickly. And prompt action by the executive is likely to be applauded by the parliament itself, at least in the short run.

The characteristics of the members of parliament are an important consideration. If their skills, acquired through education and occupation, do not match those of the civil servants and of the chief executive's advisors, how capable are they of understanding complex issues and of coming to reasonable decisions? But if the members are capable of thinking about technical matters, how "representative" are they? In most parliaments the members are elected, not appointed. If they are highly trained and skilled, their social status and their economic self-

---

[8] This section is based upon several sources: Gerhard Loewenberg, "The Role of Parliaments in Modern Political Systems," in Gerhard Loewenberg (ed.), *Modern Parliaments: Change or Decline?* (Chicago: Aldine, Atherton, 1971), pp. 1–20; Robert A. Packenham, "Legislatures and Political Development," in Allan Kornberg and Lloyd D. Musolf (eds.), *Legislatures in Developmental Perspective* (Durham, N.C.: Duke University Press, 1970), pp. 521–582; Kenneth C. Wheare, *Legislatures,* 2d ed. (New York: Oxford, 1967); Ian Budge and Cornelius O'Leary "Permanent Supremacy and Perpetual Opposition: The Parliament in Northern Ireland, 1921–72," pp. 166–232, and Marvin G. Weinbaum, "The Legislator as Intermediary: Integration of the Center and Periphery in Afghanistan," pp. 95–121, both in Albert F. Eldridge (ed.), *Legislatures in Plural Societies: The Search for Cohesion in National Development* (Durham, N.C.: Duke University Press, 1977).

interest could be very different from the population who elects them and whom they represent. Furthermore, we have earlier noted a time lag between the changes in the socioeconomic composition of parliaments and changes in the social and economic structure of the nation.

There appears to be a "trade-off," or a balancing, among the potentially contradictory desired goals of democracy, representation, and effectiveness. Elections, especially if competitive, are the presumed means by which representation is achieved and democracy implemented. But if the parliament is either powerless in interacting with the executive or inadequate in coping with the nation's needs, the parliament itself could be abrogated by the executive or repudiated and distrusted by critical segments of the population.

The growth of political parties and of organized interest groups alters the relationships among executive, parliament, and society. The executive-parliament relationship is not only an interaction between two institutions as whole bodies, and the parliament-society relationship is not only between individual members and individual voters. Rather, the relationships become organized through political parties, which link together segments of electorate, parliamentary members, and executives. Parties have become the means by which legislatures, especially in "parliamentary" systems, select the chief executive and the cabinet, and in most nations parties are the means by which executives and legislators appeal for popular support through the election system.

Interest groups mediate the same relationships. Although they seldom contest elections and form governments, they do sponsor party candidates. When elected, the parliamentary members with strong ties to interest groups are likely to become members of relevant committees, which in turn relate to the government agencies that affect the groups' members. In some countries major economic decisions, especially concerning wages, are made through intergroup negotiations; these decisions in turn heavily affect the government's actions on investment, inflation, and the balance of payments.

These last comments suggest that the government as a whole exists within a larger socioeconomic environment, and that the allocation of decision-making responsibilities between the government and private sector is an important consideration. As governments, especially in the industrial democracies, have slowly become responsible for employment and for the provision of social services, the governments have also become responsible for the economic health of the whole industries. Industries have been nationalized or, more commonly, have been protected and supported by a wide range of governmental financial arrangements. But at the same time the capacity of parliaments to understand, to monitor, and to deliberate on, economic policy has been widely questioned.

Finally, the activities of a government vary with the broad socio-economic circumstances of the nation. The governments of West Germany and of Kenya, for example, face different tasks. Likewise, they are organized differently and are staffed differently. Their need, and capacity, for certain kinds of actions vary because the societies they serve and that create them differ. We would expect that, as a result, their parliaments would also contain differently trained sets of members, and the parliaments' activities and interaction with the executive and the electorate would vary accordingly.

Parliaments can—or at least have the potential to—help their nation achieve broad social goals. Parliaments can be a means by which a nation builds its economy and raises the living standards of its people. Parliaments can be a means through which population sub-groups (ethnic, religious, etc.) are integrated into the larger nation. Parliaments can be a means by which diverse regions are blended into a national unity. Parliaments can be the means by which popular knowledge about and consent toward governmental policies are gained.

Yet we have provided ample illustrations of circumstances in which parliaments have frustrated the achievement of such broad objectives. Parliaments may be ineffective institutions. The members may pursue individual or local goals in their dealings with the national government. Parliament may become a means by which a powerful majority overwhelms a minority. Parliament may be more of a forum within which government promulgates its policies than wins understanding and consent.

The future of parliaments is uncertain because their past has been checkered. Their performance has been uneven because the nations that create them are unsettled and changing. Although parliaments as institutions, and members as individuals, have an important part to play in the growth and development of their nations, they too are caught within the wider web of the nation's social and economic circumstances within a precarious international environment.

TOWARD A CLASSIFICATION OF PARLIAMENTS

As a means of drawing together the various strands of our thinking about parliaments and especially of summarizing the relationships of parliaments with their chief executives and electorates, we shall suggest a way of classifying the world's parliaments. We must acknowledge at the outset, however, that we do not know enough about parliaments in general to be able to reflect accurately in any classification system the diverse political realities among the world's nations. Neither do we have sufficiently comprehensive information about any one parliament to permit us to place it in any one category with much confidence. Thus to suggest a classification system is a means of summarizing both our knowledge and our ignorance about parliaments.

We suggest that parliaments may be (roughly) categorized along two dimensions. Both dimensions reflect parliaments' relationships with their chief executives and also permit us to characterize their relationships with their electorates. One dimension refers to the scope of parliamentary activity. The other refers to the continuity of parliaments as governmental and political institutions.

The scope of parliamentary activity is best summarized by the distinction presented in the first chapter among questions of detail, questions of intermediate importance, and questions of broad policy.[9] Within the broad-policy category we shall introduce a further distinction, largely corresponding to the formal structure of the national government. We shall distinguish between those parliaments that select a prime minister and the cabinet in a parliamentary system and those in a separation-of-powers system, which ordinarily do not select a president. Many of the world's parliaments formally have the power to select the prime minister but in fact exercise no independent power in that respect. Such parliaments, such as the Russian, will be placed in categories that more accurately—in view of our existing information—reflect their actual activity. The resulting four categories of parliaments, arranged in descending order of scope of activity, are in Table 8.1.

Along the top of the same table are the two categories that summarize another dimension of parliamentary life—its stability. Some parliaments, such as the British and the American, have had a continuous existence over decades and even centuries. They have not been threatened in a seizure of power by either the chief executive, the military, or by other forces in society. The Russian Supreme Soviet must also be regarded as a continuous and stable parliament. Numerous parliaments, however, have been discontinued and disrupted. They have been suspended by the chief executive, or the military have seized power—usually with the result that both the chief executive as well as parliament are disbanded and perhaps arrested if not also executed.[10]

The two dimensions combined provide a potential of eight different types of parliaments. We shall discuss each of the eight types in turn, and suggest some parliaments that might fit each type.

[9] Jean Blondel, *Comparative Legislatures* (Englewood Cliffs, N.J.: Prentice-Hall, 1973), chaps. 6, 8–10.

[10] This dimension has been adapted from Michael L. Mezey, *Comparative Legislatures* (Durham, N.C.: Duke University Press, 1979), chap. 2. Some of the labels for each cell within Table 8.1 are used by Mezey, but we do not use them in precisely the same way.

Table 8.1   TYPES OF NATIONAL PARLIAMENTS

	DEGREE OF STABLE EXISTENCE	
SCOPE OF ACTIVITY	DISCONTINUOUS	CONTINUOUS
BROAD POLICY:		
Parliamentary system	FRAGMENTED	COHESIVE
	Weimar Republic	Great Britain
	French IV Republic	West Germany
		Japan
BROAD POLICY:		
Separation-of-powers	VULNERABLE	ASSERTIVE
	Philippines	United States
	Chile	
MEDIUM-RANGE QUESTIONS:	DISCONTINUOUS MARGINAL	STABLE MARGINAL
Policy modification	Thailand	South Korea
		Kenya
DETAILED QUESTIONS:	DISRUPTED MINIMAL	STABLE MINIMAL
Little policy-making	Pakistan	USSR
activity	Nigeria	Poland
		Tanzania
		Mexico
		Iran

Cohesive parliaments are continuous bodies that select the government of the day and usually also have the potential for voting that government out of office. The British Parliament is the major example. Many of the Commonwealth parliaments would belong in this category, as do the contemporary West German Bundestag, the Japanese Diet, and many of the parliaments of Western Europe.

Fragmented parliaments are subject to the possibility of being eliminated, in that the whole governmental system could be overthrown and replaced. The Reichstag of the German Weimar Republic, the Cortes of the Spanish Republic, and the General Assembly of the French Fourth Republic are examples.

Although the distinction between the cohesive and fragmented categories is made primarily in terms of the duration of their existence as permitted by outside power centers, this distinction also includes the relationship of parliaments to their electorates. The cohesive parliaments have usually had either a two-party system or pronounced tendencies toward a two-coalition system. That is, their stability is related to the organization of political parties and their voting strength in the electorate. A characteristic of the disrupted parliaments is that they have also been fragmented; the many parties have been unable to forge stable governing coalitions, and the elections have often increased the strength of the opposite extreme parties at the expense of the more modern centrist parties.[11]

Those congresses that play an active part in the formulation of broad public policy also vary in their continuity. Assertive parliaments, typified by the American Congress, strive for an equality of power and function with the chief executive. The relationship between them varies both by subject matter and through time. Although they probably cooperate on most matters, they have the independence of constitutional position and the resources of information and staff to become formidable obstacles to one another on any particular matter. The assertiveness of the Congress is made possible, at least in part, by the election results. The two parties, at least since World War II, have not infrequently split control of the two political branches. Yet the diffuseness of party organization in Congress and the varied constituencies included in each party have produced cross-party voting patterns that have both supported the positions of minority presidents and opposed those of majority presidents. Even when presidents have had Congresses with a two-thirds majority held by their own party, they have had difficulties in gaining congressional support. More than once, for example, President Carter publicly threatened to veto bills being considered by the Congress in which Democrats had a two-thirds majority elected in 1976 and 1978.

Several other nations have experienced congresses in a separation of powers system which have asserted themselves against the president to the extent they have become adversaries rather than co-equal, but somewhat cooperative, partners.[12] The result, as illustrated in the Philippines and in Chile, has been the suspension and removal of parliament. These congresses were vulnerable to outside power. In the Philippines, the congress and elections were suspended by the incumbent president. In Chile, the whole governmental system was overthrown by the military. In the Chilean case, the long history of fairly stable elections and of continuous political parties had not resulted in a stable coalition among them. The last elected president was a minority president facing a reluctant congress. In the Philippines, parties were mainly labels, with elections contested by independent candidates, after which the winners loosely associated themselves under party labels within the congress. In both the vulnerable and fragmented parliaments, elections produced unstable coalitions; this condition in turn combined with hostile outside forces to disrupt and disband parliament as a governing institution.

[11] Gerhard Loewenberg, "The Influence of Parliamentary Behavior on Regime Stability," *Comparative Politics* 3 (January 1971), pp. 177–200.
[12] This distinction is made in Mezey, *Comparative Legislatures*, pp. 278–279.

To distinguish between the parliaments that handle questions of intermediate importance and those that largely are limited to matters of detail is difficult if for no other reason than the lack of sufficient information. But it would appear that many of the parliaments of the black African nations have attempted to handle questions of intermediate importance, whereas those of the Communist party states have been confined to matters of local and specific implementation of policies that themselves were not subject to question. Kenya is an example of a stable but marginal parliament; Thailand an unstable and disrupted marginal parliament.

Minimal parliaments have been confined to questions of detail but have been employed to provide endorsement and approval to the government's policies. Parliaments in this category face strong chief executives or strong single parties and are clearly controlled by them. They are permitted, perhaps mandated, to meet, to be elected, and to approve those government proposals placed before them. The government and ruling party regard parliament as useful. Elections to and meetings of parliament help the government explain and justify its existence, its procedures, and its policies. Furthermore, the members themselves are expected by the government to explain government policies to their constituents and to mediate local needs and circumstances with the central government. Such parliaments are continuous because the government and/or ruling party support them. The power of the government to eliminate parliament is not doubted, but neither is the power of the government to successfully control parliament's activities. As a result, the category of the disrupted minimal legislature does not contain many examples.

The placement of national parliaments among the eight categories of the suggested classification is a preliminary indication of where each might best fit. The categories themselves are suggestions of what now appears, given our state of knowledge, to be the most useful ways of thinking about parliaments and their place in their political environment.

Countries and their parliaments can, of course, quickly change categories. During the two-year ascendancy of Prime Minister Indira Gandhi of India, for example, that country appeared to best fit the stable minimal category, whereas, both before and since, it appeared to resemble the British in the stable-parliament category. It may be at least some of the Communist Party parliaments of Eastern Europe are becoming stable marginal parliaments rather than stable minimal ones.

Furthermore, in every country there is considerable discussion of parliament and its proper place within its government and society. Perhaps people are continuously dissatisfied with their governments and propose means of improving—as they see it—how their government functions. In Britain and West Germany, reformers argue that their committee systems should be strengthened to resemble the American system more. In the U.S. Congress, reformers argue that the parties should be strengthened to resemble the British system more. Both the House and Senate have created reform commissions, and over the past decade both have introduced important changes in their organization, in their relationship to the president, and in the organization and conduct of elections. Dissatisfaction and proposals for change—perhaps for contradictory reasons—both in the United States and abroad are likely to be continuous features of contemporary politics because, if for no other reason, such discontent and impulse to reform has been a constant feature of our past.

WORDS AND POWER

The work of a legislative body is expressed through words. Words, in the form of bills and Acts, question time and speeches, committee hearings and committee reports, are the work of a deliberative legislative body.

Their bills are not self-enforcing or self-administered. The agencies must implement the legislation, the courts may interpret it, and the citizens' behavior is usually the intended end result. But the legislative body does not implement its own legislation and does not preside over its litigation. Parliaments are dependent upon the willingness of other governmental entities to translate legislative words into actions.

In the face of the police and the army, a parliament has no recourse in the event of a physical confrontation. Parliamentary members can be jailed, as they have been in India. Members may remain in their assembly building until the troops advance and then the members disappear and go home, as occurred in Czechoslovakia. Not only parliamentary members but presidents may be shot and killed in their office, as occurred in Chile, or prime ministers deposed and imprisoned, as in Pakistan.

Parliaments are dependent upon the willingness of other political actors for their very existence. In most nations of the world that willingness is open to question. Even in stable democracies and stable one-party systems, in which the continued existence of parliaments is not endangered, the question still remains of the extent to which they are permitted to be active and influential in the life of the government.

Perhaps the chief dynamic within the governmental system, at least in an immediate sense, lies in the relationship between parliament and the chief executive. As they cooperate and dispute, as they debate and enact, the electorate is the implicit audience. The electorate can become involved in the governing process, as well as affected by it, if the political branches of government find that they each gain advantage over the other as they appeal to and win the electorate over to their side.

But it is the potential each political actor has to disrupt the plans and preferences of the other that acts as the greatest check and limitations on the other's activities. The U.S. Congress is able to inquire into most governmental programs and agencies when it wishes. It can investigate. It can use the budget and authorization process to require the president to justify his position. Furthermore, as the president seeks approval for new policies, the capacity for Congress to inquire, to delay, to publicize, and even to defeat is at its greatest.

Although perhaps most parliamentary bodies approve, or at least do not question or delay, most governmental activities, that potential is always a present and real one. Something of this potential may be illustrated by quotations from two activist American presidents. Both, not incidentally, were former members of Congress themselves.[13]

> You have got to give it all you can, that first year. . . . Doesn't matter what kind of a majority you come in with. You've got just one year when they treat you right, and before they start worrying about themselves. The third year, you lose votes. . . . The fourth year's all politics. You cannot put anything through when half the Congress is thinking how to beat you. (Lyndon Johnson)

> . . . the Congress looks more powerful sitting here than it did when I was there in the Congress. But that is because when you are in the Congress you are one of a hundred in the Senate or one of 435 in the House. So that the power is so divided. But from here I look at a Congress, and I look at the collective power of the Congress, particularly the bloc action, and it is a substantial power. (John F. Kennedy)

[13] The Johnson quote is from Harry McPherson, *A Political Education* (Boston: Little, Brown, 1972), p. 268. The Kennedy statement is from *Congressional Quarterly Weekly Report,* December 21, 1962, p. 2278.

Bibliography

I. BOOKS AND PERIODICALS

Agranoff, Robert (ed.), *The New Style in Election Campaigns* (Boston: Holbrook Press, 1972). 392 pp.

Amilon, Ingvar, "Party Leadership Conferences: A Study in Swedish Parliamentary Practice," in Herbert Hirsch and M. Donald Hancock (eds.), *Comparative Legislative Systems* (New York: Free Press, 1971), pp. 323–329.

Andrews, William G., "The Constitutional Prescription of Parliamentary Procedures in Gaullist France," *Legislative Studies Quarterly* 3 (August 1978), pp. 465–506.

Andrews, William G., "Presidentialism and Parliamentary Electoral Politics in France: A Case Study of Eureux, 1962 and 1973," *Political Studies* 21 (September 1973), pp. 311–320.

Astiz, Carlos Alberto, "The Decay of Latin American Legislatures," in Allan Kornberg (ed.), *Legislatures in Comparative Perspective* (New York: McKay, 1973), pp. 114–126.

Atkin, Charles, and Gary Heald, "Effects of Political Advertising," *Public Quarterly* 40 (Summer 1976), pp. 216–228.

Baerwald, Hans H., *Japan's Parliament* (New York: Cambridge, 1974). 155 pp.

Bailey, Sydney D., *British Parliamentary Democracy*, 3d ed. (Boston: Houghton Mifflin, 1971). 248 pp.

Barkan, Joel, "Bringing Home the Pork: Legislative Behavior, Rural Development and Political Change in East Africa," in Joel Smith and Lloyd Musolf (eds.) *Legislatures in Development* (Durham, N.C.: Duke University Press, forthcoming), chap. 10.

Bealey, Frank J., J. Blondel, and W. P. McCann, *Constituency Politics: A Study of Newcastle-under-Lyme* (New York: Free Press, 1965). 440 pp.

Becker, Robert W., et al., "Correlates of Legislative Voting: Michigan House of Representatives, 1954–1961," *Midwest Journal of Political Science* 6 (November 1962), pp. 384–396.

Bell, Charles G. and Charles M. Price, *The First Term: A Study of Legislative Socialization* (Beverly Hills: Sage Publications. Sage Library of Social Research, vol. 18, 1975). 215 pp.

Berry, Jeffrey M., "Electoral Economics: Getting and Spending," *Policy* (Fall 1974), pp. 120–129.

Bibby, John and Roger Davidson, *On Capitol Hill*, 1st and 2d ed. (New York: Holt, Rinehart and Winston, 1967 and 1972). 280 pp. and 300 pp., respectively.

Bierzanek, Remigiusz, and Andrzej Gwizdz, "Parliamentary Control over the Administration in Poland," *Polish Round Table* (Warsaw: Yearbook of the Polish Association of Political Sciences, 1967), pp. 145–170.

Binkley, Wilfred E., *President and Congress* (New York: Knopf, 1947). 312 pp.

Blondel, Jean, *Comparative Legislatures* (Englewood Cliffs, N.J.: Prentice-Hall, 1973). 173 pp.

Boynton, G. Robert, "Southern Conservatism: Constituency Opinion and Congressional Voting," *Public Opinion Quarterly* 29 (Summer 1965), pp. 259–269.

Boynton, G. Robert, Samuel C. Patterson, and Ronald D. Hedlund, "The Missing Links in Legislative Politics: Attentive Constituents," *Journal of Politics* 31 (August 1969), pp. 700–721.

Brady, David W., and Phillip Althoff, "Party Voting in the U.S. House of Representatives, 1890–1910: Elements of a Responsible Party System," *Journal of Politics* 36 (August 1974), pp. 753–775.

Brady, David W., and Naomi B. Lynn, "Switched Seat Congressional Districts: Their Effect on Party Voting and Public Policy," *American Journal of Political Science* 17 (August 1973), pp. 528–543.

Braunthal, Gerard, *The West German Legislative Process: A Case Study of Two Transportation Bills* (Ithaca: Cornell University Press, 1972). 290 pp.

Bronowski, J., *The Ascent of Man* (Boston: Little, Brown, 1973). 448 pp.

Browne, Eric C., and Mark N. Franklin, "Aspects of Coalition Payoffs in European Parliamentary Democracies," *American Political Science Review* 67 (June 1973), pp. 453–469.

Buck, J. Vincent, "Presidential Coattails and Congressional Loyalty," *Midwest Journal of Political Science* 16 (August 1972), pp. 460–472.

Budge, Ian, and Cornelius O'Leary, "Permanent Supremacy and Perpetual

Opposition: The Parliament in Northern Ireland, 1921–72," in Albert F. Eldridge (ed.), *Legislatures in Plural Societies: The Search for Cohesion in National Development* (Durham, N.C.: Duke University Press, 1977), pp. 166–232.

Bullock, Charles S., "Freshmen Committee Assignments and Reelection in the United States House of Representatives," *American Political Science Review* 66 (September 1972), pp. 996–1007.

Burda, Andrzej (ed.), *Sejm Polskiej Rzeczypospolitej Ludowej* (Warsaw: Ossolineum, 1975). 532 pp.

Burns, James MacG. *The Deadlock of Democracy* (Englewood Cliffs, N.J.: Prentice-Hall, 1963). 376 pp.

Butler, David, and Dennis Kavanagh, *The British General Election of October 1974* (New York: St. Martin's, 1975). 368 pp.

Butler, David, and Michael Pinto-Duschinsky, *The British General Election of 1970* (New York: St. Martin's, 1971). 493 pp.

Butt, Ronald, *The Power of Parliament* (New York: Walker, 1967). 468 pp.

Campbell, Angus, and Warren E. Miller, "The Motivational Basis of Straight and Split Ticket Voting," *American Political Science Review* 60 (June 1959), pp. 393–412.

Campion, Gilbert, *An Introduction to the Procedure of the House of Commons*, 3d ed. (London: Macmillan, 1958). 350 pp.

Chee, Chan Heng, "The Role of Parliamentary Politicians in Singapore," *Legislative Studies Quarterly* 1 (August 1976), pp. 423–441.

Churchward, L. G., *Contemporary Soviet Government* (New York: Elsevier, 1968). 366 pp.

Clarke, Harold D., Richard G. Price, and Robert Krause, "Constituency Service Among Canadian Provincial Legislators: Basic Findings and a Test of Three Hypotheses," *Canadian Journal of Political Science* 8 (December 1975), pp. 520–542.

Clausen, Aage R., *How Congressmen Decide: A Policy Focus* (New York: St. Martin's, 1973). 243 pp.

Clausen, Aage R., and Carl E. Van Horn, "The Congressional Response to a Decade of Change: 1963–1972," *Journal of Politics* 39 (August 1977), pp. 624–666.

Clem, Alan L., *The Making of Congressmen: Seven Campaigns of 1974* (North Scituate, Mass.: Duxbury Press, 1976). 275 pp.

Cohen, L. H., "Local Government Complaints: The MP's Viewpoint," *Public Administration (London)* 51 (Summer 1973), pp. 175–183

Congressional Quarterly, *Politics in America*, 4th ed. (Washington, D.C.: Congressional Quarterly, 1971). 156 pp.

Congressional Quarterly, *Roll Call, 1976* (Washington, D.C.: Congressional Quarterly, 1977).

Cowart, Andrew T., "Electoral Choice in the American States: Incumbency Effects, Partisan Forces, and Divergent Partisan Majorities," *American Political Science Review* 67 (September 1973), pp. 835–853.

Crick, Bernard R., *The Reform of Parliament* (London: Weidenfeld and Nicolson, 1964). 274 pp.

Criddle, B. "Distorted Representation in France," *Parliamentary Affairs* 28 (Spring 1975), pp. 154–179.

Crotty, William J., *Political Reform and the American Experiment* (New York: Crowell, 1977). 312 pp.

Cummings, Milton C., Jr., *Congressmen and the Electorate: Elections for the U.S. House and the President, 1920–1964* (New York: Free Press, 1966). 233 pp.

Cummings, Milton C., Jr., and Robert L. Peabody, "The Decision to Enlarge the Committee on Rules: An Analysis of the 1961 Vote," in Robert L. Peabody and Nelson W. Polsby (eds.), *New Perspectives on the House of Representatives* (Chicago: Rand McNally, 1963), pp. 167–194.

Dahl, Robert, *After the Revolution?* (New Haven: Yale University Press, 1970). 171 pp.

Davidson, Roger H., *The Role of the Congressman* (New York: Pegasus, 1969). 220 pp.

Davidson, Roger H., and Walter J. Oleszek, "Adaptation and Consolidation: Structural Innovation in the U.S. House of Representatives," *Legislative Studies Quarterly* 1 (February 1976), pp. 37–66.

Declercq, Eugene R., "Inter-House Differences in American State Legislatures," *Journal of Politics* 39 (August 1977), pp. 774–785.

Dickson, A. D. R., "MP's Readoption Conflicts: Their Causes and Consequences," *Political Studies* 23 (March 1975), pp. 62–70.

Dinka, Frank, and Max J. Skidmore, "The Functions of Communist One-Party Elections: The Case of Czechoslovakia, 1971," *Political Science Quarterly* 88 (September 1973), pp. 395–422.

Di Palma, Giuseppe, "Institutional Rules and Legislative Outcomes in the Italian Parliament," *Legislative Studies Quarterly* 1 (May 1976), pp. 147–180.

Dodd, Charles H., *Politics and Government in Turkey* (Berkeley: University of California Press, 1969). 335 pp.

Dodd, Lawrence C., "Party Coalitions in Multiparty Parliaments: A Game-Theoretical Analysis," *American Political Science Review* 68 (September 1974), pp. 1093–1118.

Dye, Thomas R., "A Comparison of Constituency Influences in the Upper and Lower Chambers of a State Legislature," *Western Political Quarterly* 14 (June 1961), pp. 473–480.

Edinger, Lewis J., *Politics in West Germany*, 2d ed. (Boston: Little, Brown, 1977). 375 pp.

Edwards, George C., III, "Presidential Electoral Performance as a Source of Presidential Power," *American Journal of Political Science* 22 (February 1978), pp. 152–168.

Ellwood, John W., and James A. Thurber, "The New Congressional Budget Process: The Hows and Whys of House-Senate Differences," in Lawrence C. Dodd and Bruce I. Oppenheimer (eds.), *Congress Reconsidered* (New York: Praeger, 1977), pp. 163–192.

Epstein, Leon D., *Political Parties in Western Democracies* (New York: Praeger, 1967). 374 pp.

Erikson, Robert S. "The Advantage of Incumbency in Congressional Elections," *Polity* 3 (Spring 1971), pp. 395–405.

Fenno, Richard F., Jr., *Congressmen in Committees* (Boston: Little, Brown, 1973). 302 pp.

Fenno, Richard F., Jr., *Home Style: House Members in Their Districts* (Boston: Little, Brown, 1978). 304 pp.

Fenno, Richard F., Jr., *Power of the Purse: Appropriations Politics in Congress* (Boston: Little, Brown, 1966). 704 pp.

Fenno, Richard F., Jr., "U.S. House Members in Their Constituencies," *American Political Science Review* 71 (September 1977), pp. 883–917.

Fiorina, Morris P., *Congress: Keystone of the Washington Establishment* (New Haven: Yale University Press, 1977). 101 pp.

Fiorina, Morris P., *Representatives, Roll Calls, and Constituencies* (Lexington, Mass.: Lexington Books, 1974). 143 pp.

Fishel, Jeff, *Party and Opposition* (New York: McKay, 1973). 254 pp.

Fisher, Louis, *Presidential Spending Power*. Princeton: Princeton University Press, 1975. 345 pp.

Flinn, Thomas A. "Party Responsibility in the States: Some Causal Factors," *American Political Science Review* 58 (March 1964), pp. 60–71.

Francis, Wayne L., "Coalitions in American State Legislatures: A Propositional Analysis," in Sven Groennings, E. W. Kelley, and Michael Leiserson (eds.), *The Study of Coalition Behavior* (New York: Holt, Rinehart and Winston, 1970), pp. 409–423.

Frantzich, Stephen E., "De-Recruitment: The Other Side of the Congressional Career Equation," *Western Political Quarterly* 31 (April 1978), pp. 105–126.

Fraser, Antonia, *Cromwell: The Lord Protector* (New York: Knopf, 1973). 774 pp.

Frasure, Robert, and Allan Kornberg, "Constituency Agents and British Party Politics," *British Journal of Political Science* 5 (October 1975), pp. 459–476.

Freeman, J. Leiper, *The Political Process* (New York: Doubleday, 1955). 72 pp.

Frey, Frederick W., *The Turkish Political Elite*. (Cambridge, Mass.: MIT Press, 1965). 483 pp.

Froman, Lewis A., Jr., "Inter-Party Constituency Differences and Congressional Voting Behavior," *American Political Science Review* 57 (March 1963), pp. 57–61.

Froman, Lewis A., Jr., "A Realistic Approach to Campaign Strategies and Tactics," in M. Kent Jennings and L. Harmon Zeigler (eds.), *The Electoral Process* (Englewood Cliffs, N.J.: Prentice-Hall, 1966), pp. 1–20.

Galloway, George, *History of the United States House of Representatives* (Washington, D.C.: House Committee on House Administration, House Doc. No. 250, 89th Congress, 1965). 218 pp.

Garrison, Nelson, "Partisan Patterns of House Leadership Change, 1789–1977," *American Political Science Review* 71 (September 1977), pp. 935–936.

Gerlich, Peter, "The Institutionalization of European Parliaments," in Allan Kornberg (ed.), *Legislatures in Comparative Perspective* (New York: McKay, 1973), pp. 94–111.

Glantz, Stanton A., et al., "Election Outcomes: Whose Money Matters?" *Journal of Politics* 38 (November 1976), pp. 1033–1038.

Goldey, D. B. and R. W. Johnson, "The French General Election of March 1973," *Political Studies* 21 (September 1973), pp. 321–342.

Goodin, Robert E., "The Importance of Winning Big," *Legislative Studies Quarterly* 2 (November 1977), pp. 399–407.

Gorgone, John, "Soviet Jurists in the Legislative Arena: The Reform of Criminal Procedures, 1956–58," *Soviet Union* 3 (part 1, 1976), pp. 1–35.

Hacker, Andrew, "The Elected and the Anointed: Two American Elites," *American Political Science Review* 55 (September 1961), pp. 539–549.

Hain, Paul L., and James E. Piereson, "Lawyers and Politics Revisited: Structural Advantages of Lawyer-Politicians," *American Journal of Political Science* 19 (February 1975), pp. 41–51.

Hamilton, Alexander, John Jay, and James Madison, *The Federalist: A Commentary on the Constitution of the United States* (New York: Modern Library, n.d.). 622 pp.

Hancock, M. Donald, *Sweden: The Politics of Postindustrial Change* (Hinsdale, Ill.: Dryden, 1972). 298 pp.

Heard, Kenneth A., *General Elections in South Africa, 1943–1970* (New York: Oxford, 1974). 269 pp.

Herman, Valentine, and Francoise Mendel, *Parliaments of the World* (Berlin: De Gruyter, 1976). 985 pp.

Hinckley, Barbara, "Congressional Leadership Selection and Support: A Comparative Analysis," *Journal of Politics* 32 (May 1970), pp. 268–287.

Hinckley, Barbara, "Interpreting House Midterm Elections: Toward a Measurement of the In-Party's 'Expected' Loss of Seats," *American Political Science Review* 61 (September 1967), pp. 694–700.

Hinckley, Barbara, "Seniority, 1975: Old Theories Confront New Facts," *British Journal of Political Science* 6 (October 1976), pp. 383–399.

Hinckley, Barbara, " 'Stylized' Opposition in the U.S. House of Representatives: The Effects of Coalition Behavior," *Legislative Studies Quarterly* 2 (February 1977), pp. 5–28.

Hopkins, Raymond F., "The Kenyan Legislature: Political Functions and Citizen Perceptions," in G. R. Boynton and Chong L. Kim (eds.), *Legislative Systems in Developing Countries* (Durham, N.C.: Duke University Press, 1975), pp. 207–231.

Hopkins, Raymond F., "The Role of the M.P. in Tanzania," *American Political Science Review* 64 (September 1970), pp. 754–771.

Huckshorn, Robert J., *Party Leadership in the States* (Amherst: University of Massachusetts Press, 1976). 300 pp.

Huckshorn, Robert J., and Robert C. Spencer, *The Politics of Defeat: Campaigning for Congress* (Amherst: University of Massachusetts Press, 1971). 258 pp.

Huntington, Samuel P., *Political Order in Changing Societies* (New Haven: Yale University Press, 1968). 488 pp.

Hurley, Patricia, David Brady, and Joseph Cooper, "Measuring Legislative Potential for Policy Change," *Legislative Studies Quarterly* 2 (November 1977), pp. 385–398.

Hyson, R. V. Stewart, "The Role of the Backbencher: An Analysis of Private

Members' Bills in the Canadian House of Commons," *Parliamentary Affairs* 27 (Summer 1974), pp. 262–272.

Inter-Parliamentary Union, *Parliaments: A Comparative Study on the Structure and Functioning of Representative Institutions in Forty-One Countries* (New York: Praeger, 1962). 321 pp.

Jackson, John E., *Constituencies and Leaders in Congress: Their Effects on Senate Voting Behavior* (Cambridge: Harvard University Press, 1974). 217 pp.

Jackson, Robert J., *Rebels and Whips: An Analysis of Dissension, Discipline and Cohesion in British Political Parties* (London: Macmillan, 1968). 346 pp.

Jackson, Robert J., and Michael M. Atkinson, *The Canadian Legislative System: Politicians and Policy-Making* (Toronto: Macmillan, 1974). 196 pp.

Jacobson, Gary C., "Practical Consequences of Campaign Finance Reform: An Incumbent Protection Act?" *Public Policy* 24 (Winter 1976), pp. 1–32.

Jennings, Ivor, *Parliament*, 2d ed. (New York: Cambridge, 1957). 574 pp.

Jewell, Malcolm E., "Attitudinal Determinants of Legislative Behavior: The Utility of Role Analysis," in Allan Kornberg and Lloyd D. Musolf (eds.) *Legislatures in Developmental Perspective* (Durham, N.C.: Duke University Press, 1970), pp. 460–500.

Jewell, Malcolm E., "Linkages Between Legislative Parties and External Parties," in Allan Kornberg (ed.), *Legislatures in Comparative Perspective* (New York: McKay, 1973), pp. 203–234.

Jewell, Malcolm E., and Chu Chi-hung, "Membership Movement and Committee Attractiveness in the U.S. House of Representatives, 1963–1971," *American Journal of Political Science* 18 (May 1974), pp. 433–441.

Jewell, Malcolm E., and David M. Olson, *American State Political Parties and Elections* (Homewood, Ill.: Dorsey, 1978). 358 pp.

Jewell, Malcolm E., and Samuel C. Patterson, *The Legislative Process in the United States*, 3d ed. (New York: Random House, 1977). 527 pp.

Jones, Charles O., *Every Second Year* (Washington, D.C.: Brookings, 1967). 118 pp.

Jones, Charles O., "Inter-Party Competition for Congressional Seats," *Western Political Quarterly* 17 (September 1964), pp. 461–476.

Jones, G. W., "Development of the Cabinet," in William Thornhill (ed.), *The Modernization of British Government* (Totowa, N.J.: Rowman and Littlefield, 1975), pp. 31–62.

Jones, G. W. "The Prime Minister and Parliamentary Questions," *Parliamentary Affairs* 26 (Summer 1973), pp. 260–273.

Judge, D., "Backbench Specialization—A Study in Parliamentary Questions," *Parliamentary Affairs* 27 (Spring 1974), pp. 171–186.

Jupp, James, *Australian Party Politics* (Melbourne: Melbourne University Press, 1964). 235 pp.

Katz, Richard S., "The Attribution of Variance in Electoral Returns: An Alternative Technique," *American Political Science Review* 67 (September 1973), pp. 817–828.

Keefe, William J., and Morris S. Ogul, *The American Legislative Process: Congress and the States*, 4th ed. (Englewood Cliffs, N.J.: Prentice-Hall, 1977). 497 pp.

Kernell, Samuel, "Toward Understanding 19th Century Congressional Careers: Ambition, Competition and Rotation," *American Journal of Political Science* 21 (November 1977).

Key, V. O., *American State Politics: An Introduction* (New York: Knopf, 1956). 289 pp.

Key, V. O., *Southern Politics* (New York: Knopf, 1949). 675 pp.

Kim, Chong Lim, Justin Green, and Samuel C. Patterson, "Partisanship in the Recruitment and Performance of American State Legislators," in Heinz Eulau and Moshe M. Czudnowski (eds.), *Elite Recruitment in Democratic Polities* (New York: Halsted Press, 1976), pp. 79–104.

Kimber, Richard, and John D. Lees (eds.), *Political Parties in Modern Britain* (London: Routledge, 1972). 288 pp.

King, Anthony, "Modes of Executive-Legislative Relations: Great Britain, France, and West Germany," *Legislative Studies Quarterly* 1 (February 1976), pp. 11–36.

Kingdon, John W., *Candidates for Office: Beliefs and Strategies* (New York: Random House, 1966). 176 pp.

Kingdon, John W., *Congressmen's Voting Decisions* (New York: Harper & Row, 1973). 313 pp.

Kornberg, Allan, *Canadian Legislative Behavior: A Study of the 25th Parliament* (New York: Holt, Rinehart and Winston, 1967). 166 pp.

Kornberg, Allan, "Caucus and Cohesion in Canadian Parliamentary Parties," *American Political Science Review* 60 (March 1966), pp. 83–92.

Kornberg, Allan, and Robert C. Frasure, "Policy Differences in British Parliamentary Parties," *American Political Science Review* 65 (September 1971), pp. 694–703.

Kornberg, Allan, and William Mishler, *Influence in Parliament: Canada* (Durham, N.C.: Duke University Press, 1976). 403 pp.

Kornberg, Allan, and Kenneth Pittman, "Representative and Military Bodies: Their Roles in the Survival of Political Systems of New States," in Joel Smith and Lloyd Musolf (eds.), *Legislatures in Development* (Durham: Duke University Press, forthcoming), chap. 3.

Koskiaho, Tapio, "The Parliamentary Candidates and the Candidate Selection in Finland." Paper read at International Political Science Association World Congress, Munich, 1970 (mimeo).

Kostroski, Warren L., "Party and Incumbency in Postwar Senate Elections: Trends, Patterns, and Models," *American Political Science Review* 67 (December 1973), pp. 1213–1234.

Kramer, Gerald H., "Short-Term Fluctuations in U.S. Voting Behavior, 1896–1964," *American Political Science Review* 65 (March 1971), pp. 131–143.

Kuklinski, James H., "District Competitiveness and Legislative Roll-Call Behavior: A Reassessment of the Marginality Hypothesis," *American Journal of Political Science* 21 (August 1977), pp. 627–638.

Lane, David, *Politics and Society in the USSR* (New York: Random House, 1971). 616 pp.

LaPalombara, Joseph, and Myron Weiner (eds.), *Political Parties and Political Development* (Princeton, N.J.: Princeton University Press, 1966). 487 pp.

LeBlanc, Hugh L., "Voting in State Senates: Party and Constituency Influences," *Midwest Journal of Political Science* 13 (February 1969), pp. 33–57.

Lee, Jong R., "Presidential Vetoes from Washington to Nixon," *Journal of Politics* 37 (May 1975), pp. 532–544.

Legg, Keith R., *Politics in Modern Greece* (Stanford: Stanford University Press, 1969). 367 pp.

Lehnen, Robert G., "Behavior on the Senate Floor: An Analysis of Debate in the U.S. Senate," *Midwest Journal of Political Science* 4 (November 1967), pp. 505–520.

Leiserson, Michael, "Coalition Government in Japan," in Sven Groennings, E. W. Kelley, and Michael Leiserson (eds.), *The Study of Coalition Behavior* (New York: Holt, Rinehart and Winston, 1970), pp. 80–102.

Leonardi, Robert, Raffaella Nanetti, and Gianfranco Pasquino, "Institutionalization of Parliament and Parliamentarization of Parties in Italy," *Legislative Studies Quarterly* 3 (February 1978), pp. 161–186.

Leuthold, David A., *Electioneering in a Democracy* (New York: Wiley, 1968). 150 pp.

Linz, Juan, "Legislatures in Organic Statist-Authoritarian Regimes—The Case of Spain," in Joel Smith and Lloyd Musolf (eds.), *Legislatures in Development* (Durham, N.C.: Duke University Press, forthcoming), chap. 4.

Little, D. Richard, "Legislative Authority in the Soviet Political System," *Slavic Review* 30 (March 1971), pp. 57–73.

Little, D. Richard, "Soviet Parliamentary Committees After Khrushchev: Obstacles and Opportunities," *Soviet Studies* 24 (July 1972), pp. 41–60.

Loewenberg, Gerhard, "The Influence of Parliamentary Behavior on Regime Stability," *Comparative Politics* 3 (January 1971), pp. 177–200.

Loewenberg, Gerhard, "The Institutionalization of Parliament and Public Orientation to the Political System," in Allan Kornberg (ed.), *Legislatures in Comparative Perspective* (New York: McKay, 1973), pp. 142–156.

Loewenberg, Gerhard, "The Role of Parliaments in Modern Political Systems," in Gerhard Loewenberg (ed.), *Modern Parliaments: Change or Decline?* (Chicago: Aldine, Atherton, 1971), pp. 1–20.

Loewenberg, Gerhard, *Parliament in the German Political System* (Ithaca: Cornell University Press, 1967). 463 pp.

Mabry, Donald J., "Mexico's Party Deputy System: The First Decade," *Journal of Inter-American Studies and World Affairs* 16 (May 1974), pp. 221–233.

McCarthy, Susan B., "Gate-Keeping in the Nominations Process in Yugoslavia." Paper read at Annual Meeting of American Political Science Association, Chicago, Aug. 29–Sept. 2, 1974 (mimeo).

McKenzie, Robert T., *British Political Parties* (New York: St. Martin's, 1955). 623 pp.

Maclay, William, "Journal of William Maclay," in Allen Johnson (ed.),

Readings in American Constitutional History, 1776–1876 (Boston: Houghton Mifflin, 1912), pp. 162–167.

MacMillan, Harold, *At the End of the Day, 1961–1963* (New York: Harper & Row, 1973). 572 pp.

MacMillan, Harold, *The Past Masters: Politics and Politicians 1906–1939* (New York: Harper & Row, 1975). 240 pp.

McPherson, Harry C., *A Political Education* (Boston: Little, Brown, 1972). 467 pp.

MacRae, Duncan, Jr., "The Relation Between Roll Call Votes and Constituencies in the Massachusetts House of Representatives," *American Political Science Review* 46 (December 1952), pp. 1046–1055.

Maheshwari, Shriram, "Constituency Linkage of National Legislators in India," *Legislative Studies Quarterly* 1 (August 1976), pp. 331–354.

Manley, John F., "The Conservative Coalition in Congress," *American Behavioral Scientist*, 17 (November/December 1973), pp. 223–247.

Markus, Gregory B., "Electoral Coalitions and Senate Roll Call Behavior: An Ecological Analysis," *American Journal of Political Science* (August 1974), pp. 595–607.

Marongiu, Antonio, *Medieval Parliaments: A Comparative Study* (London: Eyre & Spottiswoode, 1968). 306 pp.

Martin, Jeanne, "Presidential Elections and Administration Support Among Congressmen," *American Journal of Political Science* 20 (August 1976), pp. 483–489.

Martin, Joe, *My First Fifty Years in Politics* (New York: McGraw-Hill, 1960). 261 pp.

Matthews, Donald R., *U.S. Senators and Their World* (New York: Vintage, 1960). 303 pp.

Mayhew, David R., *Party Loyalty Among Congressmen: The Difference Between Democrats and Republicans 1947–1962* (Cambridge: Harvard University Press, 1966). 189 pp.

Merkl, Peter H., "Coalition Politics in West Germany," in Sven Groennings, E. W. Kelley, and Michael Leiserson (eds.), *The Study of Coalition Behavior* (New York: Holt, Rinehart and Winston, 1970), pp. 13–42.

Mezey, Michael L., *Comparative Legislatures* (Durham, N.C.: Duke University Press, 1979). 317 pp.

Miller, Stefania Szlek, "The 'Znak' Group: 'Priests' or 'Jesters'? (1956–1970)," *The Polish Review* 21, no. 4 (1976), pp. 69–84.

Miller, Warren E., and Donald E. Stokes, "Constituency Influence in Congress," *American Political Science Review* 57 (March 1963), pp. 45–56.

Milnor, A. J., *Elections and Political Stability* (Boston: Little, Brown, 1969). 205 pp.

Morehouse, Sarah McCally, "The State Political Party and the Policy-Making Process," *American Political Science Review* 67 (March 1973), pp. 55–72.

Morrison, Herbert, *Government and Parliament: A Survey from the Inside.* (New York: Oxford, 1954). 363 pp.

Mote, Max E., "Soviet Local and Republic Elections," in Joseph L. Nogee (ed.), *Man, State and Society in the Soviet Union* (New York: Praeger, 1972), pp. 243–259.

Murphy, Reg, and Hal Gulliver, *The Southern Strategy* (New York: Scribner, 1971). 273 pp.

Narain, Iqbal, and Shashi Lata Puri, "Legislators in an Indian State: A Study of Role Images and the Pattern of Constituency Linkages," *Legislative Studies Quarterly* 1 (August 1976), pp. 315–330.

Nelson, Daniel N., "Citizen Participation in Romania: The People's Council Deputy." Paper read at American Political Science Association, 1975 (mimeo).

Nelson, Garrison, "Partisan Patterns of House Leadership Change, 1789–1977," *American Political Science Review* 71 (September 1977), pp. 918–939.

Neustadt, Richard E., *Presidential Power: The Politics of Leadership* (New York: Wiley, 1960). 224 pp.

Norton, Philip, "Intra-Party Dissent in the House of Commons: The Parliament of 1974," *The Parliamentarian* 58 (October 1977), pp. 240–245.

Obler, Jeffrey, "Intraparty Democracy and the Selection of Parliamentary Candidates: The Belgian Case," *British Journal of Political Science* 4 (April 1974), pp. 163–185.

Ogul, Morris S., "Congressional Oversight: Structures and Incentives," in Lawrence C. Dodd and Bruce I. Oppenheimer (eds.), *Congress Reconsidered* (New York: Praeger, 1977), pp. 207–221.

Oleszek, Walter J., "Party Whips in the United States Senate," *Journal of Politics* 33 (November 1971), pp. 955–979.

Olson, David M., "Congressmen and Their Diverse Congressional District Parties," *Legislative Studies Quarterly* 3 (May 1978), pp. 239–264.

Olson, David M., and Cynthia T. Nonidez, "Measures of Legislative Performance in the U.S. House of Representatives," *Midwest Journal of Political Science* 16 (May 1972), pp. 269–277.

Ong, Michael, "The Member of Parliament and His Constituency: The Malaysian Case," *Legislative Studies Quarterly* 1 (August 1976), pp. 405–422.

Opello, Walter C., "The New Parliament in Portugal," *Legislative Studies Quarterly* 3 (May 1978), pp. 309–334.

Ornstein, Norman J., "Causes and Consequences of Congressional Change: Subcommittee Reforms in the House of Representatives, 1970–73," in Norman J. Ornstein (ed.), *Congress in Change: Evolution and Reform* (New York: Praeger, 1975), pp. 88–114.

Ornstein, Norman J., "Congress: The Democrats Reform Power in the House of Representatives, 1969–75," in Allan P. Sindler (ed.), *America in the Seventies: Problems, Policies and Politics* (Boston: Little, Brown, 1977), pp. 2–48.

Packenham, Robert A., "Legislatures and Political Development," in Allan Kornberg and Lloyd D. Musolf (eds.), *Legislatures in Developmental Perspective* (Durham, N.C.: Duke University Press, 1970), pp. 521–582.

Patterson, Samuel C., "American State Legislatures and Public Policy," in

Herbert Jacob and Kenneth N. Vines (eds.), *Politics in the American States*, 3d ed. (Boston: Little, Brown, 1976), pp. 139–195.

Peabody, Robert L., "The Enlarged Rules Committee," in Robert L. Peabody and Nelson W. Polsby (eds.), *New Perspectives on the House of Representatives* (Chicago: Rand McNally, 1963), pp. 129–164.

Peabody, Robert L., *Leadership in Congress: Stability, Succession and Change* (Boston: Little, Brown, 1976). 522 pp.

Pederson, Mogens N., "Lawyers in Politics: The Danish Folketing and United States Legislatures," in Samuel C. Patterson and John C. Wahlke (eds.), *Comparative Legislative Behavior: Frontiers of Research* (New York: Wiley-Interscience, 1972), pp. 25–63.

Pesonen, Pertti, "Close and Safe Elections in Massachusetts," *Midwest Journal of Political Science* 7 (February 1963), pp. 54–70.

Peters, B. Guy, *The Politics of Bureaucracy: A Comparative Perspective* (New York: Longman, 1978). 246 pp.

Pois, Joseph, "Trends in General Accounting Office Audits," in Bruce L. R. Smith (ed.), *The New Political Economy: The Public Use of the Private Sector* (New York: Halsted Press, 1975), pp. 245–277.

Price, David E., "Policy Making in Congressional Committees: The Impact of 'Environmental' Factors," *American Political Science Review* 72 (June 1978), pp. 548–574.

Punnett, Robert M., *Front Bench Opposition: The Role of the Leader of the Opposition, the Shadow Cabinet and Shadow Government in British Politics* (New York: St. Martin's, 1973). 500 pp.

Putnam, Robert D., "Bureaucrats and Politicians: Contending Elites in the Policy Process," in William B. Gwyn and George C. Edwards, III (eds.), *Perspectives on Public Policy-Making* (New Orleans: Tulane Studies in Political Science, vol. 15, 1975), pp. 179–202.

Putnam, Robert D., *The Comparative Study of Political Elites* (Englewood Cliffs, N.J.: Prentice-Hall, 1976). 246 pp.

Rabushka, Alvin, and Kenneth Shepsle, *Politics in Plural Societies: A Theory of Democratic Instability* (Columbus, Ohio: Merrill, 1972). 232 pp.

Ranney, Austin, "The Concept of 'Party,'" in Oliver Garceau (ed.), *Political Research and Political Theory* (Cambridge, Mass.: Harvard University Press, 1968), pp. 143–162.

Ranney, Austin, *Pathways to Parliament* (Madison: University of Wisconsin Press, 1965). 298 pp.

Riccards, Michael P., "The Presidency and the Ratification Controversy," *Presidential Studies Quarterly* 7 (Winter 1977), pp. 37–46.

Rice, George W., "The Electoral Prospects for Non-Ruling Communist Parties," *Midwest Journal of Political Science* 17 (August 1973), pp. 597–610.

Ripley, Randall B., *Majority Party Leadership in Congress* (Boston: Little, Brown, 1969). 194 pp.

Ripley, Randall B., *Party Leaders in the House of Representatives* (Washington, D.C.: Brookings, 1967). 221 pp.

Ripley, Randall B., "The Party Whip Organizations in the United States

House of Representatives," *American Political Science Review* 58 (September 1964), pp. 561–576.

Rose, Richard, *Influencing Voters: A Study of Campaign Rationality* (New York: St. Martin's, 1967). 288 pp.

Rosenstone, Steven J., Raymond E. Wolfinger, and Richard A. McIntosh, "Voter Turnout in Midterm Elections." Paper presented at American Political Science Association, New York, N.Y., 1978.

Rosenthal, Alan, "Legislative Committee Systems: An Exploratory Analysis," *Western Political Quarterly* 26 (June 1973), pp. 252–262.

Rosenthal, Alan, *Legislative Performance in the States: Explorations of Committee Behavior* (New York: Free Press, 1974). 215 pp.

Rosenthal, Howard, "The Electoral Politics of Gaullists in the Fourth French Republic: Ideology or Constituency Interest?" *American Political Science Review* 63 (June 1969), pp. 476–487.

Rosenthal, Howard, and Subrata Sen, "Spatial Voting Models for the French Fifth Republic," *American Political Science Review* 71 (December 1977), pp. 1447–1466.

Rustow, Dankwart A., "The Development of Parties in Turkey," in Joseph LaPalombara and Myron Weiner (eds.), *Political Parties and Political Development* (Princeton, N.J.: Princeton University Press, 1966), pp. 107–133.

Rustow, Dankwart A., *The Politics of Compromise: A Study of Parties and Cabinet Government in Sweden* (Princeton, N.J.: Princeton University Press, 1955). 257 pp.

Ryle, M. T., "Developments in the Parliamentary System," in William Thornhill (ed.), *The Modernization of British Government* (Totowa, N.J.: Rowman and Littlefield, 1975), pp. 7–30.

Sartori, Giovanni, "European Political Parties: The Case of Polarized Pluralism," in Joseph LaPalombara and Myron Weiner (eds.), *Political Parties and Political Development* (Princeton, N.J.: Princeton University Press, 1966), pp. 137–176.

Sartori, Giovanni, "Will Democracy Kill Democracy? Decision Making by Majorities and by Committees," *Government and Opposition* 10 (Spring 1975), pp. 131–158.

Scher, Seymour, "Conditions for Legislative Control," *Journal of Politics* 25 (August 1963), pp. 526–551.

Schlesinger, Joseph A., *Ambition and Politics: Political Careers in the United States* (Chicago: Rand McNally, 1966). 226 pp.

Schlesinger, Joseph A., "Political Careers and Party Leadership," in Lewis J. Edinger (ed.), *Political Leadership in Industrialized Societies* (New York: Wiley, 1967), pp. 226–293.

Schlesinger, Joseph A., "Political Party Organization," in James C. March (ed.), *Handbook of Organizations* (Chicago: Rand McNally, 1964), pp. 764–801.

Schuck, Peter H., *The Judiciary Committees* (New York: Grossman, The Ralph Nader Congress Project, 1975). 446 pp.

Schwarz, John E., and Barton Fenmore, "Presidential Election Results and Congressional Roll Call Behavior: The Cases of 1964, 1968, and 1972," *Legislative Studies Quarterly* 2 (November 1977), pp. 409–422.

Schwarz, John E., and L. Earl Shaw, *The United States Congress in Comparative Perspective* (Hinsdale, Ill.: Dryden, 1976). 421 pp.

Searing, Donald, and Chris Game, "Horses for Courses: The Recruitment of Whips in the British House of Commons," *British Journal of Political Science* 7 (July 1977), pp. 361–385.

Seligman, Lester G., et al., *Patterns of Recruitment* (Chicago: Rand McNally, 1974).

Seroka, James H., "Legislative Recruitment, Nominations and Elective Procedures, and Political Change in Yugoslavia." Paper read at the Southern Political Science Association, New Orleans, November 1977 (mimeo).

Shannon, W. Wayne, *Party, Constituency and Congressional Voting* (Baton Rouge: Louisiana State University Press, 1968). 202 pp.

Sharkansky, Ira, "Agency Requests, Gubernatorial Support and Budget Success in State Legislatures," *American Political Science Review* 62 (December 1968), pp. 1220–1231.

Sharkansky, Ira, "The Politics of Auditing," in Bruce L. R. Smith (ed.), *The New Political Economy: The Public Use of the Private Sector* (New York: Halsted Press, 1975), pp. 278–318.

Shaw, Malcolm, and John D. Lees, *Committees* (Durham, N.C.: Duke University Press, forthcoming).

Sickels, Robert J., *Presidential Transactions* (Englewood Cliffs, N.J.: Prentice-Hall, 1974). 184 pp.

Sinclair, Barbara D., "Electoral Marginality and Party Loyalty in House Roll Call Voting," *American Journal of Political Science* 20 (August 1976), pp. 469–481.

Sinclair, Barbara D., "Party Realignment and the Transformation of the Political Agenda: The House of Representatives, 1925–1938," *American Political Science Review* 71 (September 1977), pp. 940–953.

Sinclair, Barbara D., "The Policy Consequences of Party Realignment—Social Welfare Legislation in the House of Representatives, 1933–1954," *American Journal of Political Science* 22 (February 1978), pp. 83–105.

Sinclair, Barbara D., "Political Upheaval and Congressional Voting: The Effects of the 1960s on Voting Patterns in the House of Representatives," *Journal of Politics* 38 (May 1976), pp. 326–345.

Sisson, Richard, and Leo Snowiss, "Legislative Viability and Political Development," in Joel Smith and Lloyd Musolf (eds.), *Legislatures in Development* (Durham, N.C.: Duke University Press, forthcoming), chap. 2.

Smith, Bruce L. R. (ed.), *The New Political Economy: The Public Use of the Private Sector* (New York: Halsted Press, 1975). 344 pp.

Snowiss, Leo, "Congressional Recruitment and Representation," *American Political Science Review* 60 (September 1966), pp. 627–639.

Sorauf, Frank, *Party and Representation* (New York: Atherton, 1963). 178 pp.

Stedman, Murray S., Jr., *State and Local Governments* (Cambridge, Mass.: Winthrop, 1976). 419 pp.

Stehle, Hansjakob, *The Independent Satellite: Society and Politics in Poland Since 1945* (New York: Praeger, 1965). 361 pp.

Stevens, Arthur J., Jr., Arthur H. Miller, and Thomas E. Mann, "Mobilization of Liberal Strength in the House: 1950–1970: The Democratic Study Group," *American Political Science Review* 68 (June 1974), pp. 667–681.

Stokes, Donald E., "Parties and the Nationalization of Electoral Forces," in William N. Chambers and W. Dean Burnham (eds.), *The American Party Systems*, 2d ed. (New York: Oxford, 1975), pp. 182–202.

Strom, Gerald S., and Barry S. Rundquist, "A Revised Theory of Winning in House-Senate Conferences," *American Political Science Review* 71 (June 1977), pp. 448–453.

Stultz, Newell M., "The National Assembly in the Politics of Kenya," in Allan Kornberg and Lloyd D. Musolf (eds.), *Legislatures in Developmental Perspective* (Durham, N.C.: Duke University Press, 1970), pp. 303–333.

Sullivan, John L., and Daniel R. Minns, "Ideological Distance Between Candidates: An Empirical Examination," *American Journal of Political Science* 20 (August 1976), pp. 439–468.

Sundquist, James L., *Politics and Policy: The Eisenhower, Kennedy, and Johnson Years* (Washington, D.C.: Brookings, 1968). 560 pp.

Taylor, Michael, and V. M. Herman, "Party Systems and Government Stability," *American Political Science Review* 65 (March 1971), pp. 28–37.

Thurber, James A., "The Impact of Party Recruitment Activity upon Legislative Role Orientations: A Path Analysis," *Legislative Studies Quarterly* 1 (November 1976), pp. 533–550.

Toma, Peter A., and Ivan Volgyes, *Politics in Hungary* (San Francisco: Freeman, 1977). 188 pp.

Tordoff, William, *Government and Politics in Tanzania* (Nairobi: East African Publishing House, 1967). 257 pp.

Tufte, Edward R., "The Relationship Between Seats and Votes in Two-Party Systems," *American Political Science Review* 67 (June 1973), pp. 540–554.

Turner, Julius, "Primary Elections as the Alternative to Party Competition in 'Safe' Districts," *Journal of Politics* 15 (May 1953), pp. 197–210.

Ulc, Otto, "Political Participation in Czechoslovakia," *Journal of Politics* 33 (May 1971), pp. 422–447.

Valen, Henry, and Daniel Katz, *Political Parties in Norway* (Oslo: Universitetsforlaget, 1964). 383 pp.

Valentine, Herman, and Francoise Mendel, *Parliaments of the World* (Berlin: De Gruyter and International Parliamentary Union, 1976). 985 pp.

Valenzuela, Arturo, and Alexander Wilde, "Presidential Politics and the Decline of the Chilean Congress," in Joel Smith and Lloyd Musolf (eds.), *Legislatures in Development* (Durham, N.C.: Duke University Press, forthcoming), chap. 7.

Vanneman, Peter, *The Supreme Soviet: Politics and the Legislative Process in the Soviet System* (Durham, N.C.: Duke University Press, 1977). 256 pp.

Wahlke, John C., Heinz Eulau, William Buchanan, and LeRoy C. Ferguson, *The Legislative System: Explorations in Legislative Behavior* (New York: Wiley, 1962). 517 pp.

Waldman, Loren, "Liberalism of Congressmen and the Presidential Vote in Their Districts," *Midwest Journal of Political Science* 11 (February 1967), pp. 73–85.

Wayne, Stephen J., *The Legislative Presidency* (New York: Harper & Row, 1978). 240 pp.

Weinbaum, Marvin G., "The Legislator as Intermediary: Integration of the Center and Periphery in Afghanistan," in Albert F. Eldridge (ed.), *Legislatures in Plural Societies: The Search for Cohesion in National Development* (Durham, N.C.: Duke University Press, 1977), pp. 95–121.

Wheare, Kenneth C., *Legislatures*, 2d ed. (New York: Oxford, 1967). 166 pp.

Wheeler, Christopher, *White-Collar Power: Changing Patterns of Interest Group Behavior in Sweden* (Urbana: University of Illinois Press, 1975). 210 pp.

Wiatr, Jerzy J., "The Hegemonic Party System in Poland," in Jerzy Wiatr and Jacek Tarkowski (eds.), *Studies in Polish Political System* (Warsaw: Polish Academy of Sciences Press, 1967), pp. 108–123.

Wildavsky, Aaron, *Budgeting: A Comparative Theory of Budgetary Processes* (Boston: Little, Brown, 1975). 432 pp.

Williams, Philip, *The French Parliament* (New York: Praeger, 1968). 136 pp.

Wilson, James Q., *Political Organization* (New York: Basic Books, 1973). 359 pp.

Wolfinger, Raymond E., and Joan Heifetz, "Safe Seats, Seniority, and Power in Congress," *American Political Science Review* 59 (June 1965), pp. 337–349.

Woshinsky, Oliver H., *The French Deputy: Incentives and Behavior in the National Assembly* (Lexington, Mass.: Lexington Books, 1973). 232 pp.

II. GOVERNMENT DOCUMENTS

Poland. Polish Interpress Agency, "Polish Parliamentary and Local Government Elections," Warsaw, February 1976 (mimeo). 8 pp.

Poland. Polish United Workers' Party, Central Committee, Political Bureau, "Development and Consolidation of the Nation's Patriotic Unity, Consolidation of the State and Development of Socialist Democracy." Polish Interpress Agency, Warsaw, March 1976 (mimeo).

United Kingdom, British Information Service, *The British Parliament* (London: HMSO, 1973). 56 pp.

United Kingdom, House of Commons, *Parliamentary Debates (Hansard)*, 1973–1978.

U.S. Bureau of the Census, *Congressional District Data Book, 1972* (Washington, D.C.: Government Printing Office).

U.S. Bureau of the Census, *Historical Statistics of the U.S.: Colonial Times to 1970*, Bicentennial ed., part I (Washington, D.C.: Government Printing Office), 1975.

U.S. Bureau of the Census, *Statistical Abstract of the United States: 1977*, 98th ed. (Washington, D.C.: Government Printing Office, 1977).

U.S. Congress, *Congressional Directory*, 1972–1978 (Washington, D.C.: Government Printing Office.)

U.S. Congress, *Congressional Record*, 1961–1978.

U.S. Congress. General Accounting Office, *Requirements for Recurring Reports to the Congress* (Washington, D.C.: Government Printing Office, 1978).

U.S. Congress. House. Ad Hoc Committee on Energy, *National Energy Act: Report of the Committee* (Washington, D.C.: House Report 95–543, 95th Congress, 1st Session, July 27, 1977).

U.S. Congress. House. Commission on Administrative Review, *Administrative Reorganization and Legislative Management*, vol. 2: *Work Management* (Washington, D.C.: Government Printing Office, House Doc. 95–232, 1977). 274 pp.

U.S. Congress. House. Commission on Administrative Review, *Background Information on Administrative Units, Members' Offices and Committees and Leadership Offices: Communication from the Chairman* (Washington, D.C.: Government Printing Office, House Doc. 95–178, June 30, 1977). 110 pp.

U.S. Congress. House. Committee on Interstate and Foreign Commerce, *Hearings: National Energy Act* (Washington, D.C.: Serial 95–22, May 9–16, 1977).

U.S. Congress. Senate. Commission on the Operation of the Senate, *Toward a Modern Senate: Final Report* (Washington, D.C.: Government Printing Office, December 1970).

USSR, *Constitution (Fundamental Law) of the Union of Soviet Socialist Republics* (Moscow: Novosti Press Agency Publishing House, 1977). 127 pp.

III. NEWSPAPERS AND GOVERNMENT REPORTS

Campaign Practices Reports, Washington, D.C., 1977.

Congressional Index (New York: Commerce Clearing House, 1971–1976).

Congressional Quarterly Almanac (Washington, D.C.: Congressional Quarterly, Inc., 1953–1978).

Congressional Quarterly Weekly Report (Washington, D.C.: Congressional Quarterly, Inc., 1972–1978).

Congressional Quarterly, "Committees and Subcommittees, 95th Congress," supplement to *Weekly Report*, April 30, 1977.

Facts on File (New York), 1977.

Keesing's Contemporary Archive (London), 1971–1978.

London Times, 1978.
New York Times, 1976–1978.
Radio Free Europe, "Polish Press Survey," No. 2355, February 7, 1972 (mimeo). 17 pp.
Wall Street Journal, 1977–1978.
Washington Post, 1977–1978.

Index

79 80 81 82 9 8 7 6 5 4 3 2 1